THE IRAQ WAR READER

History, Documents, Opinions

Edited by

Micah L. Sifry and Christopher Cerf

A TOUCHSTONE BOOK
Published by Simon & Schuster

NEW YORK LONDON TORONTO SYDNEY

TOUCHSTONE
Rockefeller Center
1230 Avenue of the Americas
New York, NY 10020

Copyright © 2003 by Micah L. Sifry and Christopher Cerf
All rights reserved,
including the right of reproduction
in whole or in part in any form.

TOUCHSTONE and colophon are registered trademarks
of Simon and Schuster, Inc.

Permissions acknowledgments appear on pages 671–676.

For information regarding special discounts for bulk purchases,
please contact Simon & Schuster Special Sales at 1-800-456-6798
or business@simonandschuster.com

Designed by Joy O'Meara-Battista

Manufactured in the United States of America

3   5   7   9   10   8   6   4   2

Library of Congress Cataloging-in-Publication Data is available.

ISBN-13: 978-0-7432-5347-5
ISBN-10:   0-7432-5347-7

To Leslie, Mira, Jesse and the memory of Robbie Friedman;
To Paige, who helped mightily, both spiritually and logistically;
And, most of all,
To a world without end.

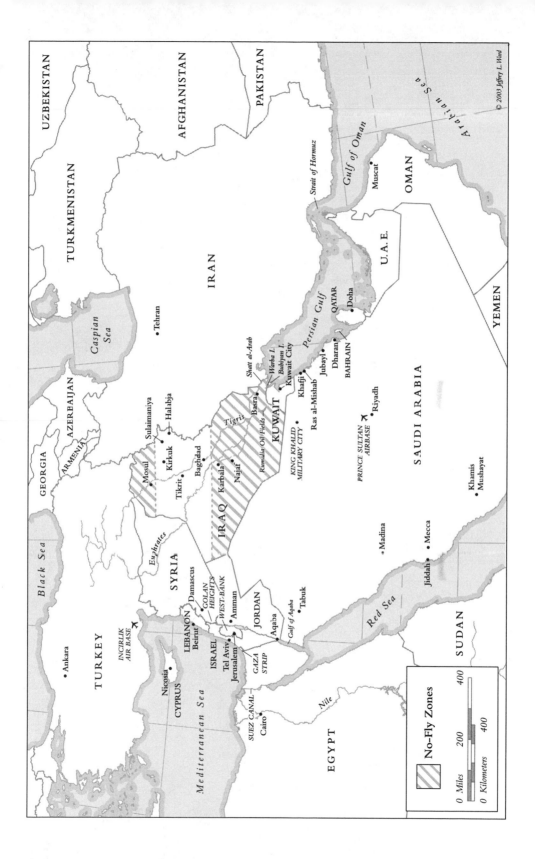

UZBEKISTAN

TURKMENISTAN

AFGHANISTAN

PAKISTAN

© 2003 Jeffrey L. Ward

GEORGIA

ARMENIA

AZERBAIJAN

Caspian
Sea

TURKEY

• Ankara

Black Sea

Nicosia •

CYPRUS

Mediterranean Sea

SUEZ CANAL

Cairo •

EGYPT

Nile

SYRIA

Damascus •

LEBANON

Beirut •

INCIRLIK
AIR BASE

ISRAEL

Tel Aviv •

Jerusalem •

GAZA
STRIP

GOLAN
HEIGHTS

WEST BANK

Amman •

JORDAN

Aqaba •

Gulf of Aqaba

• Tabuk

Red Sea

SUDAN

Euphrates

Mosul •

Tikrit •

Kirkuk •

Baghdad •

IRAQ

Karbala •

Najaf •

Tigris

Sulaimaniya •

Halabja •

Basra •

Rumaila Oil Fields

KUWAIT

Tehran •

IRAN

Shatt al-Arab

Warba I.
Bubiyan I.

Kuwait City •

Khafji •

Ras al-Mishab •

Jubayl •

Dharan •

BAHRAIN

KING KHALID
MILITARY CITY •

PRINCE SULTAN
AIRBASE

Riyadh •

SAUDI ARABIA

Madina •

Jiddah •

• Mecca

Khamis
Mushayat •

Persian Gulf

QATAR

Doha •

U. A. E.

Strait of Hormuz

Gulf of Oman

Muscat •

OMAN

Arabian Sea

YEMEN

No-Fly Zones

0   Miles   200   400

0   Kilometers   400

INTRODUCTION AND
ACKNOWLEDGMENTS

The United States and the Middle East are at a critical moment in their individual and common histories. The first international crisis of the post-Cold War era culminated in war. But despite the flood of instant information and analysis provided by television and the press during the course of the Gulf War, most Americans remain ill informed about the history of the region, the policies that brought Iraq, Kuwait, and the U.S.-led coalition to confrontation, and the complex problems that will shape the postwar Middle East. The United States has embarked upon a qualitatively new involvement with the region—a commitment that raises important questions: What is the proper role of U.S. power in the world today? Can it be guided by moral precepts, or is realpolitik and the balance of power the only choice for policymakers? What are the root causes of instability and discontent in the Middle East? Can lasting peace be brought to that tormented part of the world by the forcible intervention of outside powers? Are there other, less violent ways of resolving the disputes among the countries and peoples of the region? Can America's foreign policy be more tightly tethered to democratic debate and control? And what about the "peace dividend" and the pressing priorities back home?

With these words, we began our 1991 anthology, *The Gulf War Reader*. Sadly, or ironically, the same observations and the same questions, with minor variations, seem just as relevant today. The Gulf War, which ended in an unsettled cease-fire ordered by the first President Bush, is being finished by the second President Bush. And despite the explosion of 24-hour news coverage and the Internet, most Americans still "remain ill informed" about the history and complexity of the region. For example, polls show that about half believe one or more Iraqis helped hijack the planes of September 11th, when in fact none were involved on that terrible day that is so altering our country's self-perception. (This observation is more than merely academic: cross-tabulation shows that those who believed that were 20 to 35 percent more likely to support going to war with Saddam.) Moreover, questions about the proper role of American power and the root causes of instability and discontent have only grown more urgent since our earlier book. Today, America, and indeed much of the Western world, face a new kind of enemy, a network of angry individuals that does not appear to be deterrable through conventional means. In the face of this threat, the leaders of the United States have embraced a new doctrine of pre-emptive action that they say is needed to prevent future September 11ths. Others see it as a dangerously destabilizing and self-defeating grab at imperial dominance.

This book is meant to be a guide to the most urgent foreign policy questions of our time, as raised and interpreted by political leaders, academics, diplomats, journalists and critics. First, in Part One, "Sins of the Fathers," we examine how the West, and in particular the United States, came to clash with Saddam Hussein. What are the roots of Arab and Islamic resentment? Where did Saddam come from? How and why did the United States support him for so many years? And what happened when both sides, not quite allies but not enemies either, came to misunderstand each other's intentions over Kuwait?

In Part Two, "Aftermaths of the Gulf War," we cover the period from 1991 through 2001. How did Saddam manage to survive the Kurdish and Shiite uprisings of 1991, and what might his unlikely survival teach future rulers of Iraq? In what ways did the Pentagon and the White House succeed in manipulating the American press and public, and what lessons in skepticism may we learn as citizens judging present statements from our leaders? How did the sanctions and inspections regimes of the 1990s fall apart? How far did Iraq get in trying to develop a nuclear bomb? And who planted the seeds for the current war?

In Part Three, "War With Iraq," we endeavor to cover the whole spectrum of domestic debate over the war (with a few salient international voices as well). How should the country have responded to September 11th? Who are the authors of the new Bush Doctrine, and will their handiwork prove practicable and constructive? Is unilateral action wise or foolhardy? Did Congress abrogate its constitutional responsibility when it authorized President Bush to decide whether the nation should go to war? Was Saddam deterrable? Was he even the right target? What are the odds that regime change in Iraq will have long-term positive effects, like the liberation of long-suffering peoples and the emergence of new Arab democracies? Were U.N. inspections working, or was war the only way to enforce the Security Council's resolutions? Can countries with huge stockpiles of their own weapons of mass destruction prevent others from wanting, and getting, them too?

Finally, in Part Four, "Through a Glass Darkly," we peer forward through the fog of war into the future. There was much discussion even before the war started of how Iraq's society and government might be remade for the better after Saddam's fall; most of our authors offer cautionary notes on how difficult and dangerous a task that will be. Likewise, much was made of how this war represented a paradigm shift in America's relations with the rest of the world. Here we offer muscular and optimistic views of Pax Americana from three of its leading proponents, along with several essays presenting a more skeptical view of empire.

The Iraq War Reader was completed as the diplomatic dance in the Security Council came to an end and the war began. Whether that war was destined to be quick or drawn-out, relatively painless or truly horrifying, we cannot know, although you, dear reader, probably already do. (Visit our website at IraqWarReader.com for ongoing updates and more recommended reading.) It is our hope that our book will enrich and deepen the debates that are to come.

ASSEMBLING AN anthology like this, especially against a background of quickly changing events, would have been impossible without the extraordinary efforts of many people.

First and foremost, we'd like to thank our mutual friend Victor Navasky, who introduced us in 1991, just in time to collaborate on *The Gulf War Reader*. (Imagine our sense of déja vù— pardon the untimely use of French!— as we once again scrambled to put together a book as war clouds gathered over the Middle East.)

We are also especially grateful to Richard Butler, Joost Hiltermann, Lewis Lapham, and Kevin Phillips, who took extra time and effort to contribute newly written or adapted works to our anthology, and who offered shrewd and useful suggestions for other pieces as well.

Special thanks are due Jane Aaron, Bill Arkin, Monie Begley, John Berendt, Marc Cooper, David Corn, Bill Effros, Gloria Emerson, Louise Gikow, Hendrik Hertzberg, Christopher Hitchens, Doug Ireland, Michael Levine, John Moyers, Danny Schechter, Nermeen Shaikh, Norman Stiles, Raymond Shapiro, Bob Silvers, Ken Socha, Chris Toensing, Katrina vanden Heuvel, and (last but hardly least!) Steve Wasserman, for their friendship, patience, advice, and support. Nick Nyhart and the whole staff of Public Campaign cut one of us much valuable slack, and his colleagues Nancy Watzman and Rick Bielke deserve special appreciation for picking up that slack, as do the many generous members of the *Between the Lions* creative and production teams whose phone calls went mysteriously unanswered during the early weeks of 2003.

The writers whose works form the body of this book are, of course, the true creators of *The Iraq War Reader;* we are truly grateful for their kindness and cooperation. We owe a debt as well to several very fine resources: the Middle East Research and Information Project (MERIP), Laurie Mylroie's Iraq Daily, TheWarInContext.org, the Global Policy Forum (globalpolicy.org), the International Crisis Group (crisisweb.org), Chuck Spinney's Defense and the National Interest (d-n-i.net) and Gary Milhollin's Iraq Watch.

We offer our special thanks to our agents Ed Victor, Kim Witherspoon, and David Forrer; to Tina Fuscaldo and Lisa Weinert, who worked tirelessly on assembling and organizing our manuscript (and us!); to Brett Valley, who was always there to lend a cheerful and efficient helping hand; and to Donna Fuscaldo, whose research efforts played a critical role. We are especially grateful, too, to Cheryl Moch, our peerless permissions editor (and longtime friend); to Nancy Inglis, who shepherded our book wisely and thoughtfully through a daunting series of typesetting and copyediting deadlines; to Kelly Farley and the gallant folks at Dix Type, who excelled at an impossible typesetting task; to London King and Marcia Burch, our public relations gurus; to Francine Kass, our art director; and to Mark Gompertz, publisher of the Touchstone division of Simon & Schuster, who believed in our endeavor from the outset, and graciously smoothed the way for us whenever smoothing was required.

Were it not for Trish Todd, our editor (and the editor-in-chief of Touchstone Books), whose unexpected email message launched this project, there would have been no *Iraq War Reader.* Thanks, Trish, for getting us started, and for the vision and good humor you displayed throughout the editorial process!

Thanks as well to our families (both official and non-official), who put up with more than the usual amount of distraction and free-floating angst from us during the final weeks of this project; your love and support mean everything to us.

And, finally, we'd like to acknowledge our debt to Marcus Raskin and the late Bernard Fall, editors of *The Vietnam Reader,* and Marvin Gettleman, who edited *Vietnam: History, Documents, and Opinions on a Major World Crisis.* Their seminal works were the "mothers of all wartime anthologies," and we're honored, for the second time in twelve years, to be able to follow in their footsteps.

Micah L. Sifry and Christopher Cerf
New York City
March 27, 2003

Contents

PART THREE WAR WITH IRAQ

PART ONE

SINS OF THE FATHERS

ONE

ROOTS OF
CONFLICT:
1915–1989

"I am strongly in favor of using poisoned gas against uncivilized tribes."
—Winston Churchill, then British secretary of state for war and air, on dealing with the Arab revolt against British rule over Iraq in 1920

"We have about 50% of the world's wealth but only 6.3% of its population. . . . In this situation, we cannot fail to be the object of envy and resentment. Our real task in the coming period is to devise a pattern of relationships which will permit us to maintain this position of disparity without positive detriment to our national security. To do so, we will have to dispense with all sentimentality and day-dreaming; and our attention will have to be concentrated everywhere on our immediate national objectives. We need not deceive ourselves that we can afford today the luxury of altruism and world-benefaction."
—George Kennan, former head of the U.S. State Department Policy Planning Staff and leading architect of U.S. foreign policy after World War II, February 24, 1948

IMPERIAL LEGACY

Phillip Knightley

The new crusaders from the United States and Europe, along with their Arab auxiliaries, are gathered again in the Middle East. But their chances of a lasting victory are slim. No matter what happens to Iraq and its leader, Saddam Hussein, there will be no peace in the area until the world faces up to these historical facts: the West lied to the Arabs in the First World War; it promised them independence but then imposed imperial mandates; this ensured Arab disunity at the very moment when the West created the state of Israel.

In January 1919, Paris was a city of pomp and splendor. The most ghastly war in history had ended two months earlier in triumph for the Allies: Britain, France, and the United States. Now diplomats from these countries, grave, impressive men flanked by their military advisers, had arrived for the peace conference that would decide the fate of Germany and divide the spoils of victory.

Each night the best Paris hotels, ablaze with light from their grand chandeliers, buzzed with conversation and laughter as the delegates relaxed after their duties. In this colorful, cosmopolitan gathering, one delegate stood out. Restaurants grew quiet when he entered, and there was much behind-the-scenes jostling to meet him. For this was Lawrence of Arabia, the young Englishman who had helped persuade the Arabs to revolt against their Turkish masters, who were allies of Germany. This was the brilliant intelligence officer who had welded the warring tribes of the Middle East into a formidable guerrilla force.

This sounded sufficiently romantic in itself, but it emerged that Lawrence had appeared destined almost from birth to become the Imperial Hero. The illegitimate son of an Anglo-Irish landowner and the family governess, he became interested in archaeology as a boy and at Jesus College, Oxford, and came under the influence of D. G. Hogarth, a leading archaeologist of his time.

Hogarth imbued Lawrence with the ideals of enlightened imperialism,

Phillip Knightley, a journalist, is author of *The Secret Lives of Lawrence of Arabia* and *The First Casualty,* a history of war reporting and propaganda. This article appeared in the November 1990 issue of *M Inc.* magazine, under the title "Desert Warriors."

which, Hogarth believed, could lead to a new era of the British empire. Lawrence began to study medieval history and military tactics and to train his body to resist pain and exhaustion. He would walk his bicycle downhill and ride it up, fast; take long cross-country walks, fording streams even in the coldest weather; and spend long, lonely evenings on the Cadet Force pistol range until he became an adept shot with either hand.

During a break from Oxford, Lawrence embarked on a 1,000-mile walking tour of Syria and became fascinated by the Arabs. The Crusades became the subject of his special interest, and he dreamed of becoming a modern-day crusading knight—clean, strong, just, and completely chaste.

Just before the outbreak of war in 1914 Lawrence did a secret mapping survey of the Sinai Desert for British military intelligence, working under the cover of a historical group called the Palestine Exploration Fund. It was no surprise then that Hogarth was able to get him a wartime job with military intelligence in Cairo, where he was soon running his own agents.

But it was when the Arab revolt broke out in June 1916 that Lawrence came into his own. As Lawrence later described in his book, *Seven Pillars of Wisdom,* one of the most widely read works in the English language (and the inspiration for the film *Lawrence of Arabia*), he led his Arabs on daring raids against Turkish supply trains on the Damascus-Medina railway. They would blow up the line, derailing the engine, then charge from the hills on their camels—brave, unspoiled primitives against trained troops with machine guns.

As word of the exploits of this blue-eyed young man from Oxford spread across the desert, the Arab tribes put aside their differences. Under Lawrence, they captured the vital port of Aqaba with one glorious charge, then went on to Damascus in triumph. If the war had not ended and the politicians had not betrayed him, the story went, Lawrence might well have conquered Constantinople with half the tribes of Asia Minor at his side. Small wonder Paris was entranced.

As James T. Shotwell, a former professor of history at Columbia University and a member of the American delegation, described it, "The scene at dinner was the most remarkable I have ever witnessed. . . . Next to the Canadian table was a large dinner party discussing the fate of Arabia and the East with two American guests. . . . Between them sat that young successor of Muhammad, Colonel [T. E.] Lawrence, the twenty-eight-year-old conqueror of Damascus, with his boyish face and almost constant smile—the most winning figure, so everyone says, at the whole peace conference."

Shotwell did not know it, but Lawrence, dressed in the robes of an Arab prince, gold dagger across his chest, had dubious official status at the conference. Although usually seen in the company of Emir Faisal—who was the third son of Hussein, sharif of Mecca, a direct descendant of Muhammad and guardian of the holy places in Mecca and Medina—no one quite knew who Lawrence represented.

FAISAL, THE military leader of the revolt started by Hussein, thought Lawrence represented him. He thought that Lawrence was there to make certain that the Allies kept the promises made to the Arabs in return for their help in defeating Turkey—promises of freedom and self-government.

The British Foreign Office thought that Lawrence was there to keep Faisal amenable and to calm him down when he learned the bitter truth—that Britain and France planned to divide the Middle East between them and turn Palestine into a national home for the Jews.

Britain's India Office thought that Lawrence was there to frustrate their plan to make Iraq into a province of India, populated by Indian farmers and run from Delhi. This would be the ultimate act of revenge against the British Foreign Office for having backed Hussein during the war rather than the India Office's candidate for leader of the Arabs, King ibn Saud of Saudi Arabia.

As a British political intelligence officer, Lawrence's job had been to find the Arab leaders most suited to run the revolt against the Turks, to keep them loyal to Britain by promises of freedom that he knew Britain would never keep and to risk this fraud "on my conviction that Arab help was necessary to our cheap and speedy victory in the East and that better we win and break our word than lose."

Lawrence salved his conscience at this deception by creating a romantic notion of his own. This was that he would be able to convince his political superiors—and the Arabs—that the best compromise would be for the Arabs to become "brown citizens" within the British empire, inhabitants of a dominion entitled to a measure of self-government but owing allegiance to the British king emperor—something like Canada.

With everyone pursuing his own goal and no one really interested in what the Arabs themselves wanted, the victorious European powers proceeded to carve up the Middle East.

Did they realize that their broken promises and cynical disposition of other peoples' countries would one day bring a reckoning? Did they not recall the words of that great Arabist Gertrude Bell, who once warned that the catchwords of revolution, "fraternity" and "equality," would always have great appeal in the Middle East because they challenged a world order in which Europeans were supreme or in which those Europeans—and their client Arab leaders—treated ordinary Arabs as inferior beings? Do the ghosts of those delegates at the Paris Peace Conference—and the "tidying up" meetings that followed—now shiver as the United States and Europe gear up to impose another settlement on the Middle East?

The past will haunt the new Crusades because the Arabs have never forgotten the promises of freedom made to them in the First World War by the likes of Lawrence and President Woodrow Wilson, and the subsequent betrayal of them at Paris. It will haunt them because history in the Middle East never favors the foreigner and always takes its revenge on those who insist on seeing the region through their own eyes.

THE MESS began soon after the turn of the century. Until then the Middle East had been under 400 years of domination by the Ottoman empire, a vast and powerful hegemony extending over northern Africa, Asia, and Europe. At one stage it had stretched from the Adriatic to Aden and from Morocco to the Persian Gulf, and the skill of its generals and the bravery of its soldiers once pushed its reach into Europe as far as the outskirts of Vienna.

But by the mid–nineteenth century the impact of Western technology had started to make itself felt, and the great empire began to flake at the edges. When in 1853 Czar Nicholas called Turkey "a sick man," Britain became worried. If Turkey collapsed, Britain would have a duty to protect her own military and economic lines of communication with India, where half the British army was stationed and which was unquestionably Britain's best customer.

Others also looked to their interests. Germany wanted to turn Iraq into "a German India"; France longed for Syria, a sentiment that dated back to the Crusades: and Russia yearned to dominate Constantinople, a terminus for all caravan routes in the Middle East.

By the early 1900s all these countries were pursuing their aims by covert action. In the regions now known as Afghanistan, Iran, Iraq, Syria, and the Persian Gulf, networks of Western intelligence agents—ostensibly consuls, travelers, merchants and archaeologists—were busy influencing chieftains, winning over tribes, settling disputes, and disparaging their rivals in the hope that they would benefit from the eventual disintegration of the Ottoman empire.

When the First World War broke out in August 1914, Turkey dithered and then chose the wrong side by joining Germany. Lawrence, working for the Arab Bureau in Cairo, was part of a plan to use Arab nationalism in the service of British war aims.

The scheme was simple. The British would encourage the Arabs to revolt against their Turkish masters by the promise of independence when Turkey was defeated. How firm were these promises? Let us charitably discount those made in the heat of battle, when victory over Germany and Turkey was by no means certain, and consider only two—one made in June 1918 to seven Arab nationalist leaders in Cairo, the other part of the Anglo-French declaration made just before Germany surrendered.

The first promise was that Arab territories that were free before the war would remain so, and that in territories liberated by the Arabs themselves, the British government would recognize "the complete and sovereign independence of the inhabitants"; elsewhere governments would be based on the consent of the governed. The Anglo-French declaration promised to set up governments chosen by the Arabs themselves—in short, a clear pledge of self-determination.

The more worldly Arab nationalists warned that helping France and Britain achieve victory over Turkey might well lead merely to an exchange of one form of foreign domination for another. But these words of warning went unheeded because the hopes of the Arab masses were raised by the United States' entry into the war in April 1917.

THE ARABS thought that the American government might be more receptive than the British to their demands for self-determination. After all, the Americans knew what it was like to be under the thumb of a colonial power, and President Wilson's Fourteen Points, which advocated freedom and self-determination for races under the domination of the old multinational empires, was highly encouraging.

But the Arab skeptics turned out to be right. The Allies did not keep their promises. The Arabs did exchange one imperial ruler for another. There were forces at work of which they were ignorant. The two most powerful of these were oil and the Zionist hunger for a national home in Palestine.

The automobile had in 1919 not yet become the twentieth-century's most desirable object, but the war had made everyone realize the strategic importance of oil. Germany's oil-fired navy had been immobilized in port after the Battle of Jutland in May 1916, largely because the British blockade caused a shortage of fuel. German industrial production was hindered by a lack of lubricants, and its civilian transport almost came to a halt.

It was clear, then, that in any future conflict oil would be an essential weapon. Britain already had one source: British Petroleum, owned in part by the British government, had been pumping oil at Masjid-i-Salaman in Iran's Zagros Mountains since 1908. But it was not enough.

Even before the 1919 peace conference began to divide up the Middle East between Britain and France, some horse trading had taken place, making it unlikely that the promises made to the Arabs would be respected. France, for example, gave Britain the oil-rich area around Mosul, Iraq, in exchange for a share of the oil and a free hand in Syria. Unfortunately, Britian had already promised Syria to the Arabs. St. John Philby, the eccentric but perceptive English adviser to ibn Saud—and the man who eventually introduced American oil interests to Saudi Arabia—understood that British explanations were mere pieties: "The real crux is oil."

At the peace conference, private oil concerns pushed their governments (in the national interest, of course) to renounce all wartime promises to the Arabs. For the oilmen saw only too well that oil concessions and royalties would be easier to negotiate with a series of rival Arab states lacking any sense of unity, than with a powerful independent Arab state in the Middle East.

These old imperialist prerogatives, salted with new commercial pressures, raised few eyebrows in Europe. Sir Mark Sykes, the British side of the partnership with François Georges-Picot that in 1916 drew up the secret Sykes-Picot agreement dividing the Middle East between Britain and France, believed Arab independence would mean "Persia, poverty, and chaos."

Across the Atlantic, President Wilson looked on "the whole disgusting scramble for the Middle East" with horror. It offended everything he believed the United States stood for, and the British establishment became worried about Wilson's views. They could imperil British policy for the area. The question became, therefore, how could Britain's imperialist designs on the Middle East be reconciled with President Wilson's commitment to Middle Eastern independence? One school of thought was that Lawrence of Arabia might provide the link.

LAWRENCE OF Arabia was the creation of an American: Lowell Thomas, one-time newspaperman and lecturer in English at Princeton. When the United States entered the war in April 1917, the American people showed a marked reluctance to take up arms, so to inspire the nation to fight, President Wilson set up the Committee on Public Information under the chairmanship of a journalist, George Creel.

One of his first acts was to propose sending Thomas to gather stirring stories in Europe to stimulate enthusiasm for the war. It did not take long for Thomas to realize that there was nothing heartening or uplifting to be found in the mud and mechanized slaughter on the Western Front, so the British Department of Information guided him toward the Middle East where the British army was about to capture Jerusalem.

There Thomas found a story with powerful emotional appeal for an American audience. The war in the Middle East, militarily only a sideshow, could be presented as a modern crusade for the liberation of the Holy Land and the emancipation of its Arab, Jewish, and Armenian communities. Thomas called Lawrence "Britain's modern Coeur de Lion."

Thomas and an American newsreel photographer, Harry Chase, sought out Lawrence and did stories about this new Richard the Lion-hearted. Chase's newsreel footage was a part of Thomas's lecture on the Middle Eastern campaign, which opened at New York's Century Theatre in March 1919. Its success inspired a British impresario, Percy Burton, to bring Thomas to London, where he opened at the Royal Opera House, Covent Garden.

Thomas had refined his presentation with the help of Dale Carnegie, who later wrote *How to Win Friends and Influence People*. It was now more an extravaganza than a lecture, complete with a theater set featuring moonlight on the Nile and pyramids in the background, the Dance of the Seven Veils, the muezzin's call to prayer (adapted and sung by Mrs. Thomas), slides, newsreel footage and Thomas's commentary, accompanied by music from the band of the Welsh Guards and clouds of eastern incense wafting from glowing braziers.

Chase had devised a projection technique that used three arc-light projectors simultaneously, and a fade and dissolve facility that heightened the drama of the presentation. Thomas began by saying, "Come with me to lands of history, mystery, and romance," and referred to Lawrence as "the uncrowned king of Arabia," who had been welcomed by the Arabs for delivering them from 400 years of oppression.

It was an enormous success, later toured the world, was seen by an estimated four million people and made Thomas—whom Lawrence referred to as "the American who made my vulgar reputation, a well-intentioned, intensely crude, and pushful fellow"—into a millionaire.

But there was more to the whole business than was realized at the time. The impresario Burton was encouraged to produce the show by the English-Speaking Union, of which Thomas was a member and whose committee included such notables as Winston Churchill and the newspaper proprietor Lord Northcliffe.

The union's aim was to emphasize the common heritage of Britain and the United States, to draw the two countries closer together and forge a common sense of future destiny. If Lawrence were portrayed as an old-style British hero and, more important, a representative of the new benevolent British imperialism, then American misgivings about Britain as a greedy, oppressive power in the Middle East might be dispelled.

According to Thomas, the Arabs did not regard the fall of the Turks and the arrival of the British as a simple exchange of one ruler for another but rather as a liberation, and they were delighted when Britain agreed to run their affairs for them.

Britain's aims went further. The United States should not leave the entire burden of running the region to Britain and France. It should accept the challenge of this new imperialism and take on its own responsibilities in the Middle East. At the Paris Peace Conference Lawrence himself suggested that the United States run Constantinople and Armenia as its own mandates. The Americans were more interested, however, in what was to become of Palestine.

The second force that helped frustrate Arab aspirations was Zionism. While the European powers had seen the war with Turkey as an opportunity to divide the Ottoman empire and thus extend their imperial ambitions in the Middle East, the Zionists quickly realized that the future of Palestine was now open and that they might be able to play a large part in its future.

THE BRITISH Zionists were led by Dr. Chaim Weizmann, a brilliant chemist who contributed to the war effort by discovering a new process for manufacturing acetone, a substance vital for TNT that was until then produced only in Germany. Weizmann saw a historic opening for Zionism and began to lobby influential British politicians.

He found support from Herbert Samuel, then under secretary at the Home Office, who put the Zionist case before the cabinet in a secret memorandum. He said that the Zionists would welcome an annexation of Palestine by Britain, which "would enable England to fulfill in yet another sphere her historic part as civilizer of the backward countries."

There was not much sympathy in the cabinet at first, but the Zionists did not let the matter lapse. Early in their talks with British politicians it became clear to them that the British government felt that only a British Palestine would be a reliable buffer for the Suez Canal. Weizmann therefore assured Britain that in exchange for its support, Zionists would work for the establishment of a British protectorate there. This suited Britain better than the agreement it had already made with France for an *international* administration for Palestine.

So on November 2, 1917, Foreign Secretary Arthur Balfour made his famous and deeply ambiguous declaration that Britain would "view with favor the establishment in Palestine of a national home for the Jewish people. . . ." *

---

* Editors' note: Balfour qualified his promise with the assurance that "nothing shall be done which may prejudice the civic and religious rights of the existing non-Jewish communities or the rights and political status enjoyed by Jews in any other country."

How did the pledge to the Zionists square with what had already been promised to the Arabs in return for their support in the war against the Turks?

THIS HAS been a matter of continuing controversy, but has never been satisfactorily resolved. The first agreement between the Arabs and the British was in correspondence between the British high commissioner in Egypt and King Hussein in Mecca. The Arabs say that these letters included Palestine in the area in which Britain promised to uphold Arab independence.

The Zionists deny this. The denial has also been the official British attitude, and it was endorsed by the Palestine Royal Commission report in 1937. But an Arab Bureau report, never rescinded or corrected, puts Palestine firmly in the area promised to the Arabs.

By the time of the peace conference, with a Zionist lobby led by Weizmann and Harvard Law School professor Felix Frankfurter (later a U.S. Supreme Court justice) actively working for a national home in Palestine, the Arabs realized that they had been outmaneuvered. President Wilson, trying to be fair, insisted that a commission be dispatched to find out the wishes of the people in the whole area.

Their report made blunt reading: While there could be mandates for Palestine, Syria, and Iraq, they should only be for a limited term—independence was to be granted as soon as possible. The idea of making Palestine into a Jewish commonwealth should be dropped. This suggestion that the Zionists should forget about Palestine must have seemed quite unrealistic—their aims were too close to realization for them to be abandoned—so it surprised only the Arabs when the report was ignored, even in Washington.

It took a further two years for the Allies to tidy up the arrangements they had made for the division of the Middle East. In April 1920, there was another conference, at San Remo, Italy, to ratify earlier agreements. The whole Arab rectangle lying between the Mediterranean and the Persian frontier, including Palestine, was placed under mandates allotted to suit the imperialist ambitions of Britain and France.

There was an outburst of bitter anger. The Arabs began raiding British establishments in Iraq and striking at the French in Syria. Both insurrections were ruthlessly put down. In Iraq the British army burnt any village from which an attack had been mounted, but the Iraqis were not deterred. Lawrence weighed in from Oxford, where he was now a fellow of All Souls College, suggesting with heavy irony that burning villages was not very efficient: "By gas attacks the whole population of offending districts could be wiped out neatly; and as a method of government it would be no more immoral than the present system."

The grim truth was that something along these lines was actually being considered. Churchill, then secretary of state for war and air, asked the chief of air staff, Sir Hugh Trenchard, if he would be prepared to take over control of Iraq because the army had estimated it would need 80,000 troops and £21.5 million a year, "which is considered to be more than the country is worth." Churchill suggested that if the RAF were to take on the job, "it would . . . entail the provision of some kind of asphyxiating bombs calculated to cause disablement of some kind but not death . . . for use in preliminary operations against turbulent tribes." In the end the air force stuck to conventional high-explosive bombs, a method Britain used to control the Middle East well into the 1950s.

ARAB NATIONALIST leaders waited for American protests at this suppression in Iraq and Syria but nothing happened. What the Arabs failed to see was that with the Zionists already in the ascendancy in Palestine, America had lost interest in the sordid struggle of imperial powers in the Middle East.

The humiliation suffered by those Arabs who had allied themselves with the imperial powers was encapsulated by the experiences of Faisal, the Arab leader Lawrence had "created" and then abandoned, the Arab he had chosen as military leader of the revolt, the man to whom he had conveyed all Britain's promises. When the French kicked Faisal out of Syria, an embarrassed delegation of British officials waited on him as he passed through Palestine. One described the incident: "We mounted him a guard of honor a hundred strong. He carried himself with the dignity and the noble resignation of Islam . . . though tears stood in his eyes and he was wounded to the soul. The Egyptian sultanate did not 'recognize' him, and at Quantara station, he awaited his train sitting on his luggage."

And where was Lawrence during all this? He was at his mother's home in Oxford undergoing a major crisis of conscience. He was depressed, and according to his mother, would sometimes sit between breakfast and lunch "in the same position, without moving, and with the same expression on his face." It seems reasonable to assume that Lawrence felt guilty over the betrayal of the Arabs, both on a personal and a national level.

This would explain why he jumped at the chance to join Churchill, who had by this time moved to the Colonial Office, and was determined to do something about the Middle East. Lawrence's first job was to make amends to Faisal by offering to make him king of Iraq.

The problem was that it was not clear that the Iraqis wanted Faisal. There were other popular claimants, including ibn Saud of Saudi Arabia, whom Churchill had rejected for fear that "he would plunge the whole country into religious pandemonium." Another candidate, the nationalist leader Sayid Taleb, gained enormous popular support after threatening to revolt if the British did not allow the Iraqis to choose their leader freely.

EVER RESOURCEFUL the British sabotaged Taleb's candidacy by arranging for an armored car to pick him up as he left the British high commissioner's house in Baghdad following afternoon tea. He was then whisked on board a British ship and sent for a long holiday in Ceylon. With Sayid Taleb out of the way, Faisal was elected king by a suspiciously large majority—96.8 percent.

Because the British desired a quiet, stable state in Jordan to protect Palestine, Faisal's brother Abdullah was made king and provided with money and troops in return for his promise to suppress local anti-French and anti-Zionist activity. Their father, Hussein, the sharif of Mecca, the man who had started the Arab revolt, was offered £100,000 a year not to make a nuisance of himself, and ibn Saud received the same amount (as the strictures of the cynical Cairo accord advised, "to pay one more than the other causes jealousy") to accept the whole settlement and not attack Hussein.

And that was that. Lawrence regarded this as redemption in full of Britain's promises to the Arabs. Unfortunately, the Arabs did not see it this way and have, in one way or another, been in revolt ever since.

In Iraq, Faisal managed to obtain some measure of independence by the time of his death in 1932. But British forces intervened again in 1942 to overthrow the pro-German nationalist government of Rashid Ali and restore the monarchy. Faisal's kingdom fell for the last time in 1958, a belated casualty of the Anglo-French invasion of Egypt two years earlier.

France hung on to Syria and Lebanon until 1946 before grudgingly evacuating its forces. In the same year Britain—then coming to terms with her diminished postwar status— gave up her claim on Jordan. Abdullah reigned until 1951 when he was shot dead while entering the mosque of El Aqsa in Jerusalem in the company of his grandson, the present King Hussein. The assassin was a follower of the ex-Mufti of Jerusalem, who had accused Abdullah of having betrayed the Arabs over Palestine.

In 1958 the American Sixth Fleet stood by to save Hussein from a repetition of the coup that had just ousted his cousin, Faisal II, in Iraq. Hussein and his kingdom, shorn of the West Bank, have survived—the lasting legacy of Lawrence.

IN PALESTINE, Jewish immigration increased rapidly in the 1930s as many fled from Hitler's Europe. This influx, in turn, led in 1936—less than a year after Lawrence's death—to an Arab revolt, which was crushed by the British

Army in 1938. Unable to cope with a Jewish revolt, Britain relinquished her mandate in 1947.* In 1948, the state of Israel was established, and immediately afterward the first Arab-Israeli war occurred.

The United States held aloof from the area until oil finally locked it in. There had been some prospecting on the Saudi's eastern seaboard since 1923, but the first swallow to herald Saudi Arabia's long summer of revenue from oil was the American Charles R. Crane, who in 1931 brought in a mining engineer, Karl Twitchell, to make some mineral and water surveys.

The following year Twitchell interested the Standard Oil Company of California (SOCAL) in exploring for oil in Saudi Arabia. SOCAL negotiated a deal using St. John Philby as an intermediary and achieved commercial production in March 1938. The United States now had a strategic interest in the region.

If the new crusaders defeat and occupy Iraq, what then? A United Nations mandate, something like that imposed on the country after the First World War, allowing the victorious army to remain in control of the conquered land? Perhaps a new "Faisal" inserted as token ruler of a reluctant population? And so a new cycle of anger, frustration and bloodshed will begin because 800 years after the Crusades there will still be foreigners in Arab lands.

And Lawrence himself? Everything after his experiences in the Middle East was an anticlimax for him. He wrote *Seven Pillars of Wisdom,* undoubtedly a masterpiece, but found little further in life that really gripped him. He was consumed with guilt over the way the Arabs had been treated, had a mental breakdown and embarked on a series of homosexual sadomasochistic experiences.

He changed his name, first to John Hume Ross when he joined the Royal Air Force, and later to Thomas Edward Shaw when he joined the tank corps. He eventually went back into the RAF again and, not long after retiring, crashed his motorcycle near his home in Dorset. Six days later, on May 19, 1935, his injuries proved fatal.

Lawrence's role in the Arab revolt and his deceit on behalf of Britain left him an emotionally damaged man. He was, as one sympathetic American biographer wrote, "a prince of our disorder." But the conclusion must be that the continuing tragic history of the Middle East is largely due to the likes of Lawrence, servants in the imperial mold.

An incident during the Cairo Conference in 1921 sums up the Arab attitude toward Western intervention in their affairs—one which may not have

---

* Editors' note: In November of 1947, the U.N. voted to partition Palestine into two states—one Jewish and one Arab—but the Arab states rejected the plan.

changed over the years. One day while Lawrence and Churchill were touring Palestine their party got caught up in an anti-Zionist riot. Lawrence, in his neat suit and Homburg hat, conducted Churchill through the crowd of gesticulating Arabs. "I say, Lawrence," Churchill offered, looking rather worried, "are these people dangerous? They don't seem too pleased to see us."

THE RISE OF SADDAM HUSSEIN

Judith Miller and Laurie Mylroie

Saddam Hussein loves *The Godfather*. It is his favorite movie, one he has seen many times. He is especially fascinated by Don Corleone, a poor boy made good, whose respect for family is exceeded only by his passion for power. The iron-willed character of the Don may perhaps be the most telling model for the enigmatic figure that rules Iraq. Both come from dirt-poor peasant villages; both sustain their authority by violence; and for both, family is key, the key to power. Family is everything, or "almost" everything, because Saddam, like the Godfather, ultimately trusts no one, not even his next of kin. For both, calculation and discipline, loyalty, and ruthlessness are the measure of a man's character.

There is, however, a difference. Where the Don was a private man, obsessed with secrecy, seeking always to conceal his crimes behind a veil of anonymity, Saddam is a public figure who usurped political power and seizes every opportunity to advertise his might in order to impress upon his countrymen that there is no alternative to his rule. To visit Iraq is to enter the land of Big Brother. Enormous portraits of Saddam Hussein, black-haired and mustachioed, full of power and a strange serenity, stare down all over Baghdad. His photograph is everywhere—even on the dials of gold wristwatches. In the land where the Sumerians invented writing, discourse has been degraded to a single ubiquitous image.

But perhaps this difference matters not at all. For both the Don and Saddam relish power and seek respect, the more so because each knows what it means to have none. Neither ever forgot any insult, however trivial or imagined, both secure in the knowledge that, as Mario Puzo observed of his fictional character, "in this world there comes a time when the most humble of men, if he keeps his eyes open, can take his revenge on the most powerful." And in this likeness there perhaps lies the key to understanding Saddam Hussein's ambition.

Saddam Hussein was born sixty-six years ago on April 28, 1937, to a miser-

---

Judith Miller is a veteran correspondent for *The New York Times* and coauthor, most recently, of *Germs: Biological Weapons and America's Secret War*. Laurie Mylroie is Adjunct Scholar at the American Enterprise Institute and author of *Study of Revenge: Saddam Hussein's Unfinished War Against Iraq*. In 1990, they coauthored the bestselling *Saddam Hussein and the Crisis in the Gulf*. This excerpt is adapted from chapters 3 and 4 of their book.

ably poor, landless peasant family in the village of al-Auja, near the town of Tikrit, on the Tigris River, a hundred miles north of Baghdad. (Although Muslims do not generally share the Western custom of celebrating birthdays, Saddam has made his a national holiday in Iraq.) The Arab town of Tikrit lies in the heart of the Sunni Muslim part of Iraq. But in Iraq, the Sunnis are a minority. More than half the country is Shiite, the Sunnis' historical and theological rivals. Tikrit had prospered in the nineteenth century, renowned for the manufacture of *kalaks*, round rafts made of inflated animal skins. But as the raft industry declined, so did the fortunes of the town. By the time Saddam was born, it had little to offer its inhabitants.

Communication with the outside world was difficult. While the Baghdad-Mosul railway ran through Tikrit, the town had but one paved road. Saddam's nearby village was even worse off. It had only dirt roads. Its people, including Saddam and his family, lived in huts made of mud and reeds and burned cow dung for fuel. No one—either in Tikrit or in al-Auja—had electricity or running water. The central government in Baghdad seemed far away, its authority limited to the presence of some local policemen.

Iraq was then a seething political cauldron, governed by a people who knew little of government. The Ottoman Turks had ruled Iraq for 500 years, before a brief decade of British rule. Britain's mandate over Iraq ended in 1932, only five years before Saddam was born. Within four years of Iraq's independence, hundreds of Assyrians, an ancient Christian people, would perish at the hands of the Iraqi army. Five years later, similar atrocities would be committed in Baghdad's ancient Jewish quarter. Between independence and Saddam's first breath of life, the Iraqi army had doubled in size. It saw itself as the embodiment of the new Iraqi state, "the profession of death" that would forge a nation out of the competing religious, tribal, and ethnic factions tearing at one another's throat. It was into this volatile world that Saddam Hussein was born.

Accounts of Saddam's early years are murky. Official hagiographies shed little light. The unsavory aspects of Saddam's harsh and brutal childhood are not something he wants known. It is usually said that Saddam's father, Hussein al-Majid, died either before Saddam's birth or when he was a few months old. But a private secretary of Saddam's, who later broke with him, has suggested that Saddam's father abandoned his wife and young children. Whatever the truth, after her husband was gone, Saddam's mother, Subha, was on her own until she met Ibrahim Hassan, a married man. Eventually she convinced him to get rid of his wife, and to marry her instead. By Muslim law, Ibrahim was permitted four wives, but Subha insisted on being the only one.

Saddam's stepfather was a crude and illiterate peasant who disliked his stepson and treated him abusively. Years later, Saddam would bitterly recall how his stepfather would drag him out of bed at dawn, barking, "Get up, you son of a whore, and look after the sheep." Ibrahim often fought with Subha over Saddam, complaining, "He is a son of a dog. I don't want him." Still, Ibrahim found some use for the boy, often sending Saddam to steal chickens and sheep, which he then resold. When Saddam's cousin, Adnan Khayrallah, who would become Iraq's defense minister, started to go to school, Saddam wanted to do the same. But Ibrahim saw no need to educate the boy. He wanted Saddam to stay home and take care of the sheep. Saddam finally won out. In 1947, at the age of ten, he began school.

He went to live with Adnan's father, Khayrallah Tulfah, his mother's brother, a schoolteacher in Baghdad. Several years before, Khayrallah had been cashiered from the Iraqi army for supporting a pro-Nazi coup in 1941, which the British suppressed, instilling in Khayrallah a deep and lasting hatred for Britain and for "imperialism." Whether Saddam's stepfather kicked him out of the house or whether he left at his own initiative for his uncle's home in Baghdad is unclear. What is certain is that Khayrallah Tulfah—who would later become mayor of Baghdad—would come to wield considerable influence over Saddam.

Having started elementary school when he went to live with Khayrallah, Saddam was sixteen when he finished intermediary school, roughly the equivalent of an American junior high school. Like his uncle, he wanted to become an army officer, but his poor grades kept him out of the prestigious Baghdad Military Academy. Of the generation of Arab leaders who took power in the military coups of the 1950s and 1960s, only Saddam Hussein had no army experience, though his official biography notes his love of guns starting at the age of ten. In 1976, he would correct the deficiency by getting himself appointed lieutenant general, a rank equal to chief of staff. When Saddam became president in 1979 he would promote himself to field marshal and would insist on personally directing the war against Iran.

Baghdad was utterly different from the world he had left behind in al-Auja. Yet Saddam still lived with Tikritis. Khayrallah's home was on the western bank of the Tigris, in the predominantly lower-class Tikriti district of al-Karkh. As in most Middle Eastern cities, peasants from the same region tended to cluster in certain neighborhoods when they moved to the city, giving each other support and maintaining their rural clan connections.

Times were unusually turbulent when Saddam was a student in Baghdad. In 1952, Lieutenant Colonel Gamal Abdel Nasser led a coup that toppled Egypt's monarchy. Though there had been considerable sympathy in the United States for the Egyptian officers, Nasser and the West were soon at odds. Nasser's purchase in 1955 of huge amounts of Soviet arms and his nationalization of the Suez Canal in 1956 led France, Britain, and Israel to attack Egypt that year. Most Egyptians—indeed, most Arabs— believed that Arab nationalism, through Nasser, won a tremendous victory when the invasion was halted, Israel forced to withdraw from the Sinai, and the canal returned to Egyptian control. That the United States was almost single-handedly responsible for that outcome did not reduce the tremendous popular enthusiasm for Nasser among the Arabs.

Saddam soon found himself swept up in a world of political intrigue whose seductions were far more compelling than the tedium of schoolwork. In 1956, Saddam participated in an abortive coup against the Baghdad monarchy. The next year, at the age of twenty, he joined the Baath party, one of several radical nationalist organizations that had spread throughout the Arab world. But the Baath in Iraq were a tiny and relatively powerless band of about 300 members in those days.

In 1958, a non-Baathist group of nationalist army officers, led by General Abdul Karim Qassim, succeeded in overthrowing King Faisal II. The fall of the monarchy intensified plotting among Iraq's rival dissident factions. A year after Qassim's coup, the Baath tried to seize power by machine-gunning Qassim's car in broad daylight. Saddam (whose name translates as "the one who confronts") was a member of the hit team. He had already proven his mettle, or in the jargon of the American underworld had "made his bones," by murdering a Communist supporter of Qassim in Takrit. The Communists were the Baath's fierce rivals—in fact, the man Saddam killed was his brother-in-law. There had been a dispute in the family over politics, and his uncle Khayrallah had incited Saddam to murder him. Although Saddam and Khayrallah were arrested, they were soon released. In the anarchic confusion of Baghdad after the monarchy's fall, political crimes were common and often unpunished.

Iraqi propaganda embellishes Saddam's role in the attempt on Qassim's life, portraying him as a bold and heroic figure. He is said to have been seriously wounded in the attack. Bleeding profusely, he orders a comrade to dig a bullet out of his leg with a razor blade, an operation so painful it causes him to faint. He then disguises himself as a Bedouin tribesman, swims across the Tigris River, steals a donkey, and flees to safety across the desert to Syria.

The truth is less glamorous. Iraqi sources present at the time insist that Saddam's role in the failed assassination attempt was minor, that he was only lightly wounded, and that the wound was inadvertently inflicted by his own comrades. A sympathetic doctor treated Saddam and several others much more seriously hurt at a party safe house. Saddam would later have the opportunity to reward him for his help. When the Baath party finally succeeded in taking power in 1968, the doctor was made dean of the Medical College of Baghdad University, a post he held until he broke with Saddam in 1979.

From Syria, Saddam went to Cairo, where he would spend the next four years. The stay in Egypt was to be his only extended experience in another country. Supported by an Egyptian government stipend, he resumed his political activities, finally finishing high school at the age of twenty-four. In Cairo he was arrested twice, and both times quickly released. The first arrest occurred after he threatened to kill a fellow Iraqi over political differences. He was arrested again when he chased a fellow Baathist student through the streets of Cairo with a knife. The student was later to serve as Jordan's information minister.

Saddam entered Cairo University's Faculty of Law in 1961. He eventually received his law degree not in Cairo, but in Baghdad in 1970, after he became the number two man in the regime. It was an honorary degree.

While in Cairo, Saddam married his uncle Khayrallah's daughter, Sajida, in 1963. His studies in Egypt ended abruptly in February when Baathist army officers and a group of Arab nationalist officers together succeeded in ousting and killing General Qassim, a figure of considerable popularity, particularly among the poor of Iraq. Of Qassim, Hanna Batatu, the author of an authoritative history of Iraq, has written: "The people had more genuine affection for him than for any other ruler in the modern history of Iraq."

Many people refused to believe that Qassim was dead. It was rumored that he had gone into hiding and would soon surface. The Baathists found a macabre way to demonstrate Qassim's mortality. They displayed his bullet-riddled body on television, night after night. As Samir al-Khalil,* in his excellent book *Republic of Fear,* tells it: "The body was propped upon a chair in the studio. A soldier sauntered around, handling its parts. The camera would cut to scenes of devastation at the Ministry of Defense where Qassim had made his last stand. There, on location, it lingered on the mutilated corpses of Qassim's entourage (al-Mahdawi, Wasfi Taher, and others). Back to the studio and close-ups now of the entry and exit points of each bullet hole. The whole macabre sequence closes with a scene that must forever remain etched on the memory of all those who saw it: the soldier grabbed the lolling head by the hair, came right up close, and spat full face into it."

Saddam was elated. He hurried back to Baghdad to assume his part in the revolution. He was twenty-six years old.

---

* Editors' note: Samir al-Khalil is the former pseudonym for the Iraqi opposition activist Kanan Makiya, who has two articles in this reader.

Saddam quickly found his place in the new regime. He became an interrogator and torturer in the Qasr-al-Nihayyah, or "Palace of the End," so called because it was where King Faisal and his family were gunned down in 1958. Under the Baath the palace was used as a torture chamber.

Few in the West are aware of Saddam's activities there. But an Iraqi arrested and accused of plotting against the Baath has told of his own torture at the palace by Saddam himself: "My arms and legs were bound by rope. I was hung on the rope to a hook on the ceiling and I was repeatedly beaten with rubber hoses filled with stones." He managed to survive his ordeal; others were not so lucky. When the Baath, riven by internal splits, was ousted nine months later in November 1963 by the army, a grisly discovery was made. "In the cellars of al-Nihayyah Palace," according to Hanna Batatu, whose account is based on official government sources, "were found all sorts of loathsome instruments of torture, including electric wires with pincers, pointed iron stakes on which prisoners were made to sit, and a machine which still bore traces of chopped-off fingers. Small heaps of blooded clothing were scattered about, and there were pools on the floor and stains over the walls."

During the party split in 1963, Saddam had supported Michel Aflaq, a French-educated Syrian, the party's leading ideologue and co-founder of the party. Saddam was rewarded the next year when Aflaq sponsored him for a position in the Baath regional command, the party's highest decision-making body in Iraq. With this appointment, Saddam began his rapid ascent within the party.

His growing prominence was also due to the support of his older cousin, General Ahmad Hassan al-Bakr, the party's most respected military figure and a member of the party from its earliest days. It is said that Saddam's wife helped to cement Saddam's relations with Bakr by persuading Bakr's son to marry her sister, and by promoting the marriage of two of Bakr's daughters to two of her brothers. The party's affairs were rapidly becoming a family business. In 1965, Bakr became secretary-general of the party. The next year, Saddam was made deputy secretary-general.

During the period of his initial rise in the party, Saddam spent a brief interlude in prison, from October 1964 to his escape from jail sometime in 1966. There, as Saddam later recounted, in the idleness of prison life he reflected on the mistakes that had led to the party's split and its fall from power. He became convinced that the "Revolution of 1963" was stolen by a "rightist military aristocracy" in alliance with renegade elements of the Baath party. Divisions within the party, which had less than 1,000 full members at that time, had to end. Unity was essential for power, even if it had to be purchased by purge and blood. He determined to build a security force within the party, to create cells of loyalty which answered to no one but himself, to ensure that victory once won would be kept.

Upon his escape from prison, Saddam quickly set about building the party's internal security apparatus, the Jihaz Haneen, or "instrument of yearning." Those deemed "enemies of the party" were to be killed; unfriendly factions intimidated. Saddam's reputation as an architect of terror grew.

Two years later, on July 30, 1968, Saddam and his Baathist comrades succeeded in seizing and holding state power. Bakr became president and commander in chief in addition to his duties as secretary-general of the Baath party and the chairman of its Revolutionary Command Council. Saddam was made deputy chairman of the council, in charge of internal security. He quickly moved to strengthen control and expand his base within the party. The security services graduated hundreds of Saddam's men from their secret training schools, among them his half brothers, Barzan, Sabawi, and Wathban; another graduate, his cousin Ali Hassan al-Majid, would earn notoriety years later for his genocidal suppression of the Kurds during the Iran-Iraq war and his leading role in the invasion of Kuwait; another graduate was Arshad Yassin, his cousin and brother-in-law, whom the world would come to know as the bodyguard who repeatedly stroked the head of Stuart Lockwood, the young British "guest," as Saddam tried to get him to talk about milk and cornflakes.

Saddam was thirty-one. His penchant for asserting his authority by title— today he holds six—was evident even then. He insisted on being called "Mr. Deputy." No one else in Iraq was Mr. Deputy. It was Saddam's title, his alone. Although he would remain Mr. Deputy for a decade, he was increasingly regarded as the regime's real strongman.

The hallmarks of the new regime soon became apparent. Barely three months after the coup, the regime announced on October 9, 1968, that it had smashed a major Zionist spy ring. Fifth columnists were denounced before crowds of tens of thousands. On January 5, 1969, seventeen "spies" went on trial. Fourteen were hung, eleven of whom were Jewish, their bodies left to dangle before crowds of hundreds of thousands in Baghdad's Liberation Square. Even the Egyptian newspaper *al-Ahram* condemned the spectacle: "The hanging of fourteen people in the public square is certainly not a heartwarming sight, nor is it the occasion for organizing a festival." Baghdad radio scoffed at the international condemnation, of which there was shockingly little, by declaring, "We hanged spies, but the Jews crucified Christ." Over the next year and a half, a tapestry of alleged treason was unraveled, providing a steady spectacle of denunciation and execution. The victims were no longer primarily Jews. Very soon they were mostly Muslims. The Jews had been but a stepping-stone to the regime's real target, its political rivals. The Baath began their rule with an inauguration of blood.

Saad al-Din Ibrahim, a respected Egyptian scholar, was later to call such regimes "new monarchies in republican garb." Disillusioned with what he regarded as the failure of the new breed of "revolutionary leaders" to deliver on the radical promises they had made for transforming Arab society when they seized power, Ibrahim concluded: "Despite the presence of a political party, popular committees, and the president's claim that he is one of the people . . . the ruler in his heart of hearts does not trust to any of this nor to his fellow strugglers of all those years. The only people he can trust are first, the members of his family; second, the tribe; third, the sect, and so we have arrived at the neomonarchies in the Arab nation.

"The matter is not restricted to the appointment of relatives in key positions, but to how those relatives commit all sorts of transgressions, legal, financial, and moral without accounting, as if the country were a private estate to do what they like."

From the beginning Saddam's base was the security services. Through them he controlled the party. Saddam established the financial autonomy of his power base early on, in an innovative way. Although Islam forbids gambling, horse racing had been a popular sport under the monarchy. Qassim had banned horse races; Saddam reintroduced them. He used the funds that betting generated to provide an unfettered, independent source of revenue. After 1973, when the price of oil quadrupled, Saddam's resources rose accordingly. He began to stash away considerable sums for the party and security services, often in accounts outside the country, which are today frozen because of international sanctions imposed in response to the invasion of Kuwait.

If Bakr continued to live modestly after 1968, Saddam and his associates were bent on reversing a lifetime of personal indignities, real and imagined. He used his new political power to acquire the social and economic standing he had long coveted. Years of struggle and deprivation filled him with a measure of greed far greater than those whom he had usurped. It made him far more ruthless in his determination to hold on to power and to break all who stood in his way or who might one day challenge his rule.

NO EPISODE better reveals the essence of Saddam's regime than the baptism of blood that accompanied his ascension to absolute power in July 1979. For eleven years Saddam had waited, working in apparent harmony with his older cousin, head of the Baath party, and president of the republic, Ahmad Hassan al-Bakr. For years Saddam had worked to build a loyal and ruthless secret police apparatus. On the surface, all was well. Behind the scenes, trouble was brewing for Saddam.

The triumph of the Ayatollah Ruhollah Khomeini over the shah of Iran in January 1979 had aroused Iraq's Shiites, politically powerless, although they comprised fifty-five percent of the population. Deadly riots had erupted in a huge Shiite slum in east Baghdad, after the government had arrested the Shiites' foremost religious leader. The Baath party organization had collapsed in that sector of the city. The disturbances were so serious that Bakr concluded that it would be unwise to defy Shiite opinion within the party. But Saddam opposed any concessions. The party's Shiites, he felt, had failed to control their co-religionists. He suspected them of leniency toward the rioters, and he felt they must be purged and punished. Shiites within the party, who had been associated with Saddam, began to gather around Bakr. They were joined by some non-Shiites and army officers. They began to cast about for a way to check Saddam.

Ironically, Saddam himself had provided them a way. In the fall of 1978, Iraq and Syria, ruled by murderously rival Baath parties, suddenly announced that they would unite. Saddam was the architect of that policy. He wanted the Arab states to break their ties with Egypt, ostensibly to punish Cairo for the peace treaty it was about to sign with Israel. If he could force the Arabs to ostracize Egypt, the most important and populous Arab state, he could open the way for Iraq's dominance of the Arab world. Saddam succeeded, at least in his first step. At the November 1978 Arab summit in Baghdad, Saddam threatened to attack Kuwait, while Syrian president Hafez al-Assad warned the Saudis, "I will transfer the battle to your bedrooms." The Arab states agreed to break all ties with Egypt.

Unity with Syria, however, threatened to undermine Saddam within Iraq. It soon became apparent that Bakr could become president of a Syrian-Iraqi federation, Assad could be vice president, and Saddam would be number three. His rivals urged unity with Syria as a way of blunting his ambitions, while Saddam became increasingly apprehensive that they might succeed.

While Saddam saw the danger to himself in the proposed union, the Takritis saw their monopoly of power threatened, along with their immense privileges. Saddam decided to press the sixty-four-year-old Bakr to resign so that he could become president and leaned heavily on the family to support him. According to Iraqi sources, Khayrallah Tulfah, backed by his son Adnan, urged Bakr to step down for the good of the clan. Reluctantly, Bakr came to agree, although not before sending Assad a secret request to hasten union negotiations because "there is a current here which is anxious to kill the union in the bud before it bears fruit," according to British journalist Patrick Seale.

On July 16, 1979, President Bakr's resignation was announced, officially for reasons of health. Saddam Hussein was named president, as well as secretary-general of the Iraqi Baath party, commander in chief, head of the government, and chairman of the Revolutionary Command Council.

Saddam had succeeded in carrying out his putsch. On July 22 he staged an astonishing spectacle to inaugurate his presidency when he convened a top-level party meeting of some 1,000 party cadres. This meeting was recorded and the videotape distributed to the party. A few minutes of that tape have appeared on American television and it has been briefly described elsewhere, but no full account of that extraordinary meeting has been published before. The following account is based on an audiotape made available to the authors and the testimony of an individual who has seen the video.

The meeting begins with Muhyi Abdul Hussein al-Mashhadi, secretary of the Revolutionary Command Council and a Shiite party member for over twenty years, reading a fabricated confession detailing his participation in a supposed Syrian-backed conspiracy. Muhyi reads hurriedly, with the eager tone of a man who believes that his cooperation will win him a reprieve. (It did not.) Then Saddam, after a long, rambling statement about traitors and party loyalty, announces: "The people whose names I am going to read out should repeat the slogan of the party and leave the hall." He begins to read, stopping occasionally to light and relight his cigar. At one point he pronounces a first name, "Ghanim," but then changes his mind and goes on to the next name.

After Saddam finishes reading the list of the condemned, the remaining members of the audience begin to shout, "Long live Saddam," and "Let me die! Long live the father of Uday [Saddam's eldest son]." The cries are prolonged and hysterical. When the shouting dies down, Saddam begins to speak, but stops suddenly to retrieve a handkerchief. Tears stream down his face. As he dabs his eyes with the handkerchief, the assembly breaks into loud sobbing.

Recovering himself, Saddam speaks: "I'm sure many of our comrades have things to say, so let us discuss them." Party members call for a wider purge. One man rises, and says, "Saddam Hussein is too lenient. There has been a problem in the party for a long time. . . . There is a line between doubt and terror, and unbalanced democracy. The problem of too much leniency needs to be addressed by the party." Then Saddam's cousin, Ali Hassan al-Majid, declares: "Everything that you did in the past was good and everything that you will do in the future is good. I say this from my faith in the party and your leadership." After more appeals from the party faithful to search out traitors, Saddam brings the discussion to a close. More than twenty men, some of the most prominent in Iraq, have been taken from the hall. Saddam concludes,

"We don't need Stalinist methods to deal with traitors here. We need Baathist methods." The audience erupts into tumultuous applause.

In the days following, Saddam obliges senior party members and government ministers to join him in personally executing the most senior of their former comrades. The murdered include Mohammed Mahjoub, a member of the ruling Revolutionary Command Council; Mohammed Ayesh, head of the labor unions, and Biden Fadhel, his deputy; Ghanim Abdul Jalil, a Shiite member of the council and once a close associate of Saddam's; and Talib al-Suweleh, a Jordanian. Saddam's two most powerful opponents were dispatched before the July 22 meeting took place: General Walid Mahmoud Sirat, a senior army officer and the core of the opposition to Saddam, was tortured and his body mutilated; Adnan Hamdani, deputy prime minister, who had been in Syria on government business, was taken from the airport on his return and promptly murdered. Some sources believe that as many as 500 people may have been executed secretly in Saddam's night of the long knives. The true figure may never be known.

The savagery of Saddam's victory was meant to make him seem invincible. His rivals had been smashed; his primacy as absolute leader secured. He had replaced the state with the party, and now the party with himself, the giver of life and death. The terror that was his to dispense would make people fearful, but it would also inspire awe, and in a few, the appearance of mercy would even evoke gratitude. Saddam had made good his promise of 1971 when he had declared that "with our party methods, there is no chance for anyone who disagrees with us to jump on a couple of tanks and overthrow the government." From 1920 until 1979, Iraq had experienced thirteen coups d'état. Saddam was determined that his would be the last.

The key to understanding Saddam's rule, in the opinion of Samir al-Khalil, author of *Republic of Fear,* lies in the sophisticated way the regime has implicated ordinary people in the violence of the party by absorbing them into the repressive organs of the state. As Khalil writes: "Success is achieved by the degree to which society is prepared to police itself. Who is an informer? In Baathist Iraq the answer is anybody." A European diplomat stationed in Baghdad once told a reporter from *The New York Times* that "there is a feeling that at least three million Iraqis are watching the eleven million others."

His assessment may not be exaggerated. The Ministry of Interior is the largest of twenty-three government ministries. Khalil estimates that "the combined numbers of police and militia . . . greatly exceed the size of the standing army, and [are] in absolute terms twice as large as anything experienced in Iran under the shah." And this in a nation whose population is just under one-third the size of Iran's.

In 1984, about 25,000 people were full members of the Baath party; another 1.5 million Iraqis were sympathizers or supporters. The former are generally prepared to embrace the party line; the latter are often in the party for some peripheral reason. Party membership may be a requirement for their jobs. However lukewarm their attachment to the party, and it is for many of these, they are still part of the system, obliged to attend the weekly party meetings. If one multiplies each member by four or five dependents, the Baath can be said to have implicated slightly under half the entire population. About thirty percent of the eligible population is employed by the government. If one includes the army and militia, the figure jumps to fifty percent of the urban work force—this in a society in which sixty-five percent of its citizens now live in urban areas. For all practical purposes, state and party are synonymous.

THE INQUISITION Saddam has loosed on his people is perhaps difficult to understand. After all, with Iraq's immense oil wealth, why squander the nation's youth, its resources, and its future in a self-inflicted bloodletting extreme even by the standards of the Middle East? There is something elemental in Saddam's behavior. Robert Conquest, the author of *The Great Terror,* the classic work on Stalin's Gulag, has perhaps described one part of the answer: "One does not establish a dictatorship in order to safeguard a revolution; one makes the revolution in order to establish the dictatorship. The object of persecution is persecution. The object of torture is torture. The object of power is power."

WHAT WASHINGTON GAVE
SADDAM FOR CHRISTMAS

Murray Waas

The Reagan administration, in apparent violation of federal law, engaged in a massive effort to supply arms and military supplies to the regime of Saddam Hussein during the Iran-Iraq war. Some of these efforts to supply arms to Iraq appear not only to have violated federal law but in addition, a U.S. arms embargo then in effect against Iraq. The arms shipments were also clearly at odds with the Reagan administration's stated policy of maintaining strict U.S. neutrality in the Iran-Iraq war. And, in the light of the current conflict, they were certainly wrong-headed. Some of these American weapons were made available to Iraq through third countries that, with secret U.S. approval, would simply transfer the arms to then-embargoed Iraq, according to classified documents and sources close to the program.

There is no evidence that President George Bush—then serving as vice president—knew of the covert efforts to arm Saddam Hussein. But several sources, including senior White House officials, say Bush was a key behind-the-scenes proponent in the Reagan administration of a broader policy that urged tilting toward Iraq during the war. Bush and other White House insiders feared a military victory by the Ayatollah Khomeini, and they came to see Saddam as a bulwark against the fundamentalist Islamic fervor Khomeini was spreading throughout the Mideast. After he was elected president, Bush pursued this policy even further, attempting to develop closer business, diplomatic, and intelligence ties between Iraq and the United States.

The secret history of U.S. government approval of potentially illegal arms sales to Saddam Hussein is the story of how the Reagan and Bush administrations aided and abetted the Iraqi regime, allowing Saddam Hussein to build up the fourth-largest military arsenal in the world. It is the story of how two American presidencies assisted Saddam in obtaining chemical and biological weapons and the means of delivering them, threatening entire cities.

And it is the story of how, as the Reagan and Bush administrations carried

Murray Waas is a veteran freelance writer whose work has appeared in *The Village Voice, The New Yorker, Salon.com, Harper's,* and *The Nation.* This article originally appeared, in slightly longer form, in the December 18, 1990, issue of *The Village Voice.*

out their ill-conceived policy of tilting toward Iraq, there was no lack of American citizens willing to profit from it. Major U.S.-based corporations such as AT&T, United Technologies, General Motors, and Philip Morris were only too glad to explore expanded trade with Saddam Hussein—as long as he paid his bills on time.

AMERICA'S EFFORTS to secretly arm Saddam Hussein began in the early years of the first term of the Reagan administration. In March of 1982, reports began filtering back to the State Department from the U.S. embassy in Amman that Jordan's King Hussein was pressing for the U.S. to militarily assist Iraq. Iraq was suffering serious reverses in its war with Iran: The Ayatollah's forces had leveled many of Iraq's major oil facilities and were laying siege to Basra, Iraq's second-largest city and only port. King Hussein urged that the U.S. find some way to help arm Iraq in order to prevent a total victory by Iran.

Shortly thereafter William Eagleton, then the U.S. chargé d'affaires in Baghdad and the senior U.S. diplomat in Iraq, recommended to his superiors that the Reagan administration reverse its policy and allow shipments of U.S. arms to Iraq through third countries. Officials throughout the Reagan administration favoring the Iraqi tilt supported the recommendation.

To carry out Eagleton's plan, the U.S. would have to lift its arms embargo against Iraq, something Congress, outraged by Saddam's record on human rights and terrorism, certainly would never allow. A more likely option was to arm Iraq secretly, without lifting the embargo—but this, too, had its drawbacks, chief among them the Arms Export Control Act, which makes it illegal to transfer U.S. arms through third countries to regimes officially prohibited from receiving them. Countries that import arms from the U.S. pledge before any sale is made that they will not transfer the arms to another country without official, written approval from the U.S. government. The law also makes it a crime for U.S. citizens—including government officials—to arrange arms sales to a third country for the purpose of transferring them to a prohibited country.

Still, Eagleton pressed his case, stopping short of advocating deliberately breaking the law. In October 1983, Eagleton cabled his superiors, recommending: "We can selectively lift restrictions on third party transfers of U.S. licensed military equipment to Iraq." Later, in the same highly classified cable, he made the suggestion that "We go ahead and we do it through Egypt."

High-level U.S. intelligence sources say that the Reagan administration shortly thereafter adapted the Eagleton scenario, sending arms through third party countries, despite the fact that some of the transactions appear on their face to violate the Arms Export Control Act.

These sources say that U.S. arms shipments were made regularly to Jordan, Egypt, and Kuwait—with advance White House knowledge and approval of their transshipment to Iraq. Like the arms-for-hostages deal with Iran engineered by the Reagan administration, these third country shipments while a congressional arms embargo was in effect were apparently against the law. Among the weapons made available to Saddam, with White House approval, were top-of-the-line HAWK anti-aircraft missiles, originally sent to Jordan's King Hussein and quietly passed along to Iraq.

SADDAM'S MILITARY machine is partly a creation of the Western powers. Margaret Thatcher, perhaps the most bellicose Western leader, allowed British arms concerns to sell billions of dollars worth of tanks, missile parts, and artillery to Iraq. The French have sold Saddam Mirage fighter jets and Exocet missiles (like the one that took the lives of thirty-seven sailors aboard the U.S.S. *Stark* during the Iran-Iraq war). The West Germans have been the chief supplier to six Iraqi plants producing nerve and mustard gases.

The U.S. had an arms embargo against Iraq all during this time, making direct American sales illegal. But after the Reagan administration decided to tilt toward Iraq, the arms embargo had little effect. Besides making their own sales via Jordan, Kuwait, and Egypt, the Americans simply encouraged other nations to send arms to Saddam in their place.

"The billions upon billions of dollars of shipments from Europe would not have been possible without the approval and acquiescence of the Reagan administration," recalls a former high-level intelligence official.

One good example of the sort of arms transfer encouraged by the Americans was a $1.4 billion sale—brokered by Miami-based arms-dealer Sarkis Soghanalian, and perhaps the largest legal deal of his career—of howitzers to Iraq by the French government. U.S. intelligence sources say the Iraqis first approached the Reagan administration about purchasing long-range 175 mm artillery from the U.S. directly. But because of the arms embargo, the White House instead encouraged the Iraqis to ask private arms traffickers—like Sarkis Soghanalian—to make the deal happen.

Soghanalian was put in charge of obtaining the artillery by the Iraqis in 1981, and he approached several European governments before French President François Mitterrand agreed to sell 155 mm howitzers to Iraq. The Reagan administration, through a diplomatic back channel, encouraged the French to finalize the sale. The French agreed to supply the howitzers, Soghanalian said in a sworn deposition, only if they could keep their role secret. The Iranian government was holding several French hostages, and France didn't want to antagonize the Ayatollah. Soghanalian agreed to mask the real source of the arms through a series of complicated transactions known to those involved by the codeword "Vulcan."

Two reliable law enforcement officials who have been able to review highly classified U.S. intelligence files on the French howitzer sale—including documents from the CIA, the National Security Agency, the Pentagon, and the State Department—say those files show that the U.S. intelligence agencies had extensive prior knowledge of and monitored the massive howitzer sale to Iraq. It is also clear from those same files that the Reagan administration did nothing to discourage the sales.

WHILE THE Reagan administration was busy encouraging its European allies to ship arms to Iraq, it was simultaneously engaging in a high-level campaign to stop those same countries from arming its opponent, Iran. The effort was codenamed "Operation Staunch." Some officials associated with Operation Staunch say that, without it, Iran might have prevailed in the Iran-Iraq war.

The U.S. government official in charge of the operation was Richard Fairbanks. A longtime diplomat who served as assistant secretary of state before being named President Reagan's special envoy to the Middle East in 1982, Fairbanks had played key roles in attempts to resolve the civil war in Lebanon and build on the Camp David accords.

Fairbanks quietly made several trips to European capitals, with letters of introduction from Reagan himself, appealing to high-level officials to stop selling arms to the Khomeini regime. He had some major successes: South Korea, Italy, Portugal, Spain, and Argentina all canceled plans to sell arms to Iran after talking with Fairbanks.

When Fairbanks left the State Department in the fall of 1985, he called Operation Staunch a success: "It might not have been a 100 percent success," he told an interviewer, "but we definitely managed to stop most major weapons systems from reaching Iran from U.S. allies. By the time I returned to private law practice in September 1985, Iran's major suppliers were almost all Soviet bloc countries."

Within months of formulating and executing the U.S. tilt to Iraq as a senior State Department official, Fairbanks went to work as a paid lobbyist and adviser to the Iraqi government. Fairbanks's new employer was the Washington law firm of Paul, Hastings, Janofsky, and Walker.

According to the firm's registration form as a foreign agent, it had been retained by the Iraqi government "to provide counseling and analysis relevant to the United States' policies of interest to the government of Iraq and . . . to assist in arranging and preparing for meetings with United States elected officials." The registration statement does not list who those elected officials might have been—although the law clearly states all such contacts must be publicly disclosed.

The Justice Department record does disclose, however, that the regime of Saddam Hussein paid Fairbanks and his firm some $334,885 between early 1986 and March 1990. The records do not indicate further activities after that date. Among other things, Fairbanks provided Saddam with public relations advice free of charge in June 1987, after the Iraqis accidentally hit the U.S.S. *Stark* with a French-made Exocet missile, killing thirty-seven American sailors.

Assisting Fairbanks with the Iraqi account at the law firm was another former State Department official, James Plack. While Plack was former deputy assistant secretary of state for Near Eastern affairs, he had been an architect of the policy to tilt toward Iraq.

At the same time that Fairbanks was on the Iraqi payroll, he also served as a key foreign policy adviser to the presidential campaign of George Bush. Throughout 1988, Fairbanks was co-chairman of a group of Middle East experts who advised Bush during the campaign.

One member of the advisory group, who requested that his name not be used, said he recalls Fairbanks arguing during one panel discussion that, should Bush be elected president, "he should stay the course of the Reagan administration and work to develop stronger relations with Iraq." The panel member says he was unaware that Fairbanks was a paid lobbyist for the Iraqi government at the time. "I don't think anyone else on the panel was any more aware than I was."

After the election, Bush rewarded Fairbanks—then still on the Iraqi payroll—with an appointment as a member of the U.S. Trade Representative's Investment Policy Advisory Committee Group. At first glance, that is only a part-time position on a panel of private citizens who advise the president on trade policy; but members of the panel are routinely provided access to highly classified intelligence information, and are required to have security clearances.

MEANWHILE, THE Iraqis were also able to receive hundreds of millions of dollars of military equipment from the U.S. directly, using a loophole in the arms embargo. Between 1985 and 1990, the Iraqis purchased from the U.S. some $782 million in "dual use" goods—matériel, ostensibly intended for civilian uses, that has military applications as well. Many of the sales were allowed by the Reagan and Bush administrations over the objections of the Pentagon, which argued they would inevitably be used for military purposes.

Commerce Department records indicate that the agency approved 273 transfer licenses for "dual use" matériel sent to Iraq between 1985 and 1990. In 1982, for example, Iraq purchased sixty Hughes Helicopters—a civilian version of the familiar, dragonfly-like chopper widely used in Vietnam by the U.S. Army—that the Iraqi government promised would only be used for civilian transport. However, an eyewitness account appearing in *Aviation Week and Space Technology* reported that at least thirty of the helicopters were being used to train military pilots. The Reagan administration did not even mount a diplomatic protest.

Sources in the defense industry familiar with the sale say that Soghanalian brokered the deal for Hughes—and received a large commission.

Despite the broken pledge of two years earlier, in 1984 the State Department approved an additional sale of forty-five Bell 214 helicopters to the Hussein regime. The Bell 214 can be converted to military purposes at a minimal cost. Iraq pledged that the helicopters would only be used for "recreation"; Soghanalian again served as the broker.

"It is beyond belief that Iraq . . . would purchase forty-five helicopters at $5 million apiece simply to transport civilian VIPs," Representative Howard Berman wrote then secretary of state George Shultz in November 1984. "The helicopter which Iraq wishes to purchase, the 214ST, was originally designed for military purposes."

The State Department wrote back, arguing, "We believe that increased American penetration of the extremely competitive civilian aircraft market would serve the United States' interests by improving our balance of trade and lessening unemployment in the aircraft industry."

Sure enough, evidence surfaced that the helicopters were being used for military purposes. In October 1988, a *Washington Post* reporter given a tour by Iraqi authorities of the Iranian front witnessed Iraqi military pilots flying the Bell 214s. He also observed other Bells lined up at three Iraqi military air bases alongside Soviet MIGs.

The Reagan administration once again did not muster a word of protest with the Iraqi government. Privately, State Department officials defended the Iraqis, claiming the planes were only being used to transport military officials to the front. Only if they had been used in combat, the Iraqis said, would it be a violation.

Things did not improve once George Bush took office—in fact, the matériel with potential military applications sold to Iraq actually shifted into a far more alarming area—the prerequisites of weapons of mass destruction. According to confidential Pentagon documents, between 1985 and 1990 the Commerce Department ignored explicit Pentagon objections and approved more than a dozen exports to Iraq—including precursor chemicals necessary for the manufacture of nerve gas—that would be used by Saddam Hussein to enhance his ability to make chemical and nuclear war.

Stephen Bryen, who as the Pentagon's under secretary of defense for trade security policy from 1985 to 1988 oversaw the exports for the Defense Department, said: "It was routine for our recommendations to be ignored. They disregarded five years of thorough technical and intelligence evaluations by Defense and CIA. The key to all this I believe is the businessmen and corporations who were making huge profits from all this."

Once you've made a mass-death weapon, you need some means of delivering it to your target. On February 23, 1990, the Commerce Department allowed Internal Imaging Systems, a California company, to ship computer and related equipment to Iraq that is designed for infrared imaging enhancement. The export license was allowed despite the fact that three years earlier, CIA technical evaluations determined that the imaging system could be used for near real-time tracking of missiles.

Then the Pentagon attempted to halve the size of a shipment by Electronic Associates, a New Jersey firm that wanted to send $449,000 worth of hybrid analog computer systems used in missile wind-tunnel experiments. Indeed, the Pentagon uses the same type of system at its White Sands missile range in New Mexico.

A White House meeting was scheduled to discuss the matter. But unknown to these Pentagon officials, the hardware had already been sent to Iraq seven months earlier—with Commerce Department approval.

Only two days before the Iraqi invasion of Kuwait, a Pennsylvania firm, Homestead Engineering, obtained a Commerce Department license to export forges and computer equipment that can be used in the manufacture of 16-inch gun barrels. Such guns could deliver huge payloads to targets hundreds of miles away.

If the Iran-Iraq war served as the pretext for the U.S. tilt toward Iraq, its end did not lead the Reagan and Bush administrations to rethink the policy. The U.S. backing of Saddam, including the covert arms sales, did not moderate the dictator's behavior; it only seemed to encourage more brutality.

On August 20, 1988, the day the Iran-Iraq cease-fire went into effect, Saddam Hussein did not see a need to end the terror. Now he could mass his military forces against the troublesome Kurdish population in northern Iraq. Only five days later, Iraqi warplanes and helicopters dropped chemical weapons on villages throughout Iraqi Kurdistan.

"As described by the villagers, the bombs that fell on the morning of August 25 did not produce a large explosion," a report by the Senate Foreign Relations Committee would later relate. "Only a weak sound could be heard and then a yellowish cloud spread out from the center of the explosion and became a thin mist. The air became filled with a mixture of smells—'bad garlic,' 'rotten onions,' and 'bad apples.'

"Those who were very close to the bombs died almost instantly. Those who did not die instantly found it difficult to breathe and began to vomit. The gas stung their eyes, skin and lungs . . . Many suffered temporary blindness. Those who could not run from the growing smell, mostly the very old, the very young, died.

"The survivors who saw the dead reported that blood could be seen trickling out of the mouths of some of the bodies. A yellowish fluid could also be seen oozing out the noses and mouths of some of the dead." Ahmad Mohammed, a Kurd, recalled that day. "My mother and father were burnt; they just died and turned black."

Bashir Shemessidin testified: "In our village, 200 to 300 people died. All the animals and birds died. All the trees dried up. It smelled like something burned. The whole world turned yellow."

In the first week of September, Iraqi Minister of State Saadoun Hammadi, a member of Saddam Hussein's inner circle, came to Washington to meet with Secretary of State Shultz. The State Department, uncharacteristically, condemned the use of gas. "The Secretary today conveyed to Iraqi Minister of State Hammadi our view that Iraq's use of chemical weapons . . . is unjustifi able and abhorrent." Such violence, the statement went on to say, was "unacceptable to the civilized world." It was one of the few public condemnations of Iraq by the Reagan administration.

But the administration did not match its rhetoric with action. The very next day, the U.S. Senate passed a tough trade sanctions bill against Iraq. The Reagan administration and Secretary Shultz lobbied vehemently against the sanctions, and they were never enacted.

Nor did the administration even make a symbolic gesture of its displeasure, such as recalling the newly arrived U.S. ambassador in Baghdad. Only a few days later, the U.S. ambassador to Bulgaria was recalled after that country's ethnic Turkish minority was mistreated—but the first use of nerve gas in history to slaughter innocent civilians merited no such rebuke.

George Bush took office a short time later. Not only did Bush fail to speak out against Iraqi human rights abuses, his policy favored Saddam's regime even more than Reagan's. Through 1988, Iraq had been provided $2.8 billion in U.S. agricultural products under the Commodity Credit Corporation (CCC) credit-guarantee program. In his first days in office, Bush *doubled* the amount of the guarantees, to about $1 billion a year.

Soon thereafter, the United Nations Human Rights Commission passed a resolution calling on Iraq to account for its use of chemical weapons against the Kurds. Twelve European nations, including Ireland, Britain, and France, were among those who sponsored the resolution for the appointment of a special rapporteur to "make a thorough study of the human rights situation in Iraq." Not only did the Bush administration not join in sponsoring the resolution; it even worked against its passage.

THE UNITED States and Iraq had an almost nonexistent relationship before Ronald Reagan became president. The Baath rule of terror required foreign enemies—and America was a popular one. As late as 1980, Saddam vowed that Americans "were the enemies of the Arab nation and the enemies of Iraq," swearing that someday he would destroy them.

Soon the Reagan administration was providing Iraq billions of dollars in U.S. credit guarantees for the purchase of agricultural and industrial goods. In 1983, the president moved to ease Iraq's ever-burgeoning war debt by providing loans through the Commodity Credit Corporation credit guarantee program, allowing Saddam's regime to purchase American grain and farm products. Through 1988, Reagan's last year in office, Saddam was awarded $2.8 billion in agricultural credits.

Next, the administration started to pressure the Export-Import Bank, a congressionally funded bank charged with promoting foreign trade, to extend loan guarantees to the Iraqis. To become eligible for the Export-Import Bank's loan guarantees, Iraq had to first be taken off the State Department's list of countries accused of sponsoring terrorism. Iraq was removed from the list in 1982 after announcing the expulsion of Abu Nidal, an official of the Popular Front for the Liberation of Palestine.

Intelligence officials say the expulsion was merely cosmetic: Abu Nidal continued to use Iraq as a base of operations.

"All the intelligence I saw indicated that the Iraqis continued to support terrorism to much the same degree they had in the past," Noel Koch, then in charge of the Pentagon's counterterrorism program, said. "We took Iraq off the list and shouldn't have done it. We did it for political reasons. The purpose had to do with the policy to tilt toward Iraq in the Iran-Iraq war."

Koch says he personally objected to the decision, as did his counterpart at the State Department, Ambassador Robert Sayre, the coordinator of counterterrorism. But it did little good. "He told me his recommendation was overruled at a higher level," Koch said.

In 1984, formal diplomatic relations were restored between the U.S. and Iraq. The following year, the two nations exchanged ambassadors for the first time in nearly two decades.

Also in 1984, the U.S. Export-Import Bank began extending Iraq short-term loan guarantees for the purchase of U.S.-manufactured goods, reversing a previous ban.

Beyond the troubling questions about Saddam's support of terrorism, the Export-Import Bank also had reservations about lending to Iraq because of its immense war debts. The bank only restored loan guarantees to Iraq after what one official calls "immense political pressure" to do so from senior Reagan administration officials.

In 1984 and 1985, the bank made some $35 million in short-term loan guarantees to Iraq. But after Iraq borrowers failed to pay back the loans on time, the bank discontinued further dealings with Saddam. Despite this, in 1987, the Reagan administration once again pressured the bank to provide an additional $135 million in short-term credit guarantees for U.S. purchases.

LAST OCTOBER 15 during a campaign stop in Dallas, President Bush held his audience captive with tales of Iraqi atrocities in Kuwait. He told of "newborn babies thrown off incubators"* and "dialysis patients ripped from their machines." He spoke passionately of "the story of two young kids passing out leaflets: Iraqi troops rounded up their parents and made them watch while these two kids were shot to death—executed before their eyes."

"Hitler revisited. But remember, when Hitler's war ended, there were the Nuremberg trials."

The president, appearing decisive and defiant, told the crowd, "America will not stand aside."

But in April 1989—long before the invasion of Kuwait but long after George Bush had assumed the presidency—Amnesty International had found the torture of children so pervasive in Iraq that it devoted an entire report to the subject. Iraqi children were routinely subjected to "extractions of fingernails, beatings, whippings, sexual abuse, and electrical shock treatment" as well as "beatings with metal cables while naked and suspended by the wrists from the ceiling." Young girls had "been found hung upside down from the feet during menstruation" with "objects inserted into their vaginas." The report told of the summary execution of twenty-nine young children from one village. When the bodies of those children were returned to their families, "some of the victims had their eyes gouged out."

What did George Bush have to say then? Nothing; he made no public comment on the report.

Just six months later, Bush assistant secretary for Near Eastern and South

---

* Editors' note: See John MacArthur's article on page 135 for a full debunking of this story.

Asian affairs John Kelly gave a major policy address on Iraq. He, too, did not have a single word to say about Iraq's torture of children, or even the more general topic of human rights. Rather, reflecting the policy of his president, he simply stated, "Iraq is an important state with great potential. We want to deepen and broaden our relationship."

THE MEN WHO HELPED THE MAN WHO GASSED HIS OWN PEOPLE

Joost R. Hiltermann

In calling for regime change in Iraq, George W. Bush has accused Saddam Hussein of being a man who gassed his own people. Bush is right, of course. The public record shows Saddam's regime repeatedly spread poisonous gases on Kurdish villages in 1987 and 1988 in an attempt to put down a persistent rebellion.

The biggest such attack was against the town of Halabja in March 1988. According to local organizations providing relief to the survivors, some 6,800 Kurds were killed, the vast majority of them civilians.

It is a good thing that Bush has highlighted these atrocities by a regime that is more brutal than most. Yet it is cynical to use them as a justification for American plans to terminate the regime. By any measure, the American record on Halabja is shameful.

Analysis of thousands of captured Iraqi secret police documents and declassified U.S. government documents, as well as interviews with scores of Kurdish survivors, senior Iraqi defectors, and retired U.S. intelligence officers, show (1) that Iraq carried out the attack on Halabja; (2) that the United States, fully aware it was Iraq, accused Iran, Iraq's enemy in a fierce war, of being partly responsible for the attack; and (3) that the State Department instructed its diplomats to propagate Iran's partial culpability.

The result of this stunning act of sophistry was that the international community failed to muster the will to condemn Iraq strongly and unambiguously for an act as heinous as the terrorist strike on the World Trade Center.

This was at a time when Iraq was launching what proved to be the final battles of the 8-year war against Iran. Its wholesale use of poison gas against Iranian troops and Iranian Kurdish towns, and its threat to place chemical warheads on the missiles it was lobbing at Tehran, brought Iran to its knees.

Iraq had also just embarked on a counterinsurgency campaign, called the Anfal, against its rebellious Kurds. In this effort, too, the regime's resort to

Joost Hiltermann is the former director of the Iraqi Documents Project at Human Rights Watch (1992–1994), and the former executive director of that organization's Arms Division (1994–2002). He is writing a book on U.S. policy toward Iraq with partial support from the Open Society Institute and the John D. and Catherine T. MacArthur Foundation. This article is based on that research.

chemical weapons gave it a decisive edge, enabling the systematic killing of an estimated 100,000 men, women, and children.

The deliberate American prevarication on Halabja was the logical outcome of a pronounced six-year tilt toward Iraq, seen as a bulwark against the perceived threat posed by Iran's zealous brand of politicized Islam. The United States began the tilt after Iraq, the aggressor in the war, was expelled from Iranian territory by a resurgent Iran, which then decided to pursue its own, fruitless version of regime change in Baghdad. There was little love for what virtually all of Washington recognized as an unsavory regime, but Iraq was considered the lesser evil. Sealed by National Security Decision Directive 114 in 1983, the tilt funneled billions of dollars in loan guarantees and other credits to Iraq.

The tilt included not only material (though largely non-military) support of the Iraqi war effort, but also a deliberate closing of the eyes to atrocities committed by the Iraqi military in a war that saw unspeakable brutalities on both sides. Some of the facts about this shameful episode in American history have only recently come to light.

In warning against a possible Iraqi chemical or biological strike against American troops, Secretary of Defense Donald Rumsfeld remarked in November 2002 that "there's a danger that Saddam Hussein would do things he's done previously—he has in the past used chemical weapons."

Rumsfeld should know. Declassified State Department documents show that when he had an opportunity to raise the issue of chemical weapons with the Iraqi leadership in 1983, he failed to do so in any meaningful way. Worse, he may well have given a signal to the Iraqis that the United States would close its eyes to Iraq's use of chemical weapons during its war with Iran, providing an early boost to Iraq's plans to develop weapons of mass destruction. As President Ronald Reagan's special envoy for the Middle East, Rumsfeld in December 1983 made the first visit by an American official of his seniority to Baghdad, where he met President Saddam Hussein and Foreign Minister Tariq Aziz. Iraq had broken off diplomatic relations with the United States in June 1967. Now both sides hoped that the talks in Baghdad would facilitate a resumption of formal ties.

The visit came at a time when Iraq was facing Iranian "human wave" assaults that posed a serious threat to the regime. In response, Iraq had started to use chemical weapons on the battlefield—primarily mustard gas, a blister agent that can kill. This was known in Washington at least as early as October 1983. State Department officials had raised the alarm, suggesting ways of deterring further Iraqi use. But they faced resistance because of the tilt, which had just begun to gather bureaucratic momentum.

As talking points and minutes of the meetings show, the aim of Rumsfeld's mission was to inform the Iraqi leadership of America's shifting policy in the Middle East. It was also intended to explore a proposal to run an oil pipeline from Iraq to the Jordanian port of Aqaba (an American business interest involving the Bechtel Corporation), and to caution the Iraqis not to escalate the war in the Gulf through air strikes against Iranian oil facilities and tankers (which Washington feared might draw the United States into the war).

There is no indication that Rumsfeld raised American concerns about Iraq's use of poison gas with Saddam Hussein. But in a private meeting with Tariq Aziz, he made a single brief reference to "certain things" that made it difficult for the United States to do more to help Iraq. These things included "chemical weapons, possible escalation in the Gulf, and human rights." There is no record of further discussion of chemical weapons or human rights at these meetings, which covered the length and breadth of the warming relationship. Rumsfeld did, however, place considerable emphasis on the need for Iraq to prevent an escalation in the Gulf conflict via attacks on Iranian oil installations and tankers. Certainly nothing suggests that he told the Iraqi leadership to take care of "certain things" before diplomatic relations could be restored.

The senior U.S. diplomat in Baghdad reported a few days later with evident delight that "Ambassador Rumsfeld's visit has elevated U.S.-Iraqi relations to a new level." But, he noted, "during and following the Rumsfeld visit we have received no commitment from the Iraqis that they will refrain from military moves toward escalation in the Gulf."

To the contrary. The record of the war suggests that, flush with their new confidence in American backing, the Iraqis may have felt that they were now less restrained. They attacked Iranian oil facilities and ended up drawing United States into the war, in 1987.

Moreover, sensing correctly that it had carte blanche, Saddam's regime escalated its resort to gas warfare, graduating to ever more lethal agents. In the first Iranian offensive after Rumsfeld's visit, in February 1984, Iraq used not only large amounts of mustard gas but also the highly lethal nerve agent tabun. It was the first recorded use of the nerve agent in history. In November 1984, shortly after Reagan's reelection, diplomatic relations between the Washington and Baghdad were restored.

In February 2003 Rumsfeld made a statement that he was concerned about "Saddam Hussein using weapons of mass destruction against his own people and blaming it on us, which would fit a pattern." I can't think of many, or any, instances in which Iraq pinned chemical attacks on the United States, but the one pattern that is clearly discernible is the regime's escalating use of gas warfare as the American tilt toward Iraq intensified.*

After 1984 Iraq made increasing use of chemical weapons on the battle-field and even against civilians. Because of the strong western animus against Iran, few paid heed. Then came Halabja. Unfortunately for Iraq's sponsors, Iran rushed western reporters to the blighted town. The horrifying scenes they filmed were presented on prime time television a few days later. Soon Ted Koppel could be seen putting the Iraqi ambassador's feet to the fire on Nightline.

In response, Washington launched the "Iran too" gambit. The story was cooked up in the Pentagon, interviews with the principals show. Newly de-classified State Department documents demonstrate that American diplo-mats then received instructions to press this line with Washington's allies, and to decline to discuss the details.

It took seven weeks for the United Nations Security Council to censure the Halabja attack. Even then, its choice of neutral language (condemning the "continued use of chemical weapons in the conflict between the Islamic Republic of Iran and Iraq," and calling on "both sides to refrain from the fu-ture use of chemical weapons") diffused the effect of its belated move. Iraq, still reading the signals, proceeded to step up its use of gas until the end of the war and even afterward, during the final stage of the Anfal campaign, to dev-astating effect.

When I visited Halabja in the spring of 2002, the town, razed by successive Iranian and Iraqi occupiers, had been rebuilt, but the physical and psycholog-ical wounds remained.

Some of those who engineered the tilt today are back in power in the Bush administration. They have yet to account for their judgment that it was Iran, not Iraq, that posed the primary threat to the Gulf; for building up Iraq so that it thought it could invade Kuwait and get away with it; for encouraging Iraq's weapons of mass destruction programs by giving the regime a de facto green light on chemical weapons use; and for turning a blind eye to Iraq's worst atrocities, and then lying about it.

---

* Editors' note: At a September 19, 2002 hearing of the Senate Armed Services Committee, Senator Robert Byrd asked Defense Secretary Rumsfeld about a report in *Newsweek* that the U.S. helped Iraq "acquire the building blocks of biological weapons during the Iran-Iraq war," and gave it satellite photos of Iranian troop deployments, along with sundry "dual-use" materials. Rumsfeld responded first by recalling his service as Reagan's Middle East envoy, saying "I did meet with Mr. Tariq Aziz [Iraq's Foreign Minister]. And I did meet with Saddam Hussein and spent some time visiting with them about the war they were engaged in with Iran." Answering Byrd's question, he said, "I have never heard anything like what you've read, I have no knowledge of it whatsoever, and I doubt it."

TWO

THE FIRST GULF WAR

"Access to Persian Gulf oil and the security of key friendly states in the area are vital to U.S. national security. . . . Normal relations between the United States and Iraq would serve our longer-term interests and promote stability in both the Gulf and the Middle East."
—*President George H. W. Bush, National Security Directive 26, October 2, 1989 (paving the way for $1 billion in new U.S. loan guarantees to Iraq, despite the fact that the international banking community had stopped lending money to the country because of its unpaid debts from the Iran-Iraq war)*

"We never expected they would take all of Kuwait."
—*April Glaspie, U.S. Ambassador to Iraq, after Saddam's army invaded and occupied Kuwait on August 2, 1990*

"Access to Persian Gulf oil and the security of key friendly states are vital to U.S. national security. Consistent with NSD 26 of October 2, 1989 . . . and as a matter of long-standing policy, the United States remains committed to defending its vital interests in the region, if necessary through the use of military force, against any power with interests inimical to our own. Iraq, by virtue of its unprovoked invasion of Kuwait on August 2, 1990, and its subsequent brutal occupation, is clearly a power with interests inimical to our own."
—*President George H. W. Bush, National Security Directive 54, January 15, 1991, launching the Gulf War*

REALPOLITIK IN THE GULF:
A GAME GONE TILT

Christopher Hitchens

On the morning before Yom Kippur late this past September, I found myself standing at the western end of the White House, watching as the color guard paraded the flag of the United States (and the republic for which it stands) along with that of the Emirate of Kuwait. The young men of George Bush's palace guard made a brave showing, but their immaculate uniforms and webbing could do little but summon the discomforting contrasting image— marching across our TV screens nightly—of their hot, thirsty, encumbered brothers and sisters in the Saudi Arabian desert. I looked away and had my attention fixed by a cortege of limousines turning in at the gate. There was a quick flash of dark beard and white teeth, between burnoose and kaffiyeh, as Sheikh Jabir al-Ahmad al-Sabah, the exiled Kuwaiti emir, scuttled past a clutch of photographers and through the portals. End of photo op, but not of story.

Let us imagine a photograph of the emir of Kuwait entering the White House, and let us see it as a historian might years from now. What might such a picture disclose under analysis? How did this oleaginous monarch, whose very name was unknown just weeks before to most members of the Bush administration and the Congress, never mind most newspaper editors, reporters, and their readers, become a crucial visitor—perhaps *the* crucial visitor—on the president's autumn calendar? How did he emerge as someone on whose behalf the president was preparing to go to war?

We know already, as every historian will, that the president, in having the emir come by, was not concerned with dispelling any impression that he was the one who had "lost Kuwait" to Iraq in early August. The tiny kingdom had never been understood as "ours" to lose, as far as the American people and their representatives knew. Those few citizens who did know Kuwait (human-rights monitors, scholars, foreign correspondents) knew it was held together by a relatively loose yet unmistakably persistent form of feudalism. It could have been "lost" only by its sole owners, the al-Sabah family, not by the United States or by the "Free World."

Christopher Hitchens is a columnist for *Vanity Fair*. He is the author of several books, most recently, *Why Orwell Matters*. This article was originally published in the January 1991 issue of *Harper's*.

What a historian might make of our imaginary photo document of this moment in diplomatic history that most citizens surely would not is that it is, in fact, less a discrete snapshot than a still from an epic movie—a dark and bloody farce, one that chronicles the past two decades of U.S. involvement in the Persian Gulf. Call the film *Rules of the Game of Nations* or *Metternich of Arabia*—you get the idea. In this particular scene, the president was meeting at the White House with the emir to send a "signal" to Iraqi President Saddam Hussein that he, Bush, "stood with" Kuwait in wanting Iraq to pull out its troops. After the meeting, Bush emerged to meet the press, not alone but with his national security adviser, Brent Scowcroft. This, of course, was a signal, too: Bush meant business, of a potentially military kind. In the game of nations, however, one does not come right out and *say* one is signaling (that would, by definition, no longer be signaling); one waits for reporters to ask about signals, one denies signaling is going on, and then one trusts that unnamed White House aides and State Department officials will provide the desired "spin" and perceptions of "tilt."

On ordinary days the trivial and empty language of Washington isn't especially awful. The drizzle of repetitive key words—"perception," "agenda," "address," "concern," "process," "bipartisan"—does its job of masking and dulling reality. But on this rather important day in an altogether unprecedented process—a lengthy and deliberate preparation for a full-scale ground and air war in a faraway region—there was not a word from George Bush—not a *word*—that matched the occasion. Instead, citizens and soldiers alike would read or hear inane questions from reporters, followed by boilerplate answers from their president and interpretations by his aides, about whether the drop-by of a feudal potentate had or had not signaled this or that intent.

There is a rank offense here to the idea of measure and proportion. Great matters of power and principle are in play, and there does in fact exist a chance to evolve a new standard for international relations rather than persist in the old follies of superpower *raisons d'état;* and still the official tongue stammers and barks. Behind all the precious, brittle, Beltway in-talk lies the only idea young Americans will die for in the desert: the idea that in matters of foreign policy, even in a democratic republic, the rule is "leave it to us." Not everybody, after all, can be fitted out with the wildly expensive stealth equipment that the political priesthood requires to relay and decipher the signal flow.

THE WORD concocted in the nineteenth century for this process—the shorthand of Palmerston and Metternich—was "realpolitik." Maxims of cynicism and realism—to the effect that great states have no permanent friends or permanent principles, but only permanent interests—became common currency in post-Napoleonic Europe. Well, there isn't a soul today in Washington who doesn't pride himself on the purity of his realpolitik. And an organization supposedly devoted to the study and promulgation of such nineteenth-century realism—the firm of Henry Kissinger Associates—has furnished the Bush administration with several of its high officers, including Brent Scowcroft and Deputy Secretary of State Lawrence Eagleburger, along with much of its expertise.

Realpolitik, with its tilts and signals, is believed by the faithful to keep nations from war, balancing the powers and interests, as they say. Is what we are witnessing in the Persian Gulf, then, the breakdown and failure of realpolitik? Well, yes and no. Yes, in the sense that American troops have been called upon to restore the balance that existed before August 2, 1990. But that regional status quo has for the past two decades known scarcely a day of peace—in the Persian Gulf, it has been a balance of terror for a long time. Realpolitik, as practiced by Washington, has played no small part in this grim situation.

To even begin to understand this, one must get beyond today's tilts and signals and attempt to grasp a bit of history—something the realpoliticians are loath for you to do. History is for those clutching values and seeking truths; realpolitik has little time for such sentiment. The world, after all, is a cold place requiring hard calculation, detachment.

LEAFING THROUGH the history of Washington's contemporary involvement in the Gulf, one might begin to imagine the cool detachment in 1972 of arch-realpolitician Henry Kissinger, then national security adviser to Richard Nixon. I have before me as I write a copy of the report of the House Select Committee on Intelligence Activities chaired by Congressman Otis Pike, completed in January 1976, partially leaked, and then censored by the White House and the CIA. The committee found that in 1972 Kissinger had met with the shah of Iran, who solicited his aid in destabilizing the Baathist regime of Ahmad Hassan al-Bakr in Baghdad. Iraq had given refuge to the then-exiled Ayatollah Khomeini and used anti-imperialist rhetoric while coveting Iran's Arabic-speaking Khuzistan region. The shah and Kissinger agreed that Iraq was upsetting the balance in the Gulf; a way to restore the balance— or, anyway, to find some new balance—was to send a signal by supporting the landless, luckless Kurds, then in revolt in northern Iraq.

Kissinger put the idea to Nixon, who loved (and loves still) the game of nations and who had already decided to tilt toward Iran and build it into his most powerful regional friend, replete with arms purchased from U.S. manufacturers—not unlike Saudi Arabia today, but more on that later. Nixon authorized a covert-action budget and sent John Connally, his former Treasury secretary, to Teheran to cement the deal. (So the practice of conducting American Middle East policy by way of the free-masonry of the shady oilmen did not originate with James Baker or George Bush. As the U.S. ambassador to Iraq, April Glaspie, confided to Saddam Hussein in her now-famous meeting last July 25, almost as though giving a thumbnail profile of her bosses: "We have many Americans who would like to see the price go above $25 because they come from oil-producing states." Much more later on *that* tête-à-tête.)

The principal finding of the Pike Commission, in its study of U.S. covert intervention in Iraq and Iran in the early 1970s, is a clue to a good deal of what has happened since. The committee members found, to their evident shock, the following:

> Documents in the Committee's possession clearly show that the President, Dr. Kissinger and the foreign head of state [the shah] hoped that our clients [the Kurds] would not prevail. They preferred instead that the insurgents simply continue a level of hostilities sufficient to sap the resources of our ally's neighboring country [Iraq].

Official prose in Washington can possess a horror and immediacy of its own, as is shown by the sentence that follows:

> This policy was not imparted to our clients, who were encouraged to continue fighting.

"Not imparted." "*Not imparted*" to the desperate Kurdish villagers to whom Kissinger's envoys came with outstretched hands and practiced grins. "Not imparted," either, to the American public or to Congress. "Imparted," though, to the shah and to Saddam Hussein (then the Baathists' number-two man), who met and signed a treaty temporarily ending their border dispute in 1975—thus restoring balance in the region. On that very day, all U.S. aid to the Kurds was terminated—a decision that, of course, "imparted" itself to Saddam. On the next day he launched a search-and-destroy operation in Kurdistan that has been going on ever since and that, in the town of Halabja in 1988, made history by marking the first use of chemical weaponry by a state against its own citizens.

By the by, which realpolitician was it who became director of the CIA in the period—January 1976—when the Kurdish operation was being hastily interred, the Kurds themselves were being mopped up by Saddam, and the Pike Commission report was restricted? He happens to be the same man who now

wants you to believe Saddam is suddenly "worse than Hitler." But forget it;
everybody else has.

SOMETHING OF the same application of superpower divide-and-rule principles—no war but no peace, low-intensity violence yielding no clear victor or
loser, the United States striving for a policy of Mutual Assured Destabilization—seems to turn up in Persian Gulf history once again four years later.
Only now the United States has tilted away from Iran and is signaling Saddam
Hussein. Iranians of all factions are convinced that the United States actively
encouraged Iraq to attack their country on September 22, 1980. It remains
unclear exactly what the U.S. role was in this invasion; but there is ample evidence of the presence of our old friends, wink and nod.

Recently, I raised the matter of September 1980 tilts and signals with Admiral Stansfield Turner, who was CIA director at the time, and with Gary
Sick, who then had responsibility for Gulf policy at the National Security
Council. Admiral Turner did not, he said, have any evidence that the Iraqis
had cleared their invasion of Iran with Washington. He could say, however,
that the CIA had known of an impending invasion and had advised President
Jimmy Carter accordingly. Sick recalled that Iraq and the United States had
broken diplomatic relations in 1967 during the Arab-Israeli Six-Day War, so
that no official channels of communication were available.

Such contact as there was, Sick told me, ran through Saudi Arabia and, interestingly enough, Kuwait. This, if anything, gave greater scope to those who
like dealing in tilts and signals. Prominent among them was realpol (by way of
Trilateralism) Zbigniew Brzezinski, who was then Carter's national security
adviser. As Sick put it: "After the hostages were taken in Teheran [in November 1979], there was a very strong view, especially from Brzezinski, that in effect Iran should be punished from all sides. He made public statements to the
effect that he would not mind an Iraqi move against Iran." A fall 1980 story in
London's *Financial Times* took things a little further, reporting that U.S. intelligence and satellite data—data purporting to show that Iranian forces would
swiftly crack—had been made available to Saddam through third-party Arab
governments.

All the available evidence, in other words, points in a single direction. The
United States knew that Iraq was planning an assault on a neighboring country and, at the very least, took no steps to prevent it. For purposes of comparison, imagine Washington's response if Saddam Hussein had launched an
attack when the shah ruled Iran. Or, to bring matters up to date, ask yourself
why Iraq's 1980 assault was not a violation of international law or an act of
naked aggression that "would not stand."

Sick cautioned me not to push the evidence too far because, as he said, the actual scale of the invasion came as a surprise. "We didn't think he'd take all of Khuzistan in 1980," he said of Saddam. But nobody is suggesting that anyone expected an outright Iraqi victory. By switching sides, and by supplying arms to both belligerents over the next decade, the U.S. national security establishment may have been acting consistently rather than inconsistently. A market for weaponry, the opening of avenues of influence, the creation of superpower dependency, the development of clientele among the national security forces of other nations, and a veto on the emergence of any rival power—these were the tempting prizes.

How else to explain the simultaneous cosseting of both Iran and Iraq during the 1980s? The backstairs dealing with the Ayatollah is a matter of record. The adoption of Saddam Hussein by the power worshipers and influence peddlers of Washington, D.C., is less well remembered. How many daily readers of *The New York Times* recall that paper's 1975 characterization of Iraq as "pragmatic, cooperative," with credit for this shift going to Saddam's "personal strength"? How many lobbyists and arms peddlers spent how many evenings during the eighties at the Washington dinner table of Iraq's U.S. ambassador, Nizar Hamdoon? And how often, do you imagine, was Hamdoon asked even the most delicately phrased question about his government's continued killing of the Kurds, including unarmed women and children; its jailing and routine torturing of political prisoners during the 1980s; its taste for the summary trial and swift execution?

It can be amusing to look up some of Saddam's former fans. Allow me to open for you the April 27, 1987, issue of *The New Republic,* where we find an essay engagingly entitled "Back Iraq," by Daniel Pipes and Laurie Mylroie. These two distinguished Establishment interpreters, under the unavoidable subtitle "It's time for a U.S. 'tilt,' " managed to anticipate the recent crisis by more than three years. Sadly, they got the name of the enemy wrong:

> The fall of the existing regime in Iraq would enormously enhance Iranian influence, endanger the supply of oil, threaten pro-American regimes throughout the area, and upset the Arab-Israeli balance.

But they always say that, don't they, when the think tanks start thinking tanks? I could go on, but mercy forbids—though neither mercy nor modesty has inhibited Pipes from now advocating, in stridently similar terms, the prompt obliteration of all works of man in Iraq.

EVEN AS the Iraqi ambassador in Washington was cutting lucrative swaths through "the procurement community," and our policy intellectuals were convincing one another that Saddam Hussein could be what the shah had been until he suddenly was not, other forces (nod, wink) were engaged in bribing Iran and irritating Iraq. Take the diary entry for May 15, 1986, made by Oliver North in his later-subpoenaed notebook. The childish scrawl reads:

- —Vaughan Forrest
- —Gene Wheatin w/Forrest
- —SAT flights to
- —Rob/Flacko disc. of Remington
- —Sarkis/Cunningham/Cline/Secord
- —Close to Sen. Hugh Scott
- —TF 157, Wilson, Terpil et al blew up Letier
- —Cunningham running guns to Baghdad for CIA, then weaps, to Teheran
- —Secord running guns to Iran

This tabulation contains the names of almost every senior Middle East gunrunner. The penultimate line is especially interesting, I think, because it so succinctly evokes the "two track" balancing act under way in Iran and Iraq. That tens of thousands of young Arabs and Persians were actually dying on the battlefield . . . but forget that too.

We now understand from sworn testimony that when North and Robert McFarlane, President Reagan's former national security adviser, went with cake and Bible to Teheran in May 1986, they were pressed by their Iranian hosts to secure the release of militant Shiite prisoners held in Kuwait. Their freedom had been the price demanded by those who held American hostages in Beirut. Speaking with the authority of his president, North agreed with the Iranians, explaining later that "there is a need for a non-hostile regime in Baghdad" and noting that the Iranians knew "we can bring our influence to bear with certain friendly Arab nations" to get rid of Saddam Hussein.

Bringing influence to bear, North entered into a negotiation on the hostage exchange, the disclosure of which, Reagan's Secretary of State George Shultz said later, "made me sick to my stomach." North met the Kuwaiti foreign minister and later told the Iranians that the Shiite prisoners in Kuwait would be released if Iran dropped its support for groups hostile to the emir. When Saddam learned of the deed, which took place at the height of his war with Iran, he must have been quite fascinated.

It's at about this point, I suspect, that eyes start to glaze, consciences start to coarsen, and people start to talk about "ropes and sand" and the general impenetrability of the Muslim mind. This reaction is very convenient to those who hope to keep the waters muddy. It is quite clear that Saddam Hussein had by the late 1980s learned, or been taught, two things. The first is that the United States will intrigue against him when he is weak. The second is that it will grovel before him when he is strong. The all-important corollary is: The United States is a country that deals only in furtive signals.

IT IS AGAINST this backdrop—one of signals and nods and tilts and intrigues—and *not* against that of Bush's anger at Iraqi aggression (he is angry, but only because realpolitik has failed him) that one must read the now-famous transcript of the Glaspie-Saddam meeting last July. Keep in mind, too, that at this point, just a bit more than a week before Iraqi troops marched into Kuwait, Glaspie is speaking under instructions, and the soon-to-be "Butcher of Baghdad" is still "Mr. President."

The transcript has seventeen pages. For the first eight and a half of these, Saddam Hussein orates without interruption. He makes his needs and desires very plain in the matter of Kuwait, adding two things that haven't been noticed in the general dismay over the document. First, he borrows the method of a Coppola godfather to remind Glaspie that the United States has shown sympathy in the near past for his land and oil complaints against Kuwait:

In 1974, I met with Idriss, the son of Mullah Mustafa Barzani [the Kurdish leader]. He sat in the same seat as you are sitting now. He came asking me to postpone implementation of autonomy in Iraqi Kurdistan, which was agreed on March 11, 1970. My reply was: We are determined to fulfill our obligation. You also have to stick to your agreement.

After carrying on in this vein, and making it clear that Kuwait may go the way of Kurdistan, Saddam closes by saying he hopes that President Bush will read the transcript himself, "and will not leave it in the hands of a gang in the State Department. I exclude the secretary of state and [Assistant Secretary of State John] Kelly, because I know him and I exchanged views with him."

Now, the very first thing that Ambassador Glaspie says, in a recorded discussion that Saddam Hussein has announced he wishes relayed directly to the White House and the non-gang elements at Foggy Bottom, is this:

I clearly understand your message. We studied history at school. They taught us to say freedom or death. I think you know well that we as a people have our experience with the colonialists.

The confused semiotics of American diplomacy seem to have compelled Glaspie to say that she gets his "message" (or signal) rather than that she simply understands him. But the "message" she *conveys* in that last sentence is surely as intriguing as the message she receives. She is saying that she realizes (as many Americans are finally beginning to) that one large problem with the anomalous borders of the Gulf is the fact that they were drawn to an obsolete British colonial diagram. That fact has been the essence of Iraq's grudge against Kuwait at least since 1961. For Saddam Hussein, who has been agitating against "the colonialists" for most of his life, the American ambassador's invocation of Patrick Henry in this context had to be more than he hoped for.

But wait. She goes even further to assure him:

> We have no opinion on the Arab-Arab conflicts, like your border disagreement with Kuwait. I was in the American embassy in Kuwait during the late 60s. The instruction we had during this period was that we should express no opinion on this issue, and that the issue is not associated with America. *James Baker has directed our official spokesmen to emphasize this instruction.* [Italics mine.]

I used to slightly know Ambassador Glaspie, who is exactly the type of foreign-service idealist and professional that a man like James Baker does not deserve to have in his employ. Like Saddam, Baker obviously felt more comfortable with John Kelly as head of his Middle East department. And why shouldn't he? Kelly had shown the relevant qualities of sinuous, turncoat adaptability—acting as a "privacy channel" worker for Oliver North while ostensibly U.S. ambassador to Beirut and drawing a public reprimand from George Shultz for double-crossing his department and his undertaking, to say nothing of helping to trade the American hostages in that city. Raw talent of this kind—a man to do business with—evidently does not go unnoticed in either the Bush or Saddam administration.

Baker did not have even the dignity of a Shultz when, appearing on a Sunday morning talk show shortly after the Iraqi invasion, he softly disowned Glaspie by saying that his clear instructions to her in a difficult embassy at a crucial time were among "probably 312,000 cables or so that go out under my name." Throughout, the secretary has been as gallant as he has been honest.

The significant detail in Ambassador Glaspie's much more candid postinvasion interview with *The New York Times* was the disclosure that "we never expected they would take all of Kuwait." This will, I hope, remind you that Gary Sick and his Carter-team colleagues did not think Iraq would take all of Iran's Khuzistan region. And those with a medium-term grasp of history might recall as well how General Alexander Haig was disconcerted by General Ariel Sharon's 1982 dash beyond the agreed-upon southern portion of Lebanon all the way to Beirut. In the world of realpolitik there is always the risk that those signaled will see nothing but green lights.

A revised border with Kuwait was self-evidently part of the price that Washington had agreed to pay in its long-standing effort to make a pet of Saddam Hussein. Yet ever since the fateful day when he too greedily took Washington at its word, and the emir of Kuwait and his extended family were unfeelingly translated from yacht people to boat people, Washington has been waffling about the rights of the Kuwaiti (and now, after all these years, Kurdish) victims. Let the record show, via the Glaspie transcript, that the Bush administration had a chance to consider these rights and these peoples in advance, and coldly abandoned them.

And may George Bush someday understand that a president cannot confect a principled call to war—"hostages," "Hitler," "ruthless dictator," "naked aggression"—when matters of principle have never been the issue for him and his type. On August 2, Saddam Hussein opted out of the game of nations. He'd had enough. As he told Glaspie:

> These better [U.S.-Iraqi] relations have suffered from various rifts. The worst of these was in 1986, only two years after establishing relations, with what was known as Irangate, which happened during the year that Iran occupied [Iraq's] Fao peninsula.

Saddam quit the game—he'd had it with tilt and signal—and the president got so mad he could kill and, with young American men and women as his proxies, he killed.

Today, the tilt is toward Saudi Arabia. A huge net of bases and garrisons has been thrown over the Kingdom of Saud, with a bonanza in military sales and a windfall (for some) in oil prices to accompany it. This tilt, too, has its destabilizing potential. But the tilt also has its compensations, not the least being that the realpoliticians might still get to call the global shots from Washington. Having taken the diplomatic lead, engineered the U.N. Security Council resolutions, pressured the Saudis to let in foreign troops, committed the bulk of these troops, and established itself as the only credible source of intelligence and interpretation of Iraqi plans and mood, the Bush administration publicly hailed a new multilateralism. Privately, Washington's realpols gloated: *We* were the superpower—deutsche marks and yen be damned.

GENERALLY, IT must be said that realpolitik has been better at dividing than at ruling. Take it as a whole since Kissinger called on the shah in 1972, and see what the harvest has been. The Kurds have been further dispossessed, further reduced in population, and made the targets of chemical experiments. Perhaps half a million Iraqi and Iranian lives have been expended to no purpose on and around the Fao peninsula. The Iraqis have ingested (or engulfed) Kuwait. The Syrians, aided by an anti-Iraqi subvention from Washington, have now ingested Lebanon. The Israeli millennialists are bent on ingesting the West Bank and Gaza. In every country mentioned, furthermore, the forces of secularism, democracy, and reform have been dealt appalling blows. And all of these crimes and blunders will necessitate future wars.

That is what U.S. policy has done, or helped to do, to the region. What has the same policy done to America? A review of the Pike Commission, the Iran-Contra hearings, even the Tower Report and September's perfunctory House inquiry into the Baker-Kelly-Glaspie fiasco, will disclose the damage done by official lying, by hostage trading, by covert arms sales, by the culture of secrecy, and by the habit of including foreign despots in meetings and decisions that are kept secret from American citizens. The Gulf buildup had by Election Day brought about the renewal of a moribund consensus on national security, the disappearance of the bruited "peace dividend" ("If you're looking for it," one Pentagon official told a reporter this past fall, "it just left for Saudi Arabia"), and the re-establishment of the red alert as the preferred device for communicating between Washington and the people.

The confrontation that opened on the Kuwaiti border in August 1990 was neither the first nor the last battle in a long war, but it was a battle that now directly, overtly involved and engaged the American public and American personnel. The call was to an exercise in peace through strength. But the cause was yet another move in the policy of keeping a region divided and embittered, and therefore accessible to the franchisers of weaponry and the owners of black gold.

An earlier regional player, Benjamin Disraeli, once sarcastically remarked that you could tell a weak government by its eagerness to resort to strong measures. The Bush administration uses strong measures to ensure weak government abroad and has enfeebled democratic government at home. The reasoned objection must be that this is a dangerous and dishonorable pursuit, in which the wealthy gamblers have become much too accustomed to paying their bad debts with the blood of others.

U.S. SENATORS CHAT
WITH SADDAM

This is an excerpt from the transcript of a meeting on April 12, 1990, between Iraqi President Saddam Hussein and five U.S. senators—Robert Dole, Alan Simpson, Howard Metzenbaum, James McClure, and Frank Murkowski. U.S. Ambassador April Glaspie also attended. The American delegation met President Hussein in Mosul, Iraq, at a time when Hussein had come under criticism in the Western media for his human-rights record, his threats to attack Israel with chemical weapons, and his government's hanging of a British reporter accused of espionage. In addition, Congress was considering imposing trade sanctions against Iraq. The transcript was originally released by the Iraqi embassy in Washington.

PRESIDENT SADDAM HUSSEIN: Daily the Arabs hear scorn directed at them from the West, daily they bear insults. Why? Has the Zionist mentality taken control of you to the point that it has deprived you of your humanity? . . .

SENATOR DOLE: There are fundamental differences between our countries. We have free media in the U.S. When you say "Western," Mr. President—I don't know what you mean when you say "the West." I don't know whether or not you mean the government. There is a person who did not have the authority to say anything about . . . [your] government. He was a commentator for the VOA (the Voice of America, which represents the government only) and this person was removed from it. Please allow me to say that only 12 hours earlier President Bush had assured me that he wants better relations, and that the U.S. government wants better relations with Iraq. We believe—and we are leaders in the U.S. Congress—that the Congress also does not represent Bush or the government. I assume that President Bush will oppose sanctions, and he might veto them, unless something provocative were to happen, or something of that sort.

AMBASSADOR GLASPIE: As the ambassador of the U.S., I am certain that this is the policy of the U.S.

SENATOR DOLE: We in the Congress are also striving to do what we can in this direction. The president may differ with the Congress, and if there is a divergent viewpoint, he has the right to express it, and to exercise his authority concerning it . . .

SENATOR SIMPSON: I enjoy meeting candid and open people. This is a trademark of those of us who live in the "Wild West." . . . One of the reasons that we telephoned President Bush yesterday evening was to tell the President that our visit to Iraq would cost us a great deal of popularity, and that many people would attack us for coming to Iraq. . . . But President Bush said, "Go there. I want you there. . . . If you are criticized because of your visit to Iraq, I will defend you and speak on your behalf." . . . Democracy is a very confusing issue. I believe that your problems lie with the Western media and not with the U.S. government. As long as you are isolated from the media, the press— and it is a haughty and pampered press; they all consider themselves political geniuses, that is, the journalists do; they are very cynical—what I advise is that you invite them to come here and see for themselves.*

HUSSEIN: They are welcome. We hope that they will come to see Iraq and, after they do, write whatever they like . . . [But] I wonder, as you may wonder, if governments, for example, the U.S. government, were not behind such reports [negative news stories about Iraq]. How else could all of this [negative media coverage of Iraq] have occurred in such a short period of time?

SIMPSON: It's very easy. . . . They all live off one another. Everyone takes from the other. When there is a major news item on the front page of *The New York Times*, another journalist takes it and publishes it. . . .

SENATOR METZENBAUM: Mr. President, perhaps you have been given some information on me beforehand. I am a Jew and a staunch supporter of Israel. I did have some reservations on whether I should come on this visit.

HUSSEIN: You certainly will not regret it afterward.

METZENBAUM: I do not regret it. Mr. President, you view the Western media in a very negative light. I am not the right person to be your public-relations man, but allow me to suggest a few things, as I am more concerned about peace than I am about any other particular factor. I do not want to talk about whether the entire West Bank should be given up, or half of Jerusalem, or any

---

* Editors' note: These sentiments did not prevent Senator Simpson from calling CNN correspondent Peter Arnett, who reported from Baghdad during the Gulf War, an Iraqi "sympathizer" with a relative who was "active in the Vietcong."

other parts [of Israel]. This issue should be left to the parties concerned. However, I have been sitting here and listening to you for about an hour, and I am now aware that you are a strong and intelligent man and that you want peace. But I am also convinced that if . . . you were to focus on the value of the peace that we greatly need to achieve in the Middle East then there would not be a leader to compare with you in the Middle East. I believe, Mr. President, that you can be a very influential force for peace in the Middle East. But, as I said, I am not your public-relations man.

THE GLASPIE TRANSCRIPT: SADDAM MEETS THE U.S. AMBASSADOR

On July 25, 1990, President Saddam Hussein of Iraq summoned the United States Ambassador, April Glaspie, to his office in the last high-level contact between the two governments before the Iraqi invasion of Kuwait on August 2. Here is the complete transcript of the meeting, which also included the Iraqi Foreign Minister, Tariq Aziz, as released by Baghdad. The State Department has neither confirmed nor denied its accuracy. After this episode, Glaspie was never again offered a post requiring Senate confirmation. In 1993, then–U.N. Ambassador Madeleine Albright ordered Glaspie to leave the U.S. Mission to the U.N. on short notice. She later served as consul general in South Africa and recently retired from the foreign service.

President Saddam Hussein: I have summoned you today to hold comprehensive political discussions with you. This is a message to President Bush:

You know that we did not have relations with the U.S. until 1984 and you know the circumstances and reasons which caused them to be severed. The decision to establish relations with the U.S. were taken in 1980 during the two months prior to the war between us and Iran.

When the war started, and to avoid misinterpretation, we postponed the establishment of relations hoping that the war would end soon.

But because the war lasted for a long time, and to emphasize the fact that we are a nonaligned country, it was important to re-establish relations with the U.S. And we chose to do this in 1984.

It is natural to say that the U.S. is not like Britain, for example, with the latter's historic relations with Middle Eastern countries, including Iraq. In addition, there were no relations between Iraq and the U.S. between 1967 and 1984. One can conclude it would be difficult for the U.S. to have a full understanding of many matters in Iraq. When relations were re-established we hoped for a better understanding and for better cooperation because we too do not understand the background of many American decisions.

We dealt with each other during the war and we had dealings on various levels. The most important of those levels were with the foreign ministers.

We had hoped for a better common understanding and a better chance of cooperation to benefit both our peoples and the rest of the Arab nations.

But these better relations have suffered from various rifts. The worst of these was in 1986, only two years after establishing relations, with what was known as Irangate, which happened during the year that Iran occupied the Fao peninsula.

It was natural then to say that old relations and complexity of interests could absorb many mistakes. But when interests are limited and relations are not that old, then there isn't a deep understanding and mistakes could leave a negative effect. Sometimes the effect of an error can be larger than the error itself.

Despite all of that, we accepted the apology, via his envoy, of the American president regarding Irangate, and we wiped the slate clean. And we shouldn't unearth the past except when new events remind us that old mistakes were not just a matter of coincidence.

Our suspicions increased after we liberated the Fao peninsula. The media began to involve itself in our politics. And our suspicions began to surface anew, because we began to question whether the U.S. felt uneasy with the outcome of the war when we liberated our land.

It was clear to us that certain parties in the United States—and I don't say the president himself—but certain parties who had links with the intelligence community and with the State Department—and I don't say the secretary of state himself—I say that these parties did not like the fact that we liberated our land. Some parties began to prepare studies entitled, "Who will succeed Saddam Hussein?" They began to contact Gulf states to make them fear Iraq, to persuade them not to give Iraq economic aid. And we have evidence of these activities.

Iraq came out of the war burdened with a $40 billion debt, excluding the aid given by Arab states, some of whom consider that too to be a debt although they knew—and you knew too—that without Iraq they would not have had these sums and the future of the region would have been entirely different.

We began to face the policy of the drop in the price of oil. Then we saw the United States, which always talks of democracy but which has no time for the other point of view. Then the media campaign against Saddam Hussein was started by the official American media. The United States thought that the situation in Iraq was like Poland, Romania or Czechoslovakia. We were disturbed by this campaign but we were not disturbed too much because we had hoped that, in a few months, those who are decisionmakers in America would have a chance to find the facts and see whether this media campaign had had any effect on the lives of Iraqis. We had hoped that soon the American authorities would make the correct decision regarding their relations with Iraq. Those with good relations can sometimes afford to disagree.

But when planned and deliberate policy forces the price of oil down without good commercial reasons, then that means another war against Iraq. Because military war kills people by bleeding them, and economic war kills their humanity by depriving them of their chance to have a good standard of living. As you know, we gave rivers of blood in a war that lasted eight years, but we did not lose our humanity. Iraqis have a right to live proudly. We do not accept that anyone could injure Iraqi pride or the Iraqi right to have high standards of living.

Kuwait and the U.A.E. were at the front of this policy aimed at lowering Iraq's position and depriving its people of higher economic standards. And you know that our relations with the Emirates and Kuwait had been good. On top of all that, while we were busy at war, the state of Kuwait began to expand at the expense of our territory.

You may say this is propaganda, but I would direct you to one document, the Military Patrol Line, which is the borderline endorsed by the Arab League in 1961 for military patrols not to cross the Iraq-Kuwait border.

But go and look for yourselves. You will see the Kuwaiti border patrols, the Kuwaiti farms, the Kuwaiti oil installations—all built as closely as possible to this line to establish that land as Kuwaiti territory.

Since then, the Kuwaiti government has been stable while the Iraqi government has undergone many changes. Even after 1968 and for ten years afterwards, we were too busy with our own problems. First in the north, then the 1973 war, and other problems. Then came the war with Iran which started ten years ago.

We believe that the United States must understand that people who live in luxury and economic security can reach an understanding with the United States on what are legitimate joint interests. But the starved and the economically deprived cannot reach the same understanding.

We do not accept threats from anyone because we do not threaten anyone. But we say clearly that we hope that the U.S. will not entertain too many illusions and will seek new friends rather than increase the number of its enemies.

I have read the American statements speaking of friends in the area. Of course, it is the right of everyone to choose their friends. We can have no objections. But you know you are not the ones who protected your friends during the war with Iran. I assure you, had the Iranians overrun the region, the American troops would not have stopped them, except by the use of nuclear weapons.

I do not belittle you. But I hold this view by looking at the geography and nature of American society into account. Yours is a society which cannot accept 10,000 dead in one battle.

You know that Iran agreed to the cease-fire not because the United States had bombed one of the oil platforms after the liberation of the Fao. Is this Iraq's reward for its role in securing the stability of the region and for protecting it from an unknown flood?

So what can it mean when America says it will now protect its friends? It can only mean prejudice against Iraq. This stance plus maneuvers and statements which have been made has encouraged the U.A.E. and Kuwait to disregard Iraqi rights.

I say to you clearly that Iraq's rights, which are mentioned in the memorandum, we will take one by one. That might not happen now or after a month or after one year, but we will take it all. We are not the kind of people who will relinquish their rights. There is no historic right, or legitimacy, or need, for the U.A.E. and Kuwait to deprive us of our rights. If they are needy, we too are needy.

The United States must have a better understanding of the situation and declare who it wants to have relations with and who its enemies are. But it should not make enemies simply because others have different points of view regarding the Arab-Israeli conflict.

We clearly understand America's statement that it wants an easy flow of oil. We understand America saying that it seeks friendship with the states in the region, and to encourage their joint interests. But we cannot understand the attempt to encourage some parties to harm Iraq's interests.

The United States wants to secure the flow of oil. This is understandable and known. But it must not deploy methods which the United States says it disapproves of—flexing muscles and pressure.

If you use pressure, we will deploy pressure and force. We know that you can harm us although we do not threaten you. But we too can harm you. Everyone can cause harm according to their ability and their size. We cannot come all the way to you in the United States, but individual Arabs may reach you.

You can come to Iraq with aircraft and missiles but do not push us to the point where we cease to care. And when we feel that you want to injure our pride and take away the Iraqis' chance of a high standard of living, then we will cease to care and death will be the choice for us. Then we would not care if you fired 100 missiles for each missile we fired. Because without pride life would have no value.

It is not reasonable to ask our people to bleed rivers of blood for eight years then to tell them, "Now you have to accept aggression from Kuwait, the U.A.E. or from the U.S. or from Israel "

We do not put all these countries in the same boat. First, we are hurt and upset that such disagreement is taking place between us and Kuwait and the U.A.E. The solution must be found within an Arab framework and through direct bilateral relations. We do not place America among the enemies. We place it where we want our friends to be and we try to be friends. But repeated American statements last year made it apparent that America did not regard us as friends. Well the Americans are free.

When we seek friendship we want pride, liberty and our right to choose.

We want to deal according to our status as we deal with the others according to their status.

We consider the others' interests while we look after our own. And we expect the others to consider our interests while they are dealing with their own. What does it mean when the Zionist war minister is summoned to the United States now? What do they mean, these fiery statements coming out of Israel during the past few days and the talk of war being expected now more than at any other time?

We don't want war because we know what war means. But do not push us to consider war as the only solution to live proudly and to provide our people with a good living.

We know that the United States has nuclear weapons. But we are determined either to live as proud men, or we all die. We do not believe that there is one single honest man on earth who would not understand what I mean.

We do not ask you to solve our problems. I said that our Arab problems will be solved amongst ourselves. But do not encourage anyone to take action which is greater than their status permits.

I do not believe that anyone would lose by making friends with Iraq. In my opinion, the American president has not made mistakes regarding the Arabs, although his decision to freeze dialogue with the PLO was wrong. But it appears that this decision was made to appease the Zionist lobby or as a piece of strategy to cool the Zionist anger, before trying again. I hope that our latter conclusion is the correct one. But we will carry on saying it was the wrong decision.

You are appeasing the usurper in so many ways—economically, politically and militarily as well as in the media. When will the time come when, for every three appeasements to the usurper, you praise the Arabs just once?

When will humanity find its real chance to seek a just American solution that would balance the human rights of two hundred million human beings with the rights of three million Jews? We want friendship, but we are not running for it. We reject harm by anybody. If we are faced with harm, we will resist. This is our right, whether the harm comes from America or the U.A.E. or Kuwait or from Israel. But I do not put all these states on the same level. Israel stole the Arab land, supported by the U.S. But the U.A.E. and Kuwait do not support Israel. Anyway, they are Arabs. But when they try to weaken Iraq, then they are helping the enemy. And then Iraq has the right to defend itself.

In 1974, I met with Idriss, the son of Mullah Mustafa Barzani [the late Kurdish leader]. He sat in the same seat as you are sitting now. He came asking me to postpone implementation of autonomy in Iraqi Kurdistan, which was agreed on March 11, 1970. My reply was: we are determined to fulfil our obligation. You also have to stick to your agreement. When I sensed that Barzani had evil intention, I said to him: give my regards to your father and tell him that Saddam Hussein says the following. I explained to him the balance of power with figures exactly the way I explained to the Iranians in my open letters to them during the war. I finished this conversation with the result summarized in one sentence: if we fight, we shall win. Do you know why? I explained all the reasons to him, plus one political reason—you [the Kurds in 1974] depended on our disagreement with the shah of Iran [Kurds were financed by Iran]. The root of the Iranian conflict is their claim of half of the Shatt al-Arab waterway. If we could keep the whole of Iraq with Shatt al-Arab, we will make no concessions. But if forced to choose between half of Shatt al-Arab or the whole of Iraq, then we will give the Shatt al-Arab away, to keep the whole of Iraq in the shape we wish it to be.

We hope that you are not going to push events to make us bear this wisdom in mind in our relations with Iran. After that [meeting with Barzani's son], we gave half of Shatt al-Arab away [1975 Algeria agreement]. And Barzani died and was buried outside Iraq and he lost his war.

[At this point, Saddam Hussein ends his message to Bush, and turns to Ambassador Glaspie]

We hope we are not pushed into this. All that lies between relations with Iran is Shatt al-Arab. When we are faced with a choice between Iraq living proudly and Shatt al-Arab then we will negotiate using the wisdom we spoke of in 1975. In the way Barzani lost his historic chance, others will lose their chance too.

With regards to President Bush, I hope the president will read this himself and will not leave it in the hands of a gang in the State Department. I exclude the secretary of state and Kelly because I know him and I exchanged views with him.

AMBASSADOR GLASPIE: I thank you, Mr. President, and it is a great pleasure for a diplomat to meet and talk directly with the president. I clearly understand your message. We studied history at school. They taught us to say freedom or death. I think you know well that we as a people have our experience with the colonialists.

Mr. President, you mentioned many things during this meeting which I cannot comment on on behalf of my Government. But with your permission, I will comment on two points. You spoke of friendship and I believe it was clear from the letters sent by our president to you on the occasion of your national day that he emphasizes—

HUSSEIN: He was kind and his expressions met with our regard and respect.

GLASPIE: As you know, he directed the United States administration to reject the suggestion of implementing trade sanctions.

HUSSEIN (SMILING): There is nothing left for us to buy from America. Only wheat. Because every time we want to buy something, they say it is forbidden. I am afraid that one day you will say, "You are going to make gunpowder out of wheat."

GLASPIE: I have a direct instruction from the president to seek better relations with Iraq.

HUSSEIN: But how? We too have this desire. But matters are running contrary to this desire.

GLASPIE: This is less likely to happen the more we talk. For example, you mentioned the issue of the article published by the American Information Agency and that was sad. And a formal apology was presented.

HUSSEIN: Your stance is generous. We are Arabs. It is enough for us that someone says, "I am sorry, I made a mistake." Then we carry on. But the media campaign continued. And it is full of stories. If the stories were true, no one would get upset. But we understand from its continuation that there is a determination [to harm relations].

GLASPIE: I saw the Diane Sawyer program on ABC. And what happened in that program was cheap and unjust. And this is a real picture of what happens in the American media—even to American politicians themselves. These are the methods the Western media employs. I am pleased that you add your voice to the diplomats who stand up to the media. Because your appearance in the media, even for five minutes, would help us to make the American people understand Iraq. This would increase mutual understanding. If the American president had control of the media, his job would be much easier.

Mr. President, not only do I want to say that President Bush wanted better and deeper relations with Iraq, but he also wants an Iraqi contribution to peace and prosperity in the Middle East. President Bush is an intelligent man. He is not going to declare an economic war against Iraq.

You are right. It is true what you say that we do not want higher prices for oil. But I would ask you to examine the possibility of not charging too high a price for oil.

HUSSEIN: We do not want too high prices for oil. And I remind you that in 1974 I gave Tariq Aziz the idea for an article he wrote which criticized the policy of keeping oil prices high. It was the first Arab article which expressed this view.

TARIQ AZIZ: Our policy in OPEC opposes sudden jumps in oil prices.

HUSSEIN: Twenty-five dollars a barrel is not a high price.

GLASPIE: We have many Americans who would like to see the price go above $25 because they come from oil-producing states.

HUSSEIN: The price at one stage had dropped to $12 a barrel and a reduction in the modest Iraqi budget of $6 billion to $7 billion is a disaster.

GLASPIE: I think I understand this. I have lived here for years. I admire your extraordinary efforts to rebuild your country. I know you need funds. We understand that and our opinion is that you should have the opportunity to rebuild your country. But we have no opinion on the Arab-Arab conflicts, like your border disagreement with Kuwait.

I was in the American embassy in Kuwait during the late '60s. The instruction we had during this period was that we should express no opinion on this issue and that the issue is not associated with America. James Baker has directed our official spokesmen to emphasize this instruction. We hope you can solve this problem using any suitable methods via Klibi or via President Mubarak. All that we hope is that these issues are solved quickly. With regard to all of this, can I ask you to see how the issue appears to us?

My assessment after twenty-five years' service in this area is that your objective must have strong backing from your Arab brothers. I now speak of oil. But you, Mr. President, have fought through a horrific and painful war. Frankly, we can only see that you have deployed massive troops in the south.

Normally that would not be any of our business. But when this happens in the context of what you said on your national day, then when we read the details in the two letters of the foreign minister, then when we see the Iraqi point of view that the measures taken by the U.A.E. and Kuwait is, in the final analysis, parallel to military aggression against Iraq, then it would be reasonable for me to be concerned. And for this reason, I received an instruction to ask you, in the spirit of friendship—not in the spirit of confrontation—regarding your intentions.

I simply describe the concern of my government. And I do not mean that the situation is a simple situation. But our concern is a simple one.

HUSSEIN: We do not ask people not to be concerned when peace is at issue. This is a noble human feeling which we all feel. It is natural for you as a superpower to be concerned. But what we ask is not to express your concern in a way that would make an aggressor believe that he is getting support for his aggression.

We want to find a just solution which will give us our rights but not deprive others of their rights. But at the same time, we want the others to know that our patience is running out regarding their action, which is harming even the milk our children drink, and the pensions of the widow who lost her husband during the war, and the pensions of the orphans who lost their parents.

As a country, we have the right to prosper. We lost so many opportunities, and the others should value the Iraqi role in their protection. Even this Iraqi [the president points to the interpreter] feels bitter like all other Iraqis. We are not aggressors but we do not accept aggression either. We sent them envoys and handwritten letters. We tried everything. We asked the Servant of the Two Shrines—King Fahd—to hold a four-member summit, but he suggested a meeting between the oil ministers. We agreed. And as you know, the meeting took place in Jidda. They reached an agreement which did not express what we wanted, but we agreed.

Only two days after the meeting, the Kuwaiti oil minister made a statement that contradicted the agreement. We also discussed the issue during the Baghdad summit. I told the Arab kings and presidents that some brothers are fighting an economic war against us. And that not all wars use weapons and we regard this kind of war as a military action against us. Because if the capability of our army is lowered then, if Iran renewed the war, it could achieve goals which it could not achieve before. And if we lowered the standard of our defenses, then this could encourage Israel to attack us. I said that before the Arab kings and presidents. Only I did not mention Kuwait and U.A.E. by name, because they were my guests.

Before this, I had sent them envoys reminding them that our war had included their defense. Therefore the aid they gave us should not be regarded as a debt. We did no more than the United States would have done against someone who attacked its interests.

I talked about the same thing with a number of other Arab states. I explained the situation to brother King Fahd a few times, by sending envoys and on the telephone. I talked with brother King Hussein and with Sheikh Zaid after the conclusion of the summit. I walked with the sheikh to the plane when he was leaving Mosul. He told me, "Just wait until I get home." But after he had reached his destination, the statements that came from there were very bad—not from him, but from his minister of oil.

Also after the Jidda agreement, we received some intelligence that they were talking of sticking to the agreement for two months only. Then they would change their policy. Now tell us, if the American president found himself in this situation, what would he do? I said it was very difficult for me to talk about these issues in public. But we must tell the Iraqi people who face economic difficulties who was responsible for that . . .

GLASPIE: I spent four beautiful years in Egypt.

HUSSEIN: The Egyptian people are kind and good and ancient. The oil people are supposed to help the Egyptian people, but they are mean beyond belief. It is painful to admit it, but some of them are disliked by Arabs because of their greed.

GLASPIE: Mr. President, it would be helpful if you could give us an assessment of the effort made by your Arab brothers and whether they have achieved anything.

HUSSEIN: On this subject, we agreed with President Mubarak that the prime minister of Kuwait would meet with the deputy chairman of the Revolution Command Council in Saudi Arabia, because the Saudis initiated contact with us, aided by President Mubarak's efforts. He just telephoned me a short while ago to say the Kuwaitis have agreed to that suggestion.

GLASPIE: Congratulations.

HUSSEIN: A protocol meeting will be held in Saudi Arabia. Then the meeting will be transferred to Baghdad for deeper discussion directly between Kuwait and Iraq. We hope we will reach some result. We hope that the long-term view and the real interests will overcome Kuwaiti greed.

GLASPIE: May I ask you when you expect Sheikh Saad to come to Baghdad?

HUSSEIN: I suppose it would be on Saturday or Monday at the latest. I told brother Mubarak that the agreement should be in Baghdad Saturday or Sunday. You know that brother Mubarak's visits have always been a good omen.

GLASPIE: This is good news. Congratulations.

HUSSEIN: Brother President Mubarak told me they were scared. They said troops were only twenty kilometers north of the Arab League line. I said to him that regardless of what is there, whether they are police, border guards or army, and regardless of how many are there, and what they are doing, assure the Kuwaitis and give them our word that we are not going to do anything until we meet with them. When we meet and when we see that there is hope, then nothing will happen. But if we are unable to find a solution, then it will be natural that Iraq will not accept death, even though wisdom is above everything else. There you have good news.

AZIZ: This is a journalistic exclusive.

GLASPIE: I am planning to go to the United States next Monday. I hope I will meet with President Bush in Washington next week. I thought to postpone my trip because of the difficulties we are facing. But now I will fly on Monday.

THE EXPERTS SPEAK ON THE COMING GULF WAR

Edited by Christopher Cerf and Victor Navasky

On June 18, 1990, reports surfaced that Iraq, who had accused its neighbor Kuwait of creating a glut on the world oil market and driving down prices, had begun massing troops along the Kuwait border. When these reports proved accurate, Washington sought to show its support for Kuwait by conducting what Reuters News Service called "a small scale, short-notice naval exercise with the United Arab Emirates," and warned Iraqi president Saddam Hussein, through a statement by State Department spokesperson Margaret Tutwiler, that "there is no place for coercion and intimidation in a civilized world." The experts had a field day with the resulting events.

"[Saddam has] no intention to attack Kuwait or any other party."
—Hosni Mubarak (President of Egypt), July 25, 1990

"We don't want war because we know what war means."
—Saddam Hussein (President of Iraq), statement to U.S. Ambassador
April Glaspie at a meeting in Baghdad, July 25, 1990

"His emphasis that he wants a peaceful settlement is surely sincere."
—April Glaspie, cable to Washington after her
meeting with Saddam, July 25, 1990

"It would be crazy to think that if . . . Iraq . . . sends its five hundred thousand troops in that we're going to send troops over there and defend Kuwait."
—Fred Barnes (Senior Editor: *The New Republic*),
The McLaughlin Group, July 27, 1990

"We can't stop Iraq if it moves into Kuwait. . . . What could we do?"
—Patrick Buchanan (syndicated newspaper columnist),
The McLaughlin Group, July 27, 1990

Christopher Cerf is a coeditor of this book. Victor Navasky is the editorial director of *The Nation* and Delacorte Professor of Journalism at the Columbia University Graduate School of Journalism. This piece is excerpted from their book, *The Experts Speak.*

On August 2, 1990, Iraqi troops and tanks invaded Kuwait and seized control of the sheikdom.

"President Bush appears to have few good military options in responding to the Iraqi invasion of Kuwait."

—Kirk Spitzer (defense correspondent),
Gannett News Service, August 2, 1990

"I don't think we have a military option."

—Sam Nunn (U.S. Senator from Georgia and Chairman
of the Senate Armed Services Committee),
quoted in *The New York Times*, August 3, 1990

"Effectively, the military planning in Washington has written off Kuwait, most sources agree."

—Nicholas M. Horrock (Washington Editor),
Chicago Tribune, August 5, 1990

"[T]he Persian Gulf has . . . become the very symbol of the impotence of power, a graphic lesson in how limited the vast U.S. military establishment really is."

—Nicholas M. Horrock, *Chicago Tribune*, August 5, 1990

"If military options refer to some way of dislodging Hussein from Kuwait, then there are no military options."

—James Schlesinger (former Director of the Central Intelligence Agency and
former U.S. Secretary of Defense), quoted in *USA Today*, August 6, 1990

"An attack wouldn't change the situation at all."

—William Colby (former Director of the Central Intelligence Agency),
quoted in *USA Today*, August 6, 1990

"We couldn't drive Iraq out of there with air power. And using ground forces would be Vietnam all over again—only worse."

—Eugene LaRocque (retired U.S. Navy Admiral and Director of the Center
for Defense Information), quoted in *USA Today*, August 6, 1990

On August 8, 1990, President George Bush announced that he was deploying "elements of the 82d Airborne Division as well as key elements of the United States Air Force . . . to assist the Saudi Arabian government in the defense of its homeland."

"The mission of our troops is wholly defensive. . . . [It] is not the mission, to drive the Iraqis out of Kuwait."

—George Bush (President of the United States),
speech and ensuing press conference, August 8, 1990

"[S]ending ground troops is wrong. They can't fight in that terrain . . ."
—Arthur Schlesinger, Jr. (historian and former adviser to U.S. President John F. Kennedy), quoted in the *Dallas Morning News*, August 8, 1990

"President George Bush's decision to send troops to Saudi Arabia and to launch an economic boycott of Iraq is both naive and wildly optimistic. . . . [T]he best that Bush can expect from his policy is a confrontation stretching into years . . . And as time goes on, Bush's support in the Arab world, among the other Western powers, and in America will steadily erode."
—Roger Hilsman (Professor of International Politics at Columbia University, and former U.S. Assistant Secretary of State), *Newsday*, August 16, 1990

"Saddam Hussein's army will trample under the feet of its heroes the heads of Bush's soldiers, crush their bones and send them to America wrapped in miserable coffins."
—*Al Jumhouriya* (Iraq's state-run newspaper), editorial, January 6, 1991

"[If the U.S. attacks Iraq, it will find itself virtually alone in a bitter and bloody war that will not be won quickly or without heavy casualties."
—Cyrus R. Vance (former U.S. Secretary of State),
testimony before the Senate Foreign Relations Committee,
quoted in *The New York Times*, January 9, 1991

"It'll be brutal and costly. . . . [T]he 45,000 body bags the Pentagon has sent to the region are all the evidence we need of the high price in lives and blood we will have to pay."
—Edward Kennedy (U.S. Senator from Massachusetts), speech on the
Senate floor urging defeat of a resolution to authorize
President Bush to use force against Iraq, January 10, 1991

On January 16, 1991, the United States launched an all-out air and missile attack on Iraq, followed, on February 24, by a massive ground assault. By February 26, Kuwait City had been liberated, and, on February 28, barely 100 hours after the land offensive had begun, President Bush announced a cease-fire. Total U.S. military casualties: 383

Editors' postscript:
How many Iraqis were killed in the first Gulf War? There has never been an official accounting, either by the Pentagon or by Iraqi authorities. As the war ended, General Norman Schwarzkopf

told reporters "there were a very, very large number of dead" soldiers on the battlefield, but refused to give any exact number or estimate. In May 1991, the Pentagon's Defense Intelligence Agency (DIA) released this statement: "An analysis of very limited information leads DIA to tentatively state the following (with an error factor of 50 per cent or higher):

Killed in action: Approx. 100,000
Wounded in action: Approx. 300,000
Deserters: Approx. 150,000"

These numbers are probably too high by a factor of anywhere from 3 to 10, as John Heidenrich, a former DIA military analyst, explained in a careful article in the March 1993 issue of *Foreign Policy* magazine. He points out that these estimates do not come anywhere close to conforming with what coalition forces found on the battlefield. Only about 2,000 of the 71,000 Iraqi soldiers taken prisoner were wounded. He asks, "Where were DIA's missing 298,000" wounded troops? If they fled during the 100-hour ground war, their injuries would have tended to immobilize them, leading to their capture. Heidenrich further argues that, given the historical ratio of three wounded soldiers for every one killed, that "Iraq could not have suffered 100,000 dead but only a few thousand wounded."

In May 1992, the House Armed Service Committee estimated that the Gulf War air campaign killed 9,000 Iraqis and wounded another 17,000. In *Triumph Without Victory,* a 1992 book by the staff of *U.S. News and World Report,* a low-end estimate of 8,000 killed and 24,000 is offered. As Heidenrich points out, one of the difficulties involved in deriving an estimate is the lack of precise information on how many Iraqi troops were in the war theater in the first place. While the U.S. military assumed there were at least 500,000, later reports from Iraqi prisoners suggest that far fewer actually deployed with their units and as many as 30 percent deserted once the air campaign began. Heidenrich suggests the number of Iraqi troops may have been below 200,000 by the time of the ground assault. On the basis of reports from captured Iraqi commanders, who said their own casualty rates were very low, Heidenrich argues that "the range of Iraqi bombing casualties in the [Kuwait Theater of Operations] fell between 700 and 3,000 dead; with somewhere between 2,000 and 7,000 wounded," numbers that conform more closely with the actual number of injured taken prisoner. He adds another 6,500 killed and 19,500 wounded during the ground war, based on the observed number of Iraqi armored vehicles destroyed.

(There is reason to suspect that there were never as many as 500,000 Iraqi troops in Kuwait. Satellite photographs taken by the Soviet Union in mid-September 1990 show "no sign of a significant Iraqi presence in Kuwait," Florida's *St. Petersburg Times* reported. Satellite-imaging experts retained by the paper, including a former DIA specialist, also said there was no indication that Iraqi troops were massed on the Kuwait border with Saudi Arabia—a puzzling finding given that America was rushing troops to the region to defend Saudi Arabia from what it said was the danger that Iraq would move on that country's oil fields.)

As for the number of civilian casualties, such estimates are even more difficult to make. Four hundred Iraqis, many of them women and children, were incinerated when coalition forces bombed the Amariya bunker in Baghdad on February 13, 1991. The director of Yarmuk Hospital, the city's primary surgical center, told Erika Munk of *The Nation* that they treated 1,000 civilians for injuries suffered during the bombing, and that between 100 and 200 died. Iraqi authorities claimed much higher death tolls, but never showed reporters evidence to back up their claims. There were probably more Iraqi civilians killed in the suppression of the Shiite and Kurdish uprisings that followed the war than were killed by coalition forces during the war itself. Finally, there are the deaths that occurred during the 1990s as a result of the destruction of much of Iraqi civilian infrastructure and the imposition of economic sanctions by the U.N. In 1999, UNICEF reported that the country's mortality rate for children under 5 had doubled, meaning the premature deaths of 500,000 children had occurred. Responsibility for that atrocity has to be shared by Saddam Hussein's regime and the international community.

HOW SADDAM MISREAD THE UNITED STATES

Kenneth Pollack

The Iraqi invasion was a nasty shock for the Bush administration. It represented a serious threat to America's principal objectives in the Persian Gulf region, to ensure the free flow of oil and prevent an inimical power from establishing hegemony over the region. If Saddam were allowed to retain possession of Kuwait, leaving him with roughly 9 percent of global oil production, his economic clout would rival that of Saudi Arabia, which accounted for about 11 percent of global production. In addition, his military force, if left intact and occupying Kuwait, would allow him to so threaten the Saudis themselves that they would be effectively "Finlandized"—forced to follow foreign and oil-pricing policies dictated by Baghdad. This combination could effectively allow Saddam to control the global price of oil. In time of crisis, Baghdad could threaten to undermine the global economy by withholding Iraqi oil, thereby sending oil prices soaring. Even if Saddam chose to follow a policy of high production and low oil prices, the enormous revenues he would be collecting would allow him almost limitless spending on his WMD programs, terrorism, and other pet projects. It was simply a matter of time before the world would have to confront a nuclear-armed Saddam (and not very much time, as the U.N. inspectors discovered after the war). Moreover, the invasion of Kuwait demonstrated that the U.S. administration's policy of constructive engagement and its assessment that Saddam was "pragmatic" and "moderate" in his aims were mistaken.

These fears were driven home on Sunday, August 5, three days after the Iraqi invasion. That morning I was at the CIA bright and early when we began to receive ominous intelligence reports. The vast logistical tail that had supported the Iraqi invasion of Kuwait (and contained supplies for more than a

From 1995 to 2001, Kenneth M. Pollack served as director for Gulf affairs at the National Security Council, where he was the principal working-level official responsible for implementation of U.S. policy toward Iraq. Prior to his time in the Clinton administration, he spent seven years as a Persian Gulf military analyst for the Central Intelligence Agency. He is currently the director of research at the Saban Center for Middle East Policy at the Brookings Institution and Director of National Security Studies for the Council on Foreign Relations, and is author of the best-selling book, *The Threatening Storm: The Case for Invading Iraq,* from which this article is excerpted.

month of high-intensity combat) had been discovered deep in southern Kuwait, where it had no business being if it was only supporting an occupation of Kuwait, but where it was perfectly placed for an invasion of Saudi Arabia. Likewise, we found Iraqi artillery pieces deployed far forward, close to the Saudi border. During the night there had been an incursion by Iraqi tanks from western Kuwait into Saudi Arabia. Meanwhile, other reports provided unmistakable evidence that the Iraqis were loading CW munitions onto strike aircraft at several of their airfields in southern Kuwait. Four of the best heavy divisions of the regular army were reinforcing the eight Republican Guard divisions in Kuwait as fast as they could. And several brigades of Republican Guard armor were reported heading south toward the Saudi border from their previous positions in southern Kuwait. Although it would later turn out that these last reports were exaggerated—the Iraqi units were battalions, not brigades—the combination of these reports set off alarm bells all over Washington. I wrote up a report warning that these events could be signs of an imminent Iraqi attack on Saudi Arabia, and Bruce Riedel took it along with him when he joined Director of Central Intelligence William Webster at a meeting of the National Security Council (NSC) that afternoon. Judge Webster convinced the NSC that the Iraqi threat to the kingdom was very real (if not imminent) and would be disastrous to U.S. interests. Although no one could be sure that this was the start of an Iraqi invasion of Saudi Arabia, the NSC agreed that it could not afford to be wrong again. At the meeting, they decided to send Secretary of Defense Richard Cheney to Saudi Arabia immediately to convince Saudi King Fahd to let the United States defend the kingdom. The next day, President Bush declared to the world that Iraq's invasion of Kuwait "would not stand," and after meeting with Cheney, King Fahd agreed to Operation Desert Shield, bringing 250,000 American troops in to defend Saudi Arabia.

As best we can tell, Saddam did not intend to invade Saudi Arabia on August 5. Instead, it now appears that his actions were meant to deter an American counterattack—like a blowfish, he was puffing himself up to look big and tough, to try to convince Washington that if we wanted to retake Kuwait from him we were going to have a terrific fight on our hands. Other events, such as the forward positioning of Iraq's artillery and logistics, were accidental, caused by the dislocation that had accompanied the invasion. That said, there is no question that Saddam would have used his dominant military position in Kuwait to blackmail the Saudis on various scores and, given how easy his invasion of Kuwait had been, might at some point have chosen to simply achieve his long-cherished goal of making himself the Gulf's hegemon by invading the kingdom and seizing its oil fields outright. Indeed, Saddam's then chief of intelligence, Wafiq al-Samarra'i, told an interviewer, "I believe that Saddam did not, and would not have been satisfied with only Kuwait. Had his invasion of Kuwait been without reprisals, he would have continued to take the Eastern part of Saudi Arabia."

Over time, however, when it became clear that Saddam did not intend to attack Saudi Arabia immediately, Washington began to see the invasion as an opportunity. Saddam had now been revealed as an extremely dangerous leader, and the administration recognized that the past revelations regarding Iraq's unshakable pursuit of weapons of mass destruction and outrageous violations of human rights were further proof that the Baghdad regime was a force for real instability in the vital Persian Gulf region. Increasingly in the months after the Iraqi invasion, Bush administration officials saw the crisis as an opportunity to smash Iraq's military power, eliminate its WMD programs, and reduce or eliminate it as a threat to the region.

The evolution of Washington's strategy for dealing with the crisis demonstrated this shift. Initially, the Bush administration had only one thought: defend Saudi Arabia. After obtaining Riyadh's agreement, U.S. Central Command (CENTCOM)—the military command with responsibility for the Persian Gulf—began pouring forces into Saudi Arabia and the Gulf to defend it against a subsequent Iraqi attack. By early September, enough American forces had arrived that Washington could breathe a sigh of relief. Meanwhile, the Bush administration had played its diplomatic hand skillfully and—with some help from Iraq's aggressiveness and diplomatic bungling—had persuaded the U.N. Security Council to pass a series of resolutions condemning the Iraqi invasion, demanding that Iraq withdraw, and imposing severe sanctions on Iraq for failing to comply. This in turn made possible the fashioning of a coalition of Western and Arab states willing to defend Saudi Arabia. When Saddam proved that the sanctions alone were not going to convince him to withdraw from Kuwait, the Bush administration resolved to do the job militarily and in so doing destroy Iraq's conventional forces and WMD. The United States doubled the size of the American military force in the Gulf and elicited additional contributions from the coalition members to build an offensive capability to enforce the U.N. resolutions against Saddam's will.

REGARDLESS OF any illusions he had held before the invasion of Kuwait, afterward Saddam discerned fairly quickly that the United States was not going to accept his conquest. Initially, Baghdad tried to cover up its actions by inventing the excuse that Iraq had simply been responding to a request for intervention by "popular forces" in Kuwait. But for reasons of secrecy, Iraq had not taken any steps to contact Kuwaiti oppositionists before the invasion, so that after the fact, Baghdad could not find any Kuwaiti leader willing to serve as a quisling. By August 8, Saddam simply announced that he was annexing Kuwait as Iraq's nineteenth province. At roughly the same time, the first American ground and air forces began arriving in the Persian Gulf as part of Operation Desert Shield. Baghdad recognized that it was locked in a confrontation with the United States, and Saddam and his advisers refashioned their grand strategy around four critical assumptions:

1. Iraq believed that the multinational coalition the United States had put together was politically fragile and would collapse if pressure were applied to its weakest links, primarily the Arab members of the coalition. Baghdad believed that many of the Arab states were ambivalent about the fate of Kuwait, unhappy with U.S. support for Israel, and sensitive to charges of allowing "imperialist" forces to regain a foothold in the Middle East.

2. Saddam took it as an article of faith that the United States would be unwilling to tolerate high costs, and particularly heavy casualties, to liberate Kuwait. He believed that Kuwait was not very important to the West—especially if he promised to keep the oil flowing—and believed that the lessons of U.S. experience in Vietnam and Lebanon were that America would throw in the towel if American units began to suffer heavy casualties.

3. Saddam was also certain that in a war with Iraqi forces for Kuwait, the United States would take serious losses. Saddam failed to appreciate the vast disparity in the quality of equipment, tactics, and personnel between the Iraqi and Western militaries. Thus, he was certain that if he could not prevent a war by fracturing the political cohesion of the coalition, his army would be able to inflict a bloody stalemate on the coalition in battle that would force them to the bargaining table. What's more, Saddam was counting on the threat of this scenario to convince the Americans not to go to war in the first place.

4. Last, Saddam believed that air power would play only a minimal role in a war with the coalition. In a radio address on August 30, Saddam reassured his people that "The United States depends on the air force. The air force has never decided a war in the history of wars. In the early days of the war between us and Iran, the Iranians had an edge in the air. They had approximately 600 aircraft, all U.S.-made and whose pilots received training in the United States. They flew to Baghdad like black clouds, but they did not determine the outcome of the battle. In later years, our air force gained supremacy, and yet it was not our air force that settled

the war. The United States may be able to destroy cities, factories, and to kill, but it will not be able to decide the war with the air force."

Iraq's strategy followed logically from these assumptions. Baghdad launched a public relations offensive to undermine the coalition's political will. Iraq threatened that a war with Iraq would be the "Mother of All Battles" in which thousands of troops would be killed. It threatened to destroy Kuwait's oil infrastructure, as well as that of Saudi Arabia, hoping this would convince oil-dependent Western nations to avoid a military showdown. Tariz Aziz, among others, stated that Iraq would drag Israel into the conflict to turn it into a new Arab-Israeli war that would force the Arab members of the coalition to choose between fighting their Iraqi Arab brothers or their Zionist enemy. Iraq called on the Arab masses to revolt against their corrupt regimes who were handing over Islam's sacred lands to armies of infidels from the West.

Meanwhile, the Iraqi armed forces remained on the defensive and prepared for a knock-down, drag-out fight. Iraq chose not to attack Saudi Arabia or the coalition forces building up there because Saddam felt that doing so would simply ensure the war that he preferred to deter. Instead, Baghdad stuffed as many units as it possibly could into the Kuwaiti Theater of Operations (KTO) to try to convince the coalition that a war would be long and bloody. By the start of Operation Desert Storm in January 1991, Iraq had deployed fifty-one of its sixty-six divisions to the KTO, a force that probably numbered somewhere around 550,000 men at its peak, and fielded 3,475 tanks, 3,080 armored personnel carriers (APCs), and 2,475 artillery pieces. Iraq built extensive defensive fortifications to defend those troops, like the defenses it had constructed to stymie the Iranian offensives throughout the Iran-Iraq War. It dispersed the components of its WMD programs and heavily bunkered and reinforced what could not be hidden.

Saddam was so confident that his strategy would work that he never really took seriously the international efforts to negotiate a settlement to the crisis. Throughout the fall of 1990, a procession of officials—from the United Nations, the Arab League, France, Russia, and many other countries and organizations—came to Baghdad to try to resolve the dispute short of war. However, right up to the start of Operation Desert Shield (and for a month after it), Baghdad refused to accept any of the U.N. Security Council resolutions or to negotiate except on its own terms. Instead, the Iraqis attempted to turn each effort to negotiate a solution into an opportunity to score propaganda points. Moreover, by the end of August, Baghdad had concluded a sort of rapprochement with Tehran at the price of conceding virtually all of Iran's demands, including giving up the remaining Iranian land under Iraqi control and agreeing to some of the terms of the old Algiers Accord. The deal secured Iraq's eastern flank, allowing Baghdad to concentrate virtually all of its forces on the defense of Kuwait, but meant that Saddam now had absolutely nothing to show for the eight years of war against Iran. It meant that he was staking everything on winning the war for Kuwait.

The problem for Saddam was that the four assumptions underpinning his grand strategy all turned out to be wrong. The coalition never fell apart. It is an open debate just how close to collapse it ever came or how long it might have held together if Washington had had to delay the start of the war, but this is now a question for scholars: for Iraq it was a decisive failure. Similarly, who knows how many casualties the United States and its allies would have been willing to tolerate—although before the war, polls showed strong support even if a war resulted in 10,000 American casualties, and the administration never wavered. However, Iraq's armed forces found themselves hopelessly outmatched against the full might of the United States' armed forces and inflicted pitifully little damage on the coalition's Western militaries.

Starting on January 17, 1991, the U.S.-led coalition unleashed the forty-three days of Operation Desert Storm. The coalition air forces quickly disrupted Iraq's command and control network and tore up its extensive air defenses. American fighters quickly found that Iraqi pilots were poor dogfighters (many could barely fly, let alone fight) and shot down nearly three dozen Iraqi jets with only one coalition loss. Coalition strike aircraft shut down much of the country's electricity, water, and oil production, as well as destroying bridges and railroads, impeding movement on Iraq's roads, and hammering Iraq's military forces themselves. In addition, the coalition mounted a fierce campaign on Saddam's known WMD and arms production factories. Iraq did fight back, launching volleys of al-Hussein modified Scud missiles at Israel, Saudi Arabia, and Bahrain, but U.S. diplomacy (and the reassuring—if ultimately ineffective—presence of American Patriot surface-to-air missiles in Israel and Saudi Arabia) succeeded in keeping the Israelis out of the war and the Saudis in. When the Scuds failed to do the trick, Saddam tried other approaches. He threatened the international oil market by setting Kuwait's oil wells on fire. He tried to create an ecological catastrophe by dumping Kuwaiti oil into the Persian Gulf. He tried to mount several terrorist operations against the coalition, but these were easily thwarted by Western intelligence services. Finally, he mounted a surprise offensive by two of Iraq's best regular army divisions to maul some of the coalition Arab units in the hope that this would force the coalition high command to cut short the air campaign and get on with the ground campaign (in which, Saddam still believed, Iraq would be able to inflict heavy casualties on the coalition). But the attack had to be called off on its second day when the two divisions came under murderous fire from coalition air forces.

Very shortly, the Iraqis began to realize that things were not going according to their plan. As the weeks passed, Saddam concluded that many of his assumptions had been badly off base. Saddam's military advisers had expected that the coalition's air campaign would last three to seven days at most; even the most pessimistic among them had not believed it could go on more than ten days. It never occurred to the Iraqi leadership that the coalition would sit back and bomb them for thirty-nine days before making a move on the ground. By mid-February, Saddam had become very concerned, in particular because the coalition air campaign was doing more damage to his army in the KTO than he had ever expected. As best we understand it, Saddam's concern was not that the air strikes themselves would destroy the Iraqi Army or drive it out of Kuwait, but that they were so weakening his army in the Kuwaiti Theater that it would not be able to stand up to the coalition ground forces when they finally did attack. Coalition air strikes probably destroyed around 1,200 Iraqi armored vehicles. Of far greater importance, the coalition air campaign had effectively shut down Iraq's logistical system in the KTO and was demolishing the morale of the army, leading to widespread desertions. Indeed, by the time the coalition ground offensive did kick off on February 24, Iraqi forces in the Kuwaiti Theater had fallen from their high of around 550,000 to about 350,000 because of these morale and logistical problems.

At that point, Saddam finally began to try to negotiate his way out of Kuwait, using the Russians as intermediaries. Although initially Saddam may simply have been trying to trick the coalition into suspending its military operations, within a week he had become so desperate that he was genuinely trying to get his army out of Kuwait intact. By then he appears to have become convinced that his army was melting away and the coalition ground offensive could destroy it altogether—a catastrophe that would almost certainly produce challenges to his rule, perhaps even a full-scale revolution—and he calculated that if the army and Republican Guard were destroyed, he might not have the strength to defend himself. In mid-February, there were demonstrations in the southern Iraqi cities of al-Basrah and ad-Diwaniyyah in which the protesters shouted anti-Saddam slogans and killed several Baath Party officials, and Saddam may have seen this as a portent of things to come if he could not rescue the army in Kuwait. Although Baghdad's first offers were little more than propaganda positions it had trotted out before the onset of Desert Storm (such as making one condition for Iraqi withdrawal from Kuwait a simultaneous Israeli withdrawal from the West Bank, the Gaza

Strip, and the Golan Heights), by February 22 Iraq had agreed to begin with-drawing from Kuwait in twenty-four hours if the coalition would agree to sus-pend its military operations immediately and lift the U.N. sanctions. To the coalition, this Iraqi offer was just another hoax—what incentive would Sad-dam have to comply if the coalition ceased its military operations and lifted the sanctions? But from Saddam's perspective this was tantamount to surren-der. As Saddam's previous discussion with Soviet envoy Yevgeny Primakov had indicated, his greatest fear was that as Iraqi forces pulled out of their fortifica-tions and withdrew from Kuwait, the coalition would launch its ground offen-sive and catch the Iraqis when they were most vulnerable. He was asking only that his army be allowed to survive and the status quo ante be restored in re-turn for his withdrawing from Kuwait.

Having rejected Saddam's final offer, the coalition launched its long-awaited ground campaign on February 24. When it came, Iraq's frontline in-fantry divisions disintegrated in a mass of surrenders and flight. The coalition strategy consisted of a diversionary attack by U.S. Marines into southeastern Kuwait, coupled with a vast outflanking maneuver to the west of the Iraqi lines (the famed "Left Hook") by the U.S. VII Corps, the most powerful armored concentration in history. On the second day of the ground war Bagh-dad realized two important facts. First, that morning they had counterat-tacked the Marines with one of their best regular army mechanized divisions, only to have it wiped out in a few hours of fighting, having done virtually no damage to the Marines. This let Baghdad know that even its best formations could not hope to defeat the coalition army. Second, after several Iraqi units were destroyed by huge American armored formations in the far west of the Kuwaiti Theater, Baghdad recognized the Left Hook. It must have been a ter-rible shock to the Iraqis to realize that powerful U.S. armored forces were moving to cut off the entire Iraqi Army in Kuwait. In response, Saddam issued a general retreat order to try to get as much of his army out as fast as he could. Meanwhile, the Iraqi General Staff shifted five Republican Guard divisions and three armored and mechanized divisions of the regular army to form up defensive screens to the west and south, behind which the army was sup-posed to retreat. They also pulled several other Republican Guard and regular army heavy divisions back to defend Baghdad and al-Basrah against a possible coalition move to overthrow the regime.

On the third and fourth days of the ground campaign, coalition forces smashed into the Iraqi defensive screen and fought the hardest battles of the war. In southeastern Kuwait, the Iraqi First Mechanized and Third Armored Divisions put up a desultory fight around Kuwait International Airport and the Matlah Pass that kept the Marines occupied but never endangered them.

However, in the west of the Kuwaiti Theater, the Republican Guards fought to the death. On February 26, three U.S. armored and mechanized divisions and one armored cavalry regiment (a combined force of more than one thousand M-1A1 tanks) plowed into the lines of the Iraqi Tawakalnah 'alla Allah Mechanized Division of the Republican Guard. In roughly twelve hours of vicious combat, the Americans obliterated the Tawakalnah—destroying nearly every one of the division's three hundred operable tanks and APCs—but the Americans came away with a great deal of respect for the Republican Guards, who fought on despite being outnumbered, outgunned, and outmatched in every way. The story was the same on February 27, when other American armored units crushed a brigade of the Madinah Munawrah Armored Division and the Adnan and Nebuchadnezzar Infantry Divisions. The Guards did not fight well and inflicted minimal damage on the Americans, but they fought hard.

Meanwhile, the fog of war had descended over the American political and military leadership, prompting the most controversial decision of the war. By the end of February 27, the U.S. Central Command believed that the Republican Guard had largely been destroyed. This was based on reports from American combat units claiming to have engaged with and wiped out Iraqi Republican Guard formations, reports that U.S. troops were already at the outskirts of al-Basrah, and the assumption that coalition air forces had sealed all the lines of retreat out of the Kuwaiti Theater. Added to this were reports of a massacre by coalition aircraft of Iraqi soldiers fleeing Kuwait (mostly in stolen Kuwaiti vehicles and piled high with loot). The president was already feeling domestic pressure to end the war and the "slaughter" of Iraqi forces. Consequently, with the advice of the Pentagon and CENTCOM, President Bush ordered a halt to the ground offensive during the morning of February 28.

The reality was somewhat different. Of the eight Republican Guard divisions deployed to the Kuwaiti Theater, only three (Nebuchadnezzar, Adnan, and Tawakalnah) had been destroyed, and a fourth (Madinah) had lost about half of its strength. CENTCOM actually did not know where many American units were, believing them to be farther forward than was actually the case. Nor were the exits from the Kuwaiti Theater cut off: at least two Republican Guard divisions—the Baghdad Infantry and the Special Forces Divisions— had already escaped across the Euphrates River and were moving to defend the capital. Finally, the Hammurabi Armored Division and al-Faw Infantry Division remained largely intact and, along with the remnants of the Madinah, were taking up positions to defend al-Basrah. Even the reported "slaughter" on what was becoming called the "Highway of Death" turned out to have been wrong: in fact, the vast majority of the Iraqis fled their vehicles when the first aircraft appeared, and only a few dozen bodies were found among the hundreds of wrecked vehicles. As a result, it was a rude surprise for the administration in the first days of March when we at the CIA began to write about the 842 Iraqi tanks that had survived Desert Storm (about 400 of which were Republican Guard T-72s) and the steps that the surviving Republican Guard divisions were taking to put down the revolts against Saddam's regime.

PART TWO

AFTERMATHS OF THE GULF WAR

THREE

SADDAM SURVIVES

"There's another way for the bloodshed to stop, and that is for the Iraqi military and the Iraqi people to take matters into their own hands, to force Saddam Hussein, the dictator, to step aside."

—*President George H. W. Bush, February 15, 1991*

"What has befallen us of defeat, shame, and humiliation, Saddam, is the result of your follies, your miscalculations, and your irresponsible actions!"

—*Iraqi tank commander, addressing a large portrait of Saddam next to Baath party headquarters in downtown Basra, on February 28, 1991. Moments later, he fired several shells at Saddam's face, setting off the shortlived post-Gulf War Iraqi uprising.*

"In 1991 Iraq was not defeated. In fact, our Army withdrew from Kuwait according to a decision taken by us."

—*Saddam Hussein to CBS anchor Dan Rather, February 26, 2003*

"WE HAVE SADDAM HUSSEIN STILL HERE"

Andrew Cockburn and Patrick Cockburn

Three months to the day after the allied guns fell silent in Kuwait, a highly classified letter landed on the desk of Frank Anderson, a gray-haired senior official at CIA headquarters in Langley, Virginia. Anderson looked at it glumly and then scribbled "I don't like this" in the margin.

The letter was a formal "finding," signed by President Bush, authorizing the CIA to mount a covert operation to "create the conditions for the removal of Saddam Hussein from power." Anderson, as chief of the Near East division of the agency's Directorate of Operations, was the man who would have to carry it out. He was being asked to succeed where seven hundred thousand allied soldiers had failed and he did not think it could be done. "We didn't have a single mechanism or combination of mechanisms with which I could create a plan to get rid of Saddam at that time," he said later.

CIA officials faced with peremptory orders to deal with some foreign irritant—as in "Get rid of Khomeini"—like to quote an aphorism coined by a former director, Richard Helms: "Covert action is frequently a substitute for a policy." Anderson was paying the price for the war planners' failure to think about the future of Iraq after an allied victory in Kuwait.

George Bush himself had been the first to express the notion that the war might have been a triumph without a victory. "To be very honest with you, I haven't yet felt this wonderfully euphoric feeling that many of the American people feel," he said the day after his armies ceased fire. "I think it's that I want to see an end. And now we have Saddam Hussein still here."

Bush had ordered the cease-fire because his armies had overrun Kuwait in a headline-friendly 100 hours with minimal casualties. It appeared to have been the military equivalent of a perfect game in baseball and the American generals were not anxious to mar the record with any further fighting. In any event, the White House had been assured that the Republican Guard,

---

Patrick Cockburn is a visiting fellow at the Center for Strategic and International Studies in Washington and a veteran Middle East correspondent for the *Financial Times* and the London *Independent*. Andrew Cockburn is the author of several books on defense and international affairs. He has also written about the Middle East for *The New Yorker* and coproduced the 1991 PBS documentary on Iraq, "The War We Left Behind." This article is excerpted from their book *Out of the Ashes: The Resurrection of Saddam Hussein*.

Saddam's most loyal and accomplished troops, were trapped without the possibility of escape—one of the principal wartime objectives of the U.S. military command.

In fact, even before Bush called a halt, the bulk of the Republican Guard had already eluded the planned allied encirclement with relative ease, moving out of the intended area of entrapment on February 27. By March 1, they were sixty miles north of Basra, therefore a delay of twenty-four hours in announcing the cease-fire would have made no difference. It was only one of many miscalculations by the U.S. war planners. Other objectives wrongly thought to have been achieved included the severing of Saddam's communication links with his troops and the destruction of Iraq's nuclear, biological, and chemical warfare programs. "Saddam Hussein is out of the nuclear business," Defense Secretary Richard Cheney had confidently asserted to a closed hearing of the Senate Foreign Relations Committee after weeks of bombing. Like many other assumptions about the consequences of the Iraq campaign, this boast was soon to be revealed as embarrassingly false.

Years later, Bush would still be haunted by the recurring question: Why had he not "gone all the way to Baghdad" and settled the Saddam problem when he had had the chance? Each time he would patiently explain that the United Nations resolutions under which he had launched the war authorized only the liberation of Kuwait and he could not legally have gone further. Iraqi resistance would have stiffened. And anyway, if the Americans had gotten to Baghdad, they would have had to occupy the place for months afterward.

That was not quite the whole story. As British diplomats from the Gulf had forcefully pointed out in a secret meeting before the war, if the allies displaced Saddam and occupied Baghdad, they would eventually have to hold elections for a new government before pulling out. This would have led to all sorts of problems for Anglo-American allies among the semifeudal monarchies of the region, especially Saudi Arabia. No one wanted to encourage democracy in Iraq. It might prove catching. It had been a conservative war to keep the Middle East as it was, not to introduce change.

Militarily, an advance on Baghdad might not have been difficult. General Steven Arnold, the U.S. Army's chief operations officer in Saudi Arabia, actually drew up a secret plan after the cease-fire entitled "The Road to Baghdad," which he calculated could easily be carried out with a fraction of the forces available. Arnold's commanding officer, horrified at such an implicit admission that the victory was less than complete, put the plan under lock and key. Unfortunately, neither the military nor the White House had as yet any other plan for dealing with Iraq once the issue of Kuwait had been settled.

According to Chas. Freeman, wartime ambassador to Saudi Arabia, this lack of forethought was deliberate. "The White House was terrified of leaks about any U.S. plans that might unhinge the huge and unwieldy coalition that George Bush had put together to support the war," he recalled later. "So officials were discouraged from writing, talking, or even thinking about what to do next."

Faced with such awkward considerations, the conduct of the war had been left largely to the military, whose vision had its limitations. Before the bombing started, an air force general paid a call on Ambassador James Akins, a distinguished former diplomat with a wealth of experience in Iraq. The general explained that he wished to consult the ambassador on the selection of suitable bombing targets. Akins suggested that the Pentagon might find it more useful to draw on his knowledge of Iraqi politics and of Saddam, whom he had known for years. "Oh, no, Mr. Ambassador," said his visitor. "You see, this war has no political overtones."

During the war itself, the U.S. high command pursued a straightforward approach to Iraqi politics: Kill the president of Iraq. The chosen weapons were laser-guided bombs aimed at Saddam's command posts, meticulously charted by the targeters. Since the United States has officially foresworn assassination as an instrument of foreign policy, the scheme was cloaked in euphemisms about targeting "command and control" centers. Nevertheless, the killing was scheduled from the day in August 1990 when air force planners wrote "Saddam" as the main priority in the first bombing plan. The air force chief of staff was fired a month later for publicly admitting that the Iraqi leader was "the focus of our efforts."

Brent Scowcroft, Bush's National Security Adviser and trusted confidant, conceded afterward that "We don't do assassinations, but yes, we targeted all the places where Saddam might have been."

"So you deliberately set out to kill him if you possibly could?" he was asked.

"Yes, that's fair enough," replied the man who had approved the hit. In fact, the Iraqi leadership, anticipating the Americans' intentions, knew full well that the most dangerous place to be during the war was inside a bunker. Most stayed in suburban houses in Baghdad. "They weren't huddled in a bunker," says a senior Iraqi officer, "because we were well aware that they were well known to the allies. We also knew that there were weapons that could destroy them."

The hunt petered out after one of the places targeters thought their quarry might be turned out to be the Amariya civilian bomb shelter and over four hundred people, mostly women and children, were incinerated. The generals' fixation on targets was unfortunate because, while U.S. intelligence knew a great deal about Iraq—buildings, communications systems, power plants, bunkers—it knew very little about Iraqis. For many years there was no U.S. embassy in Baghdad and, in any case, the country and its people were screened from the outside world by an efficient and ruthless regime. Even when Saddam Hussein needed the help of U.S. intelligence, he had done his best to keep the Americans in the dark as much as possible about events in his ruthlessly efficient police state.

In the 1980s, the two countries had been de facto allies—full diplomatic relations were restored in 1984—in the war with Iran, and the CIA sent a liaison team to Baghdad to deliver satellite photos and other useful intelligence. It was a handsome gift, but Saddam, the seasoned conspirator, was highly sensitive to the perils of such a relationship.

From 1986 on, General al-Samarrai, then deputy head of the Istikbarat, military intelligence, was one of only three officers permitted by the dictator to meet with the CIA. Just to be on the safe side, Saddam put al-Samarrai himself under intensive surveillance by the Amn al-Khass, the special security organization that reported directly to the presidential palace.

"The CIA used to send us a lot of information about Iran," al-Samarrai remembers. In addition, when preparing for an attack, his service would routinely request specific intelligence from the Americans. "I used to say, for example, 'Give us information on the Basra sector.' Saddam would say: 'Don't tell them like that, ask them to give us information from the north of Iraq to the south, because if we tell them it's only Basra, they would tell the Iranians.'" al-Samarrai would sometimes get memos on his U.S. contacts back from his master with cautionary notes scribbled in the margins: "Be careful, Americans are conspirators."

(Saddam's suspicions were not without merit. In 1986, during the infamous Iran-Contra episode, the United States gave the Iranians intelligence on the Iraqi order of battle. Coincidentally or not, Iraq then suffered a stunning defeat in the Fao peninsula.)

Late in 1989, the war with Iran won, Saddam decided that the relationship had outlived its usefulness, and expelled the CIA officials stationed in Baghdad. Diplomats who remained until the invasion of Kuwait were hardly better situated to collect information, since all contacts with ordinary Iraqis were tightly restricted. Even maids and chauffeurs catering to the diplomats' domestic needs tended to be foreign workers, Egyptians or Palestinians. In any case, all contacts with foreigners were subject to suspicious scrutiny by the Mukhabarat.

After the invasion of Kuwait, the various U.S. intelligence agencies speedily accumulated a vast quantity of information from surveillance satellites and spy planes. A massive CIA program to interview the foreign contractors who had helped build the bunkers, radar sites, communications links, and other physical infrastructure for Saddam's war machine produced further mountains of reports. Sometimes the methods used were ingenious, as when the CIA analyzed the clothes of former American hostages who had been held at the Tuwaitha nuclear plant and found telltale flecks of highly enriched uranium, a clear indication of an Iraqi bomb program.

The most secret component of the collection effort was the small group of agents recruited and infiltrated into Iraq. Given the consequences of being caught, these were courageous individuals. Communication was difficult; the radios with which they were provided did not always work efficiently, and some among the spies were reluctant even to take the risk of switching the devices on. "One or two of them were very useful," recalls one former CIA official involved in the program. On the other hand, the high command in Riyadh gave the final order to attack the Amariya shelter only after a "reliable" agent reported that it was being used for military purposes.

Astonishingly, one potentially fruitful source of intelligence was off limits. In 1988, the Iraqi and Turkish governments had complained when a mid-level State Department official received a Kurdish opposition leader to hear complaints about Saddam's use of poison gas against his subjects in Kurdistan. Any implicit recognition of Kurdish nationalism was anathema to either regime, so in deference to the sensitivities of these two allies, Secretary of State George Shultz had thereupon forbidden all further contact by any official of the U.S. government with any member of the Iraqi opposition.

The "no contacts" rule still applied during the war, which was why, for example, an offer of timely military intelligence from the Kurdish underground in northern Iraq was spurned by the Pentagon. Eventually, a system was improvised by which reports collected by Kurds were radioed to their office in Iran, thence to Damascus, thence by phone to another office in Detroit, and then faxed to Peter Galbraith, the sympathetic staff director of the Senate Foreign Relations Committee. "This was not stupid stuff," remembers Galbraith. "One of them was about what happened to an allied pilot who had been shot down. But they were picked up by a bored lieutenant from naval intelligence who couldn't have been less interested."

On the day that the allied forces ceased fire, February 28, 1991, the Kurdish leader Jalal Talabani tried to enter the State Department, intending to brief officials on the imminent uprising in northern Iraq. Thanks to the bar on contacts, no official dared speak with him, and he and his party never got beyond the department's lobby. The following day, Richard Haass, director for Middle East Affairs on the National Security Council staff, phoned Galbraith to complain about the Senate staffer's sponsorship of the unwelcome Kurds.

Surely, protested Galbraith, the Kurds were allies in the fight against the Baghdad regime. "You don't understand," fumed the powerful White House official. "Our policy is to get rid of Saddam, not his regime."

The word "policy" was misused. In lieu of intelligence about the political situation in Iraq, the White House was acting on the basis of assumptions. Principal among these was a deeply ingrained belief that Saddam would inevitably be displaced by a military coup. A veteran of CIA operations in Iraq explains it this way: "All the analysts in State, CIA, DIA, NSA were in agreement with the verdict that Saddam was going to fall. There wasn't a single dissenting voice. The only trouble was, they had no hard data at all. Their whole way of thinking really was conditioned on a Western way of looking at things: A leader such as Saddam who had been defeated and humiliated would have to leave office. Just that. Plus," sighs the former covert operator, "none of these analysts had ever set foot inside Iraq. Not one."

"A collective mistake," agrees one former very high-ranking CIA official. "Everybody believed that he was going to fall. Everybody was wrong."

Nothing illustrates the lack of understanding of the situation on the ground in Iraq better than the notorious call by Bush that helped incite the uprising. According to sources familiar with the background of the speech, the original intent had been to send a message of encouragement to any potential coup plotters in Baghdad. Accordingly, Richard Haass drafted a call for the Iraqi military to "take matters into their own hands" and force Saddam from power. The appeal was due to be delivered by the president in the course of a speech on February 15.

Early on the morning of the appointed day, Saddam gave the first hint that he might be prepared to withdraw from Kuwait. Network news pictures of Iraqis enthusiastically celebrating the possibility of peace by firing guns in the air made a considerable impression on the White House. It seemed there was a public opinion in Iraq after all. A few extra words were added to Bush's script. Speaking to the American Association for the Advancement of Science later that morning, Bush now referred to the "celebratory atmosphere in Baghdad" reflecting the Iraqi people's desire to see the war end. Then he moved on to appeal to "the Iraqi military and the Iraqi people to take matters into their own hands—to force Saddam Hussein the dictator to step aside . . . and rejoin the family of nations." Just to make sure the message got across, Bush repeated it, word for word, in a second address that day at the Raytheon missile plant in Massachusetts.

As intended, the call for revolt got wide play on the international news channels avidly consumed by Iraqis. The audience, however, missed the nuanced references to "the Iraqi military *and* the Iraqi people." They took the

American leader's words at face value, drawing the reasonable conclusion that they were being called upon to join the fight against Saddam.

The supreme irony is that Bush and his advisers, in trying to promote a coup, instead encouraged an uprising that may have prevented the very coup they so devoutly desired. An Iraqi source, privy to the highest levels of the military at that time, has assured us that there was indeed a coup being planned by senior generals from some time during the war and after. But the plotters were deterred from taking action by the Shia uprising. As members of the ruling Sunni minority, they feared the consequences of Shia success and thought it more expedient, for the time being, to rally around Saddam. What their attitude might have been had the United States signaled support for the rebellion is not recorded.

George Bush himself later sensed part of the truth. In 1994, he wrote that "I did have a strong feeling that the Iraqi military, having been led to such a crushing defeat by Saddam, would rise up and rid themselves of him. We were concerned that the uprisings would sidetrack the overthrow of Saddam by causing the Iraqi military to rally around him to prevent the breakup of the country. That may have been what actually happened."

There is, however, another irony that Bush evidently fails to appreciate. In that first crucial week of March 1991, Saddam's fate hung in the balance. Many ranking military commanders as well as other officials in the regime were contemplating abandoning the sinking ship and throwing in their lot with the rebels. But this was still a highly risky gamble, since the consequences of picking the losing side would inevitably be terminally unpleasant. For anyone making the choice, the attitude of the Americans was crucial. To tip the balance, Bush did not have to launch his armies on the road to Baghdad; a hint of support or even encouragement to the rebels would probably have been enough. Instead, Washington and the U.S. military command in Riyadh not only gave indications, such as allowing Saddam's helicopters to fly, that they were less than interested in the rebels' success, but also explicitly told rebel emissaries that there would be no support—as Saddam quickly discovered. In Baghdad and elsewhere, the waverers drew the appropriate conclusions.

This adamant repudiation of the rebel cause was based on another ironclad assumption on the part of the Washington policy makers: a deeply ingrained belief that civil disorder would inevitably sunder Iraq. Since before the war, classified memos had hurtled around the national security bureaucracy, replete with ominous warnings of the consequences that would follow an Iraqi breakup, up to and including, as one Pentagon missive suggested, "the Iranian occupation of any part of Iraqi territory . . . Iraqi disintegration will improve prospects for Iranian domination of the Gulf and remove a restraint on Syria." Reports that portraits of Ayatollah Khomeini were being put up in liberated areas did not help matters. No one was going to assist what appeared to be surrogates for the dreaded fundamentalist Iranians.

As a result, the U.S. forces in the large portion of Iraq occupied during the ground offensive at the end of the war not only made no move to assist the insurgents, they actually gave tacit assistance to Saddam's forces by preventing rebels from taking desperately needed arms and ammunition in abandoned Iraqi stores. Much of these captured stocks were destroyed, but, paradoxically, the CIA took possession of an appreciable quantity and shipped it off to fundamentalists in Afghanistan, favored agency clients in the civil war in that country.

Since the president had publicly encouraged the uprising on which they were now turning their backs, the White House was embarrassed enough to draft their Saudi allies as an alibi. The Saudis, murmured officials in background briefings, were adamantly opposed to aiding the Shia, since they were in such mortal terror of Iran. Bush himself may even have believed this explanation. "It was never our goal to break up Iraq," he wrote later. "Indeed, we did not want this to happen, and most of our coalition partners (especially the Arabs) felt even stronger on the issue."

This was not, in fact, the attitude of the Saudis at the time. "The idea that the Saudi tail was wagging our dog is just bullshit," says one official who visited Riyadh in mid-March. He had been closely cross-questioned by Prince Turki bin Feisel, head of Saudi intelligence, about ways to aid the opposition (about whom the prince was woefully ignorant).

"The behavior of the Iraqi Shia in the Iran-Iraq war convinced the Saudis that the Shia were not Iranian surrogates," says Ambassador Freeman. "Washington was obsessed by that idea, and attributed it to the Saudis. I don't know where all this panic about the breakup of Iraq came from. After all, Mesopotamia has been there for quite a while—about six thousand years. Iraq is not a flimsy construction."

On March 26, 1991, Bush convened a meeting of his most senior advisers at the White House to make a final decision on help for the rebels. There was no public pressure to do so—the country was in "yellow ribbon mode," as one official remarked—and Bush himself had now joined in the general euphoria. A few days earlier, at the Gridiron Club's chummy annual get-together of politicians and media, the "agony" of the president's wartime experience had been compared to that of Abraham Lincoln by a fawning member of the press.

At the White House meeting, a hard-and-fast decision to leave Iraq to its own devices was approved by all. Of those present, only Vice President Dan

Quayle showed the slightest concern about allowing Saddam Hussein to go on slaughtering the insurgents without hindrance. No one appears to have challenged the presumption that a rebel victory would inevitably have led to Iran seizing a piece of Iraq.

Following the meeting, as Bush's spokesman announced that "We don't intend to involve ourselves in the internal conflict in Iraq," Brent Scowcroft and Richard Haass boarded a plane for Riyadh to spread the word in the field. The Saudis were still in a mood to help the rebels—a senior Kurdish representative was in Riyadh when the Americans landed. They needed to be told to get in step with policy.

In Washington, a "senior official" was briefing reporters on the fact that Bush believed "Saddam will crush the rebellions and, after the dust settles, the Baath military establishment and other elites will blame him for not only the death and destruction from the war but the death and destruction from putting down the rebellion. They will emerge then and install a new leadership." That was not quite the picture of White House policy the Saudis got from their high-powered visitors, as Sayid Majid al-Khoie soon discovered.

Al-Khoie had been held under comfortable house arrest at the Saudi border ever since he had escaped from Iraq, the promise of his meeting with Schwarzkopf still unmet. He was there when George Bush was asked, on the day after the crucial March 26 meeting, if any rebel groups had asked the United States for help.

"Not that I know of," the president blithely replied. "No, I don't believe that they have. If they have, it hasn't come to me."

After finally being allowed to travel to Riyadh, al-Khoie had his first chance to meet with the Saudi intelligence chief Prince Turki bin Feisel on March 30, three days after the two emissaries had arrived from Washington.

Al-Khoie recorded the two-hour meeting in his diary: "Why are you so worried about the Shia?" he asked.

"We can't do anything to help you," replied the prince. "The Americans don't want to remove Saddam. They say, 'Saddam is under control. This is better than somebody we don't know about. We are worried about Iran.'"

Twenty-four hours after al-Khoie heard that the Americans now wanted Saddam to stay in power, Peter Galbraith was fleeing for his life from the Kurdish city of Dohuk. The energetic Senate aide had been touring the war-torn region and had gone to bed late the night before after telling a crowd of Kurdish notables that, as the first representative of the U.S. government in a free Kurdistan, he was proud to address them. Now he was running from a vengeful Iraqi army on the verge of retaking the city. An angry red-haired Peshmerga stuck his head through the car window. "Damn Bush," he said.

The 2 million Kurds who joined Galbraith in flight were about to upset the White House's determined disengagement from Iraqi affairs. The Shia in the south had fled in equal terror, but without attracting much attention or sympathy in the outside world. The Kurds fared better, being easily accessible to the media army that speedily materialized on the Turkish border and telegenic besides. "They look middle class," murmured a Senate staffer watching TV pictures of doctors and lawyers in three-piece suits shivering on the bleak mountain sides. "I never realized they were like us." Influential figures such as the columnist William Safire, a champion of their cause since the days of their betrayal by the CIA in the 1970s, weighed in on their behalf. Galbraith, safely over the border, threw in his own bitter and well-informed denunciations of the whole postwar policy on Iraq.

With unseemly reluctance, the White House bent to public opinion and began to assist the Kurds. At first Bush sent food and medicine and then, on April 16, he ordered U.S. troops into northern Iraq to create a "safe haven" from Saddam's forces for returning refugees.

It was a momentous turning point. Although Bush stressed that the troop deployment was merely temporary, the president had now, however unwillingly, accepted a military role for the United States inside the borders of Iraq itself. Bending to force majeure, Saddam made no effort to resist. Although the allied troops were withdrawn within three months, the Iraqi army did not permanently reassert the government's control over Kurdistan. U.S. warplanes based at Incirlik, just across the Turkish border, were now assigned to "Operation Provide Comfort"—protective air cover for the Kurds and a tangible deterrent to any effort by Saddam to crush these rebellious subjects once more.

Announcing the April decision to dispatch troops into Kurdistan, the president was defensive about his famous call to the Iraqi people, now coming back to haunt him. "Do I think that the United States should bear guilt because of suggesting that the Iraqi people take matters into their own hands, with the implication being given by some that the United States would be there to support them militarily?" he replied to one aggressive questioner. "That was not true. We never implied that." Displaying a certain economy with the truth, he went on to insist that the wartime objectives had "never included the demise and destruction of Saddam personally."

WHY WE DIDN'T GO
TO BAGHDAD

George Bush and Brent Scowcroft

The end of effective Iraqi resistance came with a rapidity which surprised us all, and we were perhaps psychologically unprepared for the sudden transition from fighting to peacemaking. True to the guidelines we had established, when we had achieved our strategic objectives (ejecting Iraqi forces from Kuwait and eroding Saddam's threat to the region) we stopped the fighting. But the necessary limitations placed on our objectives, the fog of war, and the lack of a "battleship *Missouri*" surrender unfortunately left unresolved problems, and new ones arose.

We soon discovered that more of the Republican Guard survived the war than we had believed or anticipated. Owing to the unexpected swiftness of the Marine advance into Kuwait, the Guard reserves were not drawn south into the battle—and into the trap created by the western sweep around and behind Kuwait as we had planned. While we would have preferred to reduce further the threat Saddam posed to the region—and help undermine his hold on power—by destroying additional Guard divisions, in truth he didn't need those forces which escaped destruction in order to maintain internal control. He had more than twenty untouched divisions in other parts of Iraq. One more day would not have altered the strategic situation, but it would have made a substantial difference in human terms. We would have been castigated for slaughtering fleeing soldiers after our own mission was successfully completed.

We were disappointed that Saddam's defeat did not break his hold on power, as many of our Arab allies had predicted and we had come to expect. The abortive uprising of the Shi'ites in the south and the Kurds in the north did not spread to the Sunni population of central Iraq, and the Iraqi military remained loyal. Critics claim that we encouraged the separatist Shi'ites and

George Bush was the 41st president of the United States, serving from 1989 to 1993. He is currently a senior adviser to the Carlyle Group, a global private equity firm specializing in aerospace, defense, energy, and telecommunications buyouts and investments. Lieutenant General Brent Scowcroft (USAF, Retired) was national security adviser to Presidents Gerald Ford and George Bush, Sr. The former vice chairman of Kissinger Associates, he is the founder and president of The Scowcroft Group, an international business consulting firm. This article is excerpted from President Bush's and General Scowcroft's memoir of the Bush presidency, *A World Transformed*.

Kurds to rebel and then reneged on a promise to aid them if they did so. President Bush repeatedly declared that the fate of Saddam Hussein was up to the Iraqi people. Occasionally, he indicated that removal of Saddam would be welcome, but for very practical reasons there was never a promise to aid an uprising. While we hoped that a popular revolt or coup would topple Saddam, neither the United States nor the countries of the region wished to see the breakup of the Iraqi state. We were concerned about the long-term balance of power at the head of the Gulf. Breaking up the Iraqi state would pose its own destabilizing problems. While Ozal put the priority on Saddam and had a more tolerant view of Kurds than other Turkish leaders before or since, Turkey—and Iran—objected to the suggestion of an independent Kurdish state. However admirable self-determination for the Kurds or Shi'ites might have been in principle, the practical aspects of this particular situation dictated the policy. For these reasons alone, the uprisings distressed us, but they also offered Saddam an opportunity to reassert himself and rally his army. Instead of toppling him as the cause of its humiliating defeat, the Iraqi military was put to work to suppress the rebellions. It was a serious disappointment.

Trying to eliminate Saddam, extending the ground war into an occupation of Iraq, would have violated our guideline about not changing objectives in midstream, engaging in "mission creep," and would have incurred incalculable human and political costs. Apprehending him was probably impossible. We had been unable to find Noriega in Panama, which we knew intimately. We would have been forced to occupy Baghdad and, in effect, rule Iraq. The coalition would instantly have collapsed, the Arabs deserting it in anger and other allies pulling out as well. Under those circumstances, there was no viable "exit strategy" we could see, violating another of our principles. Furthermore, we had been self-consciously trying to set a pattern for handling aggression in the post–Cold War world. Going in and occupying Iraq, thus unilaterally exceeding the United Nations' mandate, would have destroyed the precedent of international response to aggression that we hoped to establish. Had we gone the invasion route, the United States could conceivably still be an occupying power in a bitterly hostile land. It would have been a dramatically different—and perhaps barren—outcome.

WHY THE UPRISINGS FAILED

Faleh A. Jabar

In March 1991, following Iraq's defeat in the Gulf War, the Kurds of northern Iraq and Arabs of the south rose up against the Baath regime. For two
brief weeks, the uprisings were phenomenally successful. Government administration in the towns was overthrown and local army garrisons were left in
disarray. Yet by the end of the month the rebellions had been crushed and the
rebels scattered, fleeing across the nearest borders or into Iraq's southern
marshes. Those who could not flee did not survive summary executions.

Despite the calls made during the war by Western leaders for Iraqis to rise
up and dispose of Saddam Hussein, these dramatic and tragic events were the
last thing any outside powers anticipated. Did the uprising also take the Iraqi
people by surprise? There is good cause to think so. Iraqi opposition leaders
had long been calling for a "popular uprising" which would end the war with
Iran and the deprivation and tyranny foisted upon them by Saddam's regime.
Yet when the moment did arrive, the opposition was totally unprepared.

Saddam's state of mind during the countdown to war, and the outlines of
his strategic thinking, have been the subject of intense speculation. It appears
he was truly convinced that he had scored a great victory over Khomeini during his previous adventure. A transcript of a secret meeting of senior officers
inside Kuwait in October 1990 reveals that many of them were surprised to
find the president there—a clear indication of Saddam's lack of trust in his
generals. In the course of the meeting, Saddam claimed he was given orders
from heaven to invade Kuwait: "May God be my witness, that it is the Lord
who wanted what happened to happen," Saddam declared. "This decision we
received almost ready made from God. . . . Our role in the decision was almost zero."

Predicting that the war would start with allied air raids, Saddam coun-
selled his commanders to "stay motionless under the ground just a little time.
If you do this, their shooting will be in vain. . . . On the ground the battle will
be another story. On the ground the Americans will not be able to put forces
as strong as you are." In the final analysis, he said, the power of oil would pre-

Faleh A. Jabar is an Iraqi writer and opposition activist living in London and the author of several books in Arabic on
modern Islamic thought. This article is excerpted from the May–June, 1992 issue of *Middle East Report*.

vail: "We have 20 percent of world reserves. Sanctions will be lifted not for the sake of our eyes, but for the sake of our oil."

If the generals could not do other than murmur their assent, the opposition was also finding it difficult to set out a strong dissenting position. Still licking their wounds from their failure to gauge the strength of patriotic feeling in the first war [with Iran] too isolated now to know how far the needle had swung the other way, they did not want to make the same mistake again. All of them had denounced the invasion and annexation of Kuwait, and demanded Iraqi withdrawal. None had lost their hope that Saddam might be displaced. But most feared they would lose their moral right to oppose the regime if they did not side with "Iraq" against the West.

In a communique from Beirut after the air war began (January 19, 1991) Muhammad Bakr al-Hakim ordered his followers in the Supreme Council for the Islamic Revolution in Iraq (SCIRI) to join the "Recruitment Forces," his organization's military wing, and instructed those based near Iran's border with Iraq to stand firm against "United States aggression." The ICP [Iraqi Communist Party] also denounced US aggression. Massoud Barzani, leader of the KDP [Kurdistan Democratic Party], opposed both the war option and the Western military build-up; and the Kurdistan Front, a coalition of Kurdish parties and the Kurdish section of the ICP, halted all military actions against the Iraqí army in Kurdistan so as not to "stab the army in the back." As the situation ripened towards a mass uprising, the opposition parties had ceased to expect any such thing. [See Appendix 2 for a Who's Who of the Iraqi Opposition.]

ASSUMING SADDAM'S true "strategy" was the one he outlined at the meeting in Kuwait—there is no evidence of any other—it was a colossal blunder. The air campaign, which he thought would last two or three days, lasted more than a month. The Israelis did not react. The Europeans stood fast alongside the Bush administration. No oil famine occurred. The ground battle Saddam so confidently awaited never materialized. Instead there was a rout. The Iraqi army would not have fought even if the order had been given. The devastation wreaked upon the country surpassed imagination.

From the ruins Baghdad radio spoke of the war as "a great achievement," and called the withdrawal "heroic." Baghdad's official version of the events reminded Iraqis of the story of an Italian general defeated at al-Alamain by General Montgomery. When reproached for having allowed whole sections of his forces to flee the battle, he solemnly remarked: "Yes, we ran away—but like lions." To the peasant conscripts who made up the vast bulk of the Iraqi armed forces, no such implausible irony was possible. For them the experience of flight ended in carnage such as that on the "highway of death" at al-Mutla.

Amidst this chaos the Iraqi people rose up to defy the dictator. In the throes of a devastating battlefield defeat they reached out for victory inside their own wrecked and wretched nation. It was the "popular uprising" for which every opposition leader, from modern leftist to traditional cleric, had been calling throughout the Iran-Iraq war. Yet most had given up hope of it ever happening and none were remotely prepared for putting it into practice.

The most common opposition scenarios involved a running series of political demonstrations at a time of crisis, when the ruling party and the security services were politically isolated and structurally ruptured. These mass protests would unify the people, further isolate the regime, and win over the army rank and file. Only then would the stage of armed revolt occur, culminating in a battle for the capital. Such an enterprise would require a field leadership with extensive networks of cadres and supporters to gather intelligence, react swiftly to developments, carefully assess the mood of the civilians and the military, and plan the positioning and actions of various units. It would need a sober and highly disciplined leadership to overcome the ethnic, religious and communal fragmentation of the Iraqi nation.

The crisis did not arrive as expected. The army, which had lost a third of its troops, disintegrated. More important, so did the security services, which had suddenly lost all control of the situation. The popular explosion, building since 1988, was detonated by the retreating soldiers and officers who had survived the horrors of al-Mutla.

The first sparks of the rebellion were in the Sunni towns of Abu'l Khasib and Zubair, about 60–70 kilometers south of Basra. It was the last day of February 1991, three days before the formal Iraqi surrender to General Schwarzkopf at Safwan. The revolt gained momentum immediately, and other cities followed suit: Basra, March 1; Suq al-Shuyukh, March 2; Nasiriyya, Najaf and Kufa, March 4; Karbala, March 7; and then Amara, Hilla, Kut, and on throughout the south. In the north the sequence was: Raniyya and Chawar Qurna, March 5; Koi Sanjaq, March 6; Sulaimaniyya, March 7 and 8; Halabja and Arabat, March 9; Arbil, March 11; D'hok, Zakhu and other small townships, March 10 and 13; and finally Kirkuk, March 20.

A detailed account of what happened in each city and township is impossible, but reports in various outlawed Iraqi publications speak of a series of events remarkably similar in every case. Masses would gather in the streets to denounce Saddam Hussein and Baathist rule, then march to seize the mayor's office, the Baath Party headquarters, the secret police (*mukhabarat*) building, the prison and the city's garrison (if there was one). People shot as they went at every poster or wall relief of the dictator. As the cities came under rebel control, the insurgents cleaned out Baathists and *mukhabarat*.

This is the general picture, but details, where known, often differed. These inconsistencies were a result of the extreme novelty of the situation and the lack of communication and the limited transportation. Not only nearby towns but frequently adjacent neighborhoods within the same town could not know what was going on in each other's quarter.

Even with hindsight, any assessment of the uprisings must be cautious. Many of the *dramatis personae* were either killed or are now in hiding in Saudi Arabia or Iraq, fearful that their families will be brutalized if they do not remain anonymous. Those who carried the burden of the uprisings, especially in the first days, were ordinary people whose accounts were often neglected by the opposition press. The situation is even further complicated: the opposition parties first claimed credit for this or that mutiny during the early days, but when failure set in they distanced themselves by saying it had been the spontaneous work of the masses.

DESPITE THESE problems, we have enough evidence to set down an approximate record of the uprisings, dividing Iraq into three zones: the south, the mostly Shi'i sector; the north, comprising the Kurdish sector; and the middle swath made up of Baghdad and its environs, together with the towns of the so-called "Sunni triangle" running from Baghdad north along the Tigris River to Mosul west to the Syrian border. Each zone is distinguished not only by its own ethnic, religious and communal identity but also, and this is important to our scheme, by the degree of political awareness, the amount of free-flowing information, the extent of organizational capacity, and the balance of military forces.

In the south, the hypothetical scenario of the uprising which the opposition parties had once sketched out was stood on its head. Armed mutiny was the first, not the last, link in the chain. Following the revolt in Zubair and Abu'l Khasib, Basra too took up arms, led by the angry retreating soldiers and followed by a mass of equally angry civilians.

"The Iraqi army cannot bear the responsibility of the defeat because it did not fight. Saddam is responsible," charged Khalil Juwaibar, an armored vehicle driver who was among the soldiers who left Zubair for Basra to stoke the fires of revolt. An officer described the mood in Zubair and Abu'l Khasib: "We were anxious to withdraw, to end the mad adventure, when Saddam announced withdrawal within 24 hours—but without any formal agreement with the allies to ensure the safety of the retreating forces. We understood that he wanted the allies to wipe us out: he had already withdrawn the Republican Guard to safety. We had to desert our tanks and vehicles to avoid aerial attacks. We walked 100 kilometers towards the Iraqi territories, hungry, thirsty and exhausted. In Zubair we decided to put an end to Saddam and his regime. We shot at Saddam's posters. Hundreds of retreating soldiers came to the city and joined the revolt: by the afternoon, we were thousands. Civilians supported us and demonstrations started. We attacked the party building and the security headquarters. In a matter of hours, the uprising spread to Basra, at exactly three o'clock on the morning of March 1.''

The Basra revolt was led at first by Muhammad Ibrahim Wali, an Iraqi officer who gathered a force of tanks, armored vehicles and trucks to attack the mayor's office, Baath Party offices and security headquarters. The vast majority of the Basra population backed the revolt. Most of the active participants in the clashes were between 14 and 35 years old. Almost all the soldiers took part, including Mechanized Regiment No. 24 stationed near Tannuma. Below the BATA shoe company premises, opposite the mayor's office, they found a secret prison. Hundreds of prisoners were released, some shouting "Down with al-Bakr," referring to Ahmad Hasan al-Bakr, who had been forced to resign as president of Iraq in 1979!

This spontaneous rebellion in Basra did not have a well-forged leadership, an integrated organization, or a political or military program. Many brave soldiers lamented the fact that cannons, tanks and other weapons were scattered here and there with no plan to move to Baghdad and no contact with other officers and soldiers in other units who as yet had no idea what had happened in Kuwait, apart from the cease-fire. Indeed, when the first officer sent to crush the uprising hoisted a white flag and entered the city to join its ranks, he was humiliated and expelled.

The Basra rebellion detonated the Iraqi uprising in general. The people of Suq al-Shuyukh were the next to rise. Three groups of armed men attacked the city, backed by the marsh tribes of Hawr al-Hammar and led by the chieftains of Albu Hijam and Albu Gassid. Virtually all citizens took to the streets and joined the battle for the centers of power. 'Abd al-Shabacha, a member of the National Assembly and an ex-Baathist, led the movement in its first days.

As THE revolt spread, it became clear that the south was up against some critical disadvantages. First, it was close to the front lines where some Republican Guard units were still stationed. Second, while the conscripted military was ripe for rebellion, it was politically immature. And thirdly, the Islamists, in the euphoria of early apparent success, joined in and raised a disastrous slogan: Ja'fari (Shi'i) rule.

The rebellion had been taking place under the watchful eyes of Iraqi Shi'i dissidents living in Iran. At SCIRI headquarters in a school in Khorramshahr, where his followers hoisted aloft both his photo and that of the late Ayatollah Khomeini, Muhammad Bakr al-Hakim told Western reporters that he looked forward to a general election in which the Iraqi people would choose their own government, adding that he had no intention of imposing Islamic rule. Inside Iraq, events told another story. "In Suq al-Shuykh Islamic slogans and posters . . . had been erected where giant portraits of Saddam Hussein once stood." With Basra and Amara open cities after the rebellion, it was easy for Iraqi dissidents to cross the borders and return home, and many did arrive in Nasiriyya, Amara, Najaf and Karbala to see their families again. Many were bent on revenge, and as a result many unnecessary killings took place in the south.

Although the SCIRI veterans were only one element of the forces who seized the cities in the south, they spoke and acted as if they were the decision makers. Al-Hakim's military command issued directions stating that "all Iraqi armed forces should submit to and obey [SCIRI] orders. . . . No action outside this context is allowed; all parties working from the Iranian territories should also obey al-Hakim's orders; no party is allowed to recruit volunteers; no ideas except the rightful Islamic ones should be disseminated . . ."

According to Dr. Muwafak al-Ruba'i, a Da'wa Party leader based in London, those who returned to the south bearing posters of al-Hakim and Khomeini achieved only the abortion of the intifada. They concentrated their efforts in the holy cities of Najaf and Karbala, "but by this they gave the uprising a very narrow character, as if it were a family affair." The successful rebels, al-Ruba'i admitted, were a disparate crew, including elements of the Sunni military, Baathists, leftists and people from all walks of life.

Al-Hakim should have known that the prospect of Islamist rule is a nightmare for all their opposition allies (whether Kurds, Communists or Arab nationalists), not to mention for Saudi Arabia and the U.S. In addition, the notion of Islamist rule in Iraq carries connotations of communal strife. It provided an opportunity for Saddam to garner domestic support and regain implicit if undeclared international sympathy.

IN THE north the political landscape was different. Sulaimaniyya was more than 1,000 kilometers from the front line, but its links with the nationalist and leftist parties made it better placed than most northern cities to know what had occurred on the battlefield. The Kurds en masse quickly grasped the meaning of the army's defeat, the subsequent disintegration of the *mukhabarat,* and the rapidly spreading rebellion. This was the moment of reckoning. The battle for Sulaimaniyya erupted within a few days of the Basra insurrection. Negative international and regional responses—U.S. fears of Iranian intervention, the alarm signals sent out by Ankara—were still tentative. The Kurds opened a second front and did so with greater boldness, cunning and discipline than the southern people.

Tension had been growing for some days. Security agents were hunting down deserters in Raniyya, a township near Sulaimaniyya, and provoking armed clashes. Demonstrations followed, police and security units opened fire and civilians defended themselves. Armed masses took control of Raniyya within an hour, but the intelligence service held out for another eight hours before collapsing, losing 34 men in the process. Crucially, the Salah al-Din Forces (the Kurds called them *jash*—donkeys), went over to the side of the people. Division No. 24, stationed at Chawar Qurna, did not fire a single bullet at the rebels and surrendered peacefully. The peshmerga helped the rebels by occupying the hills overlooking the town.

The news spread to Koi Sanjaq, where a fierce battle was fought against the special commando units backed by Qasim Agha, chief of the *jash*. It took two days to capture the town on March 6. Bazian and Basloja followed suit. By now, Sulaimaniyya itself was on the verge of an explosion. Thousands of young deserters were discussing the situation, criticizing Saddam Hussein publicly, and vandalizing his posters. On March 6 authorities announced a curfew; security and army units patrolled the town, backed by light armored vehicles. But on March 7 the city was filled with demonstrators, with women and children in the forefront. One by one the official centers of power surrendered. The battle for the headquarters of the Baath and the Popular Army in the Bakhtiari neighborhood lasted from 3 to 7:30 in the evening, when the building was razed to the ground. Fighting then shifted to the Aqari neighborhood, site of the new security service directorate. More than 900 *mukhabarat* were killed, including the director, Col. Khalaf al-Hadithi, along with some 150 rebels.

Arbil, the capital of Kurdistan, was simultaneously preparing for rebellion. This time the demonstrations were timed in coordination with the peshmerga of the Patriotic Union of Kurdistan and the Communists. On March 11, armed crowds swarmed the streets and controlled the town within three hours. A chain reaction followed in Koi, Chamchamal, Kifri, Aqra, Tuz Khurmatu, D'hok and other towns of the north.

Unlike in the south, these armed takeovers were preceded by public demonstrations lasting sometimes for several days, and bearing clear political slogans: democracy for Iraq and autonomy for Kurdistan. The Kurds were in a position to forge a wider unity: Massoud Barzani, leader of the KDP, approached the Salah al-Din Forces and tens of thousands thronged to the rebels' side. Barzani also forged cordial personal relations with many high ranking commanders from the six regular army divisions deployed in Kurdistan.

The peshmerga played a more tactical role than the retreating remnants of the conscript army had been able to play in the south. Having helped to seize control of a town, the peshmerga would withdraw, leaving the townships under the control of locally selected administrations. Such a gesture delivered three messages: first, that the cities were liberated not from the outside but from within; second, that the military's pride should not be wounded; and third that the Turkish government should not fear Kurdish secession. These tactics paid off as the rebellion snowballed and reached the oil city of Kirkuk, just three hours drive from Baghdad.

More than 50,000 soldiers left their units without fighting back, and were soon seen in the streets of the Kurdish cities, welcomed, fed and sheltered by Kurdish families. The rebels' own armed actions were carefully limited to punishing security servicemen and leading Baath cadres. Revenge attacks could not be prevented everywhere as the long-awaited moment to vent the people's anger materialized, but the scale of retaliation was much smaller than in the south.

WHAT BECAME of the middle sector of the country? It was essential for any lasting success that the masses in Baghdad bridge the wide gulf separating the north and south, between which there was clearly no political, military or organizational synchronization whatsoever. But the rebels were to be disappointed. Baghdad remained idle and quiet.

One key factor was the flow of information, or rather the lack of it. Witnesses testify that it was extremely difficult even to travel across the capital itself, never mind through the countryside. Rumors were slow to arrive. The real situation at the front was not known as it was in Basra and even in Sulaimaniyya. It took five days, according to one leftist, before they could even be sure that Basra was in rebellion.

Even then the uprising only created a queer sort of passivity: Baghdadis were waiting for the revolt to come to them. This false hope was encouraged by some opposition leaders, notably Talabani, who proposed an attack on Mosul and then on Baghdad. Al-Hakim also broadcast that the revolt was on its way. From interviews with at least a dozen Baghdadis who later left Iraq, it seems that the news spread either by the opposition leaders through Tehran radio, or on the BBC and other channels, was exaggerated and sometimes unfounded. One dissident made tremendous efforts to move around Baghdad to check out each piece of news about mass unrest in, say, the Kadhimiyya or

Thawra districts (poorer neighbors of mainly Shi'i residents): "Each time I got to the place indicated only to find nothing there," he complained.

The main cause of the passivity, however, goes back to the lack of organizational structures inside the capital. It was easy to penetrate Amara, Basra and Nasiriyya across the porous borders with Iran; the Kurds could, even when times were hardest, manage to move in and out of their cities. Baghdad was a fatal exception.

Only three parties could, in theory, have filled the gap: the Communists, the Da'wa, or the pro-Syrian Baath splinter party. But the Communists had locked themselves in the mountains of Kurdistan and identified themselves closely with the Kurdish cause. From 1980 to 1989, they confined themselves to one form of armed struggle, the least effective in Iraqi conditions: Guevaran country-to-city elite warfare. Any idea of forming armed units in the cities was dismissed as heretical or anti-revolutionary. No real attempt was made to build up cells in Baghdad. When guerrilla bases were destroyed in 1988, bringing the struggle in the countryside to an end, its critics jumped to the conclusion that any form of armed struggle was irrelevant and the best way forward was to strike a deal with the regime.

The Da'wa had enough strength and expertise to build underground networks, but had been intoxicated with the reverent Islamic belief that trust in God also meant trust in the Iranian tanks, and failed to make significant preparations of its own. The pro-Syrian Baathists held similar hope in the tanks of Damascus which would one day carry them into Baghdad. As a result, there was not a single leader to give the signal to Baghdad's four million people. Additionally, the slogans of radical Islam emanating from the south caused a good deal of concern. One Shi'i dissident told how his Sunni relatives took shelter at his house as a precaution against the indiscriminate retaliations they feared would follow when the revolt arrived. Such fears were not rare and must have helped Saddam to enhance his position, especially in the more backward areas of the "Sunni Arab triangle."

This may well explain, in part, the fatal idleness in Baghdad. Two other factors help explain why any uprising had little chance of success. One is that the regime had concentrated its security efforts in the capital. The second is the evacuation of nearly one million Baghdadis before the outbreak of the war.

DEPRIVED OF the capital's support, and lacking organizational, tactical and political coordination, the rebellious towns fell one by one. True, some cities in the south changed hands several times, but in the end all were silenced.

The relative ease with which the remnants of the Iraqi army could save the regime shocked opposition leaders, but also awakened them to the fact that the U.S. was interested in reducing the Iraqi military threat in regional terms only, hence the concentration of bombing on the retreating units which were to play a vital role in the uprising. These were the very units suspected by Saddam Hussein of potential trouble.

Half of the Iraqi units were stationed in and around the Kuwaiti theater. The other, loyal, half was divided into four groups: one in Kurdistan (which gave up without much of a fight); another in Mosul (six divisions); another in Tikrit with the task of foiling any attempt in Baghdad; and the last in Baghdad itself to thwart any attempt from the south.

In the 1930s, King Faisal said the Iraqi army should be strong enough to quell two mutinies at the same time. By 1991, Saddam Hussein arranged his forces to face a three-edged threat, from the north, from the south and from inside the capital, presuming that at least one would arise in military insurrection. In *From the House of War,* BBC correspondent John Simpson expresses amazement at the sight of Tikrit on the eve of the war: It was a fortress in the strict sense of the word, although it was more than 1000 kilometers from the front lines. In short, Iraq's pre-war security arrangements were more concerned with internal enemies.

The quantitative approach pursued by the U.S. helped rather than weakened the regime's calculations. If the Iraqi military defeat helped detonate the popular revolt, the manner in which this defeat was inflicted undermined the uprising itself. The rout relieved Saddam of the most troublesome part of his army and preserved the most loyal divisions.

The Shi'i character given (in the strict sense of the term) by Western and Arab media from the beginning was further enhanced by the unwise overstatements by some Shi'i leaders themselves. In addition, unnecessary mass revenge killings of Baathists—to some extent in the north and to a great extent in the south—rallied the majority of party cadre behind Saddam Hussein. These random killings were a clear message to Baathists that they were wanted dead, not alive, and they predictably resisted to the end.

The task of the opposition forces was to divide not only the Baathists but the Tikritis as well. The Tikriti clan provides not only state, party and security service leaders and key cadre, but 2,000 or so high- and medium-ranking officers as well. In an army reduced to one third of its former size, this Tikriti elite is a decisive core. In addition to political ties, economic interests and ideological strings, kinship lends this group an almost monolithic character. Yet political differences had caused some cracks, as in 1979 when President Ahmad Hassan al-Bakr was unseated by Saddam Hussein, or the assassination in 1989 of Saddam's brother-in-law and defense minister, Adnan Tilfah. To widen such divisions and invest them with an active political significance remains one of the most vital tasks awaiting the opposition as a whole.

For Iraq's regional neighbors (apart from Iran, of course) and the U.S., the situation seemed as if it had returned to its starting point in 1980 when Iran was bent on exporting its revolution. A war had been fought for eight years to reduce that threat. A second war was just waged to remove the resulting malgrowth and new disequilibrium. The Islamist nightmare changed regional and international attitudes. Perhaps this is why the rebels were denied, according to Col. Qattan, access to Iraqi weaponry and ammunition dumps under U.S. control across the river in Nasiriyya.

By dint of their inner contradictions and peculiarities, the Iraqi uprisings were deprived of any significant international and regional support, apart from the unhelpful one-sided Iranian backing. To most ruling elites in the Middle East, the notion of "democracy" is more dangerous than Saddam's tanks, but the Iraqi uprising was the first popular upheaval unwelcomed by both Arab opposition and Arab rulers alike. The rulers feared a spread of the so-called revolutionary arson. The opposition feared divergence from their own outward-oriented, anti-Western nationalist sentiments. The reason why this divergence was so wide, so antagonistic, is a subject that needs separate elaboration.

The uprisings were drowned in blood. The scenes of brief, mass executions exhibited before the eyes of the world an Iraq that still is a wonderland of terror. Yet Arab leftists and philanthropic liberals turned a blind eye and a deaf ear to the cries of a nation victimized. Their anti-imperialist rhetoric was loudest exactly when it was necessary to listen not to oneself but to those who were asked to line up behind the patriarch, even if he was in "his autumn." The fear of a democratic demonstration effect alientated Arab rulers from the uprisings, but the passivity of the Arab and, by extension, the international left was incomprehensible. Their fatal error was to neglect the longing of the Iraqi people for democracy. This left the cause of peace and democracy to the hypocritical manipulation of the U.S. and other Western powers. The rightful condemnation of U.S. schemes and hidden agendas should have been complemented by a defence of the Iraqi people's legitimate right to democratic freedoms and their right to decide matters of peace and war.

HOW SADDAM HELD ON TO POWER

Kanan Makiya

On August 18, 1994, six weeks before President Saddam Hussein began redeploying his troops to make the world think that he was about to do the unthinkable—invade Kuwait a second time—he promulgated Law 109. It read: "According to Section 1, Article 42, of the Iraqi Constitution, the Revolutionary Command Council has decreed that . . . the foreheads of those individuals who repeat the crime for which their hand was cut off will be branded with a mark in the shape of an X. Each intersecting line will be one centimeter in length and one millimeter in width." The crimes "for which their hand was cut off" were theft and desertion. Branding with a red-hot iron was being introduced in Saddam Hussein's post–Gulf War Iraq as a new form of punishment for these crimes.

Soldiers and car thieves were singled out for prosecution on the basis of the new laws. Iraqi newspapers reported that thirty-six thousand cars had been stolen in 1993, many of them in broad daylight on the main streets of Baghdad. This, in a police state that took pride in the fact that the crime rate under its regime, especially since the middle 1970s, had plummeted.

The new law was formulated in general terms: stealing anything worth more than 5,000 dinars—worth roughly 12 dollars in 1994—by anyone who was not a minor had become punishable in Iraq by amputation in the first instance and in the second by branding. Something must have gone wrong in the case of thirty-seven-year-old 'Ali 'Abed 'Ali, because he had his hand amputated and his forehead branded with an X at the same time. His crime: stealing a television set and 250 Iraqi dinars (worth roughly 50 cents at the time). 'Ali was shown on Iraqi television on September 9, 1994, in hospital, still under anesthetic, with his bandaged arm and close-ups of his branded forehead. The new law specified that the branding had to be done at the same hospital where the hand had been amputated at the wrist, but also that it had to be for a repeat offense, which 'Ali's clearly was not.

According to military personnel who escaped to Kuwait in 1994, up to two

A native of Iraq, Kanan Makiya is now a professor of Middle East studies at Brandeis University and Director of the Iraq Research and Documentation Project at Harvard University. He is the author of several books, including the bestselling *Republic of Fear: The Politics of Modern Iraq*. This article is excerpted from the introduction to the updated 1998 edition of that book.

thousand soldiers already might have been branded on the forehead. A Kurdish opposition radio station based in northern Iraq declared that eight hundred soldiers with branded foreheads were captured by Kurdish forces along the border of the safe-haven zone in northern Iraq. Whether or not these figures are accurate, the punishments were clearly no marginal affair.

The number of ways in which the state was publicly disfiguring the bodies of its citizens was mushrooming. Depending on the crime, the foreheads of offenders got branded with a horizontal line three to five centimeters long, or with a circle, along with the X spelled out in Law 109. Some army deserters and draft dodgers, and those who sheltered them, got special treatment: the outer part of one ear was to be cut off for the first offense; a repeat offense resulted in the amputation of the other ear and a circle being branded on the forehead. (Unconfirmed rumor from inside Iraq claimed that the word *jaban,* "coward," was also being branded on some people's foreheads, and two parallel horizontal lines three to five centimeters in length.) Only after being caught for desertion a third time would a soldier be executed. This was an improvement on the situation before the passage of these new laws, when the instant and unquestioned penalty for desertion was a firing squad. The nature of crime and punishment was changing in Saddam Hussein's Iraq.

The reaction of ordinary Iraqis to the new laws was also unprecedented. Two men whose ears had been cut off immolated themselves in central Baghdad in October 1994. Following the murder of a doctor in the southern city of Nassirriyya by an amputee, and the storming of the headquarters of the Baath party in the city of 'Amara by a crowd that cut off the ears of the Baathi officials it got its hands on, several hundred doctors went on strike to protest having to carry out the new punishments. Upon being threatened with having their own ears cut off, the doctors called off their strike. Law 117 was then promptly issued, directed at the whole medical profession. It threatened immediate amputation of the ear for anyone who assisted in the cosmetic improvement of an officially disfigured body part. The law's wording ends with this strange acknowledgment of the public's outrage: "The effects" of the punishment of amputation of the hand or ear and branding "will be eliminated [by the state] if those so punished go on to perform heroic and patriotic acts."

Changing Forms of Cruelty

Since I finished writing *Republic of Fear* in 1986, the chamber of horrors that is Saddam Hussein's Iraq has grown into something that not even the most morbid imagination could have dreamed up. *Republic of Fear* is about how such horror stories became the norm inside a hitherto ordinary developing country. It describes how a new, Kafkaesque world came into being, one ruled and held together by fear. In this world, the ideal citizen became an informer. Lies and "analysis" filled public discourse to the exclusion of everything else. Fear, the book argued, was not incidental or episodic, as in more "normal" states; it had become constitutive of the Iraqi body politic. The Baath developed the politics of fear into an art form, one that ultimately served the purpose of legitimizing their rule by making large numbers of people complicit in the violence of the regime. The special problem of Baathi violence begins with the realization that hundreds of thousands of perfectly ordinary people were routinely implicated in it. In most cases they had no choice in the matter. Still, their actions had to be justified, and ended up legitimating a regime whose emergence could not be blamed on any outsider. The Iraqi Baath are a wholly indigenous phenomenon, and the longevity of their rule can be understood only against this background of public acquiescence or acceptance of their authority—until the 1991 Gulf War came along and changed everything.

At the apex of the system of punishment sat torture. Thus the problem of modernity in Iraq, I argued, became coming to terms with a polity made up of citizens who positively expected to be tortured under certain circumstances. On the eve of the outbreak of the Iraq-Iran War, in September 1980—by which time the different elements of the new system had come together—Saddam Hussein presided over a regime that had changed all the parameters affecting societal and state-organized violence in the country. Expansion of the means of violence—army, police, security apparatuses, networks of informers, party militia, party and state bureaucracies—had undergone the classic inversion: from being a means to an end, the elimination of opponents and the exercise of raw power, they became horrific ends in themselves, spilling mindlessly across the borders that had once contained them. "War, any war, it does not matter against whom, is a not unlikely outcome of the unbridled growth of the means of violence, particularly when it is so structured as to compromise literally masses of people in its terror."

Those words were written in a chapter about the Iraq-Iran War entitled "The Final Catastrophe." In retrospect the choice of words was unfortunate, because an even bigger catastrophe was in the making—the invasion, occupation, and annexation of Kuwait—whose driving logic I would sum up today in exactly the same words. The same internal imperative was at work in September 1980 as in August 1990. The system that had reached perfection on the eve of the Iraq-Iran War remained intact all through it. However, the violence it unleashed did almost get out of control. Iranian advances on the battlefield in the early years would have unseated Saddam Hussein had the West not come to his aid (by allowing him to build an arsenal of chemical weapons, the decisive weapon of mass destruction that won Iraq its war with Iran and that became such an issue in the 1991 Gulf War). At no point, however, was the Iraqi president's authority inside Iraq and among Iraqis (excluding Kurds) threatened during the 1980s.

Nothing that came out of the Iraq-Iran War, that eight-year-long meat grinder, was going to be the same as what went into it. The war had ended on terms favorable to Iraq. But did the violence stop, or even abate? On the contrary: it turned in on itself as it had done before, from 1968 to 1980, the year the war started. The day after the cease-fire came into effect, Iraqi warplanes dropped chemical bombs on Kurdish villages. Several thousand helpless civilians died between August 25 and 27, 1988, victims of a genocidal official campaign of extermination of Kurds that had begun in earnest in February 1988, long after the regime had become assured that it was well on its way to winning the war. Under the code name "Anfal operations," the military offensive continued all through September. I believe the total number killed in the Anfal operations is around a hundred thousand people. Then there are the truly grisly stories. Reports reached Amnesty International in 1989 of hundreds of children whose eyes were gouged out to force confessions from their adult relatives.

Since 1990, human-rights organizations like Amnesty International and Human Rights Watch have taken major strides in chronicling, documenting, and recording the abuses of the Iraqi Baath, which were described by Max van der Stoel, Special Rapporteur for the United Nations on Iraq, as being "of an exceptionally grave character—so grave that it has few parallels in the years that have passed since the Second World War." The world of the Iraqi Baath was Kafkaesque in 1980, but by 1997 it had become even stranger.

There is nothing irrational about this strangeness. Cruelty feeds on itself and escalates. It has shape and form, follows patterns, obeys its own rules, and has its own history. How it progresses in a polity, or why those subjected to officially sanctioned cruelty react differently at different points in their lives, is very revealing of the most fundamental questions in politics. The politics of bodily disfigurement, for instance, came out of a Baathist tradition that was established long before Saddam Hussein introduced his 1994 punishment laws. *Republic of Fear* tells the story of how this tradition evolved from cruel public show trials to torture under conditions of total secrecy.

The show trials of 1969 affirmed the power of the fledgling Baathist state by a stage-managed, intentionally excessive display of cruelty that dramatized the imbalance between victim and victimizer. This came at a time when the state was still weak. After those early experiences, all through the eight grueling years of war with Iran, few Iraqis dreamed of publicly protesting the harsh punishments to which they were routinely subjected. For nearly twenty years every Iraqi knew that he or she lived in a torturing state, but the omniscience and omnipotence of the state's repressive capability lay in the fact that all opposition to it had been crushed—in other words, it lay in the silence and deep secrecy that now surrounded all state operations. Everything was secret where punishment was concerned, from the arrest to the charges, the interrogation, the extraction of the evidence, the trial, the judgment, and the execution of the sentence. If there was a corpse, bearing in its markings that last record of the whole affair, even it was returned to the family in a sealed box. These were the rules of the game in the extraordinarily effective state system described in this book.

All this began to change after the Gulf War of 1991. Iraqis began to speak out and tell their stories like never before. Taking advantage of the regime's rout in that war, they even revolted, capturing two-thirds of the country's governorates, and holding entire cities for a period of one to three weeks. As Iraqis like to put it, *hajiz al-khawf inkiser,* "the barrier of fear was broken," in March 1991. These people who were no longer afraid then did the unthinkable: they called upon the very allied armies that had rained bombs on their cities for six weeks to help them get rid of the system that ruled over them. Nothing like this had ever happened in Arab politics before. A window of opportunity opened up for the whole region with this dramatic transformation of priorities. But it was not to be. For the insurgents stood alone, rejected by their fellow Arabs and by the Western leaders of the coalition that had expelled Iraq from Kuwait. They were crushed, and in the years that followed that wild, insurrectionary moment, the system responded by turning full circle on itself; it went back to a formula that had worked so well for it in its early days: public displays of extreme cruelty.

The difference this time around was that the absolutism of the Republic of Fear was breaking down. Rank-and-file soldiers were deserting Saddam Hussein's army in record numbers. Iraqis were speaking out and telling their stories like they had not done before. (I had to publish *Republic of Fear* under a pseudonym; I no longer have to.) Even senior officials, like the former head of military intelligence Wafiq al-Samarraie, or the army chief of staff Nazar al-Khazragi, were defecting to an opposition just beginning to operate out of the north (not to mention the defection to Jordan in August 1995 of Saddam's two sons-in-law and their wives, the president's daughters). However, urbane, educated middle-class citizens were also learning what it meant to be hungry for the first time in their lives. Desperation ruled the south, which had spearheaded the March 1991 uprising and was now paying the price for it. Law and order were collapsing in Baghdad. Under such conditions, it was neither effective nor possible to shoot and torture everybody.

Republic of Fear, therefore, describes a state system that no longer exists in post–Gulf War Iraq. The war, the uprising that followed on its heels, and seven terrible years of sanctions and economic privation have seen to that. Nothing in Iraq today is as it was in the heyday of the regime's absolutism, which reached its apogee in the late 1970s.

Yet Saddam Hussein is still in power—a tin-pot dictator by Western standards (in comparison with Stalin or Hitler), but still one who built a formidable modern system that ruled through fear. And he has outlasted a formidable array of enemies who have long since died or been voted out of office (Ayatollah Khomeini, George Bush, Margaret Thatcher). In fact the Iraqi leader has defied nearly every prediction made about the certainty of his impending demise, including my own in the early 1990s.

Dealing with Saddam Hussein

Saddam Hussein's horrific new punishment laws, promulgated in August 1994, had nothing to do with President Clinton's dispatching U.S. aircraft, ships, and troops to the Gulf in October of that year. Whether they should have had is a different question. However, they did have something to do with why the Iraqi leader was yet again engaged in a game of chicken with the American president and the international community, a game that had reached the stage of armed conflict on at least ten previous occasions since the cease-fire in the Gulf War came into effect.

The Iraqi economy had been in deep crisis for four years, with a plummeting currency, cuts in government subsidies for basic food items like rice, wheat, and sugar, and skyrocketing prices. Officially, one Iraqi dinar was still worth three U.S. dollars, the exchange rate before the sanctions. Unofficially, one U.S. dollar could be exchanged for four hundred to six hundred Iraqi dinars. You could buy anything and anybody in Iraq for very little (the perfect conditions, incidentally, for a relatively bloodless change in regime, if an outsider could be found who was interested). The police were no longer able to cope with the growing rates of burglary, theft, and rape. In a 1992 attempt to control market forces, Saddam Hussein detained 550 of Baghdad's leading merchants on charges of profiteering; 42 of them were executed, their bodies tied to telephone poles in front of their shops with signs around their necks that read "Greedy Merchant." In short, the Iraqi president was killing, maiming, and branding his citizens as he continued to pick fights with history's most reluctant superpower. With each inconclusive new confrontation, the currency continued its downward spiral, and sanctions bit deeper into the social and moral fabric of the country. But Saddam Hussein stayed on in power, each time clawing back a little bit more of his pre–Gulf War aura of invincibility vis-à-vis Iraqis—more, at least, than he had before his latest high-risk gamble with the United States. For seven years he has been edging himself back into the game of nations, utilizing a whole array of variations on this same tactic. And he has been getting away with it.

The accumulation of little victories turned into a strategic one for Saddam Hussein on Friday, August 30, 1996, the day he sent his tanks and forty thousand crack Republican Guard troops into Arbil, inside the safe-haven area set up by the allied coalition in 1991. The secret police followed in their wake, penetrating deep into Iraqi Kurdistan, killing hundreds and arresting thousands of oppositionists who had believed in American promises of protection. Files and publications were captured, and television and radio installations, which the United States had helped to finance, were blown up. Thus ended a five-year experiment in autonomy and self-rule for the Kurdish 20 percent of Iraq's population.

The whole array of arrangements by which the United States had sought to "contain" Saddam Hussein since the Gulf War came tumbling down in the summer of 1996. Neither Saudi Arabia nor Turkey, trusted allies of the United States and pillars of the Gulf War coalition, was prepared to let American planes use its territory in 1996 as a launching pad to deliver the Iraqi dictator yet another pinprick response. American policy toward Iraq, summed up in two words, "sanctions" and "containment," was left in shambles. But those Iraqis who made it their business to change the regime in Baghdad with Western assistance paid the highest price of all. Hundreds were killed; thousands were arrested or driven into exile; and the whole infrastructure of the opposition in northern Iraq was destroyed.

That is the meaning of what happened in northern Iraq in the summer of 1996. And that remained its meaning in spite of all the cruise missiles rained down on Saddam Hussein's useless and already enfeebled air-defense system, a system that has been irrelevant to his political control over the country since 1991. American policy makers seem unable or unwilling to understand that each time they spend vast sums redeploying the naval and air armadas of the world's only remaining superpower, ostensibly to deter or contain a tin-pot dictator they are supposed to have just trounced in a major war, they magnify his importance in the eyes of the whole world.

The Iraqi case has a lot to teach us about what happens to an outlaw state that is not overthrown when it consistently breaches international norms but is subjected to a combined regime of sanctions and unbridled tyranny: it corrodes and rots, devastating and impoverishing the vast majority of the population, without necessarily becoming any easier to revolt against or overthrow from the inside. Sanctions do not work the way Western policy makers claim they do. Those of us who saw them as an interim measure, pending the overthrow of the regime by an opposition that looked to the West for assistance, have now got to reassess the situation.

"This used to be a rich country," an Iraqi intellectual who described himself as having been a fervent Saddam admirer confided to Youssef Ibrahim of *The New York Times*. "Today I'd say not more than one million Iraqis are living in any real sense of the word. They are those who uphold Saddam's rule and those who protect him. They are given food and plenty of money. The rest of us are drifting into this surreal kind of poverty where university professors sell their family's possessions to eat. It is breaking down the very fabric of this society. Sometimes when I hear foreign radio broadcast assertions that the only way to salvation is to get rid of Saddam, I say to myself, 'Do they think we are some kind of video game, or what?' You are looking at a people whose energy is drained simply looking for the next meal."

In the spring of 1994, even "He Who Shocks" (or "Shakes Things Up," the literal meaning of Saddam's name) had begun to show signs of the strain involved in constantly trying to outwit American presidents. The strain could be seen on television during a March 13 speech on the occasion of the Muslim feast Eid al-Fitr. The president was uncharacteristically angry, slapping his thigh five times while fulminating against the West for the most recent renewal of the U.N. sanctions. His government had just offered a ten-thousand-dollar reward to anybody who killed a United Nations relief worker in northern Iraq. Three divisions of the elite Republican Guards had been moved northwards to threaten Iraqi Kurdistan in March (just as they were to threaten Kuwait in October of the same year). The Iraqi leader allowed himself to look exhausted before his whole country (something leaders of his ilk must never do). His speech was slurred; his eyes were puffy. Gone was the hard, cold gaze that transfixed and unnerved its audience. Stalin is said to have had such eyes—the eyes of a man who looks poised, confident, and self-assured as he destroys those closest to him who have, by accident or otherwise, triggered an adverse feeling. "I know a person will betray me before they know it themselves," Saddam has been known to say, like Stalin before him. But on Iraqi television, shortly before the new punishment laws were to be promulgated, the feelings of a less self-confident man were there on the surface for all to see.

History is littered with leaders who crumbled at moments such as these. The shah of Iran was such a leader, as was General Galtieri of Argentina in the wake of the failure of his adventure in the Falklands. Saddam Hussein may be made of sterner stuff than these men, but there is nothing inexplicable or mysterious about his longevity in office, given the importance that a bungling United States has itself chosen to lend him. In the 1980s, he was the defender of the "eastern flank of the Arab World," to cite the title of a book very influential in Washington circles in the late 1980s. In 1990–91, he was worth sending 450,000 Americans halfway across the world to fight against. All the important issues since then go back to that war's unfinished business, and a veritable American obsession with containing the adversary, as opposed to getting on with the obvious business of helping Iraqis to topple him. This clumsy, unprincipled, hands-on/hands-off policy of a musclebound superpower saved Saddam Hussein in 1994, just as it had saved him from the retribution of ordinary Iraqis at the end of the 1991 war.

That transforming moment in Iraqi politics began the moment a formal cease-fire came into effect, on February 28, 1991. A column of Iraqi tanks fleeing from Kuwait happened to roll into Sa'ad Square, a huge rectangular open space in downtown Basra, Iraq's southernmost city. The commander at the head of the column positioned his vehicle in front of a gigantic mural of Saddam in military uniform located next to the Baath Party headquarters in the middle of the square. Standing atop his vehicle and addressing the portrait, he denounced the dictator in a blistering speech: "What has befallen us of defeat, shame, and humiliation, Saddam, is the result of your follies, your miscalculations, and your irresponsible actions!" A crowd assembled. The atmosphere became highly charged. The commander jumped back into his tank and swiveled the gun turret to take aim at the portrait. He blasted Saddam's face away with several shells. Saddam lost his face, literally, in a classic revolutionary moment, one that sparked the post–Gulf War Iraqi *intifada*. Within hours there was a meltdown of authority in Iraq, and Saddam Hussein was confronted with the most serious threat ever to his power.

Losing face and the breakdown of authority have a very long history in this part of the world. One of the great treasures of ancient Mesopotamia is the headless statue of Napir-Asu, the wife of one of the most important fourteenth-century-B.C. kings of Susa. An inscription on the statue's base reads: "He who would seize my statue, who would smash it, who would destroy its inscriptions, who would erase my name, may he be smitten by the curse of Napirisha, of Kiririsha, and of Inshushinak, that his name shall become extinct, that his offspring shall be barren, that the forces of Beltia, the great goddess, shall sweep down on him." The next time Saddam Hussein tweaks an American nose, the president would be well advised, before deciding how to respond, to ponder the implications of the fact that, like the rulers of ancient Mesopotamia, Saddam Hussein is more afraid of losing face before his enemies (above all his own citizens, who are his greatest enemies) than he is of the entire military arsenal of the United States.

Not only did American policy makers not understand this; they seem even to have been terrified by what Iraqis did at the end of the civil war. The former National Security Adviser under George Bush, Brent Scowcroft, summed up his government's dismay in a special ABC News report, "Unfinished Business in Iraq." Scowcroft was asked by Peter Jennings what he thought of the insurgency that was calling upon the allied armies to help Iraqis overthrow the tyrant and finish the job that the war had started:

I frankly wished it hadn't happened—because the military were faced with the problem of maybe a revolution inside Iraq. And they put the revolution down rather than turning the wrath against Saddam Hussein.

JENNINGS: Do I state it correctly when you say that having seen the rebellion [in southern and northern Iraq] develop, you would have preferred a coup?

SCOWCROFT: Oh, yes. Yes, we clearly would have preferred a coup. There's no question of that.

JENNINGS: Did you genuinely believe at this period that somewhere in the labyrinth around . . .

SCOWCROFT: Yes. Yes. Yes.

As it happens, *Republic of Fear,* published in 1989, was to a large extent about how the Baath under Saddam Hussein had been organizing their regime since 1968 to become "coup-proof." The levels of cruelty attained actually required that the army be subordinated to the secret police in a way that had no precedent in the modern history of Iraq. Scowcroft's answers underline how little the United States understood about the country it had mobilized nearly half a million soldiers to fight in 1990–91. Jonathan Randall, senior foreign correspondent for *The Washington Post,* thinks it was deliberate:

Accumulating evidence suggests that the Bush administration purposely set its mind against grappling with the complexity of Iraqi society before, during, and after the occupation of Kuwait. That is why it refused to have anything meaningful to do with the Iraqi opposition, be it Shia, Sunni, or

Kurd. Rarely in the history of human conflict had so great a power mobilized so many allies, moved so many troops and so much materiel, yet remained so purposely incurious about the nature of the enemy's society and its bloodstained history.

Saddam Hussein is a consummate manipulator of this kind of willful ignorance. And George Bush had left him with five intact divisions of his most elite Republican Guard troops. These he used, along with that ultimate terror weapon, helicopter gunships—specifically allowed by the cease-fire terms negotiated by General Schwarzkopf at Safwan—to crush the March 1991 uprising. Having done that, the Iraqi president turned his attention to rebuilding his image, restoring what one might call his political "face," literally replastering his torn-down portraits back again all over the country. Thus it came to be that barely had the confetti from George Bush's victory celebrations settled before the official Iraqi newspaper, *al-Jumhouriya,* took to advising Bush's psychiatrists to lock the American president up as a way of ridding him of his Iraqi obsession.

Neither the military pyrotechnics of Desert Storm nor the pinprick Tomahawk missile attacks of the various Iraqi-American confrontations since the Gulf War can cover up for the failure of the American political imagination when it comes to what ought to have been done about Saddam Hussein: remove him from office, or, at the very least, relentlessly expose his criminality before his own public and in the eyes of the world. That would have entailed shifting attention to the plight of the people of Iraq, away from the banal formalities of U.N. weapons of mass destruction inspection teams and U.N. Resolution 687.

To its everlasting credit, Western public opinion, driven by the Western media, pointed the way forward. It did so in reaction to images of Kurds fleeing Saddam's vengeance and dying at the rate of a thousand a day on the mountain slopes of Iraqi Kurdistan in April 1991. A deeply reluctant Bush administration was forced to support a historic statement, U.N. Resolution 688. The resolution condemned "the repression of the Iraqi civilian population in many parts of Iraq," and demanded that Iraq allow immediate access for relief purposes. This was the first time that the Kurds had been mentioned by name in a U.N. resolution, and it was also the first time that the United Nations had asserted a right of interference in the internal affairs of a member state. A safe-haven was established in mid-April 1991, policed by coalition forces, which denied the Iraqi army access to its own territories north of the thirty-sixth parallel. One American official, who insisted on remaining anonymous, explained to Jonathan Randall his administration's reasoning: "Frankly, we wanted to wait for the civil war to be over so that our involvement would not be seen as a decision to help the rebels, but as a decision to provide humanitarian aid."

If Saddam Hussein is still in power in Iraq, it is not only because he has consistently outwitted a succession of American administrations; it is principally because the Sunni populace that he is trying to forge into his new (and considerably reduced) social base is rightly afraid of what will happen to it when he is gone. Since 1991, the tyrant has remained in power not because he is loved (never the case in Iraq), nor because he exerts genuine authority, but out of fear of what lies in store in the future.

"People are terrified of what they see," said one Iraqi intellectual residing in Baghdad, who insisted on remaining anonymous. "If the regime falls, you can imagine the chaos that will result, with the poor attacking the less poor. Nearly everyone here has arms, and the country is slipping into chaos. Sometimes I think the regime encourages the idea of a breakdown. It's like saying, 'See what could happen?' if they were no longer around."

Almost any post-Baathist future in Iraq is going to be like walking a tightrope, balancing the legitimate grievances of all those who have suffered against the knowledge that if everyone is held accountable who is in fact guilty, the country will be torn apart. Iraq after Saddam is going to be a country in which justice is both the first thing that everybody wants and the most difficult thing for anyone to deliver. Truth will be much sought after, however gray the moral universe of right and wrong, and whoever did what to whom. It is going to be impossible for a fallible species like our own to get at the truth every time.

The experience of cruelty, of seeing into the bottom of the abyss, can turn those who inflict it or who are subjected to it in on themselves, or it can help them reach outward in the urge to remake and affirm life. Such an affirmation extends civility into the very same world of cruel facts that act constantly to dismantle it. In itself, of course, cruelty does not guarantee anything, least of all the emergence of something like forgiveness or toleration. But the possibility exists of allowing it to open a window otherwise closed to us, a window through which to consider changing the rules by which our lives are organized by those with power over us.

"In a dark time, the eye begins to see," begins a poem by Theodore Roethke. Artists and poets, like many of the ancient myths and legends from which they derive their inspiration, have long exploited this presence of darkness in order to open human hearts onto the world. That is what those who would overthrow Saddam Hussein now need to do.

FOUR

CASUALTIES
OF WAR

"I do not look on the press as an asset. Frankly, I looked on it as a problem to be managed."
> —*Then–Secretary of Defense Dick Cheney, after the first Gulf War*

"It's not the job of a journalist to snap to the attention of generals."
> —*Robert Fisk of* The Independent, *March 25, 2003*

WHAT BODIES?

Patrick J. Sloyan

eon Daniel, as did others who reported from Vietnam during the 1960s, knew about war and death. So he was puzzled by the lack of corpses at the tip of the Neutral Zone between Saudi Arabia and Iraq on Feb. 25, 1991. Clearly there had been plenty of killing. The 1st Infantry Division (Mechanized) had smashed through the defensive front-line of Saddam Hussein's army the day before, Feb. 24, the opening of the Desert Storm ground war to retake Kuwait. Daniel, representing United Press International, was part of a press pool held back from witnessing the assault on 8,000 Iraqi defenders. "They wouldn't let us see anything," said Daniel, who had seen about everything as a combat correspondent.

The artillery barrage alone was enough to cause a slaughter. A 30-minute bombardment by howitzers and multiple-launch rockets scattering thousands of tiny bomblets preceded the attack by 8,400 American soldiers riding in 3,000 M1A2 Abrams main battle tanks, Bradley fighting vehicles, Humvees, armored personnel carriers and other vehicles.

It wasn't until late in the afternoon of Feb. 25 that the press pool was permitted to see where the attack occurred. There were groups of Iraqi prisoners. About 2,000 had surrendered. But there were no bodies, no stench of feces that hovers on a battlefield, no blood stains, no bits of human beings. "You get a little firefight in Vietnam and the bodies would be stacked up like cordwood," Daniel said. Finally, Daniel found the Division public affairs officer, an Army major.

"Where the hell are all the bodies?" Daniel said.

"What bodies?" the officer replied.

Daniel and the rest of the world would not find out until months later why the dead had vanished. Thousands of Iraqi soldiers, some of them alive and firing their weapons from World War I–style trenches, were buried by plows mounted on Abrams main battle tanks. The Abrams flanked the trench lines so that tons of sand from the plow spoil funneled into the trenches. Just be-

---

Patrick Sloyan is a senior correspondent for *Newsday,* where he won the Pulitzer Prize for his coverage of Desert Storm. This article was written while he was an Alicia Patterson Fellow and published in the November 2002 edition of *The Digital Journalist.*

hind the tanks, actually straddling the trench line, came M2 Bradleys pumping 7.62mm machine gun bullets into the Iraqi troops.

"I came through right after the lead company," said Army Col. Anthony Moreno, who commanded the lead brigade during the 1st Mech's assault. "What you saw was a bunch of buried trenches with people's arms and legs sticking out of them. For all I know, we could have killed thousands."

A thinner line of trenches on Moreno's left flank was attacked by the 1st Brigade commanded by Col. Lon Maggart. He estimated his troops buried about 650 Iraqi soldiers. Darkness halted the attack on the Iraqi trench line. By the next day, the 3rd Brigade joined in the grisly innovation. "A lot of people were killed," said Col. David Weisman, the unit commander.

One reason there was no trace of what happened in the Neutral Zone on those two days were the ACEs. It stands for Armored Combat Earth movers and they came behind the armored burial brigade leveling the ground and smoothing away projecting Iraqi arms, legs and equipment.

PFC Joe Queen of the 1st Engineers was impervious to small arms fire inside the cockpit of the massive earth mover. He remained cool and professional as he smoothed away all signs of the carnage. Queen won the Bronze Star for his efforts. "A lot of guys were scared," Queen said, "but I enjoyed it." Col. Moreno estimated more than 70 miles of trenches and earthen bunkers were attacked, filled in and smoothed over on Feb. 24–25.

What happened at the Neutral Zone that day has become a metaphor for the conduct of modern warfare. While political leaders bask in voter approval for destroying designated enemies, they are increasingly determined to mask the reality of warfare that causes voters to recoil. There was no more sophisticated practitioner of this art of bloodless warfare than President George H. W. Bush. As a Navy pilot during World War II, Bush knew the ugly side of war. He once recounted how a sailor wandered into an aircraft propeller on their carrier in the South Pacific. The chief petty officer in charge of the flight deck called for brooms to sweep the man's guts overboard. "I can still hear him," Bush said of the chief's orders. "I have seen the hideous face of war."

Bush was badly stung by the reality of warfare while president. After the 1989 American invasion of Panama—where reporters were also blocked from witnessing a short-lived slaughter in Panama City—Bush held a White House news conference to boast about the dramatic assault on the Central American leader, Gen. Manuel Noriega. Bush was chipper and wisecracking with reporters when two major networks shifted coverage to the arrival ceremony for American soldiers killed in Panama at the Air Force Base in Dover, Del. Millions of viewers watched as the network television screens were split: Bush bantering with the press while flag-draped coffers were carried off Air Force planes by honor guards. Dover was the military mortuary for troops killed while serving abroad. On Bush's orders, the Pentagon banned future news coverage of honor guard ceremonies for the dead. The ban was continued by President Bill Clinton.

Shortly after Iraq invaded Kuwait in August 1990, Bush summoned battle-field commanders to Camp David, Md., for a council of war. Army Gen. H. Norman Schwarzkopf, chief of Central Command with military responsi-bility for the Persian Gulf region, flew from Tampa, Fla. He and Central Command's air boss, Air Force Lt. Gen. Charles Horner, were flown from An-drews Air Force Base, Md., by helicopter to the retreat in the Catoctin Moun-tains near Thurmont, Md. Horner said golf carts took them to the president's cabin. Bush was wearing a windbreaker.

"The president was very concerned about casualties," Horner recalled. "Not just our casualties but Iraqi casualties. He was very emphatic. He wanted casualties minimized on both sides. He went around the room and asked each military commander if his orders were understood. We all said we would do our best."

According to Horner, he took a number of steps to limit the use of anti-personnel bombs used during more than 30 days of air attacks on Iraqi army positions. Schwarzkopf's psychological warfare experts littered Iraqi troops with leaflets that warned of imminent attacks by B52 Strategic Bombers. Ara-bic warnings told troops to avoid sleeping in tanks or near artillery positions which were prime targets for 400 sorties by allied aircraft attacking day and night.

"We could have killed many more with cluster munitions," Horner said of bomblets that create lethal minefields around troop emplacements once they are dropped by aircraft.

But Bush's Camp David orders were also translated into minimizing the perception—if not the reality—of Desert Storm casualties. The president's point man for controlling these perceptions was Dick Cheney, Secretary of Defense. And, to Cheney, that meant controlling the press which he saw as a collective voice that portrayed the Pentagon as a can't do agency that wasted too much money and routinely failed in its mission. "I did not look on the press as an asset," Cheney said in an interview after Desert Storm. He was in-terviewed by authors of a Freedom Forum book, "America's Team—The Odd Couple," which explored the relationship between the media and the De-fense Department. To Cheney, containing the media was his way of protect-ing the Pentagon's credibility. "Frankly, I looked on it as a problem to be managed," Cheney said of the media.

This management had two key ingredients: control the flow of information through high level briefings while impeding reporters such as Leon Daniel. According to Cheney, he and Army Gen. Colin Powell, Chairman of the Joint Chiefs of Staff, orchestrated the briefings because "the information function was extraordinarily important. I did not have a lot of confidence that I could leave that to the press." The relentless appetite of broadcasting networks made Pentagon control a simple matter. Virtually every U.S. weapon system is monitored by television cameras either on board warplanes and helicopters or hand-held by military cameramen or individual soldiers. This "gun camera" footage may be released or withheld depending on the decisions of political bosses of the military. So when the air war began in January 1991, the media was fed carefully selected footage by Schwarzkopf in Saudi Arabia and Powell in Washington, DC. Most of it was downright misleading.

Briefings by Schwarzkopf and other military officers mostly featured laser guided or television guided missiles and bombs. But of all the tons of high explosives dropped during more than a month of night and day air attacks, only six per cent were smart bombs. The vast majority were controlled by gravity, usually dropped from above 15,000 feet—35,000 feet for U.S. heavy bombers—where winds can dramatically affect accuracy. And there never was any footage of B-52 bomber strikes that carpeted Iraqi troop positions. Films of Tomahawk cruise missiles being launched by U.S. Navy ships in the Persian Gulf were almost daily fare from the military. Years later, the Navy would concede these subsonic jets with 2,000-pound warheads had limited success. These missiles are guided by on-board computers that match pre-recorded terrain maps, shifting left or right as landmarks are spotted. But the faceless desert offered few waypoints and most Tomahawks wandered off, just as the French Legion's lost platoon did in the Sahara. The only reliable landmark turned out to be the Tigris River and Tomahawks were programmed to use it as a road to Baghdad and other targets. But Iraqi antiaircraft gunners quickly blanketed the riverside. The slow moving Tomahawks were easy targets. Pentagon claims of 98 percent success for Tomahawks during the war later dwindled to less than 10 percent effectiveness by the Navy in 1999.

Just as distorted were Schwarzkopf's claims of destruction of Iraqi Scud missiles. After the war, studies by Army and Pentagon think tanks could not identify a single successful interception of a Scud warhead by the U.S. Army's Patriot antimissile system. U.S. Air Force attacks on Scud launch sites were portrayed as successful by Schwarzkopf. The Air Force had filled the night sky with F-15E bombers with radars and infrared systems that could turn night into day. Targets were attacked with laser guided warheads. In one briefing in Riyadh, Schwarzkopf showed F15E footage of what he said was a Scud missile launcher being destroyed. Later, it turned out that the suspected Scud system was in fact an oil truck. A year after Desert Storm, the official Air Force study concluded that not a single Scud launcher was destroyed during the war. The study said Iraq ended the conflict with as many Scud launchers as it had when the conflict began.

In manipulating the first and often most lasting perception of Desert Storm, the Bush administration produced not a single picture or video of anyone being killed. This sanitized, bloodless presentation by military briefers left the world presuming Desert Storm was a war without death. That image was reinforced by limitations imposed on reporters on the battlefield. Under rules developed by Cheney and Powell, journalists were not allowed to move without military escorts. All interviews had to be monitored by military public affairs escorts. Every line of copy, every still photograph, every strip of film had to be approved—censored—before being filed. And these rules were ruthlessly enforced.

When a Scud missile eventually hit American troops during the ground war, reporters raced to the scene. The 1,000-pound warhead landed on a makeshift barracks for Pennsylvania national guard troops near the Saudi seaport of Dahran. Scott Applewhite, a photographer for the Associated Press, was one of the first on the scene. There were more than 25 dead bodies and 70 badly wounded. As Applewhite photographed the carnage, he was approached by U.S. Military Police who ordered him to leave. He produced credentials that entitled him to be there. But the soldiers punched Applewhite, handcuffed him and ripped the film from his cameras. More than 70 reporters were arrested, detained, threatened at gunpoint and literally chased from the frontlines when they attempted to defy Pentagon rules. Army public affairs officers made nightly visits to hotels and restaurants in Hafir al Batin, a Saudi town on the Iraq border. Reporters and photographers usually bolted from the dinner table. Slower ones were arrested.

Journalists such as Applewhite, who played by the rules, fared no better. More than 150 reporters who participated in the Pentagon pool system failed to produce a single eyewitness account of the clash between 300,000 allied troops and an estimated 300,000 Iraqi troops. There was not one photograph, not a strip of film by pool members of a dead body—American or Iraqi. Even if they had recorded the reality of the battlefield, it was unlikely it would have been filed by the military-controlled distribution system. As the ground war began, Cheney declared a press blackout, effectively blocking distribution of battlefield press reports. While Cheney's action was challenged by Marlin Fitzwater, the White House press secretary, the ban remained in effect. Most news accounts were delayed for days, long enough to make them worthless to their editors.

Accounts of Iraqi troops escaping from Kuwait—the carnage on the High-way of Death—were recorded by journalists operating outside the pool system.

Schwarzkopf repeatedly brushed off questions about the Iraqi death toll when the ground war ended in early March. Not until 2000, during a television broadcast, would he estimate Iraq losses in the "tens of thousands." The only precise estimate came from Cheney. In a formal report to Congress, Cheney said U.S. soldiers found only 457 Iraqi bodies on the battlefield.

To Cheney, who helped Bush's approval rating soar off the charts during Desert Storm, the press coverage had been flawless. "The best-covered war ever," Cheney said. "The American people saw up close with their own eyes through the magic of television what the U.S. military was capable of doing."

REMEMBER NAYIRAH, WITNESS FOR KUWAIT?

John R. MacArthur

In his urgent arguments during the fall and winter of 1990 for military action against Saddam Hussein, President Bush made much of the Iraqi leader's cruelty toward the Kuwaiti people. Mr. Bush's allegations of atrocities by Iraqi forces generally went unchallenged. Mr. Hussein's violent disposal of dissident Iraqis was a matter of record, so few politicians, journalists or human rights investigators were prepared to question the President's campaign to paint his opponent as Adolf Hitler reborn.

Some claims were no doubt true, but the most sensational one—that Iraqi soldiers removed hundreds of Kuwaiti babies from incubators and left them to die on hospital floors—was shown to be almost certainly false by an ABC reporter, John Martin, in March 1991, after the liberation of Kuwait. He interviewed hospital doctors who stayed in Kuwait throughout the occupation.

But before the war, the incubator story seriously distorted the American debate about whether to support military action. Amnesty International believed the tale, and its ill-considered validation of the charges likely influenced the seven senators who cited the story in speeches backing the January 12 resolution authorizing war. Since the resolution passed the Senate by only five votes, the question of how the incubator story escaped scrutiny—when it really mattered—is all the more important. (Amnesty International later retracted its support of the story.)

A little reportorial investigation would have done a great service to the democratic process. Americans would have been interested to know the identity of "Nayirah," the 15-year-old Kuwaiti girl who shocked the Congressional Human Rights Caucus on October 10, 1990, when she tearfully asserted that she had watched 15 infants being taken from incubators in Al-Adan Hospital in Kuwait City by Iraqi soldiers who "left the babies on the cold floor to die." The chairmen of the Congressional group, Tom Lantos, a California Democrat, and John Edward Porter, an Illinois Republican, explained that Nayirah's

John R. MacArthur, the publisher of *Harper's* Magazine, is the author of *Second Front: Censorship and Propaganda in the Gulf War.* This article was published on *The New York Times* op-ed page on January 6, 1992.

identity would be kept secret to protect her family from reprisals in occupied Kuwait.

There was a better reason to protect her from exposure: Nayirah, her real name, is the daughter of the Kuwaiti Ambassador to the U.S., Saud Nasir al-Sabah. Such a pertinent fact might have led to impertinent demands for proof of Nayirah's whereabouts in August and September of 1990, when she said she witnessed the atrocities, as well as corroboration of her charges. The Kuwaiti Embassy has rebuffed my efforts to interview Nayirah.

Today, we are left to ask why Mr. Lantos and Mr. Porter allowed such glaring omissions. What made Nayirah so believable that no one on the caucus staff bothered to check out her story?

One explanation might lie in how Nayirah came to the Congressmen's attention. Both Congressmen have a close relationship with Hill and Knowlton, the public relations firm hired by Citizens for a Free Kuwait, the Kuwaiti-financed group that lobbied Congress for military intervention. A Hill and Knowlton vice president, Gary Hymel, helped organize the Congressional Human Rights Caucus hearing in meetings with Mr. Lantos and Mr. Porter and the chairman of Citizens for a Free Kuwait, Hassan al-Ebraheem. Mr. Hymel presented the witnesses, including Nayirah. (He later told me he knew who she was at the time.)

Until he started working on the Kuwait account, Mr. Hymel was best known to the caucus for defending the human rights record of Turkey, a Hill and Knowlton client criticized for jailing people without due process and torturing and killing them. He is also one of the firm's lobbyists for the Indonesian Government, which has killed at least 100,000 inhabitants of East Timor since 1975.

Mr. Lantos's spokesman says that Hill and Knowlton's client list doesn't concern the Congressman, who accepted a $500 contribution from the firm's political action committee in 1988. In fact, Mr. Lantos and Mr. Porter allowed the Congressional Human Rights Foundation, a group they founded in 1985, to be housed in Hill and Knowlton's Washington headquarters. The firm provides a contribution to the foundation in the form of a $3,000 annual rent reduction, and the Hill and Knowlton switchboard delivers messages to the foundation's executive director, David Phillips.

Hill and Knowlton's client, Citizens for a Free Kuwait, donated $50,000 to the foundation, sometime after Iraq's invasion of Kuwait on August 2, 1990. (The foundation's main supporter is the U.S. government–financed National Endowment for Democracy.)

Since the Gulf War, Hill and Knowlton's collaboration with the Lantos-Porter human rights enterprise has been strengthened by the naming of the firm's vice chairman, Frank Mankiewicz, to the foundation's board in October 1991. Perhaps the Congressmen and directors were impressed by the recent addition of China to Hill and Knowlton's prestigious portfolio of clients. (The firm's clients, Indonesia and Turkey, were notably absent from the foundation's 1990–91 list of human rights "activities.")

Congress and the news media deserve censure for their lack of skepticism about the incubator story. As for Representatives Lantos and Porter, they deserve a medal from the Emir for their work on behalf of the Kuwaiti cause. But their special relationship with Hill and Knowlton should prompt a Congressional investigation to find out if their actions merely constituted an obvious conflict of interest or, worse, if they knew who the tearful Nayirah really was in October 1990.

Editors' note: Doubts about Iraqis throwing babies out of Kuwaiti incubators were first raised by Alexander Cockburn in his February 4, 1991 "Beat the Devil" column in *The Nation,* and many journalists went on to thoroughly debunk the story. Nevertheless, that did not prevent HBO Films from recycling the claim as fact in its 2002 film *Live from Baghdad.* Subsequently, a correction was posted by HBO Films at http://www.hbo.com/films/livefrombaghdad/related.shtml along with a copy of MacArthur's op-ed piece.

"THANK GOD FOR THE PATRIOT MISSILE!"

Edited by Christopher Cerf and Victor Navasky

"The Patriot's success, of course, is known to everyone. It's 100 percent—so far, of 33 [Scuds] engaged, there have been 33 destroyed."
> —General Norman Schwarzkopf
> (Commander of Allied Forces in the Persian Gulf),
> Pentagon briefing, Riyadh, Saudi Arabia, January 31, 1991

"42 Scuds engaged, 41 intercepted. Thank God for the Patriot missile!"
> —George Bush (President of the United States), addressing
> assembly-line workers at Raytheon, manufacturer of the
> Patriot missile, Andover, Massachusetts, February 15, 1991

"[I]n Saudi Arabia, just under 90% of Scud missile engagements resulted in destruction of the Scud's warhead. . . . In Israel, about half of Scud engagements by Patriot resulted in confirmed destruction of the Scud warhead, as assessed by Israeli Defense Forces."
> —Raytheon Company (manufacturer of the Patriot missile),
> official corporate statement, based on an
> official U.S. Army estimate, April 25, 1991

"We are confident that over 40 percent of the engagements in Israel and over 70 percent of the engagements in Saudi Arabia were successful. These are minor changes to our conclusions."
> —Major General Jay Garner (U.S. Army spokesperson),
> testimony before a House Government Operations
> subcommittee, April 7, 1992

Christopher Cerf is a coeditor of this book. Victor Navasky is the editorial director of *The Nation* and Delacorte Professor of Journalism at the Columbia University Graduate School of Journalism. This piece is excerpted from their book *The Experts Speak.*

"[A]bout 9% of the Patriot's Operation Desert Storm engagements are supported by the strongest evidence that an engagement resulted in a warhead kill."

—U.S. General Accounting Office Review report,
September 29, 1992

"To the best of my recollection, only one Scud missile exploded in the air as a consequence of a Patriot explosion. . . ."

—General Dan Shomron (Chief of Staff of the Israeli Defense
Force at the time of the Gulf War), quoted in
The Christian Science Monitor, September 8, 1997

DID IRAQ TRY TO ASSASSINATE EX-PRESIDENT BUSH IN 1993? A CASE NOT CLOSED

Seymour M. Hersh

On Saturday, June 26, 1993, twenty-three Tomahawk guided missiles, each loaded with a thousand pounds of high explosives, were fired from American Navy warships in the Persian Gulf and the Red Sea at the headquarters complex of the Mukhabarat, the Iraqi intelligence service, in downtown Baghdad. The attack was in response to an American determination that Iraqi intelligence, under the command of President Saddam Hussein, had plotted to assassinate former President George Bush during Bush's ceremonial visit to Kuwait in mid-April. It was President Bill Clinton's first act of war.

Three of the million-dollar missiles missed their target and landed on nearby homes, killing eight civilians, including Layla al-Attar, one of Iraq's most gifted artists. The death toll was considered acceptable by the White House; after all, scores of civilians had been killed in the Reagan Administration's F-111 bombing attack on Muammar Qaddafi's housing-and-office complex in Tripoli, Libya, in 1986. Clinton Administration officials acknowledged that they had been "lucky," as one national-security aide put it, in that only three of the computer-guided missiles went off course. Nearly three hundred Tomahawks had been fired during the Gulf War, with a higher rate of inaccuracy.

The media and a majority of the American public saw the American raid on Baghdad as a success, and as evidence that the struggling new President had finally demonstrated toughness when toughness was needed. Public-opinion polls showed that Clinton's approval rating climbed by eleven percentage points on June 27th, the day after the attack; more than two-thirds of those polled approved of the bombing.

President Clinton and those aides who supported his decision may have been right: the Iraqi intelligence service may have developed and put in motion a plot to assassinate George Bush during his triumphant visit to Kuwait to

Pulitzer Prize–winning investigative reporter Seymour M. Hersh is the author of many books, including *The Samson Option: Israel's Nuclear Arsenal and American Foreign Policy*. This article was published with the title "A Case Not Closed" in the November 1, 1993 edition of *The New Yorker*.

celebrate the Gulf War victory over Iraq. And if such a plot did exist Saddam Hussein may have known of it, or should have known, and thus would have been personally responsible for not preventing it. But my own investigations have uncovered circumstantial evidence, at least as compelling as the Administration's, that suggests that the American government's case against Iraq— as it has been outlined in public, anyway—is seriously flawed.

THE ADMINISTRATION, with its well-meaning but floundering leadership, spent two months investigating and debating the alleged assassination attempt, and then ordered the bombing just one day after receiving a written intelligence report on it. That report, delivered on June 24th by the Federal Bureau of Investigation, provided what the President and his advisers concluded was compelling evidence of Iraqi complicity at the top.

A senior White House official recently told me that one of the seemingly most persuasive elements of the report had been overstated and was essentially incorrect. And none of the Clinton Administration officials I interviewed over a ten-week period this summer claimed that there was any empirical evidence—a "smoking gun"—directly linking Saddam or any of his senior advisers to the alleged assassination attempt. The case against Iraq was, and remains, circumstantial. Nonetheless, on June 24th the F.B.I.'s intelligence report was accepted at face value by the President and his senior aides, and some of those aides told me that the mere existence of the report and the expectation that it would be leaked to the press were what drove the President to act. "We had to move quickly," one diplomat said, with rancor. "Bill Safire obviously would have the report for a weekend column." Safire, the *Times* columnist and a frequent critic of Clinton policy, had bedevilled the White House that spring with his ability to obtain restricted information from the Justice Department.

The last-minute Presidential concern over press leaks was valid, for throughout the two months of internal debate over the alleged assassination attempt the White House policymakers were constantly bombarded—and eventually persuaded, perhaps—by news leaks about the evidence against Iraq. *The Wall Street Journal* and *The Washington Post* were among the many newspapers that praised the President's firm leadership in the aftermath of the bombing of Baghdad and his willingness to send potential adversaries a message of American resolve. "Mr. Clinton is learning on the job," the *Journal* said. The newspaper was not reflecting the reality of White House decision-making, however, but merely praising a decision that it and other newspapers had been manipulated to help bring about.

As it happened, the policy was driven not by Bill Clinton and his senior staff but by those men and women in the bureaucracy who from the outset viewed the alleged assassination plot as imposing a responsibility to strike hard at the hated Saddam while also providing a quick fix for the President, who was then mired in controversy over his failure to use force against the Serbs in Bosnia. These aides told everyone in Washington who would listen that bombing Baghdad would improve Clinton's political standing at home and his diplomatic standing in the Middle East. Among the officials making such arguments were two key members of the White House staff—Samuel R. (Sandy) Berger, the deputy assistant to the President for national-security affairs, and Martin Indyk, senior director of the National Security Council Division of Near East and South Asian Affairs. Both men were privately asserting by early May—long before the delivery of the official F.B.I. report—that the intelligence implicating Iraq in the assassination attempt was overwhelming; both men remained strong advocates of the use of force.

The crisis had its beginnings in the last few days of April, when the Kuwaiti government announced that it had arrested a group of seventeen Iraqis and Kuwaitis on charges of "destabilizing" Kuwait; that one Iraqi had confessed, under interrogation, to having been sent by Iraqi intelligence to assassinate George Bush; and that a powerful bomb, weighing nearly two hundred pounds and capable of killing everyone within four hundred yards, had been found hidden in a car that had been driven across the border from Iraq to Kuwait.

The announcement produced little reaction in Washington or anywhere in Europe, essentially because the Kuwaiti government was known for making self-serving pronouncements about its adversaries. Three years ago, during Iraq's six-month occupation of Kuwait, there had been an outcry when a teen-age Kuwaiti girl testified eloquently and effectively before Congress about Iraqi atrocities involving newborn infants. The girl turned out to be the daughter of the Kuwaiti Ambassador to Washington, Sheikh Saud Nasir al-Sabah, and her account of Iraqi soldiers flinging babies out of incubators was challenged as exaggerated both by journalists and by human-rights groups. (Sheikh Saud was subsequently named Minister of Information in Kuwait, and he was the government official in charge of briefing the international press on the alleged assassination attempt against George Bush.) In a second incident, in August of 1991, Kuwait provoked a special session of the United Nations Security Council by claiming that twelve Iraqi vessels, including a speedboat, had been involved in an attempt to assault Bubiyan Island, long-disputed territory that was then under Kuwaiti control. The Security Council eventually concluded that, while the Iraqis had been provocative, there had been no Iraqi military raid, and that the Kuwaiti government knew there hadn't. What did take place was nothing more than a smuggler-versus-smuggler dispute over war booty in a nearby demilitarized zone that had emerged, after the Gulf War, as an illegal marketplace for alcohol, ammunition, and livestock.

This year, leaks about Iraqi interference in Kuwait's doings began in early May. On Saturday, May 8th, *The Washington Post* quoted Administration officials and others as saying that there was credible evidence linking the Iraqi government to the assassination attempt. The officials, who were not named, provided the newspaper with three elements of that evidence. One key fact, the *Post* said, was the ease with which the alleged Iraqi assassination team had crossed the border area between Iraq and Kuwait: "U.S. officials said the transit of . . . explosives . . . would have been difficult without official sanction." The newspaper also quoted an official as explaining that the bombs and the detonator recovered in the Iraqi-owned car were "way too sophisticated, involving things too sophisticated, to be just some crazies with a complaint against the president." Finally, the newspaper quoted Clinton Administration officials as saying that they were in the process of tracing the explosives in question "to the source." To further buttress its story, which was splashed across the front page in a banner headline, the *Post* quoted Mohammed Sabah al-Sabah, the new Kuwaiti Ambassador to Washington, as saying that one of the arrested Iraqis had confessed to being "a colonel in the Iraqi secret intelligence service, the Mukhabarat, stationed in Basra." Each of those assertions has now been shown to be factually incorrect.

The *Post* article named Berger and two other high-level Clinton Administration officials—R. James Woolsey, the director of the Central Intelligence Agency, and Frank G. Wisner, now an Under-Secretary of Defense—as being among those who advocated "direct retribution" against Iraq. By this time, too, Martin Indyk was hard at work, telling selected journalists, "We've got it"—that is, highly reliable intelligence tying Iraq to a plot against Bush. Indyk also said that Saudi Arabia, which had been the most important American and Kuwaiti ally in the Gulf War, was pressuring the Administration to take harsh action. The Saudi argument to the Clinton Administration, as it was relayed by Indyk, was that "if people think they can get away with this, you'll have no credibility" in the Middle East.

A significant factor in the campaign against Saddam Hussein was simple animosity, stemming from the Iraqi leader's occupation of Kuwait in August of 1990 and his near-suicidal defiance of American pressure, which resulted in the brutal and disastrous Gulf War in early 1991. A former American ambassador in the Middle East recalled his surprise when a colleague, who holds a high post in the Clinton Administration, told him that he had started arguing for retaliation on the day after the first reports of an assassination attempt reached Washington from Kuwait. "I was shocked, because I view him as a normally very responsible and sober person, who understands about power and how to use it," the former ambassador said. "He just hates Saddam—a visceral hatred." Another former senior official said that many officials in the Pentagon and the State Department had become increasingly angry with Iraq in the early months of the Clinton Administration, feeling that Saddam Hussein had been "getting away with things" because of Washington's preoccupation with events in the former Yugoslavia.

The May 8th *Washington Post* story inevitably led to congressional pressure on the White House. Lee H. Hamilton, Democrat of Indiana, who is the chairman of the House Foreign Affairs Committee, went on NBC's "Meet the Press" on the morning of Sunday, May 9th, and said that the United States "should retaliate" if the evidence cited by the *Post* was determined to be valid. "We cannot tolerate that kind of an action against a former President of the United States," Hamilton, a political moderate, said. "It's just outrageous."

The official White House view was articulated by Thomas S. Foley, the Democratic Speaker of the House, also on "Face the Nation." Foley urged restraint and caution until there was clear evidence that an assassination attempt had taken place and had been sponsored by Iraq. "It isn't, at least in the public sphere, clear that the evidence is overwhelming or without any ambiguity," he said.

A number of senior White House aides, supporting Foley's view, told me that the President was anything but eager to plunge into a military operation against Iraq without receiving hard evidence and without carefully reviewing his options. "He always wants to see the good and the bad sides of everything," one close associate said. Like any well-trained attorney, the associate added, Clinton wanted to understand "the prosecution case and the defense case." Another presidential observer, discussing the President's attitude toward the Kuwaiti allegations, noted, "Clinton is always looking at the downside. He's a pol—a domestic-policy wonk, who does not get off on foreign policy. He was worried about what could go wrong." Clinton's approach was reflected in the official White House response to the *Washington Post* disclosures. "We're still in the middle of the investigation," George Stephanopoulos, the White House communications director, told reporters.

The President was not alone in his caution. Janet Reno, the Attorney General, also had her doubts. "The A.G. remains skeptical of certain aspects of the case," a senior Justice Department official told me in late July, a month after the bombs were dropped on Baghdad. Ms. Reno had, however, approved the F.B.I. report sent to the White House on June 24th.

Two days after Stephanopoulos made his statement, the President's instinct for caution and deliberateness was challenged by a further leak—this time to the Washington bureau of the *Times*. On Tuesday, May 11th, the *Times*, citing "American officials," reported that there was "powerful evidence" pointing to Iraqi sponsorship of the assassination attempt. According to the *Times* report, federal investigators who had travelled to Kuwait found that components of the car bomb discovered by the Kuwaiti police were "almost exactly the same" as those of Iraqi car bombs recovered by American intelligence during the Gulf War. That assertion, too, was incorrect.

Two weeks later, what amounted to open warfare broke out among various factions in the government on the issue of who had done what in Kuwait. Someone gave a *Boston Globe* reporter access to a classified C.I.A. study that was highly skeptical of the Kuwaiti claims of an Iraqi assassination attempt. The study, prepared by the C.I.A.'s Counter Terrorism Center, suggested that Kuwait might have "cooked the books" on the alleged plot in an effort to play up the "continuing Iraqi threat" to Western interests in the Persian Gulf. Neither the *Times* nor the *Post* made any significant mention of the *Globe* dispatch, which had been written by a Washington correspondent named Paul Quinn-Judge, although the story cited specific paragraphs from the C.I.A assessment. The two major American newspapers had been driven by their sources to the other side of the debate.

Also in late May, the *Post* obtained a copy of a speech that Martin Indyk delivered before the Washington Institute for Near East Policy, in which he said that the Clinton Administration's conclusion was that the leadership of Iraq would remain hostile to American interests and aims for the foreseeable future. The Administration does not "seek or expect a reconciliation with Saddam Hussein's regime," Indyk said. Before joining the White House, Indyk had served as executive director of the institute, which was established in 1985, with financial backing from the American Israel Public Affairs Committee. This organization is considered the strongest pro-Israel lobby in Washington.

On June 10th, the *Post* returned anew to the alleged Iraqi plot, reporting once again that "the Clinton Administration has found evidence implicating the Iraqi government in a plot to assassinate former President George Bush." The *Post* further quoted its sources, described as American officials and senior intelligence analysts, as saying that, despite the consensus on Iraqi involvement, no final judgment would be issued by the government until after the trial of the alleged assassination plotters, which had begun on June 5th in Kuwait.

BY LATE June, the White House had lost any semblance of control over the media debate, and it was widely known among Washington journalists that the F.B.I.'s final report would conclude that Iraq and Saddam Hussein himself were directly involved in the assassination attempt. "FOR THE PRESIDENT, IT'S DECISION TIME ON ATTACKING IRAQ," a *Wall Street Journal* headline announced on June 23rd. The story stated, correctly, "Within the next few days, a confidential report will hit President Clinton's desk, pushing him toward one of the toughest decisions of his young presidency: whether to order new military action against Iraq." In discussing the President's options, the article noted, "There are few actions against Iraq that would arouse strong domestic opposition, and little reason to think Iraqi air defenses yet pose much of a deterrent." The *Times* weighed in on the eve of the bombing, with Thomas L. Friedman, its expert on the Middle East, writing that a plot against George Bush and the arrest of Muslim militants accused of plotting terrorist attacks in New York City "are beginning to pose a serious foreign policy question for President Clinton: How long can his Administration get by with responding to these incidents by saying, 'We're looking into it.' "

WHEN CLINTON finally acted, on the afternoon of Saturday, June 26th, he was not leading the nation, as was widely assumed and reported, but merely following the path of least bureaucratic and political resistance. He had authorized the bombing the day before, barely twenty-four hours after the well-publicized F.B.I. report arrived in the White House. The President, who had served as Attorney General in Arkansas, and his aides, many of whom were experienced attorneys and experts at evaluating evidence, took the F.B.I.'s assessment at face value, although it was that agency's planning and intelligence which had given the Presidency its worst public moments in the aftermath of the ill-conceived F.B.I. tear-gas assault on the redoubt of the cult leader David Koresh, in Waco, Texas, which led to the deaths of eighty-six cult members, including twenty-four children.

In a televised speech to the nation on Saturday night, Clinton explained that he had been presented with "compelling evidence that there was in fact a plot to assassinate former President Bush. And that this plot . . . was directed and pursued by the Iraqi intelligence service." The President strongly suggested that Saddam Hussein was personally responsible: "Saddam has repeatedly violated the will and conscience of the international community, but this attempt at revenge by a tyrant against the leader of the world coalition that defeated him in war is particularly loathsome and cowardly. . . . The Iraqi attack against President Bush was an attack against our country and against all Americans."

Clinton's staff, seeking, not unnaturally, to maximize any possible political advantage from the bombing, treated the Tomahawk attack on Baghdad as a personal triumph for the President. Aides told reporters that the President, having made his address and received early damage-assessment reports, watched a movie with his wife, Hillary, and then got a solid eight hours of sleep. The President was said to be "relaxed and calm." On his way to church services the next morning, he expressed regret over the loss of life but added, "I feel quite good about what transpired. I think the American people should feel good." The White House also found cause for celebration in the fact that the Saturday-night bombing had come as a surprise to the media. "ADMINIS-TRATION FINDS JUST KEEPING A SECRET CAN BE A TRIUMPH," one headline proclaimed. There was, the article said, "a near-defiant sense of pride" among the President's staff, and a "buoyant mood." W. Anthony Lake, the President's national-security adviser, and Sandy Berger, Lake's deputy, were warmly praised for their handling of the operation.

At a background briefing in the White House late on Saturday night, Lake explained that the President had concluded that the failed assassination attempt in Kuwait, though it had taken place in mid-April—two months earlier—amounted to "a real and present danger," and that "if we failed to act and act now, the Iraqis might continue attempting such acts of state-sponsored terrorism." The American missile launchings were initiated, he said, under the self-defense provisions of Article 51 of the United Nations Charter, which give member nations the right to respond in self-defense to armed attacks. (Lake did not say, however, that most legal authorities note that the threat must be instant and overwhelming and leave no moment for deliberation.) Lake also said that the President had ordered the attack without intending "to pass individual judgment" on the Kuwaitis and Iraqis then being tried for the alleged assassination attempt. He did not try to explain how a Presidential determination that Iraq was guilty of ordering the assassination of George Bush, and the subsequent bombing of Baghdad, could fail to escape the notice of judicial officials in Kuwait.

As the briefing continued, the national-security adviser, accompanied by Philip Heymann, deputy attorney general, and Admiral William Studeman, deputy director of the C.I.A., outlined the "compelling evidence" that sealed the government's case against Iraq. And much of the material provided that night to the press was dramatically made public the next day at the United Nations by Madeleine Albright, the American Ambassador to the U.N.

Lake and his colleagues spoke first about what they said was forensic evidence tying crucial components of the bomb recovered in Kuwait, including its remote-control detonator, to bombs previously recovered by the American intelligence community and known to have been put together by the Iraqi intelligence service. Here Lake was essentially restating what the *Times* had reported in its May 11th story—that there was unmistakable evidence showing that the components recovered in Kuwait had been built by the same person or persons who built the Iraqi bombs. In other words, the soldering techniques and modifications in the Kuwaiti car bomb—a characteristic way of twisting wires, for example—amounted to a "signature" linking it to a specific designer or technician who had also worked on Iraqi bombs.

Lake and his colleagues then discussed what they said was the second key category of evidence—the suspects themselves. Early in the inquiry, the F.B.I. had sent a team of agents to Kuwait to interview the fourteen Iraqi and Kuwaiti citizens who had been formally charged in the case, and there had been at least one more follow-up visit. The F.B.I. eventually concluded that none of the defendants, including the Iraqi who confessed to having been ordered by Iraqi intelligence agents to kill Bush, had been beaten or in any other way coerced to give evidence. No physical evidence of torture was found.

In an interview in early August at the White House, a senior official told me, "When you listen to them all"—the various defendants—"it clearly establishes that the car went from Basra to Kuwait when Bush was there. I think it is beyond a reasonable doubt that the intent was to kill Bush." Basra, the largest city in southern Iraq, is a hundred miles from Kuwait City.

However, other knowledgeable officials in the Clinton Administration, as well as current and former members of the intelligence community, had provided me with information that challenged the official's confident assessment. My examination of what is known about the recovered car bombs and of the F.B.I.'s interviews with the alleged assassins in Kuwait raises fundamental questions concerning the validity of the government's evidence, how prudently and objectively it was handled, and how the President and the men around him—experienced as many of them were in making legal judgments—reached their standard of "reasonable doubt."

THE MOST glaring weakness of the Administration's case is its assertion that the remote-control firing device found in the Kuwaiti car bomb has the same "signature" as previously recovered Iraqi bombs. In making its case, the Administration released a series of color photographs comparing, among other things, the circuit boards of the radio-controlled firing device seized in Kuwait and the circuit boards of what was said to be a similar Iraqi device. The photographs were made public by Ambassador Albright. "Even an untrained eye can see that these are identical except for the serial numbers," she said, holding up one of the photographs of the two devices. "Next, we have a similar comparison of the insides of the two firing devices. . . . As you can see, the selection of the components and the construction techniques in the two devices—including soldering, the use of connectors, and the wiring techniques, et cetera—are also identical."

The Iraqi government heatedly denied the Administration's allegations, but most reporters—and the public—found the photographs, with their obvious similarity, convincing. One notable exception was the editorial page of the *Times*, which raised questions about the "compelling evidence" cited by Clinton and also about Albright's assurances that it was the "firm judgment" of the C.I.A. that Iraqi intelligence was involved in the alleged assassination attempt. The information Ms. Albright presented "was not conclusive enough for a reasonable citizen to join her in being 'highly confident' that force— rather than criminal trials and diplomatic measures—was the wisest course," the *Times* noted, and it went on, "Let's hear the evidence, rather than assertions of officials who say they have it."

The *Times* editorial led to no reassessment by the public or by the newspaper's Washington bureau, whose staff had so avidly reported the firm judgment of some members of the Administration that Iraq had sought to kill former President Bush. There is no published evidence known to me of any effort by the *Times* to verify independently the Administration's specific claims against Iraq. No reporter, for example, has written of getting in touch with any of the many independent experts in electrical engineering and bomb forensics to ask what they thought of the photographs released by the White House.

When I asked seven such experts about those photographs last summer, they all told me essentially the same thing: the remote-control devices shown in the White House photographs were mass-produced items, commonly used for walkie-talkies and model airplanes and cars, and had not been modified in any significant way. The experts, who included former police and government contract employees and also professors of electrical engineering, agreed, too, that the two devices had no "signatures." They said there was no conceivable way that the Clinton Administration, given the materials made public at the United Nations, could assert that the remote-control devices had been put together by the same Iraqi technician.

The fact that the two devices were similar is simply not that significant, I was told by Donald L. Hansen, a twenty-eight-year veteran of the bomb squad of the San Francisco Police Department. Hansen, who has served as the director of the International Association of Bomb Technicians and Investigators, is now an instructor at the State Department's school for foreign police officers, in Baton Rouge, Louisiana, and is widely considered to be one of the top forensics experts in the field. "They're very generic devices," he told me, after analyzing the photographs of the electronic circuit boards. "To establish a signature, you've got to find unique characteristics. It's not the equipment it-self—there are millions of them. You can buy instruction manuals"—for the construction of the devices—"in New York and Chicago, and the instructions could be exactly the same. But that doesn't mean that the two were built by the same man. There are no signs of modification. If these circuit boards are what they're hanging their signature issue on, they're really stretching the en-velope. All they can say is there's a strong similarity."

Another expert, Paul A. Eden, who is an electrical engineer at the Univer-sity of Miami, estimated that individual components of the devices were man-ufactured no later than 1983. He concluded that both mechanisms were mass-produced, most likely in Taiwan, or Japan, or South Korea, and were of a type sold all over the world. "I saw nothing that would make them any dif-ferent from anything bought off the shelf from any electronics store," he said. "The design is used by everybody in the world. All it does is receive a signal and decode a tone. I can't see anything that would make it say, 'Yes, this was done by the same person.' " Eden, who has nearly forty years of experience in electronics and now runs a satellite field station for the university, suggested that the Clinton Administration had been "grasping at straws" in its presenta-tion at the United Nations. He also said that he objected to the White House's notion, repeatedly expressed by Anthony Lake and others in their briefings and public statements, that the car bomb found in Kuwait was ex-tremely sophisticated. "Anybody with half an ounce of electronics training could have done what they did and make something go boom."

A third expert, Robert H. Shaw, who has worked as a computer engineer and a systems analyst in the "black," or classified, community in Washington, expressed disappointment that the Administration had relied on "signature" to justify the bombing of Iraq. "There's no signature," Shaw told me. "Just a close coincidence that worked real bad for Saddam. You couldn't make a case," he said, referring to the legal implications of a signature finding. "I wouldn't take this to the World Court. They might throw it out and make you pay court costs. I would have just said, 'We got one, and the other guy's looked like it. They're similar enough, so goodbye Saddam.' "

In interviews with me in late July, however, two law-enforcement officials who played important roles in assembling the government's case against Iraq stated emphatically that the standards used for assessing the evidence were the same as those used in criminal investigations and prosecutions. "We had a hands-on examination by our bomb expert," said Neil Gallagher, chief of the F.B.I.'s counterterrorism section, and he went on to say that the bureau had held the expert to the standards that would be used "if he were to testify in court." Similarly, Mark Richard, a deputy assistant attorney general, told me that "the F.B.I. presented its case to Justice as if it were in front of a very skep-tical A.U.S.A."—assistant United States attorney.

The problem with such statements is that the investigative findings of the F.B.I. and the Justice Department ended up being exposed only to a political process, with senior White House planners who were worried about domestic reaction, press spin, and international reaction, and were also subjected to pressure from selective leaks to the news media. The far more rigorous proce-dures associated with the federal-court process—trial by jury and questioning by opposing counsel—were not used. If they had been, the outcome might have been different. In one recent bomb-signature case in which federal bomb experts testified, the results were disastrous for the government's wit-nesses.

This happened on July 19th, when the signature issue was the focus of a hearing held, with the jury excluded, in the United States District Court trial, in Boston, of Thomas A. Shay, who was accused of conspiring in 1991 to plant a car bomb in an attempt to kill his father; a Boston policeman had been killed while attempting to defuse the device. Shay's co-defendant, Alfred W. Tren-kler, had been charged with unlawful possession of an explosive connected with a bombing in 1986. A federal bomb expert from the Treasury Depart-ment's Bureau of Alcohol, Tobacco and Firearms testified that he had been able to match the signature of the bomb that Shay was alleged to have planted to the 1986 bomb that Trenkler was alleged to have built. A second A.T.F. wit-ness claimed that a computer analysis of more than fourteen thousand bomb incidents had further established the link between the 1986 and 1991 de-vices. The defense witness for Shay was Donald Hansen, the former San Francisco bomb-squad officer, and he repeatedly made the point that the A.T.F. forensic experts had emphasized only the similarities between the two devices, ignoring the many differences. Hansen told the court that there were only generic similarities between the two bombs—that his examination found "no particular method of twisting wires or no real distinct technique em-ployed."

In a bench ruling the next morning, Judge Rya W. Zobel said that the gov-ernment could not put forward any testimony in an attempt to link the 1986 and 1991 bombings. The two devices were similar, "without question, but I am not persuaded that they are identical," Judge Zobel concluded. "That is, I do not think, and find, that it is not so unusual and distinctive as to be like a signature."

When I spoke with Nancy Gertner, Shay's attorney, this summer, she re-called that before the judge's ruling there had repeatedly been newspaper stories citing federal officials as saying "that these were signature bombs."

She added, "It's very, very frightening that foreign policy is being made on this."

IN THE spring and summer, I had a series of background conversations with an old friend who is now serving as an intelligence analyst inside the government. The analyst, who has seen much of the classified reporting on the alleged assassination attempt, conceded in our most recent talk that a stringent cross-examination of the F.B.I.'s experts would have uncovered a number of distinctions between the two bombs, the most significant being that the two-hundred-pound car bomb carefully hidden in Kuwait was dramatically different in appearance from all previously known Iraqi car bombs. Most Iraqi car bombs that have been recovered by the American intelligence community are extremely primitive devices—essentially, the analyst said, "sticks of dynamite wrapped together, with a timer and a detonator." The bomb found in Kuwait, he added, used a state-of-the-art plastic explosive that, while safer than dynamite to handle, was far more powerful.

The analyst told me that, nonetheless, he was convinced that the bomb in Kuwait was of the same manufacture as the Iraqi bombs, because they all had the same components. "Why get into signature?" he asked rhetorically. "It's a technical issue, and the people handling it in the White House didn't have the expertise. It's like you and me talking about nuclear physics. We know just enough to endanger ourselves. The White House oversold the signature issue"—in its press briefings. "They didn't understand what they were selling."

I relayed the analyst's complaints to a senior White House official in a telephone conversation in late July, and, during an extended interview a few weeks later, the official acknowledged that he had raised the signature issue anew with the F.B.I. He was subsequently informed, he went on, that "you could not judge signature on the basis of the pictures" that the White House released after the bombing.

"I'm not a forensics expert," the official went on, with a shrug. "At some point, you have to rely on the F.B.I.'s technical expertise. You have to push them hard and probe them about anything that seems to be unclear or uncertain. By the end of their investigation, there was no question in their minds that this car bomb came from Iraqi intelligence." He believed the F.B.I., the official said, and he added that there were aspects of the car bomb and its trigger mechanism that were not made public. When I asked why not, he said, "We're not going to show what parts of their bomb make it similar to bombs coming from Iraqi intelligence. Why let Iraq know where the thumbprint is?"

The F.B.I.'s Neil Gallagher had told me, similarly, "What was made public was not the best case. There are other photographs." He refused to describe the additional evidence, and said that it would be impossible to permit outsiders to view the unpublished photographs or other data.

In subsequent interviews, officials sought to explain Gallagher's cryptic comment by revealing that some of the Iraqi bombs and detonators used in the F.B.I.'s analysis of the Kuwaiti car bomb had not been obtained in Iraq, as had been widely assumed and reported; they had been retrieved by the American intelligence community during a clandestine entry into an Iraqi Embassy in the Middle East during the Gulf War. In addition, the F.B.I. had access to components from other suspected Iraqi bombs that had been recovered in recent years from the Philippines, after an explosion at an American cultural center in Manila, and from Indonesia, where an unexploded bomb was found in a flower pot at the residence of the American Ambassador in Jakarta. The detonators in those devices and in the Kuwaiti car bomb were "put together the same way," one American official said.

Of course, the fact that the Iraqi bombs were clandestinely recovered does not alter the possibility that the various components were similar because they were similarly mass-produced, or rule out the possibility that the car bomb and detonator found in Kuwait were planted there by Kuwaitis. (Iraqi-manufactured bombs and detonators surely were abandoned in large quantities, along with tanks and weapons, after the American liberation of Kuwait in early 1991.) Nor does it have any bearing on the "smoking gun" issue of the bombing of Baghdad.

In fact, an American diplomat who was involved in the discussions of Saddam's role told me in an interview this summer that the linking of high officials in the Iraqi intelligence service to the events in Kuwait was simply "a political judgment," based, in large measure, on the pattern of behavior of the men arrested in the incident. "I don't think Saddam ordered it," the diplomat said, "but it was an Iraqi-intelligence-service attempt to assassinate an American President." Mark Richard also acknowledged, in an interview, that I was in possession of "ninety-nine per cent of the facts." Richard, a distinguished career Justice Department official, who has been assigned to many of the government's most difficult international criminal cases, explained that the final determination of Iraqi complicity in the alleged assassination attempt was a result of "process"—the careful analysis of possible scenarios—and did not stem from any specific information.

Moreover, other current and former high-ranking officials with access to intelligence, whose information has been extremely reliable in the past, specifically told me that the National Security Agency, which is responsible for electronic intelligence, had produced no significant high-level intercepts from Iraq in years. American intelligence experts have concluded that the Reagan Administration's policy of providing satellite and communications intelligence to Iraq in the mid-nineteen-eighties had an unwelcome side effect: the Iraqi intelligence service learned how to hide its important communications from the N.S.A.'s many sensors.

Finally, my old friend inside the intelligence community has repeatedly expressed his amazement at the notion, suggested by the White House, that the F.B.I.'s final report to the President on June 24th contained new and definitive information. "There's a big mystery as to why we finally went Saturday," he said a few days after the bombing. "It's not as if we suddenly had more intelligence driving it. There was nothing else. What we knew Saturday night we knew two months ago."

IN ESSENCE, the Clinton Administration, by its suggestion of still secret intelligence, is saying "Trust me" in response to the lingering questions and doubts about the forensic evidence linking the Kuwaiti car bomb to Iraq. The Administration is also saying "Trust me" in its assurances that the account provided by the Kuwaiti government was accurate. Fourteen men are now on trial in Kuwait, at least ten of them facing possible death sentences, for their role in the alleged assassination attempt. In late July, the trial proceedings were suspended until the end of October.

There is now, in fact, critical information that is known to the F.B.I. and the White House and has not been made public: that there was a crucial four-day gap between the arrest of the alleged assassins and their first mention of a car bomb and a plot to kill an American President.

The key members of the alleged Iraqi assassination team were seized while they were walking in the desert on the evening of Thursday, April 15th, one day before George Bush concluded his visit to Kuwait. Some of them had spent as many as three days roaming through Kuwait City, and had spent their nights in different apartments. The suspects had smuggled whiskey across the border, and there had evidently been much drinking during that time. No alcohol is sold legally in Kuwait, a Muslim state, and there is a booming black market between Iraq and Kuwait; there is also a steady flow of people and vehicles—all illicit—between Basra and Kuwait City. At least six of the seventeen men initially arrested had simply been ferried across the border, for a fee, and were en route to visit friends and relatives in Kuwait. Such trips were routine before the Gulf War. Four days after the men were jailed, according to their defense attorneys, one of them, Wali al-Ghazali, told the Kuwaiti authorities that he had been sent into Kuwait by Iraqi intelligence to kill Bush. A second prisoner, Ra'ad al-Assadi, testified that he knew that their car, a Toyota

Land Cruiser, had been carrying a bomb. It was only at that point that the Kuwaiti authorities searched the Land Cruiser, which was in police custody, and found the bomb.

Clinton Administration officials acknowledged that the long delay between the arrests and the recovery of the bomb lent weight to the possibility of Kuwaiti duplicity—something that had been encountered more than once in the past. "It'd be foolish to suggest that these were issues that didn't occur to us," Mark Richard said. "We played it against all scenarios: Did Kuwait do it? Make it up? Did Saddam do it? Was it some rogue operation? This was not a rush to judgment." In the end, it was decided that Kuwait had more to lose by falsifying an assassination plot—and being exposed in doing so—than Saddam Hussein did by sending in a team of amateurs who might succeed or might not.

Saddam has repeatedly made moves against his best interests—his decision to invade Kuwait was one of them—and nothing can be ruled out. Yet the White House, in working through its scenarios, apparently did not include the fact that by mid-April Saddam was engaged in desperate negotiations with the United Nations concerning the U.N. ban on importing Iraqi oil. The Saddam regime was bankrupt, and could not feed its people without hard currency and credits obtained from foreign oil sales.

Another factor, also ignored in the White House deliberations, was President-elect Clinton's assertion, made shortly before he took office, that he—unlike George Bush—was not "obsessed" with Saddam Hussein. In an interview on January 13th with the *Times,* Clinton said that he could imagine maintaining a normal diplomatic relationship with the Iraqi leader. "All he has to do is change his behavior," Clinton said. He subsequently disavowed his statements, but the C.I.A.'s Counter Terrorism Center, in its debunking of the alleged assassination attempt, reported, nonetheless, that the Kuwaiti government had expressed "frustration" because of the failure of the Clinton Administration and its European allies to take a tougher line against Iraq. The Kuwait leadership also feared, the C.I.A. concluded, as cited in the *Boston Globe,* that Clinton might abandon Kuwait in favor of better relations with Saddam Hussein. Kuwait, the report said, "has a clear incentive to play up the continuing Iraqi threat."

Also open to question is the F.B.I.'s conclusion that none of the defendants were beaten or coerced after their arrest. The F.B.I. rested its case on the fact that its agents did not personally see any signs of mistreatment. No medical examinations of the men were conducted, officials conceded, nor were lie-detector tests used. The F.B.I.'s assessment may be correct, but it has to be weighed against other evidence.

On July 3rd, the fourth day of the trial in Kuwait City, Ali Khdair Baddai, who, at seventy-three, was the oldest defendant, testified that he had been severely beaten after his arrest, according to the German news agency D.P.A. In a dispatch filed with D.P.A., a freelance journalist named Miriam Amie, the only American reporter who has attended the trial regularly thus far, quoted Baddai as stating that when he was arrested the police "hit me in the head and on my side," and going on to say, "I was bleeding over my eyes. They beat me and somebody kicked me in the side." On being asked by the presiding judge why he had not complained earlier about the beatings, Baddai responded, according to Amie, "Every day I wanted to complain to you. But then I said no." Asked by the judge why he had confessed to smuggling, he said, "Since the police beat me, I told them to write anything and I would sign it." Despite his signed guilty plea, he publicly proclaimed his innocence from the witness stand. In a subsequent interview, Amie told me that Wali al-Ghazali, who has repeatedly told the court and the F.B.I. that he was ordered by Iraqi intelligence to assassinate Bush, showed up on the first day of the trial, in June, with "a fresh scar on his forehead and a blackened nail on his thumb," and she added, "No one could talk to him." Ra'ad al-Assadi, one of the two major defendants in the case (the other being al-Ghazali), told the media after Baddai's testimony that he, too, had been beaten.

The defendants' claims were repeated by Najeeb I. al-Waqayan, the attorney for two of them. "Definitely they were beaten," al-Waqayan told me during an interview in Kuwait in July. "This is the way of the Kuwaiti police." Al-Waqayan, who studied law at San Diego State University and is one of three privately retained defense attorneys in the case (the other lawyers were retained by the state), also said that he had been unable to confer privately with his clients until the first day of the trial.

Questions about the use of torture in Kuwaiti prisons and fair trials in Kuwaiti courts have been raised often since the end of the Gulf War by two of the world's leading human-rights groups—Amnesty International, whose headquarters are in London, and Human Rights Watch, of New York. In November of 1991, Amnesty International issued a statement saying that it had "received reports that many of the people being detained by the Kuwaiti authorities had been ill-treated and tortured," and adding, "Amnesty International delegates had personally interviewed and medically examined prisoners who bore signs of torture." The group has issued a number of special reports about the trial of the alleged assassins, noting that if they are convicted "twelve of the defendants may be sentenced to death," and that "the organization is also concerned that the necessary measures to protect the defendants from torture or ill-treatment during interrogation may not have been taken, and that 'confessions' extracted under duress may later be used to convict them." Similarly, Human Rights Watch, in its World Report roundup for 1992, concluded that "arbitrary arrest and detention are still prevalent" in Kuwait, and "torture remains common."

Finally, in interviews, former American diplomatic officials and intelligence officers who had served in the Middle East expressed amusement and amazement at the F.B.I.'s categorical assurances that none of the defendants were tortured. "Either the investigators were idiots or they were lying," said James E. Akins, a former United States Ambassador to Saudi Arabia, who is now a consultant in the Middle East and elsewhere. "It boggles the imagination. There's no way the Kuwaitis would not have tortured them. That's the way the Kuwaitis are, as anybody who knows the Kuwaitis or the Middle East can tell you."

PRECISELY WHAT did happen in Kuwait during George Bush's ceremonial visit remains in dispute, with senior officials in the White House, the Justice Department, and the F.B.I. acknowledging that the assassination plot had something of an Abbott-and-Costello quality. "You could say these guys were really not that well trained," one counterintelligence official told me, with a laugh. "Not exactly like Chuck Norris coming across the border. More like 'The Gang That Couldn't Shoot Straight.' "

The story begins with Wali al-Ghazali, a male nurse from the Iraqi holy city of An Najaf, who testified in the trial that he had been approached in early April—roughly a week before the scheduled Bush visit—by an Iraqi intelligence agent while at work and pressured to take part in the assassination mission against Bush. The next day, he was taken to a garage and given a briefing on the car bomb and its remote-control components, and was also provided with a suicide belt and a photograph of a building at Kuwait University where Bush was expected to make an appearance. In case all else failed, al-Ghazali said, he was to put on the belt, get as close to Bush as possible, and detonate it—blowing up both the former President and himself.

His chief collaborator, al-Ghazali testified, was Ra'ad al-Assadi, who was the owner of a coffee shop in Basra and an acknowledged longtime smuggler of alcohol, arms, and other goods into Kuwait City. Al-Assadi was also one of many people in the Basra area who operated what amounted to an informal bus service across the surprisingly open border between Iraq and Kuwait. A round trip—usually for a weekend—cost each passenger about three hundred dollars. Being a smuggler, al-Assadi, not unexpectedly, knew many Iraqi police and intelligence officials, and he testified that he was paid about four hundred and twenty dollars in advance and given merchandise—five cases of

whiskey and six kilos of what he was told was hashish—in return for participation in the al-Ghazali mission. (Kuwaiti police later determined that the
"hashish" was of dubious quality and had no resale value.) Al-Assadi testified
that he had met with Mohammed Jawad, an Iraqi intelligence agent, in his
coffee shop, and had been provided with ten sticks of explosives and a bag of
weapons and detonators. The bombs, Jawad told him, were to be used against
targets of opportunity in Kuwait City—automobile showrooms, market-
places, and the like—in an attempt to disrupt the Bush visit and embarrass
the Kuwaiti government. Al-Assadi further testified that Jawad had offered
him an American-made four-wheel-drive Jeep for the mission, but that he rejected it as substandard. Instead, he drove his own car, an eight-passenger
van, into Kuwait. The van turned out to have been stolen from Kuwait City
during the Iraqi occupation, and had Kuwaiti tags.

Al-Assadi and al-Ghazali were the only defendants to plead guilty in connection with the alleged plot; the two men were named in a six-hundred-page
indictment, along with twelve others, that accused them of car theft and of
working with the Iraqi regime, entering Kuwait illegally, transporting weapons
and alcohol, and plotting to kill former President Bush. The other defendants
in the case have consistently denied any knowledge of or connection with the
alleged plot.

There remains a serious conflict between the testimony of the Kuwaiti—
and American—government's two star witnesses. Al-Ghazali claimed, in his
confession, that al-Assadi knew everything there was to know at the outset;
before taking off for Kuwait, the two men had met in a parking lot in Basra to
talk over the plan to murder George Bush. But al-Assadi, in his testimony, insisted that no such information had been shared with him. He knew nothing
of any plan to assassinate Bush. "I am a smuggler," he said.

The account gets much murkier at this point: there is no evidence that any
of the alleged assassins took any overt steps to deploy any bombs. Sometime
before dawn on April 13th, al-Ghazali and al-Assadi, accompanied by two
Iraqi accomplices and six paying passengers, took off for Kuwait in al-Assadi's
van and in al-Ghazali's Toyota Land Cruiser, which was then allegedly carrying the Iraqi-made car bomb. They crossed the border near Salmi, where
Kuwait, Iraq, and Saudi Arabia meet. The tristate-border area is the site of a
flourishing black market. Al-Assadi claimed that once he was across the border he buried some of the bombs in the sand and threw away the bag of detonators and weapons.

At some point, al-Assadi and al-Ghazali decided to leave their paying passengers, who included al-Assadi's uncle and a cousin by marriage, and parked
the van in the desert. The uncle refused to stay behind and came along with

al-Assadi and al-Ghazali and the accomplices as they drove off in the Land Cruiser to look for sleeping accommodations. They made their way to the sheep farm of Bader al-Shimmari, a known smuggler, with a police record, and hid the whiskey, some weapons, and their vehicle in a sheep pen. Other members of the al-Shimmari family showed up, along with the passengers left in the van, and two days and nights of smoking, drinking, womanizing, driving around, and telephoning ensued. (Everyone in Kuwait has a car telephone, it appears.) According to al-Ghazali's account, he spent one of those nights in the apartment of a friend in Kuwait City, twenty miles to the east, watched a television report about Bush's planned visit to Kuwait University, and asked to be taken there. No one offered to take him, and Bush never went to the main campus of the university anyway. That act—asking for help in casing the joint—was as close as anyone came to an overt act aimed at assassinating Bush. There was also no attempt to plant a bomb in an auto showroom, a marketplace, or anywhere else in Kuwait during the Bush visit. Al-Ghazali testified that he did not even know the location of Kuwait University—allegedly the main target of opportunity in the Bush assassination plot. Al-Assadi, he told the court, "was supposed to show me how to get there."

The al-Shimmari farm—long suspected of being a depot for smugglers and their goods—was under round-the-clock surveillance by the Kuwaiti police. The police waited less than a day before seizing the two vehicles parked there—one of which, they would later learn, contained the car bomb. At some point, according to the testimony of al-Ghazali, he got rid of his suicide belt in the desert. Al-Ghazali, al-Assadi, and at least two other Iraqis, unable to get to their cars and whiskey in the surrounded sheep pen, stole a white Mercedes, apparently thinking that it would eventually get them back to Basra. They filled the car's tank with the wrong fuel, and it broke down, forcing the men to begin walking toward the Iraqi border. They were spotted by Kuwaiti citizens—walking in the desert is highly unusual—and the police were notified. The police did nothing. More citizens made calls, and the police finally began tracking the Iraqis, who were seized without a struggle on April 15th. Eleven others, including five members of the al-Shimmari family, had been arrested a day earlier. The Kuwaiti government—to the acute embarrassment of police officials—later handed out cash awards to those citizens who reported the intruders.

Complicating the basic confusion of the various stories, in which defendant contradicted defendant, was a claim by the Kuwaiti government that it had known of the assassination attempt for more than a month. That claim was made on the second day of the trial, by Police Colonel Abdul Samad al-Shatti. He told the court that the police had learned in mid-March, from "a secret source inside Iraq," that some Iraqi "terrorists" were plotting to infiltrate Kuwait and plant bombs. No evidence to support that claim has been made public, and no warnings were given by Kuwait at the time either to George Bush or to the Clinton Administration. Furthermore, a former high-ranking Kuwaiti military officer assured me during an interview in Kuwait that there had been no significant penetration of Iraqi intelligence before the Bush visit. Colonel al-Shatti's testimony, the Kuwaiti officer explained, had been concocted out of embarrassment, after public criticism of the inept performance of the police in arresting the alleged plotters.

The C.I.A., in the Counter Terrorism Center report obtained by the *Boston Globe,* noted that its investigators had been informed by Kuwaiti security officials of the infiltration of a smuggling ring—clearly tied to the al-Shimmari family—that had been transporting weapons and other goods from Iraq to Kuwait early in the year. C.I.A. analysts, in attempting to explain the origins of the alleged assassination plot, theorized that the Kuwaiti government "may have then decided to claim this [smuggling] operation was directed against Bush."

ONE AMERICAN counterintelligence official, on being asked about the abject performance of the alleged assassination team, conceded, "I don't think their heart was in what they were doing. So it might not have been the crack front-line Republican Guard"—Iraq's best-trained military force—"but their mission was to try and get a car bomb as close as possible to kill Bush. They weren't highly motivated, and they weren't real careful, and I think they performed their duty like the White House staff performs its."

Other officials, including members of the White House staff and the Justice Department's Mark Richard, have repeatedly pointed out that Wali al-Ghazali, in private interviews with the F.B.I., continued to maintain that he was recruited by Iraqi intelligence and sent into Kuwait to kill George Bush. They have further asserted that C.I.A. analysts have been able to verify al-Ghazali's descriptions of Iraqi intelligence facilities in Basra, and have apparently corroborated his identification of some known Iraqi intelligence personnel. But these officials have also acknowledged that, since al-Ghazali is facing a death sentence, he could obviously testify—as one intelligence official put it—"to being the Pope." And they concede that the Kuwaiti officials have been unable to recover the suicide belt that al-Ghazali claimed he discarded in the desert. The bombs, detonators, and weapons allegedly thrown away by al-Assadi have not been found, either.

"Yes, some elements are extremely amateurish," Mark Richard says. "But others are not." He argues that Iraqi intelligence had "nothing to lose" by using the al-Ghazali group. "It's a win-win situation. What are these guys going to give up"—if they're captured. "The operations of the Iraqi intelligence service in Basra? They don't know it." Anyway, Richard says, the operation was obviously set up to kill al-Ghazali and the other members of the assassination team who carried out their orders and detonated the bomb.

In interviews over the summer, many past and present American intelligence officials expressed little surprise that the Clinton Administration had predicated the bombing of Baghdad on such conflicting and dubious evidence. One C.I.A. analyst explained, "Of course nobody wants to say, 'There's nothing to it, Mr. President,' especially when other guys are pushing it. The President asks the intelligence analysts for the bottom line: Is this for real or not? You can't really lose by saying yes." That hard-line attitude—"hanging tough" in a crisis—has marked many of America's intelligence failures since the beginning of the Cold War.

Thus, on a Saturday in June, the President and his advisers could not resist proving their toughness in the international arena. If they had truly had full confidence in what they were telling the press and the public about Saddam Hussein's involvement in a plot to kill George Bush, they would almost certainly have ordered a far fiercer response than they did. As it was, confronted with evidence too weak to be conclusive but, in their view, perhaps not weak enough to be dismissed, they chose to fire missiles at night at an intelligence center in the middle of a large and populous city.

"What you're trying to do is go after the people responsible," Secretary of Defense Les Aspin told reporters at a Pentagon briefing after the bombing. There was no chance that Saddam Hussein would be inside the intelligence complex at the time of the attack, he said, "but it's like any intelligence building." He went on, "You've got people who are there twenty-four hours watching communications. You presumably might have some people in there who are involved in maintenance, and cleanup crews of one kind or another. I wouldn't want to guess a number."

Anthony Lake, in his briefing that night, explained, in language eerily reminiscent of the Vietnam War, that the bombing of Baghdad "is an action, I hope, that will potentially save many Muslim as well as non-Muslim lives, both in the Middle East and elsewhere." It is no longer quite permissible to speak of destroying villages in order to save them, but maintenance men and cleanup crews had better beware.

FIVE

SANCTIONS AND INSPECTIONS

"At this juncture, my view is we don't want to lift these sanctions as long as Saddam Hussein is in power."
   —*President George Bush, May 20, 1991, going beyond the language of U.N. resolutions linking sanctions to Iraq's disarmament*

Leslie Stahl: "We have heard that a half a million children have died. I mean, that's more children than died in Hiroshima. And is the price worth it?"

Ambassador Madeleine Albright (U.S. Representative to the United Nations): "I think this is a very hard choice, but the price—we think the price is worth it . . . It is a moral question, but the moral question is even a larger one. Don't we owe to the American people and to the American military and to the other countries in the region that this man not be a threat?"

Stahl: "Even with the starvation and the lack . . ."

Albright: "I think, Leslie—it is hard for me to say this because I am a humane person, but my first responsibility is to make sure that United States forces do not have to go and refight the Gulf War."
   —*CBS 60 Minutes*, "Punishing Saddam," May 12, 1996

A BACKGROUNDER ON
INSPECTIONS AND SANCTIONS

Sarah Graham-Brown & Chris Toensing

The U.N. Special Commission (UNSCOM) established to verify Iraq's compliance with the weapons provisions of United Nations Security Council Resolution (UNSC) 687 [see appendix for full text] first entered Iraq in 1991, and inspections by UNSCOM and the International Atomic Energy Agency (IAEA) continued until December 1998. Although UNSCOM succeeded in locating and destroying the majority of Iraq's weapons of mass destruction sites, its inspections were frequently contested by the Iraqis, who resisted attempts to see certain sites and withheld documents.

From 1994, a clear rift opened among the Permanent Five members of the Security Council over the progress of the inspections. France and Russia wanted to reward specific instances of Iraqi cooperation with gradual amelioration of the country's economic isolation, including a "road map" toward the lifting of sanctions, while the U.S. and Britain refused to consider such measures. The dispute was fueled by critical ambiguities in the conditions for lifting the embargo in UNSC 687, contained in paragraphs 21 and 22 of the resolution. Paragraph 22 appears to allow the embargo on international imports from Iraq—primarily oil—to be removed once Iraq had complied with all clauses relating to weapons of mass destruction. France and Russia favored a focus on this provision. Paragraph 21 was much broader: international exports to Iraq could only resume when it was judged to have complied with "all relevant UN resolutions." The U.S. and Britain took this reference to include UNSC 688, which dealt with Iraq's treatment of the Kurds and the Shia, and strove to keep sanctions in place as a first priority.

The rift between the U.S. and Britain on one side, and France and Russia on the other, widened, and weapons inspections went on in an increasingly acrimonious atmosphere. In 1997, evidence emerged that the U.S., and possibly the Israelis, had been receiving intelligence gathered in the course of

Sarah Graham-Brown is author of *Sanctioning Saddam: The Politics of Intervention in Iraq.* Chris Toensing is editor of *Middle East Report,* a publication of the Middle East Research and Information Project (www.merip.org) based in Washington, D.C. This article is excerpted from their December 2002 publication, *Why Another War? A Backgrounder on the Iraq Crisis.*

UNSCOM inspections. Rolf Ekeus, head of UNSCOM from 1991–1997, confirmed to Swedish radio in late July 2002 that U.S. inspectors sought information outside the organization's mandate, such as details on the movements of Saddam Hussein. Revelations of intelligence gathering lent credibility to Iraq's protests that inspections were infringing upon its sovereignty, and eroded international support for UNSCOM's aggressive tactics.

DESPITE POLITICAL obstacles, weapons inspections in the 1990s achieved a great deal. UNSCOM inspections revealed a clandestine nuclear program which, according to an IAEA assessment, might have produced a usable weapon by December 1992, had Iraq continued it. The final reports of UNSCOM and IAEA filed after they left Iraq stated that Iraq's nuclear stocks were gone and suggested most of its long-range delivery systems had been destroyed. Numerous outside studies, most recently one from the London-based International Institute for Strategic Studies, have concluded that while Iraq retains the scientific expertise to manufacture a nuclear bomb, it lacks the necessary fissile material.

Questions remain about Iraq's chemical and biological weapons capacity. In the 1990s, inspectors destroyed 38,500 prohibited chemical warheads and millions of liters of chemical agents. Iraq claims to have eliminated over 30,000 more weapons and tons of additional chemical agents of its own volition, but UNSCOM was unable to verify this claim before leaving the country. In August 1995, Iraq admitted having produced large volumes of weapons-grade biological materials for use in the 1990–1991 Gulf War. UNSCOM never located this stockpile, which Iraq also claimed to have destroyed. Some former inspectors, along with the U.S. and British governments, refer to these chemical and biological materials as "missing" or "unaccounted for," and believe that Iraq has successfully hidden them from scrutiny.

On the basis of IAEA reports in 1997, Russia recommended that Iraq's nuclear file be closed, again to establish a "road map" toward Iraqi compliance and the lifting of sanctions, but Washington and London refused. Successive inspections crises ensued in 1998. In February, Iraq declined to allow so-called "presidential" sites to be inspected, again on grounds of sovereignty. U.N. Secretary General Kofi Annan defused this crisis by brokering an agreement under which international diplomats would accompany inspectors to these sites. UNSCOM continued to complain of Iraqi non-cooperation, and pulled out of Iraq in November, and again in December, the second time without consulting the Security Council. From December 16 to 19, the U.S. and Britain heavily bombed alleged weapons sites throughout southern and central Iraq. This bombardment—known as Operation Desert Fox—took place without Security Council authorization, following a pattern established by the U.S. and Britain over the 1990s.*

THE U.S. and Britain have regularly resorted to military action to enforce Security Council resolutions on Iraq without express U.N. approval. In 1991, the U.S. and Britain designated a part of the Kurdish-controlled region lying above the thirty-sixth parallel as a no-fly zone for Iraqi aircraft. A second no-fly zone was established in the south up to the thirty-second parallel in August 1992, and extended to the thirty-third parallel, close to Baghdad, in 1996. The two no-fly zones were initially policed by the U.S., Britain and France. In 1996, France withdrew from the northern zone, and in 1998 from the southern zone—in protest over Desert Fox. The U.S. and Britain have continued daily patrols of the no-fly zones, with periodic attacks on Iraqi anti-aircraft emplacements and major bombing episodes triggered by alleged large-scale movements of Iraqi armor in border areas or intensified anti-aircraft fire.

Following Desert Fox, the U.S. and Britain changed the rules of engagement in the no-fly zones, allowing pilots to strike at any part of the Iraqi air defense system, not just those that directly targeted their aircraft, by firing upon them or by "locking on" radar detectors to the planes. The scale of action in the no-fly zones since that time has increased dramatically. According to British Ministry of Defense figures quoted by the *Times* (London) in June 2000, the average monthly release of bombs rose from 0.025 tons to five tons. After a lull in early 2002, air strikes increased in intensity and frequency in the fall. By October, U.S. and British planes had bombed Iraqi targets 46 times, and "clashes" in the no-fly zones picked up again after the November 8 U.N. resolution.

A year after Desert Fox, U.N. Security Council Resolution 1284 created a new arms monitoring body called UNMOVIC, headed by Hans Blix. In 2001, negotiations sporadically took place between the U.N. and Iraq over the readmission of inspectors, but Iraq did not allow UNMOVIC into the country until November 27, 2002. Pending UNMOVIC's report due in January 2003, assertions by Iraqi defectors and the U.S. and British governments that Iraq persists in developing weapons of mass destruction are impossible to confirm or rebut.

BETWEEN DESERT Fox and the crisis of 2002, international diplomacy on Iraq focused almost exclusively on the various proposals for reinvigorated,

---

* Editors' note: See p. 205 for President Bill Clinton's December 16, 1998 speech on the beginning of Desert Fox.

Under-five mortality rate — Cross-country comparison

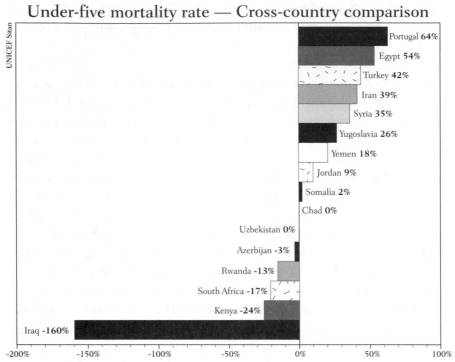

Percentage change in mortality rates among children under five, from 1990–2000. Egypt's rate was 54 percent lower in 2000 than in 1990. Iraq's rate was 160 percent higher.

"smarter" sanctions. Since their introduction in 1990, comprehensive economic sanctions on Iraq have raised substantial concerns about the impact of coercive measures against governments when the populations in question have no democratic rights. Both Security Council members and Iraq frequently allowed humanitarian issues to become bargaining chips in struggles over the fulfillment of UNSC 687. No clear definition was agreed upon for "humanitarian goods"—those commodities to be excluded from the embargo. The U.S. in particular sought to limit the definition as far as possible, initially only to include food and medicine. As time went on, the Security Council allowed the purchase of more types of goods, but contracts were frequently challenged because the sought-after items might prove to be "dual-use."

Accurate assessments of the humanitarian situation have been difficult to obtain. Most international NGOs withdrew from government-controlled areas of Iraq by mid-1992, when the Iraqi government imposed stringent restrictions on their operations. Only in 1998 was UNICEF able to carry out a nationwide survey of health and nutrition, which found, for instance, that mortality rates among children under five in central and southern Iraq had doubled from the previous decade. Most independent observers would endorse the March 1999 conclusion of the UN Security Council's Panel on Humanitarian Issues: "Even if not all suffering in Iraq can be imputed to external factors, especially sanctions, the Iraqi people would not be undergoing such deprivations in the absence of the prolonged measures imposed by the Security Council and the effects of war."

The Security Council's punitive approach was compounded by the fact that Gulf War bombing had inflicted extensive infrastructural damage, compromising the provision of clean water, sanitation and electrical power to the Iraqi population. The resulting public health emergency, rather than hunger, has been and continues to be the primary cause of increased mortality, especially among children under five. UNICEF estimated in 2002 that 70 percent of child deaths result from diarrhea and acute respiratory infections.

For its part the Iraqi government, while providing a basic food ration, placed military and security concerns over civilian needs, especially when making decisions on reconstruction. Poor planning and public education, and shortages of trained personnel caused by the catastrophic decline of real wages in the public sector, exacerbated the humanitarian crisis.

In late 1991, under pressure from U.N. agencies reporting acute humanitarian needs in Iraq, the Security Council passed Resolutions 706 and 712, designed to allow Iraq to use the proceeds of limited oil sales to purchase "humanitarian goods" outside Iraq. After prolonged negotiations, Iraq rejected the caps on its oil sales as too stringent, and called for the lifting of sanctions. By 1993, the Iraqi economy under sanctions stood at one-fifth its size in 1979, and then took a further nose dive in 1994. Meager rations lasted only about one-third to half a month. With shrinking incomes, Iraqis could not afford the spiraling prices of goods on the open market. Soon France and Russia began to float the concept of certifying Iraqi compliance with inspections, and lifting sanctions, at the Security Council. The summer 1995 defection of Hussein Kamil, Saddam Hussein's son-in-law, who came bearing detailed information on Iraq's previously unacknowledged biological weapons program, only temporarily stalled French and Russian efforts to seek an exit from sanctions.

To stymie the progress of the French-Russian proposals, the U.S. encouraged Britain to formulate U.N. Security Council Resolution 986—reviving the "oil for food" idea of UNSC 706 and 712—in early 1995. The new resolution made some concessions to Iraq's earlier objections, though Iraq initially held out for more. The Oil-for-Food program established by UNSC 986 finally came into operation at the end of 1996. Under this program, Iraq could sell specified amounts of oil during every six-month period. The proceeds, deposited in a U.N.-controlled escrow account outside Iraq, would be used to fill orders for humanitarian goods from the Iraqi government. Until 2002, a committee of all Security Council members (known as the 661 Committee) scrutinized the operation of the Oil-for-Food program. The U.S., and to a lesser extent Britain, made a common practice of placing "holds" on large numbers of orders—over $5.3 billion worth in early 2002—ostensibly because the requested items might have military uses. This practice, combined with Iraq's bureaucratic delays, interruptions of oil sales and a prolonged dispute with the Security Council over oil pricing, reduced the volume of goods getting into Iraq. Holds have disproportionately affected Iraq's ability to rebuild its water, sanitation and electricity infrastructure.

Modifications to the Oil-for-Food program later raised the ceiling on oil sales and widened the scope of goods that could be purchased, to include some items needed to refurbish Iraq's oil industry and other infrastructure. In 2001, a further resolution removed the limit on the amount of oil Iraq could sell. In 2002, Resolution 1409 shrank the role of the 661 Committee in vetting orders and placed the job of determining which items were "dual-use" in the purview of UNMOVIC, the new weapons inspection agency, and the IAEA. These "smart sanctions"—designed to deflect criticism of sanctions in general and Oil-for-Food in particular—arguably came too little, too late.

THE U.S. and Britain often present the Oil-for-Food program as a vast humanitarian relief effort, but it was intended as a stopgap measure to sustain economic sanctions while allowing more humanitarian goods into the country. It was never conceived as a full-scale program of economic rehabilitation. Oil-for-Food has brought commodities into Iraq, rather than restoring Iraqis' purchasing power or the country's infrastructure to anything approaching prewar levels.

In central and southern Iraq, where the government administers Oil-for-Food, the increase in size and caloric value of monthly rations (to 2,472 calories per person per day) has brought some improvement in nutrition, especially among young children. Market prices have also been reduced from hyperinflationary levels of the mid-1990s. Oil-for-Food, however, has also perpetuated dependence on rations, shoring up central control over food supplies. Meanwhile, systems of public transportation, water, sanitation and electricity remain in a precarious state, the last two imperiled further by several years of drought. UNICEF figures show continuing high levels of mortality and morbidity from acute respiratory infections and diarrheal diseases.

In the Kurdish-controlled areas of the north, where the U.N. implements the program, a different set of factors has influenced the humanitarian situation. Because the Iraqi regime embargoed the north, between 1992 and 1997 the Kurdish enclaves received significant amounts of humanitarian assistance via Turkey. Between 30 and 60 international NGOs worked in the north, though sporadic internal conflict and displacement between 1994 and 1997 kept the humanitarian situation unstable. Since 1997, food imports under the Oil-for-Food program have helped the Kurdish urban population, but effectively undermined the revival of the local economy, especially in the key area of agriculture. A recent survey by Save the Children–U.K. found that up to 60 percent of the northern population has nothing to fall back on should Oil-for-Food stop.

Oil-for-Food heightens the vulnerability of the whole Iraqi economy to disruption by political decisions and external factors, such as a military confrontation and the reduction or termination of oil sales. If the government of Iraq closed the de facto border with the Kurdish-controlled area, delivery of food and medical supplies purchased for the north by the Iraqi government would be interrupted. The entire ration distribution system in government areas could be disrupted if there was prolonged fighting or bombing or if large numbers of refugees fled elsewhere within the country or across the borders. In the north, because parts of the Kurdish region depend on the national grid for electricity, Baghdad is able to cut off the power supply, as it has done in the past.

AFTER THE passage of UNSC 986, Baghdad used trade to woo international support for modifying or lifting sanctions. From 1997 to 2001, companies from the Security Council member states most sympathetic to Iraq's position—France, Russia and China—garnered $5.48 billion of the $18.29 billion in contracts approved by the U.N. Firms based in Egypt and the United Arab Emirates, whose governments also moved closer to Baghdad at the end of the decade, were awarded 30 percent of Iraq's import contracts under the Oil-for-Food program in 2000.

By 2001, sanctions were crumbling around the edges. Most of Iraq's neighbors, including its adversary Syria, and countries friendly to the West, like Turkey, Jordan and some Gulf states, were involved in sanctions-busting trade with Baghdad. In comparison with the large-scale evasion of comprehensive U.N. sanctions on Rhodesia and Serbia, there has been little illegal transfer of goods in and out of Iraq, but the resulting revenues were sufficient to keep the Iraqi regime well-financed despite sanctions. Illicit trade—especially oil smuggling—also forged economic ties of mutual advantage which made Iraq's neighbors resistant to U.S. and British schemes for "enhanced containment."

Since 1997, illicit revenues amounting to roughly $2 billion per year have accrued to the regime in Baghdad. A recent report from the Coalition for International Justice, which advocates the trial of Iraqi leaders for crimes against humanity, states that 90 percent of these monies come from oil smuggling. The most remunerative smuggling route runs through Syria's pipeline to oilfields in northern Iraq, reopened on November 6, 2000 after being closed since 1982, when Hafiz al-Asad's regime backed Tehran in the Iran-Iraq war. As many as 150,000 barrels of discounted Iraqi crude per day pass through the pipeline, enabling Syria to export more of its own oil. Another third of Iraq's contraband oil finds its way to Iranian ports, where it is reportedly mixed with outgoing Iranian oil products to conserve Tehran's domestic reserves.

The Kurdish enclave bordering Turkey has benefited handsomely from imposing exit taxes on diesel and crude smuggled into Turkey, though Turkey took steps to curtail this trade beginning in March 2002, perhaps because smuggling revenue was finding its way to Iraq-based militia units of the Workers' Party of Kurdistan (PKK), which fought a separatist war against Turkey in the 1990s. Officially, Iraq exports 110,000 barrels per day of oil to Jordan, with the tacit approval of the Security Council, in return for preferential prices on Jordanian consumer goods. Jordan is particularly dependent on the Iraqi market.

THREE TIMES since the winter of 1999, the regime has halted oil exports, calculating that the resulting price spike would pressure the U.N. into concessions in reviews of the sanctions. Each time the maneuver failed, because Saudi Arabia and Kuwait filled the gap in supply to prevent the price from rising too high. Iraq has twice stopped its exports during major Israeli offensives in the Palestinian territories, rather transparently to pose as the champion of the Palestinian cause in the Arab world, also to negligible effect on the oil markets.

Smuggling and illegal surcharges on sales approved through the Oil-for-Food program have proven more effective for Iraq than direct use of the "oil weapon." Although the benefits of smuggling and sanctions-busting trade to Baghdad are well-known in Washington and London, the U.S. has been unable (or unwilling) to cut off these sources of revenue, revealing the complexity of its relations with front-line states. Turkey and Jordan have been allowed to break sanctions with impunity, arguing that their fragile economies could not afford to lose Iraqi trade, though Iran has received harsh criticism. Syria has rebuffed U.S. demands that it close down its pipeline to Iraq, and even offers of U.N. compensation for lost oil revenue, without apparent penalty. The

U.S. has backed down from calls to debate Syrian smuggling in the Security Council, because France has insisted on debating Turkish smuggling as well.

The general non-cooperation of Arab governments with U.S.-British attempts to plug holes in the embargo also signaled their displeasure with Washington's increasingly unequivocal support of Israel in its campaign to defeat the Palestinian uprising by force of arms. Arab governments, anxious about their own stability in the event of war, maintained vocal public opposition to military intervention in Iraq as the intention of the Bush administration to topple Saddam Hussein by force became clear.

Dick Cheney returned from a Middle East tour in mid-March 2002 without inducing any government to change its public line against forcible "regime change" in Iraq. The surprise rapprochement between Iraq and Kuwait at the March 2002 Arab summit—which also produced an unprecedented agreement among all Arab countries (including Iraq) to recognize the state of Israel inside its pre-1967 borders—marked the formal end of the Arab consensus behind the sanctions and containment policies of the previous decade. Iraq recognized Kuwaiti sovereignty for the first time, and the two countries issued a pledge (so far unfulfilled) to resolve Kuwaiti missing persons and stolen property claims from the Gulf War. The summit concluded with a unified call to lift the U.N. sanctions. Arab diplomats worked to persuade the Iraqi regime to accept the return of weapons inspectors.

Meanwhile, the logic of inspections and sanctions—that they would be lifted once Iraq complied with UNSC 687—has been undermined by U.S. and British statements that "regime change" is their preferred policy toward Iraq.

THE INSPECTIONS AND THE U.N.: THE BLACKEST OF COMEDIES

Richard Butler

Earlier this summer, I decided not to seek a new term as head of UNSCOM, the United Nations Special Commission formed to disarm one of the world's most dangerous, and clever, tyrants. The two years spent battling Saddam Hussein were grueling, but in the end it was not simply his recalcitrance that made it impossible for me to do my job properly. That, after all, was the predictable cost of doing business with a dictator addicted to weapons of mass destruction. Nor was it a matter of America's unwillingness to hold Saddam's feet to the fire, as one of my former UNSCOM inspectors, Scott Ritter, has famously charged.

The larger issue was that the situation inside the U.N. had grown untenable. Russia, a key member of the Security Council, had become Saddam's most aggressive advocate—and has continued in that role right up through this summer, when Moscow falsely accused me of endangering millions of Iraqis by leaving behind dangerous chemicals and explosives in our laboratory in Baghdad. Deeply alarming, too, was the behavior of the secretary-general of the U.N., Kofi Annan, who repeatedly tried to deal with the problems raised by an outlaw regime by papering them over with diplomacy. Annan and his immediate staff sought to hand Saddam the greatest possible prize: the destruction of UNSCOM, a thorn in the side of both men. Saddam wanted the thorn removed so that he could retain his weapons. Annan wanted it removed because UNSCOM was too independent to work within the mainstream of the U.N.

A year ago, Saddam put an end to all attempts to get rid of his weapons of mass destruction. Soon afterward, he went a step further, shutting down the monitoring inspections intended to deter him from building more of those weapons. It's impossible to know exactly what Saddam has been up to since then; for a year now the Security Council has struggled to reach an agreement on a successor organization to UNSCOM. But a few things are certain:

Ambassador Richard Butler led the United Nations Special Commission (UNSCOM) from July 1, 1997 until June 30, 1999. From 1992 to 1997, he was the Australian ambassador and permanent representative to the United Nations. He is the author of *The Greatest Threat: Iraq, Weapons of Mass Destruction and the Growing Crisis of Global Security.* This article was originally published with the title "Why Saddam Is Winning the War," in the September 1999 issue of *Talk* magazine.

Iraq possessed the knowledge required to make a sophisticated atomic bomb. Iraq has long-range missiles and has been hard at work on extending their range. Iraq possesses the means to make both chemical and biological weapons.

This is the disturbing reality, and not simply because it portends instability in the Middle East, serious though that is. In far graver terms, if Saddam gets away with facing down the U.N., he could destroy the world community's ability to deal with rogue states—and its capacity to stop the production of these deadly armaments.

THE FIRST evidence that Iraq possessed chemical weapons was discovered by an Australian scientist, Dr. Peter Dunn, who had been sent by the U.N. to the Iran-Iraq battle zone in 1986. Dunn found an unexploded Iraqi shell. He carefully drained the yellow-brown contents into the nearest receptacle, a Coca-Cola bottle. It was mustard gas.

In 1991, as coalition troops massed on the borders of Kuwait in the run-up to the Gulf War, Iraq sent chemical weapons encased in artillery shells and missile warheads to the front lines. All Saddam had to do was say, "Fire." James Baker, then secretary of state, took Iraqi Deputy Prime Minister Tariq Aziz aside in Geneva and warned him that if the Iraqis used chemical weapons on the coalition troops, there would be a resounding silence in the desert. Aziz understood this to mean that the U.S. would retaliate with nuclear weapons. Chemical weapons were not used during the Gulf War.

Desperate to stop the coalition bombing, Saddam quickly agreed to a cease-fire, which took the form of U.N. Security Council resolutions requiring that Iraq be stripped of its weapons of mass destruction. Iraq had 15 days to declare all of its illegal weapons and a year to destroy them. Saddam, it turned out, had an awesome array of illegal munitions. The U.N. created UNSCOM to catalog his weapons and supervise their destruction and gave UNSCOM unprecedented, far-reaching power to do so.

The policy of deceit reached its height four years later with the alleged defection of Hussein Kamel, Saddam Hussein's son-in-law and the lieutenant general in charge of his weapons programs. In August 1995 Kamel left Iraq for Jordan. Shortly thereafter, Iraqi officials pointed Rolf Ekeus, then executive chairman of UNSCOM to Kamel's chicken farm some 15 miles southeast of Baghdad, where they said UNSCOM would find what it had been looking for. They were making a preemptive strike—presumably motivated by fear of what Kamel would reveal. At the farm Ekeus discovered aluminum shipping trunks containing plans and instructions for Saddam's arsenal.

Six months later Kamel returned home amid promises that all would be forgiven. A few days after he arrived in Baghdad he was executed by members of his own family. Kamel's defection had, after all, forced Saddam to reveal the dark heart of his germ warfare program. Or had it?

Another take on the Kamel defection soon emerged inside UNSCOM. The whole thing was a setup. Shortly before Kamel left Iraq, UNSCOM had taken aerial photographs of the chicken farm, as part of its routine surveillance. The photos showed a line of a dozen very large shipping containers outside the barns. By the time Ekeus and his team arrived, these containers had disappeared. When asked to explain this discrepancy, Iraq denied the existence of these larger containers—UNSCOM's photos notwithstanding. But as UNSCOM sifted through the millions of pages of documents found on Kamel's farm, gaps were revealed; the papers had been carefully culled before Saddam's secrets were "exposed." The whole operation had been a daring ruse designed by Saddam and Kamel—who was in on every part of the play, except for the last scene: a spray of bullets to ensure his silence.

Afterwards, Ekeus strengthened the UNSCOM team investigating Iraq's attempts to conceal its weapons cache and sought intelligence assistance from U.N. member states. Iraq countered by stepping up its interference with UNSCOM inspections. Tensions mounted. In June 1996, Ekeus flew to Baghdad for an emergency meeting with Aziz. The two struck an agreement: Iraq would be permitted to severely restrict UNSCOM's access to any site the Iraqi government deemed "sensitive" for national security reasons. This was in direct violation of a Security Council resolution stating the UNSCOM should be able to go anyplace, anytime, with whatever people it needed to do its job. The cave-in had begun.

SUCH WAS the state of affairs in early 1997 when Secretary-General Annan asked me to replace Ekeus. I had been the Australian ambassador to the United Nations for five years: during the period, Annan had been head of peacekeeping at the U.N., so we were already well acquainted. I had spent most of my career formulating treaties to stop the proliferation and testing of nuclear weapons. Now I was being given the chance to do some hands-on disarmament—actually destroying weapons, not negotiating agreements.

I started on July 1. Three weeks later I flew to Baghdad to see Aziz. I was as direct as possible with him. I promised to maintain the objectivity of science and technology in all of our inspections, and I assured him we would declare Iraq disarmed just as soon as we were able to do so on the basis of hard evidence. All I required was a full and final accounting of Iraq's imported weapons and its indigenous weapons productions.

Meanwhile, I was being encouraged to move ahead quickly by senior members of the Security Council, the Russian included. Edward "Skip"

Gnehm Jr., a U.S. diplomat offered me sage advice the morning I started work. Don't give the Iraqis a finite list of UNSCOM's demands. I understood his point. If I were to tell Iraq that UNSCOM believed that it was missing ten missiles, trucks carrying 10 missiles would likely turn up at our front door in Baghdad the next day. We would never know if the real number had been fifteen.

Before long, I had my first taste of Iraqi defiance. During a routine inspection in September 1997 at what Iraq had described as a food-testing lab, the chief of our biological team glimpsed two Iraqi officials trying to run out the back door. She seized a briefcase from one, inside were biological test equipment and documents linking the headquarters of the Iraqi Special Security Organization to what appeared to be a biological weapons program. After the Iraqi generals in charge dodged my requests to explain these materials, I ordered a no-notice inspection of the Special Security headquarters building to be led by Scott Ritter, the head of our concealment staff. A small convoy of vehicles set off toward this destination. But about a half mile from the building, the convoy was stopped by armed Iraqi guards.

I telephoned Aziz, telling him to allow my people to move forward. He refused, claiming that the building in question was a "presidential site" and was therefore off-limits. It was an entirely new concept to deem these sites sanctuaries. Nothing—not even "sensitive sites"—was off-limits according to the deal Saddam had signed to put an end to the Gulf War. Besides, I pointed out, the U2 aerial picture I had on my desk in preparation for our conversation showed that the presidential palace was a mile down the road from where our motorcade had been stopped. We were still denied access. Fearing for its safety, I withdrew our team.

I reported this and similar incidents to the Security Council in October and asked the U.N. to rescind the agreement Ekeus had struck on the sensitive sites. But by then UNSCOM's political support was beginning to collapse. Russia, China, and France refused to vote for a resolution supporting the conclusions of my report of UNSCOM's work—a resolution that threatened new sanctions against Iraq unless Iraq cooperated with inspectors. The Iraqis seized on these divisions within the Security Council, formally affirming the existence of the so-called presidential sites and declaring them off-limits to UNSCOM investigators. Eight areas covering a total of 30 square miles—including 1,100 buildings, many of them warehouses and garages ideal for storage, were designated as presidential sites.

Later in the month Iraq announced that all American UNSCOM personnel would be expelled from Iraq within a week. I was determined not to allow Iraq to dictate the terms of our inspections, especially if that meant singling out a nationality. Nothing, I thought, could be more of an affront to the spirit of the United Nations. When the deadline arrived, the Americans were told to be out of Iraq by midnight. At that point, I withdrew all UNSCOM staff from Baghdad. A concerned Kofi Annan asked why we couldn't do our inspections without Americans. I was incredulous. I tried to explain that giving Iraq veto power over the composition of inspection teams would undermine the quality of the teams and set an unacceptable precedent. I prevailed, but I received my first glimpse of Annan's tendency to sacrifice substance to his notion of diplomacy.

Through all of this, Russia was playing the self-appointed role of Iraq's chief advocate in the Security Council. Russia's ambassador to the U.N., Sergei Lavrov, stopped by my office regularly to take me through the latest concessions Iraq wanted from the Security Council and UNSCOM. It was an unsettling spectacle: the ambassador of a permanent member of the Security Council working through Saddam's shopping list.

Lavrov suggested that I visit Moscow. I accepted, thinking that if I could reason with Russia's foreign minister, Yevgeny Primakov, I might be able to get things back on track. We met in a conference room in Russia's foreign ministry, where Primakov proceeded to point out that these presidential sites were deeply important to the dignity of the regime and thus should be kept out of UNSCOM's reach. I could not believe it. This was, of course, in violation of the very resolution that Russia had helped the Security Council adopt. Then he told me that it was in Russia's interest for sanctions against Iraq to be lifted so that Iraq would again be free to sell oil for profit. Why should Russia care about Iraq's economic fortunes? Primakov volunteered the answer. Iraq owed Moscow some $7 billion (for Russian tanks, helicopters, and other weapons dating back to the Iran-Iraq war), and Russia wanted the money. UNSCOM must be more "flexible," he continued. "If you can't find something, weapons, during your inspections, you should accept that it's because they don't exist." According to his logic, the onus of proof should be shifted from Iraq to UNSCOM. What more could Saddam have asked for?

When I returned to New York, Primakov's disturbing pronouncements took on a new meaning. I received intelligence reports from an outstanding source that the Russian foreign minister had been getting personal payments from Iraq. For God's sake, I thought, here we are trying to disarm a rogue regime, and a person who should be a prime mover in this grand enterprise was on the take. Since then, Russian officials have publicly denied these reports. But in intelligence circles, the report's credibility has deepened over time.

KOFI ANNAN had been secretary-general for about a year when the drama over the presidential sites started to unfold. Eager to intervene, he began communicating with Aziz. In one of their conversations, the Iraqi minister told Annan that Iraq didn't have adequate maps of its presidential sites and asked if the U.N. would send a team of surveyors to draw some up. Annan called me into his office to discuss this request. I advised him to refuse. One of our chief inspectors, I explained, had been in the Iraqi government's mapping office and had held in his hands maps of precisely the sites at issue. But Annan was determined to agree to Aziz's request, saying it was a matter of diplomacy, not truth.

Frustrated, I decided to put it to Annan in writing. In my memo I noted that Iraq had detailed maps of every inch of its territory and that he should reject Aziz's request on the grounds that he was being lied to. I said it was important to signal now that the secretary-general of the United Nations was not prepared to be played for a fool; otherwise the prospects for meaningful negotiations in Baghdad would be minimal. Annan rejected my advice, sending U.N. surveyors to Iraq to draw up the maps. Within a few weeks the maps were completed and delivered to U.N. headquarters under arrangements that suggested that they were as sacred as the Dead Sea Scrolls. The stage was now set for Annan to go to Baghdad.

On the eve of his departure in February 1998, I sent Annan and the members of the Security Council an urgent memo. This time I urged them to agree to accept special conditions for the inspection of presidential sites if—and only if—Iraq lifted the extensive restrictions it had placed on its "sensitive sites" in the earlier agreement with Ekeus. Without this trade-off, I wrote, they risked departing further from Security Council decisions.

Annan called me, clearly puzzled. "Does this mean that there's a special category of sites in addition to presidential sites?" he asked. I was shocked. For almost six months we'd been talking about this very issue—ever since I had first brought it to the Security Council. Now, hours before his departure for Iraq, it was clear that he did not understand that critical distinction. When I explained the history to him, Annan seemed concerned—in a somewhat disconsolate aside, he said that my proposal would make his negotiations very difficult.

The following week, Annan returned triumphant from Baghdad. The crisis, he said, had been averted. Iraq would allow UNSCOM inspectors into the presidential sites. But according to the fine print, our inspectors would now be accompanied by diplomatic observers. Everything else, including the sensitive site restrictions, would remain in place. "This is a man I can do business with," Annan said of Saddam at a hastily convened press conference—thus signaling a major step toward the appeasement of Iraq.

It fell to me to test the pact. I made plans to resume UNSCOM's work, ar-

ranging for several inspections at sites that I believed housed weapons or related materials. Then I went to see Annan at his Manhattan apartment to give
him an update. He was uncomfortable with my decision to press ahead so
soon after the agreement had been forged. "Couldn't you wait awhile?" he
asked. I replied that this was the only way to test the integrity of Iraq's commitment. Annan wanted to delay my going ahead.

Around this time, the Clinton administration got wind of the fact that I
was being pressured to proceed with caution. At *Time* magazine's 75th-
anniversary bash at Radio City Music Hall in March 1998, America's ambassador to the U.N. at the time, Bill Richardson, ushered my wife and me
backstage to meet President and Mrs. Clinton. The president thanked me for
my work and tried to bolster my spirits. "It's hard as hell and you're doing well
and courageously," he told me. "Don't feel threatened or dissuaded by the sort
of things that are being thrown at you. Do your job down the line. Go get those
armaments. That's what we want and we'll back you." These were encouraging words, but I knew then that the support of the United States (and, to be
fair, the United Kingdom) would not be enough in the face of weakening resolve inside the U.N.

We resumed inspections. To my surprise, Iraq decided to let us into places
to which we had never before been admitted, including the Defense Ministry,
a "sensitive site." But as our inspectors stepped inside it became clear why the
Iraqis had been willing to cooperate. The building had been emptied of its
contents.

Over the next few months the same charade would be repeated again and
again. We visited an Iraqi intelligence building only to find that the rooms had
been stripped. When we asked what the building was used for, we were told
that this was where Iraqis came for marriage licenses. Back at the U.N. I argued that showing us nothing—literally empty rooms—hardly constituted
compliance with the agreement. But Annan and his advisers insisted that the
agreement was alive and that Iraq was cooperating. Every time I saw the secretary-general he would ask how the inspections were going. The truthful answer was always "mixed at best," but no matter how I replied he would try to
put a positive spin on my words—repeatedly confusing superficial cooperation with substantive compliance.

This approach became irrelevant about six weeks after the agreement was
signed. The first inspections of presidential sites were conducted under the
terms of the agreement. Professional inspectors were overseen by diplomats.
The sites had been thoroughly sanitized, turned into Potemkin villages. It was
ludicrous. On the last day, Iraq informed the UNSCOM team leader that it
did not see a need for further inspections of the sites. With this action Iraq effectively killed the agreement.

Nonetheless, a sort of Iraq fatigue was beginning to take hold inside the Security Council. One prominent member, a man who had previously been foreign minister of his country, had even said to me, "I know [Saddam] is a homicidal dictator. I know he's cheated on you and retained weapons capability, but do we have to deal with this problem every six months?"

UNDER THESE circumstances I decided UNSCOM needed to take action. I offered the Security Council a technical briefing and a list of priority objectives—a road map to get us to the end of the disarmament task. The Council agreed that I could take the road map to Aziz in Baghdad.

We arrived in mid-June 1998 at Habbaniyah Air Base, a military airport 85 miles northwest of Baghdad. This was the only place Iraq would permit us to land. When I stepped out of our aircraft I was approached by senior members of UNSCOM's chemical weapons staff. They asked me for a word in private—and handed me a laboratory report containing the analysis of a number of destroyed missile warheads that had recently been excavated. The report showed that some of the warheads contained traces of a chemical call EMPA, a degradation product of VX nerve gas—and of no other known chemical substance. A single drop of VX can kill with an hour.

I was floored. "What the hell do we do now?" I asked the chemists.

Several years earlier Iraq had denied it had ever even produced VX. UNSCOM found evidence to the contrary; confronted with that evidence, the Iraqis tried to minimize its significance, saying they had only made 200 liters of the stuff. UNSCOM, however, proved they had actually made at least 3,900 liters, mainly at the Muthanna State Establishment, the country's vast production ground for chemical weapons. Now we had proof that they had actually loaded this deadly chemical into weapons. The extreme danger posed by such weapons was not lost on neighbors in the region.

I told Aziz that I found the VX findings disturbing but had no desire to turn them into a public fuss. I suggested that our technical advisers adjourn to a private room. In the meetings that followed, the Iraqi officials dug in, insisting that they had never loaded VX into weapons. I authorized our side to offer to run further tests on other warhead remnants in other laboratories. The Iraqis agreed. I told them, however, that whatever the results in other laboratories might be, the ones in hand would still need to be explained.

Aziz and I also talked about the road map I'd drawn up. He agreed to a version of it, pledged that his people would give us what we needed, and told me to return in six weeks to check on their progress.

IN AUGUST 1998 I flew to Baghdad for the eighth and final time. Once again my team and I took our places at the big square donut of a table in the upstairs conference room of the Iraqi foreign ministry. Aziz sat opposite me with his team, puffing on his Cohiba cigar. The Iraqis had five video cameras running, notwithstanding the brown-out illumination of the room, to record for Iraq's propaganda purposes the exchanges to come.

Aziz asked me to begin by giving my analysis of what had happened during the last six weeks. I said we'd been given virtually none of the information or materials we had sought. Aziz remained silent. I felt like an actor in a play, only it seemed that Aziz had the whole script and I had not a sheet. When I finished Aziz said in effect that he didn't agree with much of my speech, but that I'd get "the definitive answer of the leadership of the government of Iraq" at our meeting that night.

As my team and I went to our office to prepare for the evening's meeting, I had a pretty good hunch what that answer would be. I bet my deputy, Charles Duelfer, $5 that we would be thrown out of Iraq when we reconvened that evening.

We returned to the foreign ministry at about 8 p.m. Aziz got right to the point: Iraq was fed up. The country was disarmed he said, and the information we were seeking was of no importance. It was, he claimed, a deception aimed at delaying the day the Security Council would deem Iraq disarmed and lift the sanctions. "Your only duty now," Aziz told me, "is to leave this room and go back to New York and tell the Council that Iraq is disarmed." Iraq, he continued, would provide us no further information and no weapons materials, and would permit no further disarmament inspections. If I failed to deliver the message, it would be on my conscience.

"I will not do what you ask because I cannot," I replied. "This is not a question of disarmament by declaration. We need evidence—facts—and you have refused to provide them." At an impasse, we curtly shook hands and parted.

My staff and I went the brief distance down the road to the al-Rashid Hotel. It was clear to me then that Saddam was finally making a run for it. Aziz had no doubt shut us down because our road map was right. What's more, the VX discovery could potentially unravel a whole series of false statements. Worst of all, Saddam was certain that the Security Council wouldn't chase him. Upstairs, Duelfer signed and dated a $5 bill and silently handed it to me.

Later that month UNSCOM was further shaken by the resignation of Scott Ritter, who blamed the United States for the growing success of Iraq's defiance. Ritter has painted himself as a hero stabbed in the back by the boffins in Washington, a cross between John Rambo and Oliver North.

Ritter misrepresented facts and reconstructed events, conversations, and decisions in which he had played no part. But the deepest harm he did was to make allegations about UNSCOM's use of intelligence assistance provided to it by the U.S. UNSCOM used such assistance—which did not come solely from the U.S.—for disarmament purposes only; we needed to try to break the Iraqi wall of deceit. I rejected proposals that might have served or been construed to have served any other purpose. Any provider—whether it be the U.S., Russia, or France, for example—that sought to piggyback on UNSCOM for its own national intelligence purposes would damage the integrity of our efforts. I would lament that. What is truly unjust is that those who want to destroy UNSCOM have seized on Ritter's misleading and misguided posturing. Rather than stand up to Saddam, they have chosen to shoot the messenger, UNSCOM.

FROM THEN on, events moved quickly. True to Aziz's word, Iraq shut down all further disarmament work by UNSCOM; in October, we were barred from monitoring production facilities. This produced yet another crisis. The United States and the United Kingdom again increased their armed forces in the Gulf. On November 10, 1998, the acting United States ambassador to the United Nations, Peter Burleigh, conveyed to me a message from Washington. It would be prudent for me to evacuate my staff from Iraq.

Four days later the Security Council convened an emergency meeting. Members received from Aziz a last-minute pledge of cooperation with UNSCOM inspections, clearly aimed at avoiding bombing. But as the United States and the United Kingdom pointed out, the wording was ambiguous.

Lavrov, the Russian ambassador, suggested that the Security Council ask for another letter. A recess was called. As I walked out of the chamber I saw two diplomats, one Russian, one Iraqi, urgently crafting a second letter in Arabic. It was presented to the Council, but was again found deficient. Lavrov promised a third, which was also hastily drafted in the adjoining hallway.

The atmosphere had become comical. The revisions all focused on changing words, but no one had any notion whether the words corresponded to reality. It was a farce, but it worked. After the third letter, the pressure became too great. America and Britain agreed to refrain from bombing.

The next morning President Clinton announced that the bombers had been called back. He warned that this would be Saddam's last chance. The Security Council accepted Iraq's new promise of full cooperation but asked me, through UNSCOM's work, to test and report on Saddam's performance.

On November 16 I ordered all UNSCOM staff back to Baghdad to resume work. I then put together teams to conduct the full range of inspections, from the relatively ordinary to the very tough. I expected that the testing period would take a month. Two weeks into that period I accepted an invitation to go to Moscow for consultations. There my team and I had a long talk with the new foreign minister, Igor Ivanov, who wanted to know how our testing of Iraq's promise was going. I told him that it was too early to tell—that there had been elements of cooperation as well as blockage. He made clear his preference for a positive report on Iraq's behavior and stressed the great difficulty Russia would have if the West bombed Iraq. He asked me some specific questions about how long the testing period would last and how long it would take us to give Iraq a clean bill of health on disarmament if Saddam cooperated fully. I gave Ivanov factual answers to those questions. He and his representatives in New York subsequently flagrantly misrepresented those answers.

Upon my return to New York, reports from my chief inspectors in each weapons field began rolling in. Iraq was refusing to give them access to information; in some cases Iraq was seeking to impose new restrictions on our work. UNSCOM inspectors had, for instance, been blocked at the entrance to the Baath Party building where we had compelling evidence that weapons were hidden. Iraq, once again, had made a promise that it had no intention of keeping.

As I formulated my report I was contacted by the ambassadors from several Security Council nations. I told them all I would have to report was that Iraq had failed to keep its promise. The Russian ambassador was not among those who contacted me.

I did, however, speak with the United States ambassador, and on one occasion the president's national security adviser, Sandy Berger, came to New York and asked to see me. It was a private meeting, but rumors were soon circulating inside the U.N. that Berger had instructed me on what my report should say and that I had cooperated and was planning to give President Clinton an advance copy of the report. In fact, I told Berger precisely what I told the Security Council ambassadors who cared to ask: that I feared I would have to report failure.

Soon I was summoned by the United States ambassador, who told me that as a precaution I should consider removing all UNSCOM staff from Iraq. I set in motion the withdrawal procedures and spent a sleepless night while they were being carried out. I was afraid Iraq might take our people hostage and follow its past habit of placing human shields in buildings that might be targeted by American bombers. When I told the secretary-general about my evacuation decision, he agreed that it was the right thing to do. Subsequently Annan's chief of staff deleted our agreement from the record.

On December 15 I sent my report to the Security Council. The report made clear that Iraq had failed to provide the full cooperation that it had promised and that for this and other reasons I was not able to give the Security Council the assurance it required with respect to Iraq's weapons of mass destruction.

The Russian ambassador was in the middle of condemning my report when news of America's bombing of Iraq was announced in the Security Council chamber. The atmosphere, already tense, exploded. Ambassador Lavrov denounced me as a liar and stormed out. A recess was called.

The Council meeting resumed an hour and a half later. I was given the floor to respond to what Lavrov had said. Again he walked out. Since that day, the Security Council has been unable to come to agreement on how to implement its own law with respect to Iraq.

IN THINKING back on all of this, I am reminded of an experience I had at an Iraqi government guesthouse where I stayed on my first visit to Baghdad. While I was using the bathroom one day, a large cockroach came up through the drainage grate in the floor. I don't like squashing cockroaches—it seems to me that the cure is worse than the disease—so I simply turned over a small metal wastebasket and put it over the pest, thinking that it fit more or less flush to the floor might suffocate the thing. The wastebasket remained exactly where it was for three days. As I was leaving, I couldn't resist taking a final peek. The roach was still there, alive and well. It seems a fitting metaphor for Saddam—and, more to the point, the U.N.'s inability to contain him.

At stake, though, is more than just Iraq. If Saddam Hussein gets away with facing down the U.N. and retains and rebuilds his weapons of mass destruction, he will destroy the world's best shot at controlling the spread of such weapons. He will also destroy the authority of the supreme international body charged with maintaining peace and security—the Security Council of the United Nations.

The transition from the 19th to the 20th century was marked by the breakdown of a security system that had lasted some 50 years. The consequence was World War I, and at least 10 million deaths. Today's U.N. system is of a similar age.

As we turn the corner to the 21st century, we must not repeat yesterday's mistakes. We must avoid what could be the blackest of comedies: the rehabilitation of Saddam Hussein.

THE HIJACKING OF UNSCOM

Susan Wright

The work of the U.N. Special Commission (UNSCOM) charged with disarming Iraq of its chemical and biological weapons was disrupted last December. And in an exceptionally problematic way.

UNSCOM's downfall resulted not only from the use of its work to justify, without the support of the U.N. Security Council—and possibly to assist— the bombing of Iraq by the United States and Britain, but also because of the gradual blurring of organizational and operational boundaries that needed to be kept pristinely clear.

Saddam Hussein's campaign to conceal his biological and chemical weaponry was a major catalyst for UNSCOM's problems. Had Iraq fully declared its biological and chemical weapons programs under U.N. Security Council Resolutions 687 and 707, UNSCOM's role could have been restricted to confirming declarations and reporting to the U.N. Security Council.

Instead, the agency's tasks evolved from gathering information to countering an elaborate game of deception. In so doing, UNSCOM became a pawn in another game of deception being played by the United States. Details of UNSCOM's transformation have been exposed in recent months by the skillful investigative reporting of Barton Gellman and his colleagues at *The Washington Post,* as well as other journalists around the world.

UNSCOM's control over information was the first casualty of the blurring of boundaries. From its inception, UNSCOM relied on national information, particularly intelligence from the United States, to assess Iraq's chemical and biological warfare programs. It was understood—and even seen as "natural"—that the results of UNSCOM's analyses would flow back to those governments.

As Rolf Ekeus, UNSCOM's first chairman, told me in March, if governments provided intelligence, they expected feedback regarding the reliability of the information. That was "part of the game." In theory, information

Susan Wright is a research scientist at the Institute for Research on Women and Gender at the University of Michigan. Previously, she served as a senior research fellow at the U.N. Institute for Disarmament Research. She is also the editor of *Preventing a Biological Arms Race.* This article was originally published in the May/June 1999 issue of the *Bulletin of Atomic Scientists.*

was not allowed to flow to national governments without the approval of UNSCOM's chairman. In practice, it appears this safeguard was not consistently observed.

A second casualty of the blurring of organizational and operational boundaries was the means by which UNSCOM generated data. Thwarted by Iraqi concealment strategies that aimed to defeat inspections by keeping sensitive materials and equipment on the move, Ekeus initiated probes into the strategies themselves as early as 1994. An important information source was Israeli intelligence—itself problematic given the tense relations between Israel and Iraq. Following exposure of the biological weapons program in 1995 by a key defector, Hussein Kamel, Ekeus approved "special collection missions," headed by the controversial and disquietingly single-minded Scott Ritter, who later resigned to protest U.S. interference with UNSCOM's work.

Certain inspectors on these missions carried commercial scanners and recording devices into facilities to secretly intercept and record Iraqi security telecommunications. The United States, Britain, and Israel were involved in decrypting the clandestinely collected Iraqi messages.

Given the sophistication of the Iraqi concealment program, these measures seemed defensible. In mid-1996, Ekeus briefed the Security Council in a general way about the probe into Iraqi concealment methods, and about the risk that tracking the concealment of weapons might also reveal the techniques used to conceal Saddam Hussein.

Apparently no one objected. Perhaps no one imagined the shape of UNSCOM's intelligence efforts to come. (UNSCOM's future transformation may have been foreshadowed in a complaint issued by Ekeus in September 1996 to John Deutch, then director of U.S. Central Intelligence. Ekeus said that Washington had denied UNSCOM full access to the results of the special collection missions.)

Some time in the 1996–98 time frame, UNSCOM's intelligence gathering took a major turn. If *The Washington Post*'s sources are accurate, U.S. spies, working under cover as UNSCOM technicians, installed minute listening devices in innocuous-looking monitoring equipment that UNSCOM placed in Iraqi facilities. The information acquired was relayed to Baghdad and then to a CIA post in Bahrain that beamed it to National Security Agency headquarters at Fort Meade.

Britain and Israel were relieved of their decryption duties, and within UNSCOM, access to information produced by the listening devices was tightly controlled by Washington. If U.S. explanations given in March are accurate, Ekeus and his successor, Richard Butler, were not in the loop. The person with the fullest access to the information was said to be Charles

Duelfer, the deputy to both directors and a former director of the U.S. State Department's Center for Defense Industry Trade, and a person undoubtedly equipped with a high-level security clearance. Washington's "help" had turned into virtual total control of the information collected by the listening devices.

A third casualty of the blurring of UNSCOM's boundaries was the substance of the information collected. Because the same elite Iraqi security forces that protect Saddam Hussein also protect his chemical and biological weapons, U.S. officials argue that information about the former was a mere "byproduct" of gathering information about the latter. The listening devices inevitably transmitted both types of information; therefore, say the officials, there was no choice but to receive both.

But such arguments falsely portray political choices as technical imperatives. They obscure the political nature of the decisions that allowed UNSCOM to be hijacked by the United States and used to clandestinely collect data about the nature and location of Iraq's security forces. Apparently no one who knew about it questioned Washington's infiltration of UNSCOM or its appropriation of data transmitted from Iraqi sites for its own geopolitical purposes.

According to a *Washington Post* story on March 2, "U.S. government officials considered the risk of discrediting an international arms control system by infiltrating it for their own eavesdropping. They said the stakes were so high in the conflict with Iraq, and the probability of discovery so low, that they deemed the risks worth running." Thus, U.S. officials acting in secret determined that their own goals would supersede those of the Security Council.

If press reports are accurate, a final casualty of boundary-blurring may have been the use of the information generated under cover of UNSCOM to define targets for the December bombing raids during Operation Desert Fox.

It is not known if information was actually used in this way. But certainly the American and British bombing attacks did not respect any boundaries between the weapons sites claimed as the provocation for the attacks and sites associated with the regime itself. Moreover, the present uncertainty about whether or not the information was used in this way underscores the point that it certainly could have been.

Originally UNSCOM was designed as an impartial organization of experts pursuing an international effort to disarm Iraq under Security Council Resolution 687. But under strong U.S. influence, it underwent a political transformation into a cover for U.S. espionage. Whether the information collected turned out to be of any actual use to the United States is beside the point.

The crucial political problem underscored by UNSCOM's transformation is that there were no barriers to prevent either the collection of the information or its use by the United States for its own purposes, possibly including bombing raids aimed at undermining the Baath regime.

There are no obvious solutions to addressing the problems posed by Saddam Hussein's regime, but surely the path chosen by the United States has produced one of the worst possible outcomes:

Today we have a discredited monitoring agency unable to reenter Iraq and resume its responsibilities; a low-intensity, undeclared war against Iraq that has not been approved by Congress or the Security Council; a weakened Security Council; and the continuance of sanctions that are killing an unknown number of Iraqi children each month through disease and malnutrition.

In February, the Security Council appointed two panels chaired by the Brazilian ambassador to the United Nations, Celso Amorim, to address the disarmament and humanitarian dimensions of U.N. policies toward Iraq. On March 29, the 20-member disarmament panel produced a report that expresses the mixed national interests represented on it—those of Britain and the United States, who wish to retain UNSCOM and an intrusive approach to verification, and those of France, Russia, and China, who want to phase out the verification phase of the Security Council's responsibilities.

While the report does not move to radically alter or disband UNSCOM, it perhaps offers possibilities for moving beyond the December 1998 deadlock. Clearly responding to the blurring of UNSCOM's organizational and operational boundaries, it proposes that UNSCOM's "substantive relationship with intelligence providers should be one way" and that the organization "should not be used for purposes other than the ones set forth" by the Security Council. Specific measures to reinforce these conditions are, however, not proposed.

In addition, the report proposes to "revitalize" UNSCOM's role by broadening its composition to include members of the U.N. Secretariat and the Hague-based Organization for the Prohibition of Chemical Weapons in addition to representatives of national governments. This broader membership would "renovate" the inspectorate by appointing inspectors with a wider range of backgrounds and by ensuring that most inspectors were on the U.N. payroll rather than those of national governments—moves reportedly resisted by various Western representatives. Finally, the report proposes "ongoing monitoring and verification" that combines UNSCOM's disarmament function (actively ensuring that Iraq gives up its weapons of mass destruction) with the monitoring of sites previously declared to be free of weapons.

There is something for everyone in the disarmament panel's report. But at the time of this writing in late March, it remains to be seen how the Security

Council will respond when it considers the report along with that of the second panel on sanctions. The United States could remedy some of the damage it has caused by giving full support to the disarmament panel's proposals for restructuring UNSCOM and its inspectorate. (Full support should include ensuring that American commissions and inspectors have an uncompromising commitment to the United Nations.)

The Security Council itself should seek to define a "third way" that would restructure the inspection and monitoring regime in a way that prevents Iraq from producing new nuclear, chemical, and biological weapons but maintains strong safeguards against the misuse of information by national governments. Continued monitoring of dual-purpose imports for their end-uses should play an important role. A new regime should also include an emergency program to rebuild critical civilian infrastructures, especially those for water purification, agricultural production, and medical care, and it should initiate conditional, phased steps towards lifting sanctions and normalizing trade.

But for now, it is unclear just how much the United States values the United Nations when it comes to Iraq. Meanwhile—and surely with unintended irony—the compromising of UNSCOM by the United States has helped Saddam Hussein tighten his grip over the Iraqi people. And because he no longer has to worry about inspections, he has the opportunity to rebuild his nuclear, chemical, and biological arsenals.

More profoundly, hijacking a U.N. agency to pursue national geopolitical goals, including a low-intensity war, has undermined trust in all forms of international cooperation.

Will this prompt American policy makers to rethink their assumption that the Security Council can be used when it suits American purposes and circumvented when it does not? The jury is out on that one.

BEHIND THE SCENES WITH THE IRAQI NUCLEAR BOMB

Khidhir Hamza with Jeff Stein

In 1971, on the orders of Saddam Hussein, we set out to build a nuclear bomb. Our goal was to construct a device roughly equivalent to the bomb the United States dropped on Hiroshima in 1945, that is to say, with the explosive power of twenty thousand tons of TNT. The first one would be a crude device, a sphere about four feet in diameter, too big and heavy for a missile warhead but suitable for a demonstration test or, as we discovered to our horror, Saddam's plan to drop one unannounced on Israel. The crash program to build the first bomb came to an abrupt halt with the looming Allied campaign to take back Kuwait and invade Iraq. All the evidence indicates, however, that Saddam has not forsworn his goal to make Iraq a nuclear-armed power.

From the beginning, Saddam was ambitious. He set a production target of six bombs a year, which meant that Iraq would have surpassed China as a nuclear power by the end of the 1990s, and possibly sooner, had he not invaded Kuwait and triggered Desert Storm.

We had a vast number of people working in the clandestine nuclear effort. At its peak in 1993–1994, the bomb program employed more than two thousand engineers. The mechanical design team alone numbered more than two hundred engineers. We had at least three hundred employees holding Ph.D.s in such fields as physics, chemistry, biology, and chemical and nuclear engineering. More than eight hundred employees had master's degrees in the same fields. With the addition of thousands of technicians, the total workforce employed in making a bomb was in excess of twelve thousand people—twice the size of the Argonne National Laboratory, a principal U.S. nuclear weapons center. In the last three years of the 1980s, expenditures on the bomb and bomb-related programs exceeded ten billion dollars.

How close did we get to perfecting a bomb? Very. We had a device capable of producing a nuclear explosion equivalent to a few kilotons of TNT. Without a test, we could not know exactly what the yield would have been. However,

Khidhir Hamza spent twenty years developing Iraq's atomic weapon before defecting in 1994. Jeff Stein is the national security writer for *Salon*. This article is excerpted from their book *Saddam's Bombmaker: The Daring Escape of the Man Who Built Iraq's Secret Weapon*.

the engineering estimates and simulation exercises we conducted put our device in the range of from one to three kilotons.

What we lacked was a complete nuclear core. We had more than twenty-five kilograms of bomb-grade uranium fuel rescued from Osirak, the French reactor bombed by Israeli jets in 1981. Twelve kilograms were 93 percent–enriched uranium, and about fourteen kilograms were enriched to 80 percent. Additional uranium was available from the irradiated fuel of our Russian reactor (although it would have been too hot to handle). Altogether, this would have been more than sufficient to produce the eighteen to twenty kilograms needed for a bomb. The advent of Desert Storm, however, did not leave sufficient time for the uranium metal to be extracted from the fuel. Instead, Saddam ordered his Special Security Organization to take possession of the bomb components and hide them from outside inspectors.

We had adopted what's called a levitation design, which leaves a gap around the bomb core and surrounding components to create a bigger bang per kilogram than other designs we could have managed. After Desert Storm, Iraq denied that it had pursued such a design, but recent evidence suggests that it pursued levitation, experimenting with flying metal plates and materials such as plastic and foams that can be used to space the explosive gap. During my tenure as designer of the bomb, we obtained a hot isostatic press to shape these and other bomb components by gluing powders under high temperatures and pressures.

Iraq misled the inspectors in several other areas. It lied about the strength of the shaped charges, known as explosive lenses, that we had manufactured. Iraq admitted only to having RDX/TNT explosives. In fact, Iraq had imported three hundred tons of HMX, a more powerful kind of explosive, which was used to make lighter and more powerful lenses than those that were declared. In my time, we carried out several experiments using a combination of explosives that included HMX. In any case Iraq did not reveal even the lower-power lenses for inspection, nor the equipment used to manufacture them. They were hidden in military camps around the country.

Meanwhile, the bridge-wire explosive caps we manufactured to trigger the lens explosions were as good or better than those used in the Manhattan Project. The fast electronics we learned in Poland were used to supply electrical pulses to the caps. We achieved a "jitter," or total time consumed in the almost simultaneous explosions of all the caps, of 0.1 microseconds—well within the tolerances required for a successful nuclear detonation.

We also managed to cast our own uranium-metal sphere, required for the bomb core, at four inches in diameter. Iraq concealed this achievement as well from U.N. inspectors, declaring only that it had made one sphere and four hemispheres at a smaller diameter. At the same time, Iraqi officials refused to produce even these for inspection, thus masking the quality of our purified uranium metal and the precision of the casting process from our own furnace, which was also disassembled and hidden.

Because the weight and size of our device made it too big to be mounted on a missile, Iraqi scientists pursued the development of beryllium and graphite reflectors that would be many pounds lighter than the uranium metal reflectors we originally planned. This, too, was hidden from inspectors.

We were also able to manufacture our own neutron initiators from polonium produced from our Russian reactor. Because they are radioactive sources with a short shelf life, they have almost certainly expired by now, but Iraq could replace them with its own neutron generator or by buying polonium or plutonium on the international black market. Neutron generators can be manufactured by reverse engineering those used by oil companies to detect oil depths during exploration. The challenge is to turn them out on a smaller scale suitable for a deliverable bomb, which Iraq did admit was within its means. Another option for Iraq, however, would be to employ a gun-type bomb design of the kind that was used by South Africa and doesn't require a neutron initiator, but it would require more uranium for the bomb core.

Acquiring or producing bomb-grade uranium was always the biggest challenge to our program. Iraq at first maintained that it had failed to enrich uranium by the diffusion method, but after my 1994 defection, it conceded it had solved this problem. U.S. satellites could easily detect the building of full-scale diffusion plants, with four thousand stages. Therefore, Iraq would most likely pursue the short-cascade options I designed and which are more easily dispersed and hidden in a dozen or more units. Short cascades also can be combined with another enrichment method, electromagnetic isotope separation, or EMIS, to produce bomb-grade uranium. As with many other subjects, U.N. inspectors were surprised at how far along Iraq was in achieving this goal. Supposedly, the magnets manufactured for EMIS were destroyed, but more could easily be made using precision equipment that was never declared or turned over to the inspectors. Another possibility would be for Iraq to use the centrifuge technology supplied clandestinely by West German scientists in the late 1980s.

Ironically, the first lessons we got on enrichment methods came from the Manhattan Project's own reports, which were long ago declassified. I found stacks of them in the dusty archives of our own Atomic Energy Commission, on a shelf labeled "This is a gift of the U.S. Atomic Energy Commission." Apparently they were given to Iraq at the start of its peaceful energy program in 1956.

Another option for obtaining bomb-grade uranium, of course, is simply to buy it on the black market. The most likely sources are disenchanted, unemployed, underpaid, or simply corruptible officials in Russia or other nuclear-armed states. Another possible supplier is Serbia, which clandestinely aided Iraq's missile programs in the past and is now said to possess fifty kilograms of bomb-grade uranium.

The X Factor in Iraq's nuclear equation is the availability of foreign, and particularly Russian, brainpower to solve remaining technological bottlenecks, if any, and improve the state of production and manufacture of the bomb's key components. During my visit to the crumbling Soviet Union in 1990, scores of Russian nuclear scientists virtually begged me for jobs in Iraq, but the onset of Desert Storm postponed their recruitment. By the time I defected in 1994, however, some Russian scientists were at work in Iraq on chemical weapons and others were expected to join them in other programs. If some are in fact in Iraq now, they would be capable of producing a more workable system or making more powerful, and a bigger number of, atomic weapons.

In any case, I have no doubt that Iraq is pursuing the nuclear option. For a while after the Gulf War, the presence of outside inspectors and the economic embargo slowed down the pace. But at this writing, U.N. inspectors have been barred for more than a year, while oil revenues have been steadily increasing. The unity of the coalition that kicked Saddam out of Kuwait, meanwhile, has been shattered. The flow of dual-use imports to Iraq has been allowed to increase, while Russia, China, and France are pushing for a complete lifting of the embargo. If they succeed, Saddam could easily cross the nuclear bomb finish line.

This is a frightening prospect. A nuclear-armed Saddam is not only a menace to the West on his own but also a trigger for a new arms race among all the countries of the Middle East. Israel already has a nuclear stockpile; Iran is in hot pursuit of its own. With Saddam's arrival as a nuclear power, it would not be out of the question for Egypt, Syria, and even Turkey to pursue the same path.

And that is a nightmare. Saddam must be kept in a box or, better still, removed.

Editors' postscript: How far Iraq has come in its nuclear weapons program remains in dispute. In October 2002, the CIA issued a report on "Iraq's Weapons of Mass Destruction Programs" that made the following claims:

- Although Saddam probably does not yet have nuclear weapons or sufficient material to make any, he remains intent on acquiring them.
- How quickly Iraq will obtain its first nuclear weapon depends on when it acquires sufficient weapons-grade fissile material.
- If Baghdad acquires sufficient weapons-grade fissile material from abroad, it could make a nuclear weapon within a year.

- Without such material from abroad, Iraq probably would not be able to make a weapon until the last half of the decade.
- Iraq's aggressive attempts to obtain proscribed high-strength aluminum tubes are of significant concern. All intelligence experts agree that Iraq is seeking nuclear weapons and that these tubes could be used in a centrifuge enrichment program. Most intelligence specialists assess this to be the intended use, but some believe that these tubes are probably intended for conventional weapons programs.
- Based on tubes of the size Iraq is trying to acquire, a few tens of thousands of centrifuges would be capable of producing enough highly enriched uranium for a couple of weapons per year.

President Bush re-emphasized these concerns in his January 30, 2003, State of the Union address, and added one new allegation: "The British government has learned that Saddam Hussein recently sought significant quantities of uranium from Africa." Secretary of State Colin Powell further charged, in his presentation to the Security Council on February 5, that Iraqi officials "negotiated with firms in Romania, India, Russia and Slovenia for the purchase of a magnet production plant. Iraq wanted the plant to produce magnets weighing 20 to 30 grams. That's the same weight as the magnets used in Iraq's gas centrifuge program before the Gulf War," he added. "This incident linked with the tubes is another indicator of Iraq's attempt to reconstitute its nuclear weapons program," Powell concluded.

On January 27, 2003, Dr. Mohamed ElBaradei, the director general of the International Atomic Energy Agency, reported on the progress of the new round of inspections begun in late 2002 in Iraq. He told the United Nations Security Council, "We have to date found no evidence that Iraq has revived its nuclear weapons program since the elimination of the program in the 1990's. However, our work is steadily progressing and should be allowed to run its natural course. With our verification system now in place, barring exceptional circumstances, and provided there is sustained proactive cooperation by Iraq, we should be able within the next few months to provide credible assurance that Iraq has no nuclear weapons program."

As for the aluminum tubes sought by Iraq, ElBaradei said their purpose appeared to be as claimed by the Iraqis, to reverse engineer conventional rockets. He told the Security Council, "To verify this information, IAEA inspectors have inspected the relevant rocket production and storage sites, taken tube samples, interviewed relevant Iraqi personnel and reviewed procurement contracts and related documents. From our analysis to date it appears that the aluminum tubes would be consistent with the purpose stated by Iraq and, unless modified, would not be suitable for manufacturing centrifuges; however, we are still investigating this issue. It is clear, however, that the attempt to acquire such tubes is prohibited under Security Council Resolution 687." On March 7, ElBaradei went further, stating that although his investigations were continuing, his nuclear experts had found "no indication" that Iraq had tried to import high-strength aluminum tubes or specialized ring magnets for enrichment of uranium.

Furthermore, he charged that documents provided by unidentified states may have been faked to suggest that the African country of Niger sold uranium to Iraq between 1999 and 2001. According to *The Washington Post*, "Knowledgeable sources familiar with the forgery investigation described the faked evidence as a series of letters between Iraqi agents and officials in [Niger]. . . . The forgers had made relatively crude errors that eventually gave them away—including names and titles that did not match up with the individuals who held office at the time the letters were purportedly written." Said one U.S. official who reviewed the documents, "We fell for it."

Seymour Hersh points out, in an article on this controversy in the March 31, 2003 *New Yorker*, that the Bush Administration made much use of the aluminum tubes and Niger-Iraq material in its classified briefings of members of Congress in the fall of 2002. Democrats were considering alternatives to the administration's resolution authorizing Bush to wage war on Iraq, but testimony from C.I.A. Director George Tenet and Colin Powell citing this purportedly new evidence of Iraq's intentions "helped to mollify" them, Hersh writes. On March 14, 2003, Senator Jay Rockefeller asked the F.B.I. to investigate the matter, saying, "There is a possibility that the fabrication of these documents may be part of a larger deception campaign aimed at manipulating public opinion and foreign policy regarding Iraq."

SIX

NEW STORMS BREWING

"Since the sons of the land of the two holy places [eds. note: Saudi Arabia, with its two sacred cities, Mecca and Medina] feel and strong believe that *jihad* against the unbelievers in every part of the world is absolutely essential, then it follows that they will be even more enthusiastic, more powerful, and larger in number upon fighting on their own land . . . defending the greatest of their [holy places]. They know that the Muslims of the world will assist and help them to victory. To liberate their [holy places] is the greatest of issues concerning all Muslims; it is the duty of every Muslim in this world. "I say to you: These youths love death as you love life. . . . Our youths believe in paradise after death. They . . . know that their rewards in fighting you, the United States, would be double the rewards in fighting someone else not from the people of the book. They have no intention except to enter paradise by killing you. An infidel, and enemy of God like you. . . . Terrorizing you, while you are carrying arms on our land, is a legitimate and morally demanded duty."
—*Osama bin Laden, from his "Declaration of War," August 1996*

"It should be the policy of the United States to support efforts to remove the regime headed by Saddam Hussein from power in Iraq and to promote the emergence of a democratic government to replace that regime."
—*From the Iraq Liberation Act of 1998, passed 360–38*
in the House of Representatives and unanimously in the Senate

AN OPEN LETTER TO
PRESIDENT CLINTON:
"REMOVE SADDAM FROM POWER"

Project for the New American Century

JANUARY 26, 1998

The Honorable William J. Clinton
President of the United States
Washington, DC

Dear Mr. President:

We are writing you because we are convinced that current American policy toward Iraq is not succeeding, and that we may soon face a threat in the Middle East more serious than any we have known since the end of the Cold War. In your upcoming State of the Union Address, you have an opportunity to chart a clear and determined course for meeting this threat. We urge you to seize that opportunity, and to enunciate a new strategy that would secure the interests of the U.S. and our friends and allies around the world. That strategy should aim, above all, at the removal of Saddam Hussein's regime from power. We stand ready to offer our full support in this difficult but necessary endeavor.

The policy of "containment" of Saddam Hussein has been steadily eroding over the past several months. As recent events have demonstrated, we can no longer depend on our partners in the Gulf War coalition to continue to uphold the sanctions or to punish Saddam when he blocks or evades U.N. inspections. Our ability to ensure that Saddam Hussein is not producing weapons of mass destruction, therefore, has substantially diminished. Even if full inspections were eventually to resume, which now seems

199

highly unlikely, experience has shown that it is difficult if not impossible to monitor Iraq's chemical and biological weapons production. The lengthy period during which the inspectors will have been unable to enter many Iraqi facilities has made it even less likely that they will be able to uncover all of Saddam's secrets. As a result, in the not-too-distant future we will be unable to determine with any reasonable level of confidence whether Iraq does or does not possess such weapons.

Such uncertainty will, by itself, have a seriously destabilizing effect on the entire Middle East. It hardly needs to be added that if Saddam does acquire the capability to deliver weapons of mass destruction, as he is almost certain to do if we continue along the present course, the safety of American troops in the region, of our friends and allies like Israel and the moderate Arab states, and a significant portion of the world's supply of oil will all be put at hazard. As you have rightly declared, Mr. President, the security of the world in the first part of the 21st century will be determined largely by how we handle this threat.

Given the magnitude of the threat, the current policy, which depends for its success upon the steadfastness of our coalition partners and upon the cooperation of Saddam Hussein, is dangerously inadequate. The only acceptable strategy is one that eliminates the possibility that Iraq will be able to use or threaten to use weapons of mass destruction. In the near term, this means a willingness to undertake military action as diplomacy is clearly failing. In the long term, it means removing Saddam Hussein and his regime from power. That now needs to become the aim of American foreign policy.

We urge you to articulate this aim, and to turn your Administration's attention to implementing a strategy for removing Saddam's regime from power. This will require a full complement of diplomatic, political and military efforts. Although we are fully aware of the dangers and difficulties in implementing this policy, we believe the dangers of failing to do so are far greater. We believe the U.S. has the authority under existing U.N. resolutions to take the necessary steps, including military steps, to protect our vital interests in the Gulf. In any case, American policy cannot continue to be crippled by a misguided insistence on unanimity in the U.N. Security Council.

We urge you to act decisively. If you act now to end the threat of weapons of mass destruction against the U.S. or its allies, you will be acting in the most fundamental national security interests of the country. If we accept a course of weakness and drift, we put our interests and our future at risk.

Sincerely,

Elliott Abrams	William Kristol
Richard L. Armitage	Richard Perle
William J. Bennett	Peter W. Rodman
Jeffrey Bergner	Donald Rumsfeld
John Bolton	William Schneider, Jr.
Paula Dobriansky	Vin Weber, Paul Wolfowitz
Francis Fukuyama	R. James Woolsey
Robert Kagan	Robert B. Zoellick
Zalmay Khalilzad	

Editors' note: The Project for the New American Century was established in the spring of 1997 as a nonprofit educational organization "whose goal is to promote American global leadership." Of the eighteen signers of this letter to President Clinton, eleven held posts in the Bush administration as of March 2003: Elliott Abrams, Senior Director for Near East, Southwest Asian and North African Affairs on the National Security Council; Richard L. Armitage, Deputy Secretary of State; John Bolton, Under Secretary, Arms Control and International Security; Paula Dobriansky, Under Secretary of State for Global Affairs; Zalmay Khalilzad, President Bush's special envoy to Afghanistan and Ambassador-at-Large for Free Iraqis; Richard Perle, chairman of the Pentagon's Defense Policy Board; Peter W. Rodman, Assistant Secretary of Defense for International Security Affairs; Donald Rumsfeld, Secretary of Defense; William Schneider, Jr., chairman of the Pentagon's Defense Science Board; Paul Wolfowitz, Deputy Secretary of Defense; and Robert B. Zoellick, the U.S. Trade Representative. Another friend of PNAC who has signed several of the group's other statements is I. Lewis Libby, who is today Vice President Cheney's chief of staff.

STATEMENT: JIHAD AGAINST JEWS AND CRUSADERS

World Islamic Front

This February 23, 1998 statement was signed by Osama bin Laden; Ayman al-Zawahiri, leader of the Jihad Group in Egypt; Abu-Yasir Rifa'i Ahmad Taha, Egyptian Islamic Group; Sheikh Mir Hamzah, secretary of the Jamiat-ul-Ulema-e-Pakistan; and Fazlul Rahman, leader of the Jihad Movement in Bangladesh.

. . . The Arabian Peninsula [Saudi Arabia] has never—since God made it flat, created its desert, and encircled it with seas—been stormed by any forces like the crusader armies spreading in it like locusts, eating its riches and wiping out its plantations. All this is happening at a time in which nations are attacking Muslims like people fighting over a plate of food. In the light of the grave situation and the lack of support, we and you are obliged to discuss current events, and we should all agree on how to settle the matter.

No one argues today about three facts that are known to everyone, we will list them in order to remind everyone:

First, for over seven years the United States has been occupying the lands of Islam in the holiest of places, the Arabian Peninsula, plundering its riches, dictating to its rulers, humiliating its people, terrorizing its neighbors, and turning its bases in the peninsula into a spearhead through which to fight the neighboring Muslim peoples.

If some people have in the past argued about the fact of the occupation, all the people of the peninsula have now acknowledged it. The best proof of this is the Americans' continuing aggression against the Iraqi people using the peninsula as a staging post, even though all its rulers are against their territories being used to that end, but they are helpless.

Second, despite the great devastation inflicted on the Iraqi people by the

---

After Bin Laden's "Declaration of War" against the United States in 1996, this statement marks a broadening of his initial focus on overthrowing the Saudi government and forcing the United States out of that country. Here, Bin Laden gives equal attention to opposing the sanctions on Iraq and to battling Israel. Despite its grandiose name, the "World Islamic Front" was primarily the Al-Qaeda group along with smaller organizations from Egypt, Pakistan and Bangladesh. Six months after this statement was released, car bombs set by Al-Qaeda operatives exploded at the U.S. embassies in Nairobi, Kenya and Dar es Salaam, Tanzania. Over 300 people were killed, and thousands were injured.

crusader-Zionist alliance, and despite the huge number of those killed, which has exceeded one million . . . despite all this, the Americans are once again trying to repeat the horrific massacres, as though they are not content with the protracted blockade imposed after the ferocious war or the fragmentation and devastation. So here they come to annihilate what is left of this people and to humiliate their Muslim neighbors.

Third, if the Americans' aims behind these wars are religious and economic, the aim is also to serve the Jews' petty state and divert attention from its occupation of Jerusalem and murder of Muslims there. The best proof of this is their eagerness to destroy Iraq, the strongest neighboring Arab state, and their endeavor to fragment all the states of the region such as Iraq, Saudi Arabia, Egypt, and Sudan into paper statelets and through their disunion and weakness to guarantee Israel's survival and the continuation of the brutal crusader occupation of the peninsula.

All these crimes and sins committed by the Americans are a clear declaration of war on God, his messenger, and Muslims. And *ulama* [religious leaders] have throughout Islamic history unanimously agreed that the *jihad* is an individual duty if the enemy destroys the Muslim countries. This was revealed by Imam bin-Qadama in *al-Mughni*, Imam al-Kisa'i in *al-Bada'i*, al-Qurtubi in his interpretation, and the sheikh of al-Islam in his books, where he said: "As for the fighting to repulse [an enemy], it is aimed at defending sanctity and religion, and it is a duty as agreed [by the *ulama*]. Nothing is more sacred than belief except repulsing an enemy who is attacking religion and life."

On that basis, and in compliance with God's order, we issue the following *fatwa* to all Muslims:

The ruling to kill the Americans and their allies—civilians and military— an individual duty for every Muslim who can do it in any country in which it is possible to do it, in order to liberate the al-Aqsa mosque and the holy mosque [Mecca] from their grip, and in order for their armies to move out of all the lands of Islam, defeated and unable to threaten any Muslim. This is in accordance with the words of Almighty God, "And fight the pagans all together as they fight you all together," and "Fight them until there is no more tumult or oppression, and there prevail justice and faith in God."

This is in addition to the words of Almighty God: "And why should ye not fight in the cause of God and of those who, being weak, are ill-treated (and oppressed)?—women and children, whose cry is: "Our Lord, rescue us from this town, whose people are oppressors; and raise for us from thee one who will help!"

We—with God's help—call on every Muslim who believes in God and wishes to be rewarded to comply with God's order to kill the Americans and plunder their money wherever and whenever they find it. We also call on Muslim *ulama,* leaders, youths, and soldiers to launch the raid on Satan's U.S. troops and the devil's supporters allying with them, and to displace those who are behind them so that they may learn a lesson.

Almighty God said: "O ye who believe, give your response to God and his Apostle, when he calleth you to that which will give you life. And know that God cometh between a man and his heart, and that it is he to whom ye shall all be gathered."

Almighty God also says: "O ye who believe, what is the matter with you, that when ye are asked to go forth in the cause of God, ye cling so heavily to the earth! Do ye prefer the life of this world to the hereafter? But little is the comfort of this life, as compared with the hereafter. Unless ye go forth, he will punish you with a grievous penalty, and put others in your place; but him ye would not harm in the least. For God hath power over all things."

Almighty God also says: "So lose no heart, nor fall into despair. For ye must gain mastery if ye are true in faith."

TELEVISED ADDRESS TO THE NATION: "THE COSTS OF ACTION MUST BE WEIGHED AGAINST THE PRICE OF INACTION"

President Bill Clinton

On December 16, 1998, President Bill Clinton ordered the extensive bombing of Iraqi targets, a four-day campaign called Desert Fox which he told the American people about in a televised speech that evening. An abridged version of his address appears below.

President Clinton's action came after a series of confrontations between Iraq and the U.N. inspectors, Saddam's decision to prohibit fresh inspections on October 31, and the subsequent withdrawal of inspectors from Baghdad.

Earlier, on August 20, 1998, as special prosecutor Ken Starr's investigation of the president's alleged indiscretions with Monica Lewinsky was reaching a climax, cruise missiles had been fired at the Sudan and Afghanistan, aimed at punishing Osama bin Laden for the bombing of U.S. embassies in East Africa on August 7. They failed to hit bin Laden, and evidence soon surfaced that the "chemical weapons plant" they destroyed in the Sudan was not a munitions facility at all, but rather a pharmaceutical factory producing vital medicines for civilian purposes.

Three days after Clinton announced his Desert Fox campaign, the House of Representatives voted to impeach him for perjuring himself before a grand jury and obstructing justice in the Monica Lewinsky affair. In the wake of Desert Fox, the Security Council was split on determining new terms for an inspection regime. Four years were to pass before inspectors returned to Iraq.

GOOD EVENING. Earlier today, I ordered America's Armed Forces to strike military and security targets in Iraq. They are joined by British forces. Their mission is to attack Iraq's nuclear, chemical, and biological programs, and its military capacity to threaten its neighbors. Their purpose is to protect the national interest of the United States and, indeed, the interest of people throughout the Middle East and around the world. Saddam Hussein must not be allowed to threaten his neighbors or the world with nuclear arms, poison gas, or biological weapons.

I want to explain why I have decided, with the unanimous recommendation of my national security team, to use force in Iraq, why we have acted now and what we aim to accomplish.

Six weeks ago, Saddam Hussein announced that he would no longer cooperate with the United Nations weapons inspectors, called UNSCOM. They are highly professional experts from dozens of countries. Their job is to oversee the elimination of Iraq's capability to retain, create and use weapons of mass destruction, and to verify that Iraq does not attempt to rebuild that capability. The inspectors undertook this mission, first, seven and a half years ago, at the end of the Gulf War, when Iraq agreed to declare and destroy its arsenal as a condition of the cease-fire.

The international community had good reason to set this requirement. Other countries possess weapons of mass destruction and ballistic missiles. With Saddam, there's one big difference: he has used them, not once but repeatedly—unleashing chemical weapons against Iranian troops during a decade-long war, not only against soldiers, but against civilians; firing Scud missiles at the citizens of Israel, Saudi Arabia, Bahrain, and Iran—not only against a foreign enemy, but even against his own people, gassing Kurdish civilians in Northern Iraq.

The international community had little doubt then, and I have no doubt today, that left unchecked, Saddam Hussein will use these terrible weapons again.

The United States has patiently worked to preserve UNSCOM, as Iraq has sought to avoid its obligation to cooperate with the inspectors. On occasion, we've had to threaten military force, and Saddam has backed down. Faced with Saddam's latest act of defiance in late October, we built intensive diplomatic pressure on Iraq, backed by overwhelming military force in the region. The U.N. Security Council voted 15 to zero to condemn Saddam's actions and to demand that he immediately come into compliance. Eight Arab nations—Egypt, Syria, Saudi Arabia, Kuwait, Bahrain, Qatar, United Arab Emirates, and Oman—warned that Iraq alone would bear responsibility for the consequences of defying the U.N.

When Saddam still failed to comply, we prepared to act militarily. It was only then, at the last possible moment, that Iraq backed down. It pledged to the U.N. that it had made—and I quote—"a clear and unconditional decision to resume cooperation with the weapons inspectors."

I decided then to call off the attack, with our airplanes already in the air, because Saddam had given in to our demands. I concluded then that the right thing to do was to use restraint and give Saddam one last chance to prove his willingness to cooperate.

I made it very clear at that time what "unconditional cooperation" meant, based on existing U.N. resolutions and Iraq's own commitments. And along with Prime Minister Blair of Great Britain, I made it equally clear that if Saddam failed to cooperate fully, we would be prepared to act without delay, diplomacy or warning.

Now, over the past three weeks, the U.N. weapons inspectors have carried out their plan for testing Iraq's cooperation. The testing period ended this weekend, and last night, UNSCOM's Chairman, Richard Butler, reported the results to U.N. Secretary General Annan. The conclusions are stark, sobering and profoundly disturbing.

In four out of the five categories set forth, Iraq has failed to cooperate. Indeed, it actually has placed new restrictions on the inspectors. Here are some of the particulars:

Iraq repeatedly blocked UNSCOM from inspecting suspect sites. For example, it shut off access to the headquarters of its ruling party, and said it will deny access to the party's other offices, even though U.N. resolutions make no exception for them and UNSCOM has inspected them in the past.

Iraq repeatedly restricted UNSCOM's ability to obtain necessary evidence. For example, Iraq obstructed UNSCOM's effort to photograph bombs related to its chemical weapons program. It tried to stop an UNSCOM biological weapons team from videotaping a site and photocopying documents, and prevented Iraqi personnel from answering UNSCOM's questions.

Prior to the inspection of another site, Iraq actually emptied out the building, removing not just documents, but even the furniture and the equipment. Iraq has failed to turn over virtually all the documents requested by the inspectors; indeed, we know that Iraq ordered the destruction of weapons-related documents in anticipation of an UNSCOM inspection.

So Iraq has abused its final chance. As the UNSCOM report concludes—and again I quote—"Iraq's conduct ensured that no progress was able to be made in the fields of disarmament. In light of this experience, and in the absence of full cooperation by Iraq, it must, regrettably, be recorded again that the Commission is not able to conduct the work mandated to it by the Security Council with respect to Iraq's prohibited weapons program."

In short, the inspectors are saying that, even if they could stay in Iraq, their work would be a sham. Saddam's deception has defeated their effectiveness. Instead of the inspectors disarming Saddam, Saddam has disarmed the inspectors.

This situation presents a clear and present danger to the stability of the

Persian Gulf and the safety of people everywhere. The international community gave Saddam one last chance to resume cooperation with the weapons inspectors. Saddam has failed to seize the chance.

And so we had to act, and act now. Let me explain why.

First, without a strong inspections system, Iraq would be free to retain and begin to rebuild its chemical, biological, and nuclear weapons programs—in months, not years.

Second, if Saddam can cripple the weapons inspections system and get away with it, he would conclude that the international community, led by the United States, has simply lost its will. He will surmise that he has free rein to rebuild his arsenal of destruction. And some day, make no mistake, he will use it again, as he has in the past.

Third, in halting our air strikes in November, I gave Saddam a chance, not a license. If we turn our backs on his defiance, the credibility of U.S. power as a check against Saddam will be destroyed. We will not only have allowed Saddam to shatter the inspections system that controls his weapons of mass destruction program; we also will have fatally undercut the fear of force that stops Saddam from acting to gain domination in the region.

That is why, on the unanimous recommendation of my national security team, including the Vice President, Secretary of Defense, the Chairman of the Joint Chiefs of Staff, the Secretary of State, and the National Security Advisor, I have ordered a strong, sustained series of air strikes against Iraq. They are designed to degrade Saddam's capacity to develop and deliver weapons of mass destruction, and to degrade his ability to threaten his neighbors. At the same time, we are delivering a powerful message to Saddam: If you act recklessly, you will pay a heavy price.

[. . . .]

I hope Saddam will come into cooperation with the inspection system now and comply with the relevant U.N. Security Council resolutions. But we have to be prepared that he will not, and we must deal with the very real danger he poses. So we will pursue a long-term strategy to contain Iraq and its weapons of mass destruction, and work toward the day when Iraq has a government worthy of its people.

First, we must be prepared to use force again if Saddam takes threatening actions, such as trying to reconstitute his weapons of mass destruction or their delivery systems, threatening his neighbors, challenging allied aircraft over Iraq, or moving against his own Kurdish citizens. The credible threat to use force and, when necessary, the actual use of force, is the surest way to contain Saddam's weapons of mass destruction program, curtail his aggression and prevent another Gulf War.

Second, so long as Iraq remains out of compliance, we will work with the international community to maintain and enforce economic sanctions. Sanctions have cost Saddam more than $120 billion—resources that would have been used to rebuild his military. The sanctions system allows Iraq to sell oil for food, for medicine, for other humanitarian supplies for the Iraqi people. We have no quarrel with them. But without the sanctions, we would see the oil-for-food program become oil-for-tanks, resulting in a greater threat to Iraq's neighbors and less food for its people.

The hard fact is that so long as Saddam remains in power, he threatens the well-being of his people, the peace of his region, the security of the world. The best way to end that threat once and for all is with the new Iraqi government, a government ready to live in peace with its neighbors, a government that respects the rights of its people.

Bringing change in Baghdad will take time and effort. We will strengthen our engagement with the full range of Iraqi opposition forces and work with them effectively and prudently.

The decision to use force is never cost-free. Whenever American forces are placed in harm's way, we risk the loss of life. And while our strikes are focused on Iraq's military capabilities, there will be unintended Iraqi casualties. Indeed, in the past, Saddam has intentionally placed Iraqi civilians in harm's way in a cynical bid to sway international opinion. We must be prepared for these realities. At the same time, Saddam should have absolutely no doubt: If he lashes out at his neighbors, we will respond forcefully.

Heavy as they are, the costs of action must be weighed against the price of inaction. If Saddam defies the world and we fail to respond, we will face a far greater threat in the future. Saddam will strike again at his neighbors; he will make war on his own people. And mark my words, he will develop weapons of mass destruction. He will deploy them, and he will use them. Because we are acting today, it is less likely that we will face these dangers in the future.
[. . .]

PART THREE

WAR WITH IRAQ

SEVEN

THE IMPACT OF SEPTEMBER 11TH

"[Want] best info fast. Judge whether good enough hit S.H. [Saddam Hussein] at same time. Not only UBL [Usama bin Laden]. Go massive. Sweep it all up. Things related and not."

— *Defense Secretary Donald Rumsfeld's reaction to news of the September 11 attacks, as of 2:40 P.M. that day, according to notes taken by aides with him in the National Military Command Center (CBS News, "Plans for Iraq Attack Began on 9/11," report by David Martin, September 4, 2002)*

REFLECTIONS ON SEPTEMBER 11th

Susan Sontag

The disconnect between last Tuesday's monstrous dose of reality and the self-righteous drivel and outright deceptions being peddled by public figures and TV commentators is startling, depressing. The voices licensed to follow the event seem to have joined together in a campaign to infantilize the public. Where is the acknowledgement that this was not a "cowardly" attack on "civilization" or "liberty" or "humanity" or "the free world" but an attack on the world's self-proclaimed super-power, undertaken as a consequence of specific American alliances and actions? How many citizens are aware of the ongoing American bombing of Iraq? And if the word "cowardly" is to be used, it might be more aptly applied to those who kill from beyond the range of retaliation, high in the sky, than to those willing to die themselves in order to kill others. In the matter of courage (a morally neutral virtue): whatever may be said of the perpetrators of Tuesday's slaughter, they were not cowards.

Our leaders are bent on convincing us that everything is O.K. America is not afraid. Our spirit is unbroken, although this was a day that will live in infamy and America is now at war. But everything is not O.K. And this was not Pearl Harbor. We have a robotic president who assures us that America stands tall. A wide spectrum of public figures, in and out of office, who are strongly opposed to the policies being pursued abroad by this Administration apparently feel free to say nothing more than that they stand united behind President Bush. A lot of thinking needs to be done, and perhaps is being done in Washington and elsewhere, about the ineptitude of American intelligence and counterintelligence, about options available to American foreign policy, particularly in the Middle East, and about what constitutes a smart program of military defense. But the public is not being asked to bear much of the burden of reality. The unanimously applauded, self-congratulatory bromides of a Soviet Party Congress seemed contemptible. The unanimity of the sanctimonious, reality-concealing rhetoric spouted by American officials and media commentators in recent days seems, well, unworthy of a mature democracy.

Susan Sontag is a fiction writer, essayist, cultural critic and human rights activist. Her most recent books are *Regarding the Pain of Others,* and a collection of essays, *Where the Stress Falls.* This brief essay was among a series of responses to September 11th that were published in *The New Yorker* on September 24, 2001.

Those in public office have let us know that they consider their task to be a manipulative one: confidence-building and grief management. Politics, the politics of a democracy—which entails disagreement, which promotes candor—has been replaced by psychotherapy. Let's by all means grieve together. But let's not be stupid together. A few shreds of historical awareness might help us to understand what has just happened, and what may continue to happen. "Our country is strong," we are told again and again. I for one don't find this entirely consoling. Who doubts that America is strong? But that's not all America has to be.

VOICES OF MORAL OBTUSENESS

Charles Krauthammer

In the wake of a massacre that killed more than 5,000 innocent Americans in a day, one might expect moral clarity. After all, four days after Pearl Harbor, the isolationist America First Committee (which included such well-meaning young people as Gerald Ford and Potter Stewart) formally disbanded. There had been argument and confusion about America's role in the world and the intentions of its enemies. No more.

Similarly, two days after Hitler invaded Poland, it was Neville Chamberlain himself, seduced and misled by Hitler for years, who declared war on Germany.

And yet, within days of the World Trade Center massacre, an event of blinding clarity, we are already beginning to hear the voices, prominent voices, of moral obtuseness.

Susan Sontag is appalled at "the self-righteous drivel" that this was an "attack on 'civilization'" rather than on America as "a consequence of specific American alliances and actions. How many citizens are aware of the ongoing American bombing of Iraq?"

What Sontag is implying, but does not quite have the courage to say, is that because of these "alliances and actions," such as the bombing of Iraq, we had it coming. The implication is as disgusting as Jerry Falwell's blaming the attack on sexual deviance and abortion, except that Falwell's excrescences appear on loony TV, Sontag's in *The New Yorker*.

Let us look at those policies. The bombing of Iraq? First, we are not bombing Iraqi civilians. We attack antiaircraft positions that are trying to shoot down our planes. Why are our planes there? To keep Iraq from projecting its power to re-invade and re-attack its neighbors.

Why are we keeping Saddam in his box? Because we know he is developing nuclear, chemical and biological weapons and we know of what he is capable: He has already gassed 5,000 Kurds, used chemical weapons against Iran and launched missiles into Tehran, Riyadh and Tel Aviv with the explicit aim of murdering as many people as possible.

Charles Krauthammer is a columnist for *The Washington Post* and an essayist for *Time* magazine. In 1987, he won the Pulitzer Prize for distinguished commentary. This column was published in the *Post* on September 21, 2001.

Or maybe Sontag means American support for Israel. Perhaps she means that America should have abandoned Israel—after it made its astonishingly generous peace offer to the Palestinians (with explicit American assurances to support Israel as it took "risks for peace") and was rewarded with a guerrilla war employing the same terrorist savagery that we witnessed on September 11.

Let us look at American policies. America conducted three wars in the 1990s. The Gulf War saved the Kuwaiti people from Saddam. American intervention in the Balkans saved Bosnia. And then we saved Kosovo from Serbia. What do these three military campaigns have in common? In every one we saved a Muslim people.

And then there was Somalia, a military operation of unadulterated altruism. Its sole purpose was to save the starving people of Somalia. Muslims all.

For such alliances and actions, we get more than 5,000 Americans murdered, or, as Sontag puts it, "last Tuesday's monstrous dose of reality."

Moral obtuseness is not restricted to intellectuals. I witnessed a High Holiday sermon by a guest rabbi warning the congregation, exactly seven days after our generation's Pearl Harbor, against "oversimplifying" by speaking in terms of "good guys and bad guys."

Oversimplifying? Has there ever been a time when the distinction between good and evil was more clear?

And where are the Muslim clerics—in the United States, Europe and the Middle East—who should be joining together to make that distinction with loud unanimity? Where are their *fatwas* against suicide murder? Where are the authoritative communal declarations that these crimes are contrary to Islam?

President Bush said so in his visit to Washington's main mosque. But Bush is a Christian. He is a hardly an authority on Islam.

Why did the spiritual leader of the Islamic Society of North America, Dr. Muzammil Siddiqi, not say that such terrorism is contrary to Islam in his address at the national prayer service at the Washington National Cathedral? His words went out around the world. Yet he was vague and elusive. "But those that lay the plots of evil, for them is a terrible penalty." Very true. But who are the layers of plots of evil? Those who perpetrated the World Trade Center attack? Or America, as thousands of Muslims in the street claim? The imam might have made that clear. He did not.

This is no time for obfuscation. Or for agonized relativism. Or, obscenely, for blaming America first. (The habit dies hard.) This is a time for clarity. At a time like this, those who search for shades of evil, for root causes, for extenuations are, to borrow from Lance Morrow, "too philosophical for decent company."

AGAINST THE WAR METAPHOR

Hendrik Hertzberg

The catastrophe that turned the foot of Manhattan into the mouth of Hell on the morning of September 11, 2001, unfolded in four paroxysms. At a little before nine, a smoldering scar on the face of the north tower of the World Trade Center (an awful accident, like the collision of a B-25 bomber with the Empire State Building on July 28, 1945?); eighteen minutes later, the orange and gray blossoming of the second explosion, in the south tower; finally, at a minute before ten and then at not quite ten-thirty, the sickening slide of the two towers, collapsing one after the other. For those in the immediate vicinity, the horror was of course immediate and unmistakable; it occurred in what we have learned to call real time, and in real space. For those farther away—whether a few dozen blocks or halfway around the world—who were made witnesses by the long lens of television, the events were seen as through a glass, brightly. Their reality was visible but not palpable. It took hours to begin to comprehend their magnitude; it is taking days for the defensive numbness they induced to wear off; it will take months—or years—to measure their impact and meaning.

New York is a city where, however much strangers meet and mix on the streets and in the subways, circles of friends are usually demarcated by work and family. The missing and presumed dead—their number is in the thousands—come primarily from the finance, international trade, and government service workers in the doomed buildings, and from the ranks of firefighters and police officers drawn there by duty and courage. The umbra of personal grief already encompasses scores or even hundreds of thousands of people; a week or two from now, when the word has spread from friend to colleague to relative to acquaintance, the penumbra will cover millions. The city has never suffered a more shocking calamity from any act of God or man.

The calamity, of course, goes well beyond the damage to our city and to its similarly bereaved rival and brother Washington. It is national; it is international; it is civilizational. In the decade since the end of the Cold War, the human race has become, with increasing rapidity, a single organism. Every

Hendrik Hertzberg is the editorial director of *The New Yorker*. This essay was published in that magazine with the title "Tuesday and After," on September 24, 2001.

219

kind of barrier to the free and rapid movement of goods, information, and people has been lowered. The organism relies increasingly on a kind of trust—the unsentimental expectation that people, individually and collectively, will behave more or less in their rational self-interest. (Even the anti-globalizers of the West mostly embrace the underlying premises of the new dispensation; their demand is for global democratic institutions to mitigate the cruelties of the global market.) The terrorists made use of that trust. They rode the flow of the world's aerial circulatory system like lethal viruses.

With growing ferocity, officials from the President on down have described the bloody deeds as acts of war. But, unless a foreign government turns out to have directed the operation (or, at least, to have known and approved its scope in detail and in advance), that is a category mistake. The metaphor of war—and it is more metaphor than description—ascribes to the perpetrators a dignity they do not merit, a status they cannot claim, and a strength they do not possess. Worse, it points toward a set of responses that could prove futile or counterproductive. Though the death and destruction these acts caused were on the scale of war, the acts themselves were acts of terrorism, albeit on a wholly unprecedented level. From 1983 until last week, according to the *Times,* ten outrages had each claimed the lives of more than a hundred people. The worst—the destruction of an Air-India 747 in 1985—killed three hundred and twenty-nine people; the Oklahoma City bombing, which killed a hundred and sixty-eight, was the seventh worst. Last week's carnage surpassed that of any of these by an order of magnitude. It was also the largest violent taking of life on American soil on any day since the Civil War, including December 7, 1941. And in New York and Washington, unlike at Pearl Harbor, the killed and maimed were overwhelmingly civilians.

The tactics of the terrorists were as brilliant as they were depraved. The nature of those tactics and their success—and there is no use denying that what they did was, on its own terms, successful—points up the weakness of the war metaphor. Authorities estimated last week that "as many as" fifty people may have been involved. The terrorists brought with them nothing but knives and the ability to fly a jumbo jet already in the air. How do you take "massive military action" against the infrastructure of a stateless, compartmentalized "army" of fifty, or ten times fifty, whose weapons are rental cars, credit cards, and airline tickets?

The scale of the damage notwithstanding, a more useful metaphor than war is crime. The terrorists of September 11th are outlaws within a global polity. They may enjoy the corrupt protection of a state (and corruption, like crime, can be ideological or spiritual as well as pecuniary in motive). But they do not constitute or control a state and do not even appear to aspire to control one. Their status and numbers are such that the task of dealing with them should be viewed as a police matter, of the most urgent kind. As with all criminal fugitives, the essential job is to find out who and where they are. The goal of foreign and military policy must be to induce recalcitrant governments to coöperate, a goal whose attainment may or may not entail the use of force but cannot usefully entail making general war on the peoples such governments rule and in some cases (that of Afghanistan, for example) oppress. Just four months ago, at a time when the whole world was aware both of the general intentions of the terrorist Osama bin Laden and of the fact that the Afghan government was harboring him, the United States gave the Taliban a forty-three-million-dollar grant for banning poppy cultivation. The United States understands that on September 11th the line between the permissible and the impermissible shifted. The Taliban must be made to understand that, too.

As for America's friends, they have rallied around us with alacrity. On Wednesday, the NATO allies, for the first time ever, invoked the mutual-defense clause of the alliance's founding treaty, formally declaring that "an armed attack" against one—and what happened on September 11th, whether you call it terrorism or war, was certainly an armed attack—constitutes an attack against all. This gesture of solidarity puts to shame the contempt the Bush Administration has consistently shown for international treaties and instruments, including those in areas relevant to the fight against terrorism, such as small-arms control, criminal justice, and nuclear proliferation. By now, it ought to be clear to even the most committed ideologues of the Bush Administration that the unilateralist approach it was pursuing as of last Tuesday is in urgent need of reevaluation. The world will be policed collectively or it will not be policed at all.

OPEN LETTER TO
PRESIDENT BUSH:
"LEAD THE WORLD TO VICTORY"

Project for the New American Century

SEPTEMBER 20, 2001

The Honorable George W. Bush
President of the United States
Washington, DC

Dear Mr. President,

We write to endorse your admirable commitment to "lead the world to victory" in the war against terrorism. We fully support your call for "a broad and sustained campaign" against the "terrorist organizations and those who harbor and support them." We agree with Secretary of State Powell that the United States must find and punish the perpetrators of the horrific attack of September 11, and we must, as he said, "go after terrorism wherever we find it in the world" and "get it by its branch and root." We agree with the Secretary of State that U.S. policy must aim not only at finding the people responsible for this incident, but must also target those "other groups out there that mean us no good" and "that have conducted attacks previously against U.S. personnel, U.S. interests and our allies."

In order to carry out this "first war of the 21st century" successfully, and in order, as you have said, to do future "generations a favor by coming together and whipping terrorism," we believe the following steps are necessary parts of a comprehensive strategy.

Osama bin Laden

We agree that a key goal, but by no means the only goal, of the current war on terrorism should be to capture or kill Osama bin Laden, and to de-

---

The Project for the New American Century was established in the spring of 1997 as a nonprofit educational organization "whose goal is to promote American global leadership." Its chairman is William Kristol, who is the editor of *The Weekly Standard*.

stroy his network of associates. To this end, we support the necessary military action in Afghanistan and the provision of substantial financial and military assistance to the anti-Taliban forces in that country.

Iraq

We agree with Secretary of State Powell's recent statement that Saddam Hussein "is one of the leading terrorists on the face of the Earth. . . ." It may be that the Iraqi government provided assistance in some form to the recent attack on the United States. But even if evidence does not link Iraq directly to the attack, any strategy aiming at the eradication of terrorism and its sponsors must include a determined effort to remove Saddam Hussein from power in Iraq. Failure to undertake such an effort will constitute an early and perhaps decisive surrender in the war on international terrorism. The United States must therefore provide full military and financial support to the Iraqi opposition. American military force should be used to provide a "safe zone" in Iraq from which the opposition can operate. And American forces must be prepared to back up our commitment to the Iraqi opposition by all necessary means.

Hezbollah

Hezbollah is one of the leading terrorist organizations in the world. It is suspected of having been involved in the 1998 bombings of the American embassies in Africa, and implicated in the bombing of the U.S. Marine barracks in Beirut in 1983. Hezbollah clearly falls in the category cited by Secretary Powell of groups "that mean us no good" and "that have conducted attacks previously against U.S. personnel, U.S. interests and our allies." Therefore, any war against terrorism must target Hezbollah. We believe the administration should demand that Iran and Syria immediately cease all military, financial, and political support for Hezbollah and its operations. Should Iran and Syria refuse to comply, the administration should consider appropriate measures of retaliation against these known state sponsors of terrorism.

Israel and the Palestinian Authority

Israel has been and remains America's staunchest ally against international terrorism, especially in the Middle East. The United States should fully support our fellow democracy in its fight against terrorism. We should insist that the Palestinian Authority put a stop to terrorism emanating from territories under its control and imprison those planning terrorist attacks against Israel. Until the Palestinian Authority moves against terror, the United States should provide it no further assistance.

U.S. Defense Budget

A serious and victorious war on terrorism will require a large increase in defense spending. Fighting this war may well require the United States to engage a well-armed foe, and will also require that we remain capable of defending our interests elsewhere in the world. We urge that there be no hesitation in requesting whatever funds for defense are needed to allow us to win this war.

There is, of course, much more that will have to be done. Diplomatic efforts will be required to enlist other nations' aid in this war on terrorism. Economic and financial tools at our disposal will have to be used. There are other actions of a military nature that may well be needed. However, in our judgment the steps outlined above constitute the minimum necessary if this war is to be fought effectively and brought to a successful conclusion. Our purpose in writing is to assure you of our support as you do what must be done to lead the nation to victory in this fight.

Sincerely,

William Kristol, Richard V. Allen, Gary Bauer, Jeffrey Bell, William J. Bennett, Rudy Boschwitz, Jeffrey Bergner, Eliot Cohen, Seth Cropsey, Midge Decter, Thomas Donnelly, Nicholas Eberstadt, Hillel Fradkin, Aaron Friedberg, Francis Fukuyama, Frank Gaffney, Jeffrey Gedmin, Reuel Marc Gerecht, Charles Hill, Bruce P. Jackson, Eli S. Jacobs, Michael Joyce, Donald Kagan, Robert Kagan, Jeane Kirkpatrick, Charles Krauthammer, John Lehman, Clifford May, Martin Peretz, Richard Perle, Norman Podhoretz, Stephen P. Rosen, Randy Scheunemann, Gary Schmitt, William Schneider, Jr.; Richard H. Shultz, Henry Sokolski, Stephen J. Solarz, Vin Weber, Leon Wieseltier, Marshall Wittmann

A YEAR LATER: WHAT THE RIGHT AND LEFT HAVEN'T LEARNED

Marc Cooper

This first anniversary of 9/11 marks not only a horrific tragedy, but also a year of tragically missed opportunities—for both the right and the left.

For the right, September 11 offered the possibility of transcending a national case of smug insularity. I had hoped that the crumbled twin towers, like any near-death experience, would have generated some soul-searching reflection. The unprecedented attack against civilians on our own soil could have led to a realization that we, indeed, are not so different from those suffering peoples we read about "over there" or "out there"; that Americans—like Somalis or Rwandans—can also die senselessly and in massive, shocking numbers.

September 11 granted the opportunity for the American right to take a less jingoistic, less selfish, more internationalist view of the globe. Not that we had to apologize for the cowardly attack on New York, nor that we somehow provoked the assault. But rather a deeper comprehension that America, while more powerful and prosperous, is just one more country among many and in no way exempt from the travails and sacrifices that too many thought happened only in places whose names we cannot even pronounce.

The possibility existed, on the right, to at least review, if not revise, American foreign policy in the Middle East. There might have been some understanding that traditional U.S. support for autocratic, undemocratic regimes from Saudi Arabia to Egypt, while in no way justifying or producing the 9/11 attacks, allows them to resonate sympathetically with angry and desperate millions.

Domestically, the attacks produced a spontaneous outpouring of mutual solidarity and community compassion. People were ready to sacrifice and to give selflessly. Twenty years of Reaganite individualism appeared to melt overnight as millions of Americans seemed to once again believe that collective solutions could and should work—that caring could even occasionally trump greed.

Marc Cooper is a columnist for the *L.A. Weekly* and a contributing editor to *The Nation,* where he hosts the nationally syndicated program *RadioNation.* His latest book is *Pinochet and Me, A Chilean Anti-Memoir.* This article was originally published with the title "A Year Later: Only Fear and Loathing Remain" in the *L.A. Weekly* issue of September 13–19, 2002.

Not that I expected a political conversion of the conservative right, any en masse desertion from the ramparts of the free market. But maybe some sort of public-works program? Maybe rebuilding parts of our crumbling urban infrastructure or an accelerated public-health program for 50 million uninsured— if for no other reason, at least in the name of disaster preparedness or homeland security?

None of this, of course, came to pass. Instead we got more tax breaks for the wealthy, and piggish corporate handouts to the airlines and insurance companies. (Illinois Congresswoman Jan Shakowsky told me that lobbyists for the airlines were worming their way through Capitol Hill a mere 24 hours after the World Trade Center attacks.)

And when the world extended its heart to a wounded America, the Bush administration turned its back. You're either with us or against us. And either way, we really don't care. The neoconservatives who dominate the administration saw an opening to advance a unilateralist Pax Americana and have given that project their all.

The ABM treaty was ripped up, and accelerated NATO expansion—under U.S. tutelage—was shoved down the Russians' throats. (And now we are shocked to learn that President Putin is cutting long-term deals with the Iraqis.) The Strangelovian chorus around Don Rumsfeld revived the macabre principle of nuclear first strikes. Real arms control is off the table. The green light for one more binge of military spending flashes brightly.

We demanded that the entire world submit to our concept of the war on terrorism, but the U.S. has gone AWOL on the war for the environment. The Kyoto accords are just one more victim of September 11.

The just and measured military response to the attacks, the absolutely necessary move to dismember al Qaeda and to deny it further sanctuary by the Taliban, somehow slid into an undefined and unaccountable endless war. With the Middle East now at a volatile tipping point, the administration cannot find its voice to so much as criticize Israeli settlers' developments on occupied land, but instead aims to toss matches at gasoline by launching an unprovoked and unjustifiable war against Saddam Hussein.

What the political right has learned in this last year, then, is only to cynically wrap itself in the flag, to further advance its narrow political agenda at home and its reckless hegemonic vision abroad by keeping Americans shrouded in fear.

UNFORTUNATELY, THE political left has also shirked its responsibilities and just as equally avoided learning anything from this catastrophe.

September 11 revealed America, for once, as victim instead of victimizer.

The left's Manichean view that only two forces—American imperialism and appropriate reaction against it—shape world events was no longer viable.

The left might have seen that American military deployment is not a priori evil. Virtually none of the dire predictions the left made about the war in Afghanistan have come to pass. The U.S. has not (unfortunately) occupied the country. Millions were not driven out or killed or forced into famine. American ground troops have not been dragged into a Vietnam-like quagmire. The regime we have put into power is not worse than—or the same as—the Taliban. It's backward and corrupt, but it's better. Civilians were killed—as they are in all wars. (The Salvadoran guerrillas—heroes to the left—once boasted of their successful assassination of dozens of civilian mayors of poor rural towns.) But there was no targeting, no carpet-bombing, of Afghan civilians.

If it wished, the left could have seen an America that had matured and progressed over the last 50 years. It could have taken pride in an America that didn't lock up millions of Arab-Americans, where the level of hate crimes barely flickered upward. And while Attorney General Ashcroft has strained to stretch and snap constitutional guarantees, a resilient American civil society and a democratic, if flawed, court system have offered effective resistance. Two American citizens have been stripped of their legal rights and declared enemy combatants. That's two Americans too many. But it is only two. This is not martial law. This is not fascism. This is not Chile or Argentina or East Germany—not even close.

Especially for the left, September 11 offered a unique opportunity to come back home, to find commonality and identification with a society from which too many progressives and radicals have felt alienated and estranged. In the suffering of September 11, the American left might have taken the hand of its fellow Americans and together searched—at least for a moment—for what unites rather than divides us.

But American leftists are surprisingly ready to brand those who depart from their views as "fascists." The left, already tiny and isolated, has too frequently derived its industrial-strength self-righteousness from its own marginality. The left actually fears engagement with the broader society around it. It chooses self-loathing. Or, better, the loathing of all those common folk in whose name and interests it claims to be "struggling." So when millions of ordinary Americans, shocked and frightened by September 11, and moved by the scale of the human tragedy, and wanting to *do something,* put out a flag, the American left responded too often not with compassion, but with scorn.

What has been truly staggering over the past year has been the dogmatic refusal of much of the left to simply say "yes." Yes, America was attacked. Yes, we unequivocally mourn the unprovoked death of 3,000 fellow citizens. Yes, the window washers, the cooks, the secretaries and, yes, even the stockbrokers who were incinerated that morning a year ago were guilty of absolutely nothing, except showing up to work on time.

Instead, from the left, we get a steady stream of "yes/buts." Yes, to all the above—*but* we killed more people in Vietnam. Or yes, but we created Osama bin Laden (a patent lie). Or yes, but we starved more babies in Iraq. Or yes, but . . . well, you fill in the blank: But what about the oil pipelines? But what about covering for the Saudis? And so on and so forth ad nauseam. Every possible explanation from the left except the one obvious and true explanation right before our eyes: that a conspiracy of highly educated, religiously motivated zealots—as opposed to impoverished and oppressed freedom fighters—ruthlessly massacred 3,000 of us a year ago. And would have just as easily killed 10 times as many in the same barbaric onslaught. Period.

On this anniversary of September 11, without guilt or hesitation, I mourn their deaths. And I mourn a political culture whose moral compass has been driven awry by ideological rigidity from all sides.

BETTER SAFE THAN SORRY

Mona Charen

It will be interesting to see how the debate over civil liberties and the war on terror play out now that the electorate has given President Bush such a vote of confidence. Since September 11, the left has pitched fits about military commissions, alleged attorney-client privilege infringements, telephone taps, surveillance of suspected terrorists, fingerprinting and photographing of some foreign visitors, and particularly round-ups of visa violators. Each of these measures has been met with loud objections from liberals who are convinced that the Bush administration is on the verge of creating a police state.

Others see the world differently. Instead of an out-of-control government behemoth spying on you and me in complete disregard for civil liberties, they see our domestic and foreign intelligence services as defanged watchdogs, powerless to detect or stop terrorism after decades of liberal "reforms."

No one, least of all a conservative concerned about government power, should take civil liberties protection lightly. But the liberal reforms of the past generation have gone way beyond protecting the privacy rights of American citizens—they've protected the ability of international terrorists to function in this country virtually unimpeded. Everyone now knows that FBI agent Colleen Rowley pleaded with her superiors for permission to inspect the computer of Zacharias Moussaoui, only to be told that she lacked "probable cause." If investigators had searched that laptop, they would have found the name and phone number of one the ringleaders of the September 11 plot.

This bit of recent history is raised to imply that the FBI screwed up in August 2001. Yet when the suggestion is made that perhaps the "probable cause" standard be brought down a notch, say to "reasonable suspicion," the civil-liberties types go ballistic. When the Justice Department interviewed several thousand men from Arab nations, *The New York Times* decried the "vast roundup" and the American Civil Liberties Union shrilled that this "dragnet approach . . . is likely to magnify concerns of racial and ethnic profiling. In fact, as Professor Robert Turner of the University of Virginia Law School re-

Mona Charen is a syndicated columnist and political analyst living in the Washington, D.C. area. This column was originally published with the title "The War Over the War," on November 19, 2002.

lates, interviewees were treated politely and asked, among other things, whether they had encountered any acts of bigotry.

Before September 11, and thanks to a process of emasculization stretching back to the Church committee hearings of the 1970s, the FBI and CIA were forbidden to share information. Even within the FBI, thanks to "the wall" inaugurated under Attorney General Janet Reno, a counter-terrorism agent examining a terror cell in Buffalo could not walk down the hall and chat with a criminal investigator who was looking into money laundering by the same people. The FBI was forbidden to conduct general Internet searches, or to visit public places open to all.

Seventy-five percent of the American people told the Gallup organization that the Bush administration has not gone too far in restricting civil liberties. Fifty percent thought they'd gone far enough, but 25 thought they should have been tougher. Only 11 percent thought the administration had gone too far.

What liberals are now urging is that suspected terrorists, here or abroad, be accorded the full panoply of rights we give to ordinary criminal defendants. But this judicializes war. President Bill Clinton adhered to this model and accordingly turned down an opportunity to capture bin Laden because he feared we might not have proper evidence for a criminal indictment.

But the war powers of the presidency, long respected by the courts, permit special action in the case of war. Even before September 11, bin Laden had declared war on the United States and was clearly ineligible for a criminal trial. He was morally and legally an enemy combatant. Similarly, though, President Bush has not taken any action since September 11 that was not also approved overwhelmingly by the Congress.

But the key point is this: If we err on the side of civil liberties instead of on the side of security, hundreds of thousands or millions of Americans could die. If we err on the side of security, many people will be inconvenienced and a few individuals may be wrongly imprisoned for some time. In which direction would you lean?

THE ENEMY WITHIN

Daniel Pipes

The day after 9/11, Texas police arrested two Indian Muslim men riding a train and carrying about $5,000 in cash, black hair dye and boxcutters like those used to hijack four planes just one day earlier.

[The police held the pair initially on immigration charges (their U.S. visas had expired); when further inquiry turned up credit card fraud, that kept them longer in detention. But law enforcement's real interest, of course, had to do with their possible connections to Al-Qaeda.]

To investigate this matter—and here our information comes from one of the two, Ayub Ali Khan, after he was released—the authorities put them through some pretty rough treatment.

Khan says the interrogation "terrorized" him. [He recounts how "Five to six men would pull me in different directions very roughly as they asked rapid-fire questions. . . . Then suddenly they would brutally throw me against the wall." They also asked him political questions: had he, for example, "ever discussed the situation in Palestine with friends?"]

Eventually exonerated of connections to terrorism and freed from jail, Khan is—not surprisingly—bitter about his experience, saying that he and his traveling partner were singled out on the basis of profiling. This is self-evidently correct: Had Khan not been a Muslim, the police would have had little interest in him and his boxcutters.

Khan's tribulation brings to attention the single-most delicate and agonizing issue in prosecuting the War on Terror. Does singling out Muslims for additional scrutiny serve a purpose? And if so, is it legally and morally acceptable?

In reply to the first question—yes, enhanced scrutiny of Muslims makes good sense, for several reasons:

- In the course of their assaults on Americans, Islamists—the supporters of militant Islam—have killed nearly 4,000 people since 1979. No other enemy has remotely the same record.

Daniel Pipes is director of the Middle East Forum and a columnist for the *New York Post* and *The Jerusalem Post*. He is the author of many books, most recently *Militant Islam Reaches America*. This article is an abridged version of a piece he wrote for the *New York Post* on January 24, 2003.

- Islamists are plotting to kill many more Americans, as shown by the more than one-group-a-month arrests of them since 9/11.
- While most Muslims are not Islamists and most Islamists are not terrorists, all Islamist terrorists are Muslims.
- Islamist terrorists do not appear spontaneously, but emerge from a milieu of religious sanction, intellectual justification, financial support and organizational planning.

These circumstances—and this is the unpleasant part—point to the imperative of focusing on Muslims. There is no escaping the unfortunate fact that Muslim government employees in law enforcement, the military and the diplomatic corps need to be watched for connections to terrorism, as do Muslim chaplains in prisons and the armed forces. Muslim visitors and immigrants must undergo additional background checks. Mosques require a scrutiny beyond that applied to churches and temples.

Singing out a class of persons by their religion feels wrong, if not downright un-American, prompting the question: Even if useful, should such scrutiny be permitted?

If Americans want to protect themselves from Islamist terrorism, they must temporarily give higher priority to security concerns than to civil-libertarian sensitivities.

Preventing Islamists from inflicting further damage implies the regrettable step of focusing on Muslims. Not to do so is an invitation to further terrorism.

This solemn reality suggests four thoughts:

First, as Khan's experience shows, Muslims are already subjected to added scrutiny; the time has come for politicians to catch up to reality and formally acknowledge what are now quasi-clandestine practices. Doing so places these issues in the public arena, where they can openly be debated.

Second, because having to focus heightened attention on Muslims is inherently so unpleasant, it needs to be conducted with utmost care and tact, remembering, above all, that seven out of eight Muslims are not Islamists, and fewer still are connected to terrorism.

Third, this is an emergency measure that should end with the War on Terror's end.

Finally, innocent Muslims who must endure added surveillance can console themselves with the knowledge that their security, too, is enhanced by these steps.

"FIRST THEY CAME FOR
THE MUSLIMS . . ."

Anthony Lewis

The Palmer Raids were one of the most notorious episodes in American legal history. A. Mitchell Palmer, President Woodrow Wilson's attorney general from 1919 to 1921, rounded up 3,000 allegedly "subversive" aliens for deportation. Only about 300 were actually deported, but the roundup was widely deplored as crude and lawless intimidation.

In the wake of September 11, current Attorney General John Ashcroft carried out the most sweeping roundup of aliens since the Palmer Raids. Between 1,100 and 2,000 people were arrested and detained. The exact number is unknown because the Department of Justice, after criticism grew, stopped announcing a running total. The last published figure, in November 2001, was 1,147. Perhaps in part because he put a lid of secrecy on the operation, Ashcroft's roundup has not aroused the kind of outrage that Palmer's did.

David Cole, a law professor at Georgetown University and the country's foremost civil liberties advocate in the immigration field, provided the most complete discussion of the Ashcroft sweep. In the December 2002–January 2003 *Boston Review,* he describes it as a program that used thin legal pretexts to hold aliens for extended periods so that the FBI could question and investigate them.

After days or even weeks without being given a reason for their detention, Cole wrote, most detainees were charged with minor immigration-status violations—working without authorization, for example, or taking too few courses for a student visa, neither of which would ordinarily call for such draconian treatment. Many detainees who had violated the conditions of their visas agreed to leave the country voluntarily but were nonetheless held for months more until finally being allowed to leave. As of September 2002, only four detainees had been charged with crimes related to terrorism. The clear

Anthony Lewis is a former columnist for *The New York Times.* This article was published in the spring 2003 issue of *The American Prospect.*

implication is that the real purpose was to keep people incommunicado while the FBI investigated them, a form of intimidation nor ordinarily allowed under U.S. law.

Because of pervasive secrecy, little was known about how the detainees were treated until *The New York Times* published a story by David Rohde on Jan. 20, 2003. It was datelined Karachi, Pakistan. Rohde had interviewed six Pakistani men deported from the United States after being detained in Ashcroft's sweep.

One of the men, Anser Mehmood, said he was held for four months during 2002 in solitary confinement in a windowless cell in a Brooklyn federal detention center. Two overhead fluorescent lights were on at all times. "No official from the FBI and [the Immigration and Naturalization Service (INS)] came to interview me," Mehmood said. The other five men said they had been asked only cursory questions such as, "Do you like Osama bin Laden? . . . Do you pray five times a day?"

Detainees charged with deportable offenses had secret hearings that were closed to family members, the press and the public. On orders from the attorney general, the chief immigration judge, Michael Creppy, told immigration judges to close all hearings deemed of "special interest" by the government. Those cases were not to be listed on the public docket, and their existence was not to be confirmed or denied if anyone asked. As in other matters, the Bush administration asserted the need for secrecy on the unilateral—and, in the administration's view, not-to-be-challenged—initiative of the executive branch.

The order for closed deportation hearings was challenged in two lawsuits that reached the 3rd and 6th U.S. Circuit Courts of Appeals. The two courts came to opposite conclusions. A three-judge panel of the 3rd Circuit upheld the secrecy directive by a vote of 2-to-1. Chief Judge Edward Becker said that even though a Supreme Court decision had held that the First Amendment barred closed trials, because trials had been traditionally public, there was an insufficient tradition of open immigration trials to be governed by that ruling. "Although there may be no judicial remedy for these closures," he said, "there is, as always, the powerful check of political accountability on executive discretion." It was a singularly inapposite—some might say cynical—comment given that the very secrecy at issue prevented public accountability.

A panel of the 6th Circuit held unanimously that the Creppy directive violated the First Amendment rights of the press and public to attend deportation hearings. The government could move to close particular hearings, the court said, by making a showing of security concerns to the judge; but it could not simply rule a whole class of cases out of bounds without any showing of need. The opinion, written by Judge Damon Keith, had some strong language on the role of the press and the danger of secrecy. The government has very great power to establish immigration policy and law, Keith wrote. He added:

> The only safeguard on this extraordinary governmental power is the public, deputizing the press as the guardians of their liberty. Today the executive branch seeks to take this safeguard away from the public by placing its actions beyond public scrutiny. Against noncitizens, it seeks to deport a class if it unilaterally calls them 'special interest' cases. The executive branch seeks to uproot people's lives, outside the public eye and behind a closed door.
>
> Democracies die behind closed doors. The First Amendment, through a free press, protects the people's right to know that their government acts fairly, lawfully and accurately in deportation proceedings. When government begins closing doors, it selectively controls information rightfully belonging to the people. Selective information is misinformation.

The secrecy imposed by Ashcroft was challenged in a third case, brought in the District of Columbia. The government defended the secrecy rule as required by national security. Disclosing the names of those held, it argued, would give al-Qaeda clues as to how the government was searching for terrorists. Federal District Judge Gladys Kessler rejected the argument. "The first priority of the judicial branch," she said, "must be to ensure that our government always operates within the statutory and constitutional constraints which distinguish a democracy from a dictatorship. Unquestionably, the public's interest in learning the identity of those arrested and detained is essential to verifying whether the government is operating within the bounds of law." The government appealed Kessler's decision.

IN THE atmosphere of fear after 9/11 and Ashcroft's orders to use sweeping measures against possible terrorists, INS and FBI agents inevitably made mistakes—at a high human price. Muslims, citizens as well as aliens, were picked out for treatment that was often harsh and humiliating. But because of the pervasive secrecy, only occasionally did these episodes come to public attention.

Nacer Fathi Mustafa and his father, American citizens of Palestinian descent, were on their way back home to Florida on Sept. 15, 2001, after a business trip to Mexico. At the Houston airport they were stopped by immigration agents, arrested and charged with altering their passports. The implication was that they had done so because they were terrorists. For 67 days they were held in a Texas jail. Then the government decided that there was nothing wrong with their passports after all. "What bothered me most," Nacer Mustafa said in a *New York Times* interview, "was at the end, they just said I could go. Nobody ever apologized."

Ali Erikenoglu, an American-born Muslim of Turkish descent, was at home with his family in Paterson, N.J., when four FBI agents knocked at the door late one night a year after 9/11. They had questions for him: Are you anti-Semitic? What kind of American are you? Why do you have a Bible? (He had attended a Catholic high school.) Many Muslims live in Paterson, and Erikenoglu was one of hundreds questioned on the basis of his religion. He told *Newsday:* "Not only am I terrified. I am angry. You feel essentially at their mercy. For the first time I felt like I had to justify my innocence."

M. J. Alhabeeb, a professor of economics at the University of Massachusetts Amherst, was visited in his office by an FBI agent and a campus police officer. They said they had gotten a tip that Alhabeeb had anti-American views, and they asked him to explain. Alhabeeb, a U.S. citizen who came to this country from Iraq, told *The Boston Globe* that he felt obligated to prove his loyalty by saying that his brother-in-law had been executed by Saddam Hussein's regime. "I came to this country to get away from that kind of thing," the suspicion of disloyalty, he told the *Globe*. "Every Iraqi has this fear. For Americans, it's hard to comprehend."

THE FOCUS on people of Muslim religion and Middle Eastern names was not the random work of individual agents. It was Justice Department policy. Regulations approved by Ashcroft also required that all males from 25 listed countries, who were older than 16 years of age, and who were in the United States without permanent resident status had to register with the INS. All 25 countries are Arab or Muslim, except North Korea. Those rules set off the first large-scale public protest against post–9/11 security measures in which hundreds of men, mostly from Iran, were detained when they registered in southern California in December 2002. Most were said to have violated the terms of their visas.

The government of Pakistan, which has supported American policy, especially resented the inclusion of its citizens in the registration order. Pakistani Foreign Minister Khursid Mahmud Kasuri personally visited Ashcroft and Secretary of State Colin Powell in January to protest. He suggested that the rules so offended Pakistani opinion that it was now more difficult to defend U.S. military action in Iraq.

Given the identity of the 9/11 attackers, it was not surprising that U.S. authorities have kept a more careful watch on visitors from Arab and Muslim countries. But the peremptory handling of foreigners by the Justice Department, their extended detention in many cases and the sweeping together of the plainly innocent with legitimate suspects were not only offensive to American values but likely to intensify anti-American feelings.

NOT THE WAR WE NEEDED

Barbara Ehrenreich

On the morning of September 11, 2001, I turned on the TV in my hotel room to catch the latest news about the missing intern, Chandra Levy. Maybe that's not what I wanted to see, but it's all I was likely to see on CNN, which had devoted itself almost exclusively to the case since at least July. We'd had O.J., we'd had Tonya Harding and Monica Lewinsky, and now the cable news channels were, as we liked to say that summer, "All Chandra, all the time." So the images of planes crashing into buildings, followed by buildings crashing to the earth, did not, at first, compute. If anyone had a motive, I figured in my post-traumatic stupor, it had to be Gary Condit.

The events of that morning went far beyond anything that could be handled by the usual cliché of a "wake-up call." We Americans had been lazy, willfully ignorant, and self-involved to the point of solipsism. If there was an outside world, we didn't want to know about it, unless the death of a beautiful princess was involved. And now here it was: palpable, in-your-face evidence of the existence of people unlike ourselves, people who were, in fact, murderously hostile to us and clever enough to eclipse even Chandra.

We had been following, I now realized, the plot line of innumerable horror films, in which the thoughtless teenagers party hard in some ramshackle, out of the way site until one of the group shows up dead and hideously mutilated. That is the point at which it dawns on them that they are not alone, that there is someone out there—some incomprehensible Other who wants them dead. But with the beer flowing and the hormones surging, they have no way of organizing against the threat.

Many Americans responded, in those first few months after the attack, in generous and intelligent ways. They sent aid to the victims' families; they bought up books on Islam and learned to distinguish between Arabs and Muslims, moderates and fundamentalists, Sufis and Wahhabists. In some communities, good-hearted people reached out to the Arab Americans, Sikhs, and Hindus who were suddenly facing vengeful harassment from the incorrigibly

Barbara Ehrenreich is a political essayist whose commentaries have appeared in *Time* magazine, *The Progressive, The Nation, Harper's, Z Magazine* and *Mother Jones*. Among her many books are *Blood Rites: Origins and History of the Passions of War*, and most recently, *Nickel and Dimed: On (Not) Getting By in America*. This article was originally published in the October 2002 issue of *The Progressive*.

ignorant. Churches shared Ramadan feasts with mosques; students assembled for teach-ins. We were playing a desperate game of catch-up, trying to comprehend a whole world, that of Islam, we'd dismissed as too musty and backward to bother with.

But now that we were awake, we also needed to respond—a point that the brave anti-war demonstrators who briefly flourished in the fall of '01 did not always seem to grasp. When someone declares "death to Americans"—babies and old people alike, not to mention Jews, Israelis, and possibly Christians— you've got an enemy, like it or not. I, for one, did not want to earn my frequent flyer miles wrestling with suicide-killers. With great reluctance and foreboding, I had to agree with the Bush Administration that America needed to launch a "war on terror," or at least a determined effort to apprehend the terrorists.

How to go about it, though? Terrorists, by definition, lack the obvious targets, like capital cities, government buildings, and uniformed armies. They are warriors without a state or, in this case, even a clear-cut geographical point of concentration. As it soon emerged, the presumptive comrades of the 9/11 suicide-bombers are scattered around the globe—in Saudi Arabia, Egypt, Sudan, Somalia, Germany, France, Indonesia, England, Pakistan, and the Philippines. An enormous amount of intelligence, in every sense of the word, would be required to flush them out: Cells would have to be infiltrated, prospective defectors courted, investigations launched all over the world. Plus, of course, we'd have to try to understand the roots of their bitterness and the conditions—of both poverty and thwarted middle class ambitions—that nourished them. If we wanted a real "war on terror," that is.

What we got is something very different. First, there was war against Afghanistan, which at least had the advantage of being a far more familiar type of military target than a diffuse international network of terrorists. No one can mourn the fiendish Taliban whom American and British bombs quickly displaced, but other than that, it is hard to know, a full year later, what exactly the war accomplished. Are the leaders of Al Qaeda dead or merely scattered? Have their far-flung cells been rendered headless and impotent, or were they decentralized enough to carry on independently? If the goal was to crush terrorism, there is no way of knowing whether this war succeeded.

As for Afghanistan, it is in little better shape today than it was a year ago, with hunger rampant, warlords riding high in the countryside, and most women still too fearful to emerge from their burkas. Unknown numbers of civilians—somewhere between 500 and 3,000—managed to get in the way of the bombs and the bullets, earning us the lasting enmity of their survivors. Maybe all we won was the fleeting satisfaction of countering violence with violence, however misdirected—like those traditional societies in New Guinea in which even deaths by disease were "avenged" by going to war against a neighboring village.

But at least, in Afghanistan, our leaders were still ostensibly waging a war on terrorism. For reasons unclear to the rest of the world—attention deficit disorder or possibly early-stage Alzheimer's—that project is now being dropped. Al Qaeda may still be festering on three or four continents, preparing to dispatch thousands more Americans by plane-bombs or poison. But we are gearing up for war with, of all places, Iraq.

Why not Germany, where some of the pre–9/11 plotting took place, or Saudi Arabia, which supplied fifteen of the nineteen terrorists? Or, if the idea is to topple headstrong, potentially roguish leaders who have the means of mass destruction at their fingertips, why not Pakistan, North Korea, India, or Sharon's belligerent Israel? There are no known connections between Saddam Hussein and Osama bin Laden, aside from a history of mutual dislike, and no reason to start a new war when the old one is nowhere near finished. One can't help suspect that our leaders sense they've gotten nowhere at all in the war against terrorism, and are eager to change the subject.

Whatever motivates current U.S. foreign policy—oil, domestic politics, or the Oedipal rage of a lackluster son—it isn't likely to make us any safer. The war in Afghanistan, combined with Bush's meek stance toward Sharon, has already convinced Muslims throughout the world that their lives have no value to America's leaders. An invasion of Iraq and the attendant "collateral damage" will harden the impression that the United States is pursuing its own kind of jihad—against the Islamic world. Inevitably, a generation of young Muslims in Riyadh or Cairo or Hamburg will seek martyrdom by taking out some of us.

So here we are, caught inside the horror film we know so well from the screen. 9/11 awakened us briefly from our fantasies of sex and murder and weight loss to the existence of an implacably hostile Other. But like the partying teens in the movies, the people in charge can't seem to figure out a way of responding that doesn't recklessly escalate the danger.

EIGHT

THE BUSH DOCTRINE

"We have to put a shingle outside our door saying, 'Superpower Lives Here,' no matter what the Soviets do."
—*Colin Powell, then chairman of the Joint Chiefs, as the cold war was ending in 1989*

"How do you capitalize on these opportunities?"
—*Condaleezza Rice, U.S. National Security Advisor, to her staff in the wake of September 11th*

"Part of the Bush administration clearly believes that as a superpower, we must take advantage of this opportunity to change the world for the better, and we don't need to go out of our way to accommodate alliances, partnerships, or friends in the process, because that would be too constraining. . . . [But, relying almost solely on ad hoc] coalitions of the willing, is fundamentally, fatally flawed. As we've seen in the debate about Iraq, it's already given us an image of arrogance and unilateralism, and we're paying a very high price for that image. If we get to the point where everyone secretly hopes the United States gets a black eye because we're so obnoxious, then we'll be totally hamstrung in the war on terror. We'll be like Gulliver with the Lilliputians."
—*Brent Scowcroft, former U.S. National Security Advisor, March 8, 2003*

WHAT TO DO ABOUT IRAQ

Robert Kagan and William Kristol

W hat next in the war on terrorism? We hear from many corners that it is still too early to ask this question. If you mention the word Iraq, respectable folks at the State Department and on *The New York Times* op-ed page get red-faced. After all, the mission in Afghanistan is not over. The destruction of Osama bin Laden and the al Qaeda network is not finished. And even when these goals are accomplished, they say, we won't even begin to think about Iraq until we've taken care of Somalia, the Philippines, Yemen, Indonesia—and Antarctica, and the moon.

All this strikes us as an elaborate stratagem for avoiding the hard decision to confront Saddam Hussein. Yes, it is essential to capture bin Laden and destroy al Qaeda. It is necessary to stabilize Afghanistan and back a functioning government there. And, yes, we have to roll up the al Qaeda operations in other troublesome parts of the world.

But none of this precludes dealing with Iraq, or makes the obligation of dealing with Iraq less urgent. The United States can, after all, walk and chew gum at the same time. The Iraqi threat is enormous. It gets bigger with every day that passes. And it can't wait until we finish tying up all the "loose ends." For one thing, those loose ends are not just minor details. If bin Laden has left Central Asia, he'll be hard to find. Who knows how long it may take? Meanwhile, history moves on, and the clock is ticking in Iraq. If too many months go by without a decision to move against Saddam, the risks to the United States may increase exponentially. And after September 11, those risks are no longer abstract. Ultimately, what we do or do not do in the coming months about Saddam Hussein's regime in Iraq will decisively affect our future security.

And it will determine more than that. Whether or not we remove Saddam Hussein from power will shape the contours of the emerging world order, perhaps for decades to come. Either it will be a world order conducive to our lib-

Robert Kagan is a senior associate at the Carnegie Endowment for International Peace and a contributing editor at *The New Republic* and *The Weekly Standard*. He served in the State Department from 1985 to 1988. His new book is *Of Paradise and Power: America vs. Europe in the New World Order*. William Kristol is editor of *The Weekly Standard*. He coedited with Kagan the book *Present Dangers: Crisis and Opportunity in American Foreign and Defense Policy*. This article was published in the January 21, 2002 issue of *The Weekly Standard*.

eral democratic principles and our safety, or it will be one where brutal, well-armed tyrants are allowed to hold democracy and international security hostage. Not to take on Saddam would ensure that regimes implicated in terror and developing weapons of mass destruction will be a constant—and growing—feature of our world. Destroying Osama bin Laden and al Qaeda is, obviously, very important. Dealing with other sponsors of terrorism—Iran in particular—is crucial. But, in the near-future, Iraq is the threat and the supreme test of whether we as a nation have learned the lesson of September 11.

THE AMAZING thing about the current "debate" over Iraq is that no one disputes the nature of the threat. Everyone agrees that, as Al Gore's former national security adviser Leon Fuerth puts it, "Saddam Hussein is dangerous and likely to become more so," that he "is a permanent menace to his region and to the vital interests of the United States."

No one questions, furthermore, the basic facts about Saddam Hussein's weapons programs:

• According to U.N. weapons inspectors and western intelligence agencies, Iraq possesses the necessary components and technical knowledge to build nuclear bombs in the near future. A report prepared by the German intelligence services in December 2000, based on defectors' reports, satellite imagery, and aerial surveillance, predicted that Iraq will have three nuclear bombs by 2005. But that may be too optimistic. Before the Gulf War no one had a clue how far advanced Saddam's nuclear weapons program was. According to the Federation of American Scientists, even with an intrusive inspections regime, "Iraq might be able to construct a nuclear explosive before it was detected." Today, no one knows how close Saddam is to having a nuclear device. What we do know is that every month that passes brings him closer to the prize.

• The chemical weapon VX is the most toxic poison known to man. Ten milligrams—one drop—can kill a human being. In the mid-1990s, Iraq admitted producing VX in large quantities. When U.N. inspectors left Iraq at the end of 1998, they believed Iraq maintained 41 different sites capable of producing VX in a matter of weeks. They also believed Iraq possessed enough precursor materials to produce over 200 tons of the poison, enough to kill hundreds of thousands, if not millions, of people. A year ago, U.S. officials told *The New York Times* that Iraq had rebuilt "a series of factories that the United States has long suspected of producing chemical and biological weapons." A year later, who knows how many of those factories are operational?

• The Federation of American Scientists reports that Iraq possesses the equipment, the know how, and the materials to produce "350 liters of weapons-grade anthrax" a week. In the five years before Desert Storm, Iraq produced 8,500 liters of anthrax and managed to place 6,500 liters in various munitions. We can only imagine how much anthrax Saddam Hussein may have at his disposal today.

NOR IS there any doubt that, after September 11, Saddam's weapons of mass destruction pose a kind of danger to us that we hadn't fully grasped before. In the 1990s, much of the complacency about Saddam, both in Washington and in Europe, rested on the assumption that he could be deterred. Saddam was not a madman, the theory went, and would not commit suicide by actually using the weapons he was so desperately trying to obtain. Some of us, it's true, had our doubts about this logic. The issue seemed to us not so much whether we could deter Saddam, but whether he could deter us: If Saddam had had nuclear weapons in 1991, would we have gone to war to drive him from Kuwait?

But after September 11, we have all been forced to consider another scenario. What if Saddam provides some of his anthrax, or his VX, or a nuclear device to a terrorist group like al Qaeda? Saddam could help a terrorist inflict a horrific attack on the United States or its allies, while hoping to shroud his role in the secrecy of cutouts and middlemen. How in the world do we deter that? To this day we don't know who provided the anthrax for the post-September 11 attacks. We may never know for sure.

What we do know is that Saddam is an ally to the world's terrorists and always has been. He has provided safe haven to the infamous Abu Nidal. Reliable reports from defectors and former U.N. weapons inspectors have confirmed the existence of a terrorist training camp in Iraq, complete with a Boeing 707 for practicing hijackings, and filled with non-Iraqi radical Muslims. We know, too, that Mohamed Atta, the ringleader of September 11, went out of his way to meet with an Iraqi intelligence official a few months before he flew a plane into the World Trade Center. As Leon Fuerth understates, "There may well have been interaction between Mr. Hussein's intelligence apparatus and various terrorist networks, including that of Osama bin Laden."

SO THERE is no debate about the facts. No one doubts the nature of the threat Saddam poses. Most even agree that, as former national security adviser Samuel R. Berger says, "the goal . . . should be getting rid of Saddam Hussein." Leon Fuerth recently wrote that Saddam "and his government must be ripped out of Iraq if we are ever to be secure and if the sufferings of the Iraqi people are ever to abate."

Tough talk from a Clintonista. But when it comes to actually doing something about Saddam, suddenly it's a different story. Fuerth, Berger, Madeleine Albright, and Tom Daschle and a host of other Democrats (with the increasingly notable and honorable exception of Joseph Lieberman) insist over and over again that no matter how much of a threat Saddam may pose, no matter how necessary it may be to "rip" him out of Iraq—nevertheless we should not do it.

Here is Daschle, in late December: "A strike against Iraq would be a mistake. It would complicate Middle Eastern diplomacy. . . . I think we have to keep the pressure on Iraq in a collective way, with our Arab allies. Unilateralism is a very dangerous concept. I don't think we should ever act unilaterally." What's more, the Iraq doves claim, removing Saddam would be a diversion from the war against al Qaeda, and the cure would be worse than the disease.

This is nonsense. It is almost impossible to imagine any outcome for the world both plausible and worse than the disease of Saddam with weapons of mass destruction. A fractured Iraq? An unsettled Kurdish situation? A difficult transition in Baghdad? These may be problems, but they are far preferable to leaving Saddam in power with his nukes, VX, and anthrax. As for the other arguments, the effort to remove Saddam from power would no more be a "diversion" from the war on al Qaeda than the fight against Hitler was a "diversion" from the fight against Japan. Can it really be that this great American superpower, much more powerful than in 1941, cannot fight on two fronts at the same time against dangerous but second-rate enemies?

And as for the issue of unilateral versus multilateral action, we would prefer that the United States act together with friends and allies in any attack on Iraq. We believe others will indeed join us if we demonstrate our serious intention to oust Saddam—the British and some other Europeans, as well as Turkey and other states in the Middle East. But whether they join us or not, there is too much at stake for us to be deterred by the pro forma objections of, say, Saudi Arabia or France.

ON ONE point, we agree with some of the critics. We doubt that the so-called "Afghanistan model" of airstrikes combined with very limited U.S. ground troops, and dependence on a proxy force, can be counted on as sufficient for Iraq. The United States should support Ahmad Chalabi and the Iraqi National Congress—they are essential parts of any solution in Iraq. But we cannot count on the Iraqi opposition to win this war. Nor can we count on precision bombing and U.S. Special Forces alone to do the job. American ground forces in significant number are likely to be required for success in

Iraq. At the least, we need to be prepared to use such forces, and for a number of reasons.

First, there is the special problem posed by Saddam's weapons of mass destruction. Any attack on Iraq must succeed quickly. There is no time to repeat the pattern in Afghanistan of trying a little of this and a little of that and seeing what works. In the Afghan war, it was a change of strategy after three weeks that eventually turned the tide against the Taliban. We don't have the luxury of early mistakes in Iraq. As soon as any attack begins, Saddam will be sorely tempted to launch a chemical or biological attack on one of his neighbors, probably Israel. Any U.S. attack will have to move with lightning speed to destroy or secure sites from which such an Iraqi strike could be launched.

But even then, as the Gulf War demonstrated, it is almost impossible to locate every Scud missile in the Iraqi desert before it is fired. A key element of American strategy must therefore aim at affecting the decision-making process of Saddam's top commanders in the field. Whether or not they carry out an order from Saddam to launch a chemical or biological weapon at Israel may depend on their perception of whether Saddam and his regime are likely to survive. If the size and speed of an American invasion make it clear, in the first hours, that Saddam is finished, an Iraqi commander may think twice before making himself an accomplice to Saddam's genocidal plans. We believe it is essential that the effort to remove Saddam not be a drawn-out affair.

American troops on the ground will be important for another reason. The best way to avoid chaos and anarchy in Iraq after Saddam is removed is to have a powerful American occupying force in place, with the clear intention of sticking around for a while. We have already begun to see the price of not having such a force in Afghanistan. In Iraq, even more than in Afghanistan, the task of nation-building will be crucial. We don't want a vacuum of power in Iraq. We don't want Iran playing games in Iraq. We don't want Turkey worried that it will be left alone to deal with the Kurdish question. The United States will have to make a long-term commitment to rebuilding Iraq, and that commitment cannot be fulfilled without U.S. troops on the ground.

Although we hear only about the risks of such action, the benefits could be very substantial. A devastating knockout blow against Saddam Hussein, followed by an American-sponsored effort to rebuild Iraq and put it on a path toward democratic governance, would have a seismic impact on the Arab world—for the better. The Arab world may take a long time coming to terms with the West, but that process will be hastened by the defeat of the leading anti-western Arab tyrant. Once Iraq and Turkey—two of the three most important Middle Eastern powers—are both in the pro-western camp, there is a reasonable chance that smaller powers might decide to jump on the band-wagon.

WE ARE aware that many will find all this too much to stomach. Ground forces? Occupation? Nation-building? Democratization and westernization in the Arab world? Can't we just continue to "contain" Saddam? Or can't we just drop some bombs, let the Iraqis fight it out, and then beat it home? The answer is, we can't. And if we haven't learned this much from September 11, then all that we lost on that day will have been lost in vain.

It is past time for the United States to step up and accept the real respon-sibilities and requirements of global leadership. We've already tried the alternative. During the 1990s, those who argued for limiting American in-volvement overseas, for avoiding the use of ground troops, for using force in a limited way and only as a last resort, for steering clear of nation-building, for exit strategies and burden-sharing—those who prided themselves on their prudence and realism—won the day. When the World Trade Center was at-tacked in 1993, when former President Bush was almost assassinated by Sad-dam Hussein in Kuwait, when bin Laden and al Qaeda bombed U.S. embassies and the USS *Cole,* the Clinton administration took the cautious approach. A few missile strikes here and there, a few sting operations. But when confronted with the choice of using serious force against al Qaeda, or really helping the Iraqi opposition and moving to drive Saddam Hussein from power, President Clinton and his top advisers flinched. And most Republi-cans put little sustained pressure on the Clinton administration to act other-wise. The necessary actions were all deemed too risky. The administration, supported by most of the foreign policy establishment, took the "prudent" course. Only now we know that it was an imprudent course. The failure of the United States to take risks, and to take responsibility, in the 1990s paved the way to September 11.

It is a tough and dangerous decision to send American soldiers to fight and possibly die in Iraq. But it is more horrible to watch men and women leap to their deaths from flaming skyscrapers. If we fail to address the grave threats we know exist, what will we tell the families of future victims? That we were "prudent"?

The problem today is not just that failure to remove Saddam could some-day come back to haunt us. At a more fundamental level, the failure to remove Saddam would mean that, despite all that happened on September 11, we as a nation are still unwilling to shoulder the responsibilities of global leader-ship, even to protect ourselves. If we turn away from the Iraq challenge—be-cause we fear the use of ground troops, because we don't want the job of putting Iraq back together afterwards, because we would prefer not to be deeply involved in a messy part of the world   then we will have made a momentous and fateful decision. We do not expect President Bush to make that choice. We expect the president will courageously decide to destroy Saddam's regime. No step would contribute more toward shaping a world order in which our people and our liberal civilization can survive and flourish.

STATE OF THE UNION SPEECH:
THE AXIS OF EVIL

President George W. Bush

President George W. Bush introduced his concept of an "axis of evil, arming to threaten the peace of the world" during his State of the Union address before a joint session of Congress on January 29, 2002. The following is an excerpt from his address.

Our cause is just, and it continues. Our discoveries in Afghanistan confirmed our worst fears, and showed us the true scope of the task ahead. We have seen the depth of our enemies' hatred in videos, where they laugh about the loss of innocent life. And the depth of their hatred is equaled by the madness of the destruction they design. We have found diagrams of American nuclear power plants and public water facilities, detailed instructions for making chemical weapons, surveillance maps of American cities, and thorough descriptions of landmarks in America and throughout the world.

What we have found in Afghanistan confirms that, far from ending there, our war against terror is only beginning. Most of the 19 men who hijacked planes on September the 11th were trained in Afghanistan's camps, and so were tens of thousands of others. Thousands of dangerous killers, schooled in the methods of murder, often supported by outlaw regimes, are now spread throughout the world like ticking time bombs, set to go off without warning.

Thanks to the work of our law enforcement officials and coalition partners, hundreds of terrorists have been arrested. Yet, tens of thousands of trained terrorists are still at large. These enemies view the entire world as a battlefield, and we must pursue them wherever they are. So long as training camps operate, so long as nations harbor terrorists, freedom is at risk. And America and our allies must not, and will not, allow it.

Our nation will continue to be steadfast and patient and persistent in the pursuit of two great objectives. First, we will shut down terrorist camps, disrupt terrorist plans, and bring terrorists to justice. And, second, we must prevent the terrorists and regimes who seek chemical, biological or nuclear weapons from threatening the United States and the world.

Our military has put the terror training camps of Afghanistan out of business, yet camps still exist in at least a dozen countries. A terrorist underworld including groups like Hamas, Hezbollah, Islamic Jihad, Jaish i Mohammed—operates in remote jungles and deserts, and hides in the centers of large cities.

While the most visible military action is in Afghanistan, America is acting elsewhere. We now have troops in the Philippines, helping to train that country's armed forces to go after terrorist cells that have executed an American, and still hold hostages. Our soldiers, working with the Bosnian government, seized terrorists who were plotting to bomb our embassy. Our Navy is patrolling the coast of Africa to block the shipment of weapons and the establishment of terrorist camps in Somalia.

My hope is that all nations will heed our call, and eliminate the terrorist parasites who threaten their countries and our own. Many nations are acting forcefully. Pakistan is now cracking down on terror, and I admire the strong leadership of President Musharraf.

But some governments will be timid in the face of terror. And make no mistake about it: If they do not act, America will.

Our second goal is to prevent regimes that sponsor terror from threatening America or our friends and allies with weapons of mass destruction. Some of these regimes have been pretty quiet since September the 11th. But we know their true nature. North Korea is a regime arming with missiles and weapons of mass destruction, while starving its citizens.

Iran aggressively pursues these weapons and exports terror, while an unelected few repress the Iranian people's hope for freedom.

Iraq continues to flaunt its hostility toward America and to support terror. The Iraqi regime has plotted to develop anthrax, and nerve gas, and nuclear weapons for over a decade. This is a regime that has already used poison gas to murder thousands of its own citizens—leaving the bodies of mothers huddled over their dead children. This is a regime that agreed to international inspections—then kicked out the inspectors. This is a regime that has something to hide from the civilized world.

States like these, and their terrorist allies, constitute an axis of evil, arming to threaten the peace of the world. By seeking weapons of mass destruction, these regimes pose a grave and growing danger. They could provide these arms to terrorists, giving them the means to match their hatred. They could attack our allies or attempt to blackmail the United States. In any of these cases, the price of indifference would be catastrophic.

We will work closely with our coalition to deny terrorists and their state sponsors the materials, technology, and expertise to make and deliver weapons of mass destruction. We will develop and deploy effective missile defenses to protect America and our allies from sudden attack. And all nations should know: America will do what is necessary to ensure our nation's security.

We'll be deliberate, yet time is not on our side. I will not wait on events, while dangers gather. I will not stand by, as peril draws closer and closer. The United States of America will not permit the world's most dangerous regimes to threaten us with the world's most destructive weapons.

Our war on terror is well begun, but it is only begun. This campaign may not be finished on our watch—yet it must be and it will be waged on our watch.

We can't stop short. If we stop now—leaving terror camps intact and terror states unchecked—our sense of security would be false and temporary. History has called America and our allies to action, and it is both our responsibility and our privilege to fight freedom's fight.

THE NEXT WORLD ORDER

Nicholas Lemann

When there is a change of command—and not just in government—the new people often persuade themselves that the old people were much worse than anyone suspected. This feeling seems especially intense in the Bush Administration, perhaps because Bill Clinton has been bracketed by a father-son team. It's easy for people in the Administration to believe that, after an unfortunate eight-year interlude, the Bush family has resumed its governance—and about time, too.

The Bush Administration's sense that the Clinton years were a waste, or worse, is strongest in the realms of foreign policy and military affairs. Republicans tend to regard Democrats as untrustworthy in defense and foreign policy, anyway, in ways that coincide with what people think of as Clinton's weak points: an eagerness to please, a lack of discipline. Condoleezza Rice, Bush's national-security adviser, wrote an article in *Foreign Affairs* two years ago in which she contemptuously accused Clinton of "an extraordinary neglect of the fiduciary responsibilities of the commander in chief." Most of the top figures in foreign affairs in this Administration also served under the President's father. They took office last year, after what they regard as eight years of small-time flyswatting by Clinton, thinking that they were picking up where they'd left off.

Not long ago, I had lunch with—sorry!—a senior Administration foreign-policy official, at a restaurant in Washington called the Oval Room. Early in the lunch, he handed me a twenty-seven-page report, whose cover bore the seal of the Department of Defense, an outline map of the world, and these words:

Defense Strategy for the 1990s:
The Regional Defense Strategy
Secretary of Defense
Dick Cheney
January 1993

Nicholas Lemann is a staff writer at *The New Yorker*. Prior to that, he worked at the *Washington Monthly, The Washington Post*, the *Texas Monthly*, and was national correspondent of *The Atlantic Monthly* from 1983 to 1998. This article was published in *The New Yorker* on April 1, 2002.

One of the difficulties of working at the highest level of government is communicating its drama. Actors, professional athletes, and even elected politicians train for years, go through a great winnowing, and then perform publicly. People who have titles like Deputy Assistant Secretary of Defense are just as ambitious and competitive, have worked just as long and hard, and are often playing for even higher stakes—but what they do all day is go to meetings and write memos and prepare briefings. How, possibly, to explain that some of the documents, including the report that the senior official handed me, which was physically indistinguishable from a high-school term paper, represent the government version of playing Carnegie Hall?

After the fall of the Berlin Wall, Dick Cheney, then the Secretary of Defense, set up a "shop," as they say, to think about American foreign policy after the Cold War, at the grand strategic level. The project, whose existence was kept quiet, included people who are now back in the game, at a higher level: among them, Paul Wolfowitz, the Deputy Secretary of Defense; Lewis Libby, Cheney's chief of staff; and Eric Edelman, a senior foreign-policy adviser to Cheney—generally speaking, a cohesive group of conservatives who regard themselves as bigger-thinking, tougher-minded, and intellectually bolder than most other people in Washington. (Donald Rumsfeld, the Secretary of Defense, shares these characteristics, and has been closely associated with Cheney for more than thirty years.) Colin Powell, then the chairman of the Joint Chiefs of Staff, mounted a competing, and presumably more ideologically moderate, effort to reimagine American foreign policy and defense. A date was set—May 21, 1990—on which each team would brief Cheney for an hour; Cheney would then brief President Bush, after which Bush would make a foreign-policy address unveiling the new grand strategy.

Everybody worked for months on the "five-twenty-one brief," with a sense that the shape of the post-Cold War world was at stake. When Wolfowitz and Powell arrived at Cheney's office on May 21st, Wolfowitz went first, but his briefing lasted far beyond the allotted hour, and Cheney (a hawk who, perhaps, liked what he was hearing) did not call time on him. Powell didn't get to present his alternate version of the future of the United States in the world until a couple of weeks later. Cheney briefed President Bush, using material mostly from Wolfowitz, and Bush prepared his major foreign-policy address. But he delivered it on August 2, 1990, the day that Iraq invaded Kuwait, so nobody noticed.

The team kept working. In 1992, the *Times* got its hands on a version of the material, and published a front-page story saying that the Pentagon envisioned a future in which the United States could, and should, prevent any other nation or alliance from becoming a great power. A few weeks of controversy ensued about the Bush Administration's hawks being "unilateral"—controversy that Cheney's people put an end to with denials and the counter-leak of an edited, softer version of the same material.

As it became apparent that Bush was going to lose to Clinton, the Cheney team's efforts took on the quality of a parting shot. The report that the senior official handed me at lunch had been issued only a few days before Clinton took office. It is a somewhat bland, opaque document—a "scrubbed," meaning unclassified, version of something more candid—but it contained the essential ideas of "shaping," rather than reacting to, the rest of the world, and of preventing the rise of other superpowers. Its tone is one of skepticism about diplomatic partnerships. A more forthright version of the same ideas can be found in a short book titled "From Containment to Global Leadership?," which Zalmay Khalilzad, who joined Cheney's team in 1991 and is now special envoy to Afghanistan, published a couple of years into the Clinton Administration, when he was out of government. It recommends that the United States "preclude the rise of another global rival for the indefinite future." Khalilzad writes, "It is a vital U.S. interest to preclude such a development— i.e., to be willing to use force if necessary for the purpose."

When George W. Bush was campaigning for President, he and the people around him didn't seem to be proposing a great doctrinal shift, along the lines of the policy of containment of the Soviet Union's sphere of influence which the United States maintained during the Cold War. In his first major foreign-policy speech, delivered in November of 1999, Bush declared that "a President must be a clear-eyed realist," a formulation that seems to connote an absence of world-remaking ambition. "Realism" is exactly the foreign-policy doctrine that Cheney's Pentagon team rejected, partly because it posits the impossibility of any one country's ever dominating world affairs for any length of time.

One gets many reminders in Washington these days of how much the terrorist attacks of September 11th have changed official foreign-policy thinking. Any chief executive, of either party, would probably have done what Bush has done so far—made war on the Taliban and Al Qaeda and enhanced domestic security. It is only now, six months after the attacks, that we are truly entering the realm of Presidential choice, and all indications are that Bush is going to use September 11th as the occasion to launch a new, aggressive American foreign policy that would represent a broad change in direction rather than a specific war on terrorism. All his rhetoric, especially in the two addresses he has given to joint sessions of Congress since September 11th, and all the information about his state of mind which his aides have leaked, indicate that he sees this as the nation's moment of destiny—a perception that the people around him seem to be encouraging, because it enhances Bush's stature and opens the way to more assertive policymaking.

Inside government, the reason September 11th appears to have been "a transformative moment," as the senior official I had lunch with put it, is not so much that it revealed the existence of a threat of which officials had previously been unaware as that it drastically reduced the American public's usual resistance to American military involvement overseas, at least for a while. The Clinton Administration, beginning with the "Black Hawk Down" operation in Mogadishu, during its first year, operated on the conviction that Americans were highly averse to casualties; the all-bombing Kosovo operation, in Clinton's next-to-last year, was the ideal foreign military adventure. Now that the United States has been attacked, the options are much broader. The senior official approvingly mentioned a 1999 study of casualty aversion by the Triangle Institute for Security Studies, which argued that the "mass public" is much less casualty-averse than the military or the civilian élite believes; for example, the study showed that the public would tolerate thirty thousand deaths in a military operation to prevent Iraq from acquiring weapons of mass destruction. (The American death total in the Vietnam War was about fifty-eight thousand.) September 11th presumably reduced casualty aversion even further.

Recently, I went to the White House to interview Condoleezza Rice. Rice's *Foreign Affairs* article from 2000 begins with this declaration: "The United States has found it exceedingly difficult to define its 'national interest' in the absence of Soviet power." I asked her whether that is still the case. "I think the difficulty has passed in defining a role," she said immediately. "I think September 11th was one of those great earthquakes that clarify and sharpen. Events are in much sharper relief." Like Bush, she said that opposing terrorism and preventing the accumulation of weapons of mass destruction "in the hands of irresponsible states" now define the national interest. (The latter goal, by the way, is new—in Bush's speech to Congress on September 20th, America's sole grand purpose was ending terrorism.) We talked in her West Wing office; its tall windows face the part of the White House grounds where television reporters do their standups. In her bearing, Rice seemed less crisply military than she does in public. She looked a little tired, but she was projecting a kind of missionary calm, rather than belligerence.

In the *Foreign Affairs* article, Rice came across as a classic realist, putting forth "the notions of power politics, great powers, and power balances" as the proper central concerns of the United States. Now she sounded as if she had moved closer to the one-power idea that Cheney's Pentagon team proposed ten years ago—or, at least, to the idea that the other great powers are now in harmony with the United States, because of the terrorist attacks, and can be induced to remain so. "Theoretically, the realists would predict that when you have a great power like the United States it would not be long before you had other great powers rising to challenge it or trying to balance against it," Rice said. "And I think what you're seeing is that there's at least a predilection this time to move to productive and coöperative relations with the United States, rather than to try to balance the United States. I actually think that statecraft matters in how it all comes out. It's not all foreordained."

Rice said that she had called together the senior staff people of the National Security Council and asked them to think seriously about "how do you capitalize on these opportunities" to fundamentally change American doctrine, and the shape of the world, in the wake of September 11th. "I really think this period is analogous to 1945 to 1947," she said—that is, the period when the containment doctrine took shape—"in that the events so clearly demonstrated that there is a big global threat, and that it's a big global threat to a lot of countries that you would not have normally thought of as being in the coalition. That has started shifting the tectonic plates in international politics. And it's important to try to seize on that and position American interests and institutions and all of that before they harden again."

The National Security Council is legally required to produce an annual document called the National Security Strategy, stating the over-all goals of American policy—another government report whose importance is great but not obvious. The Bush Administration did not produce one last year, as the Clinton Administration did not in its first year. Rice said that she is working on the report now.

"There are two ways to handle this document," she told me. "One is to do it in a kind of minimalist way and just get it out. But it's our view that, since this is going to be the first one for the Bush Administration, it's important. An awful lot has happened since we started this process, prior to 9/11. I can't give you a certain date when it's going to be out, but I would think sometime this spring. And it's important that it be a real statement of what the Bush Administration sees as the strategic direction that it's going."

It seems clear already that Rice will set forth the hope of a more dominant American role in the world than she might have a couple of years ago. Some questions that don't appear to be settled yet, but are obviously being asked, are how much the United States is willing to operate alone in foreign affairs, and how much change it is willing to try to engender inside other countries— and to what end, and with what means. The leak a couple of weeks ago of a new American nuclear posture, adding offensive capability against "rogue states," departed from decades of official adherence to a purely defensive position, and was just one indication of the scope of the reconsideration that is going on. Is the United States now in a position to be redrawing regional maps, especially in the Middle East, and replacing governments by force? Nobody thought that the Bush Administration would be thinking in such ambitious terms, but plainly it is, and with the internal debate to the right of where it was only a few months ago.

Just before the 2000 election, a Republican foreign-policy figure suggested to me that a good indication of a Bush Administration's direction in foreign affairs would be who got a higher-ranking job, Paul Wolfowitz or Richard Haass. Haass is another veteran of the first Bush Administration, and an intellectual like Wolfowitz, but much more moderate. In 1997, he published a book titled "The Reluctant Sheriff," in which he poked a little fun at Wolfowitz's famous strategy briefing of the early nineties (he called it the "Pentagon Paper") and disagreed with its idea that the United States should try to be the world's only great power over the long term. "For better or worse, such a goal is beyond our reach," Haass wrote. "It simply is not doable." Elsewhere in the book, he disagreed with another of the Wolfowitz team's main ideas, that of the United States expanding the "democratic zone of peace": "Primacy is not to be confused with hegemony. The United States cannot compel others to become more democratic." Haass argued that the United States is becoming less dominant in the world, not more, and suggested "a revival of what might be called traditional great-power politics."

Wolfowitz got a higher-ranking job than Haass: he is Deputy Secretary of Defense, and Haass is Director of Policy Planning for the State Department—in effect, Colin Powell's big-think guy. Recently, I went to see him in his office at the State Department. On the wall of his waiting room was an array of photographs of every past director of the policy-planning staff, beginning with George Kennan, the father of the containment doctrine and the first holder of the office that Haass now occupies.

It's another indication of the way things are moving in Washington that Haass seems to have become more hawkish. I mentioned the title of his book. "Using the word 'reluctant' was itself reflective of a period when foreign policy seemed secondary, and sacrificing for foreign policy was a hard case to make," he said. "It was written when Bill Clinton was saying, 'It's the economy, stupid'—not 'It's the world, stupid.' Two things are very different now. One, the President has a much easier time making the case that foreign policy matters. Second, at the top of the national-security charts is this notion of weapons of mass destruction and terrorism."

I asked Haass whether there is a doctrine emerging that is as broad as Kennan's containment. "I think there is," he said. "What you're seeing from this Administration is the emergence of a new principle or body of ideas—I'm not sure it constitutes a doctrine—about what you might call the limits of sovereignty. Sovereignty entails obligations. One is not to massacre your own people. Another is not to support terrorism in any way. If a government fails to meet these obligations, then it forfeits some of the normal advantages of sovereignty, including the right to be left alone inside your own territory. Other governments, including the United States, gain the right to intervene. In the case of terrorism, this can even lead to a right of preventive, or peremptory, self-defense. You essentially can act in anticipation if you have grounds to think it's a question of when, and not if, you're going to be attacked."

Clearly, Haass was thinking of Iraq. "I don't think the American public needs a lot of persuading about the evil that is Saddam Hussein," he said. "Also, I'd fully expect the President and his chief lieutenants to make the case. Public opinion can be changed. We'd be able to make the case that this isn't a discretionary action but one done in self-defense."

On the larger issue of the American role in the world, Haass was still maintaining some distance from the hawks. He had made a speech not long before called "Imperial America," but he told me that there is a big difference between imperial and imperialist. "I just think that we have to be a little bit careful," he said. "Great as our advantages are, there are still limits. We have to have allies. We can't impose our ideas on everyone. We don't want to be fighting wars alone, so we need others to join us. American leadership, yes; but not American unilateralism. It has to be multilateral. We can't win the war against terror alone. We can't send forces everywhere. It really does have to be a collaborative endeavor."

He stopped for a moment. "Is there a successor idea to containment? I think there is," he said. "It is the idea of integration. The goal of U.S. foreign policy should be to persuade the other major powers to sign on to certain key ideas as to how the world should operate: opposition to terrorism and weapons of mass destruction, support for free trade, democracy, markets. Integration is about locking them into these policies and then building institutions that lock them in even more."

The first, but by no means the last, obvious manifestation of a new American foreign policy will be the effort to remove Saddam Hussein. What the United States does in an Iraq operation will very likely dwarf what's been done so far in Afghanistan, both in terms of the scale of the operation itself and in terms of its aftermath.

Several weeks ago, Ahmad Chalabi, the head of the Iraqi National Congress, the Iraqi opposition party, came through Washington with an entourage of his aides. Chalabi went to the State Department and the White House to ask, evidently successfully, for more American funding. His main public event was a panel discussion at the American Enterprise Institute. Chalabi's leading supporter in town, Richard Perle, the prominent hawk and former Defense Department official, acted as moderator. Smiling and supremely confident, Perle opened the discussion by saying, "Evidence is mounting that the Administration is looking very carefully at strategies for dealing with Saddam Hussein." The war on terrorism, he said, will not be complete "until Saddam is successfully dealt with. And that means replacing his regime. . . . That action will be taken, I have no doubt."

Chalabi, who lives in London, is a charming, suave middle-aged man with a twinkle in his eye. He was dressed in a double-breasted pin-striped suit and a striped shirt with a white spread collar. Although he and his supporters argue that the Iraqi National Congress, with sufficient American support, can defeat Saddam just as the Northern Alliance defeated the Taliban in Afghanistan, this view hasn't won over most people in Washington. It isn't just that Chalabi doesn't look the part of a rebel military leader ("He could fight you for the last petit four on the tray over tea at the Savoy, but that's about it," one skeptical former Pentagon official told me), or that he isn't in Iraq. It's also that Saddam's military is perhaps ten times the size that the Taliban's was, and has been quite successful at putting down revolts over the last decade. The United States left Iraq in 1991 believing that Saddam might soon fall to an internal rebellion; Chalabi's supporters believe that Saddam is much weaker now, and that even signs that a serious operation was in the offing could finish him off. But non–true believers seem to be coming around to the idea that a military operation against Saddam would mean the deployment of anywhere from a hundred thousand to three hundred thousand American ground troops.

Kenneth Pollack, a former C.I.A. analyst who was the National Security Council's staff expert on Iraq during the last years of the Clinton Administration, recently caused a stir in the foreign-policy world by publishing an article in *Foreign Affairs* calling for war against Saddam. This was noteworthy because three years ago Pollack and two co-authors published an article, also in *Foreign Affairs,* arguing that the Iraqi National Congress was incapable of defeating Saddam. Pollack still doesn't think Chalabi can do the job. He believes that it would require a substantial American ground, air, and sea force, closer in size to the one we used in Kuwait in 1990–91 than to the one we are using now in Afghanistan.

Pollack, who is trim, quick, and crisp, is obviously a man who has given a briefing or two in his day. When I went to see him at his office in Washington, with a little encouragement he got out from behind his desk and walked over to his office wall, where three maps of the Middle East were hanging. "The only way to do it is a full-scale invasion," he said, using a pen as a pointer. "We're talking about two grand corps, two to three hundred thousand people altogether. The population is here, in the Tigris-Euphrates valley." He pointed to the area between Baghdad and Basra. "Ideally, you'd have the Saudis on board." He pointed to the Prince Sultan airbase, near Riyadh. "You could make Kuwait the base, but it's much easier in Saudi. You need to take western Iraq and southern Iraq"—pointing again—"because otherwise they'll fire Scuds at Israel and at the Saudi oil fields. You probably want to prevent Iraq from blowing up its own oil fields, so troops have to occupy them. And you need troops to defend the Kurds in northern Iraq." Point, point. "You go in as hard as you can, as fast as you can." He slapped his hand on the top of his desk. "You get the enemy to divide his forces, by threatening him in two places at once." His hand hit the desk again, hard. "Then you crush him." Smack.

That would be a reverberating blow. The United States has already re-moved the government of one country, Afghanistan, the new government is obviously shaky, and American military operations there are not completed. Pakistan, which before September 11th clearly met the new test of national unacceptability (it both harbors terrorists and has weapons of mass destruc-tion), will also require long-term attention, since the country is not wholly under the control of the government, as the murder of Daniel Pearl demon-strated, and even parts of the government, like the intelligence service, may not be entirely under the control of the President. In Iraq, if America invades and brings down Saddam, a new government must be established—an enor-mous long-term task in a country where there is no obvious, plausible new leader. The prospective Iraq operation has drawn strong objections from the neighboring nations, one of which, Russia, is a nuclear superpower. An inva-sion would have a huge effect on the internal affairs of all the biggest Middle Eastern nations: Iran, Turkey, Saudi Arabia, and even Egypt. Events have forced the Administration to become directly involved in the Israeli-Palestinian conflict, as it hadn't wanted to do. So it's really the entire region that is in play, in much the way that Europe was immediately after the Second World War.

In September, Bush rejected Paul Wolfowitz's recommendation of imme-diate moves against Iraq. That the President seems to have changed his mind is an indication, in part, of the bureaucratic skill of the Administration's con-servatives. "These guys are relentless," one former official, who is close to the high command at the State Department, told me. "Resistance is futile." The conservatives' other weapon, besides relentlessness, is intellectualism. Colin Powell tends to think case by case, and since September 11th the conserva-tives have outflanked him by producing at least the beginning of a coherent, hawkish world view whose acceptance practically requires invading Iraq. If the United States applies the doctrines of Cheney's old Pentagon team, "shaping" and expanding "the zone of democracy," the implications would extend far beyond that one operation.

The outside experts on the Middle East who have the most credibility with the Administration seem to be Bernard Lewis, of Princeton, and Fouad Ajami, of the Johns Hopkins School of Advanced International Studies, both of whom see the Arab Middle East as a region in need of radical remediation. Lewis was invited to the White House in December to brief the senior foreign-policy staff. "One point he made is, Look, in that part of the world, nothing matters more than resolute will and force," the senior official I had lunch with told me—in other words, the United States needn't proceed gingerly for fear of inflaming the "Arab street," as long as it is prepared to be strong. The senior official also recommended as interesting thinkers on the Middle East Charles Hill, of Yale, who in a recent essay declared, "Every regime of the Arab-Islamic world has proved a failure," and Reuel Marc Gerecht, of the American Enterprise Institute, who published an article in *The Weekly Standard* about the need for a change of regime in Iran and Syria. (Those goals, Gerecht told me when we spoke, could be accomplished through pressure short of an invasion.)

Several people I spoke with predicted that most, or even all, of the nations that loudly oppose an invasion of Iraq would privately cheer it on, if they felt certain that this time the Americans were really going to finish the job. One purpose of Vice-President Cheney's recent diplomatic tour of the region was to offer assurances on that matter, while gamely absorbing all the public criticism of an Iraq operation. In any event, the Administration appears to be committed to acting forcefully in advance of the world's approval. When I spoke to Condoleezza Rice, she said that the United States should assemble "coalitions of the willing" to support its actions, rather than feel it has to work within the existing infrastructure of international treaties and organizations. An invasion of Iraq would test that policy in more ways than one: the Administration would be betting that it can continue to eliminate Al Qaeda cells in countries that publicly opposed the Iraq operation.

When the Administration submitted its budget earlier this year, it asked for a forty-eight-billion-dollar increase in defense spending for fiscal 2003, which begins in October, 2002. Much of that sum would go to improve military pay and benefits, but ten billion dollars of it is designated as an unspecified contingency fund for further operations in the war on terrorism. That's probably at least the initial funding for an invasion of Iraq.

This spring, the Administration will be talking to other countries about the invasion, trying to secure basing and overflight privileges, while Bush builds up a rhetorical case for it by giving speeches about the unacceptability of developing weapons of mass destruction. A drama involving weapons inspections in Iraq will play itself out over the spring and summer, and will end with the United States declaring that the terms that Saddam offers for the inspections, involving delays and restrictions, are unacceptable. Then, probably in the late summer or early fall, the enormous troop positioning, which will take months, will begin. The Administration obviously feels confident that the United States can effectively parry whatever aggressive actions Saddam takes during the troop buildup, and hopes that its moves will destabilize Iraq enough to cause the Republican Guard, the military key to the country, to turn against Saddam and topple him on its own. But the chain of events leading inexorably to a full-scale American invasion, if it hasn't already begun, evidently will begin soon.

Lewis (Scooter) Libby, who was the principal drafter of Cheney's future-of-the-world documents during the first Bush Administration, now works in an office in the Old Executive Office Building, overlooking the West Wing, where he has a second, smaller office. A packet of public-relations material prompted by the recent paperback publication of his 1996 novel, *The Apprentice,* quotes the *Times'* calling him "Dick Cheney's Dick Cheney," which seems like an apt description: he appears absolutely sure of himself, and, whether by coincidence or as a result of the influence of his boss, speaks in a tough, confidential, gravelly rumble. Like Condoleezza Rice and Bush himself, he gives the impression of having calmly accepted the idea that the project of war and reconstruction which the Administration has now taken on may be a little exhausting for those charged with carrying it out but is unquestionably right, the only truly prudent course.

When I went to see Libby, not long ago, I asked him whether, before September 11th, American policy toward terrorism should have been different. He went to his desk and got out a large black loose-leaf binder, filled with typewritten sheets interspersed with foldout maps of the Middle East. He looked through it for a long minute, formulating his answer.

"Let us stack it up," he said at last. "Somalia, 1993; 1994, the discovery of the Al Qaeda–related plot in the Philippines; 1993, the World Trade Center, first bombing; 1993, the attempt to assassinate President Bush, former President Bush, and the lack of response to that, the lack of a serious response to that; 1995, the Riyadh bombing; 1996, the Khobar bombing; 1998, the Kenyan embassy bombing and the Tanzanian embassy bombing; 1999, the plot to launch millennium attacks; 2000, the bombing of the *Cole.* Throughout this period, infractions on inspections by the Iraqis, and eventually the withdrawal of the entire inspection regime; and the failure to respond significantly to Iraqi incursions in the Kurdish areas. No one would say these challenges posed easy problems, but if you take that long list and you ask, 'Did we respond in a way which discouraged people from supporting terrorist activities, or activities clearly against our interests? Did we help to shape the environment in a way which discouraged further aggressions against U.S. interests?,' many observers conclude no, and ask whether it was then easier for someone like Osama bin Laden to rise up and say credibly, 'The Americans don't have the stomach to defend themselves. They won't take casualties to defend their interests. They are morally weak.' "

Libby insisted that the American response to September 11th has not been standard or foreordained. "Look at what the President has done in Afghanistan," he said, "and look at his speech to the joint session of Congress"—meaning the State of the Union Message, in January. "He made it clear that it's an important area. He made it clear that we believe in expanding the zone of democracy even in this difficult part of the world. He made it clear that we stand by our friends and defend our interests. And he had the courage to identify those states which present a problem, and to begin to build consensus for action that would need to be taken if there is not a change of behavior on their part. Take the Afghan case, for example. There are many other courses that the President could have taken. He could have waited for juridical proof before we responded. He could have engaged in long negotiations with the Taliban. He could have failed to seek a new relationship with Pakistan, based on its past nuclear tests, or been so afraid of weakening Pakistan that we didn't seek its help. This list could go on to twice or three times the length I've mentioned so far. But, instead, the President saw an opportunity to refashion relations while standing up for our interests. The problem is complex, and we don't know yet how it will end, but we have opened new prospects for relations not only with Afghanistan, as important as it was as a threat, but with the states of Central Asia, Pakistan, Russia, and, as it may develop, with the states of Southwest Asia more generally."

We moved on to Iraq, and the question of what makes Saddam Hussein unacceptable, in the Administration's eyes. "The issue is not inspections," Libby said. "The issue is the Iraqis' promise not to have weapons of mass destruction, their promise to recognize the boundaries of Kuwait, their promise not to threaten other countries, and other promises that they made in '91, and a number of U.N. resolutions, including all the other problems I listed. Whether it was wise or not—and that is the subject of debate—Iraq was given a second chance to abide by international norms. It failed to take that chance then, and annually for the next ten years."

"What's your level of confidence," I asked him, "that the current regime will, in fact, change its behavior in a way that you will be satisfied by?"

He ran his hand over his face and then gave me a direct gaze and spoke slowly and deliberately. "There is no basis in Iraq's past behavior to have confidence in good-faith efforts on their part to change their behavior."

NO MEETING IN PRAGUE

Robert Novak

Seated next to Donald Rumsfeld last Tuesday as he drank coffee at the Pentagon with reporters in the Godfrey Sperling group, I asked the secretary of defense to confirm or deny whether suicide hijacker Mohammed Atta met an Iraqi secret service operative in Prague and then returned to the U.S. to die in the Sept. 11 terrorist attacks. "I don't know whether he did or didn't," Rumsfeld replied.

In those eight words, the defense chief confirmed published reports that there is no evidence placing the presumed leader of the terrorist attacks in the Czech capital, with or without Iraqi spymaster Ahmed al-Ani. His alleged presence in Prague is the solitary piece of evidence that could link Saddam Hussein's dictatorial regime to the carnage at the World Trade Center.

Rumsfeld followed his terse response to my Atta question with an explanation of why it really doesn't matter. A connection with the Sept. 11 attacks, he made clear, is not necessary to justify U.S. military action against Iraq to remove Saddam from power. The cause for war is alleged development of weapons of mass destruction by the Baghdad regime.

Why, then, do ardent attack-Iraq advocates outside the government—William Safire, Kenneth Adelman, James Woolsey—cling to the reality of the imagined meeting in Prague? Because President Bush will be alone in the world if he orders the attack on Iraq without a casus belli tied to Sept. 11.

It is impossible to prove whether Atta was or was not in Prague in April 2001 as first claimed last October by Czech Interior Minister Stanislav Gross, but these are the facts: Atta definitely did not travel under his own name back and forth from the Czech Republic. The 9/11 terrorists always traveled in the open. For Atta to have used an assumed name would be a radically different method of operation. The sole evidence for the Prague meeting is the word of Czech officials, who are now divided and confused.

The CIA does not want to be dragged into public debate with *New York Times* columnist Safire, and its officials insist that "we don't have a dog in that fight." In truth, however, cool-headed analysts at Langley see no evi-

Robert Novak's syndicated column appears in over 300 newspapers. He is also a television commentator who is a member of CNN's *Capitol Gang* and frequently appears on *Crossfire* and other programs. This column was originally published on May 13, 2002.

dence whatever of the Prague meeting and in their gut believe it did not take place.

Is there evidence of any other Iraqi connection to 9/11? "I don't discuss intelligence information," Rumsfeld replied. In fact, there is none. Responding to my question whether it made any difference to U.S. policy on Iraq, he said, "I don't know how to answer it." He then depicted terrorist nations—"Iran, Iraq, Syria, Libya, I suppose North Korea"—working together to develop weapons of mass destruction. This could mean the death of "potentially hundreds of thousands of people."

Responding to another reporter's question, Rumsfeld asserted "the nuclear weapon . . . is somewhat more difficult to develop, maintain and use than, for example, biological weapons," adding, "I would elevate the biological risk." Indeed, nobody in the U.S. government takes seriously statements by former Israeli Prime Minister Benjamin Netanyahu on his recent visit to Washington that Iraq can deliver a nuclear bomb here in a suitcase.

Whether the Iraqis possess biological capability is unknown and debatable. Former U.N. arms inspector Scott Ritter contends Iraq's biowar factories and their equipment were destroyed. Without "acquisition of a large amount of new technology," Ritter has said, "I don't see Iraq being able to do high quality production on a large scale of bioweapons." While Ritter's detractors are many, his allegations never have been contradicted.

There is justifiable belief in the White House, the Pentagon and even the State Department that the world—not to mention Iraq—will be better and safer without Saddam Hussein in Baghdad. But that does not justify to the world the overthrowing of a government.

That is why ace reporter Bill Safire writes column after column insisting that the Prague meeting took place. That is also why national security expert Ken Adelman insisted April 29 on CNN's "Crossfire" that Atta "went 7,000 miles to meet with one of the Iraq intelligence officers in Prague." Even if it never happened, the meeting is essential to justify a U.S. attack on Iraq.

REMARKS AT WEST POINT: "NEW THREATS REQUIRE NEW THINKING"

President George W. Bush

This is an excerpted version of President George W. Bush's June 1, 2002 speech to the graduating class at the United States Military Academy at West Point, N.Y., where he laid out his vision of taking preemptive action to protect America's security.

History has [. . .] issued its call to your generation. In your last year, America was attacked by a ruthless and resourceful enemy. You graduate from this Academy in a time of war, taking your place in an American military that is powerful and is honorable. Our war on terror is only begun, but in Afghanistan it was begun well.

I am proud of the men and women who have fought on my orders. America is profoundly grateful for all who serve the cause of freedom, and for all who have given their lives in its defense. This nation respects and trusts our military, and we are confident in your victories to come.

This war will take many turns we cannot predict. Yet I am certain of this: Wherever we carry it, the American flag will stand not only for our power, but for freedom. Our nation's cause has always been larger than our nation's defense. We fight, as we always fight, for a just peace—a peace that favors human liberty. We will defend the peace against threats from terrorists and tyrants. We will preserve the peace by building good relations among the great powers. And we will extend the peace by encouraging free and open societies on every continent.

Building this just peace is America's opportunity, and America's duty. From this day forward, it is your challenge, as well, and we will meet this challenge together. You will wear the uniform of a great and unique country. America has no empire to extend or utopia to establish. We wish for others only what we wish for ourselves—safety from violence, the rewards of liberty, and the hope for a better life.

In defending the peace, we face a threat with no precedent. Enemies in the past needed great armies and great industrial capabilities to endanger the

American people and our nation. The attacks of September the 11th required a few hundred thousand dollars in the hands of a few dozen evil and deluded men. All of the chaos and suffering they caused came at much less than the cost of a single tank. The dangers have not passed. This government and the American people are on watch, we are ready, because we know the terrorists have more money and more men and more plans.

The gravest danger to freedom lies at the perilous crossroads of radicalism and technology. When the spread of chemical and biological and nuclear weapons, along with ballistic missile technology—when that occurs, even weak states and small groups could attain a catastrophic power to strike great nations. Our enemies have declared this very intention, and have been caught seeking these terrible weapons. They want the capability to blackmail us, or to harm us, or to harm our friends—and we will oppose them with all our power.

For much of the last century, America's defense relied on the Cold War doctrines of deterrence and containment. In some cases, those strategies still apply. But new threats also require new thinking. Deterrence—the promise of massive retaliation against nations—means nothing against shadowy terrorist networks with no nation or citizens to defend. Containment is not possible when unbalanced dictators with weapons of mass destruction can deliver those weapons on missiles or secretly provide them to terrorist allies.

We cannot defend America and our friends by hoping for the best. We cannot put our faith in the word of tyrants, who solemnly sign non-proliferation treaties, and then systematically break them. If we wait for threats to fully materialize, we will have waited too long.

Homeland defense and missile defense are part of stronger security, and they're essential priorities for America. Yet the war on terror will not be won on the defensive. We must take the battle to the enemy, disrupt his plans, and confront the worst threats before they emerge. In the world we have entered, the only path to safety is the path of action. And this nation will act.

Our security will require the best intelligence, to reveal threats hidden in caves and growing in laboratories. Our security will require modernizing domestic agencies such as the FBI, so they're prepared to act, and act quickly, against danger. Our security will require transforming the military you will lead—a military that must be ready to strike at a moment's notice in any dark corner of the world. And our security will require all Americans to be forward-looking and resolute, to be ready for preemptive action when necessary to defend our liberty and to defend our lives.

The work ahead is difficult. The choices we will face are complex. We must uncover terror cells in 60 or more countries, using every tool of finance, intelligence and law enforcement. Along with our friends and allies, we must oppose proliferation and confront regimes that sponsor terror, as each case requires. Some nations need military training to fight terror, and we'll provide it. Other nations oppose terror, but tolerate the hatred that leads to terror—and that must change. We will send diplomats where they are needed, and we will send you, our soldiers, where you're needed.

All nations that decide for aggression and terror will pay a price. We will not leave the safety of America and the peace of the planet at the mercy of a few mad terrorists and tyrants. We will lift this dark threat from our country and from the world.

Because the war on terror will require resolve and patience. It will also require firm moral purpose. In this way our struggle is similar to the Cold War. Now, as then, our enemies are totalitarians, holding a creed of power with no place for human dignity. Now, as then, they seek to impose a joyless conformity, to control every life and all of life.

America confronted imperial communism in many different ways—diplomatic, economic, and military. Yet moral clarity was essential to our victory in the Cold War. When leaders like John F. Kennedy and Ronald Reagan refused to gloss over the brutality of tyrants, they gave hope to prisoners and dissidents and exiles, and rallied free nations to a great cause.

Some worry that it is somehow undiplomatic or impolite to speak the language of right and wrong. I disagree. Different circumstances require different methods, but not different moralities. Moral truth is the same in every culture, in every time, and in every place. Targeting innocent civilians for murder is always and everywhere wrong. Brutality against women is always and everywhere wrong. There can be no neutrality between justice and cruelty, between the innocent and the guilty. We are in a conflict between good and evil, and America will call evil by its name. By confronting evil and lawless regimes, we do not create a problem, we reveal a problem. And we will lead the world in opposing it.

As we defend the peace, we also have an historic opportunity to preserve the peace. We have our best chance since the rise of the nation state in the 17th century to build a world where the great powers compete in peace instead of prepare for war. The history of the last century, in particular, was dominated by a series of destructive national rivalries that left battlefields and graveyards across the Earth. Germany fought France, the Axis fought the Allies, and then the East fought the West, in proxy wars and tense standoffs, against a backdrop of nuclear Armageddon.

Competition between great nations is inevitable, but armed conflict in our world is not. More and more, civilized nations find ourselves on the same side—united by common dangers of terrorist violence and chaos. America has, and intends to keep, military strengths beyond challenge—thereby, making the destabilizing arms races of other eras pointless, and limiting rivalries to trade and other pursuits of peace.

Today the great powers are also increasingly united by common values, instead of divided by conflicting ideologies. The United States, Japan and our Pacific friends, and now all of Europe, share a deep commitment to human freedom, embodied in strong alliances such as NATO. And the tide of liberty is rising in many other nations.

[. . . .]

The 20th century ended with a single surviving model of human progress, based on non-negotiable demands of human dignity, the rule of law, limits on the power of the state, respect for women and private property and free speech and equal justice and religious tolerance. America cannot impose this vision—yet we can support and reward governments that make the right choices for their own people. In our development aid, in our diplomatic efforts, in our international broadcasting, and in our educational assistance, the United States will promote moderation and tolerance and human rights. And we will defend the peace that makes all progress possible.

When it comes to the common rights and needs of men and women, there is no clash of civilizations. The requirements of freedom apply fully to Africa and Latin America and the entire Islamic world. The peoples of the Islamic nations want and deserve the same freedoms and opportunities as people in every nation. And their governments should listen to their hopes.

A truly strong nation will permit legal avenues of dissent for all groups that pursue their aspirations without violence. An advancing nation will pursue economic reform, to unleash the great entrepreneurial energy of its people. A thriving nation will respect the rights of women, because no society can prosper while denying opportunity to half its citizens. Mothers and fathers and children across the Islamic world, and all the world, share the same fears and aspirations. In poverty, they struggle. In tyranny, they suffer. And as we saw in Afghanistan, in liberation they celebrate.

America has a greater objective than controlling threats and containing resentment. We will work for a just and peaceful world beyond the war on terror.

THE NEW BUSH DOCTRINE

Richard Falk

President Bush's June graduation address to the cadets at West Point has attracted attention mainly because it is the fullest articulation, so far, of the new strategic doctrine of pre-emption. The radical idea being touted by the White House and Pentagon is that the United States has the right to use military force against any state that is seen as hostile or makes moves to acquire weapons of mass destruction—nuclear, biological or chemical. The obvious initial test case for pre-emption is Iraq, whose government the United States is continually threatening to overthrow, either on the model of the displacement of the Taliban in Afghanistan or by some other method. Washington's war plans have evidently not been finalized, and whether the intimations of war—despite the numerous objections voiced by neighboring governments and European allies—are to be taken literally is still unclear.

What is certain, and scary, is the new approach to the use of international force beneath the banner of counterterrorism and in the domestic climate of fervent nationalism that has existed since September 11. This new approach repudiates the core idea of the United Nations Charter (reinforced by decisions of the World Court in The Hague), which prohibits any use of international force that is not undertaken in self-defense after the occurrence of an armed attack across an international boundary or pursuant to a decision by the U.N. Security Council. When Iraq conquered and annexed Kuwait in 1990, Kuwait was legally entitled to act in self-defense to recover its territorial sovereignty even without any U.N. authorization. And the United States and others were able to join Kuwait in bolstering its prospects, thereby acting in what international lawyers call collective self-defense.

Back in 1956, when the American commitment to this Charter effort to limit the discretion of states to the extent possible was still strong, the U.S. government surprised its allies and adversaries by opposing the Suez war of Britain, France and Israel because it was a nondefensive use of force against Egypt, despite the provocations associated at the time with Nasser's anti-

Richard Falk, chair of the board of the Nuclear Age Peace Foundation, is the author of many books, including, most recently, *The Great Terror War*. He is Albert G. Milbank Professor Emeritus of International Law at Princeton University and Visiting Distinguished Professor in Global and International Studies at the University of California, Santa Barbara. This article was originally published in the July 15, 2002 issue of *The Nation*.

Israeli, anti-Western militancy. This legal commitment had evolved by stages in the period after World War I, and when the surviving leaders of Germany and Japan were prosecuted for war crimes, "crimes against the peace" were declared to be even worse than atrocities committed in the course of the war. The task of the Charter was to give this concept as clear limits as possible.

Pre-emption, in contrast, validates striking first—not in a crisis, as was done by Israel with plausible, if not entirely convincing, justification in the 1967 war, when enemy Arab troops were massing on its borders after dismissing the U.N. war-preventing presence, but on the basis of shadowy intentions, alleged potential links to terrorist groups, supposed plans and projects to acquire weapons of mass destruction, and anticipations of possible future dangers. It is a doctrine without limits, without accountability to the U.N. or international law, without any dependence on a collective judgment of responsible governments and, what is worse, without any convincing demonstration of practical necessity.

It is true that the reality of the mega-terrorist challenge requires some rethinking of the relevance of rules and restraints based on conflict in a world of territorial states. The most radical aspects of the Al Qaeda challenge are a result of its nonterritorial, concealed organizational reality as a multistate network. Modern geopolitics was framed to cope with conflict, and relations among sovereign states; the capacity of a network with modest resources to attack and wage a devastating type of war against the most powerful state does require acknowledgment that postmodern geopolitics needs a different structure of security.

Postmodernity refers here to preoccupations that can no longer be reduced to territorial dimensions. This contrasts with "modernity," born internationally in 1648 at the Peace of Westphalia with the emergence of the secular sovereign state, and a world politics that could be understood by reference to territorial ambitions and defense. For Osama bin Laden, the focus has been on nonterritorial empowerment via mega-terrorism, with the vision of an Islamic *umma* replacing the modern, Western-inspired structure of distinct sovereign states. For George W. Bush, the emphasis has been on carrying the retaliatory war to the networked enemy concealed in some sixty countries, and on declaring war against all those nonstate forces around the world.

To respond to the threat of mega-terrorism does require some stretching of international law to accommodate the reasonable security needs of sovereign states. Prior cross-border military reactions to transnational terrorism over the years by the United States, India, Israel and others were generally tolerated by the U.N. and international public opinion because they seemed proportionate and necessary in relation to the threats posed, and the use of force relied upon was in its essence reactive, not anticipatory. International law was bent to serve these practical imperatives of security, but not broken. But the Bush doctrine of pre-emption goes much further, encroaching on highly dangerous terrain. It claims a right to abandon rules of restraint and of law patiently developed over the course of centuries, rules governing the use of force in relation to territorial states, not networks.

To propose abandoning the core legal restraint on international force in relations among states is to misread the challenge of September 11. It permits states to use force nondefensively against their enemies, thereby creating a terrible precedent. There is every reason to think that containment and deterrence remain effective ways to approach a state that threatens unwarranted expansion. There is no evidence to suggest that Iraq cannot be deterred, and its pattern of behavior in relation to its war against Iran in the 1980s, as well as its conquest and annexation of Kuwait in 1990, were based on a rational calculation of gains that, when proved incorrect, led to a reversal of policy. Brutal and oppressive as the regime in Iraq is, it was accepted until 1990 as a geopolitical ally of sorts. As a state, it acts and behaves normally, that is, by weighing benefits and costs. It is surrounded and threatened by superior force, and any attempt to lash out at neighbors or others would almost certainly result in its immediate and total destruction. There is no reason whatsoever to think that deterrence and containment would not succeed, even should Baghdad manage to acquire biological, chemical or nuclear weapons. Deterrence and containment succeeded in relation to the Soviet Union for more than four decades, under far more demanding circumstances.

What is at stake with pre-emption, as tied to the "axis of evil" imagery, is more hidden and sinister. What is feared in Washington, I think, is not aggressive moves by these countries but their acquisition of weapons of mass destruction that might give them a deterrent capability with respect to the United States and other nations. Since the end of the cold war the United States has enjoyed the luxury of being undeterred in world politics. It is this circumstance that makes Bush's "unilateralism" particularly disturbing to other countries, and it must be understood in relation to the moves of the Pentagon, contained in a report leaked last December, to increase U.S. reliance on nuclear weapons in a variety of strategic circumstances. At West Point, Bush declared with moral fervor that "our enemies . . . have been caught seeking these terrible weapons." It never occurs to our leaders that these weapons are no less terrible when in the hands of the United States, especially when their use is explicitly contemplated as a sensible policy option. There is every reason for others to fear that when the United States is undeterred it will again become subject to "the Hiroshima temptation," in which it might threaten and use such weapons in the absence of any prospect of retaliation.

Bush goes further, combining empire with utopia, reminding his West Point audience that "the twentieth century ended with a single surviving model of human progress based on nonnegotiable demands of human dignity, the rule of law, limits on the power of the state, respect for women and private property, and free speech and equal justice and religious tolerance." The clear intention is to suggest that America is the embodiment of this model. And while Bush does concede that "America cannot impose this vision," he does propose that it "can support and reward governments that make the right choices for their own people," and presumably punish those that don't. Not only does the United States claim the right to global dominance but it also professes to have the final answers for societal well-being, seeming to forget its homeless, its crowded and expanding prisons, its urban blight and countless other domestic reminders that ours may not be the best of all possible worlds, and especially not for all possible peoples.

This vision of postmodern geopolitics is underwritten by a now-familiar strong message of evangelical moralism. Bush notes that "some worry that it is somehow undiplomatic or impolite to speak the language of right and wrong. I disagree," and adds that "moral truth is the same in every culture, in every time, and in every place." Such moral absolutism is then applied to the current global realities. Bush insists that "we are in a conflict between good and evil, and America will call evil by its name. By confronting evil and lawless regimes, we do not create a problem, we reveal a problem. And we will lead the world in opposing it." Aside from occupying the moral high ground, which exempts America from self-criticism or from addressing the grievances others have with respect to our policies, such sentiments imply a repudiation of dialogue and negotiation. As there can be no acceptable compromise with the forces of evil, there can be no reasonable restraint on the forces of good. We may lament fundamentalism in the Islamic world and decry the fulminations of Osama bin Laden, but what about our own?

In contemplating this geopolitical vision for the future, one wonders what happened to candidate Bush's rhetoric about the importance of "humility" in defining America's role in the world. Of course, he was then trying to downsize the humanitarian diplomacy attributed (mostly wrongly) to Clinton/Gore, but the contrast in tone and substance is still striking. One wonders whether the heady atmosphere of the Oval Office has fed these geopolitical dreams, or whether our President, well-known for his lack of foreign policy knowledge, has been manipulated into a crusading mode by bureaucratic hawks who seized the opportunity so tragically provided by September 11.

Many influential Americans share this dream of a borderless global empire but adopt less forthright language. For instance, the respected military commentator Eliot Cohen, writing in a recent issue of *Foreign Affairs,* suggests that "in the twenty-first century, characterized like the European Middle Ages by a universal (if problematic) high culture with a universal language, the U.S. military plays an extraordinary and inimitable role. It has become, whether Americans or others like it or not, the ultimate guarantor of international order." To make such an assertion without apology or justification is to say, in effect, that the imperial role of the United States is no longer in doubt, or even subject to useful debate. To acknowledge that it makes no difference whether Americans or others support this destiny is to reveal the fallen condition of democracy and the irrelevance of international public opinion. Along similar lines of presupposition, Stephen Biddle, in the same issue of *Foreign Affairs,* observes in relation to the problems of the Balkans, and specifically Kosovo, that "Americans do well in crusades," but then he cites Cohen and Andrew Bacevich to the effect that "they are not suited . . . to the dirty work of imperial policing to secure second- or third-tier interest." Such an outlook makes the fact of an American global empire a foregone conclusion.

But pre-emption and double standards were not the only troubling features of this postmodern geopolitical outlook outlined in the West Point speech. There is first of all the issue of global dominance, a project to transform the world order from its current assemblage of sovereign states in the direction of a postmodern (that is, nonterritorial) global empire administered from Washington. Bush misleadingly assured the graduating cadets that "America has no empire to extend or utopia to establish," and then went on to describe precisely such undertakings. The President mentioned that past rivalries among states arose because of their efforts to compete with one another, but insisted that the future will be different because of American military superiority: "America has, and intends to keep, military strengths beyond challenge, thereby making the destabilizing arms races of other eras pointless, and limiting rivalries to trade and other pursuits of peace." The ambition here is breathtaking and imperial—nothing less than to remind all states that the era of self-help security is essentially over, that America is the global gendarme, and that other states should devote their energies to economic and peaceful pursuits, leaving overall security in Washington's hands. One can only wonder at the reaction of foreign ministries around the world, say in Paris or Beijing, when confronted by this language, which dramatically diminishes traditional sovereign rights, as well as by the reinforcing moves to scrap the ABM treaty, to build a missile defense shield and to plan for the weaponization of space.

Whether it is Bush at West Point, or the more sedate writings of the foreign policy elite writing for each other, or for that matter intelligent and progressive criticism, useful analysis must proceed from the postmodern realization that we are addressing a menacing nonstate adversary concealed in a network that is simultaneously everywhere and nowhere. These new circumstances definitely call for new thinking that adapts international law and global security in an effective and constructive manner. But the adjustments called by Bush do not meet the specific challenge of mega-terrorism, and they unleash a variety of dangerous forces. What is needed is new thinking that sees the United States as part of a global community that is seeking appropriate ways to restore security and confidence, but builds on existing frameworks of legal restraints and works toward a more robust U.N., while not claiming for itself an imperial role to make up the rules of world politics as it goes along. Given the bipartisan gridlock that has gripped the country since September 11, positive forms of new thinking will almost certainly come, if they come, from pressures exerted by the citizenry outside the Beltway. We as citizens have never faced a more urgent duty.

INSIDE THE SECRET WAR COUNCIL

Mark Thompson

If you could slip past the soldiers toting M-16s at the door, the Pentagon's 17 miles of corridors might remind you a little of an inner-city apartment building: every other door is plastered with alarms, fortified latches and ugly combination locks. You would buzz past signs bearing mysterious acronyms— WELCOME ABOARD J3/SMOO—that blur rather than clarify what's cooking behind those doors. Asked what goes on inside, officers get that "Don't ask, don't tell" look—and don't even reply.

So it was alarming when one secret agency's work spilled into the open recently, only to be dismissed by almost everyone involved. Meeting last month in Defense Secretary Donald Rumsfeld's private conference room, a group called the Defense Policy Board heard an outside expert, armed only with a computerized PowerPoint briefing, denounce the Saudis for being "active at every level of the terror chain, from planners to financiers, from cadre to foot soldier, from ideologist to cheerleader." Such claims have been on the rise since September 11, when 15 of the 19 hijackers were Saudis. Relatives of those killed in the attacks filed suit last week seeking $1 trillion from, among others, three Saudi princes who allegedly gave money to groups supporting the terrorists. But the Pentagon briefer's solution to the Saudi problem was provocative in the extreme: Washington should declare the Saudis the enemy, he said, and threaten to take over the oil wells if the kingdom doesn't do more to combat Islamic terrorism. "I though the briefing was ridiculous," a board member said, "a waste of time, and the quicker he left the better." When the briefing leaked to the press, it sent diplomatic tremors ricocheting to Riyadh.

This is the kind of outside-the-Pentagon-box thinking that routinely takes place inside the Defense Policy Board, the Secretary's private think tank in a building where helmets often trump thinking caps. Chaired by Richard Perle—a Reagan Pentagon official whose hard-line views won him the title "Prince of Darkness"—the board gives its 31 unpaid members something every Washington player wants: unrivaled access without accountability. Perle uses his post as a springboard for his unilateralist, attack-Iraq views to

Mark Thompson covers the Pentagon, the CIA, and arms-control issues as national security correspondent for *Time* magazine. This article was originally published on August 26, 2002 in *Time*.

try to whip the Bush Administration into action. But despite its name, the board does not make policy. As the Saudi episode shows, it can do something far scarier: give a false impression of it.

That wasn't the point when the Pentagon set up the board in 1985 to advise the Defense Secretary on key issues of the day. Unlike many of the department's ancillary agencies, it toils in the shadows. Its classified sessions combine outsiders' briefings with internal discussions on military deep-think. Is the Pentagon buying the right weapons? Is the U.S. cozying up to the right nations? Is the U.S. military pivoting properly in the wake of Sept. 11? Each member's access to top-secret U.S. intelligence gives the board's opinions a cachet not enjoyed by Washington's public think tanks, which chum out reports on such topics.

Beneath the brass plating, the board's impact is harder to discern. Though its quarterly, two-day sessions take place in Rumsfeld's inner sanctum, the board's two full-time employees run the operation from another floor. Perle sets the agenda and briefers. The members take no votes, do not strive to reach a consensus and write no reports. Instead, they wrap up each session sharing what they have learned with Rumsfeld, who is free to ignore what he is told.

Rumsfeld has given some of the Republican right's most outspoken (and forsaken) hawks a place to nest. Among them: former Vice President Dan Quayle, former House Speaker Newt Gingrich and ex-CIA and Pentagon boss James Schlesinger. True, there are also centrist Republican members, like Henry Kissinger. But the board has an undeniably hard-nosed tilt: seven of the 31 members have ties to the conservative Hoover Institution at Stanford University. Previous boards had at least a few members with views sharply opposed to the incumbent Administration—Perle was on the board through Clinton's two terms—but this one lacks Democratic firepower. The sprinkling of Democrats includes token moderates and those, like former CIA chief James Woolsey, who are hawks within their own party.

In effect, the board has become Perle's podium. It rarely achieved any notice before he assumed the chairmanship last year, but now his position there lends weight to his public pronouncements. His recent column in the *London Daily Telegraph* titled "Why the West Must Strike First Against Saddam Hussein" identified him as "chairman of the Defence Policy Board."

But board members, serving at Rumsfeld's pleasure, are like a choir preaching to the pastor. The board "is just another p.r. shop for Rumsfeld," says Michael O'Hanlon, a defense expert with the Brookings Institution. "It gives his ideas more currency." O'Hanlon admits, though, that he would "jump at the chance" to serve on it for the access to the nation's top Defense officials. But Lawrence Korb, a Reagan-era Pentagon official, thinks the board is "a net loss for the Administration because many people think it represents the Administration's views."

That's why when Perle invited Laurent Murawiec, a senior Rand Corp. analyst, to give a briefing on the kingdom, it stirred up such a fuss. "I didn't know what he was going to say, but he had done some serious research on Saudi Arabia," Perle told *Time*. In fact, Murawiec's work for Rand has not focused on Saudi Arabia.

Perle's ignorance of Murawiec's talking points matched his unfamiliarity with his briefer's past. Back in the 1980s, Murawiec worked for political extremist and perpetual presidential aspirant Lyndon LaRouche as an editor of LaRouche's magazine, *Executive Intelligence Review.* By the end of last week, LaRouche was denouncing both his former associate and "suspected Israeli agent Richard Perle" for pushing the U.S. toward war with the Islamic world.

None of Murawiec's arguments were relayed to Rumsfeld, Perle said last week from his vacation home in France. While Perle considers such unvarnished views important "to stimulate discussion," he points out that the board also received a more mainline briefing from U.S. intelligence officials.

When the substance of Murawiec's briefing leaked to *The Washington Post,* U.S. officials tried to pretend it had never happened. Rumsfeld dismissed it as the musings of "a French national, a resident alien," and Secretary of State Colin Powell phoned the Saudi Foreign Minister to calm down his government. Rand issued a statement distancing itself from its analyst's comments. Murawiec wasn't talking.

Rumsfeld made clear last week that despite the Saudi embarrassment, he values the board's advice. "I have always benefited from a competition of ideas," he said. But in a Pentagon known for marching in lockstep to Rumsfeld's orders, the surreal Saudi briefing left some thinking that Perle's board should focus next on picking its targets—and the weapons used against them—more wisely.

Editors' note: Starting in March 2003, questions arose surrounding Richard Perle's business dealings as an advisor to Global Crossing, the telecommunications firm; Autonomy, a software developer doing work for the Defense and Homeland Security Departments; and Trireme Partners, a venture capital firm that invests in companies related to national security. As a "special government employee," Perle is subject to government ethics rules prohibiting him from using public office for private gain. After Democratic Congressman John Conyers called for an official investigation, Perle announced, on March 27, that he was stepping down as chairman of the Defense Policy Board, but vowed to stay on as a member. Conyers called that move "a small step in the right direction." According to the Center for Public Integrity, a watchdog group, at least ten of the board's thirty-one members are executives or lobbyists with private companies that have tens of billions worth of contracts with the Defense Department and other government agencies.

NINE

THE COUNTRY DEBATES GOING TO WAR

"The problem here is that there will always be some uncertainty about how quickly he can acquire nuclear weapons. But we don't want the smoking gun to be a mushroom cloud."
—*Condoleezza Rice, U.S. National Security Advisor, Sept. 8, 2002*

"The way Mr. Bush and Mr. Blair are conducting their campaign against Iraq means doomed if you do, doomed if you don't."
—*Tariq Aziz, Iraqi deputy prime minister, Sept. 15, 2002*

"If we go in unilaterally, or without the full weight of international organizations behind us, if we go in with a very sparse number of allies, if we go in without an effective information operation . . . we're likely to supercharge recruiting for al-Qaeda."
—*retired Gen. Wesley Clark, former NATO Supreme Commander, September 9, 2002*

"It's pretty interesting that all the generals see it the same way, and all the others who have never fired a shot, and are hot to go to war, see it another. . . . We are about to do something that will ignite a fuse in this region. . . . [W]e will rue the day we ever started."
—*Marine Gen. Anthony Zinni, former head of U.S. Central Command, October 17, 2002*

THE WAR ON WHAT? THE WHITE HOUSE AND THE DEBATE ABOUT WHOM TO FIGHT NEXT

Nicholas Lemann

Just a few hours after the terrorist attacks of September 11th, President Bush made a brief appearance at Barksdale Air Force Base, in Louisiana. "Make no mistake," he said, "the United States will hunt down and punish those responsible for these cowardly acts." It was a clear, specific reaction to the attacks. Nine days later, when Bush came to the Capitol to give his first full speech about the attacks, before a joint session of Congress, he identified Al Qaeda as their perpetrator and laid out a detailed course of action: the United States would go after Al Qaeda all over the world; Al Qaeda's chief governmental protector, the Taliban, would have to coöperate fully, or it would be removed from power in Afghanistan. Then he added two memorable, but less specific, sentences: "Our war on terror begins with Al Qaeda, but it does not end there. It will not end until every terrorist group of global reach has been found, stopped, and defeated."

The difference between retaliating against Al Qaeda and declaring war on terror is the difference between a response and a doctrine. Beginning with that first speech, Bush has steadily upped the doctrinal ante. The next time Bush addressed a joint session of Congress—when he delivered his State of the Union Message, in January—he said, "Our nation will continue to be steadfast and patient and persistent in the pursuit of two great objectives. First, we will shut down terrorist camps, disrupt terrorist plans, and bring terrorists to justice. And, second, we must prevent the terrorists and regimes who seek chemical, biological, or nuclear weapons from threatening the United States and the world." So now there was a second doctrine: Bush was broadening the United States' understanding of being at war, extending it from international terrorist organizations to governments that were not necessarily connected to Al Qaeda or involved in the September 11th attacks. In three less noticed speeches, at military universities—The Citadel, last De-

Nicholas Lemann is a staff writer at *The New Yorker*. Prior to that, he worked at *The Washington Monthly*, *The Washington Post*, the *Texas Monthly*, and was national correspondent of *The Atlantic Monthly* from 1983 to 1998. This article was published in *The New Yorker* on September 9, 2002.

cember; Virginia Military Institute, in April; and West Point, in June—Bush has made it clear that the United States intends to remove from power more governments than just Afghanistan's. In the West Point speech, the most significant of the three, he said that the "Cold War doctrines of deterrence and containment" are no longer sufficient for the United States, and that from now on "we must take the battle to the enemy, disrupt his plans, and confront the worst threats before they emerge"—in other words, wage war on other states preventively.

All these formulations are important, but "war on terror" is the one that has caught on. It isn't just Bush who uses it constantly; the press and his Democratic opposition do, too. The phrase meets the basic test of Presidential rhetoric: it has entered the language so fully, and framed the way people think about how the United States is reacting to the September 11th attacks so completely, that the idea that declaring and waging war on terror was not the sole, inevitable, logical consequence of the attacks just isn't in circulation.

During the drafting of Bush's first speech, there was debate even within the Administration about the use of the word "war" (although since practically the first thing Bush said on hearing that a second plane had flown into the World Trade Center was "We're at war," it was probably beside the point). Presidents have been declaring metaphoric war on non-traditional enemies— that is, not sovereign states or alliances—at least since Lyndon Johnson declared war on poverty, in 1964. Doing so has clear advantages. It promises the public a dramatic effort to solve a terrible problem, while implicitly asking in return for the kind of support that politicians get only in extraordinary circumstances. But there are disadvantages, too. Traditional wars are fought by military means and have definite endings. Metaphoric wars don't. Terror, like poverty and inflation and drugs, will never sit at a desk and sign an unconditional surrender in front of television cameras. The public can tire of a war that lasts for years. The war metaphor can become a trap: a single successful terrorist attack on the United States, even a relatively minor one, would surely open up a discourse about having "lost" the war on terror. The Administration is aware of these difficulties—that's why Bush declared war on terror with caveats about the war's not being likely to have a neat conclusion and requiring great patience on the public's part, and why other officials, especially Attorney General John Ashcroft, have talked about future attacks as a virtual certainty. Still, over the past year the Administration has succeeded in convincing the country that it is notionally at war.

Although Bush qualified his initial declaration of war on terrorists with the phrase "of global reach," he was still, in effect, promising to wipe out not just Al Qaeda but every other jihad organization that operates across national borders. He was also inviting countries to ask—as Israel, Russia, India, and others have done—for more American help in their own struggles against violent political opposition that, because it attacks civilians, qualifies as terrorism. The commitment is enormous.

The second most resonant passage in that first Bush speech—"Every nation, in every region, now has a decision to make. Either you are with us or you are with the terrorists"—represents another daunting undertaking by the United States, because fitting "every nation, in every region" into the Procrustean bed of being "with us" and against "the terrorists" is more complicated than Bush made it sound. The most obvious example of a nation that sided with us against the terrorists, Pakistan, quite clearly continues to violate Bush's injunction that "from this day forward, any nation that continues to harbor or support terrorism will be regarded by the United States as a hostile regime," since Pakistan is the home base of terrorists who operate in Kashmir. The reason Pakistan's President, Pervez Musharraf, doesn't adhere more strictly to the Bush doctrine is that if he did he'd be overthrown by Islamists, and then Pakistan would be much less "with us" than it is now. In recent months, Bush and other members of the Administration have begun talking about supporting democracy in the Middle East, and Musharraf, who took office in a coup and has altered Pakistan's constitution so as to make its elections as minimally significant as possible, is a reminder that, in many places, American policy is an imperfect fit with the situation on the ground. The standard that Bush has proposed for preventive military action against threatening regimes, if carried out literally, would represent yet another huge project, since perhaps a dozen governments that are not formal, reliable allies of the United States have some chemical- or biological-weapons capability. If one takes the President at his word, the United States has assumed, under the rubric of the war on terror, a new set of foreign-policy commitments that are much more ambitious, complicated, and difficult to realize than Bush's successful catchphrase would indicate.

For months after September 11th, there was no real debate about the war on terror. That's understandable—we've begun to forget how profoundly the terrorists terrorized us and how necessary cohesion felt after an attack that was beyond the imaginings not just of ordinary citizens but of even the leading experts on terrorism. What little dissent there was in those early days seemed as if it must have been ordered up by a covert wartime National Recovery Administration that had become concerned about the problem of underemployment among patriotic political commentators. Then, after the first of the year, leading Democrats—and only leading Democrats; the position of most Democratic congressional candidates today is one of unwavering support for the

President—began to voice a carefully delimited critique of Bush's conduct of the war, and to propose a different way of conducting it. The critique varies from person to person, but it would be fair to call the vision underlying it something like "war on terror: the enhanced edition."

In a speech at the Council on Foreign Relations, in New York, in February, Al Gore said that he no longer felt constrained, as he had in the fall and early winter, from criticizing Bush's conduct of the war. But he specifically endorsed the two main ideas Bush had put forth at that point: war on terror and American opposition to rogue regimes. His criticism was that Bush wasn't doing more to pursue these goals through liberal means like foreign aid and diplomacy.

Most of the other Democrats at the possible Presidential-candidate level have since given foreign-policy speeches touching on some of the same themes. They have said, variously, that Bush was acting unilaterally, was undercommitted to the reconstruction effort in Afghanistan, wasn't adequately funding non-fundamentalist education efforts in the Middle East, wasn't adding enough new intelligence capability, and wasn't upgrading the Office of Homeland Security to the status of a Cabinet department (Bush has since adopted the Democratic position on that issue). Words like "commitment," "engagement," "involvement," and "coöperation" came up a lot in these speeches. Bill Clinton made a foreign-policy appearance in June, also under the auspices of the Council on Foreign Relations, at which he got closer to a workable slogan than the others had: he said that he supported a strategy of "more partners and fewer terrorists" (or, alternatively, "fewer enemies and more friends"), featuring worldwide health-and-education aid, foreign-debt relief, and more international peacekeeping efforts. Senator John Kerry, of Massachusetts, who has the best military combat credentials among the Democrats who are thinking about running for President, opened a second front at the beginning of the summer, by criticizing Bush as a Commander-in-Chief, especially for permitting the escape of top Al Qaeda leaders, including possibly Osama bin Laden, by relying on Afghan soldiers as proxy ground forces in the Battle of Tora Bora, in December.

Kerry's position was consistent with that of the other Democrats: they all want more of the war on terror, not less; in Kerry's case, more American troops on the ground in Afghanistan. Most of the leading figures in Washington, it seems, are avid participants in what might be called the Kennan Games: the winner will be the person who has most successfully used September 11th as the basis for a new American grand strategy as durable and memorable as the one George Kennan proposed in 1946—containment of the Soviet bloc. The Democrats do disagree internally about Bush's idea of the United States' replacing regimes, particularly Iraq. But they agree about declaring war on terror and about using September 11th as the occasion to try to extend America's overwhelming power even further. One Administration foreign-policy official told me, a little smugly but not without justice, that the foreign-policy debate inside the Bush Administration is a lot more interesting and impassioned than the debate outside it.

The official was talking about the struggle between the Administration's hawks and moderates—a struggle that the press usually describes as an argument between Donald Rumsfeld, the Secretary of Defense (the hawk), and Colin Powell, the Secretary of State (the moderate). The description is accurate as far as it goes, but the hawks, who believe that the United States should remain the world's sole great power for many decades and that force, rather than international coöperation, is the best means to that end, are nested in places other than the Pentagon. Vice-President Cheney is a hawk who spends much more time with Bush than Rumsfeld does, and there are important hawks who are one or two levels down on Cheney's staff, on the National Security Council staff, and even at the State Department (chiefly John R. Bolton, the Under-Secretary for Arms Control and International Security), as well as at Defense.

One reason the hawks are so interesting is that they seem to break all the rules and get away with it. The foreign-policy world prides itself on maintaining a bipartisan consensus, so being outside the consensus should, theoretically, rob you of influence. But the hawks have defied the consensus for thirty years, ever since they turned against détente with the Soviet Union during the Nixon Administration, and today they have more influence than ever. President Bush is supposed to insist on absolute personal loyalty and on keeping all debate strictly internal, but the hawks plainly have goals other than just Bush's reëlection; they announce or leak positions in advance of Bush (Paul Wolfowitz, the Deputy Secretary of Defense, declared less than a week after September 11th that the United States would be "ending states who sponsor terrorism"), and their circle includes people who misbehaved during the 2000 campaign, like William Kristol, the editor of *The Weekly Standard,* who was a John McCain supporter. Washington's attitude toward the hawks seems to be official disapproval tinged with sneaking admiration. They have an incaution that usually makes holding office impossible, and yet they have gained high-ranking jobs and kept them. Their operational persistence and their intellectual boldness give them disproportionate influence—the origins of just about all of Bush's doctrinal statements over the last year clearly can be traced to the hawks.

A good place to find the mainstream Democratic counter-argument to the hawks is a book published in March called *The Paradox of American Power: Why the World's Only Superpower Can't Go It Alone,* by Joseph S. Nye, Jr., the dean of Harvard's Kennedy School of Government and someone who might well have turned up in a high-ranking foreign-policy job in a Gore Administration. Nye acknowledges that the United States is supremely powerful right now, but he says that it is a temporary condition to be taken advantage of, and not something that can become permanent. We should pursue "soft power," a complex web of alliances and aid agreements that bind the rest of the world to our interests and give us a more benign reputation abroad. Another person who would almost certainly be shaping American foreign policy in a Gore Administration, Richard Holbrooke, the former United Nations Ambassador, argued, when I spoke with him recently, that the hawks around Bush fundamentally misunderstand the role being played by the international organizations that the United States helped create after the Second World War. "The entire system was created by statesmen like Roosevelt, Truman, and Acheson to bind other countries to our interests—to prevent rogue states," Holbrooke said. "True, some international organizations got taken over, like UNESCO. But on the whole the international system was much more favorable to us than to others. Remember that Bush's father was Ambassador to the U.N. He understands this."

During the Clinton Administration, Joseph Nye was an Assistant Secretary of Defense. After he returned to Harvard, he became a member, along with hawks like Wolfowitz and Richard Perle, of an advisory group called the Defense Policy Board, whose members are briefed periodically at the Pentagon. When the Bush Administration came into office, Perle was made the board's chairman, Nye and other Democratic members were not reappointed, and the board became Hawk Central. I went to see Nye not long ago, and he said, "There's more difference between the traditionalists and the hawks in the Administration than between the traditionalists and the Democrats, especially on the question of to what extent we should pay attention to the views of others."

The contrast between the Democrats' faith in international treaties and organizations and the hawks' mistrust of them couldn't be more deep-seated; it reflects fundamentally different views of human nature. Do you get people to behave the way you'd like them to through power and force, or by encouragement and friendship? The hawks would say, Clearly the former, especially in the Arab world. They see the tough, threatening messages that Bush has been sending to other governments, through his rhetoric and through his refusal to participate in international organizations, as having already paid off in the form of increased influence for the United States. A lot of the conversation in foreign-policy circles is about articles in small-circulation periodicals. The article that prompted the most buzz this summer was an essay in *Policy Review*, a conservative publication affiliated with the Hoover Institution, called "Power and Weakness," by Robert Kagan, another prominent hawk. Kagan is currently enduring one of the cruellest fates that can be visited on one of his kind: because of his wife's job, he lives in Brussels, in the bosom of the "international community." Kagan says, with good-humored condescension, that of course the Europeans believe in international law and multilateralism. Who can blame them? Weak nations, lacking the resources and the will to maintain military power, always have.

To the extent that the supremely confident hawks take seriously anyone who disagrees with them, it wouldn't be the multilateralists, whom they regard as sentimental and naïve, but old-fashioned foreign-policy realists, people who think of themselves as being hardheaded enough to conduct their discussion of American foreign policy on the ground of practical matters like national interest and balance of power. Moral campaigns to remake the world don't cut it with the realists. To them it's the hawks who are sentimental and naïve, and also dangerously incautious, because they overestimate the extent to which the United States can impose its will abroad without suffering unforeseen consequences. For the past year, the realists have been the dog that hasn't barked. (There is a left-wing argument against the war on terror, which proceeds from a suspicion of American power; it counts as a loudly barking dog because commentators who object to it have given it so much publicity.) The realists are practically reverential toward American power, but, unlike just about everybody in Washington—Administration hawks and moderates, Democrats and Republicans in Congress—they don't think there should be a war on terror.

Over the summer, foreign-policy elder statesmen like Brent Scowcroft, James Baker, and Zbigniew Brzezinski got a lot of attention for publicly expressing realist doubts about the prospective American invasion of Iraq, and Vice-President Cheney responded with a speech making the case for war, but the broader realist argument about the war on terror has been absent from the national discussion. I went to see some of the leading realists recently, with the idea of giving their opinions a public airing. The people I interviewed are well-known figures in international relations, professors at major universities—John Mearsheimer, of the University of Chicago; Stephen Van Evera and Barry Posen, of M.I.T.; and Stephen Walt, of Harvard—but they reported that they haven't been seriously in touch with anybody in government over the past year. Evidently, their point of view isn't being considered in Washington.

The consensus among the realists is that the United States should have declared war on Al Qaeda, not on terrorism. If it had, then all foreign-policy projects would be evaluated on the basis of how well they served the worldwide struggle against Al Queda. The realists are minimalists. They often say things like "do less" and "reduce the American footprint." Using the September 11th attacks as the occasion to remake America's role in the world is exactly what they don't want. They revere tough-minded diplomacy and suspect military adventurism—another of their favorite formulations is that it's better to display the velvet glove than the mailed fist. In the nineteen-nineties, they opposed United States military involvement in the Balkans, and today they oppose the idea of invading Iraq and of seeking "regime change" in other countries. The hawks believe that anti-Americanism springs from pure irrational hatred and can best be dealt with through shows of force; the realists believe anti-Americanism varies with the extent of visible, bellicose American behavior, and that is why they want to reduce the footprint.

"I think the Al Qaeda threat is very serious," Stephen Van Evera told me. We were a long, long way from the corridors of power—sitting on a park bench in Lexington, Massachusetts. "We used to believe there was no such thing as Al Qaeda"—a terrorist organization capable of inflicting mass casualties. "They're very skillful. They combine high patience and training capacity and motivation. I was very shocked by 9/11. We're in a struggle to the death with these people. They'd bring in nuclear weapons here, if they could. I think this could be the highest threat to our national security ever: a non-deterrable enemy that may acquire weapons of mass destruction."

He went on, "Defining it as a broad war on terror was a tremendous mistake. It should have been a war on Al Qaeda. Don't take your eye off the ball. Subordinate every other policy to it, including the policies toward Russia, the Arab-Israeli conflict, and Iraq. Instead, the Administration defined it as a broad war on terror, including groups that have never taken a swing at the United States and never will. It leads to a loss of focus. Al Qaeda escapes through the cracks. And you make enemies of the people you need against Al Qaeda. There are large risks in a war against Iraq. There could be a lengthy, televised public slaughter of Muslims by Americans. A wide imperial rampage through the Middle East—what do you do after you win? We're not out of Bosnia and Kosovo yet, and Iraq is much bigger. It's a huge occupation and reconstruction. We aren't good at this."

The realists agreed wholeheartedly with the Administration's decision to use American military forces to remove the Taliban government in Afghanistan from power, because the Taliban was harboring Al Qaeda, our attacker. And they agreed that the campaign against the Taliban was a big success. But they were not particularly sanguine about American progress against Al

Qaeda in Afghanistan since the fall of the Taliban. "When I put together the evidence, it's not going very well," Van Evera said. "We've nailed eight of the top twenty-five Al Qaeda leaders. We need to roll up the entire leadership. They're still capable of launching attacks. They've attempted about a dozen since 9/11."

Barry Posen, Van Evera's colleague at M.I.T., who specializes in military analysis, maintained that the mop-up campaign in Afghanistan had been severely hampered by American unwillingness to use ground forces, because of fear of casualties and because current American military doctrine overstresses the benefits of air power. "It looks like we missed a number of opportunities," he said, "and the reason was that we didn't want to take risks. Tora Bora was a disaster, universally acknowledged as such, and never explained. The idea that casualty aversion could play a role here—it's extraordinary. If that's true, something's really wrong. The American people would have paid hundreds of dead to get the Al Qaeda leaders. Or it was pure incompetence—using drones and a bunch of mercenaries and bombs in a cordon operation. We couldn't have done a worse job. We should have put in every Ranger in range. There's no excuse. This is very weird. Then they have this second chance, Operation Anaconda"—the American effort to encircle Al Qaeda and Taliban forces in the Shah-i-Kot valley, in eastern Afghanistan, last March. "My sense is, it was the toughest of the Al Qaeda hard cases, very good and gutsy. The commander"—Major General Franklin Hagenbeck—"didn't know what he was doing. He didn't send enough forces. He didn't take enough artillery. And there was too much reliance on the Afghans. And, it's clear, they were kerfuffled afterward. They went to the Brits for more troops"—England flew in seventeen hundred marines as reinforcements—"and the commander was relieved," by Lieutenant General Dan McNeill. "They knew something was wrong. Opportunity No. 2 was missed. My guess is, most of them got away. So this is disturbing—a war on terror that doesn't focus on the terrorists."

From now on, the realists say, the pursuit of Al Qaeda will be an intelligence and police operation, not a military one: the big problem isn't that of physically conquering the dozens of cells from which terrorist operations are launched; it's locating them. The continuing use of American military power—especially on not strictly related projects, like invading Iraq—will do more harm than good, by alienating governments whose coöperation America will need in eliminating Al Qaeda cells on their soil, and by creating the kind of instability in the region that has in the past provided Al Qaeda with its best opportunities to establish bases of operations. "Military power is not necessary to wiping out Al Qaeda," Stephen Walt said. "It's a crude instrument, and it almost always has effects you can't anticipate. We're seeing that now. We didn't get Mullah Omar and Osama bin Laden. We're killing civilians. We're killing friendly forces. This is ultimately a battle for the hearts and minds of people around the world. When your village just got levelled by an American mistake, the conclusions you draw will be rather different from what we'd want them to be."

He went on, "Americans do not yet perceive a cost to having a freewheeling foreign policy. We stayed in the Persian Gulf for ten years, and lost fewer than three hundred people. We knocked off the Taliban in a few weeks. But imagine going into Iraq. If things go badly, we end up there for a long time. There's a point where the costs start adding up. It will generate higher and higher levels of resentment. Empires start generating a lot of resentment. I'd leave Saddam right where he is. Keep him bottled up. Wait for him to die. What do we do if we're successful? How many coups were there in Iraq between 1958 and 1968? It's a country riven with internal divisions. That's why the Bush people didn't go to Baghdad in 1991. Iran is much more powerful and important than Iraq—how do Iranians react? I have limited confidence in our ability to run countries we don't understand. Why, in the middle of pursuing Al Qaeda, would you decide, 'Oh, let's take a big country and invade it and create a giant political mess there!' We've seen people attempting this in the Middle East before, and it hasn't worked. You never know how these operations will go. History is not on the side of the advocates here."

Al Qaeda was obviously helped by Afghanistan's descent into warlordism following the withdrawal of Soviet forces (and of American support for the opposition to them), in 1989. After September 11th, "failed states" looked like a pressing threat to American national security, because they provide terrorists with territory. The realists would therefore put far above the threat to the United States posed by Saddam Hussein's weapons programs the threat posed by instability in Afghanistan and Pakistan—countries whose pro-American Presidents, Hamid Karzai and Pervez Musharraf, respectively, are behaving like men who believe that their lives are increasingly in danger, and whose remote areas provide haven for Al Qaeda members. Saddam may be trying to develop nuclear weapons, but Pakistan has nuclear weapons already, and its military and intelligence services are full of Al Qaeda sympathizers. "We may lose Pakistan," John Mearsheimer told me, "and that would be a huge blow, because Al Qaeda would be able to operate in Pakistan, and it could get its hands on nuclear weapons. It's clear that Musharraf is in a precarious position. In Afghanistan, Karzai is in much less control than Musharraf. Pakistan is a coherent state. Afghanistan is not. There's no Army, it's run by warlords. It's almost impossible to maintain order." To the realists, the precariousness of the region is another reason not to invade Iraq: quite often, when war comes to one country it destabilizes the governments of neighboring countries. (The Administration recently announced that Al Qaeda is now also operating across Iraq's eastern border, in Iran.) And if, after an invasion of Iraq, some parts of that country are no longer controlled by Saddam Hussein but are not controlled by the United States either, Al Qaeda would have another place where it could establish itself.

The realists, along with many other foreign-policy experts who aren't necessarily in their camp on all issues, are also worried that Al Qaeda might get its hands on fissile material, or even nuclear weapons, that may be available in the southeastern regions of the old Soviet empire. In 1991, two of the United States Senate's foreign-policy eminences—Sam Nunn, of Georgia, and Richard Lugar, of Indiana—wrote and passed legislation that provided American funding for the safe storage and destruction of the old Soviet nuclear weapons in Russia and three former Soviet republics. Last December, Nunn (now an ex-senator) and Lugar went to the White House to pitch the idea of extending the program, in light of the threat from Al Qaeda, to other countries in the region. The officials they met with, a high-level group including Condoleezza Rice, the national-security adviser, and Vice-President Cheney, who participated by videoconference from the secure location where he spent much of the fall, seemed interested. But the Administration wound up adopting only a small version of the idea, and in the spring it suspended funding for the Nunn-Lugar program. This was taken to be another sign of the influence of the hawks and of their suspicion of international agreements, especially in the area of arms reduction.

The realists all noted that thus far in the war on terror President Bush's speeches have been bold but his actions have been cautious. While steadily laying out a case for something close to a world war, he has stationed fewer than ten thousand American troops in Afghanistan (many fewer than President Clinton stationed in the Balkans) and has deployed them sparingly in combat. He did not achieve the one policy change that would probably be most helpful in promoting American interests in Pakistan—a substantial lifting of the barriers on imports of Pakistani textiles, which would have made the United States look like the midwife of prosperity there—because of opposition from domestic textile manufacturers. He has not yet succeeded in creating a Department of Homeland Security. He has not imposed on the public the usual wartime tax increases and military call-ups.

Bush is a prudent politician. As governor of Texas, he almost always chose adept compromise over confrontation, even though he had been elected and reelected with healthy majorities. He is certainly aware that (if you judge by election results, not polls) he has been much less popular as a national politician than as a local one—that's why he spends so much time visiting states that were close in the 2000 election, and offering them policy sweeteners like steel-import tariffs. Since 2000, the Republicans have lost governors' races in Virginia and New Jersey. Bush has a thin majority in the House of Representatives. He lost his majority in the Senate when he came out of the gate as a strong conservative. With the sole exception of his big early tax cut, legislatively he has either met the Democrats partway (as in his education bill) or been unable to pass his program (as in his energy bill). The Bushes may seem like a dynasty, but a glance at the electoral won-lost records of the President and his kin—former President Bush, and Governor Jeb Bush, of Florida—demonstrates that they're not politically invincible in the way that Ronald Reagan or the Kennedy brothers were. It is difficult to imagine that the President feels supremely confident about being reëlected. So he would appear to have neither the inclination nor the means to put through a daring new foreign-policy program.

But the war on terrorism and the ideas associated with it strike a very deep chord in Bush, aside from whatever political advantages they may offer. During the campaign, when Bush promised to restore honor and dignity to the Presidency, he really meant it—and he meant more by it than just forswearing hanky-panky in the Oval Office. Republicans, and particularly Bush, seem to have a view of Clinton and Gore that goes something like this: O.K., those guys may be more intellectually agile than we are, but we're tougher, more disciplined, more mature. We understand how precious the prestige of the United States is, and we won't squander it in loose talk and half-cocked action. The September 11th attacks gave Bush a chance to display what, to his mind, would be his competitive advantage over his predecessor and his chief rival; all the comments by his aides about how he had found his destiny were in effect admissions both of the extent of Bush's ambition and of a feeling that conditions before September 11th hadn't been propitious for a display of his strengths.

The realists are right when they say that Bush's talk and his actions have been out of synch. The President and his people may be praying that their sabre rattling will bring about a coup or a revolution in Iraq that will obviate the need for an invasion. That Bush so far has said more than he's done doesn't necessarily mean, however, that the really consequential decisions following from September 11th still lie before him. It's important to Bush to be a man of his word—that's the essence of his non-Clintonism. He has rhetorically committed the Presidency to a series of ideas that in turn commit the United States to a course of action. It seems as if the big decisions have already been made.

DON'T ATTACK SADDAM

Brent Scowcroft

Our nation is presently engaged in a debate about whether to launch a war against Iraq. Leaks of various strategies for an attack on Iraq appear with regularity. The Bush administration vows regime change, but states that no decision has been made whether, much less when, to launch an invasion.

It is beyond dispute that Saddam Hussein is a menace. He terrorizes and brutalizes his own people. He has launched war on two of his neighbors. He devotes enormous effort to rebuilding his military forces and equipping them with weapons of mass destruction. We will all be better off when he is gone.

That said, we need to think through this issue very carefully. We need to analyze the relationship between Iraq and our other pressing priorities—notably the war on terrorism—as well as the best strategy and tactics available were we to move to change the regime in Baghdad.

SADDAM'S STRATEGIC objective appears to be to dominate the Persian Gulf, to control oil from the region, or both.

That clearly poses a real threat to key U.S. interests. But there is scant evidence to tie Saddam to terrorist organizations, and even less to the Sept. 11 attacks. Indeed Saddam's goals have little in common with the terrorists who threaten us, and there is little incentive for him to make common cause with them.

He is unlikely to risk his investment in weapons of mass destruction, much less his country, by handing such weapons to terrorists who would use them for their own purposes and leave Baghdad as the return address. Threatening to use these weapons for blackmail—much less their actual use—would open him and his entire regime to a devastating response by the U.S. While Saddam is thoroughly evil, he is above all a power-hungry survivor.

Saddam is a familiar dictatorial aggressor, with traditional goals for his aggression. There is little evidence to indicate that the United States itself is an object of his aggression. Rather, Saddam's problem with the U.S. appears to

Lieutenant General Brent Scowcroft (USAF, Retired) was national security adviser to Presidents Gerald Ford and George Bush, Sr.. The former vice chairman of Kissinger Associates, he is the founder and president of The Scowcroft Group, an international business consulting firm. This article was published on August 15, 2002 in *The Wall Street Journal*.

be that we stand in the way of his ambitions. He seeks weapons of mass destruction not to arm terrorists, but to deter us from intervening to block his aggressive designs.

Given Saddam's aggressive regional ambitions, as well as his ruthlessness and unpredictability, it may at some point be wise to remove him from power. Whether and when that point should come ought to depend on overall U.S. national security priorities. Our pre-eminent security priority—underscored repeatedly by the president—is the war on terrorism. An attack on Iraq at this time would seriously jeopardize, if not destroy, the global counterterrorist campaign we have undertaken.

The United States could certainly defeat the Iraqi military and destroy Saddam's regime. But it would not be a cakewalk. On the contrary, it undoubtedly would be very expensive—with serious consequences for the U.S. and global economy—and could as well be bloody. In fact, Saddam would be likely to conclude he had nothing left to lose, leading him to unleash whatever weapons of mass destruction he possesses.

Israel would have to expect to be the first casualty, as in 1991 when Saddam sought to bring Israel into the Gulf conflict. This time, using weapons of mass destruction, he might succeed, provoking Israel to respond, perhaps with nuclear weapons, unleashing an Armageddon in the Middle East. Finally, if we are to achieve our strategic objectives in Iraq, a military campaign very likely would have to be followed by a large-scale, long-term military occupation.

BUT THE central point is that any campaign against Iraq, whatever the strategy, cost and risks, is certain to divert us for some indefinite period from our war on terrorism. Worse, there is a virtual consensus in the world against an attack on Iraq at this time. So long as that sentiment persists, it would require the U.S. to pursue a virtual go-it-alone strategy against Iraq, making any military operations correspondingly more difficult and expensive. The most serious cost, however, would be to the war on terrorism. Ignoring that clear sentiment would result in a serious degradation in international cooperation with us against terrorism. And make no mistake, we simply cannot win that war without enthusiastic international cooperation, especially on intelligence.

Possibly the most dire consequences would be the effect in the region. The shared view in the region is that Iraq is principally an obsession of the U.S. The obsession of the region, however, is the Israeli-Palestinian conflict. If we were seen to be turning our backs on that bitter conflict—which the region, rightly or wrongly, perceives to be clearly within our power to resolve—in order to go after Iraq, there would be an explosion of outrage against us. We would be seen as ignoring a key interest of the Muslim world in order to satisfy what is seen to be a narrow American interest.

Even without Israeli involvement, the results could well destabilize Arab regimes in the region, ironically facilitating one of Saddam's strategic objectives. At a minimum, it would stifle any cooperation on terrorism, and could even swell the ranks of the terrorists. Conversely, the more progress we make in the war on terrorism, and the more we are seen to be committed to resolving the Israel-Palestinian issue, the greater will be the international support for going after Saddam.

IF WE are truly serious about the war on terrorism, it must remain our top priority. However, should Saddam Hussein be found to be clearly implicated in the events of Sept. 11, that could make him a key counterterrorist target, rather than a competing priority, and significantly shift world opinion toward support for regime change.

In any event, we should be pressing the United Nations Security Council to insist on an effective no-notice inspection regime for Iraq—any time, anywhere, no permission required. On this point, senior administration officials have opined that Saddam Hussein would never agree to such an inspection regime. But if he did, inspections would serve to keep him off balance and under close observation, even if all his weapons of mass destruction capabilities were not uncovered. And if he refused, his rejection could provide the persuasive casus belli which many claim we do not now have. Compelling evidence that Saddam had acquired nuclear-weapons capability could have a similar effect.

In sum, if we will act in full awareness of the intimate interrelationship of the key issues in the region, keeping counterterrorism as our foremost priority, there is much potential for success across the entire range of our security interests—including Iraq. If we reject a comprehensive perspective, however, we put at risk our campaign against terrorism as well as stability and security in a vital region of the world.

"THE RISKS OF INACTION ARE FAR GREATER THAN THE RISK OF ACTION"

Vice President Dick Cheney

The following is an excerpted version of Vice President Dick Cheney's August 26, 2002 address to the 103rd National Convention of the Veterans of Foreign Wars in Nashville, Tennessee. It marked the beginning of the Bush Administration's aggressive campaign to convince the American public of the need to take preemptive action against Saddam Hussein.

America in the year 2002 must ask careful questions, not merely about our past, but also about our future. The elected leaders of this country have a responsibility to consider all of the available options. And we are doing so. What we must not do in the face of a mortal threat is give in to wishful thinking or willful blindness. We will not simply look away, hope for the best, and leave the matter for some future administration to resolve. As President Bush has said, time is not on our side. Deliverable weapons of mass destruction in the hands of a terror network, or a murderous dictator, or the two working together, constitutes as grave a threat as can be imagined. The risks of inaction are far greater than the risk of action.

Now and in the future, the United States will work closely with the global coalition to deny terrorists and their state sponsors the materials, technology, and expertise to make and deliver weapons of mass destruction. We will develop and deploy effective missile defenses to protect America and our allies from sudden attack. And the entire world must know that we will take whatever action is necessary to defend our freedom and our security.

As former Secretary of State Kissinger recently stated: "The imminence of proliferation of weapons of mass destruction, the huge dangers it involves, the rejection of a viable inspection system, and the demonstrated hostility of Sad-

---

Richard B. Cheney is the Vice President of the United States. He was White House Chief of Staff during the Ford Administration, and was President George Bush, Sr.'s Secretary of Defense, overseeing U.S. military forces during Operation Just Cause in Panama and Operation Desert Storm in the Persian Gulf region. He served six consecutive terms in the House as a Republican representative from Wyoming, and, from 1995 until August 2000, he was CEO of Halliburton, the world's leading oil-field supply, engineering, and construction company.

dam Hussein combine to produce an imperative for preemptive action." If the United States could have preempted 9/11, we would have, no question. Should we be able to prevent another, much more devastating attack, we will, no question. This nation will not live at the mercy of terrorists or terror regimes.

I am familiar with the arguments against taking action in the case of Saddam Hussein. Some concede that Saddam is evil, power-hungry, and a menace—but that, until he crosses the threshold of actually possessing nuclear weapons, we should rule out any preemptive action. That logic seems to me to be deeply flawed. The argument comes down to this: yes, Saddam is as dangerous as we say he is, we just need to let him get stronger before we do anything about it.

Yet if we did wait until that moment, Saddam would simply be emboldened, and it would become even harder for us to gather friends and allies to oppose him. As one of those who worked to assemble the Gulf War coalition, I can tell you that our job then would have been infinitely more difficult in the face of a nuclear-armed Saddam Hussein. And many of those who now argue that we should act only if he gets a nuclear weapon, would then turn around and say that we cannot act because he has a nuclear weapon. At bottom, that argument counsels a course of inaction that itself could have devastating consequences for many countries, including our own.

Another argument holds that opposing Saddam Hussein would cause even greater troubles in that part of the world, and interfere with the larger war against terror. I believe the opposite is true. Regime change in Iraq would bring about a number of benefits to the region. When the gravest of threats are eliminated, the freedom-loving peoples of the region will have a chance to promote the values that can bring lasting peace. As for the reaction of the Arab "street," the Middle East expert Professor Fouad Ajami predicts that after liberation the streets in Basra and Baghdad are "sure to erupt in joy in the same way the throngs in Kabul greeted the Americans." Extremists in the region would have to rethink their strategy of Jihad. Moderates throughout the region would take heart. And our ability to advance the Israeli-Palestinian peace process would be enhanced, just as it was following the liberation of Kuwait in 1991.

The reality is that these times bring not only dangers but also opportunities. In the Middle East, where so many have known only poverty and oppression, terror and tyranny, we look to the day when people can live in freedom and dignity and the young can grow up free of the conditions that breed despair, hatred, and violence.

In other times the world saw how the United States defeated fierce enemies, then helped rebuild their countries, forming strong bonds between our peoples and our governments. Today in Afghanistan, the world is seeing that America acts not to conquer but to liberate, and remains in friendship to help the people build a future of stability, self-determination, and peace.

We would act in that same spirit after a regime change in Iraq. With our help, a liberated Iraq can be a great nation once again. Iraq is rich in natural resources and human talent, and has unlimited potential for a peaceful, prosperous future. Our goal would be an Iraq that has territorial integrity, a government that is democratic and pluralistic, a nation where the human rights of every ethnic and religious group are recognized and protected. In that troubled land all who seek justice, and dignity, and the chance to live their own lives, can know they have a friend and ally in the United States of America.

Great decisions and challenges lie ahead of us. Yet we can and we will build a safer and better world beyond the war on terror.

DRAIN THE SWAMP AND THERE WILL BE NO MORE MOSQUITOES

Noam Chomsky

September 11 shocked many Americans into an awareness that they had better pay much closer attention to what the U.S. government does in the world and how it is perceived. Many issues have been opened for discussion that were not on the agenda before. That's all to the good.

It is also the merest sanity, if we hope to reduce the likelihood of future atrocities. It may be comforting to pretend that our enemies "hate our freedoms," as President Bush stated, but it is hardly wise to ignore the real world, which conveys different lessons.

The president is not the first to ask: "Why do they hate us?" In a staff discussion 44 years ago, President Eisenhower described "the campaign of hatred against us [in the Arab world], not by the governments but by the people." His National Security Council outlined the basic reasons: the U.S. supports corrupt and oppressive governments and is "opposing political or economic progress" because of its interest in controlling the oil resources of the region.

Post–September 11 surveys in the Arab world reveal that the same reasons hold today, compounded with resentment over specific policies. Strikingly, that is even true of privileged, Western-oriented sectors in the region.

To cite just one recent example: in the August 1 issue of *Far Eastern Economic Review,* the internationally recognised regional specialist Ahmed Rashid writes that in Pakistan "there is growing anger that U.S. support is allowing [Musharraf's] military regime to delay the promise of democracy."

Today we do ourselves few favours by choosing to believe that "they hate us" and "hate our freedoms." On the contrary, these are attitudes of people who like Americans and admire much about the U.S., including its freedoms. What they hate is official policies that deny them the freedoms to which they too aspire.

For such reasons, the post–September 11 rantings of Osama bin Laden— for example, about U.S. support for corrupt and brutal regimes, or about the

Noam Chomsky is Institute Professor of Linguistics at the Massachusetts Institute of Technology and author of many books, most recently *Understanding Power.* This article was published in the *Guardian* (London) on September 9, 2002.

U.S. "invasion" of Saudi Arabia—have a certain resonance, even among those who despise and fear him. From resentment, anger and frustration, terrorist bands hope to draw support and recruits.

We should also be aware that much of the world regards Washington as a terrorist regime. In recent years, the U.S. has taken or backed actions in Colombia, Nicaragua, Panama, Sudan and Turkey, to name a few, that meet official U.S. definitions of "terrorism"—that is, when Americans apply the term to enemies.

In the most sober establishment journal, *Foreign Affairs*, Samuel Huntington wrote in 1999: "While the U.S. regularly denounces various countries as 'rogue states,' in the eyes of many countries it is becoming the rogue superpower . . . the single greatest external threat to their societies."

Such perceptions are not changed by the fact that, on September 11, for the first time, a western country was subjected on home soil to a horrendous terrorist attack of a kind all too familiar to victims of Western power. The attack goes far beyond what's sometimes called the "retail terror" of the IRA, FLN or Red Brigades.

The September 11 terrorism elicited harsh condemnation throughout the world and an outpouring of sympathy for the innocent victims. But with qualifications.

An international Gallup poll in late September found little support for "a military attack" by the U.S. in Afghanistan. In Latin America, the region with the most experience of U.S. intervention, support ranged from 2% in Mexico to 16% in Panama.

The current "campaign of hatred" in the Arab world is, of course, also fuelled by U.S. policies toward Israel-Palestine and Iraq. The U.S. has provided the crucial support for Israel's harsh military occupation, now in its 35th year.

One way for the U.S. to lessen Israeli-Palestinian tensions would be to stop refusing to join the long-standing international consensus that calls for recognition of the right of all states in the region to live in peace and security, including a Palestinian state in the currently occupied territories (perhaps with minor and mutual border adjustments).

In Iraq, a decade of harsh sanctions under U.S. pressure has strengthened Saddam Hussein while leading to the death of hundreds of thousands of Iraqis—perhaps more people "than have been slain by all so-called weapons of mass destruction throughout history," military analysts John and Karl Mueller wrote in *Foreign Affairs* in 1999.

Washington's present justifications to attack Iraq have far less credibility than when President Bush Sr. was welcoming Saddam as an ally and a trading partner after he had committed his worst brutalities—as in Halabja, where Iraq attacked Kurds with poison gas in 1988 At the time, the murderer Saddam was more dangerous than he is today.

As for a U.S. attack against Iraq, no one, including Donald Rumsfeld, can realistically guess the possible costs and consequences. Radical Islamist extremists surely hope that an attack on Iraq will kill many people and destroy much of the country, providing recruits for terrorist actions.

They presumably also welcome the "Bush doctrine" that proclaims the right of attack against potential threats, which are virtually limitless. The president has announced: "There's no telling how many wars it will take to secure freedom in the homeland." That's true.

Threats are everywhere, even at home. The prescription for endless war poses a far greater danger to Americans than perceived enemies do, for reasons the terrorist organisations understand very well.

Twenty years ago, the former head of Israeli military intelligence, Yehoshaphat Harkabi, also a leading Arabist, made a point that still holds true. "To offer an honourable solution to the Palestinians respecting their right to self-determination: that is the solution of the problem of terrorism," he said. "When the swamp disappears, there will be no more mosquitoes."

At the time, Israel enjoyed the virtual immunity from retaliation within the occupied territories that lasted until very recently. But Harkabi's warning was apt, and the lesson applies more generally.

Well before September 11 it was understood that with modern technology, the rich and powerful will lose their near monopoly of the means of violence and can expect to suffer atrocities on home soil.

If we insist on creating more swamps, there will be more mosquitoes, with awesome capacity for destruction.

If we devote our resources to draining the swamps, addressing the roots of the "campaigns of hatred," we can not only reduce the threats we face but also live up to ideals that we profess and that are not beyond reach if we choose to take them seriously.

QUESTIONS THAT WON'T BE ASKED ABOUT IRAQ

Congressman Ron Paul

Soon we hope to have hearings on the pending war with Iraq. I am concerned there are some questions that won't be asked—and maybe will not even be allowed to be asked. Here are some questions I would like answered by those who are urging us to start this war.

1. Is it not true that the reason we did not bomb the Soviet Union at the height of the Cold War was because we knew they could retaliate?

2. Is it not also true that we are willing to bomb Iraq now because we know it cannot retaliate—which just confirms that there is no real threat?

3. Is it not true that those who argue that even with inspections we cannot be sure that Hussein might be hiding weapons, at the same time imply that we can be more sure that weapons exist in the absence of inspections?

4. Is it not true that the U.N.'s International Atomic Energy Agency was able to complete its yearly verification mission to Iraq just this year with Iraqi cooperation?

5. Is it not true that the intelligence community has been unable to develop a case tying Iraq to global terrorism at all, much less the attacks on the United States last year? Does anyone remember that 15 of the 19 hijackers came from Saudi Arabia and that none came from Iraq?

6. Was former CIA counter-terrorism chief Vincent Cannistraro wrong when he recently said there is no confirmed evidence of Iraq's links to terrorism?

7. Is it not true that the CIA has concluded there is no evidence that a Prague meeting between 9/11 hijacker Atta and Iraqi intelligence took place?

8. Is it not true that northern Iraq, where the administration claimed al-Qaeda were hiding out, is in the control of our "allies," the Kurds?

9. Is it not true that the vast majority of al-Qaeda leaders who escaped appear to have safely made their way to Pakistan, another of our so-called allies?

Representative Ron Paul (R-Texas) has been a member of Congress from 1976 to 1984 and from 1996 to present. In 1988 he ran for president as the candidate of the Libertarian Party. This is the text of a speech he made on the floor of the U.S. House of Representatives on September 10, 2002.

10. Has anyone noticed that Afghanistan is rapidly sinking into total chaos, with bombings and assassinations becoming daily occurrences; and that according to a recent U.N. report the al-Qaeda "is, by all accounts, alive and well and poised to strike again, how, when, and where it chooses"?

11. Why are we taking precious military and intelligence resources away from tracking down those who did attack the United States—and who may again attack the United States—and using them to invade countries that have not attacked the United States?

12. Would an attack on Iraq not just confirm the Arab world's worst suspicions about the U.S., and isn't this what bin Laden wanted?

13. How can Hussein be compared to Hitler when he has no navy or air force, and now has an army 1/5 the size of twelve years ago, which even then proved totally inept at defending the country?

14. Is it not true that the constitutional power to declare war is exclusively that of the Congress? Should presidents, contrary to the Constitution, allow Congress to concur only when pressured by public opinion? Are presidents permitted to rely on the U.N. for permission to go to war?

15. Are you aware of a Pentagon report studying charges that thousands of Kurds in one village were gassed by the Iraqis, which found no conclusive evidence that Iraq was responsible, that Iran occupied the very city involved, and that evidence indicated the type of gas used was more likely controlled by Iran not Iraq?*

16. Is it not true that anywhere between 100,000 and 300,000 U.S. soldiers have suffered from Persian Gulf War syndrome from the first Gulf War, and that thousands may have died?

17. Are we prepared for possibly thousands of American casualties in a war against a country that does not have the capacity to attack the United States?

18. Are we willing to bear the economic burden of a 100 billion dollar war against Iraq, with oil prices expected to skyrocket and further rattle an already shaky American economy? How about an estimated 30 years occupation of Iraq that some have deemed necessary to "build democracy" there?

19. Iraq's alleged violations of U.N. resolutions are given as reason to initiate an attack, yet is it not true that hundreds of U.N. Resolutions have been ignored by various countries without penalty?

20. Did former President Bush not cite the U.N. Resolution of 1990 as the reason he could not march into Baghdad, while supporters of a new attack assert that it is the very reason we can march into Baghdad?

---

* Editors' note: See p. 41 for Joost Hiltermann's debunking of this unfortunate piece of disinformation.

21. Is it not true that, contrary to current claims, the no-fly zones were set up by Britain and the United States without specific approval from the United Nations?

22. If we claim membership in the international community and conform to its rules only when it pleases us, does this not serve to undermine our position, directing animosity toward us by both friend and foe?

23. How can our declared goal of bringing democracy to Iraq be believable when we prop up dictators throughout the Middle East and support military tyrants like Musharraf in Pakistan, who overthrew a democratically elected president?

24. Are you familiar with the 1994 Senate Hearings that revealed the U.S. knowingly supplied chemical and biological materials to Iraq during the Iran-Iraq war and as late as 1992—including after the alleged Iraqi gas attack on a Kurdish village?

25. Did we not assist Saddam Hussein's rise to power by supporting and encouraging his invasion of Iran? Is it honest to criticize Saddam now for his invasion of Iran, which at the time we actively supported?

26. Is it not true that preventive war is synonymous with an act of aggression, and has never been considered a moral or legitimate U.S. policy?

27. Why do the oil company executives strongly support this war if oil is not the real reason we plan to take over Iraq?

28. Why is it that those who never wore a uniform and are confident that they won't have to personally fight this war are more anxious for this war than our generals?

29. What is the moral argument for attacking a nation that has not initiated aggression against us, and could not if it wanted?

30. Where does the Constitution grant us permission to wage war for any reason other than self-defense?

31. Is it not true that a war against Iraq rejects the sentiments of the time-honored Treaty of Westphalia, nearly 400 years ago, that countries should never go into another for the purpose of regime change?

32. Is it not true that the more civilized a society is, the less likely disagreements will be settled by war?

33. Is it not true that since World War II Congress has not declared war and—not coincidentally—we have not since then had a clear-cut victory?

34. Is it not true that Pakistan, especially through its intelligence services, was an active supporter and key organizer of the Taliban?

35. Why don't those who want war bring a formal declaration of war resolution to the floor of Congress?

THE WAR PARTY'S IMPERIAL PLANS

Pat Buchanan

The fires had not yet gone out at the World Trade Center and the Pentagon, a year ago, before the War Party had introduced its revised plans for American empire. What many saw as a horrific atrocity and tragedy, they saw instantly as an opportunity to achieve U.S. hegemony over an alienated Islamic world.

President Bush initially directed America's righteous wrath and military power at al-Qaeda. But in his "axis-of-evil" address, he signed on to the War Party's agenda.

What lies ahead? When America invades Iraq, it will have to destroy Saddam and all his weapons of mass destruction. Else, the war will have been a failure. And to ensure destruction of those weapons, we must occupy Iraq. If you would see what follows, pull out a map.

With Americans controlling Iraq, Syria is virtually surrounded by hostile powers: Israel on the Golan, Turks and Kurds to the north, U.S. power to the west in Iraq and south in Jordan. Syrian President Assad will be forced to pull his army out of Lebanon, leaving Israel free to reinvade Lebanon to settle accounts with Hezbollah.

Now look to Iran. With Americans occupying Iraq, Iran is completely surrounded: Americans and Turks to the west, U.S. power in the Gulf and Arabian Sea to the south, in Afghanistan to the east and in the old Soviet republics to the north. U.S. warplanes will be positioned to interdict any flights to Lebanon to support Hezbollah.

Iraq is the key to the Middle East. As long as we occupy Iraq, we are the hegemonic power in the region. And after we occupy it, a window of opportunity will open—to attack Syria and Iran before they acquire weapons of mass destruction.

This is the vision that enthralls the War Party—"World War IV," as they call it—a series of "cakewalks," short sharp wars on Iraq, Syria and Iran to eliminate the Islamic terrorist threat to us and Israel for generations.

No wonder Ariel Sharon and his Amen Corner are exhilarated. They see

---

Patrick J. Buchanan is a syndicated columnist and television commentator who worked for Presidents Nixon, Ford, and Reagan and ran for president himself in 1992, 1996 and 2000 (when he was the Reform Party's nominee). He currently hosts MSNBC's daily news program *Buchanan & Press*, appears on *The McLaughlin Group*, and is the editor of *The American Conservative*. This column was published on September 11, 2002.

America's war on Iraq as killing off one enemy and giving Israel freedom to deal summarily with two more: Hezbollah and the Palestinians. Two jumps ahead of us, the Israelis are already talking up the need for us to deal with Libya, as well.

Anyone who believes America can finish Saddam and go home deceives himself. With Iraq's military crushed, the country will come apart. Kurds in the north and Shi'ites in the south will try to break away, and Iraq will be at the mercy of its mortal enemy, Iran. U.S. troops will have to remain to hold Iraq together, to find and destroy those weapons, to democratize the regime, and to deter Iran from biting off a chunk and dominating the Gulf.

Recall: After we crushed Germany and Japan in World War II, both were powerless to reassume their historic roles of containing Russia and China. So, America, at a cost of 100,000 dead in Vietnam and Korea, had to assume those roles. With Iraq in ruins, America will have to assume the permanent role of Policeman of the Persian Gulf.

But is this not a splendid vision, asks the War Party. After all, is this not America's day in the sun, her moment in history? And is not the crushing of Islamism and the modernization of the Arab world a cause worthy of a superpower's investment of considerable treasure and blood?

What is wrong with the War Party's vision?

Just this: Pro-American regimes in Cairo, Amman and Riyadh will be shaken to their foundations by the cataclysm unleashed as Americans smash Iraq, while Israelis crush Palestinians. Nor is Iran likely to passively await encirclement. Terror attacks seem certain. Nor is a militant Islam that holds in thrall scores of millions of believers from Morocco to Indonesia likely to welcome infidel America and Israel dictating the destiny of the Muslim world.

As for the pro-American regimes in Kabul and Pakistan, they are but one bullet away from becoming anti-American. And should the Royal House of Saud come crashing down, as the War Party ardently hopes, do they seriously believe a Vermont-style democracy will arise?

Since Desert Storm, America has chopped its fleets, air wings and ground troops by near 50 percent, while adding military commitments in the Balkans, Afghanistan, the Gulf and Central Asia. Invading and occupying Iraq will require hundreds of thousands of more troops.

We are running out of army. And while Americans have shown they will back wars fought with no conscripts and few casualties, the day is not far off when they will be asked to draft their sons to fight for empire, and many of those sons will not be coming home. That day, Americans will tell us whether they really wish to pay the blood tax that is the price of policing the War Party's empire.

"I STAND BEFORE YOU TODAY A MULTILATERALIST"

U.N. Secretary General Kofi Annan

Following is the text of a speech delivered by U.N. Secretary-General Kofi Annan to the General Assembly on September 12, 2002. Annan took the unusual step of releasing the full text of his remarks to the press in advance of his speech, as he hoped to influence the rising debate over what kind of action to take vis-à-vis Iraq.

We cannot begin today without reflecting on yesterday's anniversary— and on the criminal challenge so brutally thrown in our faces on 11 September 2001.

The terrorist attacks of that day were not an isolated event. They were an extreme example of a global scourge, which requires a broad, sustained and global response.

Broad, because terrorism can be defeated only if all nations unite against it.

Sustained, because the battle against terrorism will not be won easily, or overnight. It requires patience and persistence.

And global, because terrorism is a widespread and complex phenomenon, with many deep roots and exacerbating factors.

Mr. President, I believe that such a response can only succeed if we make full use of multilateral institutions.

I stand before you today as a multilateralist—by precedent, by principle, by Charter and by duty.

I also believe that every government that is committed to the rule of law at home, must be committed also to the rule of law abroad. And all States have a clear interest, as well as clear responsibility, to uphold international law and maintain international order.

Our founding fathers, the statesmen of 1945, had learnt that lesson from the bitter experience of two world wars and a great depression.

They recognized that international security is not a zero-sum game. Peace, security and freedom are not finite commodities—like land, oil or gold— which one State can acquire at another's expense. On the contrary, the more peace, security and freedom any one State has, the more its neighbours are likely to have.

And they recognized that, by agreeing to exercise sovereignty together, they could gain a hold over problems that would defeat any one of them acting separately.

If those lessons were clear in 1945, should they not be much more so today, in the age of globalization?

On almost no item on our agenda does anyone seriously contend that each nation can fend for itself. Even the most powerful countries know that they need to work with others, in multilateral institutions, to achieve their aims.

Only by multilateral action can we ensure that open markets offer benefits and opportunities to all.

Only by multilateral action can we give people in the least developed countries the chance to escape the ugly misery of poverty, ignorance and disease.

Only by multilateral action can we protect ourselves from acid rain, or global warming; from the spread of HIV/AIDS, the illicit trade in drugs, or the odious traffic in human beings.

That applies even more to the prevention of terrorism. Individual States may defend themselves, by striking back at terrorist groups and at the countries that harbour or support them. But only concerted vigilance and cooperation among all States, with constant, systematic exchange of information, offers any real hope of denying the terrorists their opportunities.

On all these matters, for any one State—large or small—choosing to follow or reject the multilateral path must not be a simple matter of political convenience. It has consequences far beyond the immediate context.

When countries work together in multilateral institutions—developing, respecting, and when necessary enforcing international law—they also develop mutual trust, and more effective cooperation on other issues.

The more a country makes use of multilateral institutions—thereby respecting shared values, and accepting the obligations and restraints inherent in those values—the more others will trust and respect it, and the stronger its chance to exercise true leadership.

And among multilateral institutions, this universal Organization has a special place.

Any State, if attacked, retains the inherent right of self-defence under Article 51 of the Charter. But beyond that, when States decide to use force to deal with broader threats to international peace and security, there is no substitute for the unique legitimacy provided by the United Nations.

Member States attach importance, great importance in fact, to such legitimacy and to the international rule of law. They have shown—notably in the action to liberate Kuwait, 12 years ago—that they are willing to take actions under the authority of the Security Council, which they would not be willing to take without it.

The existence of an effective international security system depends on the Council's authority—and therefore on the Council having the political will to act, even in the most difficult cases, when agreement seems elusive at the outset. The primary criterion for putting an issue on the Council's agenda should not be the receptiveness of the parties, but the existence of a grave threat to world peace.

Let me now turn to four current threats to world peace, where true leadership and effective action are badly needed.

First, the Israeli-Palestinian conflict. Recently, many of us have been struggling to reconcile Israel's legitimate security concerns with Palestinian humanitarian needs.

But these limited objectives cannot be achieved in isolation from the wider political context. We must return to the search for a just and comprehensive solution, which alone can bring security and prosperity to both peoples, and indeed to the whole region.

The ultimate shape of a Middle East peace settlement is well known. It was defined long ago in Security Council Resolutions 242 and 338, and its Israeli-Palestinian components were spelt out even more clearly in Resolution 1397: land for peace; end to terror and to occupation; two States, Israel and Palestine, living side by side within secure and recognized borders.

Both parties accept this vision. But we can reach it only if we move rapidly and in parallel on all fronts. The so-called "sequential" approach has failed.

As we agreed at the Quartet meeting in Washington last May, an international peace conference is needed without delay, to set out a roadmap of parallel steps: steps to strengthen Israel's security, steps to strengthen Palestinian economic and political institutions, and steps to settle the details of the final peace agreement. Meanwhile, humanitarian steps to relieve Palestinian suffering must be intensified. The need is urgent.

Second, the leadership of Iraq continues to defy mandatory resolutions adopted by the Security Council under Chapter VII of the Charter.

I have engaged Iraq in an in-depth discussion on a range of issues, including the need for arms inspectors to return, in accordance with the relevant Security Council resolutions.

Efforts to obtain Iraq's compliance with the Council's resolutions must continue. I appeal to all those who have influence with Iraq's leaders to impress on them the vital importance of accepting the weapons inspections. This is the indispensable first step towards assuring the world that all Iraq's weapons of mass destruction have indeed been eliminated, and—let me stress—towards the suspension and eventual ending of the sanctions that are causing so many hardships for the Iraqi people.

I urge Iraq to comply with its obligations—for the sake of its own people, and for the sake of world order. If Iraq's defiance continues, the Security Council must face its responsibilities.

Third, permit me to press all of you, as leaders of the international community, to maintain your commitment to Afghanistan.

I know I speak for all in welcoming President Karzai to this Assembly, and congratulating him on his escape from last week's vicious assassination attempt—a graphic reminder of how hard it is to uproot the remnants of terrorism in any country where it has taken root. It was the international community's shameful neglect of Afghanistan in the 1990s that allowed the country to slide into chaos, providing a fertile breeding ground for Al Qaeda.

Today, Afghanistan urgently needs help in two areas. The Government must be helped to extend its authority throughout the country. Without this, all else may fail. And donors must follow through on their commitments to help with rehabilitation, reconstruction and development. Otherwise the Afghan people will lose hope—and desperation, we know, breeds violence.

And finally, in South Asia the world has recently come closer than for many years past to a direct conflict between two countries with nuclear capability. The situation may now have calmed a little, but it remains perilous. The underlying cause must be addressed. If a fresh crisis erupts, the international community might have a role to play; though I gladly acknowledge—and indeed, strongly welcome—the efforts made by well-placed Member States to help the two leaders find a solution.

Excellencies, let me conclude by reminding you of your pledge two years ago, at the Millennium Summit, "to make the United Nations a more effective instrument" in the service of the peoples of the world.

Today I ask all of you to honour that pledge.

Let us all recognize, from now on—in each capital, in every nation, large and small—that the global interest is our national interest.

"A GRAVE AND GATHERING DANGER . . ."

President George W. Bush

On September 12, 2002, President Bush went to the United Nations General Assembly and challenged the nations of the world to enforce the Security Council's resolutions on Iraq. This is an edited version of his speech.

Mr. Secretary General, Mr. President, distinguished delegates, and ladies and gentlemen: We meet one year and one day after a terrorist attack brought grief to my country, and brought grief to many citizens of our world. Yesterday, we remembered the innocent lives taken that terrible morning. Today, we turn to the urgent duty of protecting other lives, without illusion and without fear.

We've accomplished much in the last year—in Afghanistan and beyond. We have much yet to do—in Afghanistan and beyond. Many nations represented here have joined in the fight against global terror, and the people of the United States are grateful.

The United Nations was born in the hope that survived a world war—the hope of a world moving toward justice, escaping old patterns of conflict and fear. The founding members resolved that the peace of the world must never again be destroyed by the will and wickedness of any man. We created the United Nations Security Council, so that, unlike the League of Nations, our deliberations would be more than talk, our resolutions would be more than wishes. After generations of deceitful dictators and broken treaties and squandered lives, we dedicated ourselves to standards of human dignity shared by all, and to a system of security defended by all.

Today, these standards, and this security, are challenged.

[. . . .]

Our common security is challenged by regional conflicts—ethnic and religious strife that is ancient, but not inevitable. In the Middle East, there can be no peace for either side without freedom for both sides. America stands committed to an independent and democratic Palestine, living side by side with Israel in peace and security. Like all other people, Palestinians deserve a government that serves their interests and listens to their voices. My nation

313

will continue to encourage all parties to step up to their responsibilities as we seek a just and comprehensive settlement to the conflict.

Above all, our principles and our security are challenged today by outlaw groups and regimes that accept no law of morality and have no limit to their violent ambitions. In the attacks on America a year ago, we saw the destructive intentions of our enemies. This threat hides within many nations, including my own. In cells and camps, terrorists are plotting further destruction, and building new bases for their war against civilization. And our greatest fear is that terrorists will find a shortcut to their mad ambitions when an outlaw regime supplies them with the technologies to kill on a massive scale.

In one place—in one regime—we find all these dangers, in their most lethal and aggressive forms, exactly the kind of aggressive threat the United Nations was born to confront.

Twelve years ago, Iraq invaded Kuwait without provocation. And the regime's forces were poised to continue their march to seize other countries and their resources. Had Saddam Hussein been appeased instead of stopped, he would have endangered the peace and stability of the world. Yet this aggression was stopped—by the might of coalition forces and the will of the United Nations.

To suspend hostilities, to spare himself, Iraq's dictator accepted a series of commitments. The terms were clear, to him and to all. And he agreed to prove he is complying with every one of those obligations.

He has proven instead only his contempt for the United Nations, and for all his pledges. By breaking every pledge—by his deceptions, and by his cruelties—Saddam Hussein has made the case against himself.

In 1991, Security Council Resolution 688 demanded that the Iraqi regime cease at once the repression of its own people, including the systematic repression of minorities—which the Council said, threatened international peace and security in the region. This demand goes ignored.

Last year, the U.N. Commission on Human Rights found that Iraq continues to commit extremely grave violations of human rights, and that the regime's repression is all pervasive. Tens of thousands of political opponents and ordinary citizens have been subjected to arbitrary arrest and imprisonment, summary execution, and torture by beating and burning, electric shock, starvation, mutilation, and rape. Wives are tortured in front of their husbands, children in the presence of their parents—and all of these horrors concealed from the world by the apparatus of a totalitarian state.

In 1991, the U.N. Security Council, through Resolutions 686 and 687, demanded that Iraq return all prisoners from Kuwait and other lands. Iraq's regime agreed. It broke its promise. Last year the Secretary General's high-level coordinator for this issue reported that Kuwait, Saudi, Indian, Syrian,

Lebanese, Iranian, Egyptian, Bahraini, and Omani nationals remain unaccounted for—more than 600 people. One American pilot is among them.

In 1991, the U.N. Security Council, through Resolution 687, demanded that Iraq renounce all involvement with terrorism, and permit no terrorist organizations to operate in Iraq. Iraq's regime agreed. It broke this promise. In violation of Security Council Resolution 1373, Iraq continues to shelter and support terrorist organizations that direct violence against Iran, Israel, and Western governments. Iraqi dissidents abroad are targeted for murder. In 1993, Iraq attempted to assassinate the Emir of Kuwait and a former American President.* Iraq's government openly praised the attacks of September the 11th. And al Qaeda terrorists escaped from Afghanistan and are known to be in Iraq.

In 1991, the Iraqi regime agreed to destroy and stop developing all weapons of mass destruction and long-range missiles, and to prove to the world it has done so by complying with rigorous inspections. Iraq has broken every aspect of this fundamental pledge.

From 1991 to 1995, the Iraqi regime said it had no biological weapons.† After a senior official in its weapons program defected and exposed this lie, the regime admitted to producing tens of thousands of liters of anthrax and other deadly biological agents for use with Scud warheads, aerial bombs, and aircraft spray tanks. U.N. inspectors believe Iraq has produced two to four times the amount of biological agents it declared, and has failed to account for more than three metric tons of material that could be used to produce biological weapons. Right now, Iraq is expanding and improving facilities that were used for the production of biological weapons.

---

* Editors' note: This is one of the only times President Bush has made public reference to the alleged plot to assassinate his father. Only once, later in September during a Republican fundraiser in Houston, did the President use a more personal wording, calling Saddam "a guy that tried to kill my dad." It has been little reported that the former president's entourage during that 1993 Kuwait visit also included Laura Bush, the current First Lady; Neil Bush, his brother; and Neil's wife, Sharon—all of whom might also have been killed. Doubts remain, however, over whether there ever was a serious plot to assassinate former President Bush, and if the purported bomb can be linked to Iraq, or if the whole episode was conjured up by the Kuwaitis to reinforce the U.S. alliance with Kuwait. See Seymour Hersh's article on p. 140 for more details.

† Editors' note: Iraq has consistently said that it destroyed its remaining chemical and biological weapons stocks after the Gulf War, but it has so far been unable to provide documentary or other proof of doing so. President Bush's reference to "a senior official in [Iraq's] weapons program" presumably refers to Hussein Kamel, Saddam's brother-in-law, who defected in 1995 after running Iraq's WMD programs for ten years. According to *Newsweek* (March 3, 2003), Kamel "told CIA and British intelligence officers and U.N. inspectors in the summer of 1995 that after the Gulf War, Iraq destroyed all its chemical and biological weapons stocks and the missiles to deliver them." The U.N. inspectors did not take Kamel's statement as verification of Iraq's claim. Instead, *Newsweek* reports that Kamel's revelations "were hushed up by the U.N. inspectors" who wanted to "bluff Saddam into disclosing still more." Kamel's tale raises serious questions about whether the unaccounted-for Iraqi stockpile of chemical and biological weapons referred to by President Bush still exists. In February 2003, Iraq gave U.N. inspectors a list of people to interview who it said had participated in the destruction of the WMD stocks. But the question may never ultimately be settled. According to *Newsweek*, Kamel also told investigators that Iraq had not abandoned its WMD ambitions. Technical materials, design, and engineering details, and even missile-warhead molds were retained, sometimes in people's homes. The reason for doing so, said Kamel: "It is the first step to return to production" after the U.N. inspections were over.

United Nations' inspections also revealed that Iraq likely maintains stockpiles of VX, mustard and other chemical agents, and that the regime is rebuilding and expanding facilities capable of producing chemical weapons.

And in 1995, after four years of deception, Iraq finally admitted it had a crash nuclear weapons program prior to the Gulf War. We know now, were it not for that war, the regime in Iraq would likely have possessed a nuclear weapon no later than 1993.

Today, Iraq continues to withhold important information about its nuclear program—weapons design, procurement logs, experiment data, an accounting of nuclear materials and documentation of foreign assistance. Iraq employs capable nuclear scientists and technicians. It retains physical infrastructure needed to build a nuclear weapon. Iraq has made several attempts to buy high-strength aluminum tubes used to enrich uranium for a nuclear weapon. Should Iraq acquire fissile material, it would be able to build a nuclear weapon within a year. And Iraq's state-controlled media has reported numerous meetings between Saddam Hussein and his nuclear scientists, leaving little doubt about his continued appetite for these weapons.

Iraq also possesses a force of Scud-type missiles with ranges beyond the 150 kilometers permitted by the U.N. Work at testing and production facilities shows that Iraq is building more long-range missiles that it can inflict mass death throughout the region.

[. . . .]

As we meet today, it's been almost four years since the last U.N. inspectors set foot in Iraq, four years for the Iraqi regime to plan, and to build, and to test behind the cloak of secrecy.

We know that Saddam Hussein pursued weapons of mass murder even when inspectors were in his country. Are we to assume that he stopped when they left? The history, the logic, and the facts lead to one conclusion: Saddam Hussein's regime is a grave and gathering danger. To suggest otherwise is to hope against the evidence. To assume this regime's good faith is to bet the lives of millions and the peace of the world in a reckless gamble. And this is a risk we must not take.

Delegates to the General Assembly, we have been more than patient. We've tried sanctions. We've tried the carrot of oil for food, and the stick of coalition military strikes. But Saddam Hussein has defied all these efforts and continues to develop weapons of mass destruction. The first time we may be completely certain he has nuclear weapons is when, God forbid, he uses one. We owe it to all our citizens to do everything in our power to prevent that day from coming.

The conduct of the Iraqi regime is a threat to the authority of the United Nations, and a threat to peace. Iraq has answered a decade of U.N. demands with a decade of defiance. All the world now faces a test, and the United Nations a difficult and defining moment. Are Security Council resolutions to be honored and enforced, or cast aside without consequence? Will the United Nations serve the purpose of its founding, or will it be irrelevant?

The United States helped found the United Nations. We want the United Nations to be effective, and respectful, and successful. We want the resolutions of the world's most important multilateral body to be enforced. And right now those resolutions are being unilaterally subverted by the Iraqi regime. Our partnership of nations can meet the test before us, by making clear what we now expect of the Iraqi regime.

If the Iraqi regime wishes peace, it will immediately and unconditionally forswear, disclose, and remove or destroy all weapons of mass destruction, long-range missiles, and all related material.

If the Iraqi regime wishes peace, it will immediately end all support for terrorism and act to suppress it, as all states are required to do by U.N. Security Council resolutions.

If the Iraqi regime wishes peace, it will cease persecution of its civilian population, including Shi'a, Sunnis, Kurds, Turkomans, and others, again as required by Security Council resolutions.

If the Iraqi regime wishes peace, it will release or account for all Gulf War personnel whose fate is still unknown. It will return the remains of any who are deceased, return stolen property, accept liability for losses resulting from the invasion of Kuwait, and fully cooperate with international efforts to resolve these issues, as required by Security Council resolutions.

If the Iraqi regime wishes peace, it will immediately end all illicit trade outside the oil-for-food program. It will accept U.N. administration of funds from that program, to ensure that the money is used fairly and promptly for the benefit of the Iraqi people.

If all these steps are taken, it will signal a new openness and accountability in Iraq. And it could open the prospect of the United Nations helping to build a government that represents all Iraqis—a government based on respect for human rights, economic liberty, and internationally supervised elections.

The United States has no quarrel with the Iraqi people; they've suffered too long in silent captivity. Liberty for the Iraqi people is a great moral cause, and a great strategic goal. The people of Iraq deserve it; the security of all nations requires it. Free societies do not intimidate through cruelty and conquest, and open societies do not threaten the world with mass murder. The United States supports political and economic liberty in a unified Iraq.

[. . . .]

My nation will work with the U.N. Security Council to meet our common challenge. If Iraq's regime defies us again, the world must move deliberately, decisively to hold Iraq to account. We will work with the U.N. Security Council for the necessary resolutions. But the purposes of the United States should not be doubted. The Security Council resolutions will be enforced—the just demands of peace and security will be met—or action will be unavoidable. And a regime that has lost its legitimacy will also lose its power.

Events can turn in one of two ways: If we fail to act in the face of danger, the people of Iraq will continue to live in brutal submission. The regime will have new power to bully and dominate and conquer its neighbors, condemning the Middle East to more years of bloodshed and fear. The regime will remain unstable—the region will remain unstable, with little hope of freedom, and isolated from the progress of our times. With every step the Iraqi regime takes toward gaining and deploying the most terrible weapons, our own options to confront that regime will narrow. And if an emboldened regime were to supply these weapons to terrorist allies, then the attacks of September the 11th would be a prelude to far greater horrors.

If we meet our responsibilities, if we overcome this danger, we can arrive at a very different future. The people of Iraq can shake off their captivity. They can one day join a democratic Afghanistan and a democratic Palestine, inspiring reforms throughout the Muslim world. These nations can show by their example that honest government, and respect for women, and the great Islamic tradition of learning can triumph in the Middle East and beyond. And we will show that the promise of the United Nations can be fulfilled in our time.

Neither of these outcomes is certain. Both have been set before us. We must choose between a world of fear and a world of progress. We cannot stand by and do nothing while dangers gather. We must stand up for our security, and for the permanent rights and the hopes of mankind. By heritage and by choice, the United States of America will make that stand. And, delegates to the United Nations, you have the power to make that stand, as well.

Thank you very much.

PEACE PUZZLE

Michael Berube

Halfway through George W. Bush's term of office, one year since 9/11, and the ideal of moral clarity in U.S. foreign policy couldn't be murkier. According to Donald Rumsfeld, Paul Wolfowitz, Dick Cheney, and Richard Perle, every moment we postpone war with Iraq damages our credibility; according to Brent Scowcroft, General Anthony Zinni, Lawrence Eagleburger, and James Baker III, nothing would damage our credibility so much as a unilateral, preemptive war on Iraq.

The Bush administration is trying to persuade "allies" like Saudi Arabia to sign up for Gulf War II, but somebody keeps dropping hints to *The Washington Post* that when Iraq goes down, the Rand Corp. will advise the president that the kingdom should go next. On Tuesdays, Thursdays, and Saturdays, they tell the world that they desire nothing more than the liberation of oppressed Iraqis, but on Mondays, Wednesdays, and Fridays, their cheerleaders in the press bellow that what the Islamic world needs now is a crushing, humiliating military defeat that will bring a useful chaos to the part of the world running roughly from the West Bank to Islamabad. Such is the position of the war party. To gauge by the president's speech to the United Nations Thursday, the administration actually has a serious case to make against Saddam Hussein's violations of U.N. resolutions; but then again, the administration does not always hold U.N. resolutions in such high regard, and according to the White House chief of staff, Andrew Card, has waited so long to make its case because August is a bad time for new product placement. And you would think that if the president was having a hard time making his case to the Republican policy elite, let alone the U.N., it would be a simple matter for the American left to rally popular opposition to the war as well.

You might think that, but you'd be wrong. Most liberals in Congress are either mumbling under their breath or speaking up only to call for a "debate" they themselves are unwilling to begin; the progressive left has been noisier, but the progressive left has its own problems, mired as it is in an Afghanistan quagmire of its own making. It would be a positive service to democracy

Michael Berube is a professor of American literature at Penn State and the author of *Life As We Know It*. This article was published in *The Boston Globe* on September 15, 2002.

if left-wing public intellectuals would take the lead where elected liberals cannot or will not, urging their fellow Americans that the war on terrorism requires many things—peace in Israel and Palestine, an end to the United States' long-term addiction to oil—before it requires any regime change in Iraq. But the left is having some trouble providing that service, because one wing of it actually supports military intervention in Iraq, while another wing opposes all military interventions regardless of their objectives.

The left has been divided before, but rarely has it been at once so vehement and so incoherent as this. On one side are the internationalists who find themselves emboldened by laudable military interventions in Kosovo and Afghanistan, which used U.S. air power—but not ground troops—to overthrow two of the worst regimes on the planet. Some, like Michael Walzer of *Dissent* magazine, have already signed on for another Mission for Good in Iraq, becoming even more hawkish than most of the first Bush administration; others, like *The Nation* columnist Christopher Hitchens, have tentatively suggested that the United States might do well to consider that "you can't subject the Iraqi people to the cruelty of sanctions for so long while leaving the despot in place." (Hitchens notes that since the United States has intervened on Saddam Hussein's behalf in the past, "there is at least a potential argument that an intervention to cancel such debts would be justifiable." Who could have imagined that Hitchens and his lifelong nemesis Henry Kissinger would wind up sitting on the same fence, each refusing to look at the other?

On the other side are the anti-imperialists who opposed the war in Afghanistan in stark and unyielding terms. They did not cheer the collapse of the World Trade Center; that is simple slander. But they did argue, to their shame, that the U.S. military response was even more morally odious than the hijackers' deliberate slaughter of civilians. Some antiwar protesters were 19-year-old anarchists, some were devout Quakers, and some were Trotskyite diehards; but some were America's most distinguished dissidents at home and abroad, like Howard Zinn and Gore Vidal. And the antiwar left's arguments against war were simply astonishing. As Z *Magazine* contributor Cynthia Peters wrote last October, the operation that wrested control of Afghanistan from Al Qaeda and the Taliban was a "calculated crime against humanity that differs from September 11th only in scale; that is: it is many times larger." Obtuse arguments like these, combined with the paranoid insistence that the United States had long planned strikes against the Taliban in order to secure an Afghan oil pipeline (a claim thoroughly debunked by Ken Silverstein in *The American Prospect*), have damaged the anti-imperialists' cause immeasurably. The anti-imperialist left correctly believes, for instance, that the American bombing of Kakrak in early July (a massive "intelligence failure" that killed about 50 Afghans attending a wedding party) was an atrocity; but it cannot admit that, on balance, the routing of the Taliban might have struck a blow, however ambiguous and poorly executed, for human freedom.

Accordingly, *The Nation,* the most mainstream of journals on the progressive left, has become remarkably ambivalent about what it means to be a progressive leftist. On one page of its Sept. 2 issue, an unsigned editorial titled "Iraq: The Doubters Grow" asks whether we will leave Iraq in chaos "as we have done in Afghanistan." On the very next page, an editorial by Anthony Borden and John West of the Institute for War and Peace Reporting details the chaos of Kabul yet acknowledges that "conditions are vastly improved from the circumstances of only a few months ago—when the country was plagued by severe persecution and increasing food shortages with seemingly no hope." Perhaps we have not brought disaster to Afghanistan after all; it's hard to tell here. Still further left, the *Counterpunch* and *Z Magazine* stalwarts have kept their self-assurance but have lost their credibility—not with the Bush administration, of course, which had no plans to read Noam Chomsky's complete works before settling on an Iraq policy, but with much of the rest of the progressive left, among whose ranks I include myself.

For leftists like me who had long considered Chomsky as our own beacon of moral clarity, it is hard to say which development is more catastrophic: the fact that Chomsky-bashing has become a major political pastime, or the fact that Chomsky has become so very difficult to defend. Chomsky's response to the war in Afghanistan offered a repellent mix of hysteria and hauteur, as in this early interview: "The U.S. has already demanded that Pakistan terminate the food and other supplies that are keeping at least some of the starving and suffering people of Afghanistan alive. If that demand is implemented, unknown numbers of people who have not the remotest connection to terrorism will die, possibly millions. Let me repeat: the U.S. has demanded that Pakistan kill possibly millions of people who are themselves victims of the Taliban. This has nothing to do even with revenge. It is at a far lower moral level even than that. The significance is heightened by the fact that this is mentioned in passing, with no comment, and probably will hardly be noticed. We can learn a great deal about the moral level of the reigning intellectual culture of the West by observing the reaction to this demand." By the same token, we can learn a great deal about the moral level of the antiwar left by observing its willingness to debate claims like these; over the past year, unfortunately, Chomsky and his followers have demonstrated rather little capacity for self-criticism. It is not permissible, apparently, to argue that Chomsky was right about Vietnam, Nicaragua, and East Timor but wrong about Afghanistan; those who fail to acknowledge Chomsky's infallibility about Afghanistan are guilty of thought-crime or conservatism, whichever is worse.

Most likely the hard left's myopia and intransigence will not matter to most Americans—that is, those who never trusted the judgment of Chomsky or Z *Magazine* in the first place and don't see why it matters now that anti-imperialists have lost a "credibility" they never had in some quarters. But the reason it should matter, even in parts of America where there are no campuses, no anti-Sharon rallies, and no subscribers to *Counterpunch,* is that the United States cannot be a beacon of freedom and justice to the world if it conducts itself as an empire. Nor can we fight Al Qaeda networks in 60 countries if we alienate our allies in Europe, who so far seem to be much more capable of finding and arresting members of Al Qaeda than is our own Justice Department.

The antiwar left once knew well that its anti-imperialism was in fact a form of patriotism—until it lost its bearings in Kosovo and Kabul, insisting beyond all reason that those military campaigns were imperialist wars for oil or regional power. And why does that matter? Because in the agora of public opinion, the antiwar left never claimed to speak to pragmatic concerns or political contingencies: for the antiwar left, the moral ground was the only ground there was. So when the antiwar left finds itself on shaky moral ground, it simply collapses.

In foreign affairs both left and right claim to speak for the conscience of America, but on Iraq the right has no moral clarity and the left has lost its moral compass. This is not a problem for the masters of realpolitik, who have long since inured themselves to the task of doing terrible things to human beings in the course of pursuing the national interest; but it is utterly devastating to those few souls who still dream that the course of human events should be judged—and guided—by principles common to many nations rather than by policies concocted by one. The emergence of the antiwar right, however, may yet hold a lesson for the left, insofar as it relies on Brent Scowcroft's internationalism rather than Pat Buchanan's isolationism: The challenge, clearly, is to learn how to be strenuously anti-imperialist without being indiscriminately antiwar. It is a lesson the American left has never had to learn—until now.

STUCK TO THE U.N. TAR BABY

George Will

A contemporary said of Chief Justice John Marshall—the most consequential American never to be president—that "he hit the Constitution much as the Lord hit the chaos, at a time when everything needed creating." President Bush is struggling to do something comparably ambitious in international affairs.

One reason it is such a struggle is that new technologies of menace are in the hands of regimes that can—as Iraq is doing with its letter proposing renewed weapons inspections—manipulate the United Nations. The dominant thought of the "international community"—wishful thinking—invests the United Nations with the responsibility for coping with the menace.

The president touched that tar baby, the United Nations, in November when he improvidently proposed the return of U.N. weapons inspectors, and he was not unstuck from the tar baby by Vice President Cheney's recent insistence that inspectors could provide only "false comfort." There is a domestic constituency that favors staying stuck. It favors it for various reasons, but one has a particularly long pedigree.

Chief Justice Marshall, a great definer of American nationhood, was opposed by Jeffersonians, with their anti-nationalist vision of the nation as only a confederation produced by a compact (implicitly revocable; see 1861) among states. Today Bush's defense of American national autonomy is opposed, among Americans, mainly by members of the party that traces its lineage to Jefferson.

Many Democrats have more than a merely banal political reason—they believe they prosper when focusing on domestic matters—for pushing this nation deeper into the tar baby's embrace. Their desire is to avoid having to assert what many of them believe: that the use of U.S. force in preemptive self-defense requires permission from the not altogether savory collection of regimes that is misnamed the United Nations.

It is perverse, and profoundly dangerous, that the United Nations is being encouraged to place upon its own brow a garland of laurels it has woven for it-

George Will is a syndicated columnist, ABC television commentator, and author whose work appears in more than 450 newspapers and regularly in *Newsweek*. This column was published on September 19, 2002.

self as the sole legitimizer of force in international affairs. Even NATO, an alliance of democracies, is said to be morally bound to defer. The United Nations' overweening vanity is made possible by the acquiescence of formerly formidable European nations. They now are eager to disguise decadence as a moral gesture, that of sloughing off sovereignty—and with it, responsibilities.

The United Nations' prestige is at an apogee and its performance is at a nadir. The composition of its Security Council is anachronistic—a historical accident. If the United Nations were being founded today, France would not be a permanent member of the Security Council and India would be. India's population is 17 times that of France and three times that of all 15 members of the European Union; India will account for one-fifth of the world's population growth this year, and by 2050 it will have a population almost as large as the world had in 1900.

No wonder France celebrates deference to the United Nations, which is a mirror with a frozen reflection of the world in 1945. That is why another shadow of a great power, Russia, with a GDP of $300 billion (smaller than the Netherlands') is a permanent member of the Security Council, and Japan, with a GDP of $2.9 trillion, is not.

In Iraq, the United Nations is meeting its Abyssinia. That is what Ethiopia was called in October 1935, when Mussolini's Italy invaded it and the United Nations' predecessor, the League of Nations, proved to be impotent as an instrument of international order.

When the president told the United Nations that Iraq's race for weapons of mass destruction is a "grave and gathering danger," he echoed the title of the first volume of Churchill's history of the Second World War, "The Gathering Storm." The president's substitution of the phrase "grave and gathering danger" for the common phrase "clear and present danger" is freighted with significance.

Some critics seem to say that in order for the president to "make the case" for proving that the danger is present, its presence must be evidenced by a "smoking gun." But that means America cannot act against Iraq until acting is much more dangerous, when Iraq has nuclear weapons.

With America's political culture increasingly colored by the legal culture, and with Democrats increasingly the party of trial lawyers, there is a growing tendency to treat foreign policy crises as episodes of "Law & Order," crises to be discussed in televisioncourtroom patois, such as "smoking gun." As Condoleezza Rice has said, let us hope the smoking gun is not a mushroom cloud.

AGAINST A DOCTRINE OF PRE-EMPTIVE WAR

Former Vice President Al Gore

On September 23, 2002, former Vice-President and Democratic Presidential candidate Al Gore spoke out on the Bush administration's Iraq policy in a speech to the Commonwealth Club of California. Following is an abridged transcript of his remarks.

Like all Americans I have been wrestling with the question of what our country needs to do to defend itself from the kind of intense, focused and enabled hatred that brought about September 11th, and which at this moment must be presumed to be gathering force for yet another attack. I'm speaking today in an effort to recommend a specific course of action for our country which I believe would be preferable to the course recommended by President Bush. Specifically, I am deeply concerned that the policy we are presently following with respect to Iraq has the potential to seriously damage our ability to win the war against terrorism and to weaken our ability to lead the world in this new century.

To begin with, I believe we should focus our efforts first and foremost against those who attacked us on September 11th and have thus far gotten away with it. The vast majority of those who sponsored, planned and implemented the cold blooded murder of more than 3,000 Americans are still at large, still neither located nor apprehended, much less punished and neutralized. I do not believe that we should allow ourselves to be distracted from this urgent task simply because it is proving to be more difficult and lengthy than predicted. Great nations persevere and then prevail. They do not jump from one unfinished task to another.

We are perfectly capable of staying the course in our war against Osama bin Laden and his terrorist network, while simultaneously taking those steps necessary to build an international coalition to join us in taking on Saddam Hussein in a timely fashion.

I don't think that we should allow anything to diminish our focus on avenging the 3,000 Americans who were murdered and dismantling the network of terrorists who we know to be responsible for it. The fact that we don't know where they are should not cause us to focus instead on some other enemy whose location may be easier to identify.

Nevertheless, President Bush is telling us that the most urgent requirement of the moment—right now—is not to redouble our efforts against Al Qaeda, not to stabilize the nation of Afghanistan after driving his host government from power, but instead to shift our focus and concentrate on immediately launching a new war against Saddam Hussein. And he is proclaiming a new, uniquely American right to pre-emptively attack whomsoever he may deem represents a potential future threat.

Moreover, he is demanding in this high political season that Congress speedily affirm that he has the necessary authority to proceed immediately against Iraq and for that matter any other nation in the region, regardless of subsequent developments or circumstances. The timing of this sudden burst of urgency to take up this cause as America's new top priority, displacing the war against Osama bin Laden, was explained by the White House Chief of Staff in his now well known statement that "from an advertising point of view, you don't launch a new product line until after Labor Day."

Nevertheless, Iraq does pose a serious threat to the stability of the Persian Gulf and we should organize an international coalition to eliminate his access to weapons of mass destruction. Iraq's search for weapons of mass destruction has proven impossible to completely deter and we should assume that it will continue for as long as Saddam is in power. Moreover, no international law can prevent the United States from taking actions to protect its vital interests, when it is manifestly clear that there is a choice to be made between law and survival. I believe, however, that such a choice is not presented in the case of Iraq. Indeed, should we decide to proceed, that action can be justified within the framework of international law rather than outside it. In fact, though a new U.N. resolution may be helpful in building international consensus, the existing resolutions from 1991 are sufficient from a legal standpoint.

We also need to look at the relationship between our national goal of regime change in Iraq and our goal of victory in the war against terror. In the case of Iraq, it would be more difficult for the United States to succeed alone, but still possible. By contrast, the war against terror manifestly requires broad and continuous international cooperation. Our ability to secure this kind of cooperation can be severely damaged by unilateral action against Iraq. If the Administration has reason to believe otherwise, it ought to share those reasons with the Congress—since it is asking Congress to endorse action that might well impair a more urgent task: continuing to disrupt and destroy the international terror network.

[. . . .]

President George H. W. Bush purposely waited until after the mid-term elections of 1990 to push for a vote at the beginning of the new Congress in January of 1991. President George W. Bush, by contrast, is pushing for a vote in this Congress immediately before the election. Rather than making efforts to dispel concern at home and abroad about the role of politics in the timing of his policy, the President is publicly taunting Democrats with the political consequences of a "no" vote—even as the Republican National Committee runs pre-packaged advertising based on the same theme—in keeping with the political strategy clearly described in a White House aide's misplaced computer disk, which advised Republican operatives that their principal game plan for success in the election a few weeks away was to "focus on the war." Vice President Cheney, meanwhile, indignantly described suggestions of political motivation "reprehensible." The following week he took his discussion of war strategy to the Rush Limbaugh show.

The foreshortening of deliberation in the Congress robs the country of the time it needs for careful analysis of what may lie before it. Such consideration is all the more important because of the Administration's failure thus far to lay out an assessment of how it thinks the course of a war will run—even while it has given free rein to persons both within and close to the administration to suggest that this will be an easy conquest. Neither has the Administration said much to clarify its idea of what is to follow regime change or of the degree of engagement it is prepared to accept for the United States in Iraq in the months and years after a regime change has taken place.

By shifting from his early focus after September 11th on war against terrorism to war against Iraq . . . the President has somehow squandered the international outpouring of sympathy, goodwill and solidarity that followed the attacks of September 11th and converted it into anger and apprehension aimed much more at the United States than at the terrorist network—much as we manage to squander in one year's time the largest budget surpluses in history and convert them into massive fiscal deficits. He has compounded this by asserting a new doctrine—of pre-emption.

The doctrine of pre-emption is based on the idea that in the era of proliferating WMD, and against the background of a sophisticated terrorist threat, the United States cannot wait for proof of a fully established mortal threat, but should rather act at any point to cut that short.

The problem with pre-emption is that in the first instance it is not needed in order to give the United States the means to act in its own defense against terrorism in general or Iraq in particular. But that is a relatively minor issue compared to the longer-term consequences that can be foreseen for this doctrine. To begin with, the doctrine is presented in open-ended terms, which means that if Iraq is the first point of application, it is not necessarily the last. In fact, the very logic of the concept suggests a string of military engagements against a succession of sovereign states: Syria, Libya, North Korea, Iran, etc., wherever the combination exists of an interest in weapons of mass destruction together with an ongoing role as host to or participant in terrorist operations. It means also that if the Congress approves the Iraq resolution just proposed by the Administration it is simultaneously creating the precedent for pre-emptive action anywhere, anytime this or any future president so decides.

The Bush Administration may now be realizing that national and international cohesion are strategic assets. But it is a lesson long delayed and clearly not uniformly and consistently accepted by senior members of the cabinet. From the outset, the Administration has operated in a manner calculated to please the portion of its base that occupies the far right, at the expense of solidarity among Americans and between America and her allies.

On the domestic front, the Administration, months before conceding the need to create an institution outside the White House to manage homeland defense, has been willing to see progress on the new department held up, for the sake of an effort to coerce the Congress into stripping civil service protections from tens of thousands of federal employees.

Far more damaging, however, is the Administration's attack on fundamental constitutional rights. The idea that an American citizen can be imprisoned without recourse to judicial process or remedies, and that this can be done on the say-so of the President or those acting in his name, is beyond the pale.

Regarding other countries, the Administration's disdain for the views of others is well documented and need not be reviewed here. It is more important to note the consequences of an emerging national strategy that not only celebrates American strengths, but appears to be glorifying the notion of dominance. If what America represents to the world is leadership in a commonwealth of equals, then our friends are legion; if what we represent to the world is empire, then it is our enemies who will be legion.

[. . . .]

The events of the last eighty-five years provide ample evidence that our approach to winning the peace that follows war is almost as important as winning the war itself. The absence of enlightened nation building after World War I led directly to the conditions which made Germany vulnerable to fascism and the rise of Adolf Hitler and made all of Europe vulnerable to his evil designs. By contrast the enlightened vision embodied in the Marshall plan, NATO, and the other nation building efforts in the aftermath of World War II led directly to the conditions that fostered prosperity and peace for most of the years since this city gave birth to the United Nations.

Two decades ago, when the Soviet Union claimed the right to launch a preemptive war in Afghanistan, we properly encouraged and then supported the resistance movement which, a decade later, succeeded in defeating the Soviet Army's efforts. Unfortunately, when the Russians left, we abandoned the Afghans and the lack of any coherent nation building program led directly to the conditions which fostered Al Qaeda terrorist bases and Osama bin Laden's plotting against the World Trade Center. Incredibly, after defeating the Taliban rather easily, and despite pledges from President Bush that we would never again abandon Afghanistan we have done precisely that. And now the Taliban and Al Qaeda are quickly moving back to take up residence there again. A mere two years after we abandoned Afghanistan the first time, Saddam Hussein invaded Kuwait. Following a brilliant military campaign, the U.S. abandoned the effort to destroy Saddam's military prematurely and allowed him to remain in power.

What is a potentially even more serious consequence of this push to begin a new war as quickly as possible is the damage it can do not just to America's prospects to winning the war against terrorism but to America's prospects for continuing the historic leadership we began providing to the world fifty-seven years ago, right here in this city by the bay.

I believe, therefore, that the resolution that the President has asked Congress to pass is much too broad in the authorities it grants, and needs to be narrowed. The President should be authorized to take action to deal with Saddam Hussein as being in material breach of the terms of the truce and therefore a continuing threat to the security of the region. To this should be added that his continued pursuit of weapons of mass destruction is potentially a threat to the vital interests of the United States. But Congress should also urge the President to make every effort to obtain a fresh demand from the Security Council for prompt, unconditional compliance by Iraq within a definite period of time. If the Council will not provide such language, then other choices remain open, but in any event the President should be urged to take the time to assemble the broadest possible international support for his course of action. Anticipating that the President will still move toward unilateral action, the Congress should establish now what the administration's thinking is regarding the aftermath of a U.S. attack for the purpose of regime change.

Specifically, Congress should establish why the President believes that unilateral action will not severely damage the fight against terrorist networks, and that preparations are in place to deal with the effects of chemical and biological attacks against our allies, our forces in the field, and even the homefront. The resolution should also require commitments from the President that action in Iraq will not be permitted to distract from continuing and improving work to reconstruct Afghanistan, and that the United States will commit to stay the course for the reconstruction of Iraq.

The Congressional resolution should make explicitly clear that authorities for taking these actions are to be presented as derivatives from existing Security Council resolutions and from international law: not requiring any formal new doctrine of pre-emption, which remains to be discussed subsequently in view of its gravity.

Last week President Bush added a troubling new element to this debate by proposing a broad new strategic doctrine that goes far beyond issues related to Iraq and would affect the basic relationship between the United States and the rest of the world community. Article 51 of the United Nations charter recognizes the right of any nation to defend itself, including the right in some circumstances to take pre-emptive actions in order to deal with imminent threats. President Bush now asserts that we will take pre-emptive action even if we take the threat we perceive as not imminent. If other nations assert the same right then the rule of law will quickly be replaced by the reign of fear—any nation that perceives circumstances that could eventually lead to an imminent threat would be justified under this approach in taking military action against another nation. An unspoken part of this new doctrine appears to be that we claim this right for ourselves—and only for ourselves. It is, in that sense, part of a broader strategy to replace ideas like deterrence and containment with what some in the administration call "dominance."

This is because President Bush is presenting us with a proposition that contains within itself one of the most fateful decisions in our history: a decision to abandon what we have thought was America's mission in the world—a world in which nations are guided by a common ethic codified in the form of international law—if we want to survive.

We have faced such a choice once before, at the end of the Second World War. At that moment, America's power in comparison to the rest of the world was if anything greater than it is now, and the temptation was clearly to use that power to assure ourselves that there would be no competitor and no threat to our security for the foreseeable future. The choice we made, however, was to become a co-founder of what we now think of as the post-war era, based on the concepts of collective security and defense, manifested first of all in the United Nations. Through all the dangerous years that followed, when we understood that the defense of freedom required the readiness to put the existence of the nation itself into the balance, we never abandoned our belief that what we were struggling to achieve was not bounded by our own physical security, but extended to the unmet hopes of humankind. The issue before us is whether we now face circumstances so dire and so novel that we must choose one objective over the other.

So it is reasonable to conclude that we face a problem that is severe, chronic, and likely to become worse over time.

But is a general doctrine of pre-emption necessary in order to deal with this problem? With respect to weapons of mass destruction, the answer is clearly not. The Clinton Administration launched a massive series of air strikes against Iraq for the stated purpose of setting back his capacity to pursue weapons of mass destruction. There was no perceived need for new doctrine or new authorities to do so. The limiting factor was the state of our knowledge concerning the whereabouts of some assets, and a concern for limiting conse-quences to the civilian populace, which in some instances might well have suffered greatly.

Does Saddam Hussein present an imminent threat, and if he did would the United States be free to act without international permission? If he presents an imminent threat we would be free to act under generally accepted under-standings of Article 51 of the U.N. Charter which reserves for member states the right to act in self-defense.

If Saddam Hussein does not present an imminent threat, then is it justifi-able for the Administration to be seeking by every means to precipitate a con-frontation, to find a cause for war, and to attack? There is a case to be made that further delay only works to Saddam Hussein's advantage, and that the clock should be seen to have been running on the issue of compliance for a decade: therefore not needing to be reset again to the starting point. But to the extent that we have any concern for international support, whether for its political or material value, hurrying the process will be costly. Even those who now agree that Saddam Hussein must go, may divide deeply over the wisdom of presenting the United States as impatient for war.

At the same time, the concept of pre-emption is accessible to other countries. There are plenty of potential imitators: India/Pakistan; China/Taiwan; not to forget Israel/Iraq or Israel/Iran. Russia has already cited it in anticipation of a possible military push into Georgia, on grounds that this state has not done enough to block the operations of Chechen rebels. What this doctrine does is to destroy the goal of a world in which states con-sider themselves subject to law, particularly in the matter of standards for the use of violence against each other. That concept would be displaced by the notion that there is no law but the discretion of the President of the United States.

I believe that we can effectively defend ourselves abroad and at home without dimming our principles. Indeed, I believe that our success in defending ourselves depends precisely on not giving up what we stand for.

WHY WE HATE THEM

Ann Coulter

I've been too busy fretting about "why they hate us" to follow the Democrats' latest objections to the war on terrorism. So it was nice to have Al Gore lay out their full traitorous case this week. To show we really mean business, Gore said we should not get sidetracked by a madman developing weapons of mass destruction who longs for our annihilation.

Rather, Gore thinks the U.S. military should spend the next 20 years sifting through rubble in Tora Bora until they produce Osama bin Laden's DNA. "I do not believe that we should allow ourselves to be distracted from this urgent task," he said, "simply because it is proving to be more difficult and lengthy than predicted."

Al Bore wants to put the war on terrorism in a lockbox.

Gore also complained that Bush has made the "rest of the world" angry at us. Boo hoo hoo. He said foreigners are not worried about "what the terrorist networks are going to do, but about what we're going to do."

Good. They should be worried. They hate us? We hate them. Americans don't want to make Islamic fanatics love us. We want to make them die. There's nothing like horrendous physical pain to quell angry fanatics. So sorry they're angry—wait until they see American anger. Japanese kamikaze pilots hated us once too. A couple of well-aimed nuclear weapons, and now they are gentle little lambs. That got their attention.

Stewing over the "profound and troubling change in the attitude of the German electorate toward the United States," Gore ruefully noted that the German-American relationship is in "a dire crisis." Alas, the Germans hate us.

That's not all. According to Gore, the British hate us, too. Gore said Prime Minister Tony Blair is getting into "what they describe as serious trouble with the British electorate" because of his alliance with the U.S. ("Serious trouble" is British for "serious trouble.")

That same night, James Carville—the heart and soul of the Democratic

Ann Coulter is a political analyst, attorney, and self-described "bomb thrower" who has been dubbed "the Abbie Hoffman of the Right" for her no-holds-barred commentaries on the Washington scene. After September 11th, in her column for *National Review Online*, she wrote of "the ones cheering and dancing right now" that "we should invade their countries, kill their leaders and convert them to Christianity." The resulting controversy led to a break between her and *National Review.* Her column now appears in *FrontPageMagazine.com,* where this article was published on September 26, 2002.

Party—read from the identical talking points on "Crossfire": "The Koreans hate us. Now the Germans—you know that's one against Germany. You know what? You know what? If we had a foreign policy that tried to get people to like us, as opposed to irritating everybody in the damn world, it would be a lot better thing." (Hillary Clinton on James Carville: "Great human being.")

Perhaps we could get Djibouti to like us if we legalized clitorectomies for little girls. America is fighting for its survival and the Democrats are obsessing over why barbarians hate us.

The Democrats' scrolling series of objections to the war is utterly contradictory. On one hand, liberals say Bush is trying to build an "empire." But on the other hand, they are cross that we haven't turned Afghanistan into the 51st state yet. This follows their earlier argument that Afghanistan would be another Vietnam "quagmire."

The "empire" argument is wildly popular among the anti-American set. Maureen Dowd said Dick Cheney and "Rummy" were seeking "the perks of empire," hoping to install "lemon fizzes, cribbage and cricket by the Tower of Babel." She warned that invading Iraq would make them hate us: "How long can it be before the empire strikes back?"

Ah yes—we must mollify angry fanatics who seek our destruction because otherwise they might get mad and seek our destruction.

Gore, too, says America will only create more enemies if "what we represent to the world is an empire." But then he complained that we have "abandoned almost all of Afghanistan"—rather than colonizing it, evidently. He seems to think it is our responsibility to "stabilize the nation of Afghanistan" and recommends that we "assemble a peacekeeping force large enough to pacify the countryside."

And then we bring in the lemon fizzes, cribbage and cricket?

After tiring themselves out all summer yapping about how Bush can't invade Iraq without first consulting Congress, now the Democrats are huffy that they might actually have to vote. On "Meet the Press" a few weeks ago, Sen. Hillary Clinton objected to having to vote on a war resolution before the November elections, saying, "I don't know that we want to put it in a political context."

Yes, it would be outrageous for politicians to have to inform the voters how they stand on important national security issues before an election.

Minority Whip Nancy Pelosi, D-Calif., the ranking Democrat on the House intelligence committee, said the Democrats would not have enough information to make an informed decision on Iraq—until January. The war will have to take back seat to urgent issues like prescription drugs and classroom size until then. The Democratic Party simply cannot rouse itself to battle.

Instead of obsessing over why angry primitives hate Americans, a more fruitful area for Democrats to examine might be why Americans are beginning to hate Democrats.

WHAT'S MISSING IN THE IRAQ DEBATE

Peggy Noonan

The battle is joined, the debate begun in earnest. In the past 48 hours we have witnessed Bush vs. Daschle, Hitchens vs. Cockburn, Democrats vs. Republicans, *The American Conservative* vs. *The Weekly Standard* and *National Review,* paleocons vs. neocons, compassionate conservatives vs. the left. In New York we debate whether strong criticism of Israeli policy is prima facie evidence of anti-Semitism. In Washington it's two questions: Who owns conservatism, and is the modern left more than a collection of depressives, America-lasters and anti-Semites?

The background music to all this has underscored the drama of the moment: It is the plaintive wilderness fiddle of PBS's "The Civil War," repeated each night all week. You can walk the dog in the evening in the upscale neighborhoods of the East and hear the fiddle's lonely tune coming from the screened windows of neighbor after neighbor. It's what you hear as you walk along, wondering how the question of war will be resolved.

We wanted interesting lives, and we got them.

WHAT IS at issue as we discuss war on Iraq? The safety of America, of untold numbers of people, the position of our country in the Mideast and elsewhere—and that's just the beginning. The debate has already become personal. This one is "a repulsive character," that one is "another middle-aged porker of the right." Personal viciousness is probably inevitable, but this fight should be serious.

It should be epochal.

One question has already been settled. The war will be the great issue of the 2002 elections. Some Democrats says this is Karl Rove's plan to restrict the national conversation to foreign policy, where Republicans are traditionally strong, and away from the economy. Maybe that is Mr. Rove's plan, and if it is, it's not without logic—what *is* more important than war?

Peggy Noonan is a contributing editor of *The Wall Street Journal* and the author, most recently, of *When Character Was King: A Story of Ronald Reagan.* This article was published on September 27, 2002 in the *Journal.*

But as plans go it's not without danger. Opponents of the war will now gather their forces, their resources, their arguments and data. They'll be all over trying to make their case. They'll have no trouble being heard.

So far they've not done well. They have argued that there are grave risks to action, but this is not an argument. There are grave risks to inaction, too. They have argued that America will have a hard time establishing a new Iraqi government. Well, yes. That doesn't mean it must not or cannot be attempted.

More is needed from the opposition.

The Bush administration says Saddam Hussein is sinister and vicious. Let me, with confidence and admitted presumption, assert on behalf of the majority of Americans: We believe it. Saddam has used poison gas, has already invaded two neighboring countries, has murdered people in the coldest of blood. The administration says Saddam is gathering weapons of mass destruction, and again: We believe it. There is plenty of evidence, and there is also proof. They say he is pursuing nuclear arms. Again: We believe it. He would.

The opponents of war, it seems to me, must face the questions that flow from what we know.

If you know Saddam is wicked, know he's gathering weapons of mass murder, know madmen are likely to ultimately use the weapons they stockpile, and know, finally, that he wishes America ill, then why not move against him? And why not now? Wouldn't inaction be irresponsible?

BUT THE administration still has questions to face, too. Among them: What has stopped Saddam from using the weapons he has, and has had for some time? Isn't it deterrence—the sure knowledge that if he launches missiles weighted with weapons of mass murder he can wave goodbye to Baghdad, to his own life and those of many, many of his countrymen? The era of Saddam the Great would end.

If we move against Saddam now, this inhibiting incentive is lessened or removed. What will stop Saddam from going out in a great blaze of "glory"? He can kill millions.

Why is deterrence no longer operable?

The Democrats on Capitol Hill have so far failed to mount a principled, coherent opposition. I am not shocked by this, are you? One senses they are looking at the whole question merely as a matter of popular positioning: *Will they like me if I say take out Saddam? Will they get mad at me if we try to take him out and it's a disaster? Will they like me if I say there's no reason to go to war? Have I focus-grouped this?* Such unseriousness is potentially deeply destructive. It is certainly irresponsible. And here's the funny thing: If some Demo-

crat stood up and spoke thoughtfully and without regard for political consequences about what is right for us to do, he'd likely garner enhanced respect
and heightened standing. He'd seem taller than his colleagues. At any rate,
more than usual, I am missing Pat Moynihan and Sam Nunn.

Members of the administration, on the other hand, seem lately almost ine-
briated with a sense of mission. And maybe that's inevitable when the stakes
are high and you're sure you're right. But in off-the-cuff remarks and unprepared moments the president and some of his men often seem to have missing within them a sense of the tragic. Which is odd because we're talking
about war, after all. Leaders can't lead by moping, but a certain, well, solem-
nity, I suppose, might be well received by many of us.

AT ANY RATE, the battle is joined. It will be waged over the next six weeks. It is
going to be hot. It is going to dominate public discourse. This is good. We
need and deserve a debate that is worthy of the moment, and worthy of the
people—the millions of them—who could be affected by America's decision
one way or another.

And by the way, it is not bad for a critical world to see how a great democracy, the world's oldest, goes about resolving questions of the utmost gravity.
This is a good time to remind them who, and what, we are.

WARS ARE NEVER FOUGHT FOR ALTRUISTIC REASONS

Arundhati Roy

Recently, those who have criticised the actions of the U.S. government (myself included) have been called "anti-American." Anti-Americanism is in the process of being consecrated into an ideology. The term is usually used by the American establishment to discredit and, not falsely—but shall we say inaccurately—define its critics. Once someone is branded anti-American, the chances are that he or she will be judged before they're heard and the argument will be lost in the welter of bruised national pride.

What does the term mean? That you're anti-jazz? Or that you're opposed to free speech? That you don't delight in Toni Morrison or John Updike? That you have a quarrel with giant sequoias? Does it mean you don't admire the hundreds of thousands of American citizens who marched against nuclear weapons, or the thousands of war resisters who forced their government to withdraw from Vietnam? Does it mean that you hate all Americans?

This sly conflation of America's music, literature, the breathtaking physical beauty of the land, the ordinary pleasures of ordinary people with criticism of the U.S. government's foreign policy is a deliberate and extremely effective strategy. It's like a retreating army taking cover in a heavily populated city, hoping that the prospect of hitting civilian targets will deter enemy fire.

There are many Americans who would be mortified to be associated with their government's policies. The most scholarly, scathing, incisive, hilarious critiques of the hypocrisy and the contradictions in U.S. government policy come from American citizens. (Similarly, in India, not hundreds, but millions of us would be ashamed and offended, if we were in any way implicated with the present Indian government's fascist policies.)

To call someone anti-American, indeed, to be anti-American, is not just racist, it's a failure of the imagination. An inability to see the world in terms other than those that the establishment has set out for you: If you don't love

Arundhati Roy is the author of the novel *The God of Small Things,* for which she received the 1997 Booker Prize. She has also written three nonfiction books, *The Cost of Living, Power Politics,* and *War Talk.* This article was published on September 27, 2002 in *The Guardian* (London).

us, you hate us. If you're not good, you're evil. If you're not with us, you're with the terrorists.

Last year, like many others, I too made the mistake of scoffing at this post-September 11 rhetoric, dismissing it as foolish and arrogant. I've realised that it's not. It's actually a canny recruitment drive for a misconceived, dangerous war. Every day I'm taken aback at how many people believe that opposing the war in Afghanistan amounts to supporting terrorism. Now that the initial aim of the war—capturing Osama bin Laden—seems to have run into bad weather, the goalposts have been moved. It's being made out that the whole point of the war was to topple the Taliban regime and liberate Afghan women from their burqas. We're being asked to believe that the U.S. marines are actually on a feminist mission. (If so, will their next stop be America's military ally, Saudi Arabia?) Think of it this way: in India there are some pretty reprehensible social practices, against "untouchables," against Christians and Muslims, against women. Pakistan and Bangladesh have even worse ways of dealing with minority communities and women. Should they be bombed?

Uppermost on everybody's mind, of course, particularly here in America, is the horror of what has come to be known as 9/11. Nearly 3,000 civilians lost their lives in that lethal terrorist strike. The grief is still deep. The rage still sharp. The tears have not dried. And a strange, deadly war is raging around the world. Yet, each person who has lost a loved one surely knows that no war, no act of revenge, will blunt the edges of their pain or bring their own loved ones back. War cannot avenge those who have died. War is only a brutal desecration of their memory.

To fuel yet another war—this time against Iraq—by manipulating people's grief, by packaging it for TV specials sponsored by corporations selling detergent or running shoes, is to cheapen and devalue grief, to drain it of meaning. We are seeing a pillaging of even the most private human feelings for political purpose. It is a terrible, violent thing for a state to do to its people.

The U.S. government says that Saddam Hussein is a war criminal, a cruel military despot who has committed genocide against his own people. That's a fairly accurate description of the man. In 1988, he razed hundreds of villages in northern Iraq and killed thousands of Kurds. Today, we know that that same year the U.S. government provided him with $500m in subsidies to buy American farm products. The next year, after he had successfully completed his genocidal campaign, the U.S. government doubled its subsidy to $1bn. It also provided him with high-quality germ seed for anthrax, as well as helicopters and dual-use material that could be used to manufacture chemical and biological weapons.

It turns out that while Saddam was carrying out his worst atrocities, the U.S. and UK governments were his close allies. So what changed?

In August 1990, Saddam invaded Kuwait. His sin was not so much that he had committed an act of war, but that he acted independently, without orders from his masters. This display of independence was enough to upset the power equation in the Gulf. So it was decided that Saddam be exterminated, like a pet that has outlived its owner's affection.

A decade of bombing has not managed to dislodge him. Now, almost 12 years on, Bush Jr. is ratcheting up the rhetoric once again. He's proposing an all-out war whose goal is nothing short of a regime change. Andrew H. Card Jr., the White House chief of staff, described how the administration was stepping up its war plans for autumn: "From a marketing point of view," he said, "you don't introduce new products in August." This time the catchphrase for Washington's "new product" is not the plight of people in Kuwait but the assertion that Iraq has weapons of mass destruction. Forget "the feckless moralising of the 'peace' lobbies," wrote Richard Perle, chairman of the Defence Policy Board. The U.S. will "act alone if necessary" and use a "pre-emptive strike" if it determines it is in U.S. interests.

Weapons inspectors have conflicting reports about the status of Iraq's weapons of mass destruction, and many have said clearly that its arsenal has been dismantled and that it does not have the capacity to build one. What if Iraq does have a nuclear weapon? Does that justify a pre-emptive U.S. strike? The U.S. has the largest arsenal of nuclear weapons in the world. It's the only country in the world to have actually used them on civilian populations. If the U.S. is justified in launching a pre-emptive attack on Iraq, why, any nuclear power is justified in carrying out a pre-emptive attack on any other. India could attack Pakistan, or the other way around.

Recently, the U.S. played an important part in forcing India and Pakistan back from the brink of war. Is it so hard for it to take its own advice? Who is guilty of feckless moralising? Of preaching peace while it wages war? The U.S., which Bush has called "the most peaceful nation on earth," has been at war with one country or another every year for the last 50 years.

Wars are never fought for altruistic reasons. They're usually fought for hegemony, for business. And then, of course, there's the business of war. In his book on globalisation, *The Lexus and the Olive Tree*, Tom Friedman says: "The hidden hand of the market will never work without a hidden fist. McDonald's cannot flourish without McDonnell Douglas. And the hidden fist that keeps the world safe for Silicon Valley's technologies to flourish is called the U.S. Army, Air Force, Navy and Marine Corps." Perhaps this was written in a moment of vulnerability, but it's certainly the most succinct, accurate description of the project of corporate globalisation that I have read.

After September 11 and the war against terror, the hidden hand and fist have had their cover blown—and we have a clear view now of America's other weapon—the free market—bearing down on the developing world, with a clenched, unsmiling smile. The Task That Never Ends is America's perfect war, the perfect vehicle for the endless expansion of American imperialism. In Urdu, the word for profit is fayda. Al-qaida means the word, the word of God, the law. So, in India, some of us call the War Against Terror, Al-qaida vs Al-fayda—The Word vs The Profit (no pun intended). For the moment it looks as though Al-fayda will carry the day. But then you never know . . .

In the past 10 years, the world's total income has increased by an average of 2.5% a year. And yet the numbers of the poor in the world has increased by 100 million. Of the top 100 biggest economies, 51 are corporations, not countries. The top 1% of the world has the same combined income as the bottom 57%, and the disparity is growing. Now, under the spreading canopy of the war against terror, this process is being hustled along. The men in suits are in an unseemly hurry. While bombs rain down, contracts are being signed, patents registered, oil pipelines laid, natural resources plundered, water privatised and democracies undermined.

But as the disparity between the rich and poor grows, the hidden fist of the free market has its work cut out. Multinational corporations on the prowl for "sweetheart deals" that yield enormous profits cannot push them through in developing countries without the active connivance of state machinery—the police, the courts, sometimes even the army. Today, corporate globalisation needs an international confederation of loyal, corrupt, preferably authoritarian governments in poorer countries, to push through unpopular reforms and quell the mutinies. It needs a press that pretends to be free. It needs courts that pretend to dispense justice. It needs nuclear bombs, standing armies, sterner immigration laws, and watchful coastal patrols to make sure that its only money, goods, patents and services that are globalised—not the free movement of people, not a respect for human rights, not international treaties on racial discrimination or chemical and nuclear weapons, or greenhouse gas emissions, climate change, or, God forbid, justice. It's as though even a gesture towards international accountability would wreck the whole enterprise.

Close to one year after the war against terror was officially flagged off in the ruins of Afghanistan, in country after country freedoms are being curtailed in the name of protecting freedom, civil liberties are being suspended in the name of protecting democracy. All kinds of dissent are being defined as "terrorism." Donald Rumsfeld said that his mission in the war against terror was to persuade the world that Americans must be allowed to continue their way of life. When the maddened king stamps his foot, slaves tremble in their quarters. So, it's hard for me to say this, but the American way of life is simply not sustainable. Because it doesn't acknowledge that there is a world beyond America.

Fortunately, power has a shelf life. When the time comes, maybe this mighty empire will, like others before it, overreach itself and implode from within. It looks as though structural cracks have already appeared. As the war against terror casts its net wider and wider, America's corporate heart is haemorrhaging. A world run by a handful of greedy bankers and CEOs whom nobody elected can't possibly last.

Soviet-style communism failed, not because it was intrinsically evil but because it was flawed. It allowed too few people to usurp too much power: 21st-century market-capitalism, American-style, will fail for the same reasons.

WE DON'T NEED NO STINKIN' PROOF!

Arianna Huffington

We all know who attacked us on September 11, 2001, don't we? No, not Osama bin Laden. God, that is so last year. It never turns out to be the person you first suspect. It was Saddam Hussein. For some reason we couldn't find him when we went after him in Afghanistan, bringing that magic elixir of regime change along with us. But now we've got a better idea: track him down where he actually lives, in Baghdad, and punish him right in his own backyard. It's the only way to obtain justice for the thousands he killed on 9/11.

At least that's the way the White House is now pitching the story.

In this latest rewrite of history, Osama has suddenly lost his beard and grown a mustache, morphing into the Butcher of Baghdad—or one of the look-alike stand-ins Saddam has been using for public appearances since 1998.

"You can't distinguish between Al-Qaeda and Saddam when you talk about the war on terror," said President Bush in the Oval Office last week.

Really? He can't differentiate between a group of evil ultra-radical Islamic fundamentalists that carried out the Sept. 11 attacks and an evil secular nationalist who, despite the frantic efforts of the Bush administration, has not been directly linked to 9/11? He'd better start making such distinctions—and fast. When every expert who knows anything about the Mideast can distinguish between the two, is it too much to ask that a President who's ready to go to war look a bit more closely?

People under stress often regress to earlier stages of development. It appears that Bush is so intent on getting Saddam, so obsessively tightly gripped by a need to succeed where his war hero dad failed, so obsessively determined to lay the murderous 9/11 assault at Baghdad's door, that he's regressed to that level of childhood development where fantasy, reality and wish fulfillment are

Arianna Huffington is a nationally syndicated columnist and author of many books, most recently *Pigs at the Trough: How Corporate Greed and Political Corruption are Undermining America*. This column was published on September 30, 2002.

all mixed up. Except that this time, things like nuclear weapons and the safety of the world for the next few decades are involved.

Now, I'm no psychologist, but I believe there is a clinical term for this condition: going off the deep end.

How else to explain the president's bizarre response to a reporter's straightforward query last week about who poses a bigger threat to America, Saddam or Al-Qaeda?

"That's an interesting question," he replied. "I'm trying to think of something humorous to say but I can't when I think about Al-Qaeda and Saddam Hussein."

When did the president take over the "Tonight Show?" Why would the idea that he should make a joke about such a deadly serious subject even cross his mind? It would be like asking Danielle van Dam's parents about the trial of their daughter's murderer and having them apologize for not being ready with a humorous quip.

No, Mr. President, you needn't apologize—your inability to treat serious subjects lightly is not one of your deficiencies. So rather than struggling to come up with a wan witticism, why don't you just answer the question? Especially since it appears by your actions that you've already come up with one.

Instead of bothering to give the least defense of his sudden fusion of Saddam and Osama, Bush launched into a fantasy-fueled diatribe: "The danger is, is that they work in concert. The danger is, is that Al-Qaeda becomes an extension of Saddam's madness and his hatred and his capacity to extend weapons of mass destruction around the world."

The president's regressed condition is spreading like the West Nile virus throughout the West Wing and beyond.

Witness the symptomatic blurring of fact and fantasy exhibited by Defense Secretary Donald Rumsfeld. When asked at an Armed Services Committee hearing about what is now compelling us to "take precipitous actions" against Iraq, Rumsfeld barked: "What's different? What's different is 3,000 people were killed." Yeah, by Mohammed Atta and company—not Saddam Hussein. But why quibble over details when there is a propaganda war to be won?

National Security Adviser Condoleezza Rice continued the assault on reality when she vaguely yet ominously claimed: "There clearly are contacts between Al-Qaeda and Iraq that can be documented." Well, then why not document them? We've documented contacts between Al-Qaeda and our oil dealers in Saudi Arabia and Al-Qaeda and our new best friends in Pakistan. But I don't see any B-2s powering up for raids over Riyadh or Karachi.

As is the White House custom, Rice simply refused to back up her claims. So did Rumsfeld, who memorably rebuffed a reporter late last week by saying,

"That happens to be a piece of intelligence that either we don't have or we don't want to talk about." In other words: Proof? We don't need no stinking proof! And just because I'm asking your sons and daughters to possibly sacrifice their lives for it doesn't mean you deserve to know whether it even exists.

It would be nice if we could just take them all at their word and let the bombs fall where they may. But Sen. Bob Graham, who, as chairman of the Senate Intelligence Committee is privy to the inside scoop, says he's seen no evidence of any link between Al-Qaeda and Saddam Hussein

So we're left with the fevered, infantile imaginings of the president and his pals. "We had dots before," said Anna Perez, Rice's spokeswoman. "Now we have a higher density of dots. Have we connected those dots? No."

Perhaps the president should put down his saber-rattle, pick up his crayons and connect them before drawing us into a bloody war.

THE PRESIDENT'S REAL GOAL IN IRAQ

Jay Bookman

The pieces just didn't fit. Something else had to be going on; something was missing.

In recent days, those missing pieces have finally begun to fall into place. As it turns out, this is not really about Iraq. It is not about weapons of mass destruction, or terrorism, or Saddam, or U.N. resolutions.

This war, should it come, is intended to mark the official emergence of the United States as a full-fledged global empire, seizing sole responsibility and authority as planetary policeman. It would be the culmination of a plan 10 years or more in the making, carried out by those who believe the United States must seize the opportunity for global domination, even if it means becoming the "American imperialists" that our enemies always claimed we were.

Once that is understood, other mysteries solve themselves. For example, why does the administration seem unconcerned about an exit strategy from Iraq once Saddam is toppled?

Because we won't be leaving. Having conquered Iraq, the United States will create permanent military bases in that country from which to dominate the Middle East, including neighboring Iran.

In an interview Friday, Defense Secretary Donald Rumsfeld brushed aside that suggestion, noting that the United States does not covet other nations' territory. That may be true, but 57 years after World War II ended, we still have major bases in Germany and Japan. We will do the same in Iraq.

And why has the administration dismissed the option of containing and deterring Iraq, as we had the Soviet Union for 45 years? Because even if it worked, containment and deterrence would not allow the expansion of American power. Besides, they are beneath us as an empire. Rome did not stoop to containment; it conquered. And so should we.

Among the architects of this would-be American Empire are a group of brilliant and powerful people who now hold key positions in the Bush admin-

Jay Bookman is the deputy editorial page editor of the *Atlanta Journal-Constitution,* where this article was published on September 29, 2002.

istration: They envision the creation and enforcement of what they call a worldwide "Pax Americana," or American peace. But so far, the American people have not appreciated the true extent of that ambition.

Part of it's laid out in the National Security Strategy, a document in which each administration outlines its approach to defending the country. The Bush administration plan, released September 20, marks a significant departure from previous approaches, a change that it attributes largely to the attacks of September 11.

To address the terrorism threat, the president's report lays out a newly aggressive military and foreign policy, embracing pre-emptive attack against perceived enemies. It speaks in blunt terms of what it calls "American internationalism," of ignoring international opinion if that suits U.S. interests. "The best defense is a good offense," the document asserts.

It dismisses deterrence as a Cold War relic and instead talks of "convincing or compelling states to accept their sovereign responsibilities."

In essence, it lays out a plan for permanent U.S. military and economic domination of every region on the globe, unfettered by international treaty or concern. And to make that plan a reality, it envisions a stark expansion of our global military presence.

"The United States will require bases and stations within and beyond Western Europe and Northeast Asia," the document warns, "as well as temporary access arrangements for the long-distance deployment of U.S. troops."

The report's repeated references to terrorism are misleading, however, because the approach of the new National Security Strategy was clearly not inspired by the events of September 11. They can be found in much the same language in a report issued in September 2000 by the Project for the New American Century, a group of conservative interventionists outraged by the thought that the United States might be forfeiting its chance at a global empire.

"At no time in history has the international security order been as conducive to American interests and ideals," the report said, stated two years ago. "The challenge of this coming century is to preserve and enhance this 'American peace.'"

Familiar Themes

Overall, that 2000 report reads like a blueprint for current Bush defense policy. Most of what it advocates, the Bush administration has tried to accomplish. For example, the project report urged the repudiation of the anti-ballistic missile treaty and a commitment to a global missile defense system. The administration has taken that course.

It recommended that to project sufficient power worldwide to enforce Pax Americana, the United States would have to increase defense spending from 3 percent of gross domestic product to as much as 3.8 percent. For next year, the Bush administration has requested a defense budget of $379 billion, almost exactly 3.8 percent of GDP.

It advocates the "transformation" of the U.S. military to meet its expanded obligations, including the cancellation of such outmoded defense programs as the Crusader artillery system. That's exactly the message being preached by Rumsfeld and others.

It urges the development of small nuclear warheads "required in targeting the very deep, underground hardened bunkers that are being built by many of our potential adversaries." This year the GOP-led U.S. House gave the Pentagon the green light to develop such a weapon, called the Robust Nuclear Earth Penetrator, while the Senate has so far balked.

That close tracking of recommendation with current policy is hardly surprising, given the current positions of the people who contributed to the 2000 report.

Paul Wolfowitz is now deputy defense secretary. John Bolton is undersecretary of state. Stephen Cambone is head of the Pentagon's Office of Program, Analysis and Evaluation. Eliot Cohen and Devon Cross are members of the Defense Policy Board, which advises Rumsfeld. I. Lewis Libby is chief of staff to Vice President Dick Cheney. Dov Zakheim is comptroller for the Defense Department.

"Constabulary Duties"

Because they were still just private citizens in 2000, the authors of the project report could be more frank and less diplomatic than they were in drafting the National Security Strategy. Back in 2000, they clearly identified Iran, Iraq and North Korea as primary short-term targets, well before President Bush tagged them as the Axis of Evil. In their report, they criticize the fact that in war planning against North Korea and Iraq, "past Pentagon wargames have given little or no consideration to the force requirements necessary not only to defeat an attack but to remove these regimes from power."

To preserve the Pax Americana, the report says U.S. forces will be required to perform "constabulary duties"—the United States acting as policeman of the world—and says that such actions "demand American political leadership rather than that of the United Nations."

To meet those responsibilities, and to ensure that no country dares to challenge the United States, the report advocates a much larger military presence spread over more of the globe, in addition to the roughly 130 nations in which U.S. troops are already deployed.

More specifically, they argue that we need permanent military bases in the Middle East, in Southeast Europe, in Latin America and in Southeast Asia, where no such bases now exist. That helps to explain another of the mysteries of our post–September 11 reaction, in which the Bush administration rushed to install U.S. troops in Georgia and the Philippines, as well as our eagerness to send military advisers to assist in the civil war in Colombia.

The 2000 report directly acknowledges its debt to a still earlier document, drafted in 1992 by the Defense Department. That document had also envisioned the United States as a colossus astride the world, imposing its will and keeping world peace through military and economic power. When leaked in final draft form, however, the proposal drew so much criticism that it was hastily withdrawn and repudiated by the first President Bush.

Effect on Allies

The defense secretary in 1992 was Richard Cheney; the document was drafted by Wolfowitz, who at the time was defense undersecretary for policy.

The potential implications of a Pax Americana are immense.

One is the effect on our allies. Once we assert the unilateral right to act as the world's policeman, our allies will quickly recede into the background. Eventually, we will be forced to spend American wealth and American blood protecting the peace while other nations redirect their wealth to such things as health care for their citizenry.

Donald Kagan, a professor of classical Greek history at Yale and an influential advocate of a more aggressive foreign policy—he served as co-chairman of the 2000 New Century project—acknowledges that likelihood.

"If [our allies] want a free ride, and they probably will, we can't stop that," he says. But he also argues that the United States, given its unique position, has no choice but to act anyway.

"You saw the movie 'High Noon'? he asks. "We're Gary Cooper."

Accepting the Cooper role would be an historic change in who we are as a nation, and in how we operate in the international arena. Candidate Bush certainly did not campaign on such a change. It is not something that he or others have dared to discuss honestly with the American people. To the contrary, in his foreign policy debate with Al Gore, Bush pointedly advocated a more humble foreign policy, a position calculated to appeal to voters leery of military intervention.

For the same reason, Kagan and others shy away from terms such as empire, understanding its connotations. But they also argue that it would be naive and dangerous to reject the role that history has thrust upon us. Kagan, for example, willingly embraces the idea that the United States would establish permanent military bases in a post-war Iraq.

"I think that's highly possible," he says. "We will probably need a major concentration of forces in the Middle East over a long period of time. That will come at a price, but think of the price of not having it. When we have economic problems, it's been caused by disruptions in our oil supply. If we have a force in Iraq, there will be no disruption in oil supplies."

Costly Global Commitment

Rumsfeld and Kagan believe that a successful war against Iraq will produce other benefits, such as serving an object lesson for nations such as Iran and Syria. Rumsfeld, as befits his sensitive position, puts it rather gently. If a regime change were to take place in Iraq, other nations pursuing weapons of mass destruction "would get the message that having them . . . is attracting attention that is not favorable and is not helpful," he says.

Kagan is more blunt.

"People worry a lot about how the Arab street is going to react," he notes. "Well, I see that the Arab street has gotten very, very quiet since we started blowing things up."

The cost of such a global commitment would be enormous. In 2000, we spent $281 billion on our military, which was more than the next 11 nations combined. By 2003, our expenditures will have risen to $378 billion. In other words, the *increase* in our defense budget from 1999 to 2003 will be more than the total amount spent annually by China, our next largest competitor.

The lure of empire is ancient and powerful, and over the millennia it has driven men to commit terrible crimes on its behalf. But with the end of the Cold War and the disappearance of the Soviet Union, a global empire was essentially laid at the feet of the United States. To the chagrin of some, we did not seize it at the time, in large part because the American people have never been comfortable with themselves as a New Rome.

Now, more than a decade later, the events of Sept. 11 have given those advocates of empire a new opportunity to press their case with a new president. So in debating whether to invade Iraq, we are really debating the role that the United States will play in the years and decades to come.

Are peace and security best achieved by seeking strong alliances and international consensus, led by the United States? Or is it necessary to take a more unilateral approach, accepting and enhancing the global dominance that, according to some, history has thrust upon us?

If we do decide to seize empire, we should make that decision knowingly, as a democracy. The price of maintaining an empire is always high. Kagan and others argue that the price of rejecting it would be higher still.

That's what this is about.

Editors' postscript: After Bookman's article was published, Yale historian Donald Kagan wrote an op–ed in response, entitled "Comparing America to Ancient Empires is 'Ludicrous.' " "I think it would be a very bad idea and entirely inconsistent with the kind of nation the United States is and should continue to be," Kagan wrote. "All comparisons between America's current place in the world and anything legitimately called an empire in the past reveal ignorance and confusion about any reasonable meaning of the concept empire, especially the comparison with the Roman Empire, which Bookman makes."

Bookman replied in a later column, writing that "Kagan . . . is arguing with himself. This is the same Donald Kagan who, in an interview with George Will, said, 'I think you have to go all the way back, nearly 2,000 years, to the Roman Empire, to find a single power so pre-eminent compared to all others.' And it was Kagan and his colleagues, not I, who adopted and embraced the term 'Pax Americana' with its deliberate and provocative echo of 'Pax Romana,' the Roman peace. Furthermore, Kagan's most recent book, *While America Sleeps,* is a 435-page, explicit, detailed comparison between the position of the British Empire in the 1920s with the position of the United States today.

THE IMPERIALISM CANARD

Andrew Sullivan

At some point, given the increasing desperation of the antiwar polemicists, the code word "imperialism" had to come up. And so it has. In what is to me a deeply clarifying alliance, the hard right and the hard left agree on this: The war on Iraq is an imperialist war.

In the inaugural issue of his new magazine, *American Conservative,* Pat Buchanan bemoans the history of imperialism, and how overreach undid "the Ottoman, Russian, Austro-Hungarian, and German empires in World War I, the Japanese in World War II, the French and the British the morning after." Which leads Buchanan to the following prediction: "We will soon launch an imperial war on Iraq with all the 'On-to-Berlin!' bravado with which French poilus and British Tommies marched in August 1914."

Not to be outdone, Gary Kamiya, yet another *Salon* lefty boomer, vies with Buchanan in his isolationist fears: "By word and deed—breaking treaties, disdaining allies, declaring America exempt from international law, announcing a new doctrine of preemptive force—the Bush administration has shown its desire to establish the United States as, in effect, an imperial power, the new Rome. After September 11, an angry and triumphalist America is to be answerable to no one. Flaunting our 3,000 dead like a crusader's banner, we will march against foes wherever we may find them, our unchallengeable military and invincible rectitude giving us the right and might to do whatever we want. Deus lo volt!"

The political corollary to this fast-accelerating meme is Rep. Jim McDermott, D-Wash, fresh from his tour of Baghdad, where he did all he could to give aid and comfort to one of the most brutal dictators in world history. "This president is trying to bring to himself all the power to become an emperor—to create Empire America," McDermott pronounced last Sunday. He was referring to Bush, not Saddam, natch.

But is the United States these days anything like an actual empire? Being an empire, after all, does not merely mean that you are extremely powerful,

---

Andrew Sullivan, a former editor of *The New Republic* (1991–1996), has written two books and also worked as a contributing writer and columnist for *The New York Times Magazine,* a regular contributor to *The New York Times Book Review,* and a weekly columnist for the *Sunday Times* of London. This article was published on October 8, 2002 in *Salon.com.*

militarily, economically or culturally. It means, if it is to mean anything concrete, the appropriation of others' territory, goods and people at the barrel of a gun. Even one of the milder empires in world history, the British Empire, was essentially an imposition of brute force on large parts of the globe in order to generate wealth and cheap goods for the domestic market. The people subject to such imperialism have no role in their own future, no sovereignty over their own country, no right to their own goods and services. Under any viable definition of imperialism, the colonies provide tribute to the center, as the fledgling American colonies once did to London. And they have no choice.

Once you spend a couple of minutes thinking about this, you realize that the notion of "Imperial America" is dangerous nonsense. Take Afghanistan. Has the United States annexed the country, as the Soviets and British once did? Have the Americans put large numbers of troops in there to control the entire country? Did they impose a government by force? Are they busy plundering the place for its natural resources? Nope. They liberated the country from an invader, they helped set up a domestic council for a democratic Afghanistan and, far from bilking the place for treasure, they have actually spent millions rebuilding the country, with no direct quid pro quo. An exception? Hardly. Remember Germany and Japan? How many imperial powers have sunk fortunes into colonies only to allow them complete independence, even to the point of resisting American foreign policy?

Some leftists and rightists concede this but argue rather that free trade itself is a form of imperialism. But, as the 19th century protectionist and imperialist Tories could have told you, the critical point about free trade—once fiercely defended by anti-imperialist liberals—is that it's voluntary. No one is being forced to trade right now with the United States, or anyone else, for that matter. Without military coercion in order to appropriate goods, there's no imperialism by any reasonable definition of the name.

What about McDermott's implicit point: Is Bush trying to exercise powers of war and peace in ways that make him a de facto Caesar of the New World?

He is asking for no more powers to wage war than many other presidents before him, and Congress has a huge say in what emerges. Bush couldn't even get the networks to cover his major war address Monday. Somehow, I think Caesar had an easier time of it.

And remember how reluctant this president once was to wage war at all. In the campaign, he was clearly less interventionist than Gore, asked for less defense spending and urged America to be a "humble nation." He changed because war was declared on us. And his current war proposal is, if anything, explicitly anti-imperialist.

Who, after all, is Saddam? He's a man who presides over a fake nation, contrived by British imperialists; a man who tried to invade and annex Iran; and then tried to invade and annex Kuwait and Saudi Arabia. He, unlike Bush, has no constitutional authority and will never be subject to popular criticism or resistance. Deposing him is therefore the precise opposite of what Buchanan and Kamiya and McDermott claim. It's an anti-imperialist venture. And because such ventures invariably have the people on their side, this is yet another war that the anti-imperialist hegemon, America, will almost certainly win.

TEN

THE DEBATE IN CONGRESS

"Whereas naval units of the Communist regime in Vietnam, in violation of the principles of the Charter of the United Nations and of international law, have deliberately and repeatedly attacked United States naval vessels lawfully present in international waters, and have thereby created a serious threat to international peace; and

"Whereas these attacks are part of a deliberate and systematic campaign of aggression that the Communist regime in North Vietnam has been waging against its neighbors and the nations joined with them in the collective defense of their freedom; and

"Whereas the United States is assisting the peoples of Southeast Asia to protect their freedom and has no territorial, military or political ambitions in that area, but desires only that these people should be left in peace to work out their own destinies in their own way:

"Now, therefore, be it resolved by the Senate and House of Representatives of the United States of America in Congress assembled.

1. That the Congress approves and supports the determination of the President as Commander in Chief, to take all necessary measures to repel any armed attack against the forces of the United States and to prevent further aggression.

2. The United States regards as vital to its national interest and to world peace the maintenance of international peace and security in Southeast Asia. Consonant with the Constitution of the United States and the Charter of the United Nations and in accordance with its obliga-

tions under the Southeast Asia Collective Defense Treaty, the United States is, therefore, prepared, as the President determines, to take all necessary steps, including the use of armed force, to assist any member or protocol state of the Southeast Asia Collective Defense Treaty requesting assistance in defense of its freedom.

3. This resolution shall expire when the President shall determine that the peace and security of the area is reasonably assured by international conditions created by action of the United Nations or otherwise, except that it may be terminated earlier by concurrent resolution of the Congress.

—The Tonkin Gulf Resolution, which was passed by the U.S. Congress on August 7, 1964 with only two negative votes. Later, it was revealed that no North Vietnamese boats had attacked American ships. "For all I know, our Navy could have been shooting at whales out there," President Lyndon Johnson admitted.

OF PRE-EMPTION AND APPEASEMENT, BOX-CUTTERS AND LIQUID GOLD

Reps. Charles Rangel, Howard Berman, Dennis Kucinich, Nancy Pelosi, Tom DeLay, Richard Gephardt

The following are excerpts from the October 10, 2002 debate in the House of Representatives on the Hastert-Gephardt Authorization For Use of Military Force Against Iraq Resolution (H.J. Res. 114).

REP. CHARLES RANGEL (D-NY): Mr. Speaker, in June of 2000, President Clinton allowed me the great honor to take some veterans back to Korea in commemoration of the 50th anniversary of the Korean War. They were all members of the Second Infantry Division. We left Fort Lewis, Washington, in July and August of 1950, and we had left more men behind dead than came home. The raggedy group of veterans that went back, all black because we were in a segregated infantry unit, most had not gone to college, and, like myself, some had not even finished high school, we thought then that we were fighting for our country. But the more education I got, the more sophisticated I got, I realized we were fighting for the United Nations.

Then when I became a Member of Congress and I led this same group of tattered veterans back to the same battlefields, they asked, why did Congress send them to South Korea and expose them to North Korean and Chinese warfare? And I had to tell them that this Congress never did send them there. No vote was ever taken in this Congress to say that they were at war with the people of North Korea or the People's Republic of China.

I made a vow to them, and I am keeping it today, that never will I delegate the responsibility of considering the dangers of war. I will not leave it to the President, unless he brings me evidence that we are in danger. I will not give it to the United Nations, because I do not believe that this sacred responsibility should be transferred. And I do believe that each and every one of those veterans, if they thought our beloved country was in trouble, would be the first to stand up to salute the flag and be prepared to destroy what enemy we had, preemptive or not. I am against this resolution.

REP. HOWARD BERMAN (D-CA): Mr. Speaker, I was a fervent opponent of the Vietnam War and a strong supporter of sensible detente with the Soviet Union. But under today's circumstances, the best way to give peace a chance and to save the most lives, American and Iraqi, is for America to stand united and for Congress to authorize the President to use force if Saddam does not give up his weapons of mass destruction. Confront Saddam now, or pay a much heavier price later.

We dismissed the first World Trade Center bombing as an isolated incident. When two embassies were bombed, we failed to see the broader implication of those acts. When the USS *Cole* was attacked, still we did not read the handwriting on the wall. It was irrational, we thought, that madmen would grow bold enough to attack America on her own shores. We wanted to give peace a chance. But then came 9/11, and it is time to say "no more." . . . We have brought key members of the Clinton national security team to the Hill, architects of our past policy to contain Saddam. These foreign policy experts from the Democratic Party have told us to a person that containment will no longer do the job and that the policy we are asked to endorse today is the right one for a peace-loving people. . . .

As one who has watched [Saddam] for 20 years, let me pose an analogy. It is just an analogy, because I reject the unproven efforts to tie Saddam to the events of 9/11. We are on an airplane, and we know that a few passengers have smuggled box cutters on board. We know these passengers have taken courses to learn how to fly a jumbo jet. We know that their friends have already flown a small plane into a building, killing hundreds of their own neighbors. But those armed passengers have not yet lunged for the cockpit.

What should a peace loving people do? We know that people sitting near these dangerous passengers could be hurt if we take aggressive action. Should we wait until they kill the pilot and take over the airplane before we act? Of course not. We admire those with the courage to surround the armed passengers and demand that they give up their weapons under threat of force. That is what this resolution does.

Is the threat imminent? Well, surely Saddam has box cutters, Saddam has a history of using them, Saddam is in the process of upgrading the box cutters, Saddam has boarded the plane with the box cutters. Confront Saddam now, or pay a much heavier price later.

REP. DENNIS KUCINICH (D-OH): Mr. Speaker, more than two millennia ago, the world began a shift from the philosophy of an eye for an eye. We were taught a new gospel of compassion of doing unto others as you would have them do unto you. It is that teaching, that faith and compassion that has sustained the human heart and this Nation.

I believe, as did Washington and Lincoln, that America has been favored by divine providence. But what if we lose our connection to our source by an abuse of power? We are at a dangerous moment in human history when 20 centuries of moral teachings are about to be turned upside down. Instead of adherence to the Golden Rule, we are being moved toward the rule of liquid gold: do unto others before they do unto you.

No longer are we justified by our faith; we are now justified by our fear. Iraq was not responsible for 9/11, but some fear it was. There is no proof Iraq worked with al Qaeda to cause 9/11, but some fear it did. It is fear which leads us to war. It is fear which leads us to believe that we must kill or be killed, fear which leads us to attack those who have not attacked us, fear which leads us to ring our Nation and the very heavens with weapons of mass destruction.

The American people need the attention of their government today. People who have worked a lifetime are finding the American dream slipping away. People who have saved, who have invested wisely are suffering because of corruption on Wall Street, the failing economy, and the declining stock market.

People have lost their homes, they have lost their jobs, they have lost their chances for a good education for their children. The American dream is slipping away, and all the people hear from Washington, D.C., is war talk, so loud as to drown out the voices of the American people calling for help.

Seventy years ago, Franklin Roosevelt said, "We have nothing to fear but fear itself," calling America to a domestic agenda, a New Deal for America. Faith in our country calls us to that again. Faith in our country calls us to work with the world community to create peace through inspection, not destruction. Faith in our country calls us to use our talents and abilities to address the urgent concerns of America today.

REP. NANCY PELOSI (D-CA): I rise in opposition to the resolution on national security grounds. The clear and present danger that our country faces is terrorism. I say flat out that unilateral use of force without first exhausting every diplomatic remedy and other remedies and making a case to the American people will be harmful to our war on terrorism. For the past 13 months, it will be 13 months tomorrow, we have stood shoulder to shoulder with President Bush to remove the threat of terrorism posed by the al Qaeda. Our work is not done. Osama bin Laden, Mullah Omar and the other al Qaeda terrorist leaders have not been accounted for. We have unfinished business. We are risking the cooperation that we have from over 60 nations of having their intelligence and their cooperation in fighting this war on terrorism.

There are many, many costs involved in this war, and one of them is the cost to the war on terrorism. We cannot let this coalition unravel. Others have talked about this threat that is posed by Saddam Hussein. Yes, he has chemical weapons, he has biological weapons, he is trying to get nuclear weapons. This is a threat not only from him but from other countries of concern in the past.

I want to call to the attention of my colleagues a statement about Saddam's use of chemical and biological weapons that was just declassified and sent to the Chairman of the Senate Select Committee on Intelligence.

The question is: If we initiate an attack and he thought he was in extremis or otherwise, what is the likelihood in response to our attack that Saddam Hussein would use chemical and biological weapons? This is a letter from George Tenet, the head of the CIA to the committee. The response: Pretty high, if we initiate the attack.

Force protection is our top priority on the Permanent Select Committee on Intelligence. We must protect our men and women in uniform. They are courageous. They risk their lives for our freedom, for our country. We cannot put them in harm's way unless we take every measure possible to protect them. So another cost is not only the cost of the war on terrorism but in the cost of human lives of our young people by making Saddam Hussein the person who determines their fates.

Another cost is to our economy. The markets do not like war. They do not like the uncertainty of war. Our economy is fragile as it is. The President has spoken. In his speech the other night, he talked about rebuilding Iraq's economy after our invasion. We have problems with our own economy. We must focus on building our own economy before we worry about Iraq's economy after we invade Iraq.

So let us do what is proportionate, what is appropriate, which mitigates the risk for our young people. Another cost in addition to human lives, the cost of terrorism, cost to our economy, another cost is to our budget. This cost can be unlimited, unlimited. There is no political solution on the ground in Iraq. Let us not be fooled by that. So when we go in, the occupation, which is now being called liberation, could be interminable and so could the amount of money, unlimited that it will cost, $100 to $200 billion. We will pay any price to protect the American people, but is this the right way to go, to jeopardize in a serious way our young people when that can be avoided?

. . . These costs to the war on terrorism, the loss of life, the cost to our economy, the cost in dollars to our budget, these costs must be answered for.

If we go in, certainly we can show our power to Saddam Hussein. If we resolve this issue diplomatically, we can show our strength as a great country, as a great country. Let us show our greatness. Vote no on this resolution.

Rep. Tom DeLay (R-TX): Mr. Speaker, Americans have always had to summon courage to disregard the timid counsel of those who would mortgage our security to the false promises of wishful thinking and appeasement. The perils of complacency were driven home to us in September of last year. We saw in tragic detail that evil is far more than some abstract concept. No longer should America allow dangers to gather and multiply. No longer should we stand idle as terrorists and terrorist states plot to murder our citizens.

As a free society, we have to defeat dangers before they ripen. The war on terrorism will be fought here at home, unless we summon the will to confront evil before it attacks. President Bush certainly understands this imperative for action. The President is demonstrating the strong, moral leadership to find and defeat threats to the United States before they strike. Because once a madman like Saddam Hussein is able to deliver his arsenal, whether it is chemical, biological or nuclear weapons, there is no telling when an American city will be attacked at his direction or with his support.

A nuclear armed Iraq would soon become the world's largest safe haven and refuge for the world's terrorist organizations. Waiting to act until after Saddam has nuclear weapons will leave free nations with an awful dilemma. Will they, on the one hand, risk nuclear annihilation by confronting terrorists in Iraq or will they give in to fear by failing to confront these terrorist groups?

For that reason, regime change in Iraq is a central goal of the war on terror. It is vital because a war on terrorism that leaves the world's leading purveyor and practitioner of terror in power would be a bald failure.

Some call Hussein a diversion, but far from being a diversion, confronting Saddam Hussein is a defining measure of whether we still wage the war on terror fully and effectively. It is the difference between aggressive action and misguided passivity.

The question we face today is not whether to go to war, for war was thrust upon us. Our only choice is between victory or defeat. And let us just be clear about it. In the war on terror, victory cannot be secured at a bargaining table. . . . Today, the free world chooses strength over temporizing and timidity. Terrorists and tyrants will see that the fruits of their evil will be certain destruction by the forces of democracy.

Now we seek broad support, but I am telling my colleagues that fighting this war on terrorism by committee or consensus is a certain prescription for defeat. We will defend our country by defeating terrorists wherever they may flee around the world. None of us take the gravity of this vote and its ramifications lightly, but history informs us that the dangers of complacency and inaction far outweigh the calculated risks of confronting evil.

In the fullness of time, America will be proud that in our hour of testing we chose the bold path of action, not the hollow comfort of appeasement. So let us just take this stand today against tyranny. Let us take this stand against terror. Let us take this stand against fear. Let us stand with the President of the United States. I say to my colleagues, just trust the cherished principles on which we were founded. Put faith in freedom and raise our voices and send this message to the world: The forces of freedom are on the march and terrorists will find no safe harbor in this world.

MINORITY LEADER RICHARD GEPHARDT (D-MO): . . . Let me say to my colleagues and my constituents in Missouri why I have decided to vote for this resolution. First, September 11 has made all the difference. The events of that tragic day jolted us to the enduring reality that terrorists not only seek to attack our interests abroad but also to strike us here at home. We have clear evidence now that they even desire to use weapons of mass destruction against us. Before 9/11, we experienced the terrorist attacks on Khobar Towers, the USS *Cole,* on two embassies in Africa, but we did not believe it would happen here. On 9/11, it did happen here; and it can happen again.

September 11 was the ultimate wake-up call. We must now do everything in our power to prevent further terrorist attacks and ensure that an attack with a weapon of mass destruction cannot happen. The consequences of such an attack are unimaginable. We spent 50 years in a Cold War and trillions of dollars deterring a weapon of mass destruction attack on the United States by another country. Now we must prevent such an attack by terrorists who, unlike our previous adversaries, are willing to die.

In these new circumstances, deterrence well may not work. With these new dangers, prevention must work. If my colleagues worry about terrorists getting weapons of mass destruction or their components from countries, the first candidate we must worry about is Iraq. The 12-year history of the U.N. effort to disarm Iraq convinces me that Iraq is a problem that must be dealt with diplomatically if we can, militarily if we must.

I did not come to this view overnight. It has, instead, evolved over time, as we have learned the facts about the Iraqi regime with clarity. As you know, I opposed the use of force against Iraq in 1991 in favor of giving sanctions more time to work. Others supported force, but thought that by dislodging Iraq from Kuwait we would neutralize the threat. In hindsight, both of these assessments were wrong.

In 1991, no one knew the extent to which Saddam Hussein would sacrifice the needs of his people in order to sustain his hold on power, deceive the international community in order to preserve his weapons of mass destruction programs, or take hostile actions against U.S. interests in the region.

Saddam Hussein's track record is too compelling to ignore, and we know that he continues to develop weapons of mass destruction, including nuclear devices; and he may soon have the ability to use nuclear weapons against other nations. I believe we have an obligation to protect the United States by preventing him from getting these weapons and either using them himself or passing them or their components on to terrorists who share his destructive intent. . . .

At the insistence of many of us, the resolution includes a provision urging President Bush to continue his efforts to get the U.N. to effectively enforce its own resolutions against Iraq. I have told the President directly, on numerous occasions, that in my view, and in the view of a lot of us, he must do everything he possibly can to achieve our objectives with the support of the United Nations. His speech to the U.N. on September 12 was an excellent beginning to this effort.

Exhausting all efforts at the U.N. is essential. But let us remember why. We started the U.N. over 50 years ago. We remain the greatest advocate of the rule of law, both domestically and internationally. We must do everything we can to get the U.N. to succeed. It is in our own self-interest to do that. In 1945, Harry Truman told the Senate that the creation of the U.N. constituted, in his words, an expression of national necessity. He said the U.N. points down the only road to enduring peace. He said let us not hesitate to start down that road, with God's help, and with firm resolve that we can and will reach our goal: peace and security for all Americans.

Completely bypassing the U.N. would set a dangerous precedent that would undoubtedly be used by other countries in the future to our and the world's detriment. It is too high a price to pay. I am glad the President said in his speech Monday that diplomacy is the first choice for resolving this matter.

This resolution also limits the scope and duration of the President's authority to use force. It requires Presidential determinations before our Armed Forces may be used against Iraq, including assurances to Congress that he has pursued all diplomatic means to address this threat and that any military action will not undermine our ongoing efforts against terrorism.

Finally, the bill provides for regular consultation with and reporting to Congress on the administration's diplomatic and military efforts and, of great importance to all Americans, the planning for assistance, reconstruction, and regional stabilization efforts in a postconflict Iraq.

The efforts we must undertake in a postconflict Iraq could be the most enduring challenge we face in this entire endeavor, which is another reason for doing everything humanly possible to work through the U.N. to reach our goals.

Now a word on what this resolution, in my view, is not. In my view, it is not an endorsement or an acceptance of the President's new policy of preemption. Iraq is unique, and this resolution is a unique response. A full discussion of the President's new preemption policy must come at another time. But the acceptance of such a momentous change in policy must not be inferred from the language of this resolution.

It is also important to say that, thus far, the President's predominant response to 9/11 has been the use of military power. Obviously, self-defense requires the use of effective military force. But the exercise of military power is not a foreign policy. It is one means of implementing foreign policy. In the post–9/11 world, we must motivate and inform our citizens about how we construct a foreign policy that promotes universal values, improves living standards, increases freedom in all countries and, ultimately, prevents thousands and thousands of young people across this world from deciding to become terrorists. We will never defeat terrorism by dealing with its symptoms. We must get to its root causes. . . .

I want to say a final word to those watching beyond our borders. To our friends around the world, I say thank you for standing with us in our time of trial. Your support strengthens the bonds of friendship between our people and the people of the world.

To our enemies, who watch this democratic debate and wonder if America speaks with one voice, I say have no doubt. We are united as a people in defending ourselves and we debate the best means for doing that. Do not mistake our resolve. Do not underestimate our determination. Do not misunderstand that we stand here today not as arguing Republicans and Democrats but as Americans, using the sacred right of free speech and thought and freedom to determine our collective course.

The Hastert-Gephardt Resolution passed by a vote of 296–133, with 3 members not voting. According to an analysis of the vote done by Public Campaign, using data provided by the Center for Responsive Politics, a nonpartisan organization that tracks money in politics, there was a clear correlation between how much money a member received from the defense industry in campaign contributions and how they voted on the Iraq resolution. Members who voted for the resolution received on average, slightly more than twice the amount from that industry in the 2001–02 election cycle than did members who voted against the resolution. Furthermore, of the 150 members of the House who had received at least $10,000 from the defense sector, 123 voted yes, and 25 voted no. There was a total of $6.9 million in defense sector contributions to House members in 2002, and another $2.6 million to the Senate. Peace oriented PACs gave a total of $396,000. Thus, the defense industry outspent peace advocates by about 23 to 1.

LETTER TO SENATOR BOB GRAHAM

CIA Director George Tenet

The following is a letter written by CIA Director George Tenet to Senator Bob Graham on October 7, 2002, in response to Senator Graham's request that he declassify the agency's judgments on the likelihood of Saddam using weapons of mass destruction against the United States. The letter had been solicited by Graham, who, through his access to classified intelligence reports, had become convinced that the Agency was being less than forthcoming with findings that failed to support President Bush's assertion that Iraq could launch an attack on the United States at any time.

---

7 OCTOBER 2002

The Honorable Bob Graham
Chairman
Select Committee on Intelligence
United States Senate
Washington, D.C. 20510

Dear Mr. Chairman:

In response to your letter of 4 October 2002, we have made unclassified material available to further the Senate's forthcoming open debate on a Joint Resolution concerning Iraq.

As always, our declassification efforts seek a balance between your need for unfettered debate and our need to protect sources and methods. We have also been mindful of a shared interest in not providing to Saddam a blueprint of our intelligence capabilities and shortcomings, or with insight into our expectation of how he will and will not act. The salience of such concerns is only heightened by the possibility for hostilities between the U.S. and Iraq.

George Tenet is the director of central intelligence of the United States. Originally appointed by President Clinton in July 1997, he became the first CIA director in 28 years to remain in office after the White House switched occupants when George W. Bush asked him, in January 2001, to continue to serve.

These are some of the reasons why we did not include our classified judgments on Saddam's decisionmaking regarding the use of weapons of mass destruction (WMD) in our recent unclassified paper on *Iraq's Weapons of Mass Destruction*. Viewing your request with those concerns in mind, however, we can declassify the following from the paragraphs you requested:

> Baghdad for now appears to be drawing a line short of conducting terrorist attacks with conventional or CBW against the United States.
>
> Should Saddam conclude that a U.S.-led attack could no longer be deterred, he probably would become much less constrained in adopting terrorist actions. Such terrorism might involve conventional means, as with Iraq's unsuccessful attempt at a terrorist offensive in 1991, or CBW.
>
> Saddam might decide that the extreme step of assisting Islamist terrorists in conducting a WMD attack against the United States would be his last chance to exact vengeance by taking a large number of victims with him.

Regarding the 2 October closed hearing, we can declassify the following dialogue:

Senator Levin: . . . If (Saddam) didn't feel threatened, did not feel threatened, is it likely that he would initiate an attack using a weapon of mass destruction?

Senior Intelligence Witness: . . . My judgment would be that the probability of him initiating an attack—let me put a time frame on it—in the foreseeable future, given the conditions we understand now, the likelihood I think would be low.

Senator Levin: Now if he did initiate an attack you've . . . indicated he would probably attempt clandestine attacks against us . . . But what about his use of weapons of mass destruction? If we initiate an attack and he thought he was in extremis or otherwise, what's the likelihood in response to our attack that he would use chemical or biological weapons?

Senior Intelligence Witness: Pretty high, in my view.

In the above dialogue, the witness's qualifications—"in the foreseeable future, given the conditions we understand now"—were intended to underscore that the likelihood of Saddam using WMD for blackmail, deterrence, or otherwise grows as his arsenal builds. Moreover, if Saddam used WMD, it would disprove his repeated denials that he has such weapons.

Regarding Senator Bayh's question of Iraqi links to al Qaeda, Senators could draw from the following points for unclassified discussions:

- Our understanding of the relationship between Iraq and al-Qaeda is evolving and is based on sources of varying reliability. Some of the information we have received comes from detainees, including some of high rank.
- We have solid reporting of senior level contacts between Iraq and al-Qaeda going back a decade.
- Credible information indicates that Iraq and al-Qaeda have discussed safe haven and reciprocal non-aggression.
- Since Operation Enduring Freedom, we have solid evidence of the presence in Iraq of al-Qaeda members, including some that have been in Baghdad.
- We have credible reporting that al-Qaeda leaders sought contacts in Iraq who could help them acquire WMD capabilities. The reporting also stated that Iraq has provided training to al-Qaeda members in the areas of poisons and gases and making conventional bombs.
- Iraq's increasing support to extremist Palestinians, coupled with growing indications of a relationship with al-Qaeda suggest that Baghdad's links to terrorists will increase, even absent U.S. military action.

Sincerely,

George J. Tenet
Director of Central Intelligence

IRAQ'S DISARMAMENT IS IMPOSSIBLE WITHOUT REGIME CHANGE

Senator John McCain

"The retention of weapons of mass destruction capabilities is self-evidently the core objective of the [Iraqi] regime, for it has sacrificed all other domestic and foreign policy goals to this singular aim." So concludes a recent report by the International Institute for Strategic Studies. The question facing all of us in this body is whether Saddam Hussein's aggressive weapons development, in defiance of the Gulf War cease-fire and a decade of U.N. Security Council resolutions, can stand, when the cost of inaction against this gathering threat could be intolerably high.

I am proud to join Senators Lieberman, Warner, and Bayh in laying down our amendment providing the President the necessary authority to defend the national security of the United States against the continuing threat posed by Iraq and enforce all relevant U.N. Security Council resolutions against Saddam Hussein's regime. I welcome this debate. I am confident it will result in a resounding vote of support for the President as he moves to confront the threat we face in Iraq. I also believe it will be a powerful signal to the world that the American people are united in their determination to meet, and to end, this menace. Our diplomacy at the United Nations will benefit from a strong and bipartisan Congressional vote in favor of this resolution. Our enemies will understand that we are united in our resolve to confront the danger posed by a dictator whose possession of the worst weapons and systematic defiance of every norm the civilized world holds dear threaten all who value freedom and law.

Congress has already spoken on this matter. On August 14, 1998, President Clinton signed into law Senate Joint Resolution 54, which declared that "the Government of Iraq is in material and unacceptable breach of its inter-

Senator John McCain, Republican of Arizona, made these remarks on October 8, 2002 on the Senate floor during debate over the Iraq resolution. He has served in Congress since 1982, when he was elected to the House of Representatives. The son and grandson of prominent Navy admirals, McCain was a naval aviator for 22 years. In 1967, he was shot down over Vietnam and held as a prisoner of war in Hanoi for five and a half years (1967–1973), much of it in solitary confinement. He retired from the Navy as a captain in 1981. In 2000, he campaigned unsuccessfully for the Republican nomination for president.

national obligations" and urged the President "to take appropriate action, in accordance with the Constitution and relevant laws of the United States, to bring Iraq into compliance with its international obligations." On October 31, 1998, the President signed into law the Iraq Liberation Act, which stated that "it should be the policy of the United States to support efforts to remove the regime headed by Saddam Hussein from power in Iraq and to promote the emergence of a democratic government to replace that regime."

Then, as now, Democrats and Republicans recognized the menace posed by Saddam Hussein's arsenal and his ambitions. Unfortunately, after four days of bombing Iraq in Operation Desert Fox in December 1998, the United States and the international community effectively walked away from the Iraq problem, freeing Iraq from a weapons inspection regime that, by that time, had become so compromised by Saddam Hussein's intransigence as to be completely ineffective. Nothing has taken its place over the past four years, even as porous sanctions and illicit oil revenues have enriched the regime. Over this time, Saddam Hussein's threat to the world has grown without hindrance. Regrettably, some of the very same permanent members of the Security Council whose vote for a new resolution on Iraq we are now courting actively conspired against rigorous weapons inspections in Iraq during the 1990s, for reasons that had more to do with their narrow commercial interests than with the world's interest in being rid of the menace posed by Saddam Hussein's weapons of terror.

This threat is not new. Saddam Hussein has been in gross violation of the terms of the cease-fire that ended the Persian Gulf War since that war's end, as a host of United Nations Security Council resolutions passed since 1991 can attest. As *The Economist* has written, "He has treated inspections as a continuation of the Gulf War by other means." After years of stymied efforts to enforce the inspections regime, the international community effectively sanctioned Saddam's impunity after it became clear he would never allow intrusive inspections, and once it became apparent to many Americans that the only way to end his defiance was to end his regime. The withering under U.N. Security Council auspices of the international inspections regime over the course of a decade, and Iraq's decision to even consider renewed inspections only under threat of force today, make clear that unvarnished faith in the ability of the U.N. Security Council or a new corps of inspectors to disarm Saddam's regime is misplaced.

Over the course of this debate, the Senate will consider amendments that would require Security Council authorization before the United States could act to enforce a decade of Security Council resolutions, and that would narrow the focus of American policy of Iraq's disarmament, rather than against the range of Saddam's offenses against his people and his neighbors and the continuing threat his regime itself poses to American national security.

These debates will be important. I believe the President's position will prevail. Congress cannot foresee the course of this conflict and should not unnecessarily constrain the options open to the President to defeat the threat we have identified in Saddam Hussein. Once Congress acts on a resolution, only the President will have to make the choices, with American forces likely deployed in the region to carry out his orders, that will end the threat Saddam Hussein's weapons and his ambitions pose to the world. Congress should give the President the authority he believes he needs to protect American national security against an often irrational dictator who has demonstrated a history of aggression outside his borders and a willingness to use weapons of mass destruction against all enemies, foreign and domestic.

This is not just another Arab despot, not one of many tyrants who repress their people from within the confines of their countries. As *New Yorker* writer Jeffrey Goldberg, who recently traveled across northern Iraq, recently wrote in *Slate*:

> There are, of course, many repugnant dictators in the world; a dozen or so in the Middle East alone. But Saddam Hussein is a figure of singular repugnance, and singular danger. To review: there is no dictator in power anywhere in the world who has, so far in his career, invaded two neighboring countries; fired ballistic missiles at the civilians of two other neighboring countries; tried to have assassinated an ex-president of the United States; harbored al Qaeda fugitives . . . ; attacked civilians with chemical weapons; attacked the soldiers of an enemy with chemical weapons; conducted biological weapons experiments on human subjects; committed genocide; and . . . [weaponized] aflotoxin, a tool of mass murder and nothing else. I do not know how any thinking person could believe that Saddam Hussein is a run-of-the-mill dictator. No one else comes close . . . to matching his extraordinary and variegated record of malevolence.

In light of Saddam Hussein's record of aggression, prohibited weapons development, and consistent rejection of every international obligation imposed on him, I believe the burden of proof in this debate must rest on those who believe inspections could actually achieve the disarmament of Iraq, rather than on those of us who are deeply skeptical that inspections alone could accomplish our common goal. History shows that we will most likely not disarm Iraq without changing the regime in Baghdad—a regime whose continued existence is predicated on possession of weapons of mass destruction. As arms control experts Gary Milhollin and Kelly Motz have noted, "Unless the Iraqi dictator should suddenly and totally reverse course on arms inspection and everything that goes with it, or be forced into early retirement—in other words, unless Saddam Hussein's Iraq ceases to be Saddam Hussein's Iraq—inspections will never work."

Similarly, given the Security Council's failure to enforce its own Article Seven resolutions against Iraq, which are backed by the threat of force and have the sanctity of international law, I believe the burden of proof in this debate must rest on those who can defend the Council's record with regard to Iraq and can convince the rest of us that the Council's judgment, rather than that of our commander in chief, should be the final authority on a matter that so directly affects American security.

Important participants in this debate support the President's determination to use military force to bring about Iraq's disarmament but would constrain the President's authority to act against Iraq to uphold Security Council resolutions related to repression within Iraq, Iraq's support for terrorism, and other issues. This approach would limit the President's authority to achieving only Iraq's disarmament and would explicitly oppose a comprehensive challenge to his tyrannical regime. I believe those who hold this view have an obligation to explain why they would constrain the President's authority to use military force in ways he believes would tie his hands and raise unacceptably high the threshold for ordering military action to defend the national security of the United States.

Others will argue that Saddam Hussein can be deterred—that he is a rational actor who understands that acting on his ambitions will threaten his regime. But deterrence has failed utterly in the past. I fail to see how waiting for some unspecified period of time, allowing Saddam's nuclear ambitions to grow unchecked, will ever result in a stable deterrence regime. Not only would deterrence condemn the Iraqi people to more unspeakable tyranny, it would condemn Saddam's neighbors to perpetual instability. And once Iraq's nuclear ambitions are realized, no serious person could expect the Iraqi threat to diminish. Again, the burden in this debate rests on those who believe American policy has actually been successful in containing the threat Saddam's regime poses to the world.

There is no greater responsibility we face as members of this body than voting to place the country on a course that could send young Americans to war in her defense. All of us must weigh our consciences carefully. Although we may hold different views of how to respond to the threat posed by Saddam Hussein's Iraq, the very fact that we are holding this free debate, and that the fate of nations and peoples other than our own will be determined by the outcome of our actions, serves as a reminder that we are a great nation, united in freedom's defense, and called once again to make the world safe for freedom's blessings to flourish. The quality of our greatness will determine the character of our response.

NO PLACE FOR KINGS IN AMERICA

Senator Robert C. Byrd

A s I have witnessed the tides that ebb and flow on the world stage over these 50 years, all the more have I come to believe that the Constitution is the principal mast to which we should rope ourselves in order to put wax in our ears to the siren calls that will lead us astray from what the Constitution says.

The Constitution very clearly says, in a nonambiguous sentence, the Congress shall have power to declare war. I am very pained to see a Congress, most of the leaders of which say we should pass this resolution—pass it now, pass it here, get it behind us before the election. Get it behind us.

Where are we looking? We are looking at Iraq. Yet there is nothing new in the evidence. I have asked the director of the CIA on two different occasions: What is different? Do not tell me anything about policy; we will make the policy. But tell me what there is by way of intelligence where you are the expert. What is there that is new today, that you know today that you did not know three months ago or six months ago?

I asked that question of the secretary of state: What is it that is new? I have asked that question of the secretary of defense. What does he say? The thing that is new is September 11. That is not so new; that is over 365 days old. So what is there that is new that requires us to make this fateful, far-reaching decision before the election?

There is nothing new. They have known it for three months, six months. A lot of it they have known for years. This is a fateful decision, and the decision ought to be made here, and this Congress ought not turn this fateful determination, this decision, over to any president, any one man, because, as James Madison said, the trust and the temptation are too great for any one man.

Here we are today; we have rubber spines, rubber legs, and we do not have backbones. This branch of government, under the Constitution, is the branch

Senator Robert Byrd, Democrat of West Virginia, spoke on the Senate floor on October 4, 2002, from which these remarks are excerpted. He has served in the Senate since 1956. He was Senate Majority Leader for six years (1977–80, 1987–88) and Senate Minority Leader six years (1981–86). His energetic opposition to the Iraq war resolution drew support from Senators Kennedy (D-MA), Sarbanes (D-MD), Durbin (D-IL), Wellstone (D-MN) and Boxer (D-CA), and an estimated 20,000 calls and 50,000 emails of support poured into his office. At the end, after the Senate voted 77–23 in favor of the resolution, Byrd lamented, "I have fought the good fight. I might as well talk to the ocean."

consisting of the immediately elected representatives of the people, and under the Constitution it is to declare war.

The framers were very wise when they determined that these two matters—the decision to go to war and the making of war—should be in two different places. The decision, the determination to declare war, should flow from this branch, the people's branch, and the matter of making war should be in the hands of a unified commander, the commander in chief.

What are we doing? In my view, if we accept this resolution as it is written, we are saying both of these vital functions would be placed in the hands of one man.

I respect the president of the United States. We should work with him, and we should support him when we can. But remember what Madison said: The trust and the temptation are too great for any one man.

We elected representatives of the people are not supposed to follow any president, whether he is a Democrat or Republican, meekly and without question. I do not believe there is a Republican in this body who knows me well who would believe for a moment, if we had a Democratic president today, I would not be saying exactly what I am saying right now.

There is no king in the American scheme of things. There is no place for kings in our constitutional system. But there is a place for men. When I say "men," of course, I am speaking of men and women.

We are voting on this new Bush doctrine of preventive strikes—preemptive strikes. There is nothing in this Constitution about preemptive strikes. Yet in this rag here, this resolution, we are about to vote to put the imprimatur of the Congress on that doctrine. That is what the Bush administration wants us to do. They want Congress to put its stamp of approval on that Bush doctrine of preemptive strikes.

That is a mistake. Are we going to present the face of America as the face of a bully that is ready to go out at high noon with both guns blazing or are we going to maintain the face of America as a country which believes in justice, the rule of law, freedom and liberty and the rights of all people to work out their ultimate destiny?

What are the ramifications around the globe? What is the image of the United States then going to be? A nation that is a rogue nation, that is determined to wipe out other nations with a preemptive strike? And what will happen if we deliver a preemptive strike? Will other nations be encouraged to do the same?

I think the president is in a much better position, ultimately, if we let the United Nations speak first and not go to the United Nations and say: Now, we would love to hear what you have to say, but regardless of what you have to say, we have made up our minds, and if you don't do it, we are going to do it.

We are committing the blood and the treasure of the American people to do what the United Nations won't do. I say, do what the president has done thus far. Put it in the lap of the United Nations and expect them to give us an answer. Then come back to the people's representatives and let them make a determination as to whether or not at that point we should strike.

[However], if we are going to make it a blank check, let's make it a blank check right upfront, without all of these flowery fig leaves of "whereas" clauses, and simply say that the president has this power. Give it to him and we will put up a sign on the top of this Capitol: "Out of business." "Gone home." "Gone fishing."

We are giving to the president of the United States a blank check, and Congress cannot do that. Congress should not do that. Where is the termination? Where is the deadline? Where is the sunset language that says after this happens this resolution shall no longer exist? There is nothing. This goes on to the next president of the United States.

Why shouldn't the leadership of this Congress say that the concerns are so great, the potential is so weighty, that we, the people's representatives, ought to go back and talk to the American people about this? Let's hear from them before we make this final decision. Why should we be forced to make this decision now?

AUTHORIZATION FOR USE OF MILITARY FORCE AGAINST IRAQ RESOLUTION OF 2002

The following is the text of the Authorization for Use of Military Force Against Iraq Resolution of 2002 (H.J.Res.114). It passed the House by a vote of 296–133 and the Senate by 77–23.

Joint Resolution

To authorize the use of United States Armed Forces against Iraq.

Whereas in 1990 in response to Iraq's war of aggression against and illegal occupation of Kuwait, the United States forged a coalition of nations to liberate Kuwait and its people in order to defend the national security of the United States and enforce United Nations Security Council resolutions relating to Iraq;

Whereas after the liberation of Kuwait in 1991, Iraq entered into a United Nations sponsored cease-fire agreement pursuant to which Iraq unequivocally agreed, among other things, to eliminate its nuclear, biological, and chemical weapons programs and the means to deliver and develop them, and to end its support for international terrorism;

Whereas the efforts of international weapons inspectors, United States intelligence agencies, and Iraqi defectors led to the discovery that Iraq had large stockpiles of chemical weapons and a large scale biological weapons program, and that Iraq had an advanced nuclear weapons development program that was much closer to producing a nuclear weapon than intelligence reporting had previously indicated;

Whereas Iraq, in direct and flagrant violation of the cease-fire, attempted to thwart the efforts of weapons inspectors to identify and destroy Iraq's weapons of mass destruction stockpiles and development capabilities, which finally resulted in the withdrawal of inspectors from Iraq on October 31, 1998;

Whereas in Public Law 105-235 (August 14, 1998), Congress concluded that Iraq's continuing weapons of mass destruction programs threatened vital United States interests and international peace and security, declared Iraq to be in 'material and unacceptable breach of its international obligations' and urged the President 'to take appropriate action, in accordance with the Constitution and relevant laws of the United States, to bring Iraq into compliance with its international obligations';

Whereas Iraq both poses a continuing threat to the national security of the United States and international peace and security in the Persian Gulf region and remains in material and unacceptable breach of its international obligations by, among other things, continuing to possess and develop a significant chemical and biological weapons capability, actively seeking a nuclear weapons capability, and supporting and harboring terrorist organizations;

Whereas Iraq persists in violating resolution of the United Nations Security Council by continuing to engage in brutal repression of its civilian population thereby threatening international peace and security in the region, by refusing to release, repatriate, or account for non-Iraqi citizens wrongfully detained by Iraq, including an American serviceman, and by failing to return property wrongfully seized by Iraq from Kuwait;

Whereas the current Iraqi regime has demonstrated its capability and willingness to use weapons of mass destruction against other nations and its own people;

Whereas the current Iraqi regime has demonstrated its continuing hostility toward, and willingness to attack, the United States, including by attempting in 1993 to assassinate former President Bush and by firing on many thousands of occasions on United States and Coalition Armed Forces engaged in enforcing the resolutions of the United Nations Security Council;

Whereas members of al Qaida, an organization bearing responsibility for attacks on the United States, its citizens, and interests, including the attacks that occurred on September 11, 2001, are known to be in Iraq;

Whereas Iraq continues to aid and harbor other international terrorist organizations, including organizations that threaten the lives and safety of United States citizens;

Whereas the attacks on the United States of September 11, 2001, underscored the gravity of the threat posed by the acquisition of weapons of mass destruction by international terrorist organizations;

Whereas Iraq's demonstrated capability and willingness to use weapons of mass destruction, the risk that the current Iraqi regime will either employ those weapons to launch a surprise attack against the United States or its Armed Forces or provide them to international terrorists who would do so, and the extreme magnitude of harm that would result to the United States and its citizens from such an attack, combine to justify action by the United States to defend itself;

Whereas United Nations Security Council Resolution 678 (1990) authorizes the use of all necessary means to enforce United Nations Security Council Resolution 660 (1990) and subsequent relevant resolutions and to compel Iraq to cease certain activities that threaten international peace and security, including the development of weapons of mass destruction and refusal or obstruction of United Nations weapons inspections in violation of United Nations Security Council Resolution 687 (1991), repression of its civilian population in violation of United Nations Security Council Resolution 688 (1991), and threatening its neighbors or United Nations operations in Iraq in violation of United Nations Security Council Resolution 949 (1994);

Whereas in the [January 14, 1991] Authorization for Use of Military Force Against Iraq Resolution (Public Law 102-1), Congress has authorized the President 'to use United States Armed Forces pursuant to United Nations Security Council Resolution 678 (1990) in order to achieve implementation of Security Council Resolution 660, 661, 662, 664, 665, 666, 667, 669, 670, 674, and 677';

Whereas in December 1991, Congress expressed its sense that it 'supports the use of all necessary means to achieve the goals of United Nations Security Council Resolution 687 as being consistent with the Authorization of Use of Military Force Against Iraq Resolution (Public Law 102-1),' that Iraq's repression of its civilian population violates United Nations Security Council Resolution 688 and 'constitutes a continuing threat to the peace, security, and stability of the Persian Gulf region,' and that Congress, 'supports the use of all necessary means to achieve the goals of United Nations Security Council Resolution 688';

Whereas the Iraq Liberation Act of 1998 (Public Law 105-338) expressed the sense of Congress that it should be the policy of the United States to support efforts to remove from power the current Iraqi regime and promote the emergence of a democratic government to replace that regime;

Whereas on September 12, 2002, President Bush committed the United States to 'work with the United Nations Security Council to meet our common challenge' posed by Iraq and to 'work for the necessary resolutions,' while also making clear that 'the Security Council resolutions will be enforced, and the just demands of peace and security will be met, or action will be unavoidable';

Whereas the United States is determined to prosecute the war on terrorism and Iraq's ongoing support for international terrorist groups combined with its development of weapons of mass destruction in direct violation of its obligations under the 1991 cease-fire and other United Nations Security Council resolutions make clear that it is in the national security interests of the United States and in furtherance of the war on terrorism that all relevant United Nations Security Council resolutions be enforced, including through the use of force if necessary;

Whereas Congress has taken steps to pursue vigorously the war on terrorism through the provision of authorities and funding requested by the President to take the necessary actions against international terrorists and terrorist organizations, including those nations, organizations, or persons who planned, authorized, committed, or aided the terrorist attacks that occurred on September 11, 2001, or harbored such person or organizations;

Whereas the President and Congress are determined to continue to take all appropriate actions against international terrorists and terrorist organizations, including those nations, organizations, or persons who planned, authorized, committed, or aided the terrorist attacks that occurred on September 11, 2001, or harbored such persons or organizations;

Whereas the President has authority under the Constitution to take action in order to deter and prevent acts of international terrorism against the United States, as Congress recognized in the joint resolution on Authorization for Use of Military Force (Public Law 107–40); and

Whereas it is in the national security interests of the United States to restore international peace and security to the Persian Gulf region: Now, therefore, be it

Resolved by the Senate and House of Representatives of the United States of America in Congress assembled,

Section 1. Short Title

This joint resolution may be cited as the 'Authorization for Use of Military Force Against Iraq Resolution of 2002'.

Sec. 2. Support For United States Diplomatic Efforts.

The Congress of the United States supports the efforts by the President to—

(1) strictly enforce through the United Nations Security Council all relevant Security Council resolutions regarding Iraq and encourages him in those efforts; and

(2) obtain prompt and decisive action by the Security Council to ensure that Iraq abandons its strategy of delay, evasion and noncompliance and promptly and strictly complies with all relevant Security Council resolutions regarding Iraq.

Sec. 3. Authorization For Use Of United States Armed Forces.

(a) AUTHORIZATION—The President is authorized to use the Armed Forces of the United States as he determines to be necessary and appropriate in order to—

(1) defend the national security of the United States against the continuing threat posed by Iraq; and

(2) enforce all relevant United Nations Security Council resolutions regarding Iraq.

(b) PRESIDENTIAL DETERMINATION—In connection with the exercise of the authority granted in subsection (a) to use force the President shall, prior to such exercise or as soon thereafter as may be feasible, but no later than 48 hours after exercising such authority, make available to the Speaker of the House of Representatives and the President pro tempore of the Senate his determination that—

(1) reliance by the United States on further diplomatic or other peaceful means alone either (A) will not adequately protect the national security of the United States against the continuing threat posed by Iraq or (B) is not likely to lead to enforcement of all relevant United Nations Security Council resolutions regarding Iraq; and

(2) acting pursuant to this joint resolution is consistent with the United States and other countries continuing to take the necessary actions against international terrorist and terrorist organizations, including those nations, organizations, or persons who planned, authorized, committed or aided the terrorist attacks that occurred on September 11, 2001.

(c) War Powers Resolution Requirements—

(1) SPECIFIC STATUTORY AUTHORIZATION—Consistent with section 8(a)(1) of the War Powers Resolution, the Congress declares that this section is intended to constitute specific statutory authorization within the meaning of section 5(b) of the War Powers Resolution.

(2)APPLICABILITY OF OTHER REQUIREMENTS—Nothing in this joint resolution supersedes any requirement of the War Powers Resolution.

Sec. 4. Reports To Congress.

(a) REPORTS—The President shall, at least once every 60 days, submit to the Congress a report on matters relevant to this joint resolution, including actions taken pursuant to the exercise of authority granted in section 3 and the status of planning for efforts that are expected to be required after such actions are completed, including those actions described in section 7 of the Iraq Liberation Act of 1998 (Public Law 105–338).

(b) SINGLE CONSOLIDATED REPORT—To the extent that the submission of any report described in subsection (a) coincides with the submission of any other report on matters relevant to this joint resolution otherwise required to be submitted to Congress pursuant to the reporting requirements of the War Powers Resolution (Public Law 93–148), all such reports may be submitted as a single consolidated report to the Congress.

(c) RULE OF CONSTRUCTION—To the extent that the information required by section 3 of the Authorization for Use of Military Force Against Iraq Resolution (Public Law 102-1) is included in the report required by this section, such report shall be considered as meeting the requirements of section 3 of such resolution.

ELEVEN

REGIME CHANGE: WHY AND WHY NOT

"The whole world focuses on us. If the United States blanches, and now fails to carry through on what has been a pretty deliberate policy, this will be an enormous encouragement to terrorists, to states that harbor them, that we are in effect a paper tiger, if you will. And, I think, it will open the floodgates to terror against us. We are simply too far down the road to recoil."

—Richard Perle, chairman, Defense Policy Board, January 25, 2003

"Some have said we must not act until the threat is imminent. Since when have terrorists and tyrants announced their intentions, politely putting us on notice before they strike? If this threat is permitted to fully and suddenly emerge, all actions, all words and all recriminations would come too late."

—President George W. Bush, State of the Union speech, January 29, 2003

"It still confuses many Americans that, in a world full of vicious slimeballs, we're about to bomb one that didn't attack us on 9/11 (like Osama); that isn't intercepting our planes (like North Korea); that isn't financing Al Qaeda (like Saudi Arabia); that isn't home to Osama and his lieutenants (like Pakistan); that isn't a host body for terrorists (like Iran, Lebanon and Syria)."

—New York Times columnist Maureen Dowd, March 9, 2003

TWO FACES, ONE TERROR

Fouad Ajami

The prospect of using force against Iraq has brought numerous demands that the U.S. establish a definitive connection between the rogue state and the events of Sept. 11. But we needn't look for a "smoking gun" that would unequivocally tie Saddam Hussein to al Qaeda. The more important link—of a more organic nature—has already been established. Iraq and al Qaeda are two main tributaries of Arab radicalism.

The men who dominate these two sinister entities cross the border between religious faith and secular politics in a seamless way. While Saddam is technically a secular leader, the border hardly exists in the contemporary world of Arab politics. As the U.N. Security Council resolved last week to convene in an emergency session should Saddam fail to satisfy a new wave of weapons inspectors, that nexus became even more volatile. One of the considerations in confronting Iraq, whether in the form of unilateral U.S. action or through U.N. coordination, is how such a move will affect the Arab street. Will any military response, however thought out, be seen as rational by Islamists?

SOME SCHOLARS have long held the view that politics and religion were always inseparable in the Muslim world. But the history of the Arab-Muslim lands does not bear this out: There was, for a good deal of the century behind us, a secular ascendancy. This trend is now in doubt.

It is out of that secular primacy that a man like Saddam emerged, although born destitute in 1937 in Tikrit, a forgotten town on the Tigris. The old order of the merchant-landlord elites which dominated his country, and that of the larger Arab world, was giving way. A new breed of restless, pitiless men stepped forth to press their claims, and they did it with terror and an authority given them by secular ideas.

Saddam Hussein has not, in the course of his brutal career, shown any

---

Fouad Ajami is the Majid Khadduri Professor and Director of Middle East Studies at the Paul H. Nitze School of Advanced International Studies at Johns Hopkins University. The author of several books, the most recent of which is *The Dream Palace of the Arabs: A Generation's Odyssey* (1998), Ajami is also a contributing editor of *U.S. News & World Report* and a member of the editorial board of *Foreign Affairs*. This article was originally published in *The Wall Street Journal* on November 16, 2002.

burning interest in Islam. One of his most faithful servants, Tariq Aziz, is a Christian Chaldean; as is his new foreign minister, Naji Sabri. This is in keeping with the origins of the party, established by two Paris-educated Syrian intellectuals, Michel Aflaq and Salah al-Din Bitar, in the 1940s—the first Greek Orthodox, the second Sunni Muslim. Rather, the ideology of the Baath derived from the National Socialism of the Third Reich. After its conquest and consolidation of political power in Iraq, the Baath party's civic religion was to become the crude cult of personality surrounding the ruler.

To the pious, this hero-worship of the dictator is a form of idolatry: There is something Babylonian about the cult of Saddam. The more austere desert world of the Arabian peninsula wouldn't have permitted such a cult. That world was intimate, and precluded the awe at the heart of the system that Saddam put together. The royal despotism, the very physical scale of the ruler's monuments, the mystery of his whereabouts, the indecipherability and surprise of his deeds (he can imprison thousands, and then release them on a whim) all bear the mark of the Iraqi setting. There is Stalinism, to be sure, and the audacity of what dictators did in the age of communism. But Saddam manipulates older sources of despotism as well.

A decade or so ago, he even claimed an affinity, a spiritual descent of sorts, from the Babylonian monarch Nebuchadnezzar; his sycophants proclaimed him a "flag bearer" and a "grandson" of that ruler. Hammurabi was also pressed into service as part of the tyrant's legend. There were sediments of civilization in the Land Between the Rivers—the Tigris and the Euphrates. And the Saddam Hussein appropriated them all.

Islam barely figured in the making of this regime. This was Iraq, and what religion was there was a matter of sectarian loyalty: In Baghdad and the belt around the Tigris, there were the Sunni Muslim Arabs (Saddam's community); in the south, there was the traditional home of Shiism. In the north, there were the Kurds, in their majority Sunnis, but set apart by ethnicity and language, and a growing sense of national separateness. The Baath glided over those communal and religious lines. Its ideologues insisted that their world was neither religious, nor sectarian. Indeed, for a time, before the Sunni Arabs emptied the Baath of all ideological pretense, and claimed power as the exclusive right of their clans, the Baath had been a natural home for the Kurds and the Shia and the remnants of the Christian communities. As the Shia were a majority of the country's population, it was convenient for the Sunni rulers to claim that they were the bearers of secularism.

It was in the name of secularism that Saddam decimated the ranks of the Shia religious class in the shrine towns of Najaf and Karbala in the late 1970s. He set out to monopolize the political world: the Shia clerics were in the way, and were shown no mercy. And it was in the name of secularism, as well, that Saddam had waged a brutal war against the Iranian Revolution of Ayatollah Khomeini. The Arab states, and powers beyond, had bought his legend, backed him as he posed as the secular, modernist sentry against the forces of the Iranian theocracy.

In a revealing illustration of Saddam's way with the faith, it was during Desert Storm that he fell back on religion. No sooner had American power broken his army, the Maximum Leader told his soldiers that "angels of mercy" would come to their rescue—this, presumably, to compensate them for the air cover they lacked. And it was in the aftermath of his staggering defeat in that campaign that the Muslim incantation, Allah Akbar, God is Great, was scribbled on the flag of the country. To the gullible, this was a son of Islam, and of the Arabs, seeking solace in the faith against the infidels. But it was not for his piety that the crowd had hailed the Iraqi upstart. He had promised revenge and power, chemical weapons with which he would torch Tel Aviv, the sacking of the pro-American regimes in the Gulf, the sharing out of the loot of oil wealth to crowds in nearby Amman and far-off Casablanca. With his defeat, these hopes came to naught, and the crowd would set out in search of a new avenger.

THE MEN who put together al Qaeda would be the new redeemers. From state terror, there was a passage now to transnational terror. Two jihadists came together to give this terror its means and its ferocity: The Saudi plotter, Osama bin Laden, and the Egyptian Islamist and physician, Ayman al Zawahiri. Unlike Saddam, who had clawed his way out of poverty, these men hailed from the apex of their societies.

That bin Laden came from considerable wealth is known, but Zawahiri, too, was born to privilege. Politics was not a means of social advancement to these two. Bin Laden had come to a sense of holy warfare in Afghanistan. Boredom with Arabia had taken him into that anti-communist fight. But in the stern Arabia of his birth, there was no room for a restless jihadist. As for Zawahiri, it was the Kingdom of God, and the rule of the Sharia (Islamic law) that beckoned. Revenge, too, was a factor. Zawahiri was picked up in the dragnet that followed the assassination of Anwar Sadat in 1981, and was tortured. He took to the road with a deep determination that the regime of the peasant-officer Hosni Mubarak would be undone, and that Mr. Mubarak's American patrons would be bloodied along the way.

What these men thought of Saddam can easily be surmised. Worldly rule by tyrants is exactly what drove Zawahiri out of Egypt. But a common cause could be made across that secular/religious divide. Anti-Americanism was a bond, as was the shared determination to destabilize the conservative Arab states.

In February 1998, when bin Laden and Zawahiri declared the creation of their "World Islamic Front," [see p. 202 for the text of this statement] and issued their incendiary fatwa authorizing the killing of "the Americans and their allies, civilian and military alike," the fate of Iraq, and the sins of the sanctions regime imposed on its people, figured prominently in the articles of indictment. "Despite the great devastation inflicted on the Iraqi people by the Crusader-Zionist alliance, and despite the huge number of those killed, which has exceeded one million, the Americans are once again trying to repeat the horrific massacres as though they are not content with the protracted blockade imposed after the ferocious war or the fragmentation and devastation." No kind words had to be said about Saddam Hussein himself; it was the Iraqi people whose sufferings were invoked. It was enough to highlight that the sanctions on Iraq were imposed with the connivance of rulers in the Arabian Peninsula, and that the House of Saud was doing America's bidding.

It is the hallmark of unsettled societies to believe in the man on horseback, in millennial and sudden redemption, in the pretender who would transform and empower a broken world, but without labor and effort and empirical work. For all the outward differences, Saddam and the leaders of al Qaeda offered the masses that flocked to their banners an absolution from responsibility, and a dream of revenge. In both cases, the crowd worked itself into a frenzy, and then fell into despondency when the Pied Piper was unable to deliver.

There was a wave of genuine despair, it should be recalled, when Saddam's armies were shattered in 1991. In the same vein, the satisfaction with bin Laden and the terrible deeds of al Qaeda soon gave way to the old bitter sense of Arab disappointment that the new redeemer, too, had left his world unchanged, and that the base he had secured in Afghanistan was undone.

If and when America ventures into Iraq, it should cast aside the distinction between secular and Islamist enemies. The rule of reason and practicality, the delivery of the Arabs from a culture of victimology and abdication, the need to take on the sources of the anti-Americanism that brought terror to America's shores, all entail a reckoning with the same malignancies.

It was the sparing of Saddam in 1991 that nourished al Qaeda, and gave its masterminds and foot-soldiers ammunition, and an ideological pretext, for targeting America. Saddam had been through war and had been let off the hook; that had been part of the emboldening of the new purveyors of terror. America's enemies in that region are full of cunning. They should be read right; the banners they unfurl—secular or religious—are of no great significance. It is the drive that animates them that matters. What they bring forth, be they dictators in bunkers or jihadists on the run, is a determination to extirpate American influence from their world, and a view of history that the deep sorrows and failings of the Arab world can be laid at the doorsteps of the distant American power.

DECIPHERING THE BUSH ADMINISTRATION'S MOTIVES

Michael T. Klare

The United States is about to go to war with Iraq. As of this writing, there are 60,000 U.S. troops already deployed in the area around Iraq, and another 75,000 or so are on their way to the combat zone. Weapons inspectors have found a dozen warheads, designed to carry chemical weapons. Even before this discovery, senior U.S. officials were insisting that Saddam was not cooperating with the United Nations and had to be removed by force. Hence, there does not seem to be any way to stop this war, unless Saddam Hussein is overthrown by members of the Iraqi military or is persuaded to abdicate his position and flee the country.

It is impossible at this point to foresee the outcome of this war. Under the most optimistic scenarios—the ones advanced by proponents of the war—Iraqi forces will put up only token resistance and American forces will quickly capture Baghdad and remove Saddam Hussein from office (by killing him or placing him under arrest). This scenario further assumes that the Iraqis will decline to use their weapons of mass destruction (WMD) or will be prevented from doing so by U.S. military action; that civilian casualties will be kept low and that most Iraqis will welcome their "liberation" from Saddam; that a new, pro-U.S. government will quickly and easily be put into place; that fighting between competing ethnic factions will be limited and easily brought under control; that anti-American protests in other Muslim countries will not get out of hand; and that American forces will be withdrawn after a relatively short occupation period of six months to a year.

It is not difficult, however, to imagine less optimistic scenarios. In these scenarios, the Iraqis could put up stiff resistance and conduct house-to-house fighting in Baghdad, thereby producing significant U.S. casualties and lead-

Michael T. Klare is the Five College Professor of Peace and World Security Studies (a joint appointment at Amherst College, Hampshire College, Mount Holyoke College, Smith College, and the University of Massachusetts at Amherst). The author of numerous books and articles on U.S. defense policy, he is also the defense correspondent of *The Nation*, a contributing editor of *Current History*, and a member of the Editorial Board of the *Bulletin of the Atomic Scientists*. This article first appeared in the January 16, 2003 issue of *Foreign Policy in Focus*.

ing, in turn, to heavy U.S. air and missile strikes on populated areas, resulting in high civilian casualties. Under these scenarios, the Iraqis will use their chemical and biological weapons in a final spasm of self-destruction, producing untold civilian and combatant casualties. The surviving Iraqis will turn against their American "liberators," resulting in constant sniping and acts of terrorism. The Kurds and Shiites and Sunnis will fight over the spoils of war, producing widespread carnage and trapping U.S. forces in the middle. American troops will remain in Iraq for a generation, or more, producing hatred and resistance throughout the Muslim world and increased levels of terrorism elsewhere.

Which scenario will prevail? Nobody can be certain at this point. Those who favor a war with Iraq tend to believe that Iraqi resistance will be light and that the rest of the optimistic scenario will fall into place. But no one can guarantee that any of this will come to pass, and there are many experts who believe that the likelihood of things going awry are very great. For example, the CIA has indicated that Iraq is most likely to use its WMD in the event that Iraq is attacked and defeat appears likely. In weighing the relative merits of going to war with Iraq, therefore, one should reckon on the worst possible outcome, not the best. One must ask: are the purported benefits of war so great as to outweigh all of the possible negative repercussions?

And this leads to the most fundamental question of all: WHY are we going to war? What is really motivating President Bush and his senior advisers to incur these enormous risks?

In their public pronouncements, President Bush and his associates have advanced three reasons for going to war with Iraq and ousting Saddam Hussein: (1) to eliminate Saddam's WMD arsenals; (2) to diminish the threat of international terrorism; and (3) to promote democracy in Iraq and the surrounding areas.

These are, indeed, powerful motives for going to war. But are they genuine? Is this what is really driving the rush to war? To answer this, we need to examine each motive in turn. In doing so, moreover, it is necessary to keep in mind that the United States cannot do everything. If we commit hundreds of thousands of American troops and hundreds of billions of dollars to the conquest, occupation, and reconstruction of Iraq, we cannot easily do the same in other countries—we simply don't have the resources to invade and occupy every country that poses a hypothetical threat to the United States or is deserving of regime change. So a decision to attack Iraq means a decision to refrain from other actions that might also be important for U.S. security or the good of the world.

1. Eliminating weapons of mass destruction: The reason most often given by the administration for going to war with Iraq is to reduce the risk of a WMD attack on the United States. To be sure, a significant WMD attack on the United States would be a terrible disaster, and it is appropriate for the President of the United States to take effective and vigorous action to prevent this from happening. If this is, in fact, Bush's primary concern, then one would imagine that he would pay the greatest attention to the greatest threat of WMD usage against the United States, and deploy available U.S. resources— troops, dollars, and diplomacy—accordingly. But is this what Bush is actually doing? The answer is no. Anyone who takes the trouble to examine the global WMD proliferation threat closely and to gauge the relative likelihood of various WMD scenarios would have to conclude that the greatest threat of WMD usage against the United States at the present time comes from North Korea and Pakistan, not Iraq.

North Korea and Pakistan pose a greater WMD threat to the United States than Iraq for several reasons. First of all, they both possess much bigger WMD arsenals. Pakistan is known to possess several dozen nuclear warheads along with missiles and planes capable of delivering them hundreds of miles away; it is also suspected of having developed chemical weapons. North Korea is thought to possess sufficient plutonium to produce one to two nuclear devices along with the capacity to manufacture several more; it also has a large chemical weapons stockpile and a formidable array of ballistic missiles. Iraq, by contrast, possesses no nuclear weapons today and is thought to be several years away from producing one, even under the best of circumstances. Iraq may possess some chemical and biological weapons and a dozen or so Scud-type missiles that were hidden at the end of the 1991 Gulf war, but it is not known whether any of these items are still in working order and available for military use. Equally important is the question of intention: how likely are these countries to actually use their WMD munitions? Nobody can answer this with any degree of certainty, of course. But there are a few things that can be said.

To begin with, Pakistani President Pervez Musharraf has publicly stated that he was prepared to employ nuclear weapons against India last year when New Delhi massed its forces on Pakistan's border and threatened to attack unless Pakistan curbed the activities of Islamic militants in Kashmir. This does not mean that Pakistan would use nuclear weapons against the United States, but it does indicate a readiness to employ such weapons as an instrument of war; it is also easy to imagine a scenario in which someone else comes to power who is far more anti-American than Musharraf.

Just as worrisome is the fact that the North Koreans have declared that they would consider any move by the United States and the U.N. to impose economic sanctions on North Korea as punishment for its pursuit of nuclear weapons as an act of war, to which they would respond accordingly, turning the United States into a "sea of fire." Again, this does not mean that they would actually choose to use their nuclear weapons, but it is not hard to imagine a scenario in which war breaks out and the North Koreans use their WMD in a desperate bid to stave off defeat.

On the other hand, the CIA has concluded that Saddam Hussein will not choose to use his country's WMD capabilities against the United States so long as his regime remains intact; it is only in the case of imminent U.S. conquest of Baghdad that he might be tempted to use these weapons.

The Bush administration has also indicated that war with Iraq is justified in order to prevent Iraq from providing WMD to anti-American terrorists. The transfer of WMD technology to terrorist groups is a genuine concern—but it is in Pakistan where the greatest threat of such transference exists, not Iraq. In Pakistan, many senior military officers are known to harbor great sympathy for Kashmiri militants and other extremist Islamic movements; with anti-Americanism intensifying throughout the region, it is not hard to imagine these officers providing the militants with some of Pakistan's WMD weapons and technology. On the other hand, the current leadership in Iraq has no such ties with Islamic extremists; on the contrary, Saddam has been a lifelong enemy of the militant Islamists and they view him in an equally hostile manner.

It follows from all this that a policy aimed at protecting the United States from WMD attacks would identify Pakistan and North Korea as the leading perils, and put Iraq in a rather distant third place. But this is not, of course, what the administration is doing. Instead, it has minimized the threat from Pakistan and North Korea and focused almost exclusively on the threat from Iraq. It is clear, then, that protecting the United States from WMD attack is not the primary justification for invading Iraq; if it were, we would be talking about an assault on Pakistan and/or North Korea, not Iraq.

2. Combating terrorism: The administration has argued at great length that an invasion of Iraq and the ouster of Saddam Hussein would constitute the culmination of and the greatest success in the war against terrorism. Why this is so has never been made entirely clear, but it is said that Saddam's hostility toward the United States somehow sustains and invigorates the terrorist threat to this country. It follows, therefore, that the elimination of Saddam would result in a great defeat for international terrorism and greatly weaken its capacity to attack the United States.

Were any of this true, an invasion of Iraq might make sense from an anti-terrorism point of view. But there simply is no evidence that this is the case; if anything, the opposite is true. From what we know of Al Qaeda and other such organizations, the objective of Islamic extremists is to overthrow any government in the Islamic world that does not adhere to a fundamentalist version of Islam and replace it with one that does. The Baathist regime in Iraq does not qualify as such a regime; thus, under Al Qaeda doctrine, it must be swept away, along with the equally deficient governments in Egypt, Jordan, and Saudi Arabia. If follows from this that a U.S. effort to oust Saddam Hussein and replace his regime with another secular government—this one kept in place by American military power—will not diminish the wrath of Islamic extremists but rather fuel it.

In addressing this matter, moreover, it is necessary to keep the Israeli-Palestinian struggle in mind. For most Arab Muslims, whatever their views of Saddam Hussein, the United States is a hypocritical power because it tolerates (or even supports) the use of state terror by Israel against the Palestinians while making war against Baghdad for the same sort of behavior. It is this perception that is fueling the anti-American current now running through the Muslim world. An American invasion of Iraq will not quiet that current, but excite it. It is thus exceedingly difficult to see how a U.S. invasion of Iraq will produce a stunning victory in the war against terrorism; if anything, it will trigger a new round of anti-American violence. Hence, it is very difficult to conclude that the administration is motivated by anti-terrorism in seeking to topple Hussein.

3. The promotion of democracy: The ouster of Saddam Hussein, it is claimed, will clear the space for the Iraqi people (under American guidance, of course) to establish a truly democratic government and serve as a beacon and inspiration for the spread of democracy throughout the Islamic world, which is said to be sadly deficient in this respect. Certainly, the spread of democracy to the Islamic world would be a good thing, and should be encouraged. But is there any reason to believe that the administration is motivated by a desire to spread democracy in its rush to war with Iraq?

There are several reasons to doubt this. First of all, many of the top leaders of the current administration, particularly Donald Rumsfeld and Dick Cheney, were completely happy to embrace the Saddam Hussein dictatorship in the 1980s when Iraq was the enemy of our enemy (that is, Iran) and thus considered our de facto friend. Under the so-called tilt toward Iraq, the Reagan-Bush administration decided to assist Iraq in its war against Iran during the Iran-Iraq War of 1980–88. As part of this policy, Reagan removed Iraq from the list of countries that support terrorism, thus permitting the provision of billions of dollars' worth of agricultural credits and other forms of assistance to Hussein. The bearer of this good news was none other than Donald Rumsfeld, who traveled to Baghdad and met with Hussein in December 1983 as a special representative of President Reagan. At the same time, the Department of Defense, provided Iraq with secret satellite data on Iranian military positions. This information was provided to Saddam even though U.S. leaders were informed by a senior State Department official on November 1, 1983 that the Iraqis were using chemical weapons against the Iranians "almost daily," and were aware that U.S. satellite data could be used by Baghdad to pinpoint CW attacks on Iranian positions. Dick Cheney, who took over as Secretary of Defense in 1989, continued the practice of supplying Iraq with secret intelligence data. Not once did Messrs. Rumsfeld and Cheney speak out against Iraqi CW use or suggest that the United States discontinue its support of the Hussein dictatorship during this period. So there is no reason whatsoever to believe that the current leadership has a principled objection to dictatorial rule in Iraq—it is only when Saddam is threatening us instead of our enemies that they care about his tyrannical behavior.

There is another reason to be skeptical about the Bush administration's commitment to democracy in this part of the world, and that is the fact that the administration has developed close relationships with a number of other dictatorial or authoritarian regimes in the area. Most notably, the United States had developed close ties with the post-Soviet dictatorships in Azerbaijan, Kazakhstan, and Uzbekistan. Each of these countries is ruled by a Stalinist dictator who once served as a loyal agent of the Soviet empire: Heydar Aliyev in Azerbaijan, Nursultan Nazarbaev of Kazakhstan, and Islam Karimov of Uzbekistan. Only slightly less odious than Saddam Hussein, these tyrants have been welcomed to the White House and showered with American aid and support. And there certainly is nothing even remotely democratic about Kuwait or Saudi Arabia, two of America's other close allies in the region. So it is hard to believe that the Bush administration is motivated by a love of democracy, when it has been so quick to embrace patently undemocratic regimes that have agreed to do its bidding.

So, if concern over WMD proliferation, or the reduction of terrorism, or a love of democracy do not explain the administration's determination to oust Saddam Hussein, what does?

I believe that the answer is a combination of three factors, all related to the pursuit of oil and the preservation of America's status as the paramount world power. Ever since the end of the cold war, American policymakers (whether Democratic or Republican) have sought to preserve America's "sole superpower" status and to prevent the rise of a "peer competitor" that could challenge U.S. paramountcy on anything approaching equal terms. At the same time, American leaders have become increasingly concerned over the country's growing dependence on imported oil, especially oil from the Persian Gulf. The United States now relies on imported oil for 55% of its requirements, and this percentage is expected to rise to 65% in 2020 and keep growing thereafter. This dependency is the "Achilles heel" for American power: unless Persian Gulf oil can be kept under American control, our ability to remain the dominant world power would be put into question.

These concerns undergird the three motives for a U.S. invasion of Iraq. The first derives from America's own dependence on Persian Gulf oil and from the principle, formally enshrined in the Carter Doctrine, that the United States will not permit a hostile state from ever coming into a position where it can threaten America's access to the Gulf. The second is the pivotal role played by the Persian Gulf in supplying oil to the rest of the world: whoever controls the Gulf automatically maintains a stranglehold on the global economy, and the Bush administration wants that to be the United States and no one else. And the third is anxiety about the future availability of oil: the United States is becoming increasingly dependent on Saudi Arabia to supply its imported petroleum, and Washington is desperate to find an alternative to Saudi Arabia should it ever be the case that access to that country is curtailed—and the only country in the world with large enough reserves to compensate for the loss of Saudi Arabia is Iraq. Let us examine each of these three factors in turn.

First, on U.S. dependence on Persian Gulf oil and the Carter Doctrine. Ever since World War II, when American policymakers first acknowledged that the United States would someday become dependent on Middle Eastern petroleum, it has been American policy to ensure that the United States would always have unrestrained access to Persian Gulf oil. At first, the United States relied on Great Britain to protect American access to the Gulf, and then, when Britain pulled out of the area in 1971, the U.S. chose to rely on the Shah of Iran. But when, in 1979, the Shah was overthrown by Islamic militants loyal to the Ayatollah Khomeini, Washington decided that it would have to assume responsibility on its own to protect the oil flow. The result was the Carter Doctrine of January 23, 1980, which states that unrestricted access to Persian Gulf is a vital interest of the United States and that, in protection of that interest, the United States will employ "any means necessary, including military force."

This principle was first invoked in 1987, during the Iran-Iraq War, when Iranian gunboats fired on Kuwaiti oil tankers and the U.S. Navy began escorting Kuwaiti tankers through the Gulf. It was next invoked in August 1990, when Iraq invaded Kuwait and posed an implied threat to Saudi Arabia. President Bush the elder responded to that threat by driving the Iraqis out of Kuwait, in Operation Desert Storm; he did not, however, continue the war into Iraq proper and remove Saddam Hussein himself. Instead, the U.S. engaged in the "containment" of Iraq, entailing an air and sea blockade.

Now, President Bush the younger seeks to abandon containment and pick up Operation Desert Storm where it left off in 1991. The reason being given for this is that Saddam is making more progress in the development of WMD, but the underlying principle is still the Carter Doctrine: Iraq under Saddam poses an implied threat to U.S. access to Persian Gulf oil, and so must be removed. As noted by Vice President Dick Cheney on August 26, 2002, in his important speech before the Veterans of Foreign Wars, "Armed with these weapons of terror and a seat at the top of 10% of the world's oil reserves, Saddam Hussein could then be expected to seek domination of the entire Middle East, take control of a great portion of the world's energy supplies, directly threaten America's friends throughout the region, and subject the United States or any other nation to nuclear blackmail." Stripped to its essence, this is a direct invocation of the Carter Doctrine.

To underscore this, it is useful to compare Cheney's VFW speech to his comments 12 years earlier, following the Iraqi invasion of Kuwait, before the Senate Armed Services Committee: "Iraq controlled 10% of the world's reserves prior to the invasion of Kuwait. Once Saddam Hussein took Kuwait, he doubled that to approximately 20% of the world's known oil reserves. . . . Once he acquired Kuwait and deployed an army as large as the one he possesses [on the border of Saudi Arabia], he was clearly in a position to dictate the future of worldwide energy policy, and that gave him a stranglehold on our economy and on that of most of the other nations of the world as well." The atmospherics may have changed since 1990, but we are still dealing with the Carter Doctrine: Saddam must be removed because of the potential threat he poses to the free flow of oil from the Persian Gulf to the U.S. and its allies.

The second administration objective springs from the language employed by Cheney in his 1990 testimony before the Senate Armed Services Committee: whoever controls the flow of Persian Gulf oil has a "stranglehold" not only on our economy but also "on that of most of that of the other nations of the world as well." This is a powerful image, and perfectly describes the administration's thinking about the Gulf area, except in reverse: by serving as the dominant power in the Gulf, WE maintain a "stranglehold" over the economies of other nations. This gives us extraordinary leverage in world affairs, and explains to some degree why states like Japan, Britain, France, and Germany—states that are even more dependent on Persian Gulf oil than we are—defer to Washington on major international issues (like Iraq) even when they disagree with us.

Maintenance of a stranglehold over Persian Gulf oil is also consistent with the administration's declared goal of attaining permanent military superiority over all other nations. If you read administration statements on U.S. national security policy, you will find that one theme stands out above all others: the United States must prevent any potential rival from ever reaching the point where it could compete with the United States on something resembling equal standing. As articulated in "The National Security Strategy of the United States of America" (released by President Bush in September 2002), this principle holds that American forces must be "strong enough to dissuade potential adversaries from pursuing a military build-up in hopes of surpassing, or equaling, the power of the United States."

One way to accomplish this, of course, is to pursue advances in technology that allow the United States to remain ahead of all potential rivals in military systems—which is what the administration hopes to accomplish by adding tens of billions of dollars to the Department of Defense budget. Another way to do this is maintain a stranglehold on the economy of potential rivals, so that they will refrain from challenging us out of fear of being choked to death through the denial of vital energy supplies. Japan and the European countries are already in this vulnerable position, and will remain so for the foreseeable future; but now China is also moving into this position, as it becomes increasingly dependent on oil from the Persian Gulf. Like the U.S., China is running out of oil, and, like us, it has nowhere to go to make up the difference except the Gulf. But since WE control access to the Gulf, and China lacks the power to break our stranglehold, we can keep China in a vulnerable, subordinate position indefinitely. As I see it, then, the removal of Saddam Hussein and his replacement by someone beholden to the United States is a key part of a broader U.S. strategy aimed at assuring permanent American global dominance. Or, as Michael Ignatieff put it in his seminal essay on America's emerging empire, the concentration of so much oil in the Gulf "makes it what a military strategist would call the empire's center of gravity" ("The Burden," *The New York Times Magazine*, January 5, 2003).

And finally, there is the issue of America's long-term energy dilemma. The problem is as follows: The United States relies on oil to supply about 40% of its energy requirements, more than any other source. At one time, this country relied almost entirely on domestic oil to supply its needs; but our need for oil is growing all the time and our domestic fields—among the oldest in the world—are rapidly being exhausted. So our need for imported oil will grow with each passing year. And the more we turn to foreign sources for our oil, the more we will have to turn to the Persian Gulf, because most of the world's untapped oil—at least two-thirds of it—is located in the Gulf area. We can of course rip up Alaska and extract every drop of oil there, but that would reduce our dependence on imported oil by only about 1–2 percentage points—an insignificant amount. We could also rely for a share of our oil on non-Gulf suppliers like Russia, Venezuela, the Caspian Sea states, and Africa, but they have much less oil than the Persian Gulf countries and they are using it up faster. So, the more you look into the future, the greater will become our dependence on the Gulf.

Now, at the current time, U.S. dependence on Persian Gulf oil means, in all practical terms, American dependence on Saudi Arabia, because Saudi Arabia has more oil than everyone else—about 250 billion barrels, or one-fourth of world reserves. That gives Saudi Arabia a lot of indirect influence over our economy and our way of life. And, as you know, there are many people in this country who are resentful of the Saudis because of their financial ties to charities linked to Osama bin Laden and Al Qaeda. More to the point, Saudi Arabia is a major backer of OPEC and tends to control the global availability of oil—something that makes American officials very nervous, especially when the Saudis use their power to put pressure on the United States to alter some of its policies, for example with respect to the Israeli-Palestinian conflict.

For all of these reasons, American leaders would like to reduce America's dependence on Saudi Arabia. But there is only ONE way to permanently reduce America's reliance on Saudi Arabia: by taking over Iraq and using it as an alternative source of petroleum. Iraq is the ONLY country in the world with sufficient reserves to balance Saudi Arabia: at least 112 billion barrels in proven reserves, and as much as 200–300 billion barrels of potential reserves. By occupying Iraq and controlling its government, the United States will solve its long-term oil-dependency dilemma for a decade or more. And this, I believe, is a major consideration in the administration's decisionmaking about Iraq.

It is this set of factors, I believe, that explain the Bush administration's determination to go to war with Iraq—not concern over WMD, terrorism, or the spread of democracy. But having said this, we need to ask: do these objectives, assuming they're the correct ones, still justify a war on Iraq? Some Americans may think so. There are, indeed, advantages to being positioned on the inside of a powerful empire with control over the world's second-largest supply of untapped petroleum. If nothing else, American motorists will be able to afford the gas for their SUVs, vans, and pick-up trucks for another decade, and maybe longer. There will also be lots of jobs in the military and in the military-industrial complex, or as representatives of American multinational corporations (although, with respect to the latter, I would not advise traveling in most of the rest of the world unless accompanied by a small army of bodyguards). But there will also be a price to pay. Empires tend to require the militarization of society, and that will entail putting more people into uniform, one way or another. It will also mean increased spending on war, and reduced spending on education and other domestic needs. It will entail more secrecy and intrusion into our private lives. All of this has to be entered into the equation. And if you ask me, empire is not worth the price.

CAN WE REALLY DETER A
NUCLEAR-ARMED SADDAM?

Kenneth Pollack

Saddam Hussein is one of the most reckless, aggressive, violence-prone, risk-tolerant, and damage-tolerant leaders of modern history. While he may not be insane, he is often delusional in constructing fantastic conceptions of how his actions are likely to play out. He is driven by paranoia over his internal situation, which makes him insensitive and rash in his external actions. All of these traits have been boldly displayed throughout his years as Iraq's leader. They do not seem to make him impossible to deter, but they do appear to make him difficult to deter in most circumstances and impossible to deter in some. For example, given Saddam's concerns about his internal position and his incredible set of misconceptions about the United States, it is doubtful that he could have been deterred from invading Kuwait in 1990.

Although it is unwise to predict what Saddam Hussein will not do, it does seem unlikely that he would employ nuclear weapons as soon as he got them—to wipe out Tel Aviv, for example. Saddam generally uses violence instrumentally, rather than gratuitously—with the important exception being cases of revenge. Again, based on what we know of his thinking, he would likely understand that a nuclear attack on Tel Aviv would invite his own incineration. Some Israeli analysts have noted that the Iraqi regime has staged large-scale evacuations of Baghdad and that some Iraqi military officers have talked as if they believed they could survive a nuclear retaliation from Israel. However, if nothing else, Saddam's behavior during the Gulf War indicates that he is wary enough of nuclear weapons that he probably will not deliberately court a nuclear attack on Baghdad by launching one of his own—at least not out of the blue. Instead, as his own thinking and actions demonstrate (as best we understand them), the much greater threat is that he will believe that his possession of nuclear weapons will allow him to carry out lesser acts of ag-

From 1995 to 2001, Kenneth M. Pollack served as director for Gulf affairs at the National Security Council, where he was the principal working-level official responsible for implementation of U.S. policy toward Iraq. Prior to his time in the Clinton administration, he spent seven years as a Persian Gulf military analyst for the Central Intelligence Agency. He is currently the director of research at the Saban Center for Middle East Policy at the Brookings Institution and director of national security studies for the Council on Foreign Relations, and is author of the best-selling book, *The Threatening Storm: The Case for Invading Iraq,* from which this article is excerpted.

gression because the United States, Israel, and anyone else would themselves be deterred from responding effectively.

If Saddam had nuclear weapons, especially weapons deliverable by ballistic missiles (which is his goal), Iraq's geographic location at the head of the Persian Gulf would allow him to threaten the destruction of a number of targets of great importance to the United States. Iraq's al-Hussein missiles can reach all of Israel, Jordan, and Syria; northeastern Saudi Arabia, including Riyadh, Dhahran, and virtually all of the Saudi oil fields; western Iran, including Tehran and the Iranian oil fields in Khuzestan; and eastern Turkey. The Saudi oil fields are a particularly worrisome target. A single well-placed nuclear weapon or several less well targeted nuclear weapons could wipe out 75 to 95 percent of all Saudi oil production. Moreover, because of the extent of both the immediate damage and the long-term radiation from a nuclear blast, it is entirely unclear when that capacity could be restored: it could take decades. At present, Saudi Arabia accounts for 15 percent of global oil production (and Iraq and Kuwait together account for another 7 percent). The world has never experienced a supply shock anything like the instantaneous loss of 15 to 22 percent of global oil production. By way of comparison, the 1973 oil embargo withdrew only 2.75 percent of global oil production from the market, and the Iranian revolution withdrew 5.68 percent. Although economists and oil experts caution that we cannot foresee all of the grievous ramifications of such an event, there is widespread agreement that it would cause a global recession probably on the scale of the Great Depression of the 1930s, if not worse.

The problem is not so much U.S. dependence on Iraqi and Saudi oil (although both are now among the top five exporters to the United States) but global economic dependence on cheap oil. The loss of so much of the world's oil—and so much of the world's spare production capacity, most of which is in Saudi Arabia and Kuwait—would drive oil prices to astronomical levels in the short run, causing massive recessions in every nation's economy because oil is so critical both directly as an input into their transportation, heating, and manufacturing sectors, and also indirectly because of its importance to the advanced Western powers that dominate the world's trade. Nor could the strategic petroleum reserves of the United States, Europe, and Japan do more than cushion the blow for a brief period of time. The roughly 1 billion barrels in all of these reserve holdings would make up for the loss of Saudi, Kuwaiti, and Iraqi oil for only about two months at current production rates. Eventually, the global economy would find ways to adapt, conserve, and employ alternative fuels, but this would take years. In the meantime, the world would endure a nightmarish transition.

As Saddam's enumeration of his Gulf War mistakes makes clear, he is well aware of the importance of Persian Gulf oil production to the entire world, particularly the West. This knowledge, plus his ability to target so many other cities of important U.S. allies, would create opportunities for great mischief if he chose to hold the oil fields or those cities hostage to his designs. It is not hard to devise scenarios in which a future, nuclear-armed Iraq could pose terrible choices for the United States:

- At a future date when U.S. forces in the Gulf region have been drawn down (a likely outcome if the United States opts for deterrence because the Saudis will likely insist on it) and Gulf state politics are sensitive to charges of pandering to Washington, Saddam could again mass his forces near Kuwait, counting on the political climate to delay a Gulf Cooperation Council invitation to the United States to reinforce its presence in the region. Saddam could then invade Kuwait and perhaps continue driving on to the Saudi oil fields (assuming Iraqi logistics could handle the operation), threatening to wipe out the oil fields with one or more well-placed nuclear explosions if the United States intervened. This would certainly be in keeping with our understanding of his views regarding the mistakes he made during the Gulf War. The United States and its allies would be faced with the choice of intervening anyway and risking the loss of 22 percent of global oil production, possibly permanently, or giving Saddam control of that same share of the world's oil wealth.
- At some point, Saddam might try to take advantage of instability in the fragile Kingdom of Jordan—or manufacture it using his economic leverage and large intelligence presence—to topple the government in Amman. The new government might then invite in Iraqi troops to help it secure control. Who knows why Saddam might want to do such a thing—to gain a better position to influence the Arab-Israeli dispute, to reassert his bid to Arab leadership, or for some other reason known only to himself—but his invasions of Kuwait and Iran were equally mystifying at the time. The problem is that Jordan's current economic and political frailty creates the opportunity for him to do so. In the past, such an Iraqi move would have crossed an Israeli "red line" for the use of force and likely would have provoked an American military response as well. Saddam might again calculate that by threatening the Saudi oil fields, Tel Aviv, or other regional targets with nuclear weapons he could preclude such a response.
- Since the death of Hafiz al-Asad in 2000, the stability of the Syrian

regime has also been a question mark. If the Alawis who rule in Damascus fell to feuding, Saddam might be tempted to intervene to install a government more to his liking. Alternatively, Iraq has nurtured a long-standing rivalry with its fellow Baathists in Syria, and it is plausible that the relationship could sour again in the future, prompting a resort to force as Saddam has done so many times in the past. Although neither the United States nor many of our allies would mourn the loss of the Syrian regime, no one would be pleased to have it replaced by a pro-Iraqi government that might move Iraqi troops to the borders of Jordan and Israel, and possibly into Lebanon. Once again, if Saddam possessed nuclear weapons, the available evidence indicates that he might believe he could deter Israel and/or the United States from intervening if he chose such a course of action.

• Finally, a nuclear-armed Saddam would also raise fears for NATO ally Turkey. Ankara and Baghdad have generally enjoyed good relations over the years, but with Saddam at the helm in Iraq there is no reason to believe this might not change overnight. After all, it was widely believed that Iraq enjoyed reasonably good relations with Kuwait until the spring of 1990. Differences could arise between them over water, the Kurds, Syria, Israel (with which Turkey has an informal alliance), or U.S.-Iraqi relations, to name only the most obvious. It is conceivable that in the future if Turkey chose to draw more water from the Tigris and Euphrates to meet its own needs, Saddam might decide to respond with force—by occupying the upper reaches of the rivers or destroying some of the Turkish dams—again believing that his own nuclear arsenal would not only limit the Turkish response but also deter the United States and Israel from intervening.

Saddam was born in 1937 or 1939 and is in distressingly good health as far as anyone outside himself and his doctor knows. He could easily live to be seventy-five, eighty, or even older. Consequently, we should not expect him to die before he can either acquire nuclear weapons or make further mischief in the region.

This raises another important question: What will happen at the end of Saddam's life if he has nuclear weapons? Let us imagine that we are able to successfully deter him for the remainder of his life because he does decide not to risk his own survival by starting down the path of nuclear confrontation with the United States or Israel (or Iran, once it acquires nuclear weapons). What bizarre notions would run through his mind as he confronted his own mortality without having achieved any of his grandiose visions? We could not rule out the possibility that he would decide to choose the time and place of his own demise by ordering a nuclear strike on Tel Aviv so that he could go down in history as the Arab leader who finally obliterated the state of Israel. Saddam's former Mukhabbarat chief, Wafiq al-Samarra'i, told PBS's *Front-line,* "Perhaps now, I'm seriously considering that Saddam might use this weapon when he's about to die. Perhaps he will use it before he dies. And perhaps he would say to himself that he will be immortalized in history text-books." Just because this makes little sense to a Westerner does not mean it would not make perfect sense to "the leader of the days of Arab glory."

Saddam is unpredictable, but this is not to suggest that he is inexplicable. It is usually possible to figure out why Saddam did something after the fact, but it is hard to predict ahead of time what he might do. What's more, because the most important catalyst in his thinking is often exaggerated internal threats that the world knows nothing about—since Iraq is such a heavily guarded police state—we do not always know when Saddam is even consider-ing a momentous action. Consequently, the United States cannot always count on having time to bolster its deterrent posture to prepare for a challenge from Saddam. This is likely to be even more true in the future as Iraq takes advantage of the liberalization of the economic sanctions to restore its logisti-cal capability, thereby enhancing Saddam's ability to deploy large conven-tional forces quickly.

Would Saddam be willing to employ nuclear weapons? Would he be willing to vaporize part or all of the Saudi oil fields in pursuit of an objective? We don't know. To a Westerner, there might be little in such a course of action that would make sense. The risks might seem too great. But the key question is: Can we trust Saddam to reach the same conclusions? Given his track record, it would be foolhardy to do so. Saddam Hussein has repeatedly demonstrated that he thinks in strange and convoluted ways that often contradict what any Westerner—or even any other Iraqi—might think sensible. There is little in Saddam's personality or his history in power to suggest that he would feel a need for prudence or restraint once he acquired nuclear weapons. Instead, all of the evidence that we have indicates that he would feel emboldened by them to pursue his more grandiose objectives.

Would the United States be willing to intervene if Iraq possessed nuclear weapons and threatened one of its neighbors with a lesser degree of violence? And how would Saddam react if we did? Again, we don't know. The answers are probably irrelevant. Given Saddam's propensity to violence, constant mis-calculations, willingness to accept terrible damage in pursuit of a goal, un-willingness to back down unless he has actually suffered terrible damage, and belief in his own messianic destiny, we could not and should not rule out any reaction from him. He would be the most dangerous leader in the world with whom to get into a nuclear confrontation.

What About His Biological and Chemical Arsenals?

This article has focused principally on the threat posed by Saddam's ultimate, and probably inevitable, acquisition of nuclear weapons. The obvious "elephant in the living room" that it has so far overlooked is the arsenal of deadly biological and chemical weapons that he is believed to possess already. And the obvious question lying out there unanswered is: Don't they create similar threats for the United States and our regional allies?

Biological and chemical warfare agents in Saddam's hands are unquestionably very dangerous. It would be much, much better for the region, the United States, and the whole world if he did not possess those weapons. If employed properly, VX gas could kill thousands of people, and some of Iraq's biological agents could kill millions. Many analysts fear that at some point in time, Saddam may be able to acquire biological agents (such as smallpox) that could potentially kill far more people than could a nuclear weapon.

However, there are some important differences between the threats posed by chemical and biological agents and those posed by nuclear weapons—differences that continue to place nuclear weapons in a category by themselves. First of all, it is much harder to kill huge numbers of people with CW and BW weapons. It is not impossible, but it requires a vulnerable population under the right set of conditions and with the right mechanism to deliver the agents. Introducing VX into the air-conditioning system of a large office building or spraying a small city with BW in a crop duster on a cool day with only a mild breeze can produce catastrophic results. In addition, because of the fear they produce, CW and BW can kill a lot of people just from overreactions due to panic.

By the same token, if a would-be mass murderer lacks those conditions and that access, chemical and biological agents can produce disappointing results. CW and BW agents are dangerous to handle. Chemical warfare agents degrade over time—and in ways very dangerous to those storing or handling them—while biological warfare agents can die if not stored properly. Chemical warfare agents can evaporate if it's too hot, and both can dissipate quickly if it is too windy. Countermeasures are often possible, in the form of protective clothing for chemical warfare and vaccines or antidotes for biological warfare. What's more, both are relatively tough to deliver promptly at strategic distances (i.e., hundreds of kilometers). This is hardest to do by missile, and, as noted, Iraq is not known to have solved its problems with missile delivery of CW and BW agents. The Iraqi Air Force is in pathetic shape at present and is likely to be the last of Iraq's military services to revive. Even then, U.S. air defenses so outmatch even potential Iraqi Air Force capabilities that Saddam could not have any real confidence that a CW- or BW-armed aircraft would reach its target. Terrorist methods are the best means of delivering CW and BW, and Saddam is leery of international terrorists, who are largely beyond his control, while his own intelligence services have thus far shown little ability to perform sophisticated terrorist operations. Again, this is not to suggest that we should ignore these threats, only that the risk is appreciably less than with a nuclear weapon, which only has to be near enough people when it is detonated to kill millions.

Second, the concept of thousands of civilian deaths from chemical warfare, let alone millions from biological warfare, remains in the realm of conjecture. No one has actually ever seen this happen. It is theoretically possible, but most people also recognize that there are means of defense—gas masks and inoculations or antidotes. Gruesome as it may sound, until a chemical or biological attack does cause mass casualties, these weapons will not provoke the same degree of fear as is caused by nuclear weapons—against which no defense is possible and for which we have the legacy of Hiroshima and Nagasaki to remind us of the scale of devastation they cause. This point is important because it makes chemical and biological weapons much less useful to Saddam as deterrents of his own. As long as the world believes that nuclear weapons trump chemical and biological weapons, Saddam will be more cautious about his foreign adventures.

Saddam himself recognizes this distinction. His order to start a crash program to build a single nuclear weapon in August 1990, and his admission after the war that it was a mistake to have invaded Kuwait until he had nuclear weapons, both speak clearly to this point. Whatever his own reasoning, Saddam understands that his existing arsenal lacks the deterrent power of nuclear weapons. This is critical to U.S. policy because it strongly suggests that Saddam will be less likely to undertake new foreign adventures while all he has are his extant capabilities. Thus the potential for a crisis with Saddam is much lower if all he has is chemical and biological weapons, as is the risk that such a crisis could result in the death of millions. There is no question that the world would be better off if Saddam did not have these weapons, but the danger is considerably less than if Saddam were allowed to acquire nuclear weapons, which he believes will deter the United States and Israel and thereby would encourage him to engage in the kind of foreign aggression that would be likely to provoke a nuclear crisis.

Gambling with Our Future

Deterrence is a policy with terrible costs. It means condemning the Iraqi people to decades more terror and torture under Saddam's totalitarianism. Unlike containment, deterrence also means giving up our ability to protect the Kurds. Human Rights Watch argues that Saddam's Anfal campaign constituted genocide against the Kurds. Certainly, it was horrific, with as many as 200,000 killed, 4,000 villages razed, and widespread and indiscriminate use of chemical warfare against Kurdish civilians. If we opt for deterrence, there will be no one to restrain Saddam should he decide to solve his Kurdish "problem" once and for all.

In addition, those who argue for deterrence for fear of the costs of an invasion, and, particularly, fear of Iraqi WMD use and terrorism, are setting a very dangerous precedent. They are, in effect, suggesting that the United States is already deterred by the weak arsenal of weapons of mass destruction Saddam already possesses and his similarly weak terrorist capabilities. In other words, a policy of deterrence toward Iraq not only is based on the belief that Saddam can be deterred but starts from the assumption that the United States already is. If the United States can be deterred from taking military action against Iraq given its current modest capabilities, every rogue state in the world will have little to do to ensure its security and will likely be emboldened to greater aggression. We would be allowing our hands to be tied with very weak string.

Deterrence also runs terrible risks. Although the alternatives are considerably more costly, deterrence is the riskiest of all the policy options available to the United States. We would be betting that we could deter a man who has proven to be hard (at times, impossible) to deter and who seems to believe that if he possessed nuclear weapons, it is the United States that would be deterred. If we were to make this bet and lose, the results would be catastrophic. Moreover, while deterrence is difficult enough, we would actually be trying to employ extended deterrence to Iraq's neighbors—deterring Iraq from attacking Kuwait, Jordan, or Saudi Arabia, rather than simply protecting ourselves. Patrick Morgan, one of the architects of Cold War deterrence theory, observes that "it is hard to make an extended deterrence threat to use WMD credible, particularly if the 'challenger' is also armed with them."

The use of nuclear weapons anywhere in the world would be terrible. Their use on the Persian Gulf oil fields; against Tel Aviv, Ankara, Riyadh, or another regional city; or against U.S. military forces in the region is unimaginable. This would be no academic exercise or Pentagon war game to decide how many people one side could lose in the pursuit of victory; regardless of what else happened, such an event would be a tragedy and a disaster. Beyond this, Saddam Hussein with nuclear weapons has the potential to push the world into a second Great Depression while killing millions of people. His track record argues that if we allow him to acquire nuclear weapons, we are likely to find ourselves in a new crisis with him in which we will not be able to predict what he will do, and his personality and his history can only lead us to expect the worst. Leaving Saddam free to acquire nuclear weapons and then hoping that in spite of his track record he can be deterred would be a terrifically dangerous gamble.

WHY SADDAM WANTS
WEAPONS OF
MASS DESTRUCTION

Charles A. Duelfer

On February 22, 2002, Charles A. Duelfer, the former deputy director of the U.N. special commission charged with inspecting Iraq's suspected chemical, biological, and nuclear weapons capabilities (UNSCOM), presented his views before the Subcommittee on Emerging Threats and Capabilities of the U.S. Senate Armed Services Committee. The following is an excerpted transcript of his testimony that sheds rare direct light on the possible thinking of Iraq's leaders regarding their pursuit of weapons of mass destruction.

UNSCOM had long pressed Iraq to provide information and documents describing the requirements and operational concepts for the BW [biological weapons], CW [chemical weapons], Ballistic Missile and nuclear programs. Iraq refused until shortly after Saddam Hussein's son-in-law, Hussein Kamal defected to Jordan in August 1995. Hussein Kamal was the most senior regime official with control over these weapons programs. Baghdad was concerned about what Kamal would reveal and sought to limit the damage by a burst of controlled cooperation and admissions.

On September 18, 1995, I had a long, late night meeting with several senior Iraqi ministers and other officials. The meeting was arranged to discuss the Iraqi concepts and requirements for their WMD development and production programs. Previously, Baghdad had refused to engage in such a discussion. I remember the meeting quite well, not simply because there was an unusual amount of candor, but because I suddenly realized how unlikely it was that the government would ever comply fully with the U.N. demand to completely give up all WMD capabilities forever. Consequently, the UNSCOM inspectors had an ultimately hopeless task under the conditions it was permitted to operate.

Charles Duelfer was deputy executive chairman of the U.N. Special Commission on Iraq (UNSCOM) from 1993 until its termination in 2000. During the final months of its existence, he served as acting chairman. Before joining the commission, he was deputy assistant secretary of state for arms control and multilateral defense matters. He is currently a visiting resident scholar at the Center for Strategic and International Studies in Washington, DC.

Iraq revealed that evening how weapons of mass destruction were viewed from the position of the Presidency (They even provided selected presidential documents.) Partial descriptions of the origin of WMD efforts were discussed. They also discussed how these programs had been used and their importance to the regime. In essence, the possession of WMD had saved the regime on two occasions. The first was in the war with Iran in the 1980's when Iranian human wave infantry attacks were repelled with chemical munitions (UNSCOM learned that 101,000 were reported "consumed" during this period).

The second instance where WMD preserved the regime was more surprising. I had asked about the decision by the Iraqi leadership not to employ WMD in the 1991 Gulf War. In a carefully worded response, the impression was conveyed that the President thought if Iraq used chemical or biological weapons against the coalition, retaliation would end his regime and probably him personally. He was successfully deterred. However, my interlocutors went on to describe how they had loaded BW and CW agent into various missile warheads and bombs before hostilities began in 1991. Moreover they dispersed these weapons and *pre-delegated the authority to use them if the United States moved on Baghdad.* The Iraqis stated that these actions apparently deterred the United States from going to Baghdad.

Whether the Iraqi leadership believes this was the only reason the United States did not go to Baghdad in 1991 is unknown. However, clearly they are convinced that the possession of WMD contributed to keeping the Americans away and thus was vital to their survival.

The Iraqi WMD programs, which were begun in the mid-1970's, and consumed large material and human resources throughout the 1980's were well worth the investment from the perspective of the leadership. It was difficult then and more difficult now, to imagine circumstances under which this regime would end these programs. Deputy Prime Minister Tariq Aziz said on more than one occasion, "You are not MacArthur. You did not occupy Iraq. Therefore, there are limits to what you can do." He was absolutely correct. Inspectors would be inherently limited in what they could do and accomplish. Nevertheless, we did eventually obtain a pretty good picture of the extent of Iraq's programs. From that, and from evidence that continues to be available even now, it is possible to make a reasonable judgment about Iraq's current capabilities and intentions.

AN UNNECESSARY WAR

John J. Mearsheimer and Stephen M. Walt

In the full-court press for war with Iraq, the Bush administration deems Saddam Hussein reckless, ruthless, and not fully rational. Such a man, when mixed with nuclear weapons, is too unpredictable to be prevented from threatening the United States, the hawks say. But scrutiny of his past dealings with the world shows that Saddam, though cruel and calculating, is eminently deterrable.

Should the United States invade Iraq and depose Saddam Hussein? If the United States is already at war with Iraq when this article is published, the immediate cause is likely to be Saddam's failure to comply with the new U.N. inspections regime to the Bush administration's satisfaction. But this failure is not the real reason Saddam and the United States have been on a collision course over the past year.

The deeper root of the conflict is the U.S. position that Saddam must be toppled because he cannot be deterred from using weapons of mass destruction (WMD). Advocates of preventive war use numerous arguments to make their case, but their trump card is the charge that Saddam's past behavior proves he is too reckless, relentless, and aggressive to be allowed to possess WMD, especially nuclear weapons. They sometimes admit that war against Iraq might be costly, might lead to a lengthy U.S. occupation, and might complicate U.S. relations with other countries. But these concerns are eclipsed by the belief that the combination of Saddam plus nuclear weapons is too dangerous to accept. For that reason alone, he has to go.

Even many opponents of preventive war seem to agree deterrence will not work in Iraq. Instead of invading Iraq and overthrowing the regime, however, these moderates favor using the threat of war to compel Saddam to permit new weapons inspections. Their hope is that inspections will eliminate any

John J. Mearsheimer is the R. Wendell Harrison Distinguished Service Professor and the co-director of the Program on International Security Policy at the University of Chicago. A graduate of West Point, and a former officer in the U.S. Air Force, he is the author of several books about security issues, the most recent of which is *The Tragedy of Great Power Politics* (2001).

Stephen M. Walt is the academic dean and the Robert and Renee Belfer Professor of International Affairs at Harvard University's John F. Kennedy School of Government. He is a member of the board of directors of *The Bulletin of the Atomic Scientists* and the editorial boards of *Foreign Policy, Security Studies,* and the *Journal of Cold War Studies*

This article was originally published in the January/February 2003 issue of *Foreign Policy.*

hidden WMD stockpiles and production facilities and ensure Saddam cannot acquire any of these deadly weapons. Thus, both the hard-line preventive-war advocates and the more moderate supporters of inspections accept the same basic premise: Saddam Hussein is not deterrable, and he cannot be allowed to obtain a nuclear arsenal.

One problem with this argument: It is almost certainly wrong. The belief that Saddam's past behavior shows he cannot be contained rests on distorted history and faulty logic. In fact, the historical record shows that the United States can contain Iraq effectively—even if Saddam has nuclear weapons— just as it contained the Soviet Union during the Cold War. Regardless of whether Iraq complies with U.N. inspections or what the inspectors find, the campaign to wage war against Iraq rests on a flimsy foundation.

Is Saddam a Serial Aggressor?

Those who call for preventive war begin by portraying Saddam as a serial aggressor bent on dominating the Persian Gulf. The war party also contends that Saddam is either irrational or prone to serious miscalculation, which means he may not be deterred by even credible threats of retaliation. Kenneth Pollack, former director for Gulf affairs at the National Security Council and a proponent of war with Iraq, goes so far as to argue that Saddam is "unintentionally suicidal."

The facts, however, tell a different story. Saddam has dominated Iraqi politics for more than 30 years. During that period, he started two wars against his neighbors—Iran in 1980 and Kuwait in 1990. Saddam's record in this regard is no worse than that of neighboring states such as Egypt or Israel, each of which played a role in starting several wars since 1948. Furthermore, a careful look at Saddam's two wars shows his behavior was far from reckless. Both times, he attacked because Iraq was vulnerable and because he believed his targets were weak and isolated. In each case, his goal was to rectify Iraq's strategic dilemma with a limited military victory. Such reasoning does not excuse Saddam's aggression, but his willingness to use force on these occasions hardly demonstrates that he cannot be deterred.

The Iran-Iraq War, 1980–88

Iran was the most powerful state in the Persian Gulf during the 1970s. Its strength was partly due to its large population (roughly three times that of

Iraq) and its oil reserves, but it also stemmed from the strong support the shah of Iran received from the United States. Relations between Iraq and Iran were quite hostile throughout this period, but Iraq was in no position to defy Iran's regional dominance. Iran put constant pressure on Saddam's regime during the early 1970s, mostly by fomenting unrest among Iraq's sizable Kurdish minority. Iraq finally persuaded the shah to stop meddling with the Kurds in 1975, but only by agreeing to cede half of the Shatt al-Arab waterway to Iran, a concession that underscored Iraq's weakness.

It is thus not surprising that Saddam welcomed the shah's ouster in 1979. Iraq went to considerable lengths to foster good relations with Iran's revolutionary leadership. Saddam did not exploit the turmoil in Iran to gain strategic advantage over his neighbor and made no attempt to reverse his earlier concessions, even though Iran did not fully comply with the terms of the 1975 agreement. Ruhollah Khomeini, on the other hand, was determined to extend his revolution across the Islamic world, starting with Iraq. By late 1979, Tehran was pushing the Kurdish and Shiite populations in Iraq to revolt and topple Saddam, and Iranian operatives were trying to assassinate senior Iraqi officials. Border clashes became increasingly frequent by April 1980, largely at Iran's instigation.

Facing a grave threat to his regime, but aware that Iran's military readiness had been temporarily disrupted by the revolution, Saddam launched a limited war against his bitter foe on September 22, 1980. His principal aim was to capture a large slice of territory along the Iraq-Iran border, not to conquer Iran or topple Khomeini. "The war began," as military analyst Efraim Karsh writes, "because the weaker state, Iraq, attempted to resist the hegemonic aspirations of its stronger neighbor, Iran, to reshape the regional status quo according to its own image."

Iran and Iraq fought for eight years, and the war cost the two antagonists more than 1 million casualties and at least $150 billion. Iraq received considerable outside support from other countries—including the United States, Kuwait, Saudi Arabia, and France—largely because these states were determined to prevent the spread of Khomeini's Islamic revolution. Although the war cost Iraq far more than Saddam expected, it also thwarted Khomeini's attempt to topple him and dominate the region. War with Iran was not a reckless adventure; it was an opportunistic response to a significant threat.

The Gulf War, 1990–91

But what about Iraq's invasion of Kuwait in August 1990? Perhaps the earlier war with Iran was essentially defensive, but surely this was not true in the case of Kuwait. Doesn't Saddam's decision to invade his tiny neighbor prove he is too rash and aggressive to be trusted with the most destructive weaponry? And doesn't his refusal to withdraw, even when confronted by a superior coalition, demonstrate he is "unintentionally suicidal"?

The answer is no. Once again, a careful look shows Saddam was neither mindlessly aggressive nor particularly reckless. If anything, the evidence supports the opposite conclusion.

Saddam's decision to invade Kuwait was primarily an attempt to deal with Iraq's continued vulnerability. Iraq's economy, badly damaged by its war with Iran, continued to decline after that war ended. An important cause of Iraq's difficulties was Kuwait's refusal both to loan Iraq $10 billion and to write off debts Iraq had incurred during the Iran-Iraq War. Saddam believed Iraq was entitled to additional aid because the country helped protect Kuwait and other Gulf states from Iranian expansionism. To make matters worse, Kuwait was overproducing the quotas set by the Organization of Petroleum Exporting Countries, which drove down world oil prices and reduced Iraqi oil profits. Saddam tried using diplomacy to solve the problem, but Kuwait hardly budged. As Karsh and fellow Hussein biographer Inari Rautsi note, the Kuwaitis "suspected that some concessions might be necessary, but were determined to reduce them to the barest minimum."

Saddam reportedly decided on war sometime in July 1990, but before sending his army into Kuwait, he approached the United States to find out how it would react. In a now famous interview with the Iraqi leader, U.S. Ambassador April Glaspie told Saddam, "[W]e have no opinion on the Arab-Arab conflicts, like your border disagreement with Kuwait." The U.S. State Department had earlier told Saddam that Washington had "no special defense or security commitments to Kuwait." The United States may not have intended to give Iraq a green light, but that is effectively what it did.

Saddam invaded Kuwait in early August 1990. This act was an obvious violation of international law, and the United States was justified in opposing the invasion and organizing a coalition against it. But Saddam's decision to invade was hardly irrational or reckless. Deterrence did not fail in this case; it was never tried.

But what about Saddam's failure to leave Kuwait once the United States demanded a return to the status quo ante? Wouldn't a prudent leader have abandoned Kuwait before getting clobbered? With hindsight, the answer seems obvious, but Saddam had good reasons to believe hanging tough might work. It was not initially apparent that the United States would actually fight, and most Western military experts predicted the Iraqi army would mount a formidable defense. These forecasts seem foolish today, but many people believed them before the war began.

Once the U.S. air campaign had seriously damaged Iraq's armed forces, however, Saddam began searching for a diplomatic solution that would allow him to retreat from Kuwait before a ground war began. Indeed, Saddam made clear he was willing to pull out completely. Instead of allowing Iraq to withdraw and fight another day, then U.S. President George H.W. Bush and his administration wisely insisted the Iraqi army leave its equipment behind as it withdrew. As the administration had hoped, Saddam could not accept this kind of deal.

Saddam undoubtedly miscalculated when he attacked Kuwait, but the history of warfare is full of cases where leaders have misjudged the prospects for war. No evidence suggests Hussein did not weigh his options carefully, however. He chose to use force because he was facing a serious challenge and because he had good reasons to think his invasion would not provoke serious opposition.

Nor should anyone forget that the Iraqi tyrant survived the Kuwait debacle, just as he has survived other threats against his regime. He is now beginning his fourth decade in power. If he is really "unintentionally suicidal," then his survival instincts appear to be even more finely honed.

History provides at least two more pieces of evidence that demonstrate Saddam is deterrable. First, although he launched conventionally armed Scud missiles at Saudi Arabia and Israel during the Gulf War, he did not launch chemical or biological weapons at the coalition forces that were decimating the Iraqi military. Moreover, senior Iraqi officials—including Deputy Prime Minister Tariq Aziz and the former head of military intelligence, General Wafiq al-Samarrai—have said that Iraq refrained from using chemical weapons because the Bush Sr. administration made ambiguous but unmistakable threats to retaliate if Iraq used WMD. Second, in 1994 Iraq mobilized the remnants of its army on the Kuwait border in an apparent attempt to force a modification of the U.N. Special Commission's (UNSCOM) weapons inspection regime. But when the United Nations issued a new warning and the United States reinforced its troops in Kuwait, Iraq backed down quickly. In both cases, the allegedly irrational Iraqi leader was deterred.

Saddam's Use of Chemical Weapons

Preventive-war advocates also use a second line of argument. They point out that Saddam has used WMD against his own people (the Kurds) and against Iran and that therefore he is likely to use them against the United States. Thus, U.S. President George W. Bush recently warned in Cincinnati that the

Iraqi WMD threat against the United States "is already significant, and it only grows worse with time." The United States, in other words, is in imminent danger.

Saddam's record of chemical weapons use is deplorable, but none of his victims had a similar arsenal and thus could not threaten to respond in kind. Iraq's calculations would be entirely different when facing the United States because Washington could retaliate with WMD if Iraq ever decided to use these weapons first. Saddam thus has no incentive to use chemical or nuclear weapons against the United States and its allies—unless his survival is threatened. This simple logic explains why he did not use WMD against U.S. forces during the Gulf War and has not fired chemical or biological warheads at Israel.

Furthermore, if Saddam cannot be deterred, what is stopping him from using WMD against U.S. forces in the Persian Gulf, which have bombed Iraq repeatedly over the past decade? The bottom line: Deterrence has worked well against Saddam in the past, and there is no reason to think it cannot work equally well in the future.

President Bush's repeated claim that the threat from Iraq is growing makes little sense in light of Saddam's past record, and these statements should be viewed as transparent attempts to scare Americans into supporting a war. CIA Director George Tenet flatly contradicted the president in an October 2002 letter to Congress, explaining that Saddam was unlikely to initiate a WMD attack against any U.S. target unless Washington provoked him. Even if Iraq did acquire a larger WMD arsenal, the United States would still retain a massive nuclear retaliatory capability. And if Saddam would only use WMD if the United States threatened his regime, then one wonders why advocates of war are trying to do just that.

Hawks do have a fallback position on this issue. Yes, the United States can try to deter Saddam by threatening to retaliate with massive force. But this strategy may not work because Iraq's past use of chemical weapons against the Kurds and Iran shows that Saddam is a warped human being who might use WMD without regard for the consequences.

Unfortunately for those who now favor war, this argument is difficult to reconcile with the United States' past support for Iraq, support that coincided with some of the behavior now being invoked to portray him as an irrational madman. The United States backed Iraq during the 1980s—when Saddam was gassing Kurds and Iranians—and helped Iraq use chemical weapons more effectively by providing it with satellite imagery of Iranian troop positions. The Reagan administration also facilitated Iraq's efforts to develop biological weapons by allowing Baghdad to import disease-producing biological materials such as anthrax, West Nile virus, and botulinal toxin. A central figure in the effort to court Iraq was none other than current U.S. Defense Secretary Donald Rumsfeld, who was then President Ronald Reagan's special envoy to the Middle East. He visited Baghdad and met with Saddam in 1983, with the explicit aim of fostering better relations between the United States and Iraq. In October 1989, about a year after Saddam gassed the Kurds, President George H.W. Bush signed a formal national security directive declaring, "Normal relations between the United States and Iraq would serve our longer-term interests and promote stability in both the Gulf and the Middle East."

If Saddam's use of chemical weapons so clearly indicates he is a madman and cannot be contained, why did the United States fail to see that in the 1980s? Why were Rumsfeld and former President Bush then so unconcerned about his chemical and biological weapons? The most likely answer is that U.S. policymakers correctly understood Saddam was unlikely to use those weapons against the United States and its allies unless Washington threatened him directly. The real puzzle is why they think it would be impossible to deter him today.

Saddam With Nukes

The third strike against a policy of containment, according to those who have called for war, is that such a policy is unlikely to stop Saddam from getting nuclear weapons. Once he gets them, so the argument runs, a host of really bad things will happen. For example, President Bush has warned that Saddam intends to "blackmail the world"; likewise, National Security Advisor Condoleezza Rice believes he would use nuclear weapons to "blackmail the entire international community." Others fear a nuclear arsenal would enable Iraq to invade its neighbors and then deter the United States from ousting the Iraqi army as it did in 1991. Even worse, Saddam might surreptitiously slip a nuclear weapon to al Qaeda or some like-minded terrorist organization, thereby making it possible for these groups to attack the United States directly.

The administration and its supporters may be right in one sense: Containment may not be enough to prevent Iraq from acquiring nuclear weapons someday. Only the conquest and permanent occupation of Iraq could guarantee that. Yet the United States can contain a nuclear Iraq, just as it contained the Soviet Union. None of the nightmare scenarios invoked by preventive-war advocates are likely to happen.

Consider the claim that Saddam would employ nuclear blackmail against his adversaries. To force another state to make concessions, a blackmailer must make clear that he would use nuclear weapons against the target state if he does not get his way. But this strategy is feasible only if the blackmailer has nuclear weapons but neither the target state nor its allies do.

If the blackmailer and the target state both have nuclear weapons, however, the blackmailer's threat is an empty one because the blackmailer cannot carry out the threat without triggering his own destruction. This logic explains why the Soviet Union, which had a vast nuclear arsenal for much of the Cold War, was never able to blackmail the United States or its allies and did not even try.

But what if Saddam invaded Kuwait again and then said he would use nuclear weapons if the United States attempted another Desert Storm? Again, this threat is not credible. If Saddam initiated nuclear war against the United States over Kuwait, he would bring U.S. nuclear warheads down on his own head. Given the choice between withdrawing or dying, he would almost certainly choose the former. Thus, the United States could wage Desert Storm II against a nuclear-armed Saddam without precipitating nuclear war.

Ironically, some of the officials now advocating war used to recognize that Saddam could not employ nuclear weapons for offensive purposes. In the January/February 2000 issue of *Foreign Affairs*, for example, National Security Advisor Rice described how the United States should react if Iraq acquired WMD. "The first line of defense," she wrote, "should be a clear and classical statement of deterrence—if they do acquire WMD, their weapons will be unusable because any attempt to use them will bring national obliteration." If she believed Iraq's weapons would be unusable in 2000, why does she now think Saddam must be toppled before he gets them? For that matter, why does she now think a nuclear arsenal would enable Saddam to blackmail the entire international community, when she did not even mention this possibility in 2000?

What About Nuclear Handoff?

Of course, now the real nightmare scenario is that Saddam would give nuclear weapons secretly to al Qaeda or some other terrorist group. Groups like al Qaeda would almost certainly try to use those weapons against Israel or the United States, and so these countries have a powerful incentive to take all reasonable measures to keep these weapons out of their hands.

However, the likelihood of clandestine transfer by Iraq is extremely small. First of all, there is no credible evidence that Iraq had anything to do with the terrorist attacks against the World Trade Center and the Pentagon or more generally that Iraq is collaborating with al Qaeda against the United States. Hawks inside and outside the Bush administration have gone to extraordinary lengths over the past months to find a link, but they have come up empty-handed.

The lack of evidence of any genuine connection between Saddam and al Qaeda is not surprising because relations between Saddam and al Qaeda have been quite poor in the past. Osama bin Laden is a radical fundamentalist (like Khomeini), and he detests secular leaders like Saddam. Similarly, Saddam has consistently repressed fundamentalist movements within Iraq. Given this history of enmity, the Iraqi dictator is unlikely to give al Qaeda nuclear weapons, which it might use in ways he could not control.

Intense U.S. pressure, of course, might eventually force these unlikely allies together, just as the United States and Communist Russia became allies during World War II. Saddam would still be unlikely to share his most valuable weaponry with al Qaeda, however, because he could not be confident it would not be used in ways that place his own survival in jeopardy. During the Cold War, the United States did not share all its WMD expertise with its own allies, and the Soviet Union balked at giving nuclear weapons to China despite their ideological sympathies and repeated Chinese requests. No evidence suggests Saddam would act differently.

Second, Saddam could hardly be confident that the transfer would go undetected. Since September 11, U.S. intelligence agencies and those of its allies have been riveted on al Qaeda and Iraq, paying special attention to finding links between them. If Iraq possessed nuclear weapons, U.S. monitoring of those two adversaries would be further intensified. To give nuclear materials to al Qaeda, Saddam would have to bet he could elude the eyes and ears of numerous intelligence services determined to catch him if he tries a nuclear handoff. This bet would not be a safe one.

But even if Saddam thought he could covertly smuggle nuclear weapons to bin Laden, he would still be unlikely to do so. Saddam has been trying to acquire these weapons for over 20 years, at great cost and risk. Is it likely he would then turn around and give them away? Furthermore, giving nuclear weapons to al Qaeda would be extremely risky for Saddam—even if he could do so without being detected— because he would lose all control over when and where they would be used. And Saddam could never be sure the United States would not incinerate him anyway if it merely suspected he had made it possible for anyone to strike the United States with nuclear weapons. The U.S. government and a clear majority of Americans are already deeply suspicious of Iraq, and a nuclear attack against the United States or its allies would raise that hostility to fever pitch. Saddam does not have to be certain the United States would retaliate to be wary of giving his nuclear weapons to al Qaeda; he merely has to suspect it might.

In sum, Saddam cannot afford to guess wrong on whether he would be detected providing al Qaeda with nuclear weapons, nor can he afford to guess wrong that Iraq would be spared if al Qaeda launched a nuclear strike against the United States or its allies. And the threat of U.S. retaliation is not as far-fetched as one might think. The United States has enhanced its flexible nuclear options in recent years, and no one knows just how vengeful Americans might feel if WMD were ever used against the U.S. homeland. Indeed, nuclear terrorism is as dangerous for Saddam as it is for Americans, and he has no more incentive to give al Qaeda nuclear weapons than the United States does—unless, of course, the country makes clear it is trying to overthrow him. Instead of attacking Iraq and giving Saddam nothing to lose, the Bush administration should be signaling it would hold him responsible if some terrorist group used WMD against the United States, even if it cannot prove he is to blame.

Vigilant Containment

It is not surprising that those who favor war with Iraq portray Saddam as an inveterate and only partly rational aggressor. They are in the business of selling a preventive war, so they must try to make remaining at peace seem unacceptably dangerous. And the best way to do that is to inflate the threat, either by exaggerating Iraq's capabilities or by suggesting horrible things will happen if the United States does not act soon. It is equally unsurprising that advocates of war are willing to distort the historical record to make their case. As former U.S. Secretary of State Dean Acheson famously remarked, in politics, advocacy "must be clearer than truth."

In this case, however, the truth points the other way. Both logic and historical evidence suggest a policy of vigilant containment would work, both now and in the event Iraq acquires a nuclear arsenal. Why? Because the United States and its regional allies are far stronger than Iraq. And because it does not take a genius to figure out what would happen if Iraq tried to use WMD to blackmail its neighbors, expand its territory, or attack another state directly. It only takes a leader who wants to stay alive and who wants to remain in power. Throughout his lengthy and brutal career, Saddam Hussein has repeatedly shown that these two goals are absolutely paramount. That is why deterrence and containment would work.

If the United States is, or soon will be, at war with Iraq, Americans should understand that a compelling strategic rationale is absent. This war would be one the Bush administration chose to fight but did not have to fight. Even if such a war goes well and has positive long-range consequences, it will still have been unnecessary. And if it goes badly—whether in the form of high U.S. casualties, significant civilian deaths, a heightened risk of terrorism, or increased hatred of the United States in the Arab and Islamic world—then its architects will have even more to answer for.

SUICIDE FROM
FEAR OF DEATH?

Richard K. Betts

With war in the Middle East imminent, it is clear that the United States has painted itself—as well as Iraq—into a corner. The Bush administration's success in engineering international support for a preventive war in the Persian Gulf is impressive, both politically and diplomatically. But Washington's case rests on two crucial errors. It understates the very real risk that an assault on Iraq will trigger a counterattack on American civilians. And even when that risk is admitted, the pro-war camp conflates it with the threat of unprovoked attack by Iraq in the future.

Many Americans still take for granted that a war to topple Saddam Hussein can be fought as it was in 1991: on American terms. Even when they recognize that the blood price may prove greater than the optimists hope, most still assume it will be paid by the U.S. military or by people in the region. Until very late in the game, few Americans focused on the chance that the battlefield could extend back to their own homeland. Yet if a U.S. invasion succeeds, Saddam will have no reason to withhold his best parting shot—which could be the use of weapons of mass destruction (WMD) inside the United States. Such an Iraqi attack on U.S. civilians could make the death toll from September 11 look small. But Washington has done little to prepare the country for this possibility and seems to have forgotten Bismarck's characterization of preventive war as "suicide from fear of death."

America's political leaders have not just lost faith in deterrence as a means to contain Iraq, they have also lost sight of the fact that, when it comes to a showdown between two countries that both possess WMD, deterrence can work both ways. The United States is about to poke a snake out of fear that

Richard Betts is the Leo A. Shifrin Professor of War and Peace Studies and the Director of the Institute of War and Peace Studies at Columbia University. He is a former Senior Fellow at the Brookings Institution, and has also served on the staff of the U.S. Senate Select Committee on Intelligence, and as a consultant to the National Security Council and Central Intelligence Agency. He has authored several books, including *The Irony of Vietnam,* which won the Woodrow Wilson Prize as the best foreign policy book of 1979. This essay originally appeared in the January/February 2003 issue of *Foreign Affairs.*

the snake might strike sometime in the future, while virtually ignoring the danger that it may strike back when America pokes it. True, not everyone demanding an American attack ignores the immediate threat such an attack might raise—but even this camp misreads that threat, thinking it reinforces the urgency of preventive war. The consequences, they argue, will only get worse if Washington waits. This argument may seem like common sense at first. But it dangerously confuses two sets of odds: the chance that Iraq will eventually challenge America even without being provoked, and the risk that Baghdad will retaliate against Washington if struck first.

The probability that Iraq could bring off a WMD attack on American soil may not be high, but even a modest probability warrants concern. By mistakenly conflating the immediate and long-term risks of Iraqi attack and by exaggerating the dangers in alternatives to war, the advocates of a preventive war against Saddam have miscast a modest probability of catastrophe as an acceptable risk.

An invasion to get rid of Saddam would represent an American attempt to do what no government has ever done before: destroy a regime that possesses WMD. Countries with WMD have fought each other twice before, but these events (when China and the Soviet Union came to blows on the Ussuri River in 1969, and when India and Pakistan fought over Kargil in 2000) were mere skirmishes. In both of those limited clashes, neither side's leadership was truly threatened. The opposite is true this time, and yet the difference has not been digested by pro-war strategists.

During Congress' debate over whether to authorize the war, for example, the danger that a preventive assault might provoke Iraqi retaliation against the American heartland went almost unmentioned. In an October letter, Director of Central Intelligence George Tenet stated that Saddam would be more likely to attempt a WMD attack against the United States as "his last chance to exact vengeance" if he believed he could no longer deter an American onslaught—but this comment received scant notice. Attention focused instead on less immediate, less likely, and less dangerous threats. Hawks argued that Iraq will get nuclear weapons in the future. But the fact is that the biological weapons Iraq already has are dangerous enough to do tremendous damage—even if the worst estimates of U.S. vulnerability are excessive.

A 1993 study by the Office of Technology Assessment concluded that one plane, delivering anthrax by aerosol under good weather conditions over the Washington, D.C., area, could kill between one million and three million people. That figure is probably far too pessimistic even for an efficiently executed attack, since among other things, the medical response would be quicker and more effective today than it would have been a decade ago. So discount this estimate by, say, 90 percent. Even then, fatalities could still exceed 100,000. This reduced figure may still be excessive, since clandestine Iraqi operations to infect U.S. cities might be crude and inefficient. Yet if you reduce the death toll by another 90 percent, fatalities would still be more than triple those of September 11. Multiple attacks, even clumsy ones, could yield tens of thousands of casualties. Worst of all, Iraq may have bioengineered new pathogens for which no defense is available. Chemical weapons, although less destructive than biological ones, could also exact a dramatic toll.

But is an Iraqi counterattack on U.S. soil really plausible? Hawks argue that Saddam must be eliminated because he may decide to use WMD in the future or give them to terrorists—even if the United States threatens him with devastating retaliation. This argument assumes that Saddam would be prepared to cut his own throat without provocation. If that is true, it certainly follows that he will lash out with anything he has if Washington goes for his jugular and puts his back against the wall.

Yet Washington now seems determined to push him to that wall. Few are proposing that Saddam be retired to a villa on the Riviera next to "Baby Doc" Duvalier's. The option of a golden parachute should be considered, but it is unlikely to be accepted. Saddam would demand protection from extradition so that he could avoid joining Milosevic in court. And even Saddam knows he has too many bitter enemies to survive for long outside Iraq. Regime change in Baghdad, therefore, probably means an end to Saddam Hussein. And he will not go gently if he has nothing left to lose. If a military assault to overthrow the Iraqi regime looks likely to succeed, there is no reason to doubt Saddam will try to use biological weapons where they would hurt Americans the most.

Instead of considering the chances of a strike on the American heartland, however, war planners have tended to focus on the vulnerability of U.S. invasion forces, or on local supporters such as Israel, Saudi Arabia, and Kuwait—as if they are the only likely targets of an Iraqi WMD attack. Awful as attacks on these targets would be, the consequences would be nowhere near as large from the American perspective as those of a strike on the United States itself. The only remaining question, then, is whether Saddam would have the capability to carry out such an attack.

Maybe he won't. Saddam may not be crafty enough to figure out how to strike the American homeland. Iraqi intelligence may be too incompetent to smuggle biological weapons into the United States and set them off. Or

Saddam's underlings might disobey orders to do so. The terrorists to whom Iraq subcontracts the job might bungle it. Or perhaps American forces could find and neutralize all of Iraq's WMD before they could be detonated. But it would be reckless to bank on maybes. Washington has given Saddam more than enough time to concoct retaliation, since he has had months of notice that the Americans are coming. The Bush administration has made this war the most telegraphed punch in military history.

Is it alarmist to emphasize the danger of an Iraqi counterattack on American soil? The odds may be low—perhaps as low as the odds were on September 10, 2001, that 19 Arab civilians would level the World Trade Center and tear a chunk out of the Pentagon. Even if the odds are as high as one out of six, however, that makes the risks inherent in overthrowing Saddam look like Russian roulette. It would be one thing for Americans to hope that they can wage war without triggering effective retaliation. But it would be altogether different to blithely assume that outcome; such unwarranted optimism represents the kind of "best case" planning that should shame any self-respecting hawk.

Taking the threat of retaliation seriously means two big things: preparing to cope with it, and reconsidering the need to start the war that could bring it on. If war on Iraq is deemed necessary despite the risk of mass destruction, Washington is dangerously far behind in preparing the home front. The United States must not wait until the war begins to put homeland defense into high gear. Studies and plans to prepare for future biological or chemical attack should be implemented in advance, not left on the drawing board until American tanks start rolling into Baghdad. The American people deserve immediate, loud, clear, and detailed instructions about how to know, what to do, where to go, and how to cope if they encounter anthrax, ricin, smallpox, VX, or other pathogens or chemicals Iraq might use against them. It is already too late now to do what should have been done much earlier— to cut through the production problems and other complications in making anthrax vaccines available to civilians (much of the military has already been vaccinated). At least there should be a crash program to test and put in place mechanisms for detecting anthrax attacks promptly and dispensing antibiotics on a massive scale; these are the minimum steps the Bush administration should take before it pokes the snake. Smallpox is a less likely threat, and much planning has been done for mass vaccination in an emergency. But at a minimum, health-care workers should be immunized in advance. Until the U.S. government is ready to do all these things, it will not be ready to start a war.

Although it is already terribly late in the day, the risk of Iraqi retaliation also underlines the need to reconsider the alternative to provoking it. Why are containment and deterrence—the strategies that worked for the four decades of the Cold War—suddenly considered more dangerous than poking the snake? Proponents of war against Iraq have provided an answer—but they are wrong.

Deterrence rests on the assumption that a rational actor will not take a step if the consequences of that action are guaranteed to be devastating to him. The United States can therefore deter Iraqi aggression unless or until Saddam deliberately chooses to bring on his own demise, when he could otherwise continue to survive, scheme, and hope for an opportunity to improve his hand. Of course, Saddam's record is so filled with rash mistakes that many now consider him undeterrable. But there is no good evidence to prove that is the case. Reckless as he has been, he has never yet done something Washington told him would be suicidal.

It is true that Saddam has a bad record of miscalculation and risk-taking. But he made his worst mistake precisely because Bush the Elder did not try to deter him. In fact, Washington effectively gave Baghdad a green light prior to its 1990 invasion of Kuwait. Ambassador April Glaspie was never instructed to warn Saddam that the United States would go to war if he grabbed Kuwait. During the ensuing war, in contrast, American leaders did issue a deterrent threat, warning Saddam against using biological or chemical weapons. And that deterrent worked. (The threat in that case was only elliptical; to make future deterrence less uncertain, threats should be much more explicit.) Despite humiliating defeat, Saddam held back his high cards in 1991 because he was never forced to the wall or confronted with his own demise. That war, unlike the one now contemplated, was limited.

Bush the Younger has quite aptly compared Saddam to Stalin but has drawn the wrong lesson from that parallel. Like Saddam, Stalin miscalculated in approving the invasion of South Korea in 1950, because President Truman (like the elder Bush in 1990) had not tried to deter him in advance. In fact, Secretary of State Dean Acheson had indicated publicly that South Korea was outside the U.S. defense perimeter. On the other hand, Stalin never invaded Western Europe, where the NATO deterrent was clear. For his part, Saddam's record shows that he is foolishly self-destructive when the consequences of his gambles are unclear, but not when they are unmistakable.

Should Saddam be compared to terrorists instead of to Stalin? If the Iraqi regime is viewed as similar to al Qaeda (a conflation of threats that official rhetoric has encouraged), deterrence would indeed be impractical. But Sad-

dam and his Baath Party supporters are not religious fanatics bent on martyrdom. They are secularist thugs focused on their fortunes in this world. Nor
can they hide from the United States, as al Qaeda members can. The crucial
difference between a rogue state and a terrorist group is that the state has a return address.

None of this is meant to imply that containment and deterrence are risk-
free strategies. They are simply less risky than would be starting a war that
could precipitate the very danger it aims to prevent. Besides, what makes
hawks so sure that long-term deterrence is more dangerous than immediate
provocation? Saddam could be a greater threat in five years than he is today.
But he could also be dead. He is now 65, and although he has so far been
adept at foiling coups and assassination attempts, his continued success is
hardly guaranteed. His stocks of WMD will grow more potent over time, but
why should Saddam suddenly decide in the future that they afford him options he now lacks? And at what point in the growth of his arsenal would he
plausibly choose to bring down a decisive American assault on himself and all
his works?

It is also worth remembering that briefs made for preventive war in the past
have proved terribly wrong. Truman, for example, did not buy arguments for
attacking the Soviet Union—despite the fact that, as the historian Paul
Schroeder wrote recently in *The American Conservative*, "Stalin had nuclear
weapons, was a worse sociopath than Hussein . . . and his record of atrocities
against his own people was far worse than Hussein's." Moreover, within a few
years of Navy Secretary Francis Matthews' and others' having recommended
preventive war against him, Stalin was dead. In 1968, similarly, Robert
Lawrence and William Van Cleave (who served a dozen years later as head of
Reagan's Pentagon transition team) published a detailed rationale in *National
Review* for attacks on China's nascent nuclear facilities. It is easy today to forget that at that time, Mao was considered as fanatically aggressive and crazy
as Saddam is today. But within a few years of Lawrence and Van Cleave's article, Washington and Beijing had become tacit allies. How history could have
turned out had either of these preventive wars actually been fought is a sobering thought, and one that the White House should now consider.

Relying on deterrence indefinitely is not foolproof. Unfortunately, international politics is full of cases where the only policy choices are between risky
options and even riskier ones. In the current era of U.S. primacy, Americans
often forget this fact, mistakenly assuming that the only problems they cannot
solve satisfactorily are those about which they are inattentive or irresolute.
Overconfident in U.S. capacity to eliminate Saddam without disastrous side

effects, leaders in Washington have also become curiously pessimistic about deterrence and containment, which sustained U.S. strategy through 40 years of Cold War against a far more formidable adversary. Why has Washington lost its faith?

One explanation is psychological and moral. Many people think of deterrence as something the good guys do to the bad, not the reverse. To use the current danger of Iraqi retaliation as a reason not to attack seems dishonorable, like taking counsel from fear, a wimpy submission to blackmail. Moreover, it strikes Americans as presumptuous for a country such as Iraq to aspire to paralyze U.S. power. And it is a matter of American honor not to be deterred from suppressing evil. The cold logic of deterrence, however, has nothing to do with which side is good or evil. Deterrence depends only on the hard facts of capability, which should constrain the good as well as the bad.

Some Americans also become indignant when it is suggested that an Iraqi counterattack could be considered the fault of American initiative. This stance, they argue, is like blaming the victim. But this argument again confuses moral and material interests. If the snake strikes back when you poke it, you may blame the snake rather than yourself for being bitten. But you will still wish that you had not poked it.

Of course, Iraq has undermined its own deterrent potential by not making it explicit. Because he always denies that he possesses prohibited WMD, Saddam cannot declare a deterrent capability or doctrine. Iraq's bugs in the basement should work like Israel's bomb in the basement—as an undeclared deterrent, known about by those who need to know. But Iraq's WMD have not worked like Israel's, because, despite their potentially comparable killing power, biological weapons just do not instill the same fear as their nuclear equivalents.

At this late date, it would be awkward for Washington to step back from war—an embarrassing retreat, unless it was cushioned by apparent success in imposing inspections. (Administration leaders are correct in believing that genuinely successful inspections are nearly impossible. To work, they would have to prove a negative—that Saddam has not stashed WMD somewhere in his vast country that inspectors have not been clued in to search.) The only thing worse than such embarrassment, however, would be to go ahead with a mistaken strategy that risks retaliation against American civilians, extraordinarily bloody urban combat, and damage to the war on terrorism. No good alternatives to war exist at this point, but there are several that are less bad.

The first such option is to squeeze the box in which Saddam is currently being contained. This means selectively tightening sanctions—not those that allegedly harm civilians, but the prohibitions on imports of materials for military use and the illicit export of oil. More monitors could be deployed, and the inspection of cargoes could be increased. The squeeze would continue at least until absolutely unimpeded disarmament inspections—anytime, anywhere, undelayed, and institutionalized until the regime changes—had been under way for a long period. There would be no international enthusiasm for more serious sanctions, but reluctant allies would embrace such a course if it were offered as the alternative to war. The crumbling of sanctions was one of the motives for the Bush administration's move toward war; stepping back from the war will reinvigorate containment and disabuse Saddam of the hope that he can wriggle away from it.

Second, Washington should continue to foment internal overthrow of Iraq's regime. Saddam seems immune to covert action, but even long-shot possibilities sometimes pan out.

Third, the Bush administration could consider quasi war. U.S. forces might occupy the Kurdish area of northern Iraq (where Saddam has not exercised control for years) and build up the wherewithal to move quickly against him at some unspecified future date—to enforce inspections, to protect Iraqi garrisons that revolt against his rule, or, ultimately, to invade Baghdad.

As the noose tightens, Washington or its allies should offer Saddam safe haven if he and his henchmen step down. Of course, he is not likely to accept, and if he does, it would lead to an international chorus of clucking tongues as a heinous criminal escaped justice. But it would not hurt to leave open a bad alternative that remains better than unlimited war.

In pondering Bismarck's line about preventive war, it helps to recall the consequences of the Prussian's passing. He was soon replaced by leaders who saw more logic and necessity in the course Bismarck had derided. In 1914, such European leaders thought they had no alternative but to confront current threats with decisive preventive war, and they believed the war would be a short one. As often happens in war, however, their expectations were rudely confounded, and instead of resolving the threat, they produced four years of catastrophic carnage.

Applying Bismarck's definition of preventive war to the current case is a bit hyperbolic. Iraqi retaliation would not destroy the United States—it might not even occur. But running even a modest risk of tens of thousands of American civilian casualties is unacceptable when compared to the exaggerated risk that Iraq will court its own suicide by using or helping others use WMD without provocation, and will do so before Saddam's regime is overthrown from within.

If war is to be, the United States must win it as quickly and decisively as possible. If no catastrophic Iraqi counterattack occurs, these warnings will be seen as needless alarmism. But before deciding on waging a war, President Bush should consider that if that war results in consequences even a fraction of those of 1914, those results will thoroughly discredit his decision to start it.

BRING BACK THE DRAFT

Representative Charles B. Rangel

President Bush and his administration have declared a war against terror-ism that may soon involve sending thousands of American troops into combat in Iraq. I voted against the Congressional resolution giving the presi-dent authority to carry out this war—an engagement that would dwarf our military efforts to find Osama bin Laden and bring him to justice.

But as a combat veteran of the Korean conflict, I believe that if we are going to send our children to war, the governing principle must be that of shared sacrifice. Throughout much of our history, Americans have been asked to shoulder the burden of war equally.

That's why I will ask Congress next week to consider and support legisla-tion I will introduce to resume the military draft.

Carrying out the administration's policy toward Iraq will require long-term sacrifices by the American people, particularly those who have sons and daughters in the military. Yet the Congress that voted overwhelmingly to allow the use of force in Iraq includes only one member who has a child in the en-listed ranks of the military—just a few more have children who are officers.

I believe that if those calling for war knew that their children were likely to be required to serve—and to be placed in harm's way—there would be more caution and a greater willingness to work with the international community in dealing with Iraq. A renewed draft will help bring a greater appreciation of the consequences of decisions to go to war.

Service in our nation's armed forces is no longer a common experience. A disproportionate number of the poor and members of minority groups make up the enlisted ranks of the military, while the most privileged Americans are underrepresented or absent.

We need to return to the tradition of the citizen soldier—with alternative national service required for those who cannot serve because of physical lim-itations or reasons of conscience.

There is no doubt that going to war against Iraq will severely strain military

---

Charles B. Rangel was elected in 2002 to his 17th term as a U.S. congressman, and is the dean of the New York State Congressional Delegation. Rep. Rangel is the ranking member of the Committee on Ways and Means, and the Deputy Democratic Whip of the House of Representatives. This article was originally published on December 31, 2002 on *The New York Times* op-ed page.

resources already burdened by a growing number of obligations. There are daunting challenges facing the 1.4 million men and women in active military service and those in our National Guard and Reserve. The Pentagon has said that up to 250,000 troops may be mobilized for the invasion of Iraq. An additional 265,000 members of the National Guard and Reserve, roughly as many as were called up during the Persian Gulf War in 1991, may also be activated.

Already, we have long-term troop commitments in Europe and the Pacific, with an estimated 116,000 troops in Europe, 90,000 in the Pacific (nearly 40,000 in Japan and 38,000 in Korea) and additional troop commitments to operations in Afghanistan, Bosnia, Kosovo and elsewhere. There are also military trainers in countries across the world, including the Philippines, Colombia and Yemen.

We can expect the evolving global war on terrorism to drain our military resources even more, stretching them to the limit.

The administration has yet to address the question of whether our military is of sufficient strength and size to meet present and future commitments. Those who would lead us into war have the obligation to support an all-out mobilization of Americans for the war effort, including mandatory national service that asks something of us all.

THE UNITED STATES OF AMERICA HAS GONE MAD

John le Carré

America has entered one of its periods of historical madness, but this is the worst I can remember: worse than McCarthyism, worse than the Bay of Pigs and in the long term potentially more disastrous than the Vietnam War. The reaction to 9/11 is beyond anything Osama bin Laden could have hoped for in his nastiest dreams. As in McCarthy times, the freedoms that have made America the envy of the world are being systematically eroded. The combination of compliant U.S. media and vested corporate interests is once more ensuring that a debate that should be ringing out in every town square is confined to the loftier columns of the East Coast press.

The imminent war was planned years before bin Laden struck, but it was he who made it possible. Without bin Laden, the Bush junta would still be trying to explain such tricky matters as how it came to be elected in the first place; Enron; its shameless favouring of the already-too-rich; its reckless disregard for the world's poor, the ecology and a raft of unilaterally abrogated international treaties. They might also have to be telling us why they support Israel in its continuing disregard for U.N. resolutions.

But bin Laden conveniently swept all that under the carpet. The Bushies are riding high. Now 88 percent of Americans want the war, we are told. The U.S. defence budget has been raised by another $60 billion to around $360 billion. A splendid new generation of nuclear weapons is in the pipeline, so we can all breathe easy. Quite what war 88 percent of Americans think they are supporting is a lot less clear. A war for how long, please? At what cost in American lives? At what cost to the American taxpayer's pocket? At what cost—because most of those 88 percent are thoroughly decent and humane people—in Iraqi lives?

How Bush and his junta succeeded in deflecting America's anger from bin Laden to Saddam Hussein is one of the great public relations conjuring tricks

John le Carré is the nom de plume of David John Moore Cornwell. An accomplished novelist, he began his working career teaching at Eton from 1956 to 1958 and was a member of the British Foreign Service from 1959 to 1964, serving first as second secretary in the British Embassy in Bonn and subsequently as political consul in Hamburg. He started writing novels in 1961, and since then has published eighteen novels, the most recent of which being *The Constant Gardener*. This article was published on January 15, 2003 in the *Times* of London.

of history. But they swung it. A recent poll tells us that one in two Americans now believe Saddam was responsible for the attack on the World Trade Centre. But the American public is not merely being misled. It is being browbeaten and kept in a state of ignorance and fear. The carefully orchestrated neurosis should carry Bush and his fellow conspirators nicely into the next election.

Those who are not with Mr. Bush are against him. Worse, they are with the enemy. Which is odd, because I'm dead against Bush, but I would love to see Saddam's downfall—just not on Bush's terms and not by his methods. And not under the banner of such outrageous hypocrisy.

The religious cant that will send American troops into battle is perhaps the most sickening aspect of this surreal war-to-be. Bush has an arm-lock on God. And God has very particular political opinions. God appointed America to save the world in any way that suits America. God appointed Israel to be the nexus of America's Middle Eastern policy, and anyone who wants to mess with that idea is a) anti-Semitic, b) anti-American, c) with the enemy, and d) a terrorist.

God also has pretty scary connections. In America, where all men are equal in His sight, if not in one another's, the Bush family numbers one President, one ex-President, one ex-head of the CIA, the Governor of Florida and the ex-Governor of Texas.

Care for a few pointers? George W. Bush, 1978–84: senior executive, Arbusto Energy/Bush Exploration, an oil company; 1986–90: senior executive of the Harken oil company. Dick Cheney, 1995–2000: chief executive of the Halliburton oil company.* Condoleezza Rice, 1991–2000: senior executive with the Chevron oil company, which named an oil tanker after her. And so on. But none of these trifling associations affects the integrity of God's work.

In 1993, while ex-President George Bush was visiting the ever-democratic Kingdom of Kuwait to receive thanks for liberating them, somebody tried to

---

* Editors' Note: It is interesting to note that—Vice President Cheney's recent outspoken demands for "regime change" notwithstanding—two subsidiaries of Halliburton, the oil services conglomerate he headed for five years before resigning in 2000 to join the Bush ticket, sold millions of dollars worth of production equipment and spare parts to the Iraqis while Cheney was at the helm. According to *The Washington Post*, one of these subsidiaries, Ingersoll Dresser Pump, also signed contracts—later blocked by the Clinton Administration—to help repair the Khor al Amaya oil terminal, which allied bombers had destroyed during the First Gulf War, when Cheney was Secretary of Defense. Cheney, who says Halliburton "had a firm policy that we wouldn't do anything in Iraq, even arrangements that were supposedly legal," has denied that he knew about the Iraqi deals at the time they were made, and notes that Halliburton subsequently sold its interest in the subsidiaries.

In the meantime, *Oil Daily* reported, in late January 2003, that the State Department's "Future of Iraq" oil and gas working group was considering the possibility of "privatizing" management of Iraqi oil assets in the aftermath of a successful American-led invasion. And, on March 25, less than a week after the war in Iraq began, it was announced that the U.S. Army Corps of Engineers had contracted KBR, a unit of Halliburton, to extinguish oil well fires in Iraq, and to make emergency repairs to Iraq's oil infrastructure.

According to David Ivanovich, writing in the *Houston Chronicle*, the U.S. Department of Defense had originally kill him. The CIA believes that "somebody" was Saddam. Hence Bush Jr.'s cry: "That man tried to kill my Daddy." But it's still not personal, this war. It's still necessary. It's still God's work. It's still about bringing freedom and democracy to oppressed Iraqi people. To be a member of the team you must also believe in Absolute Good and Absolute Evil, and Bush, with a lot of help from his friends, family and God, is there to tell us which is which. What Bush won't tell us is the truth about why we're going to war. What is at stake is not an Axis of Evil—but oil, money and people's lives. Saddam's misfortune is to sit on the second biggest oilfield in the world. Bush wants it, and who helps him get it will receive a piece of the cake. And who doesn't, won't.

If Saddam didn't have the oil, he could torture his citizens to his heart's content. Other leaders do it every day—think Saudi Arabia, think Pakistan, think Turkey, think Syria, think Egypt.

Baghdad represents no clear and present danger to its neighbours, and none to the U.S. or Britain. Saddam's weapons of mass destruction, if he's still got them, will be peanuts by comparison with the stuff Israel or America could hurl at him at five minutes' notice. What is at stake is not an imminent military or terrorist threat, but the economic imperative of U.S. growth. What is at stake is America's need to demonstrate its military power to all of us—to Europe and Russia and China, and poor mad little North Korea, as well as the Middle East; to show who rules America at home, and who is to be ruled by America abroad.

The most charitable interpretation of Tony Blair's part in all this is that he believed that, by riding the tiger, he could steer it. He can't. Instead, he gave it a phoney legitimacy, and a smooth voice. Now I fear, the same tiger has him penned into a corner, and he can't get out.

It is utterly laughable that, at a time when Blair has talked himself against the ropes, neither of Britain's opposition leaders can lay a glove on him. But that's Britain's tragedy, as it is America's: as our Governments spin, lie and lose their credibility, the electorate simply shrugs and looks the other way. Blair's best chance of personal survival must be that, at the eleventh hour, world protest and an improbably emboldened U.N. will force Bush to put his gun

---

hired KBR in November 2002 to "draw up a classified contingency plan for dealing with any well fires in Iraq." The company itself was selected to implement its own plan, a Halliburton spokesperson explained, because it was "the only contractor that could commence implementing the complex contingency plan on extremely short notice."

On March 26, the day after the Halliburton deal was announced, President Bush asked Congress for $489.3 million to cover the costs of repairing damage to Iraq's oil facilities. Under the terms of its Pentagon contract, reported CNN/Money, "much or all" of the money eventually appropriated "could go to Halliburton or its subcontractors."

Observed Representative Maxine Waters (D-California): "I think there's a serious irony in the administration letting contracts to rebuild bridges that they haven't bombed yet."

back in his holster unfired. But what happens when the world's greatest cowboy rides back into town without a tyrant's head to wave at the boys?

Blair's worst chance is that, with or without the U.N., he will drag us into a war that, if the will to negotiate energetically had ever been there, could have been avoided; a war that has been no more democratically debated in Britain than it has in America or at the U.N. By doing so, Blair will have set back our relations with Europe and the Middle East for decades to come. He will have helped to provoke unforeseeable retaliation, great domestic unrest, and regional chaos in the Middle East. Welcome to the party of the ethical foreign policy.

There is a middle way, but it's a tough one: Bush dives in without U.N. approval and Blair stays on the bank. Goodbye to the special relationship. I cringe when I hear my Prime Minister lend his head prefect's sophistries to this colonialist adventure. His very real anxieties about terror are shared by all sane men. What he can't explain is how he reconciles a global assault on al-Qaeda with a territorial assault on Iraq. We are in this war, if it takes place, to secure the fig leaf of our special relationship, to grab our share of the oil pot, and because, after all the public hand-holding in Washington and Camp David, Blair has to show up at the altar.

"But will we win, Daddy?"

"Of course, child. It will all be over while you're still in bed."

"Why?"

"Because otherwise Mr. Bush's voters will get terribly impatient and may decide not to vote for him."

"But will people be killed, Daddy?"

"Nobody you know, darling. Just foreign people."

"Can I watch it on television?"

"Only if Mr Bush says you can."

"And afterwards, will everything be normal again? Nobody will do anything horrid any more?"

"Hush child, and go to sleep."

Last Friday a friend of mine in California drove to his local supermarket with a sticker on his car saying: "Peace is also Patriotic." It was gone by the time he'd finished shopping.

WHY I AM FOR REGIME CHANGE

Christopher Hitchens

Dear brothers and sisters, boys and girls, comrades and friends,
The editor of this rag told me of your upcoming "Potlucks for Peace" event and invited my comments, and at first I couldn't think of a thing to say. For one thing, why should I address a Seattle audience (or even suppose that I have a Seattle audience, for that matter)? I daresay that I can claim a tenuous connection, because I have always had a good crowd when reading at the splendid bookstores of the city, and because it was in Seattle that I stayed when grounded on September 11, 2001, a date that now makes some people yawn.

I had been speaking to the students of Whitman College in Walla Walla about the crimes of Henry Kissinger and had told them that 11 September—which was then tomorrow—was a symbolic date. On that day in 1973, the civilian government in Chile had been drowned in blood by an atrocious military coup. On the same day in 2001, a group of Chilean survivors proposed to file a lawsuit against Kissinger in a federal court in Washington, D.C. I showed a film illustrating this, made some additional remarks, and closed by saying that the date would be long remembered in the annals of the struggle for human rights. I got some pretty decent applause—and this from the alma mater of Henry "Scoop" Jackson, whose family was present. On the following morning I got a very early call from my wife, who was three hours ahead of me. She told me to turn on the TV, and she commented mordantly that the anti-Kissinger campaign might have to be on hold for a while. (Oddly enough, and as recent events have shown, she was mistaken about that.) Everyone knows what I saw when I turned on the TV.

Now hear this. Ever since that morning, the United States has been at war with the forces of reaction. May I please entreat you to reread the preceding sentence? Or perhaps you will let me restate it for emphasis. The govern-

Christopher Hitchens defines himself as "an essayist and contrarian." He writes regularly for *Slate* and is a frequent contributor to *Vanity Fair, Harper's, Granta,* and *The London Review of Books.* For two decades, he wrote *The Nation's* biweekly "Minority Report" column, an assignment he terminated in 2002 in a much-publicized dispute involving the magazine's editorial stance on Iraq. Among his many books are *Why Orwell Matters* and *No One Left to Lie To: The Triangulation of William Clinton.* This essay, originally titled "Chew on This" because it was addressed to a group of antiwar activists who were organizing potluck dinners for peace, appeared in the January 16, 2003 issue of *The Stranger,* a Seattle weekly.

ment and people of these United States are now at war with the forces of reaction.

This outcome was clearly not willed, at least on the American side. And everybody with half an education seems to know how to glibly dilute the statement. Isn't Saudi Arabia reactionary? What about Pakistani nukes? Do we bomb Sharon for his negation of Palestinian rights? Weren't we on Saddam's side when he was at his worst? (I am exempting the frantic and discredited few who think or suggest that George W. Bush fixed up the attacks to inflate the military budget and abolish the Constitution.) But however compromised and shameful the American starting point was—and I believe I could make this point stick with greater venom and better evidence than most people can muster—the above point remains untouched. The United States finds itself at war with the forces of reaction.

Do I have to demonstrate this? The Taliban's annihilation of music and culture? The enslavement of women? The massacre of Shiite Muslims in Afghanistan? Or what about the latest boast of al Qaeda—that the bomb in Bali, massacring so many Australian holidaymakers, was a deliberate revenge for Australia's belated help in securing independence for East Timor? (Never forget that the Muslim fundamentalists are not against "empire." They fight proudly for the restoration of their own lost caliphate.) To these people, the concept of a civilian casualty is meaningless if the civilian is an unbeliever or a heretic.

Confronted with such a foe—which gladly murders Algerians and Egyptians and Palestinians if they have any doubts about the true faith, or if they happen to be standing in the wrong place at the wrong time, or if they happen to be female—exactly what role does a "peace movement" have to play? A year or so ago, the "peace movement" was saying that Afghanistan could not even be approached without risking the undying enmity of the Muslim world; that the Taliban could not be bombed during Ramadan; that a humanitarian disaster would occur if the Islamic ultra-fanatics were confronted in their own lairs. Now we have an imperfect but recovering Afghanistan, with its population increased by almost two million returned refugees. Have you ever seen or heard any of those smart-ass critics and cynics make a self-criticism? Or recant?

To the contrary, the same critics and cynics are now lining up to say, "Hands off Saddam Hussein," and to make almost the same doom-laden predictions. The line that connects Afghanistan to Iraq is not a straight one by any means. But the oblique connection is ignored by the potluck peaceniks, and one can be sure (judging by their past form) that it would be ignored even if it were as direct as the connection between al Qaeda and the Taliban. Sad-

dam Hussein denounced the removal of the Sunni Muslim–murdering Slo-
bodan Milosevic, and also denounced the removal of the Shiite-murdering
Taliban. Reactionaries have a tendency to stick together (and I don't mean
"guilt by association" here. I mean GUILT). If the counsel of the peaceniks
had been followed, Kuwait would today be the 19th province of Iraq (and
based on his own recently produced evidence, Saddam Hussein would have
acquired nuclear weapons). Moreover, Bosnia would be a trampled and
cleansed province of Greater Serbia, Kosovo would have been emptied of
most of its inhabitants, and the Taliban would still be in power in Afghanistan. Yet nothing seems to disturb the contented air of moral superiority that
surrounds those who intone the "peace movement."

There are at least three well-established reasons to favor what is eu-
phemistically termed "regime change" in Iraq. The first is the flouting by Saddam Hussein of every known law on genocide and human rights, which is why
the Senate—at the urging of Bill Clinton—passed the Iraq Liberation Act
unanimously before George W. Bush had even been nominated. The second
is the persistent effort by Saddam's dictatorship to acquire the weapons of
genocide: an effort which can and should be thwarted and which was condemned by the United Nations before George W. Bush was even governor of
Texas. The third is the continuous involvement by the Iraqi secret police in
the international underworld of terror and destabilization. I could write a separate essay on the evidence for this; at the moment I'll just say that it's extremely rash for anybody to discount the evidence that we already possess.
(And I shall add that any "peace movement" that even pretends to care for
human rights will be very shaken by what will be uncovered when the Saddam
Hussein regime falls. Prisons, mass graves, weapon sites . . . just you wait.)

None of these things on their own need necessarily make a case for an intervention, but taken together—and taken with the permanent threat posed
by Saddam Hussein to the oilfields of the region—they add up fairly convinc-
ingly. Have you, or your friends, recently employed the slogan "No War for
Oil"? If so, did you listen to what you were saying? Do you mean that oil isn't
worth fighting for, or that oil resources aren't worth protecting? Do you recall
that Saddam Hussein ignited the oilfields of Kuwait when he was in retreat,
and flooded the local waterways with fire and pollution? (Should I patronize
the potluckistas, and ask them to look up the pictures of poisoned birds and
marine animals from that year?) Are you indifferent to the possibility that
such a man might be able to irradiate the oilfields next time? OF COURSE
it's about oil, stupid.

To say that he might also do all these terrible things if attacked or threatened is to miss the point. Last time he did this, or massacred the Iraqi and

Kurdish populations, he was withdrawing his forces under an international guarantee. The Iraqi and Kurdish peoples are now, by every measure we have or know, determined to be rid of him. And the hope, which is perhaps a slim one but very much sturdier than other hopes, is that the next Iraqi regime will be better and safer, not just from our point of view but from the points of view of the Iraqi and Kurdish peoples. The sanctions policy, which was probably always hopeless, is now quite indefensible. If lifted, it would only have allowed Saddam's oligarchy to re-equip. But once imposed, it was immoral and punitive without the objective of regime change. Choose. By the way, and while we are choosing, if you really don't want war, you should call for the lifting of the no-fly zones over northern and southern Iraq. These have been war measures since 1991.

What would the lifting of the no-fly zones mean for the people who live under them? I recently sat down with my old friend Dr. Barham Salih, who is the elected prime minister of one sector of Iraqi Kurdistan. Neither he nor his electorate could be mentioned if it were not for the no-fly zones imposed—as a result of democratic protest in the West—at the end of the last Gulf War. In his area of Iraq, "regime change" has already occurred. There are dozens of newspapers, numerous radio and TV channels, satellite dishes, Internet cafes. Four female judges have been appointed. Almost half the students at the University of Sulaimaniya are women. And a pro al Qaeda group, recently transferred from Afghanistan, is trying to assassinate the Kurdish leadership and nearly killed my dear friend Barham just the other day . . . Now, why would this gang want to make that particular murder its first priority?

Before you face that question, consider this. Dr. Salih has been through some tough moments in his time. Most of the massacres and betrayals of the Kurdish people of Iraq took place with American support or connivance. But the Kurds have pressed ahead with regime change in any case. Surely a "peace movement" with any principles should be demanding that the United States not abandon them again. I like to think I could picture a mass picket in Seattle, offering solidarity with Kurdistan against a government of fascistic repression, and opposing any attempt to sell out the Kurds for reasons of realpolitik. Instead, there is a self-satisfied isolationism to be found, which seems to desire mainly a quiet life for Americans. The option of that quiet life disappeared a while back, and it's only coincidence that for me it vanished in Seattle. The United States is now at war with the forces of reaction, and nobody is entitled to view this battle as a spectator. The Union under Lincoln wasn't wholeheartedly against slavery. The USA under Roosevelt had its own selfish agenda even while combating Hitler and Hirohito. The hot-and-cold war against Stalinism wasn't exactly free of blemish and stain. How much this latest crisis turns into an even tougher war with reaction, at home or abroad, could depend partly upon those who currently think that it is either possible or desirable to remain neutral. I say "could," even though the chance has already been shamefully missed. But a mere potluck abstention will be remembered only with pity and scorn.

AN UNACCEPTABLE HELPLESSNESS

Edward Said

One opens *The New York Times* on a daily basis to read the most recent article about the preparations for war that are taking place in the United States. Another battalion, one more set of aircraft carriers and cruisers, an ever-increasing number of aircraft, new contingents of officers are being moved to the Persian Gulf area. 62,000 more soldiers were transferred to the Gulf last weekend. An enormous, deliberately intimidating force is being built up by America overseas, while inside the country, economic and social bad news multiply with a joint relentlessness. The huge capitalist machine seems to be faltering, even as it grinds down the vast majority of citizens. Nonetheless, George Bush proposes another large tax cut for the one percent of the population that is comparatively rich. The public education system is in a major crisis, and health insurance for 50 million Americans simply does not exist. Israel asks for 15 billion dollars in additional loan guarantees and military aid. And the unemployment rates in the U.S. mount inexorably, as more jobs are lost every day.

Nevertheless, preparations for an unimaginably costly war continue and continue without either public approval or dramatically noticeable disapproval. A generalised indifference (which may conceal great over-all fear, ignorance and apprehension) has greeted the administration's war-mongering and its strangely ineffective response to the challenge forced on it recently by North Korea. In the case of Iraq, with no weapons of mass destruction to speak of, the U.S. plans a war; in the case of North Korea, it offers that country economic and energy aid. What a humiliating difference between contempt for the Arabs and respect for North Korea, an equally grim, and cruel dictatorship.

In the Arab and Muslim worlds, the situation appears more peculiar. For almost a year American politicians, regional experts, administration officials, and journalists have repeated the charges that have become standard fare so far as Islam and the Arabs are concerned. Most of this chorus pre-dates

Edward W. Said, the University Professor of English and Comparative Literature at Columbia University, is a cultural critic and human rights activist. He writes regularly for the *Guardian* of London, *Le Monde Diplomatique,* the Arab-language daily *al-Hayat,* and *The Nation.* A former member of the Palestine National Council, he is the author of ten books of cultural and political criticism, most recently *Power, Politics, and Culture.* This article was published in the January 16–22, 2003 issue of *Al-Ahram* (Cairo).

11 September, as I have shown in my books *Orientalism* and *Covering Islam*. To today's practically unanimous chorus has been added the authority of the United Nation's Human Development Report on the Arab world which certified that Arabs dramatically lag behind the rest of the world in democracy, knowledge, and women's rights. Everyone says (with some justification, of course) that Islam needs reform and that the Arab educational system is a disaster, in effect, a school for religious fanatics and suicide bombers funded not just by crazy imams and their wealthy followers (like Osama bin Laden) but also by governments who are supposed allies of the United States. The only "good" Arabs are those who appear in the media decrying modern Arab culture and society without reservation. I recall the lifeless cadences of their sentences for, with nothing positive to say about themselves or their people and language, they simply regurgitate the tired American formulas already flooding the airwaves and pages of print. We lack democracy, they say, we haven't challenged Islam enough, we need to do more about driving away the specter of Arab nationalism and the credo of Arab unity. That is all discredited, ideological rubbish. Only what we, and our American instructors, say about the Arabs and Islam—vague re-cycled Orientalist clichés of the kind repeated by a tireless mediocrity like Bernard Lewis—is true. The rest isn't realistic or pragmatic enough. "We" need to join modernity, modernity in effect being Western, globalised, free-marketed, democratic—whatever those words might be taken to mean. (If I had the time, there would be an essay to be written about the prose style of people like Ajami, Gerges, Makiya, Talhami, Fandy et. al., academics whose very language reeks of subservience, inauthenticity and a hopelessly stilted mimicry that has been thrust upon them).

The clash of civilisations that George Bush and his minions are trying to fabricate as a cover for a preemptive oil and hegemony war against Iraq is supposed to result in a triumph of democratic nation-building, regime change and forcible modernisation *à l'américaine*. Never mind the bombs and the ravages of the sanctions which are unmentioned. This will be a purifying war whose goal is to throw out Saddam and his men and replace them with a re-drawn map of the whole region. New Sykes Picot. New Balfour. New Wilsonian 14 points. New world altogether. Iraqis, we are told by the Iraqi dissidents, will welcome their liberation, and perhaps forget entirely about their past sufferings. Perhaps.

Meanwhile, the soul-and-body destroying situation in Palestine worsens all the time. There seems no force capable of stopping Sharon and Mofaz, who bellow their defiance to the whole world. We forbid, we punish, we ban, we break, we destroy. The torrent of unbroken violence against an entire people continues. As I write these lines, I am sent an announcement that the entire village of Al-Daba' in the Qalqilya area of the West Bank is about to be wiped out by 60-ton American-made Israeli bulldozers: 250 Palestinians will lose their 42 houses, 700 dunums of agricultural land, a mosque, and an elementary school for 132 children. The United Nations stands by, looking on as its resolutions are flouted on an hourly basis. Typically, alas, George Bush identifies with Sharon, not with the 16-year-old Palestinian kid who is used as a human shield by Israeli soldiers.

Meanwhile, the Palestinian Authority offers a return to peacemaking, and presumably, to Oslo. Having been burned for 10 years the first time, Arafat seems inexplicably to want to have another go at it. His faithful lieutenants make declarations and write opinion pieces for the press, suggesting their willingness to accept anything, more or less. Remarkably though, the great mass of this heroic people seems willing to go on, without peace and without respite, bleeding, going hungry, dying day by day. They have too much dignity and confidence in the justice of their cause to submit shamefully to Israel, as their leaders have done. What could be more discouraging for the average Gazan who goes on resisting Israeli occupation than to see his or her leaders kneel as supplicants before the Americans?

In this entire panorama of desolation, what catches the eye is the utter passivity and helplessness of the Arab world as a whole. The American government and its servants issue statement after statement of purpose, they move troops and material, they transport tanks and destroyers, but the Arabs individually and collectively can barely muster a bland refusal (at most they say, no, you cannot use military bases in our territory) only to reverse themselves a few days later.

Why is there such silence and such astounding helplessness?

The largest power in history is about to launch and is unremittingly reiterating its intention to launch a war against a sovereign Arab country now ruled by a dreadful regime, a war the clear purpose of which is not only to destroy the Baathi regime but to re-design the entire region. The Pentagon has made no secret that its plans are to re-draw the map of the whole Arab world, perhaps changing other regimes and many borders in the process. No one can be shielded from the cataclysm when it comes (if it comes, which is not yet a complete certainty). And yet, there is only long silence followed by a few vague bleats of polite demurral in response. After all, millions of people will be affected. America contemptuously plans for their future without consulting them. Do we deserve such racist derision?

This is not only unacceptable: it is impossible to believe. How can a region of almost 300 million Arabs wait passively for the blows to fall without attempting a collective roar of resistance and a loud proclamation of an alternative view? Has the Arab will completely dissolved? Even a prisoner about to be executed usually has some last words to pronounce. Why is there now no last testimonial to an era of history, to a civilisation about to be crushed and transformed utterly, to a society that despite its drawbacks and weaknesses nevertheless goes on functioning. Arab babies are born every hour, children go to school, men and women marry and work and have children, they play, and laugh and eat, they are sad, they suffer illness and death. There is love and companionship, friendship and excitement. Yes, Arabs are repressed and misruled, terribly misruled, but they manage to go on with the business of living despite everything. This is the fact that both the Arab leaders and the United States simply ignore when they fling empty gestures at the so-called "Arab street" invented by mediocre Orientalists.

But who is now asking the existential questions about our future as a people? The task cannot be left to a cacophony of religious fanatics and submissive, fatalistic sheep. But that seems to be the case. The Arab governments—no, most of the Arab countries from top to bottom—sit back in their seats and just wait as America postures, lines up, threatens and ships out more soldiers and F-16's to deliver the punch. The silence is deafening.

Years of sacrifice and struggle, of bones broken in hundreds of prisons and torture chambers from the Atlantic to the Gulf, families destroyed, endless poverty and suffering. Huge, expensive armies. For what?

This is not a matter of party or ideology or faction: it's a matter of what the great theologian Paul Tillich used to call ultimate seriousness. Technology, modernisation and certainly globalisation are not the answer for what threatens us as a people now. We have in our tradition an entire body of secular and religious discourse that treats of beginnings and endings, of life and death, of love and anger, of society and history. This is there, but no voice, no individual with great vision and moral authority seems able now to tap into that, and bring it to attention. We are on the eve of a catastrophe that our political, moral and religious leaders can only just denounce a little bit while, behind whispers and winks and closed doors, they make plans somehow to ride out the storm. They think of survival, and perhaps of heaven. But who is in charge of the present, the worldly, the land, the water, the air and the lives dependent on each other for existence? No one seems to be in charge. There is a wonderful colloquial expression in English that very precisely and ironically catches our unacceptable helplessness, our passivity and inability to help ourselves now when our strength is most needed. The expression is: will the last person to leave please turn out the lights? We are that close to a kind of upheaval that will leave very little standing and perilously little left even to record, except for the last injunction that begs for extinction.

Hasn't the time come for us collectively to demand and try to formulate a genuinely Arab alternative to the wreckage about to engulf our world? This is not only a trivial matter of regime change, although God knows that we can do with quite a bit of that. Surely it can't be a return to Oslo, another offer to Israel to please accept our existence and let us live in peace, another cringing crawling inaudible plea for mercy. Will no one come out into the light of day to express a vision for our future that isn't based on a script written by Donald Rumsfeld and Paul Wolfowitz, those two symbols of vacant power and overweening arrogance? I hope someone is listening.

WHY WE KNOW IRAQ IS LYING

Condoleezza Rice

Eleven weeks after the United Nations Security Council unanimously passed a resolution demanding—yet again—that Iraq disclose and disarm all its nuclear, chemical and biological weapons programs, it is appropriate to ask, "Has Saddam Hussein finally decided to voluntarily disarm?" Unfortunately, the answer is a clear and resounding no.

There is no mystery to voluntary disarmament. Countries that decide to disarm lead inspectors to weapons and production sites, answer questions before they are asked, state publicly and often the intention to disarm and urge their citizens to cooperate. The world knows from examples set by South Africa, Ukraine and Kazakhstan what it looks like when a government decides that it will cooperatively give up its weapons of mass destruction. The critical common elements of these efforts include a high-level political commitment to disarm, national initiatives to dismantle weapons programs, and full cooperation and transparency.

In 1989 South Africa made the strategic decision to dismantle its covert nuclear weapons program. It destroyed its arsenal of seven weapons and later submitted to rigorous verification by the International Atomic Energy Agency. Inspectors were given complete access to all nuclear facilities (operating and defunct) and the people who worked there. They were also presented with thousands of documents detailing, for example, the daily operation of uranium enrichment facilities as well as the construction and dismantling of specific weapons.

Ukraine and Kazakhstan demonstrated a similar pattern of cooperation when they decided to rid themselves of the nuclear weapons, intercontinental ballistic missiles and heavy bombers inherited from the Soviet Union. With significant assistance from the United States—warmly accepted by both countries—disarmament was orderly, open and fast. Nuclear warheads were

Condoleezza Rice is the Assistant to the President for National Security Affairs. In June 1999, she completed a six-year tenure as Stanford University's provost, where she is also a tenured professor of political science. She has served as special assistant to President George Bush, Sr., special assistant to the director of the Joint Chiefs of Staff, as a member of several boards of directors (including the University of Notre Dame and the Chevron Corporation, which named a tanker after her), and is the author of three books and numerous articles on Soviet and Eastern European foreign and defense policy. This article was originally published on January 23, 2002 on the op-ed page of *The New York Times*.

returned to Russia. Missile silos and heavy bombers were destroyed or dismantled—once in a ceremony attended by the American and Russian defense chiefs. In one instance, Kazakhstan revealed the existence of a ton of highly enriched uranium and asked the United States to remove it, lest it fall into the wrong hands.

Iraq's behavior could not offer a starker contrast. Instead of a commitment to disarm, Iraq has a high-level political commitment to maintain and conceal its weapons, led by Saddam Hussein and his son Qusay, who controls the Special Security Organization, which runs Iraq's concealment activities. Instead of implementing national initiatives to disarm, Iraq maintains institutions whose sole purpose is to thwart the work of the inspectors. And instead of full cooperation and transparency, Iraq has filed a false declaration to the United Nations that amounts to a 12,200-page lie.

For example, the declaration fails to account for or explain Iraq's efforts to get uranium from abroad, its manufacture of specific fuel for ballistic missiles it claims not to have, and the gaps previously identified by the United Nations in Iraq's accounting for more than two tons of the raw materials needed to produce thousands of gallons of anthrax and other biological weapons.

Iraq's declaration even resorted to unabashed plagiarism, with lengthy passages of United Nations reports copied word-for-word (or edited to remove any criticism of Iraq) and presented as original text.* Far from informing, the declaration is intended to cloud and confuse the true picture of Iraq's arsenal. It is a reflection of the regime's well-earned reputation for dishonesty and constitutes a material breach of United Nations Security Council Resolution 1441, which set up the current inspections program.

Unlike other nations that have voluntarily disarmed—and in defiance of Resolution 1441—Iraq is not allowing inspectors "immediate, unimpeded, unrestricted access" to facilities and people involved in its weapons program. As a recent inspection at the home of an Iraqi nuclear scientist demonstrated, and other sources confirm, material and documents are still being moved around in farcical shell games. The regime has blocked free and unrestricted use of aerial reconnaissance.

The list of people involved with weapons of mass destruction programs, which the United Nations required Iraq to provide, ends with those who worked in 1991—even though the United Nations had previously established

---

* Editors' note: One wonders if Dr. Rice feels a similar contempt for the British government, after the world discovered that whole chunks of its latest dossier on Iraq—referred to as a "fine paper" by her colleague Secretary of State Colin Powell during his February 5 speech to the Security Council—were plagiarized from several published and not so recent academic articles, typographical errors and all. See Paul Lashmar and Raymond Whitaker's article on p. 479 for more details.

that the programs continued after that date. Interviews with scientists and weapons officials identified by inspectors have taken place only in the watchful presence of the regime's agents. Given the duplicitous record of the regime, its recent promises to do better can only be seen as an attempt to stall for time.

Last week's finding by inspectors of 12 chemical warheads not included in Iraq's declaration was particularly troubling. In the past, Iraq has filled this type of warhead with sarin—a deadly nerve agent used by Japanese terrorists in 1995 to kill 12 Tokyo subway passengers and sicken thousands of others. Richard Butler, the former chief United Nations arms inspector, estimates that if a larger type of warhead that Iraq has made and used in the past were filled with VX (an even deadlier nerve agent) and launched at a major city, it could kill up to one million people. Iraq has also failed to provide United Nations inspectors with documentation of its claim to have destroyed its VX stockpiles.

Many questions remain about Iraq's nuclear, chemical and biological weapons programs and arsenal—and it is Iraq's obligation to provide answers. It is failing in spectacular fashion. By both its actions and its inactions, Iraq is proving not that it is a nation bent on disarmament, but that it is a nation with something to hide. Iraq is still treating inspections as a game. It should know that time is running out.

I'M LOSING PATIENCE WITH MY NEIGHBOURS, MR. BUSH

Terry Jones

I'm really excited by George Bush's latest reason for bombing Iraq: he's running out of patience. And so am I!

For some time now I've been really pissed off with Mr. Johnson, who lives a couple of doors down the street. Well, him and Mr. Patel, who runs the health food shop. They both give me queer looks, and I'm sure Mr. Johnson is planning something nasty for me, but so far I haven't been able to discover what. I've been round to his place a few times to see what he's up to, but he's got everything well hidden. That's how devious he is.

As for Mr. Patel, don't ask me how I know, I just know—from very good sources—that he is, in reality, a Mass Murderer. I have leafleted the street telling them that if we don't act first, he'll pick us off one by one.

Some of my neighbours say, if I've got proof, why don't I go to the police? But that's simply ridiculous. The police will say that they need evidence of a crime with which to charge my neighbours.

They'll come up with endless red tape and quibbling about the rights and wrongs of a pre-emptive strike and all the while Mr. Johnson will be finalising his plans to do terrible things to me, while Mr. Patel will be secretly murdering people. Since I'm the only one in the street with a decent range of automatic firearms, I reckon it's up to me to keep the peace. But until recently that's been a little difficult. Now, however, George W. Bush has made it clear that all I need to do is run out of patience, and then I can wade in and do whatever I want!

And let's face it, Mr. Bush's carefully thought-out policy towards Iraq is the only way to bring about international peace and security. The one certain way to stop Muslim fundamentalist suicide bombers targeting the U.S. or the UK is to bomb a few Muslim countries that have never threatened us.

That's why I want to blow up Mr. Johnson's garage and kill his wife and

---

Terry Jones first became famous as a member of Monty Python's Flying Circus. He directed three of the Python films, including *Life of Brian,* to whose script, according to fellow Python John Cleese, Jones became "forcibly attracted." ("Wow," Cleese quotes him as saying. "It was just so neatly typed out in great big pretty orange covers with punctuation, and the pages numbered in the right order and everything. I just flipped.") This article was originally published in *The Observer,* to which Jones is a frequent contributor, on January 26, 2003.

children. Strike first! That'll teach him a lesson. Then he'll leave us in peace and stop peering at me in that totally unacceptable way.

Mr. Bush makes it clear that all he needs to know before bombing Iraq is that Saddam is a really nasty man and that he has weapons of mass destruction—even if no one can find them. I'm certain I've just as much justification for killing Mr. Johnson's wife and children as Mr. Bush has for bombing Iraq.

Mr. Bush's long-term aim is to make the world a safer place by eliminating "rogue states" and "terrorism." It's such a clever long-term aim because how can you ever know when you've achieved it? How will Mr. Bush know when he's wiped out all terrorists? When every single terrorist is dead? But then a terrorist is only a terrorist once he's committed an act of terror. What about would-be terrorists? These are the ones you really want to eliminate, since most of the known terrorists, being suicide bombers, have already eliminated themselves.

Perhaps Mr. Bush needs to wipe out everyone who could possibly be a future terrorist? Maybe he can't be sure he's achieved his objective until every Muslim fundamentalist is dead? But then some moderate Muslims might convert to fundamentalism. Maybe the only really safe thing to do would be for Mr. Bush to eliminate all Muslims?

It's the same in my street. Mr. Johnson and Mr. Patel are just the tip of the iceberg. There are dozens of other people in the street who I don't like and who—quite frankly—look at me in odd ways. No one will be really safe until I've wiped them all out.

My wife says I might be going too far but I tell her I'm simply using the same logic as the President of the United States. That shuts her up.

Like Mr. Bush, I've run out of patience, and if that's a good enough reason for the President, it's good enough for me. I'm going to give the whole street two weeks—no, ten days—to come out in the open and hand over all aliens and interplanetary hijackers, galactic outlaws and interstellar terrorist masterminds, and if they don't hand them over nicely and say "Thank you," I'm going to bomb the entire street to kingdom come.

It's just as sane as what George W. Bush is proposing—and, in contrast to what he's intending, my policy will destroy only one street.

TWELVE

LAST DANCE AT THE U.N.

"I was at a celebration of India's Independence Day, and a Frenchman came walking up to me and started talking to me about Iraq, and it was obvious that we were not going to agree. And I said, 'Wait a minute. Do you speak German?' And he looked at me kind of funny and said, 'No, I don't speak German.' And I said, 'You're welcome,' turned around and walked off."
—*House Majority Leader Tom DeLay (R-TX), February 11, 2003,*
commenting on French resistance to the
U.S.-British proposal for giving Iraq an ultimatum

"To those who are wondering in anguish when and how we are going to cede to war, I would like to tell them that nothing, at any time, in this Security Council, will be done in haste, misunderstanding, suspicion or fear. In this temple of the United Nations, we are the guardians of an ideal, the guardians of a conscience. The onerous responsibility and immense honor we have must lead us to give priority to disarmament in peace. This message comes to you today from an old country, France, from a continent like mine, Europe, that has known wars, occupation and barbarity. A country that does not forget and knows everything it owes to the freedom-fighters who came from America and elsewhere. And yet has never ceased to stand upright in the face of history and before mankind. Faithful to its values, it wishes resolutely to act with all the members of the international community. It believes in our ability to build together a better world.

> —*Dominique de Villepin, France's Minister of Foreign Affairs,*
> *at the United Nations Security Council, February 14, 2003*

"If we were to be given four months, I would welcome it. There were eight years of inspections and four years of no inspections and now we have had a couple of months. And it seems to me a rather short time to close the door and say: This is it."

> —*Hans Blix, chief U.N. weapons inspector, March 5, 2003*

"Tomorrow is a moment of truth for the world."

> —*President George W. Bush, speaking at the*
> *Azores summit with Britain and Spain, March 16, 2003*

A CASE FOR CONCERN,
NOT A CASE FOR WAR

Glen Rangwala, Nathaniel Hurd
and Alistair Millar

On January 27, UNMOVIC Executive Chairman Hans Blix and IAEA Director General Mohamed ElBaradei presented to the U.N. Security Council their required updates on the progress of weapons inspections inside Iraq. The updates arrive as the differences between the overt strategies of Security Council members reach a new level of sharpness. Permanent members China, France and Russia staked out their position over the preceding week: the inspections are satisfactorily helping to provide the Council with assurances regarding Iraq's non-conventional weapons and related programs, a military assault may have grave consequences for regional stability and the prevention of international terrorism, and the inspectors themselves must declare their inability to work in Iraq before the Council can consider changes in its policy. By contrast, the United States, along with Great Britain, has acknowledged neither positive results from the inspections process nor the inspectors' prerogative to assess the continued validity of their own work. Both factions among the Security Council's Permanent Five will find much in the Blix update to substantiate their positions.

The goal of successive Security Council resolutions, and thus the inspectors' mandate under Resolution 1441 of November 8, 2002, is limited to divesting Iraq of non-conventional weapons and dismantling the related programs. Throughout the 1990s, U.S. administrations vacillated between the Security Council's goal of disarmament and Washington's goal of regime change. Under the Clinton administration, the regime change agenda persistently served to impede disarmament, most apparently for 14 days in November 1998, when Iraq withdrew all cooperation with inspections in response to the Iraq Liberation Act signed by President Bill Clinton. Shortly after George

Glen Rangwala is a lecturer in politics at Newnham and Trinity Colleges, Cambridge University. Nathaniel Hurd is a consultant on Iraq Policy to the Mennonite United Nations office. Alistair Millar is vice president and director of the Washington, D.C., office of the Fourth Freedom Forum, an independent research organization that promotes awareness of global security issues. This article was written for *Middle East Report Online*, where it first appeared on January 28, 2003.

W. Bush came into office in early 2001, his Secretary of State, Colin Powell, was faced with a rapidly eroding sanctions regime. Powell proposed a "re-energized" sanctions policy ostensibly aimed at reducing restrictions on some civilian imports while streamlining controls on Iraqi imports of proscribed military goods and dual-use goods. But, due to pressure from within the Bush administration, this new policy was short-lived. Regime change is strongly backed by Bush and by Congress, but is not the official policy of any other Security Council member. The U.S. policy of regime change in Iraq is behind the crisis within the Security Council over whether inspections or war are the way to secure Iraq's disarmament.

Toward Peaceful Disarmament

By the standard of containing Iraq's non-conventional weapons capacity and hence keeping Iraq's potential for aggression acceptably low, inspections have worked. As a result of the ceasefire agreement with Iraq in 1991, Resolutions 687 and later 715 established an ongoing long-term monitoring and verification system (OMV), with an export/import control mechanism to assure that Iraq did not reconstitute or retain its prohibited chemical and biological weapons and missiles with a range greater than 150 km. From 1991 to 1998, the implementation of the OMV was a vital element of the disarmament process, as UNSCOM personnel left tamper-resistant monitoring equipment at sites and conducted frequent follow-up visits. The inspectors collected valuable baseline information that has increased the speed and effectiveness of the current UNMOVIC and IAEA inspection teams.

Vast improvements to surveillance and detection technologies over the last five years will increase the effectiveness of a new OMV that could be established as early as February 2003. Inspectors would also conduct in-person OMV visits frequently enough to reassure the Security Council about Iraq's non-conventional weapons capabilities. Ensuring the re-establishment of an effective OMV is a more important goal than the hot pursuit of unanswered questions, as it serves to deter the Iraqi government from reconstructing its non-conventional facilities. It also provides the Security Council with assurances that Iraq is not conducting activities prohibited by Council resolutions.

Those who advocate the continuation of inspections would find much in the January 27 updates to the Council to support their position. ElBaradei told the Security Council that "we have to date found no evidence that Iraq has revived its nuclear weapons program since the elimination of the program in the 1990s." He also made his most direct pitch for a non-violent solution, ending his presentation with a direct appeal to the U.S.: "These few months would be a valuable investment in peace because they could help us avoid a war. We trust that we will continue to have your support as we make every effort to verify Iraq's nuclear disarmament through peaceful means, and to demonstrate that the inspection process can and does work, as a central feature of the international nuclear arms control regime."

Blix, too, endorsed elements of the Iraqi approach, mentioning how "Iraq has on the whole cooperated rather well," and how inspectors' "reports do not contend that weapons of mass destruction remain in Iraq." Blix did not acknowledge that large-scale production of prohibited weapons is extremely unlikely while Iraq sits in the full glare of international scrutiny. But the negative findings of inspectors inside Iraq—who have investigated all the sites named by the U.S. and Britain as potential weapons production facilities—imply that the Iraqi threat is, at least, contained.

Seizing Upon Ambiguity

But the overt goal of the Security Council—containing Iraq—has been abandoned by the U.S., most clearly in Bush's National Security Strategy launched in September 2002. The Bush team argues that even a contained Iraq can equip terrorists. Further, administration officials have explicitly articulated regime change and enhanced control over the Persian Gulf region as U.S. policy goals. Naturally, the Bush administration cannot make their case for war internationally on this basis. But it does not need to.

Instead, the Bush team can also draw upon the nature of the inspectors' mandate to justify military action. As U.S. officials argue again and again, inspections have not verified Iraq's claims to have either destroyed its proscribed weapons or refrained from resuming their production. This line of argument dovetails with the inspections process: as Blix has repeatedly stated, under the terms of the Security Council resolutions, the burden of proof is on Iraq to demonstrate that it has disposed of the weapons stocks it held before 1991, and is not developing them again.

One day before Blix's update, Powell said at the World Economic Forum in Davos: "Where is the evidence—where is the evidence—that Iraq has destroyed the tens of thousands of liters of anthrax and botulinum we know it had before it expelled the previous inspectors? [. . .] We're talking about the most deadly things one can imagine, that can kill thousands, millions of people."

Blix has been more reticent about the "missing anthrax," but has said enough to appear to endorse the administration's point. In his update, the chief inspector referred to how anthrax "might still exist" in Iraq, though the maximum possible quantities he mentioned were less than a fifth of the alleged "stockpile" of anthrax Powell had adduced in December 2002. Inspectors have to account for the possibility that the "missing anthrax" might still exist, without pronouncing judgment upon how likely that is. Seizing upon this ambiguity, the Bush administration transforms a case for concern into a case for war.

Exhibit A: Anthrax

The confusion is between what Iraq could have produced before 1991, and what it actually did produce. Iraq could have produced considerably more biological agents than it declared if, firstly, all of Iraq's claims to have lost, damaged and destroyed growth media were untrue; and, furthermore, if its claim that its fermentors (turning the growth media into weaponizable agents) were not used for certain periods of time was also untrue. Taking the maximalist position that Iraq could have fully utilized all imported growth media, without any failed or destroyed batches, and engaged its fermentors at top production continuously, UNSCOM stated in its January 1999 report that Iraq could have produced three times as many anthrax spores as it declared.

UNSCOM's calculation used a figure of 520 kg of yeast extract that was unaccounted for. This seemingly large quantity amounts to less than 11 percent of the total amount of yeast extract destroyed under UNSCOM supervision in 1996 (4,942 kg). The Iraqi government claimed that it unilaterally destroyed a quantity of growth media at a site adjacent to al-Hakam prior to the arrival of inspectors in 1991. This explanation holds some credibility, as UNSCOM was able to conclude that it "confirmed that media was burnt and buried there but the types and quantities are not known," and thus could not reduce the quantity of material still classified as unaccounted for. Therefore, whether the quantity of unaccounted-for material is within a reasonable error margin—particularly given that UNSCOM acknowledged its understanding of Iraq's destruction of its weapons in 1991 was of "considerable uncertainty"—is itself open to question. Nevertheless, it is impossible for UNMOVIC to come to a firm conclusion on this matter, leaving the way open for the Bush administration to allege that Iraq still holds a deadly stockpile.

One further problem with the U.S. argument is that any anthrax spores produced before 1991 would probably no longer be infectious. As Middle East military expert Anthony Cordesman of the Center for Strategic and International Studies wrote in a 1998 report on the status of Iraq's biological weapons programs, "the shelf-life and lethality of Iraq's weapons is unknown, but it seems likely that the shelf-life was limited. In balance, it seems probable that any agents Iraq retained after the Gulf war now have very limited lethality, if any." Even if Iraq did retain growth media for biological weapons, that growth media would long since have passed its expiry date by 1999, and would thus have a markedly reduced efficiency in producing biological agents.

Absence of Evidence

Other known aspects of the U.S.-British case for Iraqi non-compliance are similarly flawed. Allegations by Bush and British Prime Minister Tony Blair about rebuilt facilities at former nuclear sites have been effectively quashed through IAEA inspections. The U.S. claimed that Iraq was importing aluminium tubes to use in enrichment centrifuges. The IAEA has provisionally concluded that these were used to produce short-range rockets. U.S. and British claims that Iraq had attempted to import uranium from Africa have not been substantiated by the two governments, despite numerous requests from the IAEA. It seems most likely that the reference was to an attempt in 1981–82 to import uranium from Niger.*

Claims about Iraq's retention of stocks of VX nerve agent—invoked by National Security Adviser Condoleezza Rice in her January 23 op-ed in *The New York Times*—seem dubious. From 1997, UNSCOM repeatedly confirmed Iraq's claim that it had dumped its stock of VX by taking samples from the dump site. Despite the evidence of destruction, it was not able to verify the quantity of material dumped. Sites that the U.S. and Britain alleged were involved in the production of biological or chemical weapons have been repeatedly inspected by UNMOVIC. These include Falluja II, at which inspectors found the chlorine plant at the focus of concern not even in operation, and al-Dawra Foot and Mouth Disease Vaccine Facility, which appeared to journalists as having not been reconstructed since its destruction in the mid-1990s. The inspectors have not reported any evidence of the production of proscribed agents at any of these sites.

In the face of the declining credibility of U.S. claims about particular weapons programs, the Bush team has reverted to claiming that the Iraqi gov-

---

* Editors' note: As previously noted, the U.N.'s chief nuclear weapons inspector, Mohamed ElBaradei, reported on March 7, 2003 that documents supposedly showing Iraqi officials shopping for uranium from Niger were "not authentic."

ernment is inherently untrustworthy, exhibit A being Iraq's failure to unconditionally fulfill all the obligations mandated by UNSC 1441. Clearly, the Iraqis government was highly secretive about its weapons programs since the inception of the inspections process. From the 1980s, the Iraqi economy was built around the military and its ambitious development. Exposing all past activities to inspections runs up against entrenched hostility. But the habits of secrecy are not the same as continuing programs of illicit armament.

U.S. reliance on claims about full and unconditional compliance with UNSC 1441 rather than about disarmament per se demonstrates that the claim of Iraq's threat is becoming increasingly hard to justify. Throughout the period in which inspections made substantial progress from 1992 to 1997, the Clinton administration labeled extensive though incomplete compliance as non-compliance. This strategy was taken a step further by the White House spokesman on the morning of Blix's update, who reaffirmed that compliance must be absolute. "If the answer is only partially yes, then the answer is no," he said.

Survival Strategy

The British government has claimed that the Iraqi government structures its identity around non-conventional weapons. There is no evidence for this, and it seems highly unlikely. The Iraqi government has long had a survivalist strategy, by projecting an image of strength exercised to the patrimonial benefit of its support base. This strategy has served the government well, with only the briefest of hiatuses, as when Iran retook Abadan in September 1981 and made the government's terrible miscalculation to launch war against Iran apparent.

It is not at all apparent how the retention of proscribed weapons could serve this survivalist strategy. If inspectors uncover non-conventional programs, then this would lead to the government's ouster. From 1999–2002, Iraq pushed at boundaries only indirectly related to the proscribed weapons. Iraqi weapons program personnel extended the al-Samoud missile range and imported missile engines and raw material to produce solid missile fuel. The Iraqi government acknowledged these transgressions in its December 7 declaration, and since this date has agreed to halt these programs.

Instead, the Iraqi government has sought to reinforce its image by rewarding the citizenry. Examples include the prison releases of October 2002, the doubling of the food ration, extensive resource distribution through tribal networks and the prospect of political reforms. This tactic of purported munificence has been used previously by the Iraqi government, most notably in 1991 in the wake of the Iraqi uprisings. Then, the benefits were withdrawn as soon as the hold of the loyalist military was secured over south and central Iraq. The May 1991 program of political liberalization was reversed and forgotten by September.

The survivalist approach of the Iraqi government has been most manifest in its cooperation with inspectors. The relative luxury enjoyed by the regime in the 1990s—hindering inspectors while fearing no more than further justification for the continuation of economic sanctions—no longer exists. The regime's cooperation may be insincere, or "given grudgingly" in Blix's words. The key question is not whether this grudging cooperation fits the formal requirement of unconditional compliance with UNSC 1441, but whether it will lead to the effective disarmament of Iraq.

IRAQ HAS NO INTEREST IN WAR

Saddam Hussein (Interview with Tony Benn)

On February 4, 2003, Saddam Hussein granted an interview to former British Labour cabinet minister Tony Benn. Benn, a lifelong campaigner for peace, had traveled to Baghdad to talk to Hussein in the hopes that, as Benn himself phrased it, the Iraqi leader might say "something helpful and positive" that could help avoid a war. The television interview, the first Saddam had granted since the Persian Gulf War in 1991, was broadcast through the auspices of Associated Press Television News. Saddam's response to Benn's question about his "difficulties" with the U.N. inspectors is excerpted below.

"Iraq has no interest in war. No Iraqi official or ordinary citizen has expressed a wish to go to war. The question should be directed at the other side. Are they looking for a pretext so they could justify war against Iraq? If the purpose was to make sure that Iraq is free of nuclear, chemical and biological weapons then they can do that. These weapons do not come in small pills that you can hide in your pocket. These are weapons of mass destruction and it is easy to work out if Iraq has them or not. We have said many times before and we say it again today that Iraq is free of such weapons. So when Iraq objects to the conduct of the inspection teams or others, that doesn't mean that Iraq is interested in putting obstacles before them which could hinder the efforts to get to the truth. It is in our interest to facilitate their mission to find the truth. The question is does the other side want to get to the same conclusion or are they looking for a pretext for aggression? If those concerned prefer aggression then it's within their reach. The superpowers can create a pretext any day to claim that Iraq is not implementing resolution 1441. They have claimed before that Iraq did not implement the previous resolutions. However after many years it became clear that Iraq had complied with these resolutions. Otherwise, why are they focusing now on the latest resolution and not the previous ones?"

PRESENTATION TO THE U.N. SECURITY COUNCIL: A THREAT TO INTERNATIONAL PEACE AND SECURITY

Secretary of State Colin Powell

The following is an abridged transcript of Secretary of State Colin L. Powell's presentation, on Thursday, February 6, 2003, to the United Nations Security Council.

I asked for this session today for two purposes: First, to support the core assessments made by Dr. Blix and Dr. ElBaradei. As Dr. Blix reported to this council on January 27, quote, "Iraq appears not to have come to a genuine acceptance, not even today, of the disarmament which was demanded of it," unquote.

And as Dr. ElBaradei reported, Iraq's declaration of December 7, quote, "did not provide any new information relevant to certain questions that have been outstanding since 1998."

My second purpose today is to provide you with additional information, to share with you what the United States knows about Iraq's weapons of mass destruction as well as Iraq's involvement in terrorism, which is also the subject of Resolution 1441 and other earlier resolutions.

I might add at this point that we are providing all relevant information we can to the inspection teams for them to do their work.

The material I will present to you comes from a variety of sources. Some are U.S. sources. And some are those of other countries. Some of the sources are technical, such as intercepted telephone conversations and photos taken by satellites. Other sources are people who have risked their lives to let the world know what Saddam Hussein is really up to.

I cannot tell you everything that we know. But what I can share with you,

Colin Powell is the U.S. Secretary of State. He was a professional soldier for 35 years, rising to the rank of four-star general. From 1989 to 1993, he served as chairman of the Joint Chiefs of Staff, the highest military position in the Department of Defense, during which time he oversaw Operation Desert Storm in the 1991 Persian Gulf War. He is the recipient of two Presidential Medals of Freedom, and is the author of a bestselling autobiography, *My American Journey*, published in 1995.

when combined with what all of us have learned over the years, is deeply troubling.

What you will see is an accumulation of facts and disturbing patterns of behavior. The facts on Iraqis' behavior—Iraq's behavior—demonstrate that Saddam Hussein and his regime have made no effort—no effort—to disarm as required by the international community. Indeed, the facts and Iraq's behavior show that Saddam Hussein and his regime are concealing their efforts to produce more weapons of mass destruction.

Let me begin by playing a tape for you. What you're about to hear is a conversation that my government monitored. It takes place on November 26 of last year, on the day before United Nations teams resumed inspections in Iraq.

The conversation involves two senior officers, a colonel and a brigadier general, from Iraq's elite military unit, the Republican Guard.

(BEGIN AUDIOTAPE) Speaking in Arabic.

(END AUDIOTAPE) Powell: Let me pause and review some of the key elements of this conversation that you just heard between these two officers.

First, they acknowledge that our colleague, Mohamed ElBaradei, is coming, and they know what he's coming for, and they know he's coming the next day. He's coming to look for things that are prohibited. He is expecting these gentlemen to cooperate with him and not hide things.

But they're worried. "We have this modified vehicle. What do we say if one of them sees it?"

What is their concern? Their concern is that it's something they should not have, something that should not be seen.

The general is incredulous: "You didn't get a modified. You don't have one of those, do you?"

"I have one."

"Which, from where?"

"From the workshop, from the al-Kindi company?"

"What?"

"From al-Kindi."

"I'll come to see you in the morning . . . I'm worried you all have something left."

"We evacuated everything. We don't have anything left."

Note what he says: "We evacuated everything."

We didn't destroy it. We didn't line it up for inspection. We didn't turn it in to the inspectors. We evacuated it to make sure it was not around when the inspectors showed up.

"I will come to you tomorrow."

The al-Kindi company: This is a company that is well-known to have been involved in prohibited weapons systems activity.

[. . . .]

This effort to hide things from the inspectors is not one or two isolated events—quite the contrary. This is part and parcel of a policy of evasion and deception that goes back 12 years, a policy set at the highest levels of the Iraqi regime.

We know that Saddam Hussein has what is called, quote, "a higher committee for monitoring the inspections teams," unquote. Think about that. Iraq has a high-level committee to monitor the inspectors who were sent in to monitor Iraq's disarmament.

Not to cooperate with them, not to assist them, but to spy on them and keep them from doing their jobs.

The committee reports directly to Saddam Hussein. It is headed by Iraq's vice president, Taha Yassin Ramadan. Its members include Saddam Hussein's son Qusay.

This committee also includes Lieutenant General Amir al-Saadi, an adviser to Saddam. In case that name isn't immediately familiar to you, General Saadi has been the Iraqi regime's primary point of contact for Dr. Blix and Dr. ElBaradei. It was General Saadi who last fall publicly pledged that Iraq was prepared to cooperate unconditionally with inspectors. Quite the contrary, Saadi's job is not to cooperate, it is to deceive; not to disarm, but to undermine the inspectors; not to support them, but to frustrate them and to make sure they learn nothing.

[. . . .]

Our sources tell us that, in some cases, the hard drives of computers at Iraqi weapons facilities were replaced. Who took the hard drives? Where did they go? What's being hidden? Why? There's only one answer to the why: to deceive, to hide, to keep from the inspectors.

Numerous human sources tell us that the Iraqis are moving, not just documents and hard drives, but weapons of mass destruction to keep them from being found by inspectors.

While we were here in this council chamber debating Resolution 1441 last fall, we know, we know from sources that a missile brigade outside Baghdad was dispersing rocket launchers and warheads containing biological warfare agents to various locations, distributing them to various locations in western Iraq. Most of the launchers and warheads have been hidden in large groves of palm trees and were to be moved every one to four weeks to escape detection.

We also have satellite photos that indicate that banned materials have recently been moved from a number of Iraqi weapons of mass destruction facilities.

Let me say a word about satellite images before I show a couple. The photos that I am about to show you are sometimes hard for the average person to interpret, hard for me. The painstaking work of photo analysis takes experts with years and years of experience, poring for hours and hours over light tables. But as I show you these images, I will try to capture and explain what they mean, what they indicate to our imagery specialists.

Let's look at one. This one is about a weapons munition facility, a facility that holds ammunition at a place called Taji. This is one of about 65 such facilities in Iraq. We know that this one has housed chemical munitions. In fact, this is where the Iraqis recently came up with the additional four chemical weapon shells.

Here, you see 15 munitions bunkers in yellow and red outlines. The four that are in red squares represent active chemical munitions bunkers.

How do I know that? How can I say that? Let me give you a closer look. Look at the image on the left. On the left is a close-up of one of the four chemical bunkers. The two arrows indicate the presence of sure signs that the bunkers are storing chemical munitions. The arrow at the top that says security points to a facility that is the signature item for this kind of bunker. Inside that facility are special guards and special equipment to monitor any leakage that might come out of the bunker.

The truck you also see is a signature item. It's a decontamination vehicle in case something goes wrong.

This is characteristic of those four bunkers. The special security facility and the decontamination vehicle will be in the area, if not at any one of them or one of the other, it is moving around those four, and it moves as it needed to move, as people are working in the different bunkers.

Now look at the picture on the right. You are now looking at two of those sanitized bunkers. The signature vehicles are gone, the tents are gone, it's been cleaned up, and it was done on the 22nd of December, as the U.N. inspection team is arriving, and you can see the inspection vehicles arriving in the lower portion of the picture on the right.

The bunkers are clean when the inspectors get there. They found nothing.

This sequence of events raises the worrisome suspicion that Iraq had been tipped off to the forthcoming inspections at Taji. As it did throughout the 1990s, we know that Iraq today is actively using its considerable intelligence capabilities to hide its illicit activities. From our sources, we know that inspectors are under constant surveillance by an army of Iraqi intelligence operatives. Iraq is relentlessly attempting to tap all of their communications, both voice and electronics.

I would call my colleagues' attention to the fine paper that the United Kingdom distributed yesterday, which describes in exquisite detail Iraqi deception activities.*

[. . . .]

Saddam Hussein and his regime are not just trying to conceal weapons, they're also trying to hide people. You know the basic facts. Iraq has not complied with its obligation to allow immediate, unimpeded, unrestricted and private access to all officials and other persons as required by Resolution 1441.

The regime only allows interviews with inspectors in the presence of an Iraqi official, a minder. The official Iraqi organization charged with facilitating inspections announced, announced publicly and announced ominously, that, quote, "Nobody is ready to leave Iraq to be interviewed."

Iraqi Vice President Ramadan accused the inspectors of conducting espionage, a veiled threat that anyone cooperating with U.N. inspectors was committing treason.

Iraq did not meet its obligations under 1441 to provide a comprehensive list of scientists associated with its weapons of mass destruction programs. Iraq's list was out of date and contained only about 500 names, despite the fact that UNSCOM had earlier put together a list of about 3,500 names.

Let me just tell you what a number of human sources have told us.

Saddam Hussein has directly participated in the effort to prevent interviews. In early December, Saddam Hussein had all Iraqi scientists warned of the serious consequences that they and their families would face if they revealed any sensitive information to the inspectors. They were forced to sign documents acknowledging that divulging information is punishable by death.

Saddam Hussein also said that scientists should be told not to agree to leave Iraq; anyone who agreed to be interviewed outside Iraq would be treated as a spy. This violates 1441.

In mid-November, just before the inspectors returned, Iraqi experts were ordered to report to the headquarters of the special security organization to receive counterintelligence training. The training focused on evasion methods, interrogation resistance techniques and how to mislead inspectors.

Ladies and gentlemen, these are not assertions. These are facts, corroborated by many sources, some of them sources of the intelligence services of other countries.

For example, in mid-December weapons experts at one facility were replaced by Iraqi intelligence agents who were to deceive inspectors about the work that was being done there.

---

* Editors' note: This paper was soon revealed to be largely plagiarized from the work of several graduate students, and based on dated sources. See pp. 479–481 for more details.

On orders from Saddam Hussein, Iraqi officials issued a false death certificate for one scientist, and he was sent into hiding.

In the middle of January, experts at one facility that was related to weapons of mass destruction, those experts had been ordered to stay home from work to avoid the inspectors. Workers from other Iraqi military facilities not engaged in illicit weapons projects were to replace the workers who'd been sent home. A dozen experts have been placed under house arrest, not in their own houses, but as a group at one of Saddam Hussein's guest houses. It goes on and on and on.

[. . .]

Let me now turn to those deadly weapons programs and describe why they are real and present dangers to the region and to the world.

First, biological weapons. We have talked frequently here about biological weapons. By way of introduction and history, I think there are just three quick points I need to make.

First, you will recall that it took UNSCOM four long and frustrating years to pry—to pry—an admission out of Iraq that it had biological weapons.

Second, when Iraq finally admitted having these weapons in 1995, the quantities were vast. Less than a teaspoon of dry anthrax. A little bit about this amount: This is just about the amount of a teaspoon—less than a teaspoonful of dry anthrax in an envelope shut down the United States Senate in the fall of 2001. This forced several hundred people to undergo emergency medical treatment and killed two postal workers just from an amount about this quantity that was inside of an envelope.

Iraq declared 8,500 liters of anthrax, but UNSCOM estimates that Saddam Hussein could have produced 25,000 liters. If concentrated into this dry form, this amount would be enough to fill tens upon tens upon tens of thousands of teaspoons. And Saddam Hussein has not verifiably accounted for even one teaspoonful of this deadly material.

And that is my third point. And it is key. The Iraqis have never accounted for all of the biological weapons they admitted they had and we know they had. They have never accounted for all the organic material used to make them. And they have not accounted for many of the weapons filled with these agents, such as their 400 bombs. This is evidence, not conjecture. This is true. This is all well-documented.

Dr. Blix told this council that Iraq has provided little evidence to verify anthrax production and no convincing evidence of its destruction. It should come as no shock, then, that since Saddam Hussein forced out the last inspectors in 1998, we have amassed much intelligence indicating that Iraq is continuing to make these weapons.

One of the most worrisome things that emerges from the thick intelligence file we have on Iraq's biological weapons is the existence of mobile production facilities used to make biological agents.

Let me take you inside that intelligence file and share with you what we know from eyewitness accounts. We have firsthand descriptions of biological weapons factories on wheels and on rails.

The trucks and train cars are easily moved and are designed to evade detection by inspectors. In a matter of months, they can produce a quantity of biological poison equal to the entire amount that Iraq claimed to have produced in the years prior to the Gulf War.

Although Iraq's mobile production program began in the mid-1990s, U.N. inspectors at the time only had vague hints of such programs. Confirmation came later, in the year 2000.

The source was an eyewitness, an Iraqi chemical engineer who supervised one of these facilities. He actually was present during biological agent production runs. He was also at the site when an accident occurred in 1998. Twelve technicians died from exposure to biological agents.

He reported that when UNSCOM was in the country and inspecting, the biological weapons agent production always began on Thursdays at midnight because Iraq thought UNSCOM would not inspect on the Muslim holy day, Thursday night through Friday. He added that this was important because the units could not be broken down in the middle of a production run, which had to be completed by Friday evening before the inspectors might arrive again.

This defector is currently hiding in another country with the certain knowledge that Saddam Hussein will kill him if he finds him. His eyewitness account of these mobile production facilities has been corroborated by other sources.

A second source, an Iraqi civil engineer in a position to know the details of the program, confirmed the existence of transportable facilities moving on trailers.

A third source, also in a position to know, reported in summer 2002 that Iraq had manufactured mobile production systems mounted on road trailer units and on rail cars.

Finally, a fourth source, an Iraqi major who defected, confirmed that Iraq has mobile biological research laboratories, in addition to the production facilities I mentioned earlier.

[. . . .]

In 1995, an Iraqi military officer, Mujahid Sali Abdul Latif, told inspectors that Iraq intended the spray tanks to be mounted onto a MiG-21 that had been converted into an unmanned aerial vehicle, or a UAV. UAVs outfitted with spray tanks constitute an ideal method for launching a terrorist attack using biological weapons.

Iraq admitted to producing four spray tanks. But to this day, it has provided no credible evidence that they were destroyed, evidence that was required by the international community.

There can be no doubt that Saddam Hussein has biological weapons and the capability to rapidly produce more, many more. And he has the ability to dispense these lethal poisons and diseases in ways that can cause massive death and destruction. If biological weapons seem too terrible to contemplate, chemical weapons are equally chilling.

UNMOVIC already laid out much of this, and it is documented for all of us to read in UNSCOM's 1999 report on the subject.

Let me set the stage with three key points that all of us need to keep in mind: First, Saddam Hussein has used these horrific weapons on another country and on his own people. In fact, in the history of chemical warfare, no country has had more battlefield experience with chemical weapons since World War I than Saddam Hussein's Iraq.

Second, as with biological weapons, Saddam Hussein has never accounted for vast amounts of chemical weaponry: 550 artillery shells with mustard, 30,000 empty munitions and enough precursors to increase his stockpile to as much as 500 tons of chemical agents. If we consider just one category of missing weaponry—6,500 bombs from the Iran-Iraq war—UNMOVIC says the amount of chemical agent in them would be in the order of 1,000 tons. These quantities of chemical weapons are now unaccounted for.

Dr. Blix has quipped that, quote, "Mustard gas is not marmalade. You are supposed to know what you did with it."

We believe Saddam Hussein knows what he did with it, and he has not come clean with the international community. We have evidence these weapons existed. What we don't have is evidence from Iraq that they have been destroyed or where they are. That is what we are still waiting for.

[. . . .]

Just a few weeks ago, we intercepted communications between two commanders in Iraq's Second Republican Guard Corps. One commander is going to be giving an instruction to the other. You will hear as this unfolds that what he wants to communicate to the other guy, he wants to make sure the other guy hears clearly, to the point of repeating it so that it gets written down and completely understood. Listen.

(BEGIN AUDIOTAPE) Speaking in foreign language.

(END AUDIOTAPE) Powell: Let's review a few selected items of this conversation. Two officers talking to each other on the radio want to make sure that nothing is misunderstood:

"Remove. Remove."

The expression, the expression, "I got it."

"Nerve agents. Nerve agents. Wherever it comes up."

"Got it."

"Wherever it comes up."

"In the wireless instructions, in the instructions."

"Correction. No. In the wireless instructions."

"Wireless. I got it."

Why does he repeat it that way? Why is he so forceful in making sure this is understood? And why did he focus on wireless instructions? Because the senior officer is concerned that somebody might be listening.

Well, somebody was.

"Nerve agents. Stop talking about it. They are listening to us. Don't give any evidence that we have these horrible agents."

Well, we know that they do. And this kind of conversation confirms it.

Our conservative estimate is that Iraq today has a stockpile of between 100 and 500 tons of chemical weapons agent. That is enough agent to fill 16,000 battlefield rockets.

Even the low end of 100 tons of agent would enable Saddam Hussein to cause mass casualties across more than 100 square miles of territory, an area nearly five times the size of Manhattan.

[. . . .]

Let me turn now to nuclear weapons. We have no indication that Saddam Hussein has ever abandoned his nuclear weapons program.

On the contrary, we have more than a decade of proof that he remains determined to acquire nuclear weapons.

[. . . .]

Since 1998, his efforts to reconstitute his nuclear program have been focused on acquiring the third and last component, sufficient fissile material to produce a nuclear explosion. To make the fissile material, he needs to develop an ability to enrich uranium.

Saddam Hussein is determined to get his hands on a nuclear bomb. He is so determined that he has made repeated covert attempts to acquire high-specification aluminum tubes from 11 different countries, even after inspections resumed.

These tubes are controlled by the Nuclear Suppliers Group precisely because they can be used as centrifuges for enriching uranium. By now, just about everyone has heard of these tubes, and we all know that there are differences of opinion. There is controversy about what these tubes are for.

Most U.S. experts think they are intended to serve as rotors in centrifuges used to enrich uranium. Other experts, and the Iraqis themselves, argue that they are really to produce the rocket bodies for a conventional weapon, a multiple rocket launcher.

Let me tell you what is not controversial about these tubes. First, all the experts who have analyzed the tubes in our possession agree that they can be adapted for centrifuge use. Second, Iraq had no business buying them for any purpose. They are banned for Iraq.

I am no expert on centrifuge tubes, but just as an old Army trooper, I can tell you a couple of things: First, it strikes me as quite odd that these tubes are manufactured to a tolerance that far exceeds U.S. requirements for comparable rockets. Maybe Iraqis just manufacture their conventional weapons to a higher standard than we do, but I don't think so.

Second, we actually have examined tubes from several different batches that were seized clandestinely before they reached Baghdad. What we notice in these different batches is a progression to higher and higher levels of specification, including, in the latest batch, an anodized coating on extremely smooth inner and outer surfaces. Why would they continue refining the specifications, go to all that trouble for something that, if it was a rocket, would soon be blown into shrapnel when it went off?

The high-tolerance aluminum tubes are only part of the story. We also have intelligence from multiple sources that Iraq is attempting to acquire magnets and high-speed balancing machines; both items can be used in a gas centrifuge program to enrich uranium.

In 1999 and 2000, Iraqi officials negotiated with firms in Romania, India, Russia and Slovenia for the purchase of a magnet production plant. Iraq wanted the plant to produce magnets weighing 20 to 30 grams. That's the same weight as the magnets used in Iraq's gas centrifuge program before the Gulf War. This incident linked with the tubes is another indicator of Iraq's attempt to reconstitute its nuclear weapons program.

Intercepted communications from mid-2000 through last summer show that Iraq front companies sought to buy machines that can be used to balance gas centrifuge rotors. One of these companies also had been involved in a failed effort in 2001 to smuggle aluminum tubes into Iraq.

People will continue to debate this issue, but there is no doubt in my mind, these illicit procurement efforts show that Saddam Hussein is very much focused on putting in place the key missing piece from his nuclear weapons program, the ability to produce fissile material.

[. . . .]

My friends, the information I have presented to you about these terrible weapons and about Iraq's continued flaunting of its obligations under Security Council Resolution 1441 links to a subject I now want to spend a little bit of time on. And that has to do with terrorism.

Our concern is not just about these illicit weapons. It's the way that these illicit weapons can be connected to terrorists and terrorist organizations that have no compunction about using such devices against innocent people around the world.

Iraq and terrorism go back decades. Baghdad trains Palestine Liberation Front members in small arms and explosives. Saddam uses the Arab Liberation Front to funnel money to the families of Palestinian suicide bombers in order to prolong the intifada. And it's no secret that Saddam's own intelligence service was involved in dozens of attacks or attempted assassinations in the 1990s.

But what I want to bring to your attention today is the potentially much more sinister nexus between Iraq and the al Qaeda terrorist network, a nexus that combines classic terrorist organizations and modern methods of murder. Iraq today harbors a deadly terrorist network headed by Abu Musab Al-Zarqawi, an associated collaborator of Osama bin Laden and his al Qaeda lieutenants.

Zarqawi, a Palestinian born in Jordan, fought in the Afghan war more than a decade ago. Returning to Afghanistan in 2000, he oversaw a terrorist training camp. One of his specialties and one of the specialties of this camp is poisons. When our coalition ousted the Taliban, the Zarqawi network helped establish another poison and explosive training center camp. And this camp is located in northeastern Iraq.

You see a picture of this camp.

The network is teaching its operatives how to produce ricin and other poisons. Let me remind you how ricin works. Less than a pinch—imagine a pinch of salt—less than a pinch of ricin, eating just this amount in your food, would cause shock followed by circulatory failure. Death comes within 72 hours and there is no antidote, there is no cure. It is fatal.

Those helping to run this camp are Zarqawi lieutenants operating in northern Kurdish areas outside Saddam Hussein's controlled Iraq. But Baghdad has an agent in the most senior levels of the radical organization, Ansar al-Islam, that controls this corner of Iraq. In 2000 this agent offered al Qaeda safe haven in the region. After we swept al Qaeda from Afghanistan, some of its members accepted this safe haven. They remain there today.

Zarqawi's activities are not confined to this small corner of northeast Iraq. He traveled to Baghdad in May 2002 for medical treatment, staying in the capital of Iraq for two months while he recuperated to fight another day.

During this stay, nearly two dozen extremists converged on Baghdad and established a base of operations there. These al Qaeda affiliates, based in Baghdad, now coordinate the movement of people, money and supplies into and throughout Iraq for his network, and they've now been operating freely in the capital for more than eight months.

Iraqi officials deny accusations of ties with al Qaeda. These denials are simply not credible. Last year an al Qaeda associate bragged that the situation in Iraq was, quote, "good," that Baghdad could be transited quickly.

We know these affiliates are connected to Zarqawi because they remain even today in regular contact with his direct subordinates, including the poison cell plotters, and they are involved in moving more than money and material.

Last year, two suspected al Qaeda operatives were arrested crossing from Iraq into Saudi Arabia. They were linked to associates of the Baghdad cell, and one of them received training in Afghanistan on how to use cyanide. From his terrorist network in Iraq, Zarqawi can direct his network in the Middle East and beyond.

We, in the United States, all of us at the State Department, and the Agency for International Development—we all lost a dear friend with the cold-blooded murder of Mr. Lawrence Foley in Amman, Jordan, last October. A despicable act was committed that day: The assassination of an individual whose sole mission was to assist the people of Jordan. The captured assassin says his cell received money and weapons from Zarqawi for that murder.

After the attack, an associate of the assassin left Jordan to go to Iraq to obtain weapons and explosives for further operations. Iraqi officials protest that they are not aware of the whereabouts of Zarqawi or of any of his associates. Again, these protests are not credible. We know of Zarqawi's activities in Baghdad. I described them earlier.

And now let me add one other fact. We asked a friendly security service to approach Baghdad about extraditing Zarqawi and providing information about him and his close associates. This service contacted Iraqi officials twice, and we passed details that should have made it easy to find Zarqawi. The network remains in Baghdad. Zarqawi still remains at large to come and go.

[. . . .]

We are not surprised that Iraq is harboring Zarqawi and his subordinates. This understanding builds on decades-long experience with respect to ties between Iraq and al Qaeda.

Going back to the early and mid-1990s, when bin Laden was based in Sudan, an al Qaeda source tells us that Saddam and bin Laden reached an understanding that al Qaeda would no longer support activities against Baghdad. Early al Qaeda ties were forged by secret, high-level intelligence service contacts with al Qaeda, secret Iraqi intelligence high-level contacts with al Qaeda.

We know members of both organizations met repeatedly and have met at least eight times at very senior levels since the early 1990s. In 1996, a foreign security service tells us that bin Laden met with a senior Iraqi intelligence official in Khartoum, and later met the director of the Iraqi intelligence service.

Saddam became more interested as he saw al Qaeda's appalling attacks. A detained al Qaeda member tells us that Saddam was more willing to assist al Qaeda after the 1998 bombings of our embassies in Kenya and Tanzania. Saddam was also impressed by al Qaeda's attacks on the USS *Cole* in Yemen in October 2000.

Iraqis continued to visit bin Laden in his new home in Afghanistan. A senior defector, one of Saddam's former intelligence chiefs in Europe, says Saddam sent his agents to Afghanistan sometime in the mid-1990s to provide training to al Qaeda members on document forgery.

From the late 1990s until 2001, the Iraqi Embassy in Pakistan played the role of liaison to the al Qaeda organization.

Some believe, some claim these contacts do not amount to much. They say Saddam Hussein's secular tyranny and al Qaeda's religious tyranny do not mix. I am not comforted by this thought. Ambition and hatred are enough to bring Iraq and al Qaeda together, enough so al Qaeda could learn how to build more sophisticated bombs and learn how to forge documents, and enough so that al Qaeda could turn to Iraq for help in acquiring expertise on weapons of mass destruction.

[. . . .]

We know that Saddam Hussein is determined to keep his weapons of mass destruction; he's determined to make more. Given Saddam Hussein's history of aggression, given what we know of his grandiose plans, given what we know of his terrorist associations and given his determination to exact revenge on those who oppose him, should we take the risk that he will not someday use these weapons at a time and the place and in the manner of his choosing at a time when the world is in a much weaker position to respond?

The United States will not and cannot run that risk to the American people. Leaving Saddam Hussein in possession of weapons of mass destruction for a few more months or years is not an option, not in a post-September 11 world.

My colleagues, over three months ago this council recognized that Iraq continued to pose a threat to international peace and security, and that Iraq had been and remained in material breach of its disarmament obligations. Today Iraq still poses a threat and Iraq still remains in material breach.

Indeed, by its failure to seize on its one last opportunity to come clean and disarm, Iraq has put itself in deeper material breach and closer to the day when it will face serious consequences for its continued defiance of this council.

My colleagues, we have an obligation to our citizens, we have an obligation to this body to see that our resolutions are complied with. We wrote 1441 not in order to go to war, we wrote 1441 to try to preserve the peace. We wrote 1441 to give Iraq one last chance. Iraq is not so far taking that one last chance.

We must not shrink from whatever is ahead of us. We must not fail in our duty and our responsibility to the citizens of the countries that are represented by this body.

M16 AND CIA:
THE NEW ENEMY WITHIN

Paul Lashmar and Raymond Whitaker

Tony Blair and George Bush are encountering an unexpected obstacle in their campaign for war against Iraq: their own intelligence agencies.

Britain and America's spies believe that they are being politicised: that the intelligence they provide is being selectively applied to lead to the opposite conclusion from the one they have drawn, which is that Iraq is much less of a threat than their political masters claim. Worse, when the intelligence agencies fail to do the job, the politicians will not stop at plagiarism to make their case, even "tweaking" the plagiarised material to ensure a better fit.

"You cannot just cherry-pick evidence that suits your case and ignore the rest. It is a cardinal rule of intelligence," said one aggrieved officer. "Yet that is what the PM is doing." Not since Harold Wilson has a Prime Minister been so unpopular with his top spies.

The mounting tension is mirrored in Washington. "We've gone from a zero position, where presidents refused to cite detailed intel as a source, to the point now where partisan material is being officially attributed to these agencies," said one U.S. intelligence source.

Mr. Blair is facing an unprecedented, if covert, rebellion by his top spies, who last week used the politicians' own weapon—the strategic leak—against him. The BBC received a Defence Intelligence Staff (DIS) document which showed that British intelligence believes there are no current links between the Iraqi regime and the al-Qa'ida network. The classified document, written last month, said there had been contact between the two in the past, but it assessed that any fledging relationship foundered due to mistrust and incompatible ideologies.

That conclusion contradicted one of the main charges laid against Saddam Hussein by the United States and Britain, most notably in Wednesday's speech by the Secretary of State, Colin Powell, to the U.N. Security Coun-

Paul Lashmar is an investigative reporter, author and television producer. In 1986, while on the staff of *The Observer*, he was honored as Reporter of the Year by the United Kingdom Press Awards.

Raymond Whitaker is a reporter for *The Independent*, based in London.

This article was originally published in *The Independent* on February 9, 2003.

cil—that he has cultivated contacts with the group blamed for the 11 September attacks.

Such a leak of up-to-date and sensitive material reveals the depth of anger within Britain's spy community over the misuse of intelligence by Downing Street. "A DIS document like this is highly secret. Whoever leaked it must have been quite senior and had unofficial approval from within the highest levels of British intelligence," said one insider. In response the Foreign Secretary, Jack Straw, tried to play down the importance of the DIS, which he repeatedly called the Defence Intelligence Services.

No sooner had that embarrassment passed, however, than it emerged that large chunks of the Government's latest dossier on Iraq, which claimed to draw on "intelligence material," were taken from published academic articles, some of them several years old. It was this recycled material that Mr. Powell held up in front of a worldwide television audience, saying: "I would call my colleagues' attention to the fine paper that the United Kingdom distributed . . . which describes in exquisite detail Iraqi deception activities."

Now Glen Rangwala, the Cambridge University analyst who blew the whistle on the original plagiarism, has pointed out the deception did not end there. He showed that the young Downing Street team, led by Alison Blackshaw, Alastair Campbell's personal assistant, which put the document together had "hardened" the language in several places.

How selectively the work of the intelligence agencies is being used on both sides of the Atlantic is shown by a revealing clash between Senator Bob Graham and the Bush administration's top intelligence advisers. Mr. Graham, a Democrat, is chair of the Senate Intelligence Committee. Last July, baffled by the apparently contradictory assessments on Iraq by America's 13 different intelligence agencies, he asked for a report to be drawn up by the CIA that estimated the likelihood of Saddam Hussein using weapons of mass destruction.

The CIA procrastinated, but finally produced a report after Senator Graham threatened to accuse them of obstruction. The conclusions were so significant that he immediately asked for it to be declassified. The CIA concluded that the likelihood of Saddam Hussein using such weapons was "very low" for the "foreseeable future." The only circumstances in which Iraq would be more likely to use chemical weapons or encourage terrorist attacks would be if it was attacked.

After more arguments the CIA partly declassified the report. Senator Graham noted that the parts released were those that made the case for war with Iraq. Those that did not were withheld. He appealed, and the extra material was eventually released. Yet the report has largely been ignored by the U.S. media.

Last week Colin Powell made much of the presence in Iraq of Abu Musab al-Zarqawi, the man he identified as running an al-Qa'ida network from Baghdad. He drew on information from al-Zarqawi's captured deputy, but made no mention of another explosive allegation from the same detainee: that Osama bin Laden's organisation received passports and $1m (£600,000) in cash from a member of the royal family in Qatar. It is well known in U.S. intelligence circles that the CIA director, George Tenet, is angry with the Qatari government's failure to take action. But the Gulf state would be the main U.S. air operations base in any war on Iraq, and Washington does not want to air the inconvenient facts in public.

The Doctored Dossier

A British government dossier, "Iraq—its infrastructure of concealment, deception and intimidation," was largely copied—complete with poor punctuation and grammar—from an article in last September's *Middle East Review of International Affairs* and two articles in *Jane's Intelligence Review*.

But the Downing Street compilers also rounded up the numbers and inserted stronger language than in the original. In a section on a movement called Fedayeen Saddam, members are, according to the original, "recruited from regions loyal to Saddam." The Government dossier says they are "press-ganged from regions known to be loyal to Saddam."

On Fedayeen Saddam's total membership, the original says 18,000 to 40,000. The dossier says 30,000 to 40,000.

A similar bumping-up of figures occurs with the description of the Directorate of Military Intelligence.

Included among the duties of the secret police, the Mukhabarat, says the original, are "monitoring foreign embassies in Iraq" and "aiding opposition groups in hostile regimes." The dossier says the duties include "spying on foreign embassies in Iraq" and "supporting terrorist organisations in hostile regimes."

The plagiarists cannot even copy correctly, confusing two organisations called General Security and Military Security. This means that the dossier says Military Security was created in 1992, then refers to it moving to new headquarters in 1990. The head of Military Security in 1997 is named as Taha al-Ahbabi, when he was actually in charge of General Security.

"SLEEPWALKING THROUGH HISTORY"

Senator Robert Byrd

To contemplate war is to think about the most horrible of human experiences. On this February day, as this nation stands at the brink of battle, every American on some level must be contemplating the horrors of war.

Yet, this Chamber is, for the most part, silent—ominously, dreadfully silent. There is no debate, no discussion, no attempt to lay out for the nation the pros and cons of this particular war. There is nothing.

We stand passively mute in the United States Senate, paralyzed by our own uncertainty, seemingly stunned by the sheer turmoil of events. Only on the editorial pages of our newspapers is there much substantive discussion of the prudence or imprudence of engaging in this particular war.

And this is no small conflagration we contemplate. This is no simple attempt to defang a villain. No. This coming battle, if it materializes, represents a turning point in U.S. foreign policy and possibly a turning point in the recent history of the world.

This nation is about to embark upon the first test of a revolutionary doctrine applied in an extraordinary way at an unfortunate time. The doctrine of preemption—the idea that the United States or any other nation can legitimately attack a nation that is not imminently threatening but may be threatening in the future—is a radical new twist on the traditional idea of self defense. It appears to be in contravention of international law and the U.N. Charter. And it is being tested at a time of world-wide terrorism, making many countries around the globe wonder if they will soon be on our—or some other nation's—hit list. High level Administration figures recently refused to take nuclear weapons off of the table when discussing a possible attack against Iraq. What could be more destabilizing and unwise than this type of uncertainty, particularly in a world where globalism has tied the vital economic and security interests of many nations so closely together? There are huge cracks emerging in our time-honored alliances, and U.S. intentions are suddenly

Robert Byrd is the Democratic senator from West Virginia. He gave this speech on the Senate floor on February 12, 2003.

subject to damaging worldwide speculation. Anti-Americanism based on mistrust, misinformation, suspicion, and alarming rhetoric from U.S. leaders is fracturing the once solid alliance against global terrorism which existed after September 11.

Here at home, people are warned of imminent terrorist attacks with little guidance as to when or where such attacks might occur. Family members are being called to active military duty, with no idea of the duration of their stay or what horrors they may face. Communities are being left with less than adequate police and fire protection. Other essential services are also short-staffed. The mood of the nation is grim. The economy is stumbling. Fuel prices are rising and may soon spike higher.

This Administration, now in power for a little over two years, must be judged on its record. I believe that that record is dismal.

In that scant two years, this Administration has squandered a large projected surplus of some $5.6 trillion over the next decade and taken us to projected deficits as far as the eye can see. This Administration's domestic policy has put many of our states in dire financial condition, underfunding scores of essential programs for our people. This Administration has fostered policies which have slowed economic growth. This Administration has ignored urgent matters such as the crisis in health care for our elderly. This Administration has been slow to provide adequate funding for homeland security. This Administration has been reluctant to better protect our long and porous borders.

In foreign policy, this Administration has failed to find Osama bin Laden. In fact, just yesterday we heard from him again marshaling his forces and urging them to kill. This Administration has split traditional alliances, possibly crippling, for all time, international order-keeping entities like the United Nations and NATO. This Administration has called into question the traditional worldwide perception of the United States as well-intentioned peacekeeper. This Administration has turned the patient art of diplomacy into threats, labeling, and name calling of the sort that reflects quite poorly on the intelligence and sensitivity of our leaders, and which will have consequences for years to come.

Calling heads of state pygmies, labeling whole countries as evil, denigrating powerful European allies as irrelevant—these types of crude insensitivities can do our great nation no good. We may have massive military might, but we cannot fight a global war on terrorism alone. We need the cooperation and friendship of our time-honored allies as well as the newer found friends whom we can attract with our wealth. Our awesome military machine will do us little good if we suffer another devastating attack on our homeland which severely damages our economy. Our military manpower is already stretched thin and we will need the augmenting support of those nations who can supply troop strength, not just sign letters cheering us on.

The war in Afghanistan has cost us $37 billion so far, yet there is evidence that terrorism may already be starting to regain its hold in that region. We have not found bin Laden, and unless we secure the peace in Afghanistan, the dark dens of terrorism may yet again flourish in that remote and devastated land.

Pakistan as well is at risk of destabilizing forces. This Administration has not finished the first war against terrorism and yet it is eager to embark on another conflict with perils much greater than those in Afghanistan. Is our attention span that short? Have we not learned that after winning the war one must always secure the peace?

And yet we hear little about the aftermath of war in Iraq. In the absence of plans, speculation abroad is rife. Will we seize Iraq's oil fields, becoming an occupying power which controls the price and supply of that nation's oil for the foreseeable future? To whom do we propose to hand the reigns of power after Saddam Hussein?

Will our war inflame the Muslim world resulting in devastating attacks on Israel? Will Israel retaliate with its own nuclear arsenal? Will the Jordanian and Saudi Arabian governments be toppled by radicals, bolstered by Iran which has much closer ties to terrorism than Iraq?

Could a disruption of the world's oil supply lead to a world-wide recession? Has our senselessly bellicose language and our callous disregard of the interests and opinions of other nations increased the global race to join the nuclear club and made proliferation an even more lucrative practice for nations which need the income?

In only the space of two short years this reckless and arrogant Administration has initiated policies which may reap disastrous consequences for years.

One can understand the anger and shock of any President after the savage attacks of September 11. One can appreciate the frustration of having only a shadow to chase and an amorphous, fleeting enemy on which it is nearly impossible to exact retribution.

But to turn one's frustration and anger into the kind of extremely destabilizing and dangerous foreign policy debacle that the world is currently witnessing is inexcusable from any Administration charged with the awesome power and responsibility of guiding the destiny of the greatest superpower on the planet. Frankly many of the pronouncements made by this Administration are outrageous. There is no other word.

Yet this chamber is hauntingly silent. On what is possibly the eve of horrific infliction of death and destruction on the population of the nation of Iraq—a population, I might add, of which over 50% is under age 15 this chamber is silent. On what is possibly only days before we send thousands of our own citizens to face unimagined horrors of chemical and biological warfare—this chamber is silent. On the eve of what could possibly be a vicious terrorist attack in retaliation for our attack on Iraq, it is business as usual in the United States Senate.

We are truly "sleepwalking through history." In my heart of hearts I pray that this great nation and its good and trusting citizens are not in for a rudest of awakenings.

To engage in war is always to pick a wild card. And war must always be a last resort, not a first choice. I truly must question the judgment of any President who can say that a massive unprovoked military attack on a nation which is over 50% children is "in the highest moral traditions of our country." This war is not necessary at this time. Pressure appears to be having a good result in Iraq. Our mistake was to put ourselves in a corner so quickly. Our challenge is to now find a graceful way out of a box of our own making. Perhaps there is still a way if we allow more time.

THE SECOND SUPERPOWER

Micah L. Sifry

"Democracy is a beautiful thing . . . People are allowed to express their opinions, and I welcome people's right to say what they believe. . . . You know, size of protests—it's like deciding, 'Well, I'm going to decide policy based upon a focus group.' The role of a leader is to decide policy based upon the security, in this case, the security of the people."
> —President Bush, dismissing the impact of millions of people demonstrating worldwide against war with Iraq, February 18, 2003

On February 15, 2003, the antiwar movement went global. Millions of demonstrators stood on the streets of more than 300 cities. The numbers were undeniable:

2 million in London	100,000 in Brisbane
1.3 million in Barcelona	30,000–100,000 in Hollywood
1 million in Rome	70,000 in Amsterdam
800,000 in Madrid	80,000 in Toronto
100,000–500,000 in New York City	80,000 in Portugal
400,000 in Paris	60,000–75,000 in Seattle
250,000 in San Francisco	50,000 in Buenos Aires
250,000 in Sydney	50,000 in Athens
150,000 in Montreal	45,000 in Copenhagen
100,000–200,000 in Melbourne	even 50 in Antarctica
100,000 in Adelaide	

Afterward, in *The Guardian*, Madeleine Bunting wrote of that day in London: "There will be millions of people who will never forget Saturday February 15, 2003. It was an extraordinary combination of the utterly prosaic and the deeply moving: a bursting bladder and the nearest toilets several hours' walk away in Hyde Park, an aching back and blisters, and then the remarkable sight of a heaving mass of people along the Embankment converging with crowds

Micah L. Sifry is a coeditor of this book.

pouring across Waterloo bridge. Everywhere there were astonishing juxtapositions: the body-pierced peaceniks alongside the dignified Pakistani elder with white beard; the homemade placard 'The only bush I trust is my own' drawing surreptitious giggles from a group of veiled Muslim women.

"This was a day which confounded dozens of assumptions about our age. How much harder it is today than a week ago to speak of the apathy and selfish individualism of consumer society. Saturday brought the entire business of a capital city to a glorious full-stop. Not a car or bus moved in central London, the frenetic activities of shopping and spending halted across a wide swathe of the city; the streets became one vast vibrant civic space for an expression of national solidarity. Furthermore, unlike previous occasions when crowds have gathered, this was not to mark some royal pageantry, but to articulate an unfamiliar British sentiment—one of democratic entitlement: we are the people."

The swelling of street protests occurred at the same time as an unprecedented coalescing of opposition in two important social groups—labor and organized religion. In just a few weeks in January and February, a group called U.S. Labor Against the War (USLAW) gathered the backing of 11 national unions along with over a hundred regional and local organizations representing more than 4 million workers. And in just ten days, over 200 unions and 550 union leaders from 53 countries representing 130 million workers signed an International Labor Declaration circulated by USLAW and released on February 19. The declaration read, in part, "There is no evident purpose for this war that we can support. There is no convincing link between Iraq and Al Qaeda or the attacks on Sept. 11, and neither the Bush administration nor the UN inspections have demonstrated that Iraq poses a real threat to Americans and other nations. It is clear that military action in Iraq will actually increase the likelihood of retaliatory terrorist acts around the world against Western targets. This action against Iraq by the U.S. military and others nations that may join them, threatens the peaceful resolution of disputes among states, jeopardizing the safety and security of the entire world."

The AFL-CIO also passed a resolution opposing a unilateral invasion of Iraq, insisting that war must only be launched as a last resort. "America's working families and their unions fully support the efforts to disarm the dictatorial regime of Saddam Hussein," began the resolution. "This is best achieved in concert with a broad international coalition of allies and with the sanction of the United Nations. We believe there may be times when we must stand alone and act unilaterally in defense of our national security. But, in the context of the global war on terrorism, the threat posed by Saddam Hussein deserves multilateral resolve, not unilateral action."

After September 11, most of organized labor strongly supported the U.S. intervention in Afghanistan, in pursuit of Al Qaeda and the Taliban. And the union movement has a long history of patriotic, even jingoistic, support of American foreign policy, dating back to McCarthyism, red-baiting and the Cold War. Hardhats clashed with antiwar protestors during the Vietnam years. But with the exception of the Teamsters union, whose president James P. Hoffa backs the pro-administration Committee for the Liberation of Iraq, the new opposition in organized labor represents a significant shift in rank-and-file attitudes.

The same appeared to be occurring in the country's houses of worship. In addition to the Pope in Rome, who sent a personal envoy to meet with President Bush, many religious groups were voicing opposition to a unilateral strike on Iraq as well. As Laurie Goodstein reported in *The New York Times,* "The opposition goes far beyond such traditional 'peace churches' as the Mennonites, the Church of the Brethren and the Quakers. Among Christians, the opposition includes Roman Catholics and mainline Protestant and Orthodox churches. Churches whose leaders have gone on record arguing for restraint include the United Methodist Church; Presbyterian Church; Evangelical Lutheran Church in America; American Baptist Church; Christian Church (Disciples of Christ); United Church of Christ; the Greek Orthodox Archdiocese of America; the Syrian Orthodox Church of Antioch; and the Coptic Orthodox Archdiocese of America."

Goodstein noted, "There is support for a war among some leaders of large ministries and of conservative evangelical and Pentecostal churches, but little that is organized. Mr. Bush's policy has also received the backing of Richard Land, the influential president of the Ethics and Public Policy Commission of the Southern Baptist Convention, the nation's largest Protestant denomination. Among other faiths, Jewish organizations are split, with some Orthodox groups coming out unequivocally in favor of a pre-emptive strike without United Nations authorization. Some Muslim groups have voiced their opposition, as have small Buddhist organizations."

The pace of popular mobilization—which was undoubtedly aided by the networking power of the Internet and groups like MoveOn.org and United for Peace and Justice—surprised and heartened many veterans of past antiwar organizing. And all this popular ferment led Patrick Tyler to suggest, in *The New York Times,* that "there may still be two superpowers on the planet: the United States and world public opinion." Writing in mid-February 2003, he concluded, "For the moment, an exceptional phenomenon has appeared on the streets of world cities. It may not be as profound as the people's revolutions across Eastern Europe in 1989 or in Europe's class struggles of 1848, but politicians and leaders are unlikely to ignore it."

The question for the future, as a U.S.-led war against Iraq without the sanction of the U.N. Security Council has begun, is whether this antiwar sentiment will continue to develop into a broad-based and resilient force against American unilateralism. Twelve years ago, the American peace movement pretty much collapsed once the first Gulf War started, and any chance of promoting an alternate critique of American foreign policy was drowned in the patriotic euphoria that followed the successful eviction of the Iraqi army from Kuwait. The same could happen again, but the rift between the U.S. and the rest of the world, particularly Europe—along with the likelihood of terrible consequences once the bombs start falling—suggests otherwise.

Indeed, the presence of 100,000 to 200,000 people marching down Broadway in Manhattan on the Saturday after the war began was a sign that the antiwar movement was alive and kicking. But prowar rallies, many of them spontaneous and at least some of them organized and financed by Clear Channel Communications, a radio conglomerate with close ties to the Bush Administration, were also sprouting across America. Another battle for hearts and minds was under way, and it remains to be seen which superpower will win it.

THE YES-BUT PARADE

William Safire

After his resounding re-election in 1936, Franklin D. Roosevelt turned on the right wing of his Democratic Party. "He invented a new word," recalled his speech writer, Samuel Rosenman, "to describe the congressman who publicly approved a progressive objective but who always found something wrong with any specific proposal to gain that objective—a yes-but fellow."

In gaining the progressive objective of stripping a genocidal maniac of weapons capable of murdering millions, today's U.S. president is half-supported, half-obstructed by a new parade of politicians and pundits who applaud the goal but deplore the means necessary to achieve it. Count the banners of today's yes-butters:

1. Yes, Saddam Hussein is evil, a monster in power, but is it for us to assume the power to crush every cruel tyrant in the world?

2. Yes, only the threat of U.S. force enabled the U.N. inspectors to get back into Iraq, but now that they're there, why not let them poke around until they find something?

3. Yes, Saddam is probably working on germs and poison gases and maybe even nukes, but he hasn't used them lately, and what's the rush to stop him now—why not wait until inspectors find proof positive or he demonstrates his possession?

4. Yes, Iraqi weapons could someday obliterate New York, but what's the use of stopping them when North Korean missiles could even sooner take out Los Angeles?

5. Yes, Saddam has defied 17 U.N. Security Council resolutions over a dozen years to disarm, but aren't we his moral equivalent by threatening to get it done despite a French veto?

6. Yes, we have credible testimony from captives that Saddam harbors in Baghdad terrorists trained by and affiliated with Al Qaeda, but where's the

William Safire, winner of the 1978 Pulitzer Prize for distinguished commentary, has been a political columnist for *The New York Times* since 1973. He also writes a Sunday column, "On Language," which has appeared in *The New York Times Magazine* since 1979. Before joining *The Times,* Safire was a senior White House speechwriter for President Nixon. This column was originally published in the *Times* on February 20, 2003.

smoking gun that shows the ultimate nexus—that he personally ordered the attacks of Sept. 11?

7. Yes, ending Saddam's rewards to families of suicide bombers would remove an incentive to kill innocents, but wouldn't the exercise of coalition power to curtail the financing of terror create a thousand new Osama bin Ladens?

8. Yes, the liberation of 23 million oppressed and brutalized Iraqis would spread realistic hope for democratic change throughout the Arab world, but wouldn't that destabilize the Saudi monarchy and drive up oil prices?

9. Yes, we could win, and perhaps quickly, but what if we have to fight in the streets of Baghdad or have to watch scenes of civilians dying on TV?

10. Yes, cost is no object in maintaining U.S. national security, but exactly how much is war going to cost and why not break your tax-cut promises in advance?

11. Yes, the democratic nation most easily targeted by Saddam's missiles is willing to brave that risk, but doesn't such silent support prove that American foreign policy is manipulated by the elders of Zion?

12. Yes, liberation and human rights and the promotion of democracy and the example to North Korea and Iran are all fine Wilsonian concepts, but such idealism has no place in realpolitik—and can you guarantee that our servicemembers will be home for Christmas?

This is the dirty dozen of doubt, the non-rallying cry of the half-hearted. The yes-butters never forthrightly oppose, as principled pacifists do. Rather than challenge the ends, they demean the means. Rather than go up against a grand design, they play the devil with the details. Afflicted by doubt created by the potential cost of action, they flinch at calculating the far greater cost of inaction.

Haughty statesmen felt for years that "poorly brought up" Bosnians and Kosovars were unworthy of outside military defense—until hundreds of thousands of innocent Muslims embarrassingly died. Iraqi Kurds by the thousands were poison-gassed as well, their cries and exodus ignored by European leaders in the name of preserving the sovereignty of despots. These local crowd-pleasers are ready to again embrace peace at any price so long as others pay the price.

The firm opponents of a just war draw succor from the yes-butters, whose fears are expressed in dwelling on the uncertainty of great enterprises. Their fears are neither unreasoning or unjustified, but, in the words of a president who rose above paralysis, "paralyze needed efforts to turn retreat into advance."

HAWKS HAVE MY HEAD, DOVES HAVE MY HEART, GUESS WHICH WINS?

Ian McEwan

Ambivalence is not a useful sentiment on the brink of war, but my misgivings about military action have been tempered, or complicated, by the writing of various Iraqi exiles as well as the testimony of those persecuted by the regime. In the right context, with the right ambitions, it could be a moral act to remove Saddam and his hideous entourage by force and restore Iraq to its people. By the right context, I refer to an attempt to begin the process of a focused, creative and inclusive settlement to the Palestinian problem. Naturally, it would require American leadership, and at present this is a remote prospect.

But without such an initiative, and in the aftermath of the 9/11 attacks, the whole area is too unstable; it seethes with hatred. Mutual incomprehension between the Arab world and the West is at a new peak. Only last month, the mainstream Cairo press was repeating the story that the United States itself destroyed the Twin Towers in order to have a pretext to attack Islam. Meanwhile, the U.S. administration is vague about its post-invasion plans. There has been no forthright commitment to a democratic Iraq. This invites suspicion. Military action in the Middle East now could prompt any number of very undesirable, if not tragic, consequences. No one, no "expert," can know what is going to happen. But I think it is safe to assume, given the present pandemic of irrationality, that this is not the best time to be going to war against an Arab nation.

For all that, I can't say I've been much impressed by the arguments of the anti-war movement in Great Britain. Peace movements are of their nature incapable of choosing lesser evils, and it is at least conceivable that invading Iraq now will save more suffering and more lives than doing nothing. That possibility needs to be faced and reasoned through. The movement's failure to take an interest in, or engage with, Iraqi exiles, or the Iraqi National Congress

Ian McEwan is an accomplished novelist who won the prestigious Booker Prize in 1998 for his book *Amsterdam,* and his latest book, *Atonement,* won the National Book Critics Circle award for fiction. This article was originally published on February 21, 2003 in *The New York Observer.*

meeting in London recently, was a moral evasion. All the more shameful when a large part of the I N.C. embraces the liberal or libertarian and secular values that much of the anti-war movement professes.

I keep hearing the raised voices of those very same people who preferred to leave the Taliban in power, and who were prepared to let the Kosovars rot in their camps on the borders of their homeland, and to let Serbian genocidal nationalism have its way. Why should we trust these voices now? Tony Blair, vilified at the time, played a tough hand in both those campaigns, and he was proven right. Far more would have suffered if nothing had been done. The "Bush's poodle" charge this time round is lazy. It was the Blair-Powell axis of compromise that brought the U.S. to the U.N. in the first place. Another empty argument I keep hearing is that it is inconsistent to attack Iraq because we are not attacking North Korea, Saudi Arabia and China. To which I say, three dictatorships are better than four.

To the waverer, some of the reasoning from the doves seems to emerge from a warm fug of illogic. That the U.S. has been friendly to dictators before, that it cynically supported Saddam in his war against Iran, that there are vast oil reserves in the region—none of this helps us decide what specifically we are to do about Saddam now. The peace movement needs to come up with concrete proposals for containing him if he is not to be forcefully disarmed. He has obsessively produced chemical and biological weapons on an industrial scale, and has a history of bloody territorial ambition. What to do?

No one seriously disagrees about his record of genocide—perhaps a quarter of a million Kurds slaughtered, thousands of their villages destroyed, the ruthless persecution of the Shiites in the south, the cruel suppression of dissent, the widespread use of torture and summary imprisonment and execution, with the ubiquitous security services penetrating every level of Iraqi society. It is an insult to those who have suffered to suggest, as some do, that the U.S. administration is the greater evil.

Nor does it advance the cause of peace to ignore the opportunity as well as the responsibility Saddam has, even at this late stage, to avoid a war. Those in the peace camp who argue for a complete military withdrawal from the area ignore the fact that the Kurds would face further genocide without the current protection of the no-fly zones. The peace movement does not have a monopoly of the humanitarian arguments.

As for the hawks, they have evasions of their own. There is a simple piece of arithmetic which they cannot bring themselves to do in public: Given the vile nature of the regime and the threat it presents to the region, how many Iraqi civilians should we allow ourselves to kill to be rid of him? What is the unacceptable level?

The best argument for a pre-emptive invasion would be evidence of a recent nuclear-weapons program. So far, nothing has been found. Other questions do not dissolve because they are unanswerable: If nation-building is too lowly a task for this U.S. administration, what might follow from the breakup of the nation state of Iraq, an artifice devised and imposed last century by the British? What if a missile attack draws in the efficient and bellicose Israelis? Will an invasion be Al Qaeda's recruiting sergeant? And might Saddam—the "serial miscalculator," in Kenneth Pollack's memorable phrase—take everyone down with him in a final frenzy of psychosis? To choose war is to choose unknown terrifying futures. Containment by perpetual inspection might be the duller, safer option.

This is perhaps what the French have in mind. But even the doves know that inspectors are only tolerated in Iraq now by Saddam because of the U.S. and British troops massing on the borders. They cannot remain there indefinitely. The threat of invasion is what drives the inspection process.

So, the hawks have my head, the doves my heart. At a push, I count myself—just—in the camp of the latter. And yet my ambivalence remains. I defend it by reference to the fact that nothing any of us say will make any difference: Ambivalence is no less effective than passionate conviction.

At present, following the Blix and Powell reports to the U.N. Security Council, a war looks inevitable. One can only hope now for the best outcome: that the regime, like all dictatorships, rootless in the affections of its people, will crumble like a rotten tooth; that the federal, democratic Iraq that the I.N.C. committed itself to at its conference can be helped into existence by the U.N.; and that the U.S., in the flush of victory, will find in its oilman's heart the energy and optimism to begin to address the Palestinian issue. These are fragile hopes. As things stand, it is easier to conceive of innumerable darker possibilities.

PROMISES ABROAD, WHILE AT HOME PROMISES GO FORGOTTEN

Derrick Z. Jackson

Black folks do not want to invade Iraq. The question for Americans is whether to view this as unpatriotic or as a tweet of sanity that warns us we are about to walk into a horrific explosion. According to a poll by the Pew Research Center for the People and the Press, 44 percent of African-Americans support the use of military force in Iraq. That compares with 73 percent of white Americans. Other polls show black support to be far less.

Earlier this month, an *Atlanta Journal-Constitution*/Zogby America poll found that only 23 percent of African-Americans strongly or somewhat supported a war, compared with 62 percent of white Americans. In January, a Gallup poll found that 37 percent favored an invasion, compared with 58 percent of white Americans.

Back in October, the Joint Center for Political and Economic Studies, which generally does the most extensive polling of African-Americans, found that only 19 percent of African-Americans supported a war with Iraq.

The reasons are obvious. African-Americans are 12 percent of the general population but make up 21 percent of military personnel and 30 percent of Army enlistees. They made up 23 percent of the troops sent to the 1991 Gulf War. The Department of Defense recently attempted to downplay those disproportionate percentages, reporting that African-Americans were more likely to be in administrative and support jobs and therefore were less likely than white soldiers to be killed on the front lines. White soldiers made up 71 percent of the troops in the 1991 Gulf War but suffered 76 percent of the deaths.

That ignores why African-Americans go into the service in the first place. Many of them are refugees from a job and collegiate environment that is disproportionately hostile to them. President Bush recently stoked the hostility by filing a brief to the Supreme Court opposing the University of Michigan's affirmative action program.

That alone is enough to make African-Americans wonder whether they are

Derrick Z. Jackson has been a columnist for *The Boston Globe* since 1988. He was a 2001 finalist for the Pulitzer Prize in commentary, and is a five-time winner of awards for political and sports commentary from the National Association of Black Journalists. A native of Milwaukee, he was a Neiman Fellow in Journalism at Harvard University in 1984. This article was originally published in *The Boston Globe* on February 26, 2003.

495

about to relive bad history. Time after time, war after war, African-Americans fought and died for the nation's agenda only to see the nation ignore or reject their issues. Black folks fought in the Revolution and slavery lasted nearly another century. Black soldiers were promised land after the Battle of New Orleans during the War of 1812 and never got it.

In the Civil War, African-Americans, then 14 percent of the population, were 20 percent of the Union casualties. Yet segregation and second-class opportunities were the rule for almost another century. Black folks fought in World War I in the hopes of winning full citizenship. They were rewarded with white race riots. Participation in World War II and Korea further emboldened African-Americans to protest for desegregation in the military, public accommodations, school desegregation, and voting rights.

But Americans took so long to become disgusted with the lynchings and disenfranchisement of the '40s, '50s, and early '60s that the hypocrisy could not be contained. There was Martin Luther King Jr.'s 1968 lament "for the poor of America who are paying the double price of smashed hopes at home and death and corruption in Vietnam." There was Muhammad Ali's "I ain't got no quarrel with them Viet Cong" because, as he said, "no Viet Cong ever called me nigger." There were the riots.

Thirty-five years later, too many African-Americans are still having their hopes smashed. The military, which has worked harder at equality than the private sector, has undoubtedly helped put many African-Americans on the road to the middle class. But the nation has yet to truly join African-Americans on the mission to rid the United States of its quiet weapons of mass destruction: bad schools for the poor and discrimination for striving African-Americans with the same qualifications as white Americans.

African-Americans understand that there are times when all of us are under attack. They solidly supported at least the short-term military response against the terrorists of Sept. 11. But history has also taught African-Americans to be wary. That wariness could be a warning, should Americans choose to hear it. A White House that is not committed to opportunity in Illinois must be questioned about Iraq. An America that remains comfortable with discrimination in Baltimore must be questioned as to how discriminating it will be in bombing Baghdad. An America that has not been true to black patriotism might want to question just how true the White House is to them.

A lot of white Americans may not care for affirmative action, but we all care about the economy, which Bush is all but handing over to business interests. The low enthusiasm by African-Americans for a war in Iraq might be the most patriotic act yet. It ought to be the act that makes us think what our nation is promising to the rest of the world when there are promises to keep right here.

THE LONG BOMB

Thomas L. Friedman

Watching this Iraq story unfold, all I can say is this: If this were not about my own country, my own kids and my own planet, I'd pop some popcorn, pull up a chair and pay good money just to see how this drama unfolds. Because what you are about to see is the greatest shake of the dice any president has voluntarily engaged in since Harry Truman dropped the bomb on Japan. Vietnam was a huge risk, but it evolved incrementally. And threatening a nuclear war with the Soviets over the Cuban missile crisis was a huge shake of the dice by President John Kennedy, but it was a gamble that was imposed on him, not one he initiated.

A U.S. invasion to disarm Iraq, oust Saddam Hussein and rebuild a decent Iraqi state would be the mother of all presidential gambles. Anyone who thinks President Bush is doing this for political reasons is nuts. You could do this only if you really believed in it, because Mr. Bush is betting his whole presidency on this war of choice.

And don't believe the polls. I've been to nearly 20 states recently, and I've found that 95 percent of the country wants to see Iraq dealt with without a war. But President Bush is a man on a mission. He has been convinced by a tiny group of advisers that throwing "The Long Bomb"—attempting to transform the most dangerous Arab state—is a geopolitical game-changer. It could help nudge the whole Arab-Muslim world onto a more progressive track, something that coaxing simply will not do anymore. It's something that can only be accomplished by building a different model in the heart of the Arab-Muslim world. No, you don't see this every day. This is really bold. And that leads to my dilemma. I have a mixed marriage. My wife opposes this war, but something in Mr. Bush's audacious shake of the dice appeals to me. He summed it up well in his speech last week: "A liberated Iraq can show the power of freedom to transform that vital region by bringing hope and progress into the lives of millions. America's interest in security and America's belief in liberty both lead in the same direction—to a free and peaceful Iraq."

Thomas L. Friedman joined *The New York Times* in 1981, serving as Beirut bureau chief and Israel bureau chief before becoming the paper's foreign-affairs correspondent in 1995. He has won three Pulitzer Prizes, two for international reporting and one for commentary, and his book *From Beirut to Jerusalem* won the National Book Award for non-fiction in 1989. This column was originally published on March 2, 2003 in *The New York Times*.

My dilemma is that while I believe in such a bold project, I fear that Mr. Bush has failed to create a context for his boldness to succeed, a context that could maximize support for his vision—support vital to seeing it through. He and his team are the only people who would ever have conceived this project, but they may be the worst people to implement it. The only place they've been bold is in their military preparations (which have at least gotten Saddam to begin disarming).

What do I mean? I mean that if taking out Saddam and rebuilding Iraq had been my goal from the minute I took office (as it was for the Bush team), I would not have angered all of Europe by trashing the Kyoto global warming treaty without offering an alternative. I would not have alienated the entire Russian national security elite by telling the Russians that we were ripping up the ABM treaty and that they would just have to get used to it. (You're now seeing their revenge.) I would not have proposed one radical tax cut on top of another on the eve of a huge, costly nation-building marathon abroad.

I would, though, have rallied the nation for real energy conservation and initiated a Manhattan Project for alternative energies so I would not find myself with $2.25-per-gallon gasoline on the eve of this war—because OPEC capacity is nearly tapped out. I would have told the Palestinians that until they stop suicide bombing and get a more serious leadership, we're not dealing with them, but I would also have told the Israelis that every new or expanded settlement they built would cost them $100 million in U.S. aid. And I would have told the Arabs: "While we'll deal with the Iraqi threat, we have no imperial designs on your countries. We are not on a crusade—but we will not sit idle if you tolerate extremists in your midst who imperil our democracy."

No, had Mr. Bush done all these things it would not have changed everything with France, Russia and the Arabs—or my wife. But I am convinced that it would have helped generate more support to increase our staying power in Iraq and the odds that we could pull this off.

So here's how I feel: I feel as if the president is presenting us with a beautiful carved mahogany table—a big, bold, gutsy vision. But if you look underneath, you discover that this table has only one leg. His bold vision on Iraq is not supported by boldness in other areas. And so I am terribly worried that Mr. Bush has told us the right thing to do, but won't be able to do it right.

U.S.-BRITISH DRAFT
RESOLUTION ON IRAQ

Following is the text of a draft United Nations Security Council resolution on Iraq presented to the Council on February 24, 2003. It was proposed by the United States and Britain and co-sponsored by Spain.

The Security Council.

Recalling all its previous relevant resolutions, in particular its resolutions 661 (1990) of 6 August 1990, 678 (1990) of 29 November 1990, 686 (1991) of 2 March 1991, 687 (1991) of 3 April 1991, 688 (1991) of 5 April 1991, 707 (1991) of 15 August 1991, 715 (1991) of 11 October 1991, 986 (1995) of 14 April 1995, 1284 (1999) of 17 December 1999 and 1441 (2002) of 8 November 2002, and all the relevant statements of its president.

Recalling that in its Resolution 687 (1991) the Council declared that a cease-fire would be based on acceptance by Iraq of the provisions of that resolution, including the obligations on Iraq contained therein.

Recalling that its Resolution 1441 (2002), while acknowledging that Iraq has been and remains in material breach of its obligations, afforded Iraq a final opportunity to comply with its disarmament obligations under relevant resolutions.

Recalling that in its Resolution 1441 (2002) the Council decided that false statements or omissions in the declaration submitted by Iraq pursuant to that resolution and failure by Iraq at any time to comply with, and cooperate fully in the implementation of that resolution, would constitute a further material breach.

Noting, in that context, that in its Resolution 1441 (2002), the Council recalled that it has repeatedly warned Iraq that it will face serious consequences as a result of its continued violations of its obligations.

Noting that Iraq has submitted a declaration pursuant to its Resolution 1441 (2002) containing false statements and omissions and has failed to comply with, and cooperate fully in the implementation of that resolution.

Reaffirming the commitment of all member states to the sovereignty and territorial integrity of Iraq, Kuwait, and the neighboring states.

Mindful of its primary responsibility under the Charter of the United Nations for the maintenance of international peace and security.

Recognizing the threat Iraq's noncompliance with Council resolutions and proliferation of weapons of mass destruction and long-range missiles poses to international peace and security.

Determined to secure full compliance with its decisions and to restore international peace and security in the area.

Acting under Chapter VII of the Charter of the United Nations.

Decides that Iraq has failed to take the final opportunity afforded it in Resolution 1441 (2002);

Decides to remain seized of the matter.

IRAQ'S DISARMAMENT CAN BE
ACHIEVED BY PEACEFUL MEANS

The U.S.-British draft resolution of February 24 was informally rejected by the French, German and Russian governments. On March 5, Foreign Ministers Dominique de Villepin of France, Ivan S. Ivanov of Russia and Joschka Fischer of Germany released the following statement:

Our common objective remains the full and effective disarmament of Iraq, in compliance with Resolution 1441. We consider that this objective can be achieved by the peaceful means of the inspections.

We moreover observe that these inspections are producing increasingly encouraging results:

- The destruction of the Al Samoud missiles has started and is making progress.
- Iraqis are providing biological and chemical information.
- The interviews with Iraqi scientists are continuing.

Russia, Germany and France resolutely support Messrs. Blix and ElBaradei and consider the meeting of the Council on March 7 to be an important step in the process put in place.

We firmly call for the Iraqi authorities to cooperate more actively with the inspectors to fully disarm their country. These inspections cannot continue indefinitely.

We consequently ask that the inspections now be speeded up, in keeping with the proposals put forward in the memorandum submitted to the Security Council by our three countries. We must:

- Specify and prioritize the remaining issues, program by program.
- Establish, for each point, detailed time lines.

Using this method, the inspectors have to present without any delay their work program accompanied by regular progress reports to the Security Council. This program could provide for a meeting clause to enable the Council to evaluate the overall results of this process.

In these circumstances, we will not let a proposed resolution pass that would authorize the use of force.

Russia and France, as permanent members of the Security Council, will assume all their responsibilities on this point.

We are at a turning point. Since our goal is the peaceful and full disarmament of Iraq, we have today the chance to obtain through peaceful means a comprehensive settlement for the Middle East, starting with a move forward in the peace process, by:

Publishing and implementing the road map;

Putting together a general framework for the Middle East, based on stability and security, renunciation of force, arms control and trust building measures.

Editors' postscript: On March 7, the U.N. inspectors again reported on their progress to the Security Council. Mohamed ElBaradei, head of the International Atomic Energy Agency, said, "after three months of intrusive inspections, we have to date found no evidence or plausible indication of the revival of a nuclear weapons program in Iraq." ElBaradei also asserted that he had found no sign of nuclear-related activities in newly erected buildings and other sites identified by Western intelligence agencies as questionable. Hans Blix, the chief of UNMOVIC, said that his inspectors had also not been able to verify claims that Iraq was shifting its weapons by truck to avoid detection, that it was hiding weapons in underground bunkers or that it had built mobile labs to produce biological weapons.

After France, Germany and Russia made clear their opposition to the U.S.-British draft resolution, Britain offered an amendment giving Iraq until March 17 to disarm. Both countries made two last moves seeking support for their ultimatum to Iraq. First, on March 12, Britain proposed six specific conditions that Saddam would have to meet quickly to avoid war, including going on Iraqi television to admit his possession of weapons of mass destruction, allowing 30 scientists to be interviewed outside the country, with their families, within 10 days, and surrendering his stocks of and production facilities for biological and chemical weapons. And on March 14, the United States announced its intention to publish the so-called "road map" for peace in the Israeli-Palestinian conflict—something it had previously decided to delay until after any war with Iraq.

But neither of these moves changed the deadlock in the U.N. Security Council. On one side, there was the United States and Britain, with support from Spain and Bulgaria. On the other were France, Russia, China, Germany and Syria, with the French declaring their intention to veto any resolution authorizing war. In the middle were Mexico, Pakistan, Chile, Cameroon, Angola and Guinea. The U.S. and Britain had hoped to get at least nine votes to pass their resolution, which they felt would be a moral victory, even if it was vetoed by France, one of the council's five permanent members. But it quickly became clear that that would not happen. On March 16, France floated one last proposal that would have offered Saddam Hussein thirty more days to comply, but it was summarily rejected by the U.S. Diplomacy was dead.

THE WAR BEGINS:
"THE TYRANT WILL SOON BE GONE"

President George W. Bush

On March 17, 2003, President Bush spoke on television from the White House, announcing the end of his efforts to obtain a second U.N. resolution and giving Saddam Hussein 48 hours to leave his country or face war. Following are excerpts from his remarks.

My fellow citizens, events in Iraq have now reached the final days of decision.

For more than a decade, the United States and other nations have pursued patient and honorable efforts to disarm the Iraqi regime without war. That regime pledged to reveal and destroy all its weapons of mass destruction as a condition for ending the Persian Gulf War in 1991. Since then the world has engaged in twelve years of diplomacy. We have passed more than a dozen resolutions in the United Nations Security Council. We have sent hundreds of weapons inspectors to oversee the disarmament of Iraq. Our good faith has not been returned.

[. . . .]

Peaceful efforts to disarm the Iraqi regime have failed again and again because we are not dealing with peaceful men. Intelligence gathered by this and other governments leaves no doubt that the Iraq regime continues to possess and conceal some of the most lethal weapons ever devised. This regime has already used weapons of mass destruction against Iraq's neighbors and against Iraq's people. The regime has a history of reckless aggression in the Middle East. It has a deep hatred of America and our friends. And it has aided, trained and harbored terrorists, including operatives of Al Qaeda.

The danger is clear. Using chemical, biological or, one day, nuclear weapons, obtained with the help of Iraq, the terrorists could fulfill their stated ambitions and kills thousands or hundreds of thousands of innocent people in our country or any other.

The United States and other nations did nothing to deserve or invite this threat, but we will do everything to defeat it. Instead of drifting along toward tragedy, we will set a course toward safety. Before the day of horror can come, before it is too late to act, this danger will be removed.

The United States of America has the sovereign authority to use force in assuring its own national security.

That duty falls to me as commander-in-chief by the oath I have sworn, by the oath I will keep.

Recognizing the threat to our country, the United States Congress voted overwhelmingly last year to support the use of force against Iraq. America tried to work with the United Nations to address this threat because we wanted to resolve the issue peacefully. We believe in the mission of the United Nations. One reason the U.N. was founded after the Second World War was to confront aggressive dictators actively and early before they can attack the innocent and destroy the peace.

In the case of Iraq, the Security Council did act in the early 1990s. Under Resolutions 678 and 687, both still in effect, the United States and our allies are authorized to use force in ridding Iraq of weapons of mass destruction. This is not a question of authority, it is a question of will.

[. . . .]

For the last four and a half months, the United States and our allies have worked within the Security Council to enforce that council's longstanding demands. Yet some permanent members of the Security Council have publicly announced that they will veto any resolution that compels the disarmament of Iraq. These governments share our assessment of the danger, but not our resolve to meet it.

Many nations, however, do have the resolve and fortitude to act against this threat to peace, and a broad coalition is now gathering to enforce the just demands of the world. The United Nations Security Council has not lived up to its responsibilities, so we will rise to ours.

[. . . .]

All the decades of deceit and cruelty have now reached an end. Saddam Hussein and his sons must leave Iraq within 48 hours. Their refusal to do so will result in military conflict, commenced at a time of our choosing. For their own safety, all foreign nationals, including journalists and inspectors, should leave Iraq immediately.

Many Iraqis can hear me tonight in a translated radio broadcast. And I have a message for them. If we must begin a military campaign, it will be directed against the lawless men who rule your country and not against you. As our coalition takes away their power we will deliver the food and medicine you need. We will tear down the apparatus of terror. And we will help you to build a new Iraq that is prosperous and free. In a free Iraq there will be no more wars of aggression against your neighbors, no more poison factories, no more executions of dissidents, no more torture chambers and rape rooms. The tyrant will soon be gone. The day of your liberation is near.

Editors' postscript: At 9:35 P.M. Eastern Standard Time in Washington, D.C. on March 19, the first American bombs fell on Baghdad. These were not the 3,000 precision-guided weapons that U.S. military planners had talked about using to "shock and awe" the Iraqi regime into a hoped-for quick surrender. Rather, the White House had decided to act on intelligence that Iraq's top leadership had gathered in one place and had targeted them, hoping in one fell swoop to "decapitate" the regime. At 10:15 P.M., President Bush spoke from the White House to announce the beginning of hostilities and to warn the American people that "a campaign on the harsh terrain of a nation as large as California could be longer and more difficult than some predict." About two hours later, Saddam Hussein appeared on Iraqi TV where he called "the criminal, reckless junior Bush" a war criminal. He urged his army to persevere: "God willing, we will take them to the limit at which they will lose their patience and any hope to achieve what they have planned and what the Zionist criminal has pushed them to do."

The next day dawned with reports that several oil wells in southern Iraq had been set afire, and that the Iraqis had unexpectedly (if ineffectively) managed to launch a few missiles towards the invasion force massed along the Kuwaiti-Iraqi border. Amid fears that further delay might not only permit the regime to sabotage more oil facilities, but would also expose stationary coalition soldiers to additional missile attacks, the ground assault on Iraq began in earnest, ahead of schedule. At first, television reporters and camera crews "embedded" in American units showed what appeared to be a cakewalk, as thousands of tanks and armored vehicles sped unopposed across the southern Iraqi desert toward Baghdad. ("Hey, diddle diddle, it's straight up the middle!" enthused former U.S. Army Colonel David Hackworth in his role as a guest commentator on CNN.) But it soon became clear that the troops were encountering pockets of unexpectedly stiff resistance.

World reaction to the beginning of the war varied. The U.S. released a list of countries that it touted as being in its "coalition of the willing"—including Afghanistan, Albania, Azerbaijan, Colombia, Denmark, Eritrea, Ethiopia, El Salvador, Iceland, Italy, Japan, Mongolia, the Netherlands, Nicaragua, Turkey, Uzbekistan, and most of the former Eastern bloc countries of Europe, not to mention such maritime powers as Micronesia, the Marshall Islands and Palau—but only Britain and Australia were sending combat troops to fight. The British Parliament backed Prime Minister Tony Blair's decision to join the war campaign, but one-third of the members of his Labor Party voted with the opposition. The leaders of France, Germany, Russia and China all expressed their disappointment with the abandonment of diplomacy, worried that it would lead to more terrorism and argued that the American attacks lacked a legal basis in international law. At the same time, both France and Germany said they would allow overflights by American planes and the use of bases, and France said it would join the war if Iraq used chemical or biological weapons against coalition forces. Hundreds of thousands of people marched on U.S. embassies around the world, and there were violent clashes in Egypt and the Philippines. Hans Blix, the chief U.N. weapons inspector, expressed regret at what he saw as American "impatience" with the pace of his inspections. "We had made a rapid start," he said. "We did not have any obstacles from the Iraqi side in going anywhere. They gave us prompt access and we were in a great many places all over Iraq."

On the domestic front, early polls showed support for President Bush's handling of the conflict surging to over 70 percent. Most politicians expressed support for the troops and muted any criticism they might have had of the decision to go to war. One controversy erupted after Senate Democratic minority leader Tom Daschle said he was "saddened that this president failed so miserably at diplomacy that we're now forced to go to war." Republican Speaker of the House Dennis Hastert responded that Daschle's remarks "may not give comfort to our adversaries, but they come mighty close." But some Democrats seconded Daschle's lament. "Today I weep for my country," Senator Robert Byrd said on the Senate floor. "When did we become a nation that ignores and berates our friends and calls them irrelevant? When did we decide to risk undermining international order by adopting a radical doctrinaire approach to using our awesome military might?"

On Friday night, March 21, the Pentagon announced the beginning of its "Shock and Awe" bombardment of Iraq, raining an estimated 1,500 cruise missiles and precision-guided bombs down on strategic targets in Baghdad and other cities in a single 24-hour period. As spectacular pictures of the bombing of Saddam's palaces flashed on TV screens—along with news of the inevitable civilian casualties—protests in world capitals continued. By the end of the war's first weekend, with Iraqi forces and irregulars putting up strong opposition in many places, and numerous coalition soldiers killed or captured, expectations of a quick victory were rapidly lowered. As this book went to press, the southern cities of Nasariyah and Umm Qasr were not yet fully under coalition control, vital humanitarian aid had yet to be distributed in meaningful quantities to Iraqi civilians, there were unconfirmed rumors that the people of the predominantly Shiite city of Basra were rising against Saddam, and Turkish detachments were reported to be moving into northern Iraq—much to the distress of the Kurds and the U.S. Most significantly, American armored forces were approaching the far outskirts of Baghdad, and had begun to attack the Republican Guard amidst growing fears that Saddam's alleged chemical and biological weapons might soon be used against them. The world held its breath, wondering what to expect in the days—and in the weeks and months—ahead.

PRE-EMPTIVE DEFEAT, OR HOW NOT TO FIGHT PROLIFERATION

Jonathan Schell

> *"All of us have heard this term 'preventive war' since the earliest days of Hitler. I recall that is about the first time I heard it. In this day and time . . . I don't believe there is such a thing; and, frankly, I wouldn't even listen to anyone seriously that came in and talked about such a thing."*
> —*President Dwight Eisenhower, 1953, upon being presented with plans to wage preventive war to disarm Stalin's Soviet Union*

> *"Our position is that whatever grievances a nation may have, however objectionable it finds the status quo, aggressive warfare is an illegal means for settling those grievances or for altering those conditions."*
> —*Supreme Court Justice Robert Jackson, the American prosecutor at the Nuremberg trials, in his opening statement to the tribunal*

I. The Lost War

In his poem "Fall 1961," written when the cold war was at its zenith, Robert Lowell wrote:

> *All autumn, the chafe and jar*
> *of nuclear war;*
> *we have talked our extinction to death.*

This autumn and winter, nuclear danger has returned, in a new form, accompanied by danger from the junior siblings in the mass destruction family, chemical and biological weapons. Now it is not a crisis between two super-

Jonathan Schell, *The Nation*'s peace and disarmament correspondent, is the Harold Willens Peace Fellow at the Nation Institute. He is the author of several books, his newest being *The Unconquerable World: Power, Nonviolence, and the Will of the People*. This article was published with the title "The Case Against the War" on March 3, 2003 in *The Nation*.

powers but the planned war to overthrow the government of Iraq that, like a sentence of execution that has been passed but must go through its final appeals before being carried out, we have talked to death. (Has any war been so lengthily premeditated before it was launched?) Iraq, the United States insists, possesses some of these weapons. To take them away, the United States will overthrow the Iraqi government. No circumstance is more likely to provoke Iraq to use any forbidden weapons it has. In that event, the Bush Administration has repeatedly said, it will itself consider the use of nuclear weapons. Has there ever been a clearer or more present danger of the use of weapons of mass destruction?

While we were all talking and the danger was growing, strange to say, the war was being lost. For wars, let us recall, are not fought for their own sake but to achieve aims. Victory cannot be judged only by the outcome of battles. In the American Revolutionary War, for example, Edmund Burke, a leader of England's antiwar movement, said, "Our victories can only complete our ruin." Almost two centuries later, in Vietnam, the United States triumphed in almost every military engagement, yet lost the war. If the aim is lost, the war is lost, whatever happens on the battlefield. The novelty this time is that the defeat has preceded the inauguration of hostilities.

The aim of the Iraq war has never been only to disarm Iraq. George Bush set forth the full aim of his war policy in unmistakable terms on January 29, 2002, in his first State of the Union address. It was to stop the spread of weapons of mass destruction, not only in Iraq but everywhere in the world, through the use of military force. "We must," he said, "prevent the terrorists and regimes who seek chemical, biological or nuclear weapons from threatening the United States and the world." He underscored the scope of his ambition by singling out three countries—North Korea, Iran and Iraq—for special mention, calling them an "axis of evil." Then came the ultimatum: "The United States of America will not permit the world's most dangerous regimes to threaten us with the world's most destructive weapons." Other possible war aims—to defeat Al Qaeda, to spread democracy—came and went in Administration pronouncements, but this one has remained constant. Stopping the spread of weapons of mass destruction is the reason for war given alike to the Security Council, whose inspectors are now searching for such weapons in Iraq, and to the American people, who were advised in the recent State of the Union address to fear "a day of horror like none we have ever known."

The means whereby the United States would stop the prohibited acquisitions were first set forth last June 1 in the President's speech to the graduating class at West Point. The United States would use force, and use it preemptively. "If we wait for threats to fully materialize, we will have waited too long," he said. For "the only path to safety is the path of action. And this nation will act." This strategy, too, has remained constant.

The Bush policy of using force to stop the spread of weapons of mass destruction met its Waterloo last October, when Assistant Secretary of State for East Asian and Pacific Affairs James Kelly was informed by Vice Foreign Minister Kang Sok Ju of North Korea that his country has a perfect right to possess nuclear weapons. Shortly, Secretary of State Colin Powell stated, "We have to assume that they might have one or two. . . . that's what our intelligence community has been saying for some time." (Doubts, however, remain.) Next, North Korea went on to announce that it was terminating the Agreed Framework of 1994, under which it had shut down two reactors that produced plutonium. It ejected the U.N. inspectors who had been monitoring the agreement and then announced its withdrawal from the Nuclear Nonproliferation Treaty, under whose terms it was obligated to remain nuclear-weapon-free. Soon, America stated that North Korea might be moving fuel rods from existing reactors to its plutonium reprocessing plant, and that it possessed an untested missile capable of striking the western United States. "We will not permit . . ." had been Bush's words, but North Korea went ahead and apparently produced nuclear weapons anyway. The Administration now discovered that its policy of pre-emptively using overwhelming force had no application against a proliferator with a serious military capability, much less a nuclear power. North Korea's conventional capacity alone—it has an army of more than a million men and 11,000 artillery pieces capable of striking South Korea's capital, Seoul—imposed a very high cost; the addition of nuclear arms, in combination with missiles capable of striking not only South Korea but Japan, made it obviously prohibitive.

By any measure, totalitarian North Korea's possession of nuclear weapons is more dangerous than the mere possibility that Iraq is trying to develop them. The North Korean state, which is hard to distinguish from a cult, is also more repressive and disciplined than the Iraqi state, and has caused the death of more of its own people—through starvation. Yet in the weeks that followed the North Korean disclosure, the Administration, in a radical reversal of the President's earlier assessments, sought to argue that the opposite was true. Administration spokespersons soon declared that the North Korean situation was "not a crisis" and that its policy toward that country was to be one of "dialogue," leading to "a peaceful multilateral solution," including the possibility of renewed oil shipments. But if the acquisition by North Korea of nuclear arms was not a crisis, then there never had been any need to warn the world of the danger of nuclear proliferation, or to name an axis of evil, or to deliver an ultimatum to disarm it.

For the North Korean debacle represented not the failure of a good policy but exposure of the futility of one that was impracticable from the start. Nuclear proliferation, when considered as the global emergency that it is, has never been, is not now and never will be stoppable by military force; on the contrary, force can only exacerbate the problem. In announcing its policy, the United States appeared to have forgotten what proliferation is. It is not army divisions or tanks crossing borders; it is above all technical know-how passing from one mind to another. It cannot be stopped by B-2 bombers, or even Predator drones. The case of Iraq had indeed always been an anomaly in the wider picture of nonproliferation. In the 1991 Gulf War, the U.S.-led coalition waged war to end Iraq's occupation of Kuwait. In the process it stumbled on Saddam Hussein's program for building weapons of mass destruction, and made use of the defeat to impose on him the new obligation to end the program. A war fought for one purpose led to peace terms serving another. It was a historical chain of events unlikely ever to be repeated, and offered no model for dealing with proliferation.

The lesson so far? Exactly the opposite of the intended one: If you want to avoid "regime change" by the United States, build a nuclear arsenal—but be sure to do it quietly and fast. As Mohamed ElBaradei, the director general of the International Atomic Energy Agency, has said, the United States seems to want to teach the world that "if you really want to defend yourself, develop nuclear weapons, because then you get negotiations, and not military action."

Although the third of the "axis" countries presents no immediate crisis, events there also illustrate the bankruptcy of the Bush policy. With the help of Russia, Iran is building nuclear reactors that are widely believed to double as a nuclear weapons program. American threats against Iraq have failed to dissuade Iran—or for that matter, its supplier, Russia—from proceeding. Just this week, Iran announced that it had begun to mine uranium on its own soil. Iran's path to acquiring nuclear arms, should it decide to go ahead, is clear. "Regime change" by American military action in that half-authoritarian, half-democratic country is a formula for disaster. Whatever the response of the Iraqi people might be to an American invasion, there is little question that in Iran hard-liners and democrats alike would mount bitter, protracted resistance. Nor is there evidence that democratization in Iraq, even in the unlikely event that it should succeed, would be a sure path to denuclearization. The world's first nuclear power, after all, was a democracy, and of nine nuclear powers now in the world, six—the United States, England, France, India, Israel and Russia—are also democracies. Iran, within striking range of Israel, lives in an increasingly nuclearized neighborhood. In these circumstances, would the Iranian people be any more likely to rebel against nuclearization than the Indian people did—or more, for that matter, than the American people have done? And if a democratic Iran obtained the bomb, would preemption or regime change then be an option for the United States?

The collapse of the overall Bush policy has one more element that may be even more significant than the appearance of North Korea's arsenal or Iran's apparently unstoppable discreet march to obtaining the bomb. It has turned out that the supplier of essential information and technology for North Korea's uranium program was America's faithful ally in the war on terrorism, Pakistan, which received missile technology from Korea in return. The "father" of Pakistan's bomb, Ayub Qadeer Khan, has visited North Korea thirteen times. This is the same Pakistan whose nuclear scientist Sultan Bashiruddin Mahood paid a visit to Osama bin Laden in Afghanistan a few months before September 11, and whose nuclear establishment even today is riddled with Islamic fundamentalists. The BBC has reported that the Al Qaeda network succeeded at one time in building a "dirty bomb" (which may account for Osama bin Laden's claim that he possesses nuclear weapons), and Pakistan is the likeliest source for the materials involved, although Russia is also a candidate. Pakistan, in short, has proved itself to be the world's most dangerous proliferator, having recently acquired nuclear weapons itself and passed on nuclear technology to a state and, possibly, to a terrorist group.

Indeed, an objective ranking of nuclear proliferators in order of menace would place Pakistan (a possessor of the bomb that also purveys the technology to others) first on the list, North Korea second (it peddles missiles but not, so far, bomb technology), Iran (a country of growing political and military power with an active nuclear program) third, and Iraq (a country of shrinking military power that probably has no nuclear program and is currently under international sanctions and an unprecedented inspection regime of indefinite duration) fourth. (Russia, possessor of 150 tons of poorly guarded plutonium, also belongs somewhere on this list.) The Bush Administration ranks them, of course, in exactly the reverse order, placing Iraq, which it plans to attack, first, and Pakistan, which it befriends and coddles, nowhere on the list. It will not be possible, however, to right this pyramid. The reason it is upside down is that it was unworkable right side up. Iraq is being attacked not because it is the worst proliferator but because it is the weakest.

The *reductio ad absurdum* of the failed American war policy was illustrated by a recent column in the *Washington Post* by the superhawk Charles Krauthammer. Krauthammer wants nothing to do with soft measures; yet he, too, can see that the cost of using force against North Korea would be prohibitive: "Militarily, we are not even in position to bluff." He rightly understands, too, that in the climate created by pending war in Iraq, "dialogue" is scarcely likely to succeed. He has therefore come up with a new idea. He identifies

China as the solution. China must twist the arm of its Communist ally North Korea. "If China and South Korea were to cut off North Korea, it could not survive," he observes. But to make China do so, the United States must twist China's arm. How? By encouraging Japan to build nuclear weapons. For "if our nightmare is a nuclear North Korea, China's is a nuclear Japan." It irks Krauthammer that the United States alone has to face up to the North Korean threat. Why shouldn't China shoulder some of the burden? He wants to "share the nightmares." Indeed. He wants to stop nuclear proliferation with more nuclear proliferation. Here the nuclear age comes full circle. The only nation ever to use the bomb is to push the nation on which it dropped it to build the bomb and threaten others.

As a recommendation for policy, Krauthammer's suggestion is Strangelovian, but if it were considered as a prediction it would be sound. Nuclear armament by North Korea really will tempt neighboring nations—not only Japan but South Korea and Taiwan—to acquire nuclear weapons. (Japan has an abundant supply of plutonium and all the other technology necessary, and both South Korea and Taiwan have had nuclear programs but were persuaded by the United States to drop them.) In a little-noticed comment, Japan's foreign minister has already stated that the nuclearization of North Korea would justify a pre emptive strike against it by Japan. Thus has the Bush plan to stop proliferation already become a powerful force promoting it. The policy of pre-emptive war has led to pre-emptive defeat.

General Groves Redux

Radical as the Bush Administration policy is, the idea behind it is not new. Two months after the bombing of Hiroshima and Nagasaki, Gen. Leslie Groves, the Pentagon overseer of the Manhattan Project, expressed his views on controlling nuclear proliferation. He said:

> If we were truly realistic instead of idealistic, as we appear to be [sic], we would not permit any foreign power with which we are not firmly allied, and in which we do not have absolute confidence, to make or possess atomic weapons. If such a country started to make atomic weapons we would destroy its capacity to make them before it has progressed far enough to threaten us.

The proposal was never seriously considered by President Truman and, until now, has been rejected by every subsequent President. Eisenhower's views of preventive war are given in the epigraph at the beginning of this article. In 1961, during the Berlin crisis, a few of Kennedy's advisers made the surprising discovery that Russia's nuclear forces were far weaker and more vulnerable than anyone had thought. They proposed a preventive strike. Ted Sorensen, the chief White House counsel and speechwriter, was told of the plan. He shouted, "You're crazy! We shouldn't let guys like you around here." It never came to the attention of the President.

How has it happened that President Bush has revived and implemented this long-buried, long-rejected idea? We know the answer. The portal was September 11. The theme of the "war on terror" was from the start to strike pre-emptively with military force. Piece by piece, a bridge from the aim of catching Osama bin Laden to the aim of stopping proliferation on a global basis was built. First came the idea of holding whole regimes accountable in the war on terror, then the idea of "regime change" (beginning with Afghanistan), then pre-emption, then the broader claim of American global dominance. Gradually, the most important issue of the age—the rising danger from weapons of mass destruction—was subsumed as a sort of codicil to the war on terror. When the process was finished, the result was the Groves plan writ large—a reckless and impracticable idea when it was conceived, when only one hostile nuclear power (the Soviet Union) was in prospect, and a worse one today in our world of nine nuclear powers (if you count North Korea) and many scores of nuclear-capable ones.

The Administration now hints, however, that although its overall nonproliferation policy might be in trouble, the forcible disarmament of Iraq still makes sense on its own terms. Bush now claims that "different threats require different strategies"—apparently forgetting that the Iraq policy was announced with great fanfare in the context of a global policy of preserving the world from weapons of mass destruction. The mainstream argument, shared by many doubters as well as supporters of the war, is that if Iraq is shown to possess weapons of mass destruction, its regime must be attacked and destroyed. Thus the only question is whether Iraq has the weapons. A team of "realist" analysts, organized by Stephen Walt of Harvard's John F. Kennedy School of Government and John Mearsheimer of the University of Chicago, have given a convincing response: They are prepared to live with a nuclear-armed Iraq. "The United States can contain a nuclear Iraq," they write. They argue that Hussein belongs, like his idol Stalin, in the class of rational monsters. The idea that he is not deterrable is "almost certainly wrong." He wants power; he knows that to engage again in aggression is to insure his overthrow and likely his personal extinction. The record of his wars—against Iran, against Kuwait—shows him to be brutal but calculating. He is 65 years old. Time will solve the problem, as it did with the Soviet Union.

What is of most desperately immediate concern, however, is that America's pre-emptive war will lead directly to the use of the weapons whose mere possession the war is supposed to prevent. In the debate over the inspections now going on in Iraq, it sometimes seems to be forgotten that Iraq either *does* possess weapons of mass destruction (as Colin Powell has just asserted at the U.N.) or *does not* possess them, and that each alternative has consequences that go far beyond the decision whether or not to go to war. If Iraq does not have these weapons, then the war will be an unnecessary, wholly avoidable slaughter. If Iraq does have these weapons, then there is a likelihood that it will use them. Why else would Saddam Hussein, having created them, bring on the destruction of his regime and his personal extinction by hiding them from the U.N. inspectors? And if in fact he does use them, then the United States, as it has made clear, will consider using nuclear weapons in retaliation. Powell has asserted that Saddam has recently given his forces fresh orders to use chemical weapons. Against whom? In what circumstances? Is it possible that this outcome—a Hitlerian finale—is what Hussein seeks? Could it be his plan, if cornered, to provoke the United States into the first use of nuclear weapons since Nagasaki?

We cannot know, but we do know that White House Chief of Staff Andrew Card has stated that if Iraq uses weapons of mass destruction against American troops "the United States will use whatever means necessary to protect us and the world from a holocaust"—"whatever means" being diplomatese for nuclear attack. The *Washington Times* has revealed that National Security Presidential Directive 17, issued secretly on September 14 of last year, says in plain English what Card expressed obliquely. It reads, "The United States will continue to make clear that it reserves the right to respond with overwhelming force—including potentially nuclear weapons—to the use of [weapons of mass destruction] against the United States, our forces abroad, and friends and allies." Israel has also used diplomatese to make known its readiness to retaliate with nuclear weapons if attacked by Iraq. Condoleezza Rice has threatened the Iraqi people with genocide: If Iraq uses weapons of mass destruction, she says, it knows it will bring "national obliteration." (Threats of genocide are flying thick and fast around the world these days. In January, Indian Defense Minister George Fernandes threatened that if Pakistan launched a nuclear attack on India—as Pakistan's President Pervez Musharraf has threatened to do if India invades Pakistan—then "there will be no Pakistan left when we have responded.") William Arkin writes in the *Los Angeles Times* that the United States is "drafting contingency plans for the use of nuclear weapons." STRATCOM—the successor to the Strategic Air Command—has been ordered to consider ways in which nuclear weapons can be used pre-emptively, either to destroy underground facilities or to respond to the use or threats of use of weapons of mass destruction against the United States or its forces.

Oil and Democracy

Other critics of the war have concluded from the disparity in America's treatment of Iraq and North Korea that the Administration's aim is not to deal with weapons of mass destruction at all but to seize Iraq's oil, which amounts to some 10 percent of the world's known reserves. The very fact that the Bush Administration refuses even to discuss the oil question (the war "has nothing to do with oil," Defense Secretary Donald Rumsfeld has said) suggests that the influence of oil is moving powerfully in the background. One is tempted to respond to Rumsfeld that if the Administration is not thinking about the consequences of a war for the global oil regime, it is culpably neglecting the security interests of the United States. However, there is in fact no contradiction between the goals of disarming Iraq and seizing its oil. Both fit neatly into the larger scheme of American global dominance.

Still other critics place the emphasis not on oil but on political reform of Iraq and even the entire Middle East. Thomas Friedman of the *New York Times* is prepared to support Hussein's overthrow, but only if we "do it right"— which is to say that we devote the "time and effort" to creating "a self-sustaining, progressive, accountable Arab government" in Iraq. And this delightful government (can we have one at home, too, please?), in turn, must become "a progressive model for the whole region." "Our kids" can grow up in "a safer world" only "if we help put Iraq on a more progressive path and stimulate some real change in an Arab world that is badly in need of reform." Fouad Ajami, of Johns Hopkins University, likewise wants the United States to get over its "dread of nation-building" and spearhead "a reformist project that seeks to modernize and transform the Arab landscape," now mired in "retrogression and political decay." Michael Ignatieff, director of the Carr Center for Human Rights at Harvard, is also of the "do it right" school. His starting point, however, is the need to disarm Iraq. In his essay in the *New York Times Magazine* "The American Empire: The Burden," he begins by noting that if Saddam Hussein is permitted to have weapons of mass destruction, he will have a "capacity to intimidate and deter others, including the United States." Being deterred in a region of interest is evidently unacceptable for an imperial power, and forces it to remove the offending regime. Yet if the regime is to be removed, a larger imperial agenda becomes inescapable. By this reasoning Ignatieff arrives at the same destination as Friedman and Ajami: The United States must mount "an imperial operation that would commit a reluctant republic to become the guarantor of peace, stability, democratization and oil supplies in a combustible region of Islamic peoples stretching from Egypt to Afghanistan." We arrive at a new formula that has no precedent for dealing with nuclear danger: nonproliferation by forced democratization. Ignatieff acknowledges that a republic that turns into an empire risks "endangering its identity as a free people"—thus menacing democracy at home by trying to force it on others abroad. Nevertheless, he wants the United States to take on "the burden of empire."

The Bush Administration, however, has given little encouragement to the evangelists of armed democratization. Notoriously, it has kept silent regarding its plans for postwar Iraq and its neighbors. But if its actions in the "war on terror" are any guide, democracy will not be required of Washington's imperial dependencies. The Bush Administration has been perfectly happy, for example, to extend its cooperation to such allies as totalitarian Turkmenistan and authoritarian Uzbekistan and Kazakhstan—not to speak of such longstanding autocratic allies of the United States as Egypt and Saudi Arabia. The United States has in fact never insisted on democracy as a condition for good relations with other countries. Its practice during the cold war probably offers as accurate a guide to the future as any. The United States was pleased to have democratic allies, including most of the countries of Europe, but was also ready when needed to install or prop up such brutal, repressive regimes as (to mention only a few) that of Reza Pahlavi in Iran, Saddam Hussein in Iraq (until he invaded Kuwait), Mobutu Sese Seko in Zaire (now Congo), Fulgencio Batista in Cuba, Park Chung Hee in South Korea, a succession of civilian and military dictators in South Vietnam, Lon Nol in Cambodia, Suharto in Indonesia, Ferdinand Marcos in the Philippines, the colonels' junta in Greece, Francisco Franco in Spain and a long list of military dictators in Argentina, Chile, Brazil, Uruguay, Guatemala, El Salvador and Nicaragua.

The Administration has in any case made its broader conception of democracy clear in its actions both at home and abroad. In this conception, the Administration decides and others are permitted to express their agreement. (Or else they become, as the President has said threateningly to the U.N., "irrelevant"—although it's hard to imagine what it means to say that the assembled representatives of the peoples of the earth are irrelevant. Irrelevant to what?) Just as the Administration welcomed a Congressional expression of support for the Bush war policy but denied it the power to stop the war if that were to be its choice, and just as the Administration "welcomes" a vote for war in NATO and the U.N. but denies either NATO or the U.N. the right to prevent unilateral American action, so we can expect that the people of Iraq or any other country the United States might "democratize" would be "free" to support but not to oppose American policy. (Imagine, for example, that the people of Iraq were to vote, as so many other free peoples, including the American people, have done before them, to build nuclear arsenals—perhaps on the ground that their enemy Israel already has them and Iran was building them. Would the Bush Administration accept their decision?)

We do not have to wait for war in Iraq, however, to consider the likely impact of Washington's new policies on democracy's global fortunes. The question has already arisen in the period of preparation for war. The Bush Administration has not forced the world to read between the lines to discover its position. It proposes for the world at large the same two-tier system that it proposes for the decision to go to war and for the possession of weapons of mass destruction: It lays claim to absolute military hegemony over the earth. "America has, and intends to keep, military strengths beyond challenge, thereby making the destabilizing arms races of other eras pointless, and limiting rivalries to trade and other pursuits of peace," the President said in his speech at West Point. The United States alone will be the custodian of military power; others must turn to humbler pursuits. The sword will rule, and the United States will hold the sword. As the Yale historian John Lewis Gaddis has pointed out, the policies of unilateral pre-emption, overthrow of governments and overall military supremacy form an integral package (the seizure of Middle Eastern oilfields, though officially denied as a motive, also fits in). These elements are the foundations of the imperial system that Ignatieff and others have delineated.

However, empire is incompatible with democracy, whether at home or abroad. Democracy is founded on the rule of law, empire on the rule of force. Democracy is a system of self-determination, empire a system of military conquest. The fault lines are already clear, and growing wider every day. By every measure, public opinion in the world—its democratic will—is opposed to overthrowing the government of Iraq by force. But why, someone might ask, does this matter? How many divisions do these people have, as Stalin once asked of the Pope? The answer, to the extent that the world really is democratic, is: quite a few. In a series of elections—in Germany, in South Korea, in Turkey—an antiwar position helped bring the winner to power. In divided Korea, American policy may be on its way to producing an unexpected union of South and North—against the United States. Each of these setbacks is a critical defeat for the putative American empire. In January, the prime ministers of eight countries—Spain, Italy, Portugal, Denmark, Poland, the Czech Republic, Hungary and Poland—signed a letter thanking the United States for its leadership on the Iraq issue; but in every one of those countries a majority of the public opposed a war without U.N. approval. The editors of *Time's* European edition asked its readers which nation posed the greatest threat to world peace. Of the 268,000 who responded, 8 percent answered that it was North Korea, 9 percent Iraq and 83 percent said the United States. Britain's Prime Minister Tony Blair is prepared to participate in the war without U.N. support, but some 70 percent of his people oppose his position. The government of Australia is sending troops to assist in the war effort, but 92 percent of the Australian public opposes war unsanctioned by the U.N. Gaddis rightly comments that empires succeed to the extent that people under their rule welcome and share the values of the imperial power. The above election results and poll figures suggest that no such approval is so far evident for America's global pretensions. The American "coalition" for war is an alliance of governments arrayed in opposition to their own peoples.

In a defeat parallel to—and greater than—the military defeat before the fact in the field of proliferation, the American empire is thus suffering deep and possibly irreversible political losses. Democracy is the right of peoples to make decisions. Right now, the peoples of the earth are deciding against America's plans for the world. Democracy, too, has pre-emptive resources, setting up impassable roadblocks at the first signs of tyranny. The U.N. Security Council is balking. The United States' most important alliance—NATO—is cracking. Is the American empire collapsing before it even quite comes into existence? Such a judgment is premature, but if the mere approach to war has done the damage we already see to America's reputation and power, we can only imagine what the consequences of actual war will be.

II. The Atomic Archipelago

The Administration has embarked on a nonproliferation policy that has already proved as self-defeating in its own terms as it is likely to be disastrous for the United States and the world. Nevertheless, it would be a fatal mistake for those of us who oppose the war to dismiss the concerns that the Administration has raised. By insisting that the world confront the proliferation of weapons of mass destruction, President Bush has raised the right question—or, at any rate, one part of the right question—for our time, even as he has given a calamitously misguided answer. Even if it were true—and we won't really know until some equivalent of the Pentagon Papers for our period is released—that his Administration has been using the threat of mass destruction as a cover for an oil grab, the issue of proliferation must be placed at the center of *our* concerns. For example, even as we argue that containment of Iraq makes more sense than war, we must be clear-eyed in acknowledging that Iraq's acquisition of nuclear weapons or other weapons of mass destruction would be a disaster—just as we must recognize that the nuclearization of South Asia and of North Korea have been disasters, greatly increasing the likelihood of nuclear war in the near future. These events, full of peril in themselves, are points on a curve of proliferation that leads to what can only be described as nuclear anarchy.

For a global policy that, unlike the Bush policies, actually will stop—and reverse—proliferation of all weapons of mass destruction is indeed a necessity for a sane, livable twenty-first century. But if we are to tackle the problem wisely, we must step back from the current crisis long enough to carefully analyze the origins and character of the danger. It did not appear on September 11. It appeared, in fact, on July 16, 1945, when the United States detonated the first atomic bomb near Alamogordo, New Mexico.

What is proliferation? It is the acquisition of nuclear weapons by a country that did not have them before. The first act of proliferation was the Manhattan Project in the United States. (In what follows, I will speak of nuclear proliferation, but the principles underlying it also underlie the proliferation of chemical and biological weapons.) Perhaps someone might object that the arrival of the first individual of a species is not yet proliferation—a word that suggests the multiplication of an already existing thing. However, in one critical respect, at least, the development of the bomb by the United States still fits the definition. The record shows that President Franklin Roosevelt decided to build the bomb because he feared that Hitler would get it first, with decisive consequences in the forthcoming war. In October 1939, when the businessman Alexander Sachs brought Roosevelt a letter from Albert Einstein warning that an atomic bomb was possible and that Germany might acquire one, Roosevelt commented, "Alex, what you are after is to see that the Nazis don't blow us up." As we know now, Hitler did have an atomic project, but it never came close to producing a bomb. But as with so many matters in nuclear strategy, appearances were more important than the realities (which were then unknowable to the United States). Before there was the bomb, there was the fear of the bomb. Hitler's phantom arsenal inspired the real American one. And so even before nuclear weapons existed, they were proliferating. This sequence is important because it reveals a basic rule that has driven nuclear proliferation ever since: Nations acquire nuclear arsenals above all because they fear the nuclear arsenals of others.

But fear—soon properly renamed terror in the context of nuclear strategy—is of course also the essence of the prime strategic doctrine of the nuclear age, deterrence, which establishes a balance of terror. Threats of the destruction of nations—of genocide—have always been the coinage of this realm. From the beginning of the nuclear age—indeed, even before the beginning, when the atomic bomb was only a gleam in Roosevelt's eye—deterrence and proliferation have in fact been inextricable. Just as the United States made the bomb because it feared Hitler would get it, the Soviet Union built the bomb because the United States already had it. Stalin's instructions to his scientists shortly after Hiroshima were, "A single demand of you, comrades: Provide us with atomic weapons in the shortest possible time. You know that Hiroshima has shaken the whole world. The equilibrium has been destroyed. Provide the bomb—it will remove a great danger from us." England and France, like the United States, were responding to the Soviet threat; China was responding to the threat from all of the above; India was responding to China; Pakistan was responding to India; and North Korea (with Pakistan's help) was responding to the United States. Nations proliferate in order to deter. We can state: Deterrence equals proliferation, for deterrence both causes proliferation and is the fruit of it. This has been the lesson, indeed, that the United States has taught the world in every major statement, tactic, strategy and action it has taken in the nuclear age. And the world—if it even needed the lesson—has learned well. It is therefore hardly surprising that the call to nonproliferation falls on deaf ears when it is preached by possessors—all of whom were of course proliferators at one time or another.

The sources of nuclear danger, present and future, are perhaps best visualized as a coral reef that is constantly growing in all directions under the sea and then, here and there, breaks the surface to form islands, which we can collectively call the atomic archipelago. The islands of the archipelago may seem to be independent of one another, but anyone who looks below the surface will find that they are closely connected. The atomic archipelago indeed has strong similarities to its namesake, the gulag archipelago. Once established, both feed on themselves, expanding from within by their own energy and momentum. Both are founded upon a capacity to kill millions of people. Both act on the world around them by radiating terror.

India and the Bomb: The Proliferator's View

India's path to nuclear armament, recounted in George Perkovich's masterful, definitive *India's Nuclear Bomb,* offers essential lessons in the steps by which the archipelago has grown and is likely to grow in the future. India has maintained a nuclear program almost since its independence, in 1947. Although supposedly built for peaceful uses, the program was actually, if mostly secretly, designed to keep the weapons option open. But it was not until shortly after China tested a bomb in 1964 that India embarked on a concerted nuclear weapons program, which bore fruit in 1974, when India tested a bomb for "peaceful" purposes. Yet India still held back from introducing nuclear weapons into its military forces. Meanwhile, Pakistan, helped by China, was working hard to obtain the bomb. In May of 1998, India conducted five nuclear tests. Pakistan responded with at least five, and both nations promptly declared themselves nuclear powers and soon were engaged in a major nuclear confrontation over the disputed territory of Kashmir.

Indian Foreign Minister Jaswant Singh has explained the reasons for India's decision in an article in *Foreign Affairs*. India looked out upon the world and saw what he calls a "nuclear paradigm" in operation. He liked what he saw. He writes, "Why admonish India after the fact for not falling in line behind a new international agenda of discriminatory nonproliferation pursued largely due to the internal agendas or political debates of the nuclear club? If deterrence works in the West—as it so obviously appears to, since Western nations insist on continuing to possess nuclear weapons—by what reasoning will it not work in India?" To deprive India of these benefits would be "nuclear apartheid"—a continuation of the imperialism that had been overthrown in the titanic anticolonial struggles of the twentieth century. The Nuclear Nonproliferation Treaty, under which 183 nations have agreed to forgo nuclear arms, and five who have them (the United States, England, France, Russia and China) have agreed to reduce theirs until they are gone, had many successes, but in India's backyard, where China had nuclear arms and Pakistan was developing them, nuclear danger was growing. Some have charged that the Indian government conducted the 1998 tests for political rather than strategic reasons—that is, out of a desire for pure "prestige," not strategic necessity. But the two explanations are in fact complementary. It is only because the public, which observes that all the great powers possess nuclear arsenals, agrees that they are a strategic necessity that it finds them prestigious and politically rewards governments that acquire them. Prestige is merely the political face of the general consensus, ingrained in strategy, that countries lacking nuclear weapons are helpless—"eunuchs," as one Indian politician said—in a nuclear-armed world.

Curiously, the unlimited extension in 1995 of the NPT, to which India was not a signatory, pushed India to act. From Singh's point of view, the extension made the nuclear double standard it embodied permanent. "What India did in May [1998] was to assert that it is impossible to have two standards for national security—one based on nuclear deterrence and the other outside of it."

If the world was to be divided into two classes of countries, India preferred to be in the first class.

As Singh's account makes clear, India was inspired to act not merely by the hypocrisy of great powers delivering sermons on the virtues of nuclear disarmament while sitting atop mountains of nuclear arms—galling as that might be. He believed that India, with nuclear-armed China and nuclearizing Pakistan for neighbors, was living in an increasingly "dangerous neighborhood." The most powerful tie that paradoxically binds proliferator to deterrer in their minuet of genocidal hostility is not mere imitation but the compulsion to respond to the nuclear terror projected by others. The preacher against lust who turns out to take prostitutes to a motel after the sermon sets a bad example but does not compel his parishioners to follow suit. The preacher against nuclear weapons in a nation whose silos are packed with them does, however, compel other nations to follow his example, for his nuclear terror reaches and crosses their borders. The United States terrorizes Russia (and vice versa); both terrorize China; China terrorizes India; the United States terrorizes North Korea; North Korea terrorizes Japan; and so forth, forming a web of terror whose further extensions (Israel terrorizes . . . Iran? Egypt? Syria? Libya?) will be the avenues of future proliferation. It is thanks to this web that every nuclear arsenal in the world is tied, directly or indirectly, to every other, rendering any partial approach to the problem extremely difficult, if not impossible.

The devotion of nations to their nuclear arsenals has only been strengthened by the hegemonic ambition of the United States. Hitherto, the nuclear double standard lacked a context—it was a sort of anomaly of the international order, a seeming leftover from the cold war, perhaps soon to be liquidated. America's imperial ambition gives it a context. In a multilateral, democratic vision of international affairs, it is impossible to explain why one small group of nations should be entitled to protect itself with weapons of mass destruction while all others must do without them. But in an imperial order, the reason is perfectly obvious. If the imperium is to pacify the world, it must possess overwhelming force, the currency of imperial power. Equally obviously, the nations to be pacified must not. Double standards—regarding not only nuclear weapons but conventional weapons, economic advantage, use of natural resources—are indeed the very stuff of which empires are made. For empire is to the world what dictatorship is to a country. That's why the suppression of proliferation—a new imperial vocation—must be the first order of business for a nation aspiring to this exalted role.

India's Bomb: The Possessor's View

It's equally enlightening to look at India's proliferation from the point of view of a nuclear possessor, the United States. Nuclear arsenals are endowed with a magical quality. As soon as a nation obtains one it becomes invisible to the possessor. Nuclear danger then seems to emanate only from proliferation—that is, from newcomers to the nuclear club, while the dangers that emanate from one's own arsenal disappear from sight. Gen. Tommy Franks, designated as commander of the Iraq war, recently commented, "The sight of the first mushroom cloud on one of the major population centers on this planet is something that most nations on this planet are willing to go a long ways out of the way to prevent." His forgetfulness of Hiroshima and Nagasaki might seem nothing more than a slip of the tongue if it did not represent a pervasive and deeply ingrained attitude in the United States. Another revealing incident was Secretary of State Powell's comment that North Korea, by seeking nuclear weapons, was arming itself with "fool's gold." But the military establishment that Powell once led is of course stuffed to bursting with this fool's gold. Another example of the same habit of mind (I have chosen American examples, but the blindness afflicts all nuclear powers) was provided by some comments of President Bill Clinton shortly after India's tests of 1998. He said, "To think that you have to manifest your greatness by behavior that recalls the very worst events of the twentieth century on the edge of the twenty-first century, when everybody else is trying to leave the nuclear age behind, is just wrong. And they [the Indians] clearly don't need it to maintain their security." Wise words, but ones contradicted by more than a half-century of the nuclear policies, including the current ones, of the nation he led.

The reactions of some of America's most prominent thinkers on the nuclear question to India's proliferation were also instructive. Almost immediately, their belief in the virtues of nuclear arms began to surface through the antiproliferation rhetoric. Henry Kissinger, for instance, judiciously mocked Clinton's "unique insight into the nature of greatness in the twenty-first century . . . the dubious proposition that all other nations are trying to leave the nuclear world behind," and "the completely unsupported proposition that countries with threatening nuclear neighbors do not need nuclear weapons to assure their security." Kissinger, more consistent than Clinton, found India's and Pakistan's tests "equally reasonable." He thought Washington's best course was to help its new nuclear-armed friends achieve "stable mutual deterrence," and "give stabilizing reassurances about their conventional security." Kissinger even saw a silver lining for American interests in the hope that nuclear-armed India would help the United States "contain China" (the very China to which Krauthammer now turns to disarm North Korea). It was Kissinger's view, not Clinton's, that soon prevailed. America's own love affair with the bomb asserted itself. At first, the United States imposed sanctions on both countries, but soon they were lifted. In December of 2000 President Clinton paid the first visit by an American President to India since 1978, confirming that becoming a nuclear power was indeed the path to international prestige. The United States now has growing programs of military cooperation with both countries.

Kissinger merely adjusted to the irreversible *fait accompli* of South Asian proliferation, as a realist should. He saw the tension between America's love of its own nuclear bombs and its hatred of others', and understood the problems this might cause for America's own arsenal. Could nonproliferation get out of control? Might it reach America's shores? "The administration is right to resist nuclear proliferation," he wrote, "but it must not, in the process, disarm the country psychologically."

III. One Will for One World

War in Iraq has not yet begun, but its most important lesson, taught also by the long history of proliferation, including the Indian chapter just discussed, is already plain: The time is long gone—if it ever existed—when any major element of the danger of weapons of mass destruction, including above all nuclear danger, can be addressed realistically without taking into account the whole dilemma. When we look at the story of proliferation, whether from the point of view of the haves or the have-nots, what emerges is that for practical purposes any distinction that once might have existed (and even then only in appearance, not in reality) between possessors and proliferators has now been erased. A rose is a rose is a rose, anthrax is anthrax is anthrax, a thermonuclear weapon is a thermonuclear weapon is a thermonuclear weapon. The world's prospective nuclear arsenals cannot be dealt with without attending to its existing ones. As long as some countries insist on having any of these, others will try to get them. Until this axiom is understood, neither "dialogue" nor war can succeed. In Perkovich's words, after immersing himself in the history of India's bomb, "the grandest illusion of the nuclear age is that a handful of states possessing nuclear weapons can secure themselves and the world indefinitely against the dangers of nuclear proliferation *without* placing a higher priority on simultaneously striving to eliminate their own nuclear weapons."

The days of the double standard are over. We cannot preserve it and we should not want to. The struggle to maintain it by force, anachronistically represented by Bush's proposed war on Iraq, in which the United States threatens pre-emptive use of nuclear weapons to stop another country merely from getting them, can only worsen the global problem it seeks to solve. One way or another, the world is on its way to a single standard. Only two in the long run are available: universal permission to possess weapons of mass destruction or their universal prohibition. The first is a path to global nightmare, the second to safety and a normal existence. Nations that already possess nuclear weapons must recognize that nuclear danger begins with them. The shield of invisibility must be pierced. The web of terror that binds every nuclear arsenal to every other—and also to every arsenal of chemical or biological weapons—must be acknowledged.

If pre-emptive military force leads to catastrophe and deterrence is at best a stopgap, then what is the answer? In 1945, the great Danish nuclear physicist Niels Bohr said simply, in words whose truth has been confirmed by fifty-eight years of experience of the nuclear age, "We are in a completely new situation that cannot be resolved by war." In a formulation only slightly more complex than Bohr's, Einstein said in 1947, "This basic power of the universe cannot be fitted into the outdated concept of narrow nationalisms. For there is no secret and there is no defense; there is no possibility of control except through the aroused understanding and insistence of the peoples of the world." Both men, whose work in fundamental physics had perhaps done more than that of any other two scientists to make the bomb possible, favored the abolition of nuclear arms by binding international agreement. That idea, also favored by many of the scientists of the Manhattan Project, bore fruit in a plan for the abolition of nuclear arms and international control of all nuclear technology put forward by President Truman's representative Bernard Baruch in June 1946. But the time was not ripe. The cold war was already brewing, and the Soviet Union, determined to build its own bomb, said no, then put forward a plan that the United States turned down. In 1949 the Soviet Union conducted its first atomic test, and the nuclear arms race ensued.

For the short term, the inspections in Iraq should continue. If inspections fail, then containment will do as a second line of defense. But in the long term, the true alternative to pre-emptive war against Iraq, war one day against North Korea, war against an unknowable number of other possible proliferators, is to bring Bohr and Einstein's proposal up to date. A revival of worldwide disarmament negotiations must be the means, the abolition of all weapons of mass destruction the end. That idea has long been in eclipse, and today it lies outside the mainstream of political opinion. Unfortunately, historical reality is no respecter of conventional wisdom and often requires it to change course if calamity is to be avoided. But fortunately it is one element of the genius of democracy—and of U.S. democracy in particular—that encrusted orthodoxy can be challenged and overthrown by popular pressure. The movement *against* the war in Iraq should also become a movement *for* something, and that something should be a return to the long-neglected path to abolition of all weapons of mass destruction. Only by offering a solution to the problem that the war claims to solve but does not can this war and others be stopped.

The passage of time since the failure in 1946 has also provided us with some advantages. No insuperable ideological division divides the nuclear powers (with the possible exception, now, of North Korea), as the cold war did. Their substantial unity and agreement in this area can be imagined. Every other nonnuclear nation but one (the eccentric holdout is Cuba) already has agreed under the terms of the Nuclear Nonproliferation Treaty to do without nuclear weapons. Biological and chemical weapons have been banned by international conventions (although the conventions are weak, as they lack serious inspection and enforcement provisions).

The inspected and enforced elimination of weapons of mass destruction is a goal that in its very nature must take time, and adequate time—perhaps a decade, or even more—can be allowed. But the decision to embrace the goal should not wait. It should be seen not as a distant dream that may or may not be realized once a host of other unlikely prerequisites have been met but as a powerful instrument to be used immediately to halt all forms of proliferation and inspire arms reductions in the present. There can be no successful nonproliferation policy that is not backed by the concerted will of the international community. As long as the double standard is in effect, that will cannot be created. Do we need more evidence than the world's disarray today in the face of Iraq's record of proliferation? Today's world, to paraphrase Lincoln, is a house divided, half nuclear-armed, half nuclear-weapons-free. A commitment to the elimination of weapons of mass destruction would heal the world's broken will, and is the only means available for doing so. Great powers that were getting out of the mass destruction business would have very short patience with nations, such as Iraq or North Korea, getting into that business. The Security Council would act as one. The smaller powers that had never made their pact with the devil in the first place would be at the great powers' side. Any proliferator would face the implacable resolve of all nations to persuade it or force it to reverse its course.

Let us try to imagine it: one human species on its one earth exercising one will to defeat forever a threat to its one collective existence. Could any nation stand against it? Without this commitment, the international community—if

I may express it thus—is like a nuclear reactor from which the fuel rods have been withdrawn. Making the commitment would be to insert the rods, to start up the chain reaction. The chain reaction would be the democratic activity of peoples demanding action from the governments to secure their survival. True democracy is indispensable to disarmament, and vice versa. This is the power—not the power of cruise missiles and B-52s—that can release humanity from its peril. The price demanded of us for freedom from the danger of weapons of mass destruction is to relinquish our own.

PART FOUR

THROUGH A GLASS DARKLY

THIRTEEN

THE FUTURE
OF IRAQ

"We shall be greeted, I think, in Baghdad and Basra with kites and boomboxes."

—Fouad Ajami

"American soldiers will not be received by flowers; they will be received by bullets."

—Iraqi foreign minister Tarik Aziz, January 22, 2003

"The problem for the U.S. is much the same as it was in 1991 when President Saddam had been defeated in Kuwait and had lost 14 out of Iraq's 18 provinces to Shia and Kurdish rebels. While the U.S. wanted regime change and the Iraqi leader toppled, it did not want revolutionary change. But if democracy was introduced in Iraq, revolutionary change would be inevitable because Shia and Kurds make up three-quarters of the Iraqi population."

—Patrick Cockburn, reporting from Irbil,
northern Iraq, February 21, 2003

"If we go to war, it's not about oil. But the day the war ends, it has everything to do with oil."

—Larry Goldstein, president, Petroleum Industry Research Foundation,
quoted in The Wall Street Journal, *January 16, 2003*

"There is a difference between a war of liberation and a war of conquest. Liberation means Iraqis are at the forefront. Conquest means the invaders are in charge."

—*Hoshyar Zubari, an official of the Kurdish Democratic Party, speaking in Salahuddin, Iraq, on March 26, 2003*

IRAQ: THE IMPERIAL PRECEDENT

Charles Tripp

The United States seems determined to enforce regime change in Iraq, but far less certain is just what regime it wants to replace that of Saddam Hussein, or what kind of Iraq it hopes to set up after the war. But the state of Iraq as we know it is in fact the almost accidental result of the British invasion of Mesopotamia in 1914, and subsequent poor imperial choices and default decisions. History, as ever, has been here before.

In Baghdad, an authoritarian regime, backed by military force, exercises a powerful grip over Iraq and poses a direct strategic threat to the interests of the major Western power in the region. A military expedition against the regime is mounted and, after a campaign that proves more difficult and costly than anticipated, Baghdad is captured and a new political order established under Western military and political control. But just as it seems that direct foreign rule is establishing the shape of the future for Iraq, rebellion breaks out among Iraqi army officers on the streets of Baghdad and throughout the Shi'ite centre and south of the country, putting the whole enterprise in jeopardy.

The uprising is eventually crushed, but the cost of doing that leads to a radical rethink in the army of occupation and in its government back home. In place of the ambitious visions once entertained by the occupiers, a more modest, cheaper plan emerges. It recognises the existing socio-political hierarchy in Iraq and hands control of the state, under Western surveillance, to the administrative and military elites of the old regime.

This is not a prediction of the next 12 months in Iraq. It is a description of events that took place over 80 years ago, when Great Britain conquered the three Ottoman provinces of Basra, Baghdad and Mosul and welded them into the new state of Iraq. The fact that there are echoes of the present and of possible future scenarios in Iraq has less to do with some irreducible essence of Iraqi history than with the logic of imperial power. If there is a war, the United States could find itself facing choices similar to those faced by Britain be-

Charles Tripp is a professor of Near and Middle Eastern studies at the University of London. He is the author of *The History of Iraq* (updated in 2002) and *Iran and Iraq at War* (1988). This article was originally published in the January 2003 issue of *Le Monde Diplomatique*.

tween 1914 and 1921. It is worth reflecting upon those choices to understand whether the exercise of imperial power in the task of state reconstruction has a similar logic. This could throw light on the kind of Iraq which an American military occupation might bring into being.

When the British invaded Mesopotamia in 1914, they did not intend to create a state. Their immediate objective was the security of their position in the Persian Gulf. But military success led to greater ambitions and by 1918 British forces had occupied the whole of what is now modern Iraq. Throughout the territories a civil administration was established, based on the model of British India, where many of the officers and officials had gained their experience.

It was a mixture of direct and indirect rule: the enterprise was controlled by British-staffed ministries in Baghdad, but British political officers in the provinces depended upon local community leaders to guarantee social order and collect revenues. Excluded from these arrangements were the predominantly Sunni Arab or Arabised Turkish administrative and military elites of the former Ottoman state. A distinct British imperial order began to emerge, centred on Baghdad, gradually penetrating all levels of society and appearing to consolidate British interests.

But with the end of the war in 1918, different ideas about the nature of those interests surfaced in different branches of the British state. Some held to a strong imperial vision that believed that it was part of Britain's mission to practise the micro-technologies of power, to make society fit the new administrative order. Another view, influenced both by moral doubts about the imperial project and practical questions of resources and commitment, advocated a lighter touch. Here the argument was that Britain had only two basic requirements of any government in Mesopotamia: that it should be administratively competent and that it should be respectful of British strategic requirements. It was this view which triumphed and upon which the state of Iraq was founded.

Events in Iraq, as well as in the wider international sphere and in Britain, contributed to this outcome. In 1920 the principles of national self-determination created the idea of League of Nations mandates—territories of the defeated Central Powers which one of the victorious powers would bring eventually to independence as sovereign states. The idea was taken up by those in the British government who wanted to maintain its global influence and control at minimum cost, financially and militarily. Given the changing public mood in Britain in 1919–20 about the uses of public expenditure, and the alarm in government about the cost of empire, this seemed an ideal solution.

In Iraq, many people resented the mandate as a light disguise for British imperial control; by contrast, certain British imperial servants in the country saw it as a dangerous abdication of responsibility. The clash between these two views led to the Iraqi Revolt of 1920. This began in Baghdad with mass demonstrations of urban Iraqis, both Sunni and Shi'ite, and the protests of embittered ex-Ottoman officers. The revolt gained momentum when it spread to the largely Shi'ite regions of the middle and lower Euphrates. Well-armed tribesmen, outraged by the intrusions of central government and resentful of infidel rule, seized control of most of the south of the country. It took the British several months, and cost thousands of lives—British, Indian and Iraqi—to suppress the revolt and re-establish Baghdad's control

The revolt had two profound consequences. It persuaded the British that the cost of trying to rule Iraq would be too high and that it was imperative to set up a fully functioning Iraqi government, army and administration. Furthermore, it made it almost inevitable that when the British looked for the cadres to govern the new state, they should choose the Ottoman administrative and military elites displaced during the war. The British saw these men as having proven experience in running a modern state, as well as a pragmatic grasp of the importance of Britain in helping them to entrench themselves in power, and in securing Iraq in the region. The leaders of the majority Shi'ite population and of the substantial Kurdish minority were seen as potentially mutinous, as well as too encumbered by tribal and religious traditions to govern a modern state.

These considerations shaped subsequent British policy in Iraq. Amir Faisal of the Hijaz was installed as king, sustained by mainly Sunni Arab former Ottoman officers and officials. They took over the administration from departing British officials and formed the backbone of the new Iraqi officer corps. British influence continued through its advisers in the Iraqi ministries, through its two major air force bases in the country and through the multiple ties which bound the two countries together and sustained Britain's informal empire even after Iraqi independence in 1932.

In the sense of safeguarding British strategic interests, the advocates of the minimalist or indirect approach to the question of political order in Iraq appeared to have been vindicated. However, they had also laid the foundations for a distinctive form of state in Iraq. This was affected both by the authoritarian inclinations of the new governing class, as well as by their prejudices towards the diverse communities who formed the majority of the Iraqi population.

The relevance of this to the present situation is not only that Saddam Hussein's regime is a direct descendant of this pattern of government. It is also that the temptation confronting the U.S., if and when it tries to organise the future of Iraq, may be similar to that which faced the British government and its officials in 1920. In the aftermath of a military invasion and the likely overthrow of Saddam Hussein's regime, the U.S. will face a choice.

It can try to bring about a fundamental change in the way Iraq is governed and commit the time and resources necessary to make that happen. Or it can set up an Iraqi administration which will carry out the principal wishes of the U.S.—respect for American strategic interests and maintenance of order— thereby allowing an early withdrawal of U.S. forces. This would mean recognising much of the existing power structure in Iraq, as well as the narrative of Iraqi history that brought the present regime into being. Faced by internal resistance and fearful of risking American lives and resources in a project of state reconstruction increasingly remote from the interests of the American public, it is quite possible that the U.S. administration would opt for disengagement from Iraq's internal affairs.

This might contradict the present declarations being made in Washington promising a mission to transform Iraq into a beacon of democracy in the region. It would certainly cause despair among those Iraqis who have seen the U.S. as their main hope of radical political change. But for the U.S., as for the British 80 years ago, the lower risk, the lesser cost and the short-term advantages may outweigh the possible future benefits of fundamental social transformation in Iraq.

THE FIFTY-FIRST STATE?

James Fallows

O ver the past few months I interviewed several dozen people about what could be expected in Iraq after the United States dislodged Saddam Hussein. An assumption behind the question was that sooner or later the United States would go to war—and would go with at best a fraction of the support it enjoyed eleven years ago when fighting Iraq during the Gulf War. Most nations in the region and traditional U.S. allies would be neutral or hostile unless the Bush Administration could present new evidence of imminent danger from Iraq.

A further assumption was that even alone, U.S. forces would win this war. The victory might be slower than in the last war against Iraq, and it would certainly cost more American lives. But in the end U.S. tanks, attack airplanes, precision-guided bombs, special-operations forces, and other assets would crush the Iraqi military. The combat phase of the war would be over when the United States destroyed Saddam Hussein's control over Iraq's government, armed forces, and stockpile of weapons.

What then?

The people I asked were spies, Arabists, oil-company officials, diplomats, scholars, policy experts, and many active-duty and retired soldiers. They were from the United States, Europe, and the Middle East. Some firmly supported a pre-emptive war against Iraq; more were opposed. As of late summer, before the serious domestic debate had begun, most of the people I spoke with expected a war to occur.

I began my research sharing the view, prevailing in Washington this year, that forcing "regime change" on Iraq was our era's grim historical necessity: starting a war would be bad, but waiting to have war brought to us would be worse. This view depended to some degree on trusting that the U.S. government had information not available to the public about exactly how close Saddam Hussein is to having usable nuclear warheads or other weapons of mass destruction. It also drew much of its power from an analogy every member of

James Fallows is *The Atlantic Monthly's* National Correspondent, and has worked for the magazine for more than twenty years (including a long stint as its Washington editor). He is the author of numerous books, including *Breaking the News: How the Media Undermine American Democracy*, and *National Defense*, which won the American Book Award for nonfiction. This article was originally published in the November 2002 issue of *The Atlantic Monthly.*

the public could understand—to Nazi Germany. In retrospect, the only sin in resisting Hitler had been waiting too long. Thus would it be in dealing with Saddam Hussein today. Richard Perle, a Reagan-era Defense Department official who is one of the most influential members outside government of what is frequently called the "war party," expressed this thought in representative form in an August column for the London *Daily Telegraph*: "A pre-emptive strike against Hitler at the time of Munich would have meant an immediate war, as opposed to the one that came later. Later was much worse."

Nazi and Holocaust analogies have a trumping power in many arguments, and their effect in Washington was to make doubters seem weak—Neville Chamberlains, versus the Winston Churchills who were ready to face the truth. The most experienced military figure in the Bush Cabinet, Secretary of State Colin Powell, was cast as the main "wet," because of his obvious discomfort with an effort that few allies would support. His instincts fit the general sociology of the Iraq debate: As a rule, the strongest advocates of pre-emptive attack, within the government and in the press, had neither served in the military nor lived in Arab societies. Military veterans and Arabists were generally doves. For example: Paul Wolfowitz, the deputy secretary of defense and the intellectual leader of the war party inside the government, was in graduate school through the late 1960s. Richard Armitage, his skeptical counterpart at the State Department and Powell's ally in pleading for restraint, is a Naval Academy graduate who served three tours in Vietnam.

I ended up thinking that the Nazi analogy paralyzes the debate about Iraq rather than clarifying it. Like any other episode in history, today's situation is both familiar and new. In the ruthlessness of the adversary it resembles dealing with Adolf Hitler. But Iraq, unlike Germany, has no industrial base and few military allies nearby. It is split by regional, religious, and ethnic differences that are much more complicated than Nazi Germany's simple mobilization of "Aryans" against Jews. Hitler's Germany constantly expanded, but Iraq has been bottled up, by international sanctions, for more than ten years. As in the early Cold War, America faces an international ideology bent on our destruction and a country trying to develop weapons to use against us. But then we were dealing with another superpower, capable of obliterating us. Now there is a huge imbalance between the two sides in scale and power.

If we had to choose a single analogy to govern our thinking about Iraq, my candidate would be World War I. The reason is not simply the one the historian David Fromkin advanced in his book *A Peace to End All Peace*: that the division of former Ottoman Empire territories after that war created many of the enduring problems of modern Iraq and the Middle East as a whole. The Great War is also relevant as a powerful example of the limits of human imagination: specifically, imagination about the long-term consequences of war.

The importance of imagination was stressed to me by Merrill McPeak, a retired Air Force general with misgivings about a pre-emptive attack. When America entered the Vietnam War, in which McPeak flew combat missions over the jungle, the public couldn't imagine how badly combat against a "weak" foe might turn out for the United States. Since that time, and because of the Vietnam experience, we have generally overdrawn the risks of combat itself. America's small wars of the past generation, in Grenada, Haiti, and Panama, have turned out far better—tactically, at least—than many experts dared to predict. The larger ones, in the Balkans, the Persian Gulf, and Afghanistan, have as well. The "Black Hawk Down" episode in Somalia is the main exception, and it illustrates a different rule: when fighting not organized armies but stateless foes, we have underestimated our vulnerabilities.

There is an even larger realm of imagination, McPeak suggested to me. It involves the chain of events a war can set off. Wars change history in ways no one can foresee. The Egyptians who planned to attack Israel in 1967 could not imagine how profoundly what became the Six Day War would change the map and politics of the Middle East. After its lightning victory Israel seized neighboring territory, especially on the West Bank of the Jordan River, that is still at the heart of disputes with the Palestinians. Fifty years before, no one who had accurately foreseen what World War I would bring could have rationally decided to let combat begin. The war meant the collapse of three empires, the Ottoman, the Austro-Hungarian, and the Russian; the cresting of another, the British; the eventual rise of Hitler in Germany and Mussolini in Italy; and the drawing of strange new borders from the eastern Mediterranean to the Persian Gulf, which now define the battlegrounds of the Middle East. Probably not even the United States would have found the war an attractive bargain, even though the U.S. rise to dominance began with the wounds Britain suffered in those years.

In 1990, as the United States prepared to push Iraqi troops out of Kuwait, McPeak was the Air Force chief of staff. He thought that war was necessary and advocated heavy bombing in Iraq. Now he opposes an invasion, largely because of how hard it is to imagine the full consequences of America's first purely pre-emptive war—and our first large war since the Spanish-American War in which we would have few or no allies.

WE MUST use imagination on both sides of the debate: about the risks of what Saddam Hussein might do if left in place, and also about what such a war might unleash. Some members of the war party initially urged a quick in-and-out attack. Their model was the three-part formula of the "Powell doctrine": First, line up clear support—from America's political leadership, if not internationally. Then assemble enough force to leave no doubt about the outcome. Then, before the war starts, agree on how it will end and when to leave.

The in-and-out model has obviously become unrealistic. If Saddam Hussein could be destroyed by a death ray or captured by a ninja squad that sneaked into Baghdad and spirited him away, the United States might plausibly call the job done. It would still have to wonder what Iraq's next leader might do with the weapons laboratories, but the immediate problem would be solved.

Absent ninjas, getting Saddam out will mean bringing in men, machinery, and devastation. If the United States launched a big tank-borne campaign, as suggested by some of the battle plans leaked to the press, tens of thousands of soldiers, with their ponderous logistics trail, would be in the middle of a foreign country when the fighting ended. If the U.S. military relied on an air campaign against Baghdad, as other leaked plans have implied, it would inevitably kill many Iraqi civilians before it killed Saddam. One way or another, America would leave a large footprint on Iraq, which would take time to remove.

And logistics wouldn't be the only impediment to quick withdrawal. Having taken dramatic action, we would no doubt be seen—by the world and ourselves, by al Jazeera and CNN—as responsible for the consequences. The United States could have stopped the Khmer Rouge slaughter in Cambodia in the 1970s, but it was not going to, having spent the previous decade in a doomed struggle in Vietnam. It could have prevented some of the genocide in Rwanda in the 1990s, and didn't, but at least it did not trigger the slaughter by its own actions. "It is quite possible that if we went in, took out Saddam Hussein, and then left quickly, the result would be an extremely bloody civil war," says William Galston, the director of the Institute for Philosophy and Public Policy at the University of Maryland, who was a Marine during the Vietnam War. "That blood would be directly on our hands." Most people I spoke with, whether in favor of war or not, recognized that military action is a barbed hook: once it goes in, there is no quick release.

The tone of the political debate reflects a dawning awareness of this reality. Early this year, during the strange "phony war" stage of Iraq discussions, most people in Washington assumed that war was coming, but there was little open discussion of exactly why it was necessary and what consequences it would bring. The pro-war group avoided questions about what would happen after a victory, because to consider postwar complications was to weaken the case for a pre-emptive strike. Some war advocates even said, if pressed, that the details of postwar life didn't matter. With the threat and the tyrant eliminated, the United States could assume that whatever regime emerged would be less dangerous than the one it replaced.

As the swirl of leaks, rumors, and official statements made an attack seem alternately more and less imminent, the increasing chaos in Afghanistan underscored a growing consensus about the in-and-out scenario for Iraq: it didn't make sense. The war itself might be quick, perhaps even quicker than the rout of the Taliban. But the end of the fighting would hardly mean the end of America's commitment. In August, as warlords reasserted their power in Afghanistan, General Tommy Franks, the U.S. commander, said that American troops might need to stay in Afghanistan for many years.

If anything, America's involvement in Afghanistan should have been cleaner and more containable than what would happen in Iraq. In Afghanistan the United States was responding to an attack, rather than initiating regime change. It had broad international support; it had the Northern Alliance to do much of the work. Because the Taliban and al Qaeda finally chose to melt away rather than stand and fight, U.S. forces took control of the major cities while doing relatively little unintended damage. And still, getting out will take much longer than getting in.

Some proponents of war viewed the likelihood of long involvement in Iraq as a plus. If the United States went in planning to stay, it could, they contended, really make a difference there. Richard Perle addressed a major anti-war argument—that Arab states would flare up in resentment—by attempting to turn it around. "It seems at least as likely," he wrote in his *Daily Telegraph* column, "that Saddam's replacement by a decent Iraqi regime would open the way to a far more stable and peaceful region. A democratic Iraq would be a powerful refutation of the patronizing view that Arabs are incapable of democracy."

Some regional experts made the opposite point: that a strong, prosperous, confident, stable Iraq was the last thing its neighbors, who prefer it in its bottled-up condition, wanted to see. Others pooh-poohed the notion that any Western power, however hard it tried or long it stayed, could bring about any significant change in Iraq's political culture.

Regardless of these differences, the day after a war ended, Iraq would become America's problem, for practical and political reasons. Because we would have destroyed the political order and done physical damage in the process, the claims on American resources and attention would be comparable to those of any U.S. state. Conquered Iraqis would turn to the U.S. government for emergency relief, civil order, economic reconstruction, and protection of their borders. They wouldn't be able to vote in U.S. elections, of course—although they might after they emigrated. (Every American war has created a refugee-and-immigrant stream.) But they would be part of us.

During the debate about whether to go to war, each side selectively used various postwar possibilities to bolster its case. Through the course of my interviews I found it useful to consider the possibilities as one comprehensive group. What follows is a triage list for American occupiers: the biggest problems they would face on the first day after the war, in the first week, and so on, until, perhaps decades from now, they could come to grips with the long-term connections between Iraq and the United States.

The First Day

Last-minute mayhem. The biggest concern on the first day of peace would arise from what happened in the last few days of war. "I don't think that physically controlling the important parts of the country need be as difficult as many people fear," Chris Sanders, an American who worked for eighteen years in Saudi Arabia and is now a consultant in London, told me. "But of course it all depends on how one finds oneself in a victorious position—on what you had to do to win."

What would Saddam Hussein, facing defeat and perhaps death, have decided late in the war to do with the stockpiled weapons of mass destruction that were the original justification for our attack? The various Pentagon battle plans leaked to the media all assume that Iraq would use chemical weapons against U.S. troops. (Biological weapons work too slowly, and a nuclear weapon, if Iraq had one, would be more valuable for mass urban destruction than for battlefield use.) During the buildup to the Gulf War, American officials publicly warned Iraq that if it used chemical weapons against U.S. troops, we would respond with everything at our disposal, presumably including nuclear weapons. Whether or not this was a bluff, Iraq did not use chemical weapons. But if Saddam were fighting for survival, rather than for control of Kuwait, his decisions might be different.

The major chemical weapons in Iraqi arsenals are thought to be the nerve gas sarin, also called "GB," and liquid methylphosphonothioic acid, or "VX." Both can be absorbed through the lungs, the skin, or the eyes, and can cause death from amounts as small as one drop. Sarin disperses quickly, but VX is relatively nonvolatile and can pose a more lasting danger. U.S. troops would be equipped with protective suits, but these are cumbersome and retain heat; the need to wear them has been an argument for delaying an attack until winter.

Another concern is that on his way down Saddam would use chemical weapons not only tactically, to slow or kill attacking U.S. soldiers, but also strategically, to lash out beyond his borders. In particular, he could use them against Israel. Iraq's SCUD and "al-Hussein" missiles cannot reach Europe or North America. But Israel is in easy range—as Iraq demonstrated during the Gulf War, when it launched forty-two SCUDs against Israel. (It also launched more than forty against the allied troops; all these SCUDs had conventional explosive warheads, rather than chemical payloads.) During the Gulf War the Israeli government of Yitzhak Shamir complied with urgent U.S. requests that it leave all retaliation to the Americans, rather than broadening the war by launching its own attacks. Nothing in Ariel Sharon's long career suggests that he could be similarly restrained.

A U.S. occupation of Iraq, then, could begin with the rest of the Middle East at war around it. "What's the worst nightmare at the start?" a retired officer who fought in the Gulf War asked me rhetorically. "Saddam Hussein hits Israel, and Sharon hits some Arab city, maybe in Saudi Arabia. Then you have the all-out religious war that the Islamic fundamentalists and maybe some Likudniks are itching for."

This is more a worst-case prediction than a probability, so let's assume that any regional combat could be contained and that we would get relatively quickly to the challenges of the following, postwar days.

The First Week

Refugees and relief. However quick and surgical the battle might seem to the American public, however much brighter Iraq's long-term prospects might become, in the short term many Iraqis would be desperate. Civilians would have been killed, to say nothing of soldiers. Bodies would need to be buried, wounds dressed, orphans located and cared for, hospitals staffed.

"You are going to start right out with a humanitarian crisis," says William Nash, of the Council on Foreign Relations. A retired two-star Army general, Nash was in charge of post-combat relief operations in southern Iraq after the Gulf War and later served in Bosnia and Kosovo. Most examples in this article, from Nash and others, involve the occupation of Kuwait and parts of Iraq after the Gulf War, rather than ongoing operations in Afghanistan. The campaign in Afghanistan may have a rhetorical connection to a future war in Iraq, in that both are part of the general "war on terror"; but otherwise the circumstances are very different. Iraq and Afghanistan are unlike in scale, geography, history, and politics, not to mention in the U.S. objectives and military plans that relate to them. And enough time has passed to judge the effects of the Gulf War, which is not true of Afghanistan.

"In the drive to Baghdad, you are going to do a lot of damage," Nash told me. "Either you will destroy a great deal of infrastructure by trying to isolate the battlefield—or they will destroy it, trying to delay your advance." Postwar commerce and recovery in Iraq will depend, of course, on roads, the rail system, air fields, and bridges across the Tigris and the Euphrates—facilities that both sides in the war will have incentives to blow up. "So you've got to find the village elders," Nash continued, "and say, 'Let's get things going. Where are the wells? I can bring you food, but bringing you enough water is really hard.' Right away you need food, water, and shelter—these people have to survive. Because you started the war, you have accepted a moral responsibility for them. And you may well have totally obliterated the social and political structure that had been providing these services."

Most of the military and diplomatic figures I interviewed stressed the same thing. In August, Scott Feil, a retired Army colonel who now directs a study project for the Association of the United States Army on postwar reconstruction, said at a Senate hearing, "I think the international community will hold the United States primarily responsible for the outcome in the post-conflict reconstruction effort." Charles William Maynes, a former editor of *Foreign Policy* magazine and now the president of the Eurasia Foundation, told me, "Because of the allegations that we've been killing women and children over the years with the sanctions, we are going to be all the more responsible for restoring the infrastructure."

This is not impossible, but it is expensive. Starting in the first week, whoever is in charge in Iraq would need food, tents, portable hospitals, water-purification systems, generators, and so on. During the Clinton Administration, Frederick Barton directed the Office of Transition Initiatives at USAID, which worked with State and Defense Department representatives on postwar recovery efforts in countries such as Haiti, Liberia, and Bosnia. He told me, "These places typically have no revenue systems, no public funds, no way anybody at any level of governance can do anything right away. You've got to pump money into the system." Exactly how much is hard to say. Scott Feil has estimated that costs for the first year in Iraq would be about $16 billion for post-conflict security forces and $1 billion for reconstruction—presumably all from the United States, because of the lack of allies in the war.

Catching Saddam Hussein. While the refugees were being attended to, an embarrassing leftover problem might persist. From the U.S. perspective, it wouldn't really matter whether the war left Saddam dead, captured, or in exile. What would matter is that his whereabouts were known. The only outcome nearly as bad as leaving him in power would be having him at large, like Osama bin Laden and much of the al Qaeda leadership in the months after the September 11 attacks.

"My nightmare scenario," Merrill McPeak, the former Air Force chief of staff, told me, "is that we jump people in, seize the airport, bring in the 101st [Airborne Division]—and we can't find Saddam Hussein. Then we've got Osama and Saddam Hussein out there, both of them achieving mythical heroic status in the Arab world just by surviving. It's not a trivial problem to actually grab the guy, and it ain't over until you've got him in handcuffs."

During the Gulf War, McPeak and his fellow commanders learned that Saddam was using a fleet of Winnebago-like vehicles to move around Baghdad. They tried to track the vehicles but never located Saddam himself. As McPeak concluded from reading psychological profiles of the Iraqi dictator, he is not only a thug and a murderer but an extremely clever adversary. "My concern is that he is smarter individually than our bureaucracy is collectively," he told me. "Bureaucracies tend to dumb things down. So in trying to find him, we have a chess match between a bureaucracy and Saddam Hussein."

The First Month

Police control, manpower, and intelligence. When the lid comes off after a long period of repression, people may be grateful and elated. But they may also be furious and vengeful, as the post-liberation histories of Romania and Kosovo indicate. Phebe Marr, a veteran Iraq expert who until her retirement taught at the National Defense University, told a Senate committee in August, "If firm leadership is not in place in Baghdad the day after Saddam is removed, retribution, score settling, and bloodletting, especially in urban areas, could take place." William Nash, who supervised Iraqi prisoners in liberated parts of Kuwait, told me, "The victim becomes the aggressor. You try to control it, but you'll just find the bodies in the morning."

Some policing of conquered areas, to minimize warlordism and freelance justice, is an essential step toward making the postwar era seem like an occupation rather than simple chaos. Doing it right requires enough people to do the policing; a reliable way to understand local feuds and tensions; and a plan for creating and passing power to a local constabulary. Each can be more complicated than it sounds.

Simply manning a full occupation force would be a challenge. In the occupation business there are some surprising rules of thumb. Whether a country is big or small, for instance, the surrender of weapons by the defeated troops seems to take about 120 days. Similarly, regardless of a country's size, maintaining order seems to take about one occupation soldier or police officer for each 500 people—plus one supervisor for each ten policemen. For Iraq's 23 million people that would mean an occupation force of about 50,000. Scott Feil told a Senate committee that he thought the occupation would need 75,000 security soldiers.

In most of its military engagements since Vietnam the United States has enthusiastically passed many occupation duties to allied or United Nations forces. Ideally the designated occupiers of Iraq would be other Arabs—similar rather than alien to most Iraqis in language, religion, and ethnicity. But persuading other countries to clean up after a war they had opposed would be quite a trick.

Providing even 25,000 occupiers on a sustained basis would not be easy for the U.S. military. Over the past decade the military's head count has gone down, even as its level of foreign commitment and the defense budget have gone up. All the active-duty forces together total about 1.4 million people. Five years ago it was about 1.5 million. At the time of the Gulf War the total was over two million. With fewer people available, the military's "ops tempo" (essentially, the level of overtime) has risen, dramatically in the past year. Since the terrorist attacks some 40,000 soldiers who had planned to retire or leave the service have been obliged to stay, under "stop-loss" personnel policies. In July the Army awarded a $205 million contract to ITT Federal Services to provide "rent-a-cop" security guards for U.S. bases in Bosnia, sparing soldiers the need to stand guard duty. As of the beginning of September, the number of National Guard and Reserves soldiers mobilized by federal call-ups was about 80,000, compared with about 5,600 just before September 11, 2001. For the country in general the war in Central Asia has been largely a spectator event—no war bonds, no gasoline taxes, no mandatory public service. For the volunteer military on both active and reserve duty it has been quite real.

One way to put more soldiers in Iraq would be to re-deploy them from overseas bases. Before the attacks about 250,000 soldiers were based outside U.S. borders, more than half of them in Germany, Japan, and Korea. The American military now stations more than 118,000 soldiers in Europe alone.

But in the short term the occupation would need people from the civil-affairs specialties of the military: people trained in setting up courts and police systems, restoring infrastructure, and generally leading a war-recovery effort. Many are found in the Reserves, and many have already been deployed to missions in Bosnia, Kosovo, or elsewhere. "These are an odd bunch of people," James Dunnigan, the editor of Strategypage.com, told me. "They tend to be civilians who are over-educated—they like working for the government and having adventures at the same time. They're like the characters in *Three Kings*, without finding the gold."

One of the people Dunnigan was referring to specifically is Evan Brooks. In his normal life Brooks is an attorney at Internal Revenue Service headquarters. He is also an amateur military historian, and until his recent retirement was a lieutenant colonel in the Army Reserves, specializing in civil affairs. "Between 1947 and 1983," Brooks told me, "the number of civil-affairs units that were activated [from the Reserves] could be counted on one hand. Since 1987 there has not been a single Christmas where the D.C.-area civil-affairs unit has not had people deployed overseas." Brooks was the military interface with the Kuwaiti Red Crescent for several months after the Gulf War; though he is Jewish, he became a popular figure among his Muslim colleagues, and was the only American who attended Kuwaiti subcabinet meetings. "My ambition was to be military governor of Basra [the Iraqi region closest to Kuwait]," he told me, I think whimsically. "I never quite achieved it."

Wherever the occupying force finds its manpower, it will face the challenge of understanding politics and rivalries in a country whose language few Americans speak. The CIA and the Army Special Forces have been recruiting Arabic speakers and grilling Iraqi exiles for local intelligence. The Pentagon's leadership includes at least one Arabic speaker: the director of the joint staff, John Abizaid, a three-star general. As a combat commander during the Gulf War, Abizaid was able to speak directly with Iraqis. Most American occupiers will lack this skill.

Inability to communicate could be disastrous. After the Gulf War, William Nash told me, he supervised camps containing Iraqi refugees and captured members of the Republican Guard. "We had a couple of near riots—mini-riots—in the refugee camps when Saddam's agents were believed to have infiltrated," Nash said. "We brought a guy in, and a group of refugees in the camp went berserk. Somebody said, 'He's an agent!' My guys had to stop them or they were going to tear the man to shreds. We put a bag over his head and hustled him out of there, just to save his life. And when that happens, you have no idea what kind of vendetta you've just fallen in the middle of. You have no idea if it's a six-camel issue or something much more. I take that experience from 1991 and square it fifty times for a larger country. That would be a postwar Iraq."

Eventually the occupiers would solve the problem by fostering a local police force, as part of a new Iraqi government. "You have to start working toward local, civilian-led police," Frederick Barton, the former USAID official, told me. "Setting up an academy is okay, but national police forces tend to be sources of future coups and corruption. I'd rather have a hundred and fifty small forces around the country and take my chances on thirty of them being corrupt than have a centralized force and end up with one big, bad operation."

Forming a government. Tyrants make a point of crushing any challenge to their power. When a tyranny falls, therefore, a new, legitimate source of authority may take time to emerge. If potential new leaders are easy to identify, it is usually because of their family name or record of political struggle. Corazón Aquino illustrates the first possibility: as the widow of a political rival whom Ferdinand Marcos had ordered killed, she was the ideal successor to Marcos in the Philippines (despite her later troubles in office). Charles de Gaulle in postwar France, Nelson Mandela in South Africa, and Kim Dae-jung in South Korea illustrate the second. Should the Burmese military ever fall, Aung San Suu Kyi will have both qualifications for leadership.

Iraq has no such obvious sources of new leadership. A word about its political history is useful in explaining the succession problem. From the 1500s onward the Ottoman Empire, based in Istanbul, controlled the territory that is now Iraq. When the empire fell, after World War I, Great Britain assumed supervision of the newly created Kingdom of Iraq, under a mandate from the League of Nations. The British imported a member of Syria's Hashemite royal family, who in 1921 became King Faisal I of Iraq. (The Hashemites, one of whom is still on the throne in Jordan, claim descent not only from the prophet Muhammad but also from the Old Testament Abraham.) The Kingdom of Iraq lasted until 1958, when King Faisal II was overthrown and killed in a military coup. In 1963 the Baath, or "renewal," party took power in another coup—which the United States initially welcomed, in hopes that the Baathists would be anticommunist. By the late 1970s Saddam Hussein had risen to dominance within the party.

The former monarchy is too shallow-rooted to survive reintroduction to Iraq, and Saddam has had time to eliminate nearly all sources of internal resistance. The Kurdish chieftains of the northern provinces are the primary exception. But their main impulse has been separatist: they seek autonomy from the government in Baghdad and feud with one another. That leaves Iraqi exile groups—especially the Iraqi National Congress—as the likeliest suppliers of leaders.

The INC survives on money from the U.S. government. The organization and its president, a U.S.-trained businessman named Ahmad Chalabi, have sincere supporters and also detractors within the Washington policy world. The columnist Jim Hoagland, of *The Washington Post,* has called Chalabi a "dedicated advocate of democracy" who has "sacrifice[d] most of his fortune so he can risk his life to fight Saddam." The case against Chalabi involves his fortune too: he is a high-living character, and under him the INC has been dogged by accusations of financial mismanagement. "The opposition outside Iraq is almost as divided, weak, and irrelevant as the White Russians in the 1920s," says Anthony Cordesman, of the Center for Strategic and International Studies, in Washington.

"What you will need is a man with a black moustache," a retired British spy who once worked in the region told me. "Out of chaos I am sure someone will emerge. But it can't be Chalabi, and it probably won't be a democracy. Democracy is a strange fruit, and, cynically, to hold it together in the short term you need a strongman."

Several U.S. soldiers told me that the comfortable Powell doctrine, with its emphasis on swift action and a clear exit strategy, could make the inevitable difficulty and delay in setting up plausible new leadership even more frustrating.

When British administrators supervised the former Ottoman lands in the 1920s, they liked to insinuate themselves into the local culture, à la Lawrence of Arabia. "Typically, a young man would go there in his twenties, would master the local dialects, would have a local mistress before he settled down to something more respectable," Victor O'Reilly, an Irish novelist who specializes in military topics, told me. "They were to achieve tremendous amounts with minimal resources. They ran huge chunks of the world this way, and it was psychological. They were hugely knowledgeable and got deeply involved with the locals." The original Green Berets tried to use a version of this approach in Vietnam, and to an extent it is still the ideal for the Special Forces.

But in the generation since Vietnam the mainstream U.S. military has gone in the opposite direction: toward a definition of its role in strictly martial terms. It is commonplace these days in discussions with officers to hear them describe their mission as "killing people and blowing things up." The phrase is used deliberately to shock civilians, and also for its absolute clarity as to what a "military response" involves. If this point is understood, there can be no confusion about what the military is supposed to do when a war starts, no recriminations when it uses all necessary force, and as little risk as possible that soldiers will die "political" deaths because they've been constrained for symbolic or diplomatic reasons from fully defending themselves. All this is in keeping with the more familiar parts of the Powell doctrine—the insistence on political backing and overwhelming force. The goal is to protect the U.S. military from being misused.

The strict segregation of military and political functions may be awkward in Iraq, however. In the short term the U.S. military would necessarily be the government of Iraq. In the absence of international allies or U.N. support, and the absence of an obvious Iraqi successor regime, American soldiers would have to make and administer political decisions on the fly. America's two most successful occupations embraced the idea that military officials must play political roles. Emperor Hirohito remained the titular head of state in occupied Japan, but Douglas MacArthur, a lifelong soldier, was immersed in the detailed reconstruction of Japan's domestic order. In occupied Germany, General Lucius D. Clay did something comparable, though less flamboyantly. Today's Joint Chiefs of Staff would try to veto any suggestion for a MacArthur-like proconsul. U.S. military leaders in the Balkans have pushed this role onto the United Nations. Exactly who could assume it in Iraq is not clear.

In the first month, therefore, the occupiers would face a paradox: the institution best equipped to exercise power as a local government—the U.S. military—would be the one most reluctant to do so.

Territorial integrity. This is where the exercise of power might first be put to a major test.

In ancient times what is now central Iraq was the cradle of civilization, Mesopotamia ("Mespot" in Fleet Street shorthand during the British-mandate era). Under the Ottoman Empire today's Iraq was not one province but three, and the divisions still affect current politics. The province of Baghdad, in the center of the country, is the stronghold of Iraq's Sunni Muslim minority. Sunnis dominated administrative positions in the Ottoman days and have controlled the army and the government ever since, even though they make up only about 20 percent of the population. The former province of Mosul, in the mountainous north, is the stronghold of Kurdish tribes, which make up 15 to 20 percent of the population. Through the years they have both warred against and sought common cause with other Kurdish tribes across Iraq's borders in Turkey, Iran, and Syria. Mosul also has some of the country's richest reserves of oil. The former province of Basra, to the southeast, borders Iran, Kuwait, and the Persian Gulf. Its population is mainly Shiite Muslims, who make up the majority in the country as a whole but have little political power.

The result of this patchwork is a country like Indonesia or Soviet-era Yugoslavia. Geographic, ethnic, and religious forces tend to pull it apart; only an offsetting pull from a strong central government keeps it in one piece. Most people think that under the stress of regime change Iraq would be more like Indonesia after Suharto than like Yugoslavia after Tito—troubled but intact. But the strains will be real.

"In my view it is very unlikely—indeed, inconceivable—that Iraq will break up into three relatively cohesive components," Phebe Marr, the Iraq expert, told the Senate Committee on Foreign Relations. But a weakened center could mean all sorts of problems, she said, even if the country were officially whole. The Kurds could seize the northern oil fields, for example. The Turkish government has long made clear that if Iraq cannot control its Kurdish population, Turkey—concerned about separatist movements in its own Kurdish provinces—will step in to do the job. "Turkey could intervene in the north, as it has done before," Marr said. "Iran, through its proxies, could follow suit. There could even be a reverse flow of refugees as many Iraqi Shia exiles in Iran return home, possibly in the thousands, destabilizing areas in the south.

The centrifugal forces acting on postwar Iraq, even if they did not actually break up the country, would present a situation different from those surrounding past U.S. occupations. America's longest experience as an occupier was in the Philippines, which the United States controlled formally or informally for most of a century. Many ethnic, linguistic, and religious differences separated the people of the Philippine archipelago, but because the islands have no land frontier with another country, domestic tensions could be managed with few international complications. And in dealing with Japan and Germany after World War II, the United States wanted, if anything, to dilute each country's sense of distinct national identity. There was also no doubt about the boundaries of those occupied countries.

Postwar Iraq, in contrast, would have less-than-certain boundaries, internal tensions with international implications, and highly nervous neighbors. Six countries share borders with Iraq. Clockwise from the Persian Gulf, they are Kuwait, Saudi Arabia, Jordan, Syria, Turkey, and Iran. None of them has wanted Saddam to expand Iraq's territory. But they would be oddly threatened by a post-Saddam breakup or implosion. The Turks, as noted, have a particular interest in preventing any country's Kurdish minority from rebelling or forming a separatist state. The monarchies of Saudi Arabia and Jordan fear that riots and chaos in Iraq could provoke similar upheaval among their own peoples.

"In states like the United Arab Emirates and Qatar, even Saudi Arabia," says Shibley Telhami, the Anwar Sadat Professor of Peace and Development at the University of Maryland, "there is the fear that the complete demise of Iraq would in the long run play into the hands of Iran, which they see as even more of a threat." Iran is four times as large as Iraq, and has nearly three times as many people. Although it is Islamic, its population and heritage are Persian, not Arab; to the Arab states, Iran is "them," not "us."

As Arab regimes in the region assess the possible outcomes of a war, Telhami says, "they see instability, at a minimum, for a long period of time, and in the worst case the disintegration of the Iraqi state." These fears matter to the United States, because of oil. Chaos in the Persian Gulf would disrupt world oil markets and therefore the world economy. Significant expansion of Iran's influence, too, would work against the Western goal of balancing regional power among Saudi Arabia, Iran, and postwar Iraq. So as the dust of war cleared, keeping Iraq together would suddenly be America's problem. If the Kurds rebelled in the north, if the Shiite government in Iran tried to "reclaim" the southern districts of Iraq in which fellow Shiites live, the occupation powers would have to respond—even by sending in U.S. troops for follow-up battles.

The First Year

"De-Nazification" and *"loya-jirgazation."* As the months pass, an occupation force should, according to former occupiers, spend less time reacting to crises and more time undertaking long-term projects such as improving schools, hospitals, and housing. Iraq's occupiers would meanwhile also have to launch their version of "de-Nazification": identifying and punishing those who were personally responsible for the old regime's brutality, without launching a Khmer Rouge–style purge of everyone associated with the former govern-ment. Depending on what happened to Saddam and his closest associates, war-crime trials might begin. Even if the United States had carried out the original invasion on its own, the occupiers would seek international support for these postwar measures.

In the early months the occupiers would also begin an Iraqi version of *"loya-jirga*zation"—that is, supporting a "grand council" or convention like the one at which the Afghans selected the leadership for their transitional govern-ment. Here the occupation would face a fundamental decision about its goals within Iraq.

One option was described to me by an American diplomat as the "decent interval" strategy. The United States would help to set up the framework for a new governing system and then transfer authority to it as soon as possible—whether or not the new regime was truly ready to exercise control. This is more or less the approach the United States and its allies have taken in Afghanistan: once the *loya jirga* had set up an interim government and Hamid Karzai was in place as President, the United States was happy to act as if this were a true government. The situation in Afghanistan shows the contradic-tions in this strategy. It works only if the United States decides it doesn't care about the Potemkin government's lapses and limitations—for instance, an inability to suppress warlords and ethnic-regional feuds. In Afghanistan the United States still does care, so there is growing tension between the pretense of Afghan sovereignty and the reality of U.S. influence. However complicated the situation in Afghanistan is proving to be, things are, again, likely to be worse in Iraq. The reasons are familiar; a large local army, the Northern Alliance, had played a major role in the fight against the Taliban; a natural leader, Karzai, was available; the invasion itself had been a quasi-international rather than a U.S.-only affair.

The other main option would be something closer to U.S. policy in occupied Japan: a slow, thorough effort to change fundamental social and cultural values, in preparation for a sustainable democracy. Japan's version of democracy departs from the standard Western model in various ways, but a system even half as open and liberal as Japan's would be a huge step for Iraq. The transformation of Japan was slow. It required detailed interference in the day-to-day workings of Japanese life. U.S. occupation officials supervised what was taught in Japanese classrooms. Douglas MacArthur's assistants not only rewrote the labor laws but wrote the constitution itself. They broke up big estates and reallocated the land. Carrying out this transformation required an effort comparable to the New Deal. American lawyers, economists, engineers, and administrators by the thousands spent years developing and executing reform plans. Transformation did not happen by fiat. It won't in Iraq either.

John Dower, a professor of history at MIT, is a leading historian of the U.S. occupation of Japan; his book *Embracing Defeat* won the Pulitzer Prize for nonfiction in 2000. Dower points out that in Japan occupation officials had a huge advantage they presumably would not have in Iraq: no one questioned their legitimacy. The victorious Americans had not only the power to impose their will on Japan but also, in the world's eyes, the undoubted right to remake a militarist society. "Every country in Asia wanted this to be done," Dower says. "Every country in the world." The same was true in postwar Germany. The absence of international support today is one of many reasons Dower vehemently opposes a pre-emptive attack.

Oil and money. Iraq could be the Saudi Arabia of the future. Partly because its output has been constrained by ten years' worth of sanctions, and mainly because it has never embraced the international oil industry as Saudi Arabia has, it is thought to have some of the largest untapped reserves in the world. Saudi Arabia now exports much more oil than Iraq—some seven million barrels a day versus about two million. But Iraq's output could rapidly increase.

The supply-demand balance in the world's energy markets is expected to shift over the next five years. Import demand continues to rise—even more quickly in China and India than in the United States. Production in most of the world is flat or declining—in OPEC producing countries, by OPEC fiat. The role of Persian Gulf suppliers will only become more important; having two large suppliers in the Gulf rather than just one will be a plus for consumers. So in the Arab world the U.S. crusade against Saddam looks to be motivated less by fears of terrorism and weapons of mass destruction than by the wish to defend Israel and the desire for oil.

Ideally, Iraq's re-entry into the world oil market would be smooth. Production would be ramped up quickly enough to generate money to rebuild the Iraqi economy and infrastructure, but gradually enough to keep Saudi Arabia from feeling threatened and retaliating in ways that could upset the market. International oil companies, rather than an occupation authority, would do most of the work here. What would the occupiers need to think about? First, the threat of sabotage, which would become greater to the extent that Iraq's oil industry was seen in the Arab world more as a convenience for Western consumers than as a source of wealth for Iraq. Since many of the wells are in the Kurdish regions, Kurdish rebellion or dissatisfaction could put them at risk. Oil pipelines, seemingly so exposed, are in fact not the likeliest target. "Pipes are always breaking, so we know how to fix them quickly," says Peter Schwartz, of the Global Business Network, who worked for years as an adviser to Shell Oil. At greatest risk are the terminals at seaports, where oil is loaded into tankers, and the wells themselves. At the end of the Gulf War, Iraqi troops set fire to 90 percent of Kuwait's wells, which burned for months. Wellheads and terminals are the sites that oil companies protect most carefully.

Another challenge to recovery prospects in general would be Iraq's amazingly heavy burden of debt. Iraq was directed by the United Nations to pay reparations for the damage it inflicted on Kuwait during the Gulf War. That and other debts have compounded to amounts the country cannot hope to repay. Estimates vary, but the range—$200 billion to $400 billion—illustrates the problem.

"Leaving Iraq saddled with a massive debt and wartime-reparations bill because of Saddam is an act of moral and ethical cowardice," says Anthony Cordesman, of the Center for Strategic and International Studies, a military expert who is no one's idea of a bleeding heart. "We must show the Arab and Islamic worlds that we will not profiteer in any way from our victory. We must persuade the world to forgive past debts and reparations." Cordesman and others argue that as part of regime change the United States would have to take responsibility for solving this problem. Otherwise Iraq would be left in the position of Weimar Germany after the Treaty of Versailles: crushed by unpayable reparations.

This would be only part of the financial reality of regime change. The overall cost of U.S. military operations during the Gulf War came to some $61 billion. Because of the contributions it received from Japan, Saudi Arabia, and other countries in its alliance, the United States wound up in the convenient yet embarrassing position of having most of that cost reimbursed. An assault on Iraq would be at least as expensive and would all be on our tab. Add to that the price of recovery aid. It is hard to know even how to estimate the total cost.

Legitimacy and unilateralism. An important premise for the American war party is that squawks and hand-wringing from Arab governments cannot be taken seriously. The Saudis may say they oppose an attack; the Jordanians may publicly warn against it; but in fact most governments in the region would actually be glad to have the Saddam wild card removed. And if some countries didn't welcome the outcome, all would adjust to the reality of superior U.S. force once the invasion was a fait accompli. As for the Europeans, they are thought to have a poor record in threat assessment. Unlike the United States, Europe has not really been responsible since World War II for life-and-death judgments about military problems, and Europeans tend to whine and complain. American war advocates say that Europe's reluctance to confront Saddam is like its reluctance to recognize the Soviet threat a generation ago. Europeans thought Ronald Reagan was a brute for calling the Soviet Union an "evil empire." According to this view, they are just as wrong-headed to consider George W. Bush a simpleton for talking today about an "axis of evil."

Still, support from the rest of the world can be surprisingly comforting. Most Americans were moved by the outpouring of solidarity on September 11—the flowers in front of embassies, the astonishing headline in *Le Monde:* "NOUS SOMMES TOUS AMÉRICAINS." By the same token, foreigners' hatred can be surprisingly demoralizing. Think of the news clips of exaltation in Palestinian camps after the attacks, or the tape of Osama bin Laden chortling about how many people he had killed. The United States rarely turned to the United Nations from the late 1960s through the mid-1980s, because the U.N. was so often a forum for anti-American rants. Resentment against America in the Arab world has led to a partial boycott of U.S. exports, which so far has not mattered much. It has also fueled the recruitment of suicide terrorists, which has mattered a great deal.

The presence or absence of allies would have both immediate and long-term consequences for the occupation. No matter how welcome as liberators they may be at first, foreign soldiers eventually wear out their welcome. It would be far easier if this inescapably irritating presence were varied in nationality, under a U.N. flag, rather than all American. All the better if the force were Islamic and Arabic-speaking.

The face of the occupying force will matter not just in Iraq's cities but also on its borders. Whoever controls Iraq will need to station forces along its most vulnerable frontier—the long flank with Iran, where at least half a million soldiers died during the 1980–1988 Iran-Iraq war. The Iranians will notice any U.S. presence on the border. "As the occupying power, we will be responsible for the territorial integrity of the Iraqi state," says Charles William Maynes, of the Eurasia Foundation. "That means we will have to move our troops to the border with Iran. At that point Iran becomes our permanent enemy."

The longer-term consequences would flow from having undertaken a war that every country in the region except Israel officially opposed. Chris Sanders, the consultant who used to work in Saudi Arabia, says that unless the United States can drum up some Arab allies, an attack on Iraq "will accomplish what otherwise would have been impossible—a bloc of regional opposition that transcends the very real differences of interests and opinions that had kept a unified Arab bloc from arising." Sanders adds dryly, "If I were an American strategic thinker, I would imagine that not to be in my interest."

The Long Run

So far we've considered the downside—which, to be fair, is most of what I heard in my interviews. But there was also a distinctly positive theme, and it came from some of the most dedicated members of the war party. Their claim, again, was that forcing regime change would not just have a negative virtue— that of removing a threat. It would also create the possibility of bringing to Iraq, and eventually the whole Arab world, something it has never known before: stable democracy in an open-market system.

"This could be a golden opportunity to begin to change the face of the Arab world," James Woolsey, a former CIA director who is one of the most visible advocates of war, told me. "Just as what we did in Germany changed the face of Central and Eastern Europe, here we have got a golden chance." In this view, the fall of the Soviet empire really did mark what Francis Fukuyama called "the end of history": the democratic-capitalist model showed its superiority over other social systems. The model has many local variations; it brings adjustment problems; and it encounters resistance, such as the anti-globalization protests of the late 1990s. But it spreads—through the old Soviet territory, through Latin America and Asia, nearly everywhere except through tragic Africa and the Islamic-Arab lands of the Middle East. To think that Arab states don't want a democratic future is dehumanizing. To think they're incapable of it is worse. What is required is a first Arab democracy, and Iraq can be the place.

"If you only look forward, you can see how hard it would be to do," Woolsey said. "Everybody can say, 'Oh, *sure,* you're going to democratize the Middle East.'" Indeed, that was the reaction of most of the diplomats, spies, and soldiers I spoke with—"the ruminations of insane people," one British official said.

Woolsey continued with his point: "But if you look at what we and our allies have done with the three world wars of the twentieth century—two hot, one cold—and what we've done in the interstices, we've already achieved this for two thirds of the world. Eighty-five years ago, when we went into World War I, there were eight or ten democracies at the time. Now it's around a hundred and twenty—some free, some partly free. An order of magnitude! The compromises we made along the way, whether allying with Stalin or Franco or Pinochet, we have gotten around to fixing, and their successor regimes are democracies.

"Around half of the states of sub-Saharan Africa are democratic. Half of the twenty-plus non-Arab Muslim states. We have all of Europe except Belarus and occasionally parts of the Balkans. If you look back at what has happened in less than a century, then getting the Arab world plus Iran moving in the same direction looks a lot less awesome. It's not Americanizing the world. It's Athenizing it. And it is doable."

Richard Perle, Secretary of Defense Donald Rumsfeld, and others have presented similar prospects. Thomas McInerney, a retired three-star general, said at the Senate hearings this past summer, "Our longer-term objectives will be to bring a democratic government to Iraq . . . that will influence the region significantly." At a Pentagon briefing a few days later Rumsfeld asked rhetorically, "Wouldn't it be a wonderful thing if Iraq were similar to Afghanistan—if a bad regime was thrown out, people were liberated, food could come in, borders could be opened, repression could stop, prisons could be opened? I mean, it would be *fabulous.*"

The transforming vision is not, to put it mildly, the consensus among those with long experience in the Middle East. "It is so divorced from any historical context, just so far out of court, that it is laughable," Chris Sanders told me. "There isn't a society in Iraq to turn into a democracy. That doesn't mean you can't set up institutions and put stooges in them. But it would make about as much sense as the South Vietnamese experiment did." Others made similar points.

Woolsey and his allies might be criticized for lacking a tragic imagination about where war might lead, but at least they recognize that it will lead somewhere. If they are more optimistic in their conclusions than most of the other people I spoke with, they do see that America's involvement in Iraq would be intimate and would be long.

It has become a cliché in popular writing about the natural world that small disturbances to complex systems can have unpredictably large effects. The world of nations is perhaps not quite as intricate as the natural world, but it certainly holds the potential for great surprise. Merely itemizing the foreseeable effects of a war with Iraq suggests reverberations that would be felt for decades. If we can judge from past wars, the effects we can't imagine when the fighting begins will prove to be the ones that matter most.

"IRAQ IS FULLY CAPABLE OF LIVING IN FREEDOM"

George W. Bush

The following are excerpts from a speech given by President Bush at the annual dinner of the American Enterprise Institute on February 26, 2003, where he laid out his vision for the future of Iraq.

The first to benefit from a free Iraq would be the Iraqi people, themselves. Today they live in scarcity and fear, under a dictator who has brought them nothing but war, and misery, and torture. Their lives and their freedom matter little to Saddam Hussein—but Iraqi lives and freedom matter greatly to us.

Bringing stability and unity to a free Iraq will not be easy. Yet that is no excuse to leave the Iraqi regime's torture chambers and poison labs in operation. Any future the Iraqi people choose for themselves will be better than the nightmare world that Saddam Hussein has chosen for them.

If we must use force, the United States and our coalition stand ready to help the citizens of a liberated Iraq. We will deliver medicine to the sick, and we are now moving into place nearly 3 million emergency rations to feed the hungry.

We'll make sure that Iraq's 55,000 food distribution sites, operating under the Oil For Food program, are stocked and open as soon as possible. The United States and Great Britain are providing tens of millions of dollars to the U.N. High Commission on Refugees, and to such groups as the World Food Program and UNICEF, to provide emergency aid to the Iraqi people.

We will also lead in carrying out the urgent and dangerous work of destroying chemical and biological weapons. We will provide security against those who try to spread chaos, or settle scores, or threaten the territorial integrity of Iraq. We will seek to protect Iraq's natural resources from sabotage by a dying regime, and ensure those resources are used for the benefit of the owners—the Iraqi people.

The United States has no intention of determining the precise form of Iraq's new government. That choice belongs to the Iraqi people. Yet, we will ensure that one brutal dictator is not replaced by another. All Iraqis must have a voice in the new government, and all citizens must have their rights protected.

Rebuilding Iraq will require a sustained commitment from many nations, including our own: we will remain in Iraq as long as necessary, and not a day more. America has made and kept this kind of commitment before—in the peace that followed a world war. After defeating enemies, we did not leave behind occupying armies, we left constitutions and parliaments. We established an atmosphere of safety, in which responsible, reform-minded local leaders could build lasting institutions of freedom. In societies that once bred fascism and militarism, liberty found a permanent home.

There was a time when many said that the cultures of Japan and Germany were incapable of sustaining democratic values. Well, they were wrong. Some say the same of Iraq today. They are mistaken. The nation of Iraq—with its proud heritage, abundant resources and skilled and educated people—is fully capable of moving toward democracy and living in freedom.

The world has a clear interest in the spread of democratic values, because stable and free nations do not breed the ideologies of murder. They encourage the peaceful pursuit of a better life. And there are hopeful signs of a desire for freedom in the Middle East. Arab intellectuals have called on Arab governments to address the "freedom gap" so their peoples can fully share in the progress of our times. Leaders in the region speak of a new Arab charter that champions internal reform, greater politics participation, economic openness, and free trade. And from Morocco to Bahrain and beyond, nations are taking genuine steps toward politics reform. A new regime in Iraq would serve as a dramatic and inspiring example of freedom for other nations in the region.

It is presumptuous and insulting to suggest that a whole region of the world—or the one-fifth of humanity that is Muslim—is somehow untouched by the most basic aspirations of life. Human cultures can be vastly different. Yet the human heart desires the same good things, everywhere on Earth. In our desire to be safe from brutal and bullying oppression, human beings are the same. In our desire to care for our children and give them a better life, we are the same. For these fundamental reasons, freedom and democracy will always and everywhere have greater appeal than the slogans of hatred and the tactics of terror.

Success in Iraq could also begin a new stage for Middle Eastern peace, and set in motion progress towards a truly democratic Palestinian state. The passing of Saddam Hussein's regime will deprive terrorist networks of a wealthy patron that pays for terrorist training, and offers rewards to families of suicide bombers. And other regimes will be given a clear warning that support for terror will not be tolerated.

Without this outside support for terrorism, Palestinians who are working for reform and long for democracy will be in a better position to choose new leaders. True leaders who strive for peace; true leaders who faithfully serve the people. A Palestinian state must be a reformed and peaceful state that abandons forever the use of terror.

For its part, the new government of Israel—as the terror threat is removed and security improves—will be expected to support the creation of a viable Palestinian state—(applause)—and to work as quickly as possible toward a final status agreement. As progress is made toward peace, settlement activity in the occupied territories must end. And the Arab states will be expected to meet their responsibilities to oppose terrorism, to support the emergence of a peaceful and democratic Palestine, and state clearly they will live in peace with Israel.

The United States and other nations are working on a road map for peace. We are setting out the necessary conditions for progress toward the goal of two states, Israel and Palestine, living side by side in peace and security. It is the commitment of our government—and my personal commitment—to implement the road map and to reach that goal. Old patterns of conflict in the Middle East can be broken, if all concerned will let go of bitterness, hatred, and violence, and get on with the serious work of economic development, and political reform, and reconciliation. America will seize every opportunity in pursuit of peace. And the end of the present regime in Iraq would create such an opportunity.

THE POST-SADDAM PROBLEM

Dilip Hiro

After several postponements, a U.S.-sponsored meeting of Iraqi opposition groups and individuals took place in London on December 14–15, 2002.

The main resolutions adopted by some 330 delegates to the Iraqi Open Opposition Conference reiterated their often-repeated commitment to the overthrow of Saddam Hussein and the introduction of democracy in Iraq.

"It was not the opposition Iraqis but the Americans who needed this gathering, eager to show they had broad support among diverse opposition groups," says Dr. Mustafa Alani of the Royal United Services Institute, London. "Whatever show of unity the opposition leaders managed to project will be short-lived. They will go back to devoting more space in their publications to attacking one another than Saddam."

Before the conference had begun, even Kanan Makiya, chairman of the State Department-sponsored committee that issued the document "The Transition to Democracy in Iraq," acknowledged that "no Iraqi Arab political organization on the scene today has been tested and can be said to be truly representative." The assessment of most nonpartisan Iraqis in London was that the U.S.-funded exercise was a thinly disguised attempt by the White House to provide itself with a political cover for invading Iraq.

As Alani notes, "Aside from Sharif Ali bin al Hussein [of the Movement for Constitutional Monarchy], the conference did not have a single Sunni Arab leader, even though Sunnis are a third of the Arab population." The absence of Sunnis, who have ruled Iraq since 1638—first as part of the (Sunni) Ottoman Empire, and later as an independent state, from 1932 to the present—foreshadows trouble in the post-Saddam era, in which a newly empowered Shiite majority may choose to settle old scores with the Sunnis. What's more, like other ruling classes and ethnic groups throughout history, the Sunnis are unlikely to give up power without a fight—and thus they are a force that must be reckoned with in any post-Saddam Iraq.

In reality, so much of the debate in the opposition ranks—whether or not

---

Dilip Hiro is the author of many books on the Middle East, most recently, *Iraq: In the Eye of the Storm.* Born in India, he pursued his education in Britain and the United States, and now lives in London. This article was originally published on January 6, 2003, in *The Nation*.

to form a provisional government, and whether to choose its leadership on the basis of ethnicity and sect or sheer merit—was just hot air. These options are predicated on the fate of Saddam. That will be decided by the Pentagon. And gatherings such as the one in London make not an iota of difference to its plans.

How the American invasion of Iraq proceeds will determine what happens after Saddam. Consider three scenarios: optimistic, pessimistic and in-between.

The Pentagon's optimistic scenario envisages the bulk of Saddam's military surrendering or deserting en masse at the end of two to three weeks of continuous bombing, the operation costing $1.5 billion to $3 billion a week, with the population welcoming the "liberating" American soldiers. The brevity of the conflict insures unity in the opposition ranks. The loss of Iraqi oil—now 2–2.5 percent of the global total—is amply compensated for by Saudi Arabia, with its spare capacity amounting to 6 percent of the world aggregate, and Iraq's oilfields will remain unharmed.

The military logic behind this scenario, released under different guises by the Pentagon's hawkish civilian bosses and meant to reassure the American public, is based primarily on the testimony of Iraqi defectors. The unreliability of such sources is widely known, the most glaring example of this, for the United States, being the 1961 Bay of Pigs fiasco in Cuba, in which the CIA relied on false information from defectors. This is of great concern in the case of Iraq—as was explained by a British lawyer of Iraqi origin in London, the haven for more notable Iraqi exiles than all other cities and countries combined. "When these Iraqis arrive at a Western airport, they seek political asylum," he says. "For this they must show that they are important, and that they have acted so seriously against the Saddam regime that if returned, they would be jailed, tortured or executed. So these guys lie. And over time they become expert at inventing stories." It is on this foundation that the U.S.-British alliance has built the body of its "intelligence" over the past twelve years, which underlies the Pentagon's sunny scenario.

This scenario also ignores two pre-eminent facts of recent Iraqi history. One, Iraqis have a strong nationalist sense that was enhanced when they fought the eight-year war with Iran. Two, almost invariably, Iraqi civilians blame Washington for the sanctions, which have reduced them to penury. Judging from the opinions expressed to me by ordinary citizens during my visit to Iraq in 2000, so deep is the resentment and hostility toward America and Americans that for the bulk of Iraqis, it is unimaginable that any good can come to them from Washington—especially if that would be at the end of massive bombing by the Pentagon of their weakened country and society.

They are therefore unlikely to welcome conquering U.S. soldiers with the warmth the Pentagon expects.

On November 19 the "Iraqi military defects en masse" scenario received a grievous setback. That day the Danish government arrested Nizar al Khazraji, former (Sunni) Iraqi Army chief of staff, living in the town of Soroe, and charged him with crimes against humanity and war crimes for his alleged role in the 1988 Anfal campaign against the Kurds, consisting of mass executions, razing of scores of villages and use of chemical weapons, involving some 100,000 deaths. Before his defection in 1996, Khazraji was a special adviser to Saddam, after having served him as the army chief of staff during 1987–90. "His arrest will make it that much harder to encourage other [Iraqi] officers to defect if they fear they will be charged too," said an opposition leader. Though released on bail, Khazraji has been ordered to remain in Denmark so that special prosecutor Birgitte Vestberg can complete her criminal investigations. She is unmoved by Khazraji's pleas that he is a victim of false accusations by Saddam's agents or by the prospect of upsetting the Anglo-American geopolitical plans, in which Khazraji may figure as the new leader of Iraq. Her sole task, she says, is to determine whether he has committed the alleged crimes, and that could take a year or longer.

There are other problems. Gen. Najib al Salhi, leader of the U.S.-sponsored Iraqi Military Alliance, said the Pentagon's threats to destroy Iraq's conventional weapons risked alienating military elements who might otherwise be receptive to a regime change imposed by the United States. Other generals also warned against purging the army of Saddam supporters, saying there will be a backlash if senior Iraqi officers are punished arbitrarily.

At the other end of the Pentagon's spectrum is its pessimistic scenario. This envisions intense urban fighting in Iraq, where every household has a gun, with the conflict lasting several months. During the fighting, oil wells in Iraq are torched and those elsewhere in the region are damaged by Saddamist saboteurs, as unrest spreads throughout the Middle East and the body bags of U.S. soldiers fuel an antiwar movement in America.

In turn, George W. Bush takes a strong stand, true to his recent declaration to Bob Woodward that as the President he is "the calcium in the backbone" of America. His Administration decides on a long-term occupation and reconstruction of Iraq, at the cost of $160 billion a year, according to Yale economist William Nordhaus.

Even if the worst-case scenario does not come to pass, a military occupation of Iraq remains a serious option, with senior Administration officials frequently alluding to the 1945–52 U.S. occupation of Japan under Gen. Douglas MacArthur. They glibly ignore the numerous differences between postwar Japan in 1945 and postwar Iraq in 2003. Japan under Emperor Hirohito, associated with the sun by tradition and therefore revered as a demigod, surrendered unconditionally, with the Emperor personally endorsing the victors, thus allowing MacArthur to rule by fiat to implement carefully devised policies. There is no sign that Saddam will follow Hirohito's example, or that the Bush White House has put much thought into such policies. Moreover, since MacArthur inherited wholesale the administrative infrastructure of Emperor Hirohito, the reform of the political/economic/educational system progressed smoothly. Nobody expects the institutions of the Baathist regime in Iraq to survive Saddam's defeat. So any reform will be hard to implement.

Despite the fact that policing was left to the Japanese authorities, Washington deployed 100,000 troops for more than six years to implement reform in Japan. By contrast, U.S. planners now envisage the stationing of 75,000–100,000 troops at the cost of $16 billion a year. This is unrealistic. In Northern Ireland, with a population of 1.7 million, the British government stationed close to 20,000 troops with an equal number of loyal armed policemen and an army reserve of the same size, thus committing 60,000 troops and armed police to tackle about 1,000 members of the Irish Republican Army, most of them in jail at any one time. In addition, the loyalist Protestant majority outnumbered the rebellious Catholic population by 2 to 1.

Unlike highly homogeneous Japan, Iraq is a heterogeneous society. The traditional religious, ethnic and tribal animosities will break out in postwar Iraq once the iron hand of Saddam is removed, with civil conflict erupting along ethnic and sectarian lines, the deadliest one being between Sunnis and Shiites who share the Mesopotamian plain.

Last, Japan lacks natural resources and does not share land borders with neighbors. By contrast, Iraq, possessing the second-largest oil deposits in the world, is surrounded by six intrusive neighbors, each with its own agenda, and is located in a region that has been the most volatile and violent since World War II.

Turkey has its eye on the oil region of Kirkuk in the north. The Saudi royals want to insure that the contagion of "Western-style democracy" does not take root in Iraq and then spread to their kingdom. Iran wants its co-religionist Shiites to assert their power at the expense of the Sunni minority. Syria will do its utmost to see that the new rulers in Baghdad do not turn themselves into Washington's vassals.

Finally, there is the in-between scenario, in which the fighting lasts up to three months. This will strain the fragile unity among opposition groups, as the death and destruction of Iraqi Muslims, shown on Arab and Muslim television channels, will make the continued membership of the Teheran-based Supreme Council of Islamic Revolution in Iraq (SCIRI) in the U.S.-sponsored opposition untenable.

Observers agree that SCIRI's clerics have merely taken out an insurance policy: If Saddam is overthrown, they want their share of power. Alani says, "This opportunistic alliance is more embarrassing to the United States than to Iran or SCIRI, to have a body with 'Islamic Revolution' in its name in a U.S.-sponsored alliance."

But then again, those on the inside track of the Bush Jr. Administration know well that what ultimately counts is the puppet master, not the puppet. As one well-placed American observer at the London conference said, "Eighty percent of the people here won't have any role to play in a post-Hussein government." To that figure, one should probably add another 19 percent.

SADDAM'S REAL OPPONENTS

Frank Smyth

Three years ago, the influential journal *Foreign Affairs* published an article on Iraq entitled "The Rollback Fantasy." It was a typically long and sober piece, challenging the thinking of those who were arguing for a United States role in toppling Iraq's ruler, Saddam Hussein. But unfortunately, the article contained its own odd piece of fantasy: In referring to "Iraq's Sunni majority," it managed to get one of the most basic pieces of demographic information about Iraq exactly backward. There is no Sunni majority. In proclaiming that the United States should back this alleged majority in a post-Saddam Iraq, while opposing either "Kurdish or Shiite bids for hegemony over the Sunnis," the magazine garbled its analysis. The Sunni Arabs who now govern Iraq make up no more than 17 percent of the population. As *Foreign Affairs'* editors noted two issues later: "Most Iraqis are Shiites. Our apologies."

In fact, as a quick look at a good almanac will tell you, Shiite Muslims make up at least 60 percent of Iraq's population, while Sunni Muslims (including Sunni Kurds and Sunni Arabs) are no more than 37 percent. These are important distinctions—perhaps the most crucial facts to know about Iraq if one is speculating about a post-Saddam future for the country, as much of official Washington is these days.

Yet here was Henry Kissinger popping up on the op-ed page of *The Washington Post* in January referring to "the Sunni majority, which now dominates Iraq" and, for good measure, adding an observation about "the Shiite minority in the south." It seems to be a mistake that has staying power. A *Washington Post* editorial last spring also made mention of "minority Shiites from the south." And last month, *New York Times* reporter Todd S. Purdum worried in print "that a change in regime could leave Iraq's Shiite minority more empowered."

Neither the *Post* nor the *Times* has corrected the mistake, so we can surely expect to see more references in the U.S. press to a Shiite minority that does

Frank Smyth is a freelance journalist who specializes in on-the-scene reporting about foreign affairs. He has covered the civil war in El Salvador from San Salvador, the first Gulf War from Jordan and, after the war ended, the ensuing Kurdish uprising from northern Iraq itself (where he went missing for 18 days after being captured by Iraqi forces). More recently, he has reported on Al Qaeda from Sudan (he was among the first to implicate Osama bin Laden in the twin bombing of U.S. embassies in Africa), and has traveled to Colombia to report on the American role in the counter-insurgency there. This article was first published in *The American Prospect* on March 25, 2002.

not exist—not in the south of Iraq, not in the north, not in the country as a whole. *Most Iraqis are Shiites.* And it matters. For all the plans that are now being hotly discussed about turning U.S. military might against the Iraqi regime, there is widespread confusion about what political outcome is desirable and what is realistic. If Saddam were removed from power, would the United States feel compelled to prevent the majority Shiites from forming a new Islamic state? What kind of "axis of evil" would the Bush administration face if both Iran and Iraq were controlled by Shiite clerics? What are the alternatives?

The same U.S. newspapers that are misguided about Iraq's demographics have been calling the Iraqi National Congress "the Iraqi opposition." But the INC is the active opposition's least-significant part: It has not mounted any military efforts in Iraq since September 1996. The group is based in London and is made up mostly of families who fled Iraq after the fall of the British-imposed monarchy in 1958. They are mainly Sunni Arabs—just like much of Saddam's regime—and thus are not representative of the Iraqi majority.

Meanwhile, it's been Shiite rebel groups in southern Iraq that have attempted to attack the "pillars" of Saddam's regime. In December 1996, a group calling itself al-Nahda (Renaissance) wounded Saddam's eldest son and security chief, Uday, a notorious enforcer who is credibly accused of using torture against suspected dissidents. In 1998, Shiite rebels farther south threw hand grenades at Izzat Ibrahim, Saddam's second-in-command in the Baath Party's ruling Revolutionary Command Council. (The grenades missed their target.)

In fact, a quiet war has been under way between Saddam's security forces and Shiite clerics in southern Iraq. In a bloody crackdown from April 1998 to February 1999, three grand ayatollahs were killed in gangland-style assassinations. In each case, the cleric had been handpicked by Saddam to lead Iraq's Shiites. But each one had defied Saddam by encouraging Shiite Muslims to return to their local mosques to receive prayers instead of receiving them through Iraqi state television. The clerics had also asked Saddam to release other religious leaders from imprisonment.

After Grand Ayatollah Sadiq al-Sadr was gunned down with his two sons on the road to Najaf, Shiites from Beirut to Tehran marched in the streets denouncing Saddam. Inside Iraq, some brave Shiites took to the streets, even in cities as far north as "Saddam City," a Shiite slum on the south side of Baghdad. Iraqi security forces opened fire there, reportedly killing 54 people.

The Shiites could be Saddam's Achilles' heel, but what will U.S. policy be toward the enemies of our enemy? Policy makers and pundits have voiced concern about whether the instability and "fragmentation" that might follow

Saddam's overthrow would be worse than Saddam's continued rule. Neighboring Turkey fears the possibility that Iraqi Kurds in the north might attempt to secede, thus fomenting Kurdish nationalism in Turkey. The United States is concerned with the specter of Iraq's Shiites turning either all or most of Iraq into a pro-Iranian Islamic state. Yet as long as the United States remains distant from Shiite opposition groups, the opposition to Saddam will remain divided—and insignificant.

If only those troublesome Shiites really *were* a minority, as Henry Kissinger and some in the press would have us believe, the answers might be simpler. But hasn't Kissinger always insisted on "realism" in foreign policy? Or did he mean magical realism?

IN IRAQI KURDISTAN

Tim Judah

With all the debate about whether the United States should go to war with Saddam Hussein's regime, hardly anyone seems to have noticed that the war for Iraq has already begun. A few weeks ago I sat on a mountainside in northern Iraq and watched Kurdish fighters, who are known as peshmergas, trading shellfire with a group that they say is linked to al-Qaeda and that had dug into positions on the mountain opposite. The Kurdish fighters claimed that their opponents, who are mainly Kurds but include some Arabs as well, receive some support from Saddam Hussein and a lot from Iran. As the peshmergas served tea, the otherwise silent landscape reverberated with the shelling, and puffs of smoke and dust twisted and vanished with the evening breeze. This is an overture to the war.

To get to these peshmerga positions I had driven first to Halabja, the Kurdish town on which Saddam Hussein had dropped chemical weapons on March 16, 1988, killing five thousand people virtually instantly. After Halabja I had taken the road that runs through a village called Anab and beyond that to the Iranian border. When Halabja's people began to flee from the attack of Saddam's air force in 1988, Iraqi bombers targeted them on the road at Anab, killing hundreds, including eighteen members of the family of Saadiyah Hassan Yacob. I met her in Anab, and while we talked she served grapes. They looked delicious but tasted extremely bitter. I wondered whether Anab's grapes had always tasted like this or whether they were bitter because of soil contamination from Saddam's chemical bombs. I asked Saadiyah what the gas tasted like when it fell on Anab, and she said: "It was like razors on your tongue."

Saadiyah is a striking-looking woman, but at forty-four she is unlikely to get married now. Here in Iraqi Kurdistan, where, generally speaking, girls are married off young, this is not unusual. So many men have died fighting or simply been trucked away and executed by Saddam Hussein's troops over the

Tim Judah is the former Balkans correspondent for *The Times* of London and the *Economist*. He lived in Belgrade from 1990 to 1995, where he observed firsthand the horrors of ethnic cleansing and war in the former Yugoslavia. He wrote a major series on the Kosovo war for *The New York Review of Books*, and is also the author of *Kosovo: War and Revenge*, published by Yale University Press. This article, written on assignment in northern Iraq, was originally published in *The New York Review of Books* on September 26, 2002.

years that there are not enough men to go around. And now a new cycle of conflict is beginning.

1.

In 1991, after the Gulf War, President Bush encouraged Iraqis to rise up and overthrow Saddam Hussein. In the south, among the Shia Arabs who make up some 60 percent of Iraq's population, there were revolts in several towns; and there were also uprisings among northern Iraq's Kurds, who make up between 15 and 20 percent of Iraq's 23 million people. The U.S. did nothing. The administration was alarmed at the prospect that Iraq would be torn apart, that the Shias would lead a bloody Islamic revolution dominated by neighboring Shia Iran, and that the Kurds would declare independence, provoking angry and violent reactions from, among others, America's close ally Turkey, with its own restive Kurdish population. Indeed it even signaled discreetly to Saddam Hussein, who was then rallying the Sunni Arab Iraqis, who have always dominated his country's politics despite being only some 15 percent of the population, that he should go ahead and crush the rebellions. With characteristic savagery he did so.

All across Kurdish-dominated northern Iraq the Kurds had seized control, but now Saddam's forces came roaring back. Terrified that they would again be gassed, approximately a million Kurds fled toward the Iranian and Turkish borders. There they were greeted by hordes of reporters from the world press. The sight of desperate Kurds clinging to the mountainsides on U.S. television embarrassed the Bush administration, which decided it had to do something. Saddam was told to pull back his forces, and U.S. and British troops entered northern Iraq. The British and Americans then began to patrol a no-fly zone above the region, the refugees returned, and in this way an autonomous, though internationally unrecognized, Kurdish entity emerged. Today 3.6 million Kurds live here, free from Saddam's tyranny. The U.S. and British troops have gone but the no-fly zone is still enforced and much of this part of Kurdistan, which had been reduced to rubble by Saddam especially in brutal suppression campaigns in the late 1980s, has been rebuilt.

The lands inhabited by the Kurds—Kurdistan—stretch through Iraq, Turkey, Syria, and Iran. There are also small numbers of Kurds in Armenia, Azerbaijan, and Georgia. In 1920 Britain and the other world powers, including the U.S., promised the Kurds a state of their own in the Treaty of Sèvres. The next year the Kurds were betrayed by the British, who decided that their mandate on Iraq would be better served if they included the oil-rich Kirkuk region within it. The Kurds found themselves formally divided among several of the states that succeeded the Ottoman Empire, in particular Iraq and Turkey. Today there are perhaps 20 million Kurds in Turkey, 8 million in Iran, 1.5 million in Syria, and between 4 and 5 million in Iraq, including those parts of historic Kurdistan still under Saddam's control. The governments of all of these countries distrust the Kurds because they fear that they would all eventually like to break away to form an independent Kurdistan if they could. Since the Kurds never wanted to be part of these countries, least of all to be dominated by them, this fear is quite justified.

EVER SINCE the 1920s the Iraqi Kurds have lived through cycles of rebellion, repression, and then tense peace agreements with governments in Baghdad. When these regimes have been weak, they have given concessions to the Kurds only to take them back when they have been strong. During the Iran-Iraq war between 1980 and 1988 Iraqi Kurdish peshmergas sided with Iran while Iranian Kurdish peshmergas fought with Iraq. The historic principle at work here was nothing more complicated than my enemy's enemy is my friend. The problem for the Kurds is that they really have no friends at all, only shifting alliances and interests.

Today Iraqi Kurdistan is dominated by two political parties. In 1991 the two parties were united as the Kurdistan Front. They then fell out over the division of revenues from smuggling and trade and because, while both talked about democracy, their real aim was to eliminate each other. In the mid-1990s the two parties fought a desultory but bitter civil war. Based in the east, the Patriotic Union of Kurdistan (PUK) of Jalal Talabani enlisted the support of the Iranian military to help him overcome the Kurdish Democratic Party (KDP) of Massoud Barzani, the son of Mustafa Barzani, the famous Kurdish guerrilla leader who fought in the mountains for years and died in 1978. In 1996 Barzani asked the U.S. for help, but when this was not forthcoming he asked Saddam to send in his tanks to drive out the PUK. Saddam obliged, and at the same time captured and executed Iraqi Arab opposition forces and politicians who did not have enough time to flee before his blitzkrieg.

Following his successful incursion, Saddam withdrew. Today, Iraqi Kurdistan is divided into a zone run by the PUK in the east and a KDP region in the west, but the two groups now have peaceful working relations. The U.S., and indeed every other country, would like to know whether these parties, the only organized armed groups in Iraq opposed to Saddam, will fight alongside it if it goes to war. So far the responses have varied from confusing to downright cool, but this, of course, could be part of a bargaining tactic.

2.

It is easy to see why the Kurds might not want to participate in any U.S.-led attack. About half an hour's drive south of Arbil, the main city in KDP territory, is the village of Shoresh. It lies on the south bank of the Great Zab River, a tributary of the Tigris. At the edge of the village the land slopes gently upward to a line of hills. There are no barriers or signs or warnings here, nor are there any peshmerga positions. But between the village of Shoresh and the Iraqi soldiers stationed on the top of the hills less than five hundred yards away are some of the more than eight million mines that are sprinkled across Iraqi Kurdistan. The Iraqi soldiers are so close you can actually see them strolling about. Unlike Kurdish forces, they have tanks, heavy artillery, missiles, rockets, and, most probably, chemical and biological weapons. So if the U.S. attacks Iraq, the entire population of Shoresh could be dead a few minutes later.

I watched the Iraqi troops from the roof of a house belonging to the forty-year-old Stia Ahmed. In her bedroom she has a large photograph of her husband, Qassem Mohammed, who died in Saddam's army fighting the Iranians during the war. In the picture he has long hair because he was, like many in Iraqi Kurdistan, a Dervish, a believer in the Sufi-influenced interpretation of Islam. In view of the proximity of the Iraqis I asked Mrs. Ahmed what she would do if the Americans attacked. She said that if the rest of the village fled then she would go too, but if they stayed she would stay. Then, expressing a view I was to hear from many in Iraqi Kurdistan, she said that despite the risks to her village, and even her life, she still wanted America to attack. "We would prefer Saddam to be destroyed," she said. "He did nothing for us."

At a nearby shop I met a group of some twenty-five men and boys of all ages. In these conservative and rural parts, girls and women do not venture out of their houses without permission or unless they have good reason to. The men complained that none of them had anything to do because many of their fields lay in Iraqi-controlled territory and unless you paid a large bribe you could not work them. Men of military age hardly dared to cross the lines anyway for fear of being drafted into Saddam's forces, while on their own side mines infested the fields. Ibrahim Kheder Mikhail, a sixty-eight-year-old, said that because of this, "it is like a prison here." I conducted a straw poll. Bearing in mind the risk to Shoresh if the U.S. attacked, I asked who was in favor of a U.S.-led offensive and who was against. Not a single man was against. It was certainly not a scientific poll but still, judging from many other talks I had with Kurds, I suspect that even if it had been, the result would not have been much different. These men, however, were not part of any armed force.

• • •

TEN MINUTES drive from Shoresh is the checkpoint at Kalak. It lies on one of the main roads that link Kurdish-controlled territory with Saddam's Iraq. Just before the checkpoint is a line of moneychangers looking for business. In Iraqi Kurdistan they use old Iraqi banknotes known as "Swiss Prints," because that is where they were printed. In Saddam's territory they use new banknotes adorned with his image. With a couple of brick-sized blocks of cash on his little table, Ismail Jamil explained the mechanics of the Kalak money market. "If the news is about a possible attack," he said, "the Saddam dinar and the dollar go down and the 'Swiss Print' goes up. When the news suggests there may be no attack or the situation is stable then Saddam's dinar goes up." It's not so different from Wall Street.

The moneychangers do a brisk business. Thousands, mostly Kurds, cross back and forth from Saddam Hussein's territory every day. Some are visiting family and friends, some are going there to collect modest pensions, and some are seeking the more sophisticated medical treatment that they can get in the nearby big city of Mosul or in Baghdad. A large proportion of those crossing the line, however, are men of all ages in rickety old cars who drive south, fill their tanks with cheap gasoline, and cross back north again to sell it for the higher price it fetches here. They can do this several times a day. Another part of the traffic consists of trucks laden with merchandise of all sorts and tank trucks carrying oil. Some of this trade is legal, some clearly breaks U.N. sanctions, and some lies in the twilight zone between the two. What is public knowledge however is that taxes on this trade, imposed by the KDP, have until recently financed the government in KDP territory.

Among the people I met at Kalak were Dilshad and Haider, both in their twenties. Dilshad was driving a sputtering old East German motorbike, and Haider, who has only one arm, clung to the back. He told me that he had lost his arm ten years ago when he had been shot by Iraqi troops as he tried to smuggle car parts from Kurdistan into Saddam Hussein's territory. The two men had just been to Mosul, which is only forty-seven kilometers away in Saddam-controlled Iraq but takes two hours on the bike. They do this journey four times a week and stock up on items that they can sell back home in Kurdish-controlled territory. Today they had 180 brightly colored plastic dustpans stacked in their sidecar. They buy them because Iraqi Kurdistan has no plastics factory of its own. According to Dilshad, over in Mosul "things in the market are very slow, because people are afraid of American attacks." What frightens people most, Kurds and Arabs alike is the prospect of civilian casualties. Still, according to Haider, "people want America to attack because they are hungry and suffering a lot from Saddam."

3.

Among those suffering from Saddam are Kurds who still live in Iraqi-controlled regions, especially the oil-rich city of Kirkuk. The Kurds say that Kirkuk was, is, and always will be a Kurdish city. The problem is that successive Baghdad governments have tried to Arabize the town and the region by settling Arabs from other parts of Iraq there. They want it to cease being Kurdish, precisely because they want to make sure that they will control the oil. So while Saddam Hussein's Arabization policies have been brutal, he has only intensified a policy which, to varying degrees, was already in existence when he took power.

Nobody I met could tell me how many Kurds remained in the city, but I met a good many Kurds from Kirkuk who had been thrown out of the region over the last twenty years. The PUK distributes a book in English about the Iraqi Arabization policy which has statistics for 1957 and 1977. It shows that in 1957 48 percent of Kirkuk's people were Kurds, 28.2 percent Arabs, and 21.2 percent from the Turkoman minority. By 1977 however the Kurdish population had dropped to 37.6 percent, the Arab population had grown to 44.4 percent, and the proportion of Turkoman had dropped to 16.3 percent. We can safely assume that the percentage of Kurds is far lower today.

The little town of Chamchamal lies on the road to Kirkuk and is the last stop in territory under PUK control, making it the first stop of many Kurds from Kirkuk who have just been ethnically cleansed. According to Tariq Rashid Ali, who is the PUK administrator of Chamchamal, the numbers of people expelled rises and falls but recently it has risen again. At the moment, says Mr. Ali, he is receiving about thirty expelled people a day, but more are being thrown out because they don't all cross at Chamchamal. He knows the figures for his area because those who are expelled must all register with him in order to collect the monthly food parcel that every family in Iraq is supposed to get as part of the U.N.'s "food for oil" policy. The U.N. buys food and medicines and other goods for Iraq with income from Iraq's sales of oil.*

In Mr. Ali's office I met Naaman Mohammed Ali, a man in his early thirties, who had, along with his family, been expelled from Kirkuk four days earlier. He explained the various tactics used by the regime to expel Kurds. At

---

* Unfortunately I was unable to speak to anyone among the large number of U.N. officials in Iraqi Kurdistan. The reason for this is that the U.N. has agreed to a policy by which its officials will not speak to foreign journalists unless they have entered Iraq on an official Iraqi visa. But Saddam Hussein's regime gives hardly any journalists visas; and even if they did it would be virtually impossible for them to get to Iraqi Kurdistan. This disgusting policy means that Saddam Hussein has a veto on which journalists the U.N. can speak to in Iraq. I entered Iraqi Kurdistan from Iran.

times pressure has been put on them to officially change their registered nationality from Kurd to Arab and to change their names to more Arabic-
sounding ones. If you wanted to buy a house in Kirkuk and you were not
registered as an Arab, then you had to change your name and your nationality
in order to complete the formalities. More recently, a new tactic has been
used. Pressure is being put on people to join Saddam's Jerusalem Brigade, a
kind of auxiliary army being raised in Iraq, with the purported intent of "liberating Jerusalem." However, in Kirkuk I was told Kurds were being targeted for
the draft. "If you refuse," he said, "they ask you to leave. If you refuse to leave,
they order you to leave; then they put your son or your father in jail for a week
or so and then tell you to leave again." In order to get the jailed member of the
family out of prison, the family usually complies. According to Naaman Ali,
nobody believed that the Jerusalem Brigade was really about "liberating
Jerusalem"; it had more to do with "controlling people."

Close to Chamchamal is the Barda Qaraman camp, which currently
houses about 660 people expelled from Kirkuk. Ali Khaled Fathollah Mahmood had arrived a few days earlier with his family of twelve. They were all living together, in a tent. I asked Mr. Mahmood what life was like in Kirkuk and
he said, "It's hell there." The family had left after pressure had been brought to
bear on three of Mr. Mahmood's sons to join the Jerusalem Brigade. According to his nineteen-year-old daughter, Shirin, "many young people" who had
been forced to join the Jerusalem Brigade "are dead because of a lack of food
and water and because of the heat. Two of our neighbors died." Since hardly
any journalists are ever let into Saddam-controlled Iraq, and since they are
strictly controlled if they are, there is no way to confirm such stories. However, if the U.S. begins a military offensive against Iraq we are all going to hear
a lot more about Kirkuk.

4.

Whether you are in PUK or KDP territory, every government or party office
has a map of Iraqi Kurdistan. The interesting thing about this map is that the
region claimed for Kurdistan is about twice the size of the region that the two
parties control today. Today Kirkuk, with all its oil wealth, lies outside the
Kurdish-controlled region; on the map of the Kurdistan claimed by the Kurds,
it lies in the middle of it.

If you ask Kurdish officials about whether they would help any American-
led invasion force, they become evasive. They say they have good reason to be
noncommittal. The U.S. let them down in 1991 and this was only a repetition

of an earlier betrayal in 1975 when the U.S., on behalf of the Shah of Iran, had been supporting Kurdish rebels only to drop them when the Shah and Saddam Hussein signed a deal to end their various disputes. Typically officials say they can't answer because they don't know yet exactly what is being asked of them and besides they need guarantees of their security. Equally confusing are the comments of Mr. Talabani of the PUK, who was in Washington while I was in Kurdistan. At one point he said he would be happy if the U.S. were to use his territory as a base for attacks on Saddam Hussein, only to retract this the next day; but the following day he repeated his first statement to the British papers.

In fact, if there is a war, whatever they say, they cannot fail to become involved. During the uprising of 1991, for example, Kirkuk fell to the Kurds within hours, but they held it for only ten days. When Saddam Hussein rallied his troops, he drove them out. Today the Kurds, along with Iraq's exiled Arab politicians, say they are in favor of a federal system for the country. Clearly this means a federal unit for Kurdistan; but does it mean federal units for the Arab Shias and Sunnis as well? No one can say. The Arab opposition leaders have told the Kurds that they don't believe that this is the time to specify where the border between Kurdistan and the other parts of the country should be drawn. This may suit the Kurds. Almost all the officials I talked to told me they believe that in the face of a large-scale U.S. attack, the Iraqi army, including the Republican Guard, simply will not fight. The Kurds could retake Kirkuk. The army that drove them out of the city they now dismiss as impotent.

Freydoun Abdul Kheder, the PUK's minister of the interior, told me that he believed that if Saddam's communications networks were destroyed in the first wave of bombings then "in two or three days he will lose control of Iraq." Mr. Kheder, who led the uprising in the PUK capital of Sulaimaniya in 1991, told me that he based his conclusions on his numerous contacts among senior Iraqi military figures, many of whom he knew from college or from the periods when he lived in Baghdad. A major general he knew sent his sister to see him to plead for money to feed his family. Naturally, Mr. Kheder obliged and sends him a little cash every month. How, he asked, can anyone expect the Iraqi military to fight when they are so miserably poor? Mr. Kheder says he receives much interesting information in return for favors he gives Iraqis. An interesting indicator of morale, he points out, is that he now receives more intelligence from Saddam's officers than ever before because they are convinced that the regime is nearing its end. "They want," he said, "to guarantee their future" by claiming afterward to have helped the opposition. "Saddam is finished!" he says cheerfully.

If this is indeed the case then it is clear that the Kurds will have a historic opportunity to create the border of the Iraqi Kurdistan they want—by force. If the Iraqi army really won't fight—a possibility that no one can be sure of— then between 70,000 and 100,000 peshmergas can surge forward and, in concert with local uprisings, seize as much territory for themselves as possible. This will then enable them to negotiate federal borders from a position of strength. Kirkuk, with all its oil, will be the great prize. The Kurds don't expect there will be many property disputes between returning Kurds and Arab settlers, because they expect the Arabs to flee. To make sure that this operation goes smoothly, however, the Kurds, or rather the PUK, have some unfinished business to take care of first.

Among the business in question is that of Ansar al-Islam, the armed Islamic fundamentalist group holed up in the mountains on the Iranian border close to Halabja. It is here that fighting has begun. The PUK believe that Ansar has up to seven hundred men, of whom seventy are not Kurds but Iraqi Arabs, foreign Arabs, and Sudanese. The PUK claim that Ansar is linked to al-Qaeda, Iraqi intelligence, and Iran. These three make unlikely bedfellows but there is a logic here.

Ansar, also known as Jund al-Islam, appeared last September as the result of the fragmentation of a larger Kurdish fundamentalist group. Now the PUK are preparing to crush Ansar because, when the U.S. assault begins, as they fully expect it will, they don't want to have to fight on two fronts. Occupying a politically ambiguous position in the villages surrounding the Ansar enclave are two other fundamentalist groups, some of whose men may choose to fight with Ansar should the PUK mount an offensive. Together the fighters from all the fundamentalist groups add up to some two thousand men. The PUK now have three thousand peshmergas ranged against them, and many of these troops are refugees from Kirkuk. When the time comes, they want to fight in order to go home; they don't want to fight fundamentalists in the mountains.

As we peered at the Ansar front lines, Lieutenant Colonel Ahmad Chekha Omer told me that a few weeks ago these positions had been visited by American military intelligence officers, preceded by British officers. The peshmerga high command, he believed, had requested air strikes in support of a PUK attack. He said, "We only need two jets." The coming fight will be extremely risky—but not because Saddam Hussein's intelligence services are providing money and other backing to Ansar, as the peshmergas say. The real problem is Iran. According to Lieutenant Colonel Omer, "If the Iranians don't interfere we can finish them easily." He says that Iranian military trucks were spotted in the area two months ago, that Iran has supplied the fundamentalists with three Katyusha truck-mounted multiple-rocket launchers, that Iranian spotters are helping them target their artillery, and that "Iranian officers give them maps and training to use their Katyushas."

Officials from the PUK find all this acutely embarrassing. In the past the PUK has relied heavily on Iranian support, based on the principle that they were the enemy of Iran's enemy, Saddam Hussein, not to mention the PUK's need for assistance in its conflict with the KDP. But now things are changing. While Iran was happy to help the U.S. get rid of its other enemy, the Afghan Taliban, its leaders now fear that a democratic and especially a federal Iraq will emerge with a large, stable, and secular Kurdish unit within it. This, the Iranians believe, probably rightly, would only encourage their own Kurds to demand the same thing. Everyone here remembers that after World War II a short-lived breakaway Kurdish republic emerged in Iran before being crushed. Today, its legendary leader is celebrated with a large portrait in the center of Sulaimaniya.

I talked with a teacher who has a house inside the fundamentalist enclave. He told me how Ansar was enforcing a Taliban-style regime in the area under its control, ordering men and women to strictly observe fundamentalist practices, forcing women to wear full Islamic dress including covering their faces, and beating anyone in the streets at prayer time.

SOON AFTER I visited the Ansar front, U.S. officials released stories saying that Ansar had been experimenting with poison gases in the enclave and that very senior al-Qaeda men were hiding there but that the U.S. had decided not to do anything about it. What seemed to me odd about these stories was that if they were true, the peshmergas and Mr. Kheder, who would have had everything to gain from spreading such information, might have told me about them. But they did not.

The PUK did, however, let me talk to three of their prisoners. I am always skeptical about such interviews, especially in this case since prison officials were present, but the men appeared to be speaking freely. Still, they said very little that would have displeased their PUK captors. One prisoner, Muhammed Mansour Shahab Ali, said he had smuggled guns from Iraqi intelligence to Osama bin Laden in Afghanistan. He also claimed that two years ago he smuggled thirty refrigerator motors, given to him and an accomplice by a relative of Saddam Hussein, from Iraq to bin Laden; they were, he believes, filled with some sort of gas or liquid, although he didn't know what it was.

In view of Saddam's use of chemical weapons in Kurdistan and during the Iran-Iraq war, this, if true, raises the possibility that Iraq was supplying bin Laden with materials for just such weapons. Shahab Ali said he could not give any reason why Saddam Hussein would want to support al-Qaeda, which has publicly denounced secular Arab regimes such as Saddam's. But, Ali said, "bin Laden liked fighting. He only liked fighting," implying that if al-Qaeda forces would be helpful in fighting the Kurds and now the U.S., Saddam would welcome them. I asked him if he had any regrets. He thought a bit and said that his only real regret was that he had strangled his wife, the mother of his twin boys, now lost somewhere in Afghanistan.

Another prisoner told me that he had been an Ansar fighter until he was captured. Once he began talking he poured out details of meetings between Ansar leaders and bin Laden and the various training courses the Ansar leaders had taken in Afghanistan. In fact, he described in such complicated detail how al-Qaeda money was transmitted to Ansar via a contact in London that I began to suspect that he took me for a foreign intelligence agent come to debrief him, and he thought that by giving me this information he could perhaps secure his release from prison. It is unlikely that he could have been primed for the interview since I had asked to meet with an Ansar prisoner only an hour earlier.

The third prisoner, in his thirties, told me that he was a Kurd from Baghdad who had come to the region to smuggle tea to Iran and had then joined the Islamists. Before the interview, Colonel Hassan Nuri, the director of the jail, told me that he always "acted meek," that he, Nuri, was "100 percent sure" that the man was an Iraqi intelligence agent, and that he was probably an Arab. Hassan duly appeared to be meek and gently spoken. When I asked him if, as an Ansar fighter, he had had any dealings with Iraqi intelligence, he said, "Never!" But he told me that he had witnessed Ansar's most infamous deed, the massacre on September 23, 2001, in the village of Kheli Hama of forty-two peshmerga prisoners. He told me that the prisoners were standing with their hands bound. Ansar's men then slit their throats and stabbed them with bayonets. He said the killings by some twenty of the fundamentalists took fifteen minutes. I asked him to describe the scene as the massacre began. He said that the Ansar men were shouting that the prisoners were "pagans" because the PUK (and KDP) are secular organizations and that the frightened prisoners were shouting, "For the sake of God don't kill us! We have families . . . kids!"

5.

If the Kurds play their cards shrewdly, they might do well from a U.S.-led offensive against Iraq. If the future Iraq is, contrary to many expectations, both federal and democratic, then they will have a powerful voice in Baghdad and control of their own affairs. But it will not be the end of the story. For much of the last century the Kurds of northern Iraq have been rebelling against one government or another, and few make any secret of their desire to eventually achieve independence and then to join with Kurds from Iran, Syria, and Turkey in a large Kurdish state.

At one point I asked a Kurdish government official if he believed that a Kurdish federal unit in Iraq would provide an example for Kurds in Turkey and elsewhere to follow; and if they were allowed some autonomy, would they eventually, decades later perhaps, all secede and then join together. "Yes," he said, "that's the aim." Realizing what he had said, he then added hastily, "but don't write that down." A few days later I was talking to Musa Ali Bakr, who is in charge of refugees in the KDP-controlled region of Dohuk. I told him how unconvincing it sounded, especially in the KDP region, when people like Fadhil Merani, a senior official, insisted that they wanted nothing more than a federal democracy for Iraq. When Mr. Merani told me that he was "proud to be an Iraqi," I found this hard to believe in view of Saddam's attempt to destroy the Kurdish nation. I asked Mr. Bakr why Kurdish leaders didn't come out openly and say what they really wanted, which was independence. He explained patiently that if the Kurds did this, their neighbors would instantly try to punish them by shutting their already tightly controlled borders. He summed up the Kurdish dilemma perfectly: "If you are sick you visit the doctor. He prescribes the medicine. You take a spoonful three times a day and eventually you are better, you are free. However, if you drank the whole bottle all at once, it would kill you."

At the nearby military camp of Zawita, I watched some four hundred Kurdish soldiers drilling in stiff military style. The aim of the Zawita camp, according to Aziz Waice, its commanding officer, is to convert the KDP's peshmerga guerrillas into a regular army. The men, who were all wearing white gloves, marched across the drill square screaming, "Kurdistan or Death!" Their officers, dressed in British army-style uniforms, tapped their swagger sticks against their thighs and ate candy.

In view of what may be coming it is understandable that Saddam Hussein could feel nervous, but the Turks too have been making threatening noises, implying that they might intervene if the Kurds emerge from the war with too much land and power—particularly if they control the city of Kirkuk. I told Commander Waice that if I was a Turkish general and saw pictures of this parade it might give me a heart attack. "Ha!" he laughed. "That's their problem!" In view of the baleful record of Kurdish history though, he might have said the same for the Kurds in the PUK and KDP. The U.S. may need both groups if it is to succeed in Iraq, and it is far from clear just how willing they are to help the U.S.

POST-SADDAM IRAQ: LINCHPIN OF A NEW OIL ORDER

Michael Renner

Only in the most direct sense is the Bush administration's Iraq policy directed against Saddam Hussein. In contrast to all the loud talk about terrorism, weapons of mass destruction, and human rights violations, very little is being said about oil. The administration has been tight-lipped about its plans for a post-Saddam Iraq and has repeatedly disavowed any interest in the country's oil resources. But press reports indicate that U.S. officials are considering a prolonged occupation of Iraq after their war to topple Saddam Hussein. It is likely that a U.S.-controlled Iraq will be the linchpin of a new order in the world oil industry. Indeed, a war against Iraq may well herald a major realignment of the Middle East power balance.

Oil Forever

The Bush administration's ties to the oil and gas industry are beyond extensive; they are pervasive. They flow, so to speak, from the top, with a chief executive who grew up steeped in the culture of Texas oil exploration and tried his hand at it himself; and a second-in-command who came to office with a multi-million dollar retirement package in hand from his post of CEO of Halliburton Oil. Once in office, the vice president developed an energy policy under the primary guidance of a cast of oil company executives whose identities he has gone to great lengths to withhold from public view. Since taking office, the president and vice president have assembled a government peopled heavily with representatives from the oil culture they came from. These include Secretary of the Army Thomas White, a former vice president of Enron, and Secretary of Commerce Don Evans, former president of the oil explo-

Michael Renner is a senior researcher at the Washington-based Worldwatch Institute, and editor of its annual *State of the World* reports. He is a policy analyst for *Foreign Policy in Focus*, has written articles for *The Christian Science Monitor, Los Angeles Times, International Herald Tribune*, and *Le Monde Diplomatique*, and is the author of *Fighting for Survival: Environmental Decline, Social Conflict, and the New Age of Insecurity* (1996). This article first appeared as a *Foreign Policy in Focus* Policy Report in January 2003.

ration company Tom Brown, Inc., whose major stake in the company was worth $13 million by the time he took office.

The Bush administration's energy policy is predicated on ever-growing consumption of oil, preferably cheap oil. U.S. oil consumption is projected to increase by one-third over the next two decades. The White House is pushing hard for greater domestic drilling and wants to open the Arctic National Wildlife Refuge to the oil industry. Even so, the administration's National Energy Policy Development Group, led by Vice President Cheney, acknowledged in a May 2001 report that U.S. oil production will fall 12% over the next 20 years. As a result, U.S. dependence on imported oil—which has risen from one-third in 1985 to more than half today—is set to climb to two-thirds by 2020.

Since the 1970s, the U.S. has put considerable effort into diversifying its sources of supply; going largely outside of OPEC and outside the Middle East. The current administration is advocating greater efforts to expand production in such far-flung places as the Caspian area, Nigeria, Chad, Angola, and deep offshore areas in the Atlantic basin and is looking to leading Western Hemispheric suppliers like Canada, Mexico, and Venezuela. West Africa is expected to account for as much as a quarter of U.S. oil imports a decade from now.

But there is no escaping the fact that the Middle East—and specifically the Persian Gulf region—remains the world's prime oil province, for the U.S. and for other importers. Indeed, the Cheney report confirms that "by any estimation, Middle East oil producers will remain central to world oil security." The Middle East currently accounts for about 30% of global oil production and more than 40% of oil exports. With about 65% of the planet's known reserves, it is the only region able to satisfy the substantial rise in world oil demand predicted by the Bush administration. The Cheney report projects that Persian Gulf producers alone will supply 54–67% of world oil exports in 2020.

Saudi Arabia is a pivotal player. With 262 billion barrels, it has a quarter of the world's total proven reserves and is the single largest producer. More important, the Saudis have demonstrated repeatedly—after the Iranian revolution, and following Iraq's invasion of Kuwait—that they are prepared to compensate for losses from other suppliers, calming markets in times of turmoil. Today, Riyadh could raise its production of 8 million barrels per day (b/d) to 10.5 million b/d within three months, making up for any loss of Iraqi oil during a U.S. military assault.

Iraq: From Pariah to Fabulous Prize

The pariah state of Iraq, however, is a key prize, with abundant, high-quality oil that can be produced at very low cost (and thus at great profit). At 112 billion barrels, its proven reserves are currently second only to Saudi Arabia's. The Energy Information Administration (EIA) of the U.S. Department of Energy estimates that additional "probable and possible" resources could amount to 220 billion barrels. And because political instability, war, and sanctions have prevented thorough exploration of substantial portions of Iraqi territory, there is a chance that another 100 billion barrels lie undiscovered in Iraq's western desert. All in all, Iraq's oil wealth may well rival that of Saudi Arabia.

At present, of course, this is mere potential—the Iraqi oil industry has seriously deteriorated as a result of the 1980–88 Iran-Iraq War, the 1991 Gulf War, and inadequate postwar investment and maintenance. Since 1990, the sanctions regime has effectively frozen plans for putting additional fields into production. It has also caused a severe shortage of oil field equipment and spare parts (under the sanctions regime, the U.S. has prevented equipment imports worth some $4 billion). Meanwhile, questionable methods used to raise output from existing fields may have damaged some of the reservoirs and could actually trigger a decline in output in the short run.

But once the facilities are rehabilitated (a lucrative job for the oil service industry, including Vice President Cheney's former employer, Halliburton) and new fields are brought into operation, the spigots could be opened wide. To pay for the massive task of rebuilding, a post-sanctions Iraq would naturally seek to maximize its oil production. Some analysts, such as Fadhil Chalabi, a former Iraqi oil official, assert that Iraq could produce 8–10 million b/d within a decade and eventually perhaps as much as 12 million.

The impact on world markets is hard to overstate. Saudi Arabia would no longer be the sole dominant producer, able to influence oil markets single-handedly. Given that U.S.-Saudi relations cooled substantially in the wake of the September 11, 2001, terrorist attacks—rifts that may widen further—a Saudi competitor would not be unwelcome in Washington. An unnamed U.S. diplomat confided to Scotland's *Sunday Herald* that "a rehabilitated Iraq is the only sound long-term strategic alternative to Saudi Arabia. It's not just a case of swapping horses in mid-stream, the impending U.S. regime change in Baghdad is a strategic necessity."

Washington would gain enormous leverage over the world oil market. Opening the Iraqi spigot would flood world markets and drive prices down substantially. OPEC, already struggling with overcapacity and a tendency among its members to produce above allotted quotas (an estimated 3 million barrels per day above the agreed total of 24.7 million b/d), might unravel as individual exporters engage in destructive price wars against each other.

A massive flow of Iraqi oil would also limit any influence that other suppliers, such as Russia, Mexico, and Venezuela, have over the oil market. Lower prices could render Russian oil—more expensive to produce—uncompetitive, which would cloud the prospects for attracting foreign investment to tap Siberian oil deposits. Russia's weak economy is highly dependent on oil export revenues. Its federal budget is predicated on prices of $24–25 per barrel. Aleksei Arbatov, deputy chairman of the Russian parliament's defense committee, predicts that if a new Iraqi regime sells oil without limits, "our budget will collapse."

Oil Company Interests

To repair and expand its oil industry, Iraq will need substantial foreign investment. Thus, for eager oil companies, Iraq represents a huge bonanza—a "boom waiting to happen," according to an unnamed industry source.

Leading Oil Companies, 2000

	Oil Reserves (billion barrels)	Oil Production (million b/d)	Refining Capacity (million b/d)	Product Sales (million b/d)
Saudi Aramco	261.8	8.6	2.1	3.0
INOC (Iraq)	112.5	2.6	0.4	0.4
KPC (Kuwait)	96.5	1.7	1.0	0.9
NIOC (Iran)	89.7	3.8	1.5	1.3
PDV (Venezuela)	77.7	3.3	3.1	3.2
ADNOC (United Arab Emirates)	53.8	1.4	0.2	0.2
Pemex (Mexico)	28.3	3.5	1.5	2.1
NOC (Libya)	23.6	1.3	0.3	0.3
Lukoil (Russia)	14.3	1.6	0.5	0.9
NNPC (Nigeria)	13.5	1.3	0.4	0.3
ExxonMobil (U.S.)	12.2	2.6	6.2	8.0
PetroChina	11.0	2.1	1.9	1.1
Royal Dutch/Shell (UK/Netherlands)	9.8	2.3	3.2	5.6

(continued on p. 584)

	Oil Reserves (billion barrels)	Oil Production (million b/d)	Refining Capacity (million b/d)	Product Sales (million b/d)
British Petroleum	7.6	1.9	3.2	5.5
TotalFinaElf (France)	7.0	1.4	2.6	3.1
Chevron Texaco (U.S.)	8.5	2.0	2.1	4.0
Petrobras (Brazil)	8.4	1.3	1.9	2.2
Sinopec (China)	3.0	0.7	2.6	1.3
Nippon Mitsubishi (Japan)	0.05	0.05	1.3	1.4
WORLD	1,046.2	74.5	81.6	

Source: Adapted from Energy Intelligence Group.

Prior to the OPEC revolution in the early 1970s, a small number of companies (referred to as the "majors" or "Seven Sisters") called the shots in the industry, controlling activities from exploration and production to refining and product sales. But they lost much of their reserve base, as nationalization spread through the Middle East and OPEC nations. Today, state oil companies own the vast majority of the world's oil resources. Even though private companies still do much of the exploring, drilling, and pumping, in many countries they have access to the oil only under prices and conditions set by the host government. Although oil companies have managed to adjust to this situation, a directly owned concession would offer them far greater flexibility and profitability.

The dominant private companies (ExxonMobil and Chevron-Texaco of the U.S., Royal Dutch-Shell and BP of Britain and the Netherlands, TotalFinaElf of France), which are largely the result of recent megamergers, sell close to 29 million barrels per day in gasoline and other oil products. But production from fields owned by these "super-majors" came to 10.1 million barrels per day in 2001, or just 35% of their sales volume. Although these corporations have poured many billions of dollars into discovering new fields outside the Middle East, their proven reserves stood at just 44 billion barrels in 2001, 4% of the world's total and sufficient to keep producing oil for only another 12 years at current rates. The situation is similar for other oil companies. Thus, the oil-rich Middle East, and particularly Iraq, remains key to the future of the oil industry.

If a new regime in Baghdad rolls out the red carpet for the oil multinationals to return, it is possible that a broader wave of denationalization could sweep through the oil industry, reversing the historic changes of the early 1970s. Squeezed by a decade of sanctions, the current regime has already sig-

naled that it is prepared to provide more favorable terms to foreign companies. Such an invitation by Baghdad would be in tune with larger changes that
are afoot, as a growing number of oil producing countries are opening their industries to foreign direct investment.

Rivalries and Quid Pro Quos

Several European and Asian oil companies have in recent years signed deals
with Iraq that, if consummated, would give them access to reserves of at least
50 billion barrels and a potential output of 4–5 million barrels per day (another estimate says that Russian companies alone have signed deals involving
about 70 billion barrels). In addition, a number of contracts have been signed
for exploration in the western desert.

Russian, Chinese, and French companies in particular have tried to position themselves to develop new oil fields and to rehabilitate existing ones,
once U.N. sanctions are lifted. Russia's Lukoil, for instance, signed an agreement in 1997 to refurbish and develop the West Qurna field (with 15 billion
barrels of oil reserves). China's National Petroleum Corporation signed a deal
for the North Rumailah reservoir. And France's TotalFinaElf has set its eyes
on the giant Majnoon deposits (holding 20–30 billion barrels).

Iraq has sought to use the lure of oil concessions to build political support
among three permanent Security Council nations—France, Russia, and
China—for a lifting of sanctions. Although the international consensus in
favor of sanctions has badly eroded, this gamble has failed to pay off in the
face of determined U.S. and British opposition. (In December 2002, Iraq
cancelled a contract with three Russian companies, out of frustration that the
firms—in deference to sanctions—had not commenced oil exploration work.)
As long as Saddam Hussein stays in power, U.S. and British companies will
be kept out of Iraq, but ongoing sanctions will also thwart existing oil development plans.

"Regime change" in Baghdad would reshuffle the cards and give U.S. (and
British) companies a good shot at direct access to Iraqi oil for the first time in
30 years—a windfall worth hundreds of billions of dollars. U.S. companies
relish the prospect: Chevron's chief executive, for example, said in 1998 that
he'd "love Chevron to have access to" Iraq's oil reserves.

In preface to the passage of Security Council Resolution 1441 on November 8, there were thinly veiled threats that French, Russian, and Chinese
firms would be excluded from any future oil concessions in Iraq unless Paris,
Moscow, and Beijing supported the Bush policy of regime change. Ahmed

Chalabi, leader of the Iraqi National Congress (INC), an exile opposition group favored by the Bush administration, said that the INC would not feel bound by any contracts signed by Saddam Hussein's government and that "American companies will have a big shot at Iraqi oil" under a new regime. U.S. and British oil company executives have been meeting with INC officials, maneuvering to secure a future stake in Iraq's oil. Meanwhile, the State Department has been coaxing Iraqi opposition members to create an oil and gas working group involving Iraqis and Americans.

Nikolai Tokarev, general director of Russia's Zarubezhneft, a state-owned oil company, reflected in late 2002: "Do Americans need us in Iraq? Of course not. Russian companies will lose the oil forever if the Americans come." Fears of being excluded from Iraq's oil riches and losing influence in the region have fed Russian, French, and Chinese interest in constraining U.S. belligerence. These countries nonetheless are eager to keep their options open in the event that a pro-U.S. regime is installed in Baghdad, avoiding the "risk of ending up on the wrong side of Washington," as the *New York Times* put it.

Rival oil interests were a crucial behind-the-scenes factor as the permanent members of the U.N. Security Council jockeyed over the wording of Resolution 1441, intended to set the conditions for any action against Iraq. It is likely that backroom understandings regarding the future of Iraqi oil were part of the political minuet that finally led to the resolution's unanimous adoption. U.S. promises that the other powers would get a slice of the pie, hinted at in broad terms, were apparently inducement enough to win their nod. It is thus unlikely that French, Russian, and Chinese companies will be completely locked out of a post-Saddam Iraq, though they could find themselves in a junior position.

From Surrogates to Direct Control

Throughout the history of oil, sorting out who gets access to this highly prized resource and on what terms has often gone hand in hand with violence. At first it was Britain, the imperial power in much of the Middle East, that called the shots. But for half a century, the U.S.—seeking a preponderant share of the earth's resources—has made steady progress in bringing the Persian Gulf region into its geopolitical orbit. In Washington's calculus, securing oil supplies has consistently trumped the pursuit of human rights and democracy.

U.S. policy toward the Middle East has long relied on building up proxy forces in the region and generously supplying them with arms. After the Shah of Iran, the West's regional policeman, was toppled in 1979, Iraq became a surrogate of sorts when it invaded Iran. Washington aided Iraq in a variety of ways, including commodity credits and loan guarantees, indirect arms supplies, critical military intelligence in Baghdad's long battle against Iran, a pro-Iraqi tilt in the "tanker war," and attacks on Iran's navy.

Beginning in the 1970s, but particularly in the wake of the 1991 Gulf War, the U.S. supplied Saudi Arabia and allied Persian Gulf states with massive amounts of highly sophisticated armaments. After the Gulf War, U.S. forces never left the region completely. By prepositioning military equipment and acquiring access to military bases in Saudi Arabia, Kuwait, Bahrain, and Qatar, Washington prepared the ground for future direct intervention as needed.

In the Persian Gulf and adjacent regions, access to oil is usually secured by a pervasive U.S. military presence. From Pakistan to Central Asia to the Caucasus and from the eastern Mediterranean to the Horn of Africa, a dense network of U.S. military facilities has emerged—with many bases established in the name of the "war on terror."

Although the U.S. military presence is not solely about oil, oil is a key reason. In 1999, General Anthony C. Zinni, then the head of the U.S. Central Command, testified to the Senate Armed Services Committee that the Persian Gulf region is of "vital interest" to the U.S. and that the country "must have free access to the region's resources."

Bush administration officials have, however, categorically denied oil is one of the reasons why they are pushing for regime change in Iraq. "Nonsense," Defense Secretary Donald Rumsfeld told *60 Minutes'* Steve Kroft in mid-December 2002. "It has nothing to do with oil, literally nothing to do with oil."

But oil industry officials interviewed by *60 Minutes* on December 15 painted a different picture. Asked if oil is part of the equation, Phillip Ellis, head of global oil and gas operations for Boston Consulting replied, "Of course it is. No doubt."

In fact, oil company executives have been quietly meeting with U.S.-backed Iraqi opposition leaders. According to Ahmed Chalabi, head of the Iraqi National Congress, "The future democratic government in Iraq will be grateful to the United States for helping the Iraqi people liberate themselves and getting rid of Saddam." And he added that "American companies, we expect, will play an important and leading role in the future oil situation in Iraq."

OUR HOPES BETRAYED:
THE U.S. BLUEPRINT FOR
POST-SADDAM GOVERNMENT

Kanan Makiya

The United States is on the verge of committing itself to a post-Saddam plan for a military government in Baghdad with Americans appointed to head Iraqi ministries, and American soldiers to patrol the streets of Iraqi cities.

The plan, as dictated to the Iraqi opposition in Ankara last week by a United States–led delegation, further envisages the appointment by the U.S. of an unknown number of Iraqi quislings palatable to the Arab countries of the Gulf and Saudi Arabia as a council of advisers to this military government.

The plan reverses a decade-long moral and financial commitment by the U.S. to the Iraqi opposition, and is guaranteed to turn that opposition from the close ally it has always been during the 1990s into an opponent of the United States on the streets of Baghdad the day after liberation.

The bureaucrats responsible for this plan are drawn from those parts of the administration that have always been hostile to the idea of a U.S.-assisted democratic transformation of Iraq, a transformation that necessarily includes such radical departures for the region as the de-Baathification of Iraq (along the lines of the de-Nazification of post-war Germany), and the redesign of the Iraqi state as a non-ethnically based federal and democratic entity.

The plan is the brainchild of the would-be coup-makers of the CIA and their allies in the Department of State, who now wish to achieve through direct American control over the people of Iraq what they so dismally failed to achieve on the ground since 1991.

Its driving force is appeasement of the existing bankrupt Arab order, and

A native of Iraq, Kanan Makiya is now a professor of Middle East studies at Brandeis University and Director of the Iraq Research and Documentation Project at Harvard University. He is the author of several books, including the bestselling *Republic of Fear: The Politics of Modern Iraq,* excerpted elsewhere in this volume. A central figure in the Iraqi opposition and a key participant in the U.S. State Department's "The Future of Iraq" Initiative, Makiya acted, in 1992, as the convenor of the Human Rights Committee of the Iraqi National Congress, a transitional parliament based in Northern Iraq. This article was originally published, with the title "Our Hopes Betrayed: How a U.S. Blueprint for Post-Saddam Government Quashed the Hopes of Democratic Iraqis," in *The Observer* (London) on February 16, 2003.

ultimately the retention under a different guise of the repressive institutions of the Baath and the army. Hence its point of departure is, and has got to be, use of direct military rule to deny Iraqis their legitimate right to self-determine their future. In particular it is a plan designed to humiliate the Kurdish people of Iraq and their experiment of self-rule in northern Iraq of the last 10 years, an experiment made possible by the protection granted to the Kurds by the United States itself. That protection is about to be lifted with the entry into northern Iraq of much-feared Turkish troops (apparently not under American command), infamous throughout the region for their decades-long hostility to Kurdish aspirations.

All of this is very likely to turn into an unmitigated disaster for a healthy long-term and necessarily special relationship between the United States and post-Saddam Iraq, something that virtually every Iraqi not complicit in the existing Baathist order wants.

I write as someone personally committed to that relationship. Every word that I have committed to paper in the last quarter of a century is, in one way or another, an application of the universal values that I have absorbed from many years of living and working in the West to the very particular conditions of Iraq. The government of the United States is about to betray, as it has done so many times in the past, those core human values of self-determination and individual liberty.

We Iraqis hoped and said to our Arab and Middle Eastern brethren, over and over again, that American mistakes of the past did not have to be repeated in the future. Were we wrong? Are the enemies of a democratic Iraq, the "anti-imperialists" and "anti-Zionists" of the Arab world, the supporters of "armed struggle," and the upholders of the politics of blaming everything on the U.S. who are dictating the agenda of the anti-war movement in Europe and the U.S., are all of these people to be proved right?

Is the President who so graciously invited me to his Oval Office only a few weeks ago to discuss democracy, about to have his wishes subverted by advisers who owe their careers to those mistakes?

We, the democratic Iraqi opposition, are the natural friends and allies of the United States. We share its values and long-term goals of peace, stability, freedom and democracy for Iraq. We are here in Iraqi Kurdistan 40 miles from Saddam's troops and a few days away from a conference to plan our next move, a conference that some key administration officials have done everything in their power to postpone.

None the less, after weeks of effort in Tehran and northern Iraq, we have prevailed. The meeting will take place. It will discuss a detailed plan for the creation of an Iraqi leadership, one that is in a position to assume power at the appropriate time and in the appropriate place. We will be opposed no doubt by an American delegation if it chooses to attend. Whether or not they do join us in the coming few days in northern Iraq, we will fight their attempts to marginalise and shunt aside the men and women who have invested whole lifetimes, and suffered greatly, fighting Saddam Hussein.

To the President who so clearly wants to see a democratic Iraq, and to the American public that put its trust in him, I say: support us.

Editors' note: After Makiya published this broadside in the London *Observer*, Ahmad Chalabi, the president of the Iraqi National Congress (INC), went public with similar complaints in *The Wall Street Journal*. "The proposed U.S. occupation and military administration of Iraq is unworkable and unwise," he wrote on February 19. Echoing Makiya, he criticized the Bush Administration for planning to have an American general run the country through the existing Baathist government structure, keeping all but its most senior echelons intact.

It's unclear whether these concerns were heard in Washington. At the end of February, U.S. envoy Zalmay Khalilzad met with Iraqi opposition leaders in Kurdish-held northern Iraq and offered some reassurances. Khalilzad "did not budge from the idea of a military governor," one member of the opposition coordinating committee told the *Christian Science Monitor*, but he spoke of drawing opposition figures into government task forces or consultative bodies. Makiya was quoted as saying that he was "reassured" after hearing Khalilzad's references to the U.S. role in Germany and Japan and his comments on "de-Baathification." In addition, since making these remarks Makiya has written in *The New Republic* about meetings he had in Washington with top officials, including Vice President Cheney, where he was told that it was "now U.S. policy to pass over decision-making responsibilities to an all-Iraqi interim authority in stages, as quickly as it was possible for the Iraqis to manage them."

Khalilzad also said the U.S. was "opposed to a Turkish unilateral role in here," an attempt to calm fears among Kurds that the Turkish army would occupy their autonomous zone at the beginning of any attack on Iraq. The Turks want to keep the Kurds from expanding their independent base, and given the impasse between the U.S. and Turkey over whether American troops could use Turkish bases for their invasion, it was far from clear if Khalilzad's assurances were truly operable.

As the U.S. invasion neared, the Iraqi opposition was having problems sorting out its own internal affairs as well. On February 28, a conference of opposition groups in northern Iraq ended with the creation of a six-member leadership body. Its members were Chalabi, head of the INC; Jalal Talabani, the head of the Patriotic Union of Kurdistan (PUK); Massoud Barzani, head of the Kurdistan Democratic Party (KDP); Mohammed Bakir Hakim, head of the Supreme Council for the Islamic Revolution in Iraq (SCIRI), a Shi'ite group based in Iran; Ayad Alawi of the Iraqi National Accord, a Sunni Muslim organization reportedly close to the CIA; and Adnan Pachachi, a former Iraqi official reportedly favored by the State Department.

At least three of these six leaders have a questionable commitment to democracy. Pachachi is an 80-year-old Arab nationalist who only recently renounced his view that Kuwait is rightfully part of Iraq, has written that he cannot accept Israel's existence, and believes that Iraq and Syria should unite. Alawi, a senior Iraqi intelligence official who defected in 1971, boycotted the February 28 meeting. His group, which was formed with the support of Saudi Arabia, has mainly attracted dissident Iraqi military officers and has primarily been involved in trying to overthrow Saddam Hussein through coup attempts. Mohammed Bakir Hakim's SCIRI calls for Islamic rule under the leadership of a ruling Islamic jurist, à la the late Ayatollah Khoumeini.

FOURTEEN

THE FUTURE OF PAX AMERICANA

"The new imperialists think they are different. All empires do."
—*Todd Gitlin, writing in* Mother Jones, *January-February 2003*

"Has 'oderint dum metuant' ['let them hate so long as they fear'] really become our motto?"
—*Career diplomat John Brady Kiesling, in a letter explaining his resignation in protest from the U.S. foreign service, February 27, 2003*

"The impending war against Iraq represents a point of no return. Should the United States go it alone and attack Iraq without broader international support, it will cease to be a model for the world and instead be seen as a dangerous Goliath that needs to be tamed. . . . The victory will be a Pyrrhic one. Without the court of world opinion on its side, America will soon find that its long reign as the respected and trusted leader of the free world has come to an end."
—*Charles Kupchan, author of* The End of the American Era

"Two years from now only the Brits may be with us. . . . At some point, we may be the only ones left. That's okay with me. We are America."
—*President Bush, on the war on terrorism, quoted in Bob Woodward's* Bush at War

THE UNIPOLAR MOMENT REVISITED: AMERICA, THE BENEVOLENT EMPIRE

Charles Krauthammer

In late 1990, shortly before the collapse of the Soviet Union, it was clear that the world we had known for half a century was disappearing. The question was what would succeed it. I suggested then that we had already entered the "unipolar moment." The gap in power between the leading nation and all the others was so unprecedented as to yield an international structure unique to modern history: unipolarity.

At the time, this thesis was generally seen as either wild optimism or simple American arrogance. The conventional wisdom was that with the demise of the Soviet empire the bipolarity of the second half of the 20th century would yield to multipolarity. The declinist school, led by Paul Kennedy, held that America, suffering from "imperial overstretch," was already in relative decline. The Asian enthusiasm, popularized by (among others) James Fallows, saw the second coming of the Rising Sun. The conventional wisdom was best captured by Senator Paul Tsongas: "The Cold War is over; Japan won."

They were wrong, and no one has put it more forcefully than Paul Kennedy himself in a classic recantation published earlier this year. "Nothing has ever existed like this disparity of power; nothing," he said of America's position today. "Charlemagne's empire was merely western European in its reach. The Roman empire stretched farther afield, but there was another great empire in Persia, and a larger one in China. There is, therefore, no comparison." Not everyone is convinced. Samuel Huntington argued in 1999 that we had entered not a unipolar world but a "uni-multipolar world." Tony Judt writes mockingly of the "loud boasts of unipolarity and hegemony" heard in Washington today. But as Stephen Brooks and William Wohlforth argue in a recent review of the subject, those denying unipolarity can do so only by applying a

Charles Krauthammer is a columnist for *The Washington Post* and an essayist for *Time* magazine. In 1987, he won the Pulitzer Prize for distinguished commentary. This essay was the cover story in *The National Interest*'s Winter 2002/03 issue. Its original title, "The Unipolar Moment Revisited," refers to an earlier article written by the author entitled "The Unipolar Moment," which was published in *Foreign Affairs: America and the World* (1990/91).

ridiculous standard: that America be able to achieve all its goals everywhere all by itself. This is a standard not for unipolarity but for divinity. Among mortals, and in the context of the last half millennium of history, the current structure of the international system is clear: "If today's American primacy does not constitute unipolarity, then nothing ever will."

A second feature of this new post-Cold War world, I ventured, would be a resurgent American isolationism. I was wrong. It turns out that the new norm for America is not post-World War I withdrawal but post-World War II engagement. In the 1990s, Pat Buchanan gave 1930s isolationism a run. He ended up carrying Palm Beach.

Finally, I suggested that a third feature of this new unipolar world would be an increase rather than a decrease in the threat of war, and that it would come from a new source: weapons of mass destruction wielded by rogue states. This would constitute a revolution in international relations, given that in the past it was great powers who presented the principal threats to world peace.

Where are we twelve years later? The two defining features of the new post–Cold War world remain: unipolarity and rogue states with weapons of mass destruction. Indeed, these characteristics have grown even more pronounced. Contrary to expectation, the United States has not regressed to the mean; rather, its dominance has dramatically increased. And during our holiday from history in the 1990s, the rogue state/WMD problem grew more acute. Indeed, we are now on the eve of history's first war over weapons of mass destruction.

Unipolarity After September 11, 2001

There is little need to rehearse the acceleration of unipolarity in the 1990s. Japan, whose claim to power rested exclusively on economics, went into economic decline. Germany stagnated. The Soviet Union ceased to exist, contracting into a smaller, radically weakened Russia. The European Union turned inward toward the great project of integration and built a strong social infrastructure at the expense of military capacity. Only China grew in strength, but coming from so far behind it will be decades before it can challenge American primacy—and that assumes that its current growth continues unabated.

The result is the dominance of a single power unlike anything ever seen. Even at its height Britain could always be seriously challenged by the next greatest powers. Britain had a smaller army than the land powers of Europe and its navy was equaled by the next two navies combined. Today, American military spending exceeds that of the next *twenty* countries combined. Its navy, air force and space power are unrivaled. Its technology is irresistible. It is dominant by every measure: military, economic, technological, diplomatic, cultural, even linguistic, with a myriad of countries trying to fend off the inexorable march of Internet-fueled MTV English.

American dominance has not gone unnoticed. During the 1990s, it was mainly China and Russia that denounced unipolarity in their occasional joint communiqués. As the new century dawned it was on everyone's lips. A French foreign minister dubbed the United States not a superpower but a hyperpower. The dominant concern of foreign policy establishments everywhere became understanding and living with the 800-pound American gorilla.

And then September 11 *heightened* the asymmetry. It did so in three ways. First, and most obviously, it led to a demonstration of heretofore latent American military power. Kosovo, the first war ever fought and won exclusively from the air, had given a hint of America's quantum leap in military power (and the enormous gap that had developed between American and European military capabilities). But it took September 11 for the United States to unleash with concentrated fury a fuller display of its power in Afghanistan. Being a relatively pacific, commercial republic, the United States does not go around looking for demonstration wars. This one was thrust upon it. In response, America showed that at a range of 7,000 miles and with but a handful of losses, it could destroy within weeks a hardened, fanatical regime favored by geography and climate in the "graveyard of empires."

Such power might have been demonstrated earlier, but it was not. "I talked with the previous U.S. administration," said Vladimir Putin shortly after September 11,

and pointed out the bin Laden issue to them. They wrung their hands so helplessly and said, 'the Taliban are not turning him over, what can one do?' I remember I was surprised: If they are not turning him over, one has to think and do something.

Nothing was done. President Clinton and others in his administration have protested that nothing could have been done, that even the 1998 African embassy bombings were not enough to mobilize the American people to strike back seriously against terrorism. The new Bush Administration, too, did not give the prospect of mass-casualty terrorism (and the recommendations of the Hart-Rudman Commission) the priority it deserved. Without September 11, the giant would surely have slept longer. The world would have been aware of America's size and potential, but not its ferocity or its full capacities. (Paul

Kennedy's homage to American power, for example, was offered in the wake of the Afghan campaign.)

Second, September 11 demonstrated a new form of American strength. The center of its economy was struck, its aviation shut down, Congress brought to a halt, the government sent underground, the country paralyzed and fearful. Yet within days the markets reopened, the economy began its recovery, the president mobilized the nation, and a united Congress immediately underwrote a huge new worldwide campaign against terror. The Pentagon started planning the U.S. military response even as its demolished western façade still smoldered.

America had long been perceived as invulnerable. That illusion was shattered on September 11, 2001. But with a demonstration of its recuperative powers—an economy and political system so deeply rooted and fundamentally sound that it could spring back to life within days—that sense of invulnerability assumed a new character. It was transmuted from impermeability to resilience, the product of unrivaled human, technological and political reserves.

The third effect of September 11 was to accelerate the realignment of the current great powers, such as they are, behind the United States. In 1990, America's principal ally was NATO. A decade later, its alliance base had grown to include former members of the Warsaw Pact. Some of the major powers, however, remained uncommitted. Russia and China flirted with the idea of an "anti-hegemonic alliance." Russian leaders made ostentatious visits to pieces of the old Soviet empire such as Cuba and North Korea. India and Pakistan, frozen out by the United States because of their nuclear testing, remained focused mainly on one another. But after September 11, the bystanders came calling. Pakistan made an immediate strategic decision to join the American camp. India enlisted with equal alacrity, offering the United States basing, overflight rights and a level of cooperation unheard of during its half century of Nehruist genuflection to anti-American non-alignment. Russia's Putin, seeing both a coincidence of interests in the fight against Islamic radicalism and an opportunity to gain acceptance in the Western camp, dramatically realigned Russian foreign policy toward the United States. (Russia has already been rewarded with a larger role in NATO and tacit American recognition of Russia's interests in its "near abroad.") China remains more distant but, also having a coincidence of interests with the United States in fighting Islamic radicalism, it has cooperated with the war on terror and muted its competition with America in the Pacific.

The realignment of the fence-sitters simply accentuates the historical anomaly of American unipolarity. Our experience with hegemony historically is that it inevitably creates a counterbalancing coalition of weaker powers, most recently against Napoleonic France and Germany (twice) in the 20th century. Nature abhors a vacuum; history abhors hegemony. Yet during the first decade of American unipolarity no such counterbalancing occurred. On the contrary, the great powers lined up behind the United States, all the more so after September 11.

THE AMERICAN hegemon has no great power enemies, an historical oddity of the first order. Yet it does face a serious threat to its dominance, indeed to its essential security. It comes from a source even more historically odd: an archipelago of rogue states (some connected with transnational terrorists) wielding weapons of mass destruction.

The threat is not trivial. It is the single greatest danger to the United States because, for all of America's dominance, and for all of its recently demonstrated resilience, there is one thing it might not survive: decapitation. The detonation of a dozen nuclear weapons in major American cities, or the spreading of smallpox or anthrax throughout the general population, is an existential threat. It is perhaps the only realistic threat to America as a functioning hegemon, perhaps even to America as a functioning modern society.

Like unipolarity, this is historically unique. WMD are not new, nor are rogue states. Their conjunction is. We have had fifty years of experience with nuclear weapons— but in the context of bipolarity, which gave the system a predictable, if perilous, stability. We have just now entered an era in which the capacity for inflicting mass death, and thus posing a threat both to world peace and to the dominant power, resides in small, peripheral states.

What does this conjunction of unique circumstances—unipolarity and the proliferation of terrible weapons—mean for American foreign policy? That the first and most urgent task is protection from these weapons. The catalyst for this realization was again September 11. Throughout the 1990s, it had been assumed that WMD posed no emergency because traditional concepts of deterrence would hold. September 11 revealed the possibility of future WMD-armed enemies both undeterrable and potentially undetectable. The 9/11 suicide bombers were undeterrable; the author of the subsequent anthrax attacks has proven undetectable. The possible alliance of rogue states with such undeterrables and undetectables—and the possible transfer to them of weapons of mass destruction—presents a new strategic situation that demands a new strategic doctrine.

The Crisis of Unipolarity

Accordingly, not one but a host of new doctrines have come tumbling out since September 11. First came the with-us-or-against-us ultimatum to any state aiding, abetting or harboring terrorists. Then, pre-emptive attack on any enemy state developing weapons of mass destruction. And now, regime change in any such state.

The boldness of these policies—or, as much of the world contends, their arrogance—is breathtaking. The American anti-terrorism ultimatum, it is said, is high-handed and permits the arbitrary application of American power everywhere. Pre-emption is said to violate traditional doctrines of just war. And regime change, as Henry Kissinger has argued, threatens 350 years of post-Westphalian international practice. Taken together, they amount to an unprecedented assertion of American freedom of action and a definitive statement of a new American unilateralism.

To be sure, these are not the first instances of American unilateralism. Before September 11, the Bush Administration had acted unilaterally, but on more minor matters, such as the Kyoto Protocol and the Biological Weapons Convention, and with less bluntness, as in its protracted negotiations with Russia over the ABM treaty. The "axis of evil" speech of January 29, however, took unilateralism to a new level. Latent resentments about American willfulness are latent no more. American dominance, which had been tolerated if not welcomed, is now producing such irritation and hostility in once friendly quarters, such as Europe, that some suggest we have arrived at the end of the opposition-free grace period that America had enjoyed during the unipolar moment.*

In short, post-9/11 U.S. unilateralism has produced the first crisis of unipolarity. It revolves around the central question of the unipolar age: Who will define the hegemon's ends?

The issue is not one of style but of purpose. Secretary of Defense Donald Rumsfeld gave the classic formulation of unilateralism when he said (regarding the Afghan war and the war on terrorism, but the principle is universal), "the mission determines the coalition." We take our friends where we find them, but only in order to help us in accomplishing the mission. The mission comes first, and we decide it.

Contrast this with the classic case study of multilateralism at work: the

---

* A Sky News poll finds that even the British public considers George W. Bush a greater threat to world peace than Saddam Hussein. The poll was conducted September 2–6, 2002.

U.S. decision in February 1991 to conclude the Gulf War. As the Iraqi army was fleeing, the first Bush Administration had to decide its final goal: the liberation of Kuwait or regime change in Iraq. It stopped at Kuwait. Why? Because, as Brent Scowcroft has explained, going further would have fractured the coalition, gone against our promises to allies and violated the U.N. resolutions under which we were acting. "Had we added occupation of Iraq and removal of Saddam Hussein to those objectives," wrote Scowcroft in *The Washington Post* on October 16, 2001, ". . . our Arab allies, refusing to countenance an invasion of an Arab colleague, would have deserted us." The coalition defined the mission.

Who should define American ends today? This is a question of agency but it leads directly to a fundamental question of policy. If the coalition—whether NATO, the wider Western alliance, *ad hoc* outfits such as the Gulf War alliance, the U.N., or the "international community"—defines America's mission, we have one vision of America's role in the world. If, on the other hand, the mission defines the coalition, we have an entirely different vision.

Liberal Internationalism

For many Americans, multilateralism is no pretense. On the contrary: It has become the very core of the liberal internationalist school of American foreign policy. In the October 2002 debate authorizing the use of force in Iraq, the Democratic chairman of the Senate Armed Services Committee, Carl Levin, proposed authorizing the president to act only with prior approval from the U.N. Security Council. Senator Edward Kennedy put it succinctly while addressing the Johns Hopkins School of Advanced International Studies on September 27: "I'm waiting for the final recommendation of the Security Council before I'm going to say how I'm going to vote."

This logic is deeply puzzling. How exactly does the Security Council confer moral authority on American action? The Security Council is a committee of great powers, heirs to the victors in the Second World War. They manage the world in their own interest. The Security Council is, on the very rare occasions when it actually works, realpolitik by committee. But by what logic is it a repository of international morality? How does the approval of France and Russia, acting clearly and rationally in pursuit of their own interests in Iraq (largely oil and investment), confer legitimacy on an invasion?

That question was beyond me twelve years ago. It remains beyond me now. Yet this kind of logic utterly dominated the intervening Clinton years. The 1990s were marked by an obsession with "international legality" as expressed by this or that Security Council resolution. To take one long forgotten example: After an Iraqi provocation in February 1998, President Clinton gave a speech at the Pentagon laying the foundation for an attack on Iraq (one of many that never came). He cited as justification for the use of force the need to enforce Iraqi promises made under post–Gulf War ceasefire conditions that "the United Nations demanded—not the United States—the United Nations." Note the formulation. Here is the president of the most powerful nation on earth stopping in mid-sentence to stress the primacy of commitments made to the U.N. over those made to the United States.

This was not surprising from a president whose first inaugural address pledged American action when "the will and conscience of the international community is defied." Early in the Clinton years, Madeleine Albright formulated the vision of the liberal internationalist school then in power as "assertive multilateralism." Its principal diplomatic activity was the pursuit of a dizzying array of universal treaties on chemical weapons, biological weapons, nuclear testing, global environment, land mines and the like. Its trademark was consultation: Clinton was famous for sending Secretary of State Warren Christopher on long trips (for example, through Europe on Balkan policy) or endless shuttles (uncountable pilgrimages to Damascus) to consult; he invariably returned home empty-handed and diminished. And its principal objective was good international citizenship: It was argued on myriad foreign policy issues that we could not do X because it would leave us "isolated." Thus in 1997 the Senate passed a chemical weapons convention that even some of its proponents admitted was unenforceable, largely because of the argument that everyone else had signed it and that failure to ratify would leave us isolated. Isolation, in and of itself, was seen as a diminished and even morally suspect condition.

A lesson in isolation occurred during the 1997 negotiations in Oslo over the land mine treaty. One of the rare hold-outs, interestingly enough, was Finland. Finding himself scolded by his neighbors for opposing the land mine ban, the Finnish prime minister noted tartly that this was a "very convenient" pose for the "other Nordic countries" who "want Finland to be their land mine."

In many parts of the world, a thin line of American GIs is the land mine. The main reason we oppose the land mine treaty is that we need them in the DMZ in Korea. We man the lines there. Sweden and France and Canada do not have to worry about a North Korean invasion killing thousands of their soldiers. As the unipolar power and thus guarantor of peace in places where Swedes do not tread, we need weapons that others do not. Being uniquely situated in the world, we cannot afford the empty platitudes of allies not quite candid enough to admit that they live under the umbrella of American power. That often leaves us "isolated."

Multilateralism is the liberal internationalist's means of saving us from this shameful condition. But the point of the multilateralist imperative is not merely psychological. It has a clear and coherent geopolitical objective. It is a means that defines the ends. Its means—internationalism (the moral, legal and strategic primacy of international institutions over national interests) and legalism (the belief that the sinews of stability are laws, treaties and binding international contracts)—are in service to a larger vision: remaking the international system in the image of domestic civil society. The multilateralist imperative seeks to establish an international order based not on sovereignty and power but on interdependence—a new order that, as Secretary of State Cordell Hull said upon returning from the Moscow Conference of 1943, abolishes the "need for spheres of influence, for alliances, for balance of power."

Liberal internationalism seeks through multilateralism to transcend power politics, narrow national interest and, ultimately, the nation-state itself. The nation-state is seen as some kind of archaic residue of an anarchic past, an affront to the vision of a domesticated international arena. This is why liberal thinkers embrace the erosion of sovereignty promised by the new information technologies and the easy movement of capital across borders. They welcome the decline of sovereignty as the road to the new globalism of a norm-driven, legally-bound international system broken to the mold of domestic society.

The greatest sovereign, of course, is the American superpower, which is why liberal internationalists feel such acute discomfort with American dominance. To achieve their vision, America too—America especially—must be domesticated. Their project is thus to restrain America by building an entangling web of interdependence, tying down Gulliver with myriad strings that diminish his overweening power. Who, after all, was the ABM treaty or a land mine treaty going to restrain? North Korea?

This liberal internationalist vision—the multilateral handcuffing of American power—is, as Robert Kagan has pointed out, the dominant view in Europe. That is to be expected, given Europe's weakness and America's power. But it is a mistake to see this as only a European view. The idea of a new international community with self-governing institutions and self-enforcing norms—the vision that requires the domestication of American power—is the view of the Democratic Party in the United States and of a large part of the American foreign policy establishment. They spent the last decade in power fashioning precisely those multilateral ties to restrain the American Gulliver and remake him into a tame international citizen. The multilateralist project is to use—indeed, to use up—current American dominance to create a new international system in which new norms of legalism and interdependence rule in America's place—in short, a system that is no longer unipolar.

Realism and the New Unilateralism

The basic division between the two major foreign policy schools in America centers on the question of what is, and what should be, the fundamental basis of international relations: paper or power. Liberal internationalism envisions a world order that, like domestic society, is governed by laws and not men. Realists see this vision as hopelessly utopian. The history of paper treaties—from the prewar Kellogg-Briand Pact and Munich to the post–Cold War Oslo accords and the 1994 Agreed Framework with North Korea—is a history of naiveté and cynicism, a combination both toxic and volatile that invariably ends badly. Trade agreements with Canada are one thing. Pieces of parchment to which existential enemies affix a signature are quite another. They are worse than worthless because they give a false sense of security and breed complacency. For the realist, the ultimate determinant of the most basic elements of international life—security, stability and peace—is power.

Which is why a realist would hardly forfeit the current unipolarity for the vain promise of goo-goo one-worldism. Nor, however, should a realist want to forfeit unipolarity for the familiarity of traditional multipolarity. Multipolarity is inherently fluid and unpredictable. Europe practiced multipolarity for centuries and found it so unstable and bloody, culminating in 1914 in the catastrophic collapse of delicately balanced alliance systems, that Europe sought its permanent abolition in political and economic union. Having abjured multipolarity for the region, it is odd in the extreme to then prefer multipolarity for the world.

Less can be said about the destiny of unipolarity. It is too new. Yet we do have the history of the last decade, our only modern experience with unipolarity, and it was a decade of unusual stability among all major powers. It would be foolish to project from just a ten-year experience, but that experience does call into question the basis for the claims that unipolarity is intrinsically unstable or impossible to sustain in a mass democracy.

I would argue that unipolarity, managed benignly, is far more likely to keep the peace. Benignity is, of course, in the eye of the beholder. But the American claim to benignity is not mere self-congratulation. We have a track record. Consider one of history's rare controlled experiments. In the 1940s, lines were drawn through three peoples—Germans, Koreans and Chinese—one side closely bound to the United States, the other to its adversary. It turned into a controlled experiment because both states in the divided lands shared a common culture. Fifty years later the results are in. Does anyone doubt the superiority, both moral and material, of West Germany vs. East Germany, South Korea vs. North Korea and Taiwan vs. China? *

Benignity is also manifest in the way others welcome our power. It is the reason, for example, that the Pacific Rim countries are loath to see our military presence diminished: They know that the United States is not an imperial power with a desire to rule other countries—which is why they so readily accept it as a balancer. It is the reason, too, why Europe, so seized with complaints about American high-handedness, nonetheless reacts with alarm to the occasional suggestion that America might withdraw its military presence. America came, but it did not come to rule. Unlike other hegemons and would-be hegemons, it does not entertain a grand vision of a new world. No Thousand Year Reich. No New Soviet Man. It has no great desire to remake human nature, to conquer for the extraction of natural resources, or to rule for the simple pleasure of dominion. Indeed, America is the first hegemonic power in history to be obsessed with "exit strategies." It could not wait to get out of Haiti and Somalia; it would get out of Kosovo and Bosnia today if it could. Its principal aim is to maintain the stability and relative tranquility of the current international system by enforcing, maintaining and extending the current peace.

The form of realism that I am arguing for—call it the new unilateralism— is clear in its determination to self-consciously and confidently deploy American power in pursuit of those global ends. Note: global ends. There is a form of unilateralism that is devoted only to narrow American self-interest and it has a name, too: It is called isolationism. Critics of the new unilateralism often confuse it with isolationism because both are prepared to unashamedly exercise American power. But isolationists *oppose* America acting as a unipolar power not because they disagree with the unilateral means, but because they deem the ends far too broad. Isolationists would abandon the larger world and use American power exclusively for the narrowest of American in-

---

* This is not to claim, by any means, a perfect record of benignity. America has often made and continues to make alliances with unpleasant authoritarian regimes. As I argued recently in *Time* ("Dictatorships and Double Standards," September 23, 2002), such alliances are nonetheless justified so long as they are instrumental (meant to defeat the larger evil) and temporary (expire with the emergency): When Hitler was defeated, we stopped coddling Stalin. Forty years later, as the Soviet threat receded, the United States was instrumental in easing Pinochet out of power and overthrowing Marcos. We withdrew our support for these dictators once the two conditions that justified such alliances had disappeared: The global threat of Soviet communism had receded, and truly democratic domestic alternatives to these dictators had emerged.

terests: manning Fortress America by defending the American homeland and putting up barriers to trade and immigration.

The new unilateralism defines American interests far beyond narrow self-defense. In particular, it identifies two other major interests, both global: extending the peace by advancing democracy and preserving the peace by acting as balancer of last resort. Britain was the balancer in Europe, joining the weaker coalition against the stronger to create equilibrium. America's unique global power allows it to be the balancer in every region. We balanced Iraq by supporting its weaker neighbors in the Gulf War. We balance China by supporting the ring of smaller states at its periphery (from South Korea to Taiwan, even to Vietnam). Our role in the Balkans was essentially to create a microbalance: to support the weaker Bosnian Muslims against their more dominant neighbors, and subsequently to support the weaker Albanian Kosovars against the Serbs.

Of course, both of these tasks often advance American national interests as well. The promotion of democracy multiplies the number of nations likely to be friendly to the United States, and regional equilibria produce stability that benefits a commercial republic like the United States. America's (intended) exertions on behalf of pre-emptive non-proliferation, too, are clearly in the interest of both the United States and the international system as a whole.

Critics find this paradoxical: acting unilaterally but for global ends. Why paradoxical? One can hardly argue that depriving Saddam (and potentially, terrorists) of WMD is not a global end. Unilateralism may be required to pursue this end. We may be left isolated in so doing, but we would be acting nevertheless in the name of global interests—larger than narrow American self-interest and larger, too, than the narrowly perceived self-interest of smaller, weaker powers (even great powers) that dare not confront the rising danger.

What is the essence of that larger interest? Most broadly defined, it is maintaining a stable, open and functioning unipolar system. Liberal internationalists disdain that goal as too selfish, as it makes paramount the preservation of both American power and independence. Isolationists reject the goal as too selfless, for defining American interests too globally and thus too generously.

A THIRD CRITIQUE comes from what might be called pragmatic realists, who see the new unilateralism I have outlined as hubristic, and whose objections are practical. They are prepared to engage in a pragmatic multilateralism. They value great power concert. They seek Security Council support not because it confers any moral authority, but because it spreads risk. In their view, a single hegemon risks far more violent resentment than would a power that consistently acts as *primus inter pares,* sharing rule-making functions with others.

I have my doubts. The United States made an extraordinary effort in the Gulf War to get U.N. support, share decision-making, assemble a coalition and, as we have seen, deny itself the fruits of victory in order to honor coalition goals. Did that diminish the anti-American feeling in the region? Did it garner support for subsequent Iraq policy dictated by the original acquiescence to the coalition?

The attacks of September 11 were planned during the Clinton Administration, an administration that made a fetish of consultation and did its utmost to subordinate American hegemony and smother unipolarity. The resentments were hardly assuaged. Why? Because the extremist rage against the United States is engendered by the very structure of the international system, not by the details of our management of it.

Pragmatic realists also value international support in the interest of sharing burdens, on the theory that sharing decision-making enlists others in our own hegemonic enterprise and makes things less costly. If you are too vigorous in asserting yourself in the short-term, they argue, you are likely to injure yourself in the long-term when you encounter problems that require the full cooperation of other partners, such as counter-terrorism. As Brooks and Wohlforth put it, "Straining relationships now will lead only to a more challenging policy environment later on."

If the concern about the new unilateralism is that American assertiveness be judiciously rationed, and that one needs to think long-term, it is hard to disagree. One does not go it alone or dictate terms on every issue. On some issues such as membership in and support of the WTO, where the long-term benefit both to the American national interest and global interests is demonstrable, one willingly constricts sovereignty. Trade agreements are easy calls, however, free trade being perhaps the only mathematically provable political good. Others require great skepticism. The Kyoto Protocol, for example, would have harmed the American economy while doing nothing for the global environment. (Increased emissions from China, India and Third World countries exempt from its provisions would have more than made up for American cuts.) Kyoto failed on its merits, but was nonetheless pushed because the rest of the world supported it. The same case was made for the chemical and biological weapons treaties—sure, they are useless or worse, but why not give in there in order to build good will for future needs? But appeasing multilateralism does not assuage it; appeasement merely legitimizes it. Repeated acquiescence to provisions that America deems injurious reinforces the notion that legitimacy derives from international consensus, thus undermining America's future freedom of action—and thus contradicting the pragmatic realists' own goals.

America must be guided by its independent judgment, both about its own interest and about the global interest. Especially on matters of national security, war-making and the deployment of power, America should neither defer nor contract out decision-making, particularly when the concessions involve permanent structural constrictions such as those imposed by an International Criminal Court. Prudence, yes. No need to act the superpower in East Timor or Bosnia. But there is a need to do so in Afghanistan and in Iraq. No need to act the superpower on steel tariffs. But there is a need to do so on missile defense.

The prudent exercise of power allows, indeed calls for, occasional concessions on non-vital issues if only to maintain psychological good will. Arrogance and gratuitous high-handedness are counterproductive. But we should not delude ourselves as to what psychological goodwill buys. Countries will cooperate with us, first, out of their own self-interest and, second, out of the need and desire to cultivate good relations with the world's superpower. Warm and fuzzy feelings are a distant third. Take counterterrorism. After the attack on the U.S.S. *Cole,* Yemen did everything it could to stymie the American investigation. It lifted not a finger to suppress terrorism. This was under an American administration that was obsessively accommodating and multilateralist. Today, under the most unilateralist of administrations, Yemen has decided to assist in the war on terrorism. This was not a result of a sudden attack of goodwill toward America. It was a result of the war in Afghanistan, which concentrated the mind of heretofore recalcitrant states like Yemen on the costs of non-cooperation with the United States.* Coalitions are not made by superpowers going begging hat in hand. They are made by asserting a position and inviting others to join. What "pragmatic" realists often fail to realize is that unilateralism is the high road to multilateralism. When George Bush senior said of the Iraqi invasion of Kuwait, "this will not stand," and made it clear that he was prepared to act alone if necessary, that declaration—and the credibility of American determination to act unilaterally—in and of itself created a coalition. Hafez al-Asad did not join out of feelings of goodwill. He joined because no one wants to be left at the dock when the hegemon is sailing.

Unilateralism does not mean *seeking* to act alone. One acts in concert with others if possible. Unilateralism simply means that one does not allow oneself

---

* The most recent and dramatic demonstration of this newfound cooperation was the CIA killing on November 4, 2002, of an Al-Qaeda leader in Yemen using a remotely operated Predator drone.

to be hostage to others. No unilateralist would, say, reject Security Council support for an attack on Iraq. The nontrivial question that separates unilateralism from multilateralism—and that tests the "pragmatic realists"—is this: What do you do if, at the end of the day, the Security Council refuses to back you? Do you allow yourself to be dictated to on issues of vital national—and international—security?

WHEN I first proposed the unipolar model in 1990, I suggested that we should accept both its burdens and opportunities and that, if America did not wreck its economy, unipolarity could last thirty or forty years. That seemed bold at the time. Today, it seems rather modest. The unipolar moment has become the unipolar era. It remains true, however, that its durability will be decided at home. It will depend largely on whether it is welcomed by Americans or seen as a burden to be shed—either because we are too good for the world (the isolationist critique) or because we are not worthy of it (the liberal internationalist critique).

The new unilateralism argues explicitly and unashamedly for maintaining unipolarity, for sustaining America's unrivaled dominance for the foreseeable future. It could be a long future, assuming we successfully manage the single greatest threat, namely, weapons of mass destruction in the hands of rogue states. This in itself will require the aggressive and confident application of unipolar power rather than falling back, as we did in the 1990s, on paralyzing multilateralism. The future of the unipolar era hinges on whether America is governed by those who wish to retain, augment and use unipolarity to advance not just American but global ends, or whether America is governed by those who wish to give it up—either by allowing unipolarity to decay as they retreat to Fortress America, or by passing on the burden by gradually transferring power to multilateral institutions as heirs to American hegemony. The challenge to unipolarity is not from the outside but from the inside. The choice is ours. To impiously paraphrase Benjamin Franklin: History has given you an empire, if you will keep it.

AMERICA'S MISSION, AFTER BAGHDAD

Lawrence F. Kaplan and William Kristol

The United States has assumed an unprecedented position of power and influence in the world. By the traditional measures of national power, the United States holds a position unmatched since Rome dominated the Mediterranean world. American military power dwarfs that of any other nation, both in its war-fighting capabilities and in its ability to intervene in conflicts anywhere in the world on short notice. Meanwhile, the American economic precepts of liberal capitalism and free trade have become almost universally accepted as the best model for creating wealth, and the United States itself stands at the center of the international economic order. The American political precepts of liberal democracy have spread across continents and cultures as other peoples cast off or modify autocratic methods of governance and opt for, or at least pay lip service to, the American principles of individual rights and freedoms.

Moreover, unlike past imperial powers, if the United States has created a Pax Americana, it is not built on colonial conquest or economic aggrandizement. "America has no empire to extend or utopia to establish," President Bush said in his West Point speech. Rather, what upholds today's world order is America's benevolent influence—nurtured, to be sure, by American power, but also by emulation and the recognition around the world that American ideals are genuinely universal. As a consequence, when the world's sole superpower commits itself to norms of international conduct—for democracy, for human rights, against aggression, against weapons proliferation—it means that successful challenges to American power will invariably weaken those American-created norms. Were we—through humility, self-abnegation or a narrow conception of the national interest—to retreat from the position that history has bequeathed us, the turmoil that would soon follow would surely reach our shores.

Even if the threat posed by Iraq were to disappear tomorrow, that would not relieve us of the need to play a strong and active role in the world. Nor

Lawrence F. Kaplan is a senior editor of *The New Republic*. William Kristol is editor of *The Weekly Standard* and a political analyst for the Fox News Channel. This article is excerpted from their new book, *The War Over Iraq*.

would it absolve us of the responsibilities that fate has placed on our shoulders. Given the dangers that currently exist, and given the certainty that unknown perils await us over the horizon, there can be no respite from this burden. The maintenance of a decent and hospitable international order requires continued American leadership in resisting, and where possible undermining, aggressive dictators and hostile ideologies; in supporting American interests and liberal democratic principles; and in providing assistance to those struggling against the more extreme manifestations of human evil. If America refrains from shaping this order, we can be sure that others will shape it in ways that reflect neither our interests nor our values.

Absent the United States, who else could uphold decency in the world? Europe? Having engaged in fratricidal conflict twice in the twentieth century, and then taken shelter under an American umbrella during the Cold War, much of Europe has responded to the challenges of the post-Cold War era with a mixture of pettiness, impotence and moral lassitude. Having proclaimed the 1990s the "hour of Europe," its leaders spent the decade failing to deal with ethnic cleansing on their own continent, while cutting lucrative trade deals with a gallery of rogue states and refusing to boost their defense budgets or take the other necessary steps to establish an independent foreign policy. Could China assume the role? It is ruled by a dictatorship, hobbled by a dysfunctional ideology, and it inspires only fear and loathing amongst its neighbors. The United Nations? Far from existing as an autonomous entity, the organization is nothing more than a collection of states, many of them autocratic and few of them as public-spirited as America—which, in any case, provides the U.N. with most of its financial, political and military muscle.

A humane future, then, will require an American foreign policy that is unapologetic, idealistic, assertive and well funded. America must not only be the world's policeman or its sheriff, it must be its beacon and guide. "A policeman gets his assignments from higher authority," writes foreign policy analyst Joshua Muravchik, "but in the community of nations there is no authority higher than America." This sentiment is not merely an assertion of national pride. It is simple fact. The alternative to American leadership is a chaotic, Hobbesian world where there is no authority to thwart aggression, ensure peace and security or enforce international norms. This is what it means to be a global superpower with global responsibilities. It is short-sighted to imagine that a policy of "humility" is either safer or less expensive than a policy that aims to preclude and deter the emergence of new threats, that has the United States arriving quickly at the scene of potential trouble before it has fully erupted, that addresses threats to the national interest before they develop into full-blown crises. Senator Kay Bailey Hutchison expressed a common but mistaken view when she wrote a few years ago that "a superpower is more credible and effective when it maintains a measured distance from all regional conflicts." In fact, this is precisely the way for a superpower to cease being a superpower.

Still, it is fair to ask how the rest of the world will respond to a prolonged period of American dominance. Charles A. Kupchan, author of *The End of the American Era: U.S. Foreign Policy and the Geopolitics of the Twenty-first Century*, cautions that the Bush doctrine's "neo-imperialist overtones" could foster "the very countervailing coalition that the administration says it is trying to avoid." To be sure, those regimes that find an American-led world order menacing to their existence will seek to cut away at American power, form tactical alliances with other rogue states for the common purpose of unsettling the international order, and look for ways to divide the United States from its allies. None of this, however, adds up to a convincing argument against American preeminence. The issue today is not American "arrogance." It is the inescapable reality of American power in all its many forms. Those who suggest that these international resentments could somehow be eliminated by a more restrained American foreign policy are deluding themselves. Even a United States that never again intervened in a place like Iraq would still find itself the target of jealousy, resentment and in some cases even fear. A more polite but still preeminently powerful United States would continue to stand in the way of Chinese ambitions, offend Islamists and grate on French insecurities. Unless the United States is prepared to divest itself of its real power and influence, thereby allowing other nations to achieve a position of relative parity on the world stage, would-be challengers as well as the envious will still have much to resent.

But it is doubtful that any effective grouping of nations is likely to emerge to challenge American power. Much of the current international attack against American "hegemonism" is posturing. Allies such as the French may cavil about the American "hyperpower," but they recognize the benefits that their dependence on the United States as the guarantor of international order brings them. As for Russia and China and the Islamic world, the prospect of effective joint action between these forces is slight. Their long history of mutual mistrust is compounded by the fact that they do not share common strategic goals—even with regard to the United States. The unwillingness of these and other powers to gang up on the United States also has much to do with the fact that it does not pursue a narrow, selfish definition of its national interest, but generally finds its interest in a benevolent international order.

Is the task of maintaining American primacy and making a consistent effort to shape the international environment beyond the capacity of Americans?

Not if American leaders have the understanding and the political will to do what is necessary. What is required is not particularly forbidding. Indeed, much of the task ahead consists of building on already-existing strengths.

Despite its degradation during the 1990s, the United States still wields the strongest military forces in the world. It has demonstrated its prowess on several occasions since the end of the Cold War—in Panama, in Iraq, in Kosovo and in Afghanistan. Still, those victories owed their success to a legacy the United States has lived off for over a decade. It is true that despite increases in the latest Bush defense budget, the United States still spends too little on its military capabilities, in terms of both present readiness and investment in future weapons technologies. The gap between America's strategic ends and the means available to accomplish those ends is significant, a fact that becomes more evident each time the United States deploys forces abroad.

Still, the task of repairing these deficiencies and creating a force that can shape the international environment today, tomorrow and twenty years from now is manageable. It would probably require spending about $100 billion per year above current defense budgets. This price tag may seem daunting, but in historical terms it represents only a modest commitment of America's wealth. The sum is still low by the standards of the past fifty years, and far lower than most great powers have spent on their militaries throughout history. Is the aim of maintaining American primacy really not worth that much?

The United States also inherited from the Cold War a legacy of strong alliances in Europe and Asia, and with Israel in the Middle East. Those alliances are a bulwark of American power, and more important still, they comprise the heart of the liberal democratic order that the United States seeks to preserve and extend. Critics of a distinctly American internationalism often claim that it is unilateralist in its heart. In fact, a strategy aimed at preserving American preeminence would require an even greater U.S. commitment to its allies. The United States would not be merely an "offshore balancer" in actions of last resort, as many recommend. It would not be a "reluctant sheriff," rousing itself to action only when the threatened townsfolk turn to it in desperation. American preeminence cannot be maintained from a distance. The United States should instead conceive of itself as at once a European power, an Asian power and, of course, a Middle Eastern power. It would act as if threats to the interests of our allies are threats to us, which indeed they are. It would act as if the flouting of civilized rules of conduct are threats that affect us with almost the same immediacy as if they were occurring on our doorstep. To act otherwise would make the United States appear an unreliable partner in world affairs, and this would erode both American primacy and the international order itself.

A strong America capable of projecting force quickly and with devastating effect to important regions of the world would make it less likely that challengers to regional stability would attempt to alter the status quo in their favor. It might even deter such challengers from undertaking expensive efforts to arm themselves in the first place. An America whose willingness to project force is in doubt, on the other hand, can only encourage such challenges. The message we should be sending to potential foes is: "Don't even think about it." That kind of deterrence offers the best recipe for a lasting peace; it is much cheaper than fighting the wars that would follow should we fail to build such a capacity.

The ability to project force overseas, however, could increasingly be jeopardized over the coming years as smaller powers acquire weapons of mass destruction and the missiles to launch them at American forces, at our allies and at the American homeland. Oddly enough, foreign critics, who carp that missile defense will cement U.S. hegemony and make Americans "masters of the world," grasp its rationale better than critics here at home. The real rationale for missile defense is that without it, an adversary armed with long-range missiles can, as Robert Joseph, President Bush's counterproliferation specialist at the National Security Council, argues, "hold American and allied cities hostage and thereby deter us from intervention." In other words, missile defense is about preserving America's ability to wield power abroad.

No one could have predicted that Iraq would be the first test-case of the post-Cold War era, just as no one could have predicted that Berlin would be the first battlefield of the Cold War. Indeed, the test could just as easily have come elsewhere—in North Korea, the Taiwan Strait or the Golan Heights. But history has conspired to locate the first serious challenge of the twenty-first century in Iraq. The failure to defeat Saddam was a defining moment for the presidencies of George H. W. Bush and Bill Clinton. The question of what to do about Saddam is now a defining moment for George W. Bush. Having fallen short before, will the United States get the answer right this time? If the president responds to the challenge of Iraq with the policies and worldviews of his predecessors, he too will surely fail. If, however, President Bush succeeds in bringing about regime change in Iraq, he will set a historical precedent—for Iraq, which could become the first Arab democracy; for the United States, which will demonstrate to all the compatibility of its interests and its ideals; and for the world, which America will have made a safer and more just place.

The mission begins in Baghdad, but it does not end there. Were the United States to retreat after victory into complacency and self-absorption, as it did the last time it went to war in Iraq, new dangers would soon arise. Preventing this outcome will be a burden, of which war in Iraq represents but the first installment. But America cannot escape its responsibility for maintaining a decent world order. The answer to this challenge is the American idea itself, and behind it the unparalleled military and economic strength of its custodian. Duly armed, the United States can act to secure its safety and to advance the cause of liberty—in Baghdad and beyond.

AMERICA'S DREAMS OF EMPIRE

Pervez Hoodbhoy

Islamabad, Pakistan—Street opinion in Pakistan, and probably in most Muslim countries, holds that Islam is the true target of America's new wars. The fanatical hordes spilling out of Pakistan's madrasas are certain that a modern-day Richard the Lion-Hearted will soon bear down upon them. Swords in hand, they pray to Allah to grant war and send a modern Saladin, who can miraculously dodge cruise missiles and hurl them back to their launchers.

Even moderate Muslims are worried. They see indicators of religious war in such things as the profiling of Muslims by the Immigration and Naturalization Service, the placing of Muslim states on the U.S. register of rogues and the blanket approval given to Israeli bulldozers as they level Palestinian neighborhoods.

But Muslims elevate their importance in the American cosmography. The U.S. has aspirations far beyond subjugating inconsequential Muslim states: It seeks to remake the world according to its needs, preference and convenience. The war on Iraq is but the first step.

High ambition underlies today's American foreign policy, and its boosters are not just in Washington. Aggressive militarism has been openly endorsed by America's corporate and media establishment. Mainstream commentators in the U.S. press now argue that, given its awesome military might, American ambition has up to now been insufficient.

Max Boot, a member of the Council on Foreign Relations and a former *Wall Street Journal* editor, wrote in *The Weekly Standard* that "Afghanistan and other troubled lands today cry out for the sort of enlightened foreign administration once provided by self-confident Englishmen in jodhpurs and pith helmets." *Washington Post* editorial writer Sebastian Mallaby, writing in Foreign Affairs magazine, noted that the current world chaos may point to the need for an "imperialist revival," a return to the day when "orderly societies [imposed] their own institutions on disorderly ones." *Atlantic Monthly* correspondent Robert Kaplan, in his book "Warrior Politics," suggests that Ameri-

Pervez Hoodbhoy is professor of high-energy physics at Quaid-i-Azam University in Islamabad. This article was published on January 26, 2003, in the *Los Angeles Times*.

can policymakers should learn from the Greek, Roman and British empires. "Our future leaders could do worse," he writes, "than be praised for their . . . ability to bring prosperity to distant parts of the world under America's soft imperial influence."

Although many Americans still cling to the belief that their country's new unilateralism is a reasonable outgrowth of "injured innocence," a natural response to terrorist acts, empire has actually been part of the American way of life for more than a century. The difference since Sept. 11—and it is a significant one—is that, now that there is no other superpower to keep it in check, the U.S. no longer sees a need to battle for the hearts and minds of those it would dominate. In today's Washington, a U.S.-based diplomat recently confided to me, the United Nations has become a dirty term. International law is on the way to irrelevancy, except when it can be used to further U.S. goals.

So although extremists on all sides—from Islamic warriors to Christian fundamentalists like Jerry Falwell and Pat Robertson to the leaders of Israel's right-wing parties—may yearn for another crusade, the counter-evidence to a civilizational war is much stronger. Examining the list of America's Muslim foes and friends over the years makes clear that it is perceived self-interest rather than ideology that has dictated its policy toward Muslim nations.

During the 1950s and 1960s, America's primary foes in the Muslim world were secular nationalist leaders, not religious fundamentalists. Mohammed Mossadeq of Iran, who opposed international oil companies grabbing at Iran's oil resources, was overthrown in a coup aided by the CIA. President Sukarno of Indonesia, accused of being a communist, was removed by U.S. intervention. Gamal Abdul Nasser of Egypt, who had Islamic fundamentalists like Sayyid Qutb publicly executed, fell afoul of the U.S. and Britain after the Suez crisis. On the other hand, until very recently, America's friends were the sheiks of Saudi Arabia and the Persian Gulf states, who practiced highly conservative forms of Islam but were the darlings of Western oil companies.

In Afghanistan during the early 1980s, the United States aided Islamic fundamentalists on the principle that any opposition to the Soviet occupation was welcome. Then-CIA Director William Casey launched a massive covert operation after President Reagan signed National Security Decision Directive 166, which explicitly stated that Soviet forces should be driven from Afghanistan "by all means available."

Readers browsing through book bazaars in the Pakistani cities of Rawalpindi and Peshawar can, even today, find textbooks written as part of this effort. Underwritten by a multimillion-dollar U.S. Agency for International Development grant to the University of Nebraska, the books sought to counterbalance Marxism through creating enthusiasm for Islamic militancy.

They exhorted Afghan children to "pluck out the eyes of the Soviet enemy and cut off his legs." Years after the books were first printed, they were approved by the Taliban for use in madrasas, or religious schools.

Washington now acknowledges that "mission myopia," as such strategic errors have come to be known, helped contribute to the growth of a global jihad network in the early 1980s. But the cost of America's mistakes has been vastly greater than most policymakers care to acknowledge. The network of Islamic militant organizations created primarily out of the need to fight the Soviets in Afghanistan did not disappear after the immediate goal was achieved: Rather, like any good military-industrial complex, it grew stronger from its victories.

The resulting damage has been far greater to Muslims than to the Americans who unleashed it. Acts of jihad—killing tourists, bombing churches and the like—not only rob Muslims of moral authority, they are a strategic disaster. Even the Sept. 11 operation, though perfectly planned and executed, was a colossal strategic blunder. It vastly strengthened American militarism, gave Israeli Prime Minister Ariel Sharon a license to put the Palestinian territories under virtual lockdown, and allowed pogroms directed at Muslims in the Indian state of Gujarat to occur with only a hint of international condemnation.

The absence of a modern political culture and the weakness of Muslim civil society have long rendered Muslim states inconsequential players on the world stage. An encircled, enfeebled dictator is scarcely a threat to his neighbors as he struggles to save his skin. Tragically, Muslim leaders, out of fear and greed, publicly wring their hands but collude with the U.S. and offer their territory for bases as it now bears down on Iraq. Significantly, no Muslim country has proposed an oil embargo or a serious boycott of American companies.

What, then, should be the strategy for all those who believe in a just world and are appalled by America's war on the weak? While the strong can get away with anything, the weak cannot afford missteps. They must hew to a stern regard for morality. Vietnam, to my mind, offers a uniquely successful model of resistance. Even though B-52s were carpet-bombing his country, North Vietnamese leader Ho Chi Minh did not call for hijacking airliners or blowing up buses. On the contrary, the Vietnamese reached out to the American people, making a clear distinction between them and their government. The country's leaders didn't assume—as Osama bin Laden undoubtedly would—that Americans spoke with one voice. Jane Fonda, Joan Baez and other popular figures were invited to come and see for themselves what was happening in Vietnam, and they took what they learned back to the people at home. Had Ho thought and acted like bin Laden, his country would surely now be a radioactive wasteland, rather than a unique victor against imperialism.

Only a global peace movement that explicitly condemns terrorism against noncombatants can slow, and perhaps halt, George Bush's madly speeding chariot of war. Massive antiwar demonstrations in Washington, New York, London, Florence, and other Western cities have brought out tens of thousands at a time. A sense of commitment to human principles and peace—not fear or fanaticism—impelled these demonstrators.

It is time for people in my part of the world to ask themselves a question: Why are the streets of Islamabad, Cairo, Riyadh, Damascus and Jakarta empty? Why do only fanatics demonstrate in our cities? Let us hang our heads in shame.

CATASTROPHE AS THE GENERATOR OF HISTORICAL CHANGE: THE IRAQ CASE

Richard Butler

President George W. Bush has stated, with mantra-like repetition, that the reason for a United States attack upon Iraq, leading to a change in its government, is that this is designed to remove Iraq's weapons of mass destruction (WMD) and that is said to be "in the name of peace."

These are the basic facts. Iraq has had weapons of mass destruction for some twenty years. It has manufactured chemical and biological weapons at home. It has been supplied with the means and know-how to make them, when it has needed external sources, by western countries, including the United States. It was coached in how to deploy and use such weapons, particularly chemical weapons, by the same countries. In the case of its use of chemical weapons against Iran it was given advice on this by the United States. Finally, Iraq has used all of the types of WMD it came to possess, including within Iraq. In 1988, Saddam used chemical weapons, and it is thought possibly also biological weapons, in his attack against Kurdish villagers in northern Iraq. The crime of those villagers was that they had reservations about his regime. That attack left thousands dead and caused genetic mutations that continue today.

The main point to be made about Saddam's evident addiction to weapons of mass destruction is not that it exists, but rather that its existence has been widely known for a very long time. What has been done about it has varied greatly depending upon the political interests of other powers at any given time. These have fluctuated. The outstanding example of this phenomenon, obviously, was that the United States loved Saddam when he was the sworn enemy of Iran, after it had gone through its revolution and had taken the U.S. Embassy in Iran hostage. The same darling of the United States of two decades ago is now, to borrow from the Iranian lexicon, the "great Satan."

Ambassador Richard Butler led the United Nations Special Commission (UNSCOM) from July 1, 1997 until June 30, 1999. From 1992 to 1997, he was the Australian ambassador and permanent representative to the United Nations. He is the author of *The Greatest Threat: Iraq, Weapons of Mass Destruction and the Growing Crisis of Global Security.* This article was written especially for this book.

If the possession of weapons of mass destruction is supposed to be a distinguishing characteristic of nations then Iraq fails the test. Simply, it is not alone. Indeed, it lacks distinction. There are thirty or forty other countries in the world that also possess weapons of mass destruction and perhaps the largest irony of all is that the countries now most vehemently opposed to Iraq's WMD are themselves in possession of massive quantities of WMD.

When Iraq invaded Kuwait in 1990, it made history. Iraq became the first member state of the United Nations to invade and seek to absorb a fellow member state. In the then forty-year history of the U.N. there had been all manner of political breakdowns in various countries many instances of which violated international law—the provisions of the Charter of the United Nations. But a cardinal principle founded in that Charter—thou shalt not seize another member state—had never been violated previously.

The United Nations reacted very strongly against Saddam's action. But any sound understanding of that reaction would be severely incomplete if it did not recognise the extreme importance of the fact that the Iraqi invasion of Kuwait was virtually simultaneous with the collapse of the USSR and the end of the Cold War. It was for this latter reason that the Security Council was able to act with such unity and conviction on the matter. Thus, the first President Bush was able to declare that what we had on our hands was "a new world order." It was true that we had a new world on our hands. We came to see very quickly that it was hardly an order.

While Iraq made its particular, infamous, history in its invasion of Kuwait, the U.N. Security Council also made history. It imposed upon Iraq the most far-reaching economic sanctions ever seen. These were to encourage Saddam to withdraw from Kuwait. The Security Council warned him repeatedly that if that didn't work Iraq would face physical ejection from Kuwait. When, after six months, it became clear that Saddam would not comply, the United Nations authorised the deployment of the force that had been put together principally by the United States but which incorporated contributions from some thirty states. That force, Operation Desert Storm, ejected Iraq in a matter of mere days. It did not go on to remove him from government in Iraq because that was not its mandate.

When the military action was suspended, cease-fire resolutions were drawn up in the Security Council. It is crucial to understand that no resolutions involving conclusion of the conflict were adopted, only a cease-fire. Thus, technically, U.N.-sanctioned enforcement action has never been formally concluded—enabling the U.S. and Britain to argue that they can restart military action at any time so long as Iraq remains in non-compliance with Security Council resolutions.

The key such resolution, number 687, was truly remarkable. It is a long document but in essence it provides the following: sanctions upon Iraq will be maintained until its weapons of mass destruction are removed; those weapons are very specifically defined in the nuclear, missile, chemical and biological areas; a sub-organ of the Security Council (then known as UNSCOM, which I came to lead) was established to carry out the disarmament task, specifically, to "destroy, remove or render harmless" Iraq's specified WMD.

The method of work had three parts: Iraq was to declare all its proscribed weapons; UNSCOM would verify that declaration through inspections; destruction of whatever weapons or the means to make them was thus revealed would then take place.

While these arrangements were detailed and unprecedented and it was intended that they should work, for example ample funding was provided for them, one factor, one condition alone, was essential to their possible success—agreement by Iraq to cooperate with the process.

Iraq never decided to give and never gave in practice that cooperation, from 1991 until the present day. If it had done so the task of removing Iraq's WMD would have taken one year. Twelve years later at massive material and human cost it is still not completed and the future cost, such as in a war, promises to be even more massive.

That Iraq never made honest declarations of its weapons, concealed them, sent inspectors down blind alleys, is now drearily established in the historical record. On one level I have always found that a fitting, almost exquisite symbol of this is the fact that the first declaration Iraq made early in 1991 when its back was absolutely against the wall was a single page of paper it presented to the inspectorate on its chemical weapons program. This page was written in Arabic, by hand, in pencil, and purported to be Iraq's official declaration. It proved to be false. Truly, the Iraq inspection game has been the stuff of wondrous farce.

But, it has not been anything remotely resembling comedy for the twenty-two million ordinary people of Iraq. For over a decade Saddam has insisted that it was more important for him to retain his WMD than for them to be relieved of sanctions. Resolution 687 tied the two together. The moment that I was able to report to the Security Council that Iraq's WMD had been removed or simply accounted for, sanctions would have been taken away. I have seen a few dictatorships in my time and certainly some less than tasteful governments. But I have never witnessed anything as repugnant as Saddam's trade-off in favour of his weapons against the misery of so many people.

As the UNSCOM years went on, some key things became clear. It was possible to identify and then destroy a portion of Iraq's illegal weapons, in spite of Iraq's attempts to prevent that. In the event, a considerable portion of those weapons were dealt with. But it became evident that the job would never be completed totally, if Iraq continued to resist and conceal weapons. Finally, UNSCOM's ability to get the job done, the obverse of which was Iraq's ability to frustrate it, would be massively influenced by Security Council unity. If there was unity the chances of the disarmament process succeeding would be high. The moment the Security Council divided or indeed crumbled, as it did in 1998, then the prospects for Iraq's resistance improved greatly.

In 1998 I presented Iraq with a final list of disarmament requirements that, if fulfilled, could have led me to tell the Council that the task had been completed and sanctions could be relieved. The Iraqi side considered this briefly but once again decided it would prefer to keep its weapons and thus informed me that there would be no further disarmament work in Iraq. Its motive was to keep hold of its weapons. But its ability to implement that stance relied utterly on its knowledge that the Security Council was divided and specifically that the Russians would support them.

The question of why, as the UNSCOM years went on, the Security Council progressively divided over the Iraq issue is a crucial one. At the beginning of the period which, as already mentioned, was simultaneous with the end of the Cold War, there was an unprecedented degree of unity and co-operation within the Council. It is true that the Russians attempted to head off Operation Desert Storm but, in the end they supported it and even more important, participated in designing the extraordinary strictures upon Iraq that were set forth in resolution 687. The same was true of the other permanent members of the Security Council although it would be wrong to suggest that negotiations with them on laying down the law to Iraq were easy.

Iraq resisted the inspection process, from the beginning, and repeatedly tested and challenged it, perhaps most famously in the car-park stand–off where it detained a team of inspectors for four days in an attempt to prevent them from taking away documents it had discovered on Iraq's nuclear program. Iraq backed down eventually because the Security Council stood firm.

As each year in the post–Cold War period unfolded, the level of concern and in some case downright anxiety about the shape of a unipolar world and more particularly the ends to which the United States would use its power, grew. The motives and concerns of each of the other permanent members of the Security Council varied. Russia's deepest source of concern was its loss of status as a co-equal participant with the United States in the management of world affairs.

France felt almost historically uncomfortable with a world that had become diametrically opposite to worlds which had existed in the past and in which French diplomacy had run riot. For France multipolarity meant multiple opportunities to form alliances and relationships of convenience. There is also, of course, deep French antipathy to an increasingly Anglophonic world. The rise to singular dominance by the United States also brought a rising trend towards English as the preferred global language.

The Chinese remain perhaps least uncomfortable with American power because, in many respects the post–Cold War version of state power which began to develop in the United States was not dissimilar from the Chinese version having at its core the centrality of national sovereignty. For China the main measure of proposals to contain or deal with Iraq is whether or not they could be seen as establishing a precedent for interfering with state sovereignty. If they did not, then in the Chinese view, they did not matter much.

In the late 1990s as the first post–Cold War decade was coming to a close and the repeatedly costly and frustrating business of trying to disarm Iraq reached its seventh or eighth year, these other powers came to see the Iraq issue as perhaps the key one through which the deeper issues of the shape of a unipolar world were crystallised. Quite simply the question was whether or not America would always get its way. And so the splintering of the Security Council began. It continues to the present day.

When President George W. Bush stated on September 12, 2002 and continued to state, as a mantra for months thereafter, that if the Security Council would not disarm Iraq the United States would take direct action to do so, this was heard by other permanent members of the Council, with the exception of Britain, and by other great powers such as Germany as a policy which did not simply point a gun at Iraq but perhaps just as important at the Security Council as well. U.S. policy towards Iraq had become the indelible code for the burning question of how far what happened in the foreseeable future, in the 21st century, would be determined by American fiat, by American interests alone.

Aside from the political judgments and perceptions involved in this view of United States policy towards Iraq it should be recorded that what the President threatened was contrary to international law. The Charter of the United Nations expressly forbids any such action against any State unless it is sanctioned by the Security Council, as Desert Storm was, as an action directed towards "the maintenance of international peace and security." It is not legal to invade another country. That was what Saddam did to Kuwait in 1990. It is not legal to intervene and change the government of another country. Such United States past interventions, for example in Chile and Nicaragua, have been condemned.

This legal consideration adds copious fuel to the perception that the

United States' interpretation of its status as the sole superpower is that it may now use that power with maximum arrogance, that is, without regard to law and without feeling any particular necessity to consult with others. Lest this point be considered hyperbole, it should be recalled that key members of the current Bush administration have claimed publicly a notion of "exceptionalism," that is, that because of its unique status the United States can and should enjoy freedom from the strictures of international law.

It is for these reasons if the United States launches an attack upon Iraq to change the regime in that country and to occupy it for a period, even if it is leading a so-called coalition of the willing, it will jeopardise the continuation of the legal, co-operative, and other arrangements through which the world has sought to manage relations amongst nations for the whole of the half century since the end of the Second World War. Some may ask "so what?" If institutions have to change to fit contemporary circumstances, then so be it. While that argument contains a certain logic, the issues of the motivation and the reasons for the change then become of major importance. It must be understood, in this context, that many would conclude that the motivation and reason for what could prove to be the destruction of the Security Council was none other that it no longer served as a simple conduit for United States interests.

Any consideration of the role and importance of the Security Council, on the other hand, would be deficient if it did not recognise how very seriously flawed it has proven to be. The international community widely recognises a range of deficiencies which afflict the Council, chief amongst which are: it is unrepresentative of the post-colonial world; the identity and powers of its permanent members are dramatically outdated; indeed, the very concept of permanent members needs revision; finally, the decision-making methods of the Council, including in particular, decisions on its agenda has lead to whole continents and subjects being ignored.

Serious attempts to reform the Security Council have been under way for over a decade. With the exception of peripheral changes, all reforms have been blocked by the current permanent members including those, such as France, who have led the charge, of late, against the arrogance of the sole superpower. While the Security Council continues to occupy the central place in cooperative international efforts to maintain international peace and security, its performance has been sub-optimal. This lamentable fact has probably been most continually illustrated in its failure to gain implementation of its binding resolutions on Iraq. A close second, of course, would be its painful and extended failures with respect to the crimes against humanity committed in the constituent parts of the former Yugoslavia and in Rwanda. And this is not to mention the Council's failure, over some four decades, to implement its own resolutions on Israel and Palestine. Sadly, the more deeply one examines the record of the Security Council the more dismal it becomes.

The tried generator of historical change has been catastrophe. The best modern example is the establishment of the United Nations itself and its Charter, the latter being the major contemporary document of international law. The catastrophe that finally made those actions possible was the seventy million dead of the two world wars of the twentieth century. War, it seems, was the hallmark of that century and it made sense therefore that the central task of the United Nations would be, as is stated in the preamble of the Charter, "to save succeeding generations from the scourge of war."

The hallmark of the Cold War period was the proliferation of weapons of mass destruction. What is needed now, over a decade after the end of the Cold War, is a new mechanism similar to the Security Council but with a specific mandate to contain such proliferation and move on towards the eventual elimination of weapons of mass destruction. Elsewhere, I have outlined the proposal for the establishment of such a mechanism—the Council on Weapons of Mass Destruction.

A decision by the international community to truly address these problems of the post–Cold War world—control of weapons of mass destruction and the uses of power and collective responsibility for it—should be specifically and consciously designed rather than driven by catastrophe. What is not clear is whether, as many suspect, a unilateral attack by the United States on Saddam Hussein's Iraq, possibly over the dead body of the Security Council, will prove exactly to be that catastrophe.

REGIME CHANGE

Lewis H. Lapham

They that can give up essential liberty to obtain a little temporary safety deserve neither liberty nor safety.

—Benjamin Franklin

U nrelenting in its search for Osama bin Laden and the roots of all the world's evil, the Defense Department some months ago established an Information Awareness Office that took for its letterhead emblem the all-seeing eye of God. Although still in the early stages of development and for the moment funded with an annual budget of only $200 million, the new medium of mass investigation seeks to "detect and classify" every prospective terrorist (foreign, hybrid, mutant, or native born) setting foot on American soil. No door or envelope unopened, no secret unexposed, no suspicious suitcase or Guatemalan allowed to descend unnoticed from a cruise ship or a bicycle.

To give weight and form to a paranoid dream of reason not unlike the one that sustained the sixteenth-century Spanish Inquisition, the government apparently means to recruit a synod of high-speed computers capable of sifting through "ultra-large" data warehouses stocked with every electronic proof of human movement in the wilderness of cyberspace—bank, medical, and divorce records, credit-card transactions, emails (interoffice and extraterritorial), college transcripts, surveillance photographs (from cameras in hospitals and shopping malls as well as from those in airports and hotel bars), driver's licenses and passport applications, bookstore purchases, website visits, and traffic violations. Connect all the names and places to all the dates and times, and once the systems become fully operational, in four years or maybe ten, the protectors of the public health and safety hope to reach beyond "truth maintenance" and "biologically inspired algorithms for agent control" to the construction of "FutureMap"—i.e., a set of indices programmed into the fiberoptic equivalent of a crystal ball that modifies "market-based techniques for avoiding surprise" in such a way that next week's nuclear explosion can be seen as clearly as last week's pornographic movie. In the

---

Lewis Lapham is the editor of *Harper's* Magazine. He is the author of several books, most recently *Theater of War*. This article was adapted by him, especially for this book, from his January and February 2003 *Notebook* columns in *Harper's*.

meantime, while waiting for the technical upgrades with which to perform "entity extraction from natural language text," the clerks seated at the computer screens can look for inspiration to the mandala on their office stationery—an obverse of the Great Seal of the United States similar to the ornament on the back of the $1 bill, an Egyptian pyramid and mystic, Rosicrucian light buttressed by the tendering in Latin of the motto "Knowledge is power."

When reports of the IAO's existence belatedly appeared in the mainstream press in November of last year, nine months after the headquarters' staff began moving the first electronic robots into an air-conditioned basement in Virginia, the news didn't capture the attention of the Congress or excite the interest of the television networks. No politician uttered a discouraging word; no prominent historian entertained the risk of a possibly unpatriotic question. The talk-show gossip of the moment dwelled on the prospect of war in Iraq and the setting up of the Department of Homeland Security (soon to be equipped with its own domestic espionage service), and except for an occasional lawyer associated with the American Civil Liberties Union, most of the people in New York to whom I mentioned the Pentagon's gift for totalitarian fantasy were inclined to think that intelligence gathering was somehow akin to weather forecasting—a routine and necessary precaution, annoying and possibly unconstitutional but entirely appropriate in a time of trouble.

William Safire entered an objection on the opinion page of *The New York Times* ("Orwellian scenario . . . sweeping theft of privacy rights . . . exploitation of fear"), but elsewhere in the large-circulation media protests were hard to find. The general opinion so clearly favored the Bush Administration's policies of forward deterrence and preemptive strike that I wasn't surprised by the absence of commentary, much less complaint, when it was announced in early December that the FBI had been jettisoning the baggage of due process while pursuing the rumor of an underwater terrorist attack against an unknown target somewhere along the 95,000 miles of the American coastline. From hundreds of dive-shop operators everywhere in the country the FBI demanded the names of the several million swimmers who had taken diving lessons over the course of the last three years. Only two citizens refused the request, the co-owners of Reef Seekers Dive Company in Beverly Hills, California. When word of their noncooperation showed up in a newspaper story, they were besieged by vindictive telephone calls expressing the hope that their shop prove to be the next locus of a terrorist bombing.

THE INCIDENT speaks to the nervous temper of the times—hundreds of dive shops, only one refusing to give up its client list; the voice of the people tuned to the pitch of an angry mob—and illustrates the lesson in obedience well and truly learned by a once free people during the second half of a century defined in the history books as America's own. I'm old enough to remember public speeches unfettered by the dogma of political correctness, a time when it was possible to apply for a job without submitting to a blood or urine test, when people construed their freedoms as a constitutional birthright, not as favors grudgingly bestowed by a sometimes benevolent government. I also can remember the days when people weren't afraid of tobacco smoke, sexual intercourse, and saturated fats; when irony was understood and money wasn't sacred; when even men in uniform could be trusted to recognize a joke.

The spacious and once familiar atmospheres of liberty (wisecracking and open-ended, tolerant, unkempt, experimental, and democratic) didn't survive the poisoning of Hiroshima or serve the purposes of the Cold War with the Russians. The easygoing, provincial republic of fifty years ago gradually assumed the character of a world-encircling nation-state, its plow shares beaten into swords, borrowing from its enemies (first the nonexistent Communist empire, now the unseen terrorist jihad) the practice of restricting the freedom of its own citizens in the interest of what the increasingly oligarchic governments in Washington proclaim to be "the national security." Begin the narrative almost anywhere in the late 1940s or early 1950s—with the National Security Act of 1947, the hearings before the House Un-American Activities Committee in 1951, President Harry Truman's decision to build the hydrogen bomb, the composition of the Hollywood Blacklist, or Senator Joe McCarthy's search for Marxists marching in the Rose Bowl Parade—and the plot development moves briskly forward in the direction of more fear and less courage, toward the substitution of White House intrigue for congressional debate and the professions of smiling loyalty preferred to the clumsy and impolitic fumbling for the truth.

Bear in mind the conclusion of the Church committee hearings as long ago as 1976—"too many people have been spied upon by too many Government agencies and too much information has been collected"—and space permits only a brief acknowledgment of the various police powers seized by the government under the rubric of the war on drugs (the use of anonymous informants, the taking of property without conviction or arrest), of the illegal surveillance of American citizens by their own intelligence agencies (the CIA between 1953 and 1973 producing an index of 1.5 million suspicious American names, the FBI compiling a list of 26,000 individuals to be summarily rounded up in the event of "a national emergency"), of the Justice Department's long campaign against the civil rights expressed in the First, Fourth, Fifth, Sixth, and Eighth amendments to the Constitution, and of a system of public education that offers its best-attended courses of instruction to the student populations in the army and the prisons. Add to the constant threat of nuclear extinction the sum of the wiretaps infiltrated into the American consciousness across the span of three generations, and it's no wonder that by the late 1990s, even in the midst of the reassuring prosperity allied with a buoyant stock market, and well before the destruction of the World Trade Center, the public-opinion polls found the bulk of the respondents willing to give up a generous percentage of their essential liberty in return for safer streets, secure suburbs, well-lighted parking garages, and risk-free cocktail waitresses.

SINCE THE shock of September 11, 2001, the American public has quickened the pace of its retreat into the shelters of harmless speech and heavy law enforcement. If I were to measure the general level of submissiveness by my own encounters with the habit of self-censorship and the general concern with social hygiene—acquaintances reluctant to remark on the brutality of the Israeli army for fear of being thought anti-Semitic, public scolds who damn me as a terrorist for smoking a cigarette in Central Park, college students so worried about the grooming of their résumés that they avoid rock concerts on the off-chance that their faces might show up on a police-department videotape—I might be tempted to argue that America's winning of the Cold War resulted in the loss of its soul. In place of the reckless and independent-minded individual once thought to embody the national stereotype (child of nature, descendant of Daniel Boone, hard-drinking and unorthodox) we now have a quorum of nervous careerists, psalm-singing and well-behaved, happy to oblige, eager to please, trained to hold up their hands and empty their pockets when passing through airport security or entering City Hall.

John Quincy Adams understood the terms of the bargain as long ago as 1821, speaking as the secretary of state against sending the U.S. Navy to rearrange Spain's colonial empire in Colombia and Chile. America, he said, "goes not abroad, in search of monsters to destroy." Were the country to embark on such a foolish adventure,

> she would involve herself beyond the power of extrication, in all the wars of interest and intrigue, of individual avarice, envy, and ambition, which assume the colors and usurp the standard of freedom. The fundamental maxims of her policy would insensibly change from liberty to force. . . . She might become the dictatress of the world. She would no longer be the ruler of her own spirit.

The Bush Administration equates the American spirit with power, not with liberty. During the months since the fall of the twin towers it has assumed the colors and usurped the standard of freedom to jury-rig the framework of an autocratic state. If not as a concerted effort to restrict the liberties of the American people, how else does one describe the Republican agenda now in motion in the nation's capital? Backed by the specious promise of imminent economic recovery and secured by the guarantee of never-ending war, the legislative measures mobilized by the White House and the Congress suggest that what the Bush Administration has in mind is not the defense of the American citizenry against a foreign enemy but the protection of the American oligarchy from the American democracy. In every instance, and no matter what the issue immediately at hand, the bias is the same—more laws limiting the rights of individuals, fewer laws restraining the rights of property:

1. The systematic transfer of the nation's wealth from the union of the poor to the confederacy of the rich. President Bush's new plan to exclude from taxation all corporate dividends received by individuals, at the same time lowering the income-tax rates previously scheduled to take effect between now and 2009, assigns the bulk of the refund (64 percent) to the wealthiest 5 percent of the nation's taxpayers, more than half of the award to people earning at least $200,000 a year, a quarter of it to people earning more than $1 million a year.
2. The easing of environmental regulations on the energy industries in New England.
3. The opening of the national forests in the Pacific Northwest and the Arctic National Wildlife Refuge to further expropriation by the oil, gas, mining, and timber industries.
4. The persistent issuing of health-insurance regulations intended to subvert and eventually overturn the 1973 Supreme Court ruling, *Roe v. Wade,* that recognized a woman's freedom to decide whether or not she will give birth to a child.
5. The reinforcing of the monopolies held by the big media syndicates on the country's systems of communication.
6. Outfitting the banks and credit-card agencies with the privilege to sell to the highest bidders any or all of the personal data acquired from their customers.
7. A series of bills in Congress meant to reduce the nation's health-care costs by denying medical services to people too poor to pay for the upkeep of the insurance companies.

8. The nomination to the federal appeals courts of judges apt to find legal precedents in the pages of the Bible rather than in the Constitution.

9. The broad expansion of the government's police power and the Justice Department's reserving to itself the right to tap anybody's phone and open everybody's mail, to decide who is and who is not an un-American.

The Homeland Security Act runs to a length of 484 pages, and when it was presented to Congress last November Senator Robert C. Byrd of West Virginia flung the text down on his desk with a gesture that reminded a *New York Times* reporter of "the fury of Moses smashing the tablets." One of only nine senators who voted against the bill, Byrd denounced it as a foolish and unlawful seizure of power unlikely to do much harm to America's enemies but certain to do a great deal of harm to the American people. "With a battle plan like the Bush Administration is proposing," Byrd said, "instead of crossing the Delaware River to capture the Hessian soldiers on Christmas day, George Washington would have stayed on his side of the river and built a bureaucracy."

Not having read the small print in the Homeland Security Act, I can't guess at the extent to which it will further subtract from the country's store of civil liberty, but if I understand correctly its operative bias (170,000 functionaries undefended by a labor union and serving at the pleasure and sole discretion of the president of the United States), I all too easily can imagine a new department of bureaucratic control that incorporates the paranoid systems of thought engendered by the Cold War with the dogmas of political correctness meant to cure the habit of free speech, and deploys the surveillance techniques made possible by the miracles of modern telecommunications technology.

A servile Congress approves the requested legislation as eagerly as if it had been called upon to save a sinking ship with the rapid slamming of steel doors. The haste and cowardice of the non-partisan majorities comes as no surprise because Congress represents the constituency of the frightened rich—not the will or the spirit of what was once a democratic republic but the interest of a scared and selfish oligarchy anxious to preserve its comforts in the impregnable vaults of military empire. The grotesque maldistribution of the country's wealth over the last thirty years has brought forth a class system fully outfitted with the traditional accessories of complacence, stupidity, and pride. People supported by incomes of $10 or $15 million a year not only mount a different style of living than those available to an income of $50,000 or even $150,000 a year, they acquire different habits of mind—reluctant to think for themselves, afraid of the future, careful to expatriate their profits in offshore tax havens, disinclined to trust a new hairdresser or a new idea, grateful for the security of gated residential protectorates, reassured by reactionary political theorists who say that history is at an end and that if events should threaten to prove otherwise (angry mobs rising in Third World slums to beg a chance at freedom or demand a piece of the action) America will send an army to exterminate the brutes.

Not an inspiring set of attitudes, but representative of the social class that owns our news media, staffs the White House, and pays for our elections. If neither the Republicans nor the Democrats have stumbled upon a forceful or generous political idea since 1968, it's because the widening distance between the American citizenry and the American elites obliges the candidates of both parties to go for money to the same body of comfortable opinion (the few hundred thousand individuals, interest groups, or corporations that contribute more than $1,000 to any one campaign) content to think that the idealism implicit in what Benjamin Franklin recognized as the American experiment has run its course, served its purpose, gone far enough. Whether sporting lapel pins in the shape of elephants or donkeys, the members of Congress dance to the tune of the same big but nervous money, the differences in their political views reduced to a choice between the grilled or potted shrimp.

I don't count myself a believer in the dystopian futures imagined in Aldous Huxley's *Brave New World* or George Orwell's *1984,* but I think it would be a mistake to regard the trend of events as somehow favorable to the cause of liberty. President Bush likes to present himself as the embodiment of the spirit of 1776, but to the directorship of the Pentagon's new Information Awareness Office he appointed Vice Admiral John Poindexter, a royalist ideologue, a convicted felon, and a proven enemy of both the American Congress and the articles of the Constitution. As national security adviser to President Ronald Reagan in 1985, the admiral supervised what came to be known as the Iran-Contra swindle—the selling of missiles to the despotic ayatollahs in Iran in return for money with which to fund, secretly and illegally, a thuggish junta in Nicaragua. After the scheme collapsed under the weight of its criminal stupidity, the admiral repeatedly lied to the congressional committee investigating the farce (thus his convictions on five felony counts), and when called upon to account for his false testimony he said that he considered it his "duty" to conceal information too sensitive to be entrusted to loud-mouthed politicians.

Not an honest or liberal-minded man, the admiral, but unfortunately representative of the arrogant corporatists currently in charge of the government in Washington. Glimpsed in the persons of Secretary of Defense Donald Rumsfeld, Vice President Dick Cheney, and Attorney General John Ashcroft, the senior managers of the Bush Administration make no secret of their contempt for the rules of democratic procedure (inefficient, wrong-headed, and slow), their distrust of the American people (indolent and immoral, corrupted by a debased popular culture, undeserving of the truth), and their disdain for the United Nations and the principle of international law (sophomoric idealisms popular with weak nations too poor to pay for a serious Air Force). I don't for a moment doubt the eager commitment to the great and noble project of "regime change," but on the evidence of the last eighteen months they've been doing their most effective work in the United States, not in Afghanistan, Saudi Arabia, or Iraq. Better understood as radical nationalists than as principled conservatives, they borrow the logic endorsed by the American military commanders in Vietnam (who found it necessary to destroy a village in order to save it), and they offer the American people a choice similar to the one presented by the officers of the Spanish Inquisition to independent-minded heretics—give up your liberty, and we will set you free.

HEGEMONY, HUBRIS
AND OVERREACH

Kevin Phillips

L et us leave for the news analysts and cameras the short-term consequences of deploying the United States military to establish a *de facto*
U.S. protectorate or sphere of influence in the region between the Persian
Gulf, the Caspian Sea and the Khyber Pass. This inquiry is aimed at a less-
discussed subject: the long-term effects on a leading world economic power
of hubris and overreach in the projection of its power as a hegemon.

To put things in plain English, I am talking about the past powers—Britain
most recently, Holland back when New York was New Amsterdam, and Hapsburg Spain when hidalgos named Coronado, DeSoto and Ponce De Leon
were crisscrossing what is now the United States—and how they ruined their
economies by going one or two wars too far. Given the present levels of U.S.
individual, corporate, national and international debts and payments imbal-
ances, there is good reason to worry about a similar fate for the United States
developing over the next ten or twenty years.

The hubris of the Bush White House and cabinet hardly needs elaboration. Satisfaction with the republic of yesteryear is no longer enough, and talk
of empire is open in Washington. Unfortunately, this cockiness also has
precedents: the arrogance of Edwardian Britain, the smugness of Holland's
bankers to the world, the military hauteur of the Great Armada and the crack
Castilian regiments.

Readers unfamiliar with the commercial and economic circumstances of
the three can glean the attitudes, if not the cold statistics, from the following
displays of pride. A late 16th century Spaniard observed "Let London manufacture those fine fabrics . . . Holland her chambrays, Florence her cloth; the
Indies their beaver and vicuna; Milan her broaches; India and Flanders their
linens . . . so long as our capital can enjoy them. The only thing it proves is
that all nations train journeymen for Madrid and that Madrid is the queen of
parliaments, for all the world serves her, and she serves nobody."

Kevin Phillips has been a political and economic commentator for more than three decades. He is currently a regular contributor to the *Los Angeles Times* and National Public Radio. He is the author of ten books, including, most recently, *Wealth and Democracy*, which he drew on in the writing of this article especially for this book.

The most conspicuous Dutch boast was expressed in the imagery decorating the exterior of the great Amsterdam town hall begun in the glory year of 1648, which showed that city receiving the tributes of four continents—Europe, Africa, Asia, and America—while a Dutch Atlas, unaided, supported the globe on his back.

In Britain, economist W. S. Jevons caught the assurance of the Victorian Era: "The plains of North America and Russia are our cornfields: Chicago and Odessa are our granaries; Canada and the Baltic are our timber forests, Australia contains our sheep farms, and in Argentina and on the Western prairies of North America are our herds of oxen: Peru sends her silver, and the gold of South Africa and Australia flows to London; the Hindus and Chinese grow tea for us, and our coffee, sugar and spice plantations are all in the Indies, Spain and France are our vineyards, and the Mediterranean our fruit garden."

Not any longer, of course. Today's over-extended empire has its seat in Washington, where happy-talk economists write similar speeches for treasury officials and Sun Belt congressmen. But let us now return to the premise of this analysis: that nothing matches war for undoing a leading economic power that is decades past its absolute global zenith (1945–50 for us) yet is at the peak of its glorious self-perception and elite sense of global entitlement.

The 9/11 terrorist attack on the United States produced a proper and effective retaliation in Afghanistan. There is less to be said for the metamorphosis of that response into a broader ambition to subdue, dominate and reshape an area that stretches northwest from the Persian Gulf to the Caucasus and eastward to Afghanistan and Central Asia. History may describe the Balkans as a burial ground of great power ambition, but the geopolitical lessons of this part of the world have been just as brutal for would-be hegemons from Alexander the Great to Russia and Britain.

Early military results are not a reliable long-term yardstick. From European Macedonia, Alexander got as far as present-day Pakistan, Hitler almost made it to the oil-rich Caucasus in 1942, and Russian and British troops held Kabul, Afghanistan, for a number of years during their respective attempts to subdue it. Thus the irony: military success in 2003 could be a long-term minus, while defeat could have aspects of a silver lining.

The Spanish, Dutch and British experiences with war and overreach are instructive. Fifteen years ago, Yale Professor Paul Kennedy offered lessons that are still just as relevant today about the succession of mistakes made by Spain at its peak. The costly failure of the Great Armada sent against England in 1588 was followed by the royal bankruptcy of 1596. Next, the deepening decline in gold and silver shipments from the new world made an economic disaster out of Spain's lengthy, draining military embroilment in Europe's

Thirty Years War (1618–1648). By the time the war ended, the nation's hegemony in Europe was over and its economy a shambles.

It is not generally realized how far-flung was the global reach of the Dutch, whose new maritime nation succeeded Hapsburg Spain as the leading world economic power of the 17th century. At its peak in the middle of the century, the de facto empire of the Dutch Republic stretched from stations in Japan to control of Manhattan, from the Spice Islands of current-day Indonesia to Africa's Cape of Good Hope, the Caribbean and territories adjacent to Brazil.

In retrospect, the Dutch, who were already beginning to lose some territory in the 1660s and 1670s, overreached in 1688 when William of Orange, their hereditary ruler, also took the crown of England. The result was a war with France that wound up, a few intermissions notwithstanding, lasting almost a quarter of a century. By the time the Dutch emerged from the military and economic stress of that encounter, they had dissipated their onetime naval and commercial hegemony, lost vital markets, industries and more overseas possessions, and taken on enough wartime debt to double interest rates. Within a few decades, the only clear leadership they retained was in one aspect of finance—lending to foreign rulers and governments.

The chronology of British decline is more recent and better remembered. The zenith in Britain's share of world manufacturing and trade came in the 1850s and 1860s, but the man in the street did not feel the change in the tides of world industry until the 1890s and 1900s. For Britain's aristocracy and financiers, the peak of overseas investment and imperial splendor and hubris did not come until the 1900–1914 period. The Boer War of 1899–1901 had brought some military burdens and unexpected budget demands, but concerns about these were quickly pushed aside by Kipling's cultural nationalism and the battleship race with Germany.

Some forty years have passed since a hit show "Oh What a Lovely War" opened in London, but the title, and the words and music, are as evocative and appropriate today as they were then. The great conflict that was to be remembered as "the deluge" began in August 1914 with the cheers of a huge crowd in Trafalgar Square. In an intermediate stage, it was hailed as "the war to end all wars." What it ended instead was Britain's status as the leading world economic power. Even before 1914, the United States had moved ahead of Britain in manufacturing, and the First World War put New York on a level with London as an international financial center. Now, all of a sudden, the United States had become the global lender, Britain the borrower required to sell assets. World War Two, of course, completed the process. By 1947–48, the British people were living under food rationing more suited to a loser than victor, and Britain maintained its financial footing only with the assistance of the U.S. Treasury Department.

Do these Hapsburg, Dutch and British examples hold out a warning to the United States? I think so. America's first war with Iraq in 1991 was actually a money-making proposition because Washington was able to pass the hat to other members of the coalition, including Japan and Saudi Arabia. Many billions were raised this way. Of course, that was when we had a true coalition of the fiscally willing.

The possibilities discussed for 2003, by contrast, carried a steep price tag. The estimates for U.S. military outlays ranged between $50 and $200 billion. The rewards-cum-compensation offered to allies varied from $5 to 15 billion for Turkey down to relative peanuts for the *borscht* republics of Eastern Europe counting on weapons overhauls and marching-around money in return for their war endorsements. The occupation and rebuilding of Iraq was down for another $75 billion. All of this, moreover, presumed that nothing much would go wrong militarily.

The trouble is that things can go wrong *economically* even if, initially at least, they don't go wrong *militarily.* Gaining a *de facto* protectorate over such a large unstable region could turn out to be less an opportunity—to gain hegemony over Iraqi resources, expand regional oil production and lower prices—than a potential burden. Despite the difficulty in making comparisons across centuries, there is a chance that such a role could begin the U.S. equivalent of the Hapsburg, Dutch and British draining experiences of 1618–1648, 1688–1713 and 1914–1945.

Certainly the current context of U.S. indebtedness argues for caution, but one gets the sense that either the favorable petroleum calculus dominates or the supply-side theorists manning the economic battlements in Washington simply cannot stand to let the prospect of possibly limitless deficits interrupt a reverie. The extent to which debt and interest burdens were part of what choked Spain, the Netherlands and Britain in their days becomes all the more relevant when one considers that the United States is already the world's leading debtor, to the tune of some $2 trillion. The economic hubris displayed here could turn out to match the geopolitical and military hauteur.

Actually, it probably already has. The federal budget deficit is already returning to the dollar levels that worried policymakers during the 1990–1991 confrontation with Iraq. Worse, because the United States manufactures and produces less and less of what it physically requires, the U.S. current account deficit is now closing in on $500 billion a year, roughly 5% of Gross Domestic Product.

Borrowing on this level is only sustainable when foreigners want to invest in U.S. stocks, bonds, property or industry on a very large scale and when they have faith in the valuation of the U.S. dollar and the wisdom of U.S. leadership. If they turn sour on the U.S., there is the potential—no one can set the odds—for an economic disaster. The U.S. is already within fumbling distance of the record British current account deficit—in the 6–7% range—that prevailed in 1947–48 when Britain, for all practical purposes, was on a financial respirator.

Recent policies of the United States—from doctrines of pre-emptive war to insults exchanged with European allies and actions that often appear to reflect an anti-Muslim bias—have dissipated much of the international goodwill extended after 9/11 and created a new global surge of anti-Americanism that clearly adds to the threat. International support for the United States in matters of economics and in its efforts to control of global terrorism has never been more important, but military hubris and geopolitical chutzpah verging on unilateralism may put such support in jeopardy.

The United States is not *sui generis*. God does not march under the American flag. We may come to regret pretending otherwise.

APPENDICES

Appendix 1

KEY U.N. RESOLUTIONS

UN Security Council Resolution 687
(April 3, 1991)

The Security Council,

Recalling its resolutions 660 (1990) of 2 August 1990, 661 (1990) of 6 August 1990, 662 (1990) of 9 August 1990, 664 (1990) of 18 August 1990, 665 (1990) of 25 August 1990, 666 (1990) of 13 September 1990, 667 (1990) of 16 September 1990, 669 (1990) of 24 September 1990, 670 (1990) of 25 September 1990, 674 (1990) of 29 October 1990, 677 (1990) of 28 November 1990, 678 (1990) of 29 November 1990 and 686 (1991) of 2 March 1991,

Welcoming the restoration to Kuwait of its sovereignty, independence and territorial integrity and the return of its legitimate Government,

Affirming the commitment of all Member States to the sovereignty, territorial integrity and political independence of Kuwait and Iraq, and noting the intention expressed by the Member States cooperating with Kuwait under paragraph 2 of resolution 678 (1990) to bring their military presence in Iraq to an end as soon as possible consistent with paragraph 8 of resolution 686 (1991),

Reaffirming the need to be assured of Iraq's peaceful intentions in the light of its unlawful invasion and occupation of Kuwait,

Taking note of the letter dated 27 February 1991 from the Deputy Prime Minister and Minister for Foreign Affairs of Iraq addressed to the President of the Security Council and of his letters of the same date addressed to the President of the Council and to the Secretary-General, and those letters dated 3 March and 5 March he addressed to them, pursuant to resolution 686 (1991),

Noting that Iraq and Kuwait, as independent sovereign States, signed at Baghdad on 4 October 1963 "Agreed Minutes between the State of Kuwait and the Republic of Iraq regarding the restoration of friendly relations, recognition and related matters," thereby formally recognizing the boundary between Iraq and Kuwait and the allocation of islands, which Agreed Minutes were registered with the United Nations in accordance with Article 102 of the Charter of the United Nations and in which Iraq recognized the independence and complete sovereignty of the State of Kuwait with its boundaries as specified in the letter of the Prime Minister of Iraq dated 21 July 1932 and as accepted by the ruler of Kuwait in his letter dated 10 August 1932,

Conscious of the need for demarcation of the said boundary,

Conscious also of the statements by Iraq threatening to use weapons in violation of its obligations under the Protocol for the Prohibition of the Use in War of Asphyxiating, Poisonous or Other Gases, and of Bacteriological Methods of Warfare, signed at

Geneva on 17 June 1925, and of its prior use of chemical weapons, and affirming that grave consequences would follow any further use by Iraq of such weapons,

Recalling that Iraq has subscribed to the Final Declaration adopted by all States participating in the Conference of States Parties to the 1925 Geneva Protocol and Other Interested States, held in Paris from 7 to 11 January 1989, establishing the objective of universal elimination of chemical and biological weapons,

Recalling also that Iraq has signed the Convention on the Prohibition of the Development, Production and Stockpiling of Bacteriological (Biological) and Toxin Weapons and on Their Destruction, of 10 April 1972,

Noting the importance of Iraq ratifying the Convention,

Noting also the importance of all States adhering to the Convention and encouraging its forthcoming review conference to reinforce the authority, efficiency and universal scope of the Convention,

Stressing the importance of an early conclusion by the Conference on Disarmament of its work on a convention on the universal prohibition of chemical weapons and of universal adherence thereto,

Aware of the use by Iraq of ballistic missiles in unprovoked attacks and therefore of the need to take specific measures in regard to such missiles located in Iraq,

Concerned by the reports in the hands of Member States that Iraq has attempted to acquire materials for a nuclear-weapons programme contrary to its obligations under the Treaty on the Non-Proliferation of Nuclear Weapons of 1 July 1968,

Recalling the objective of the establishment of a nuclear-weapon-free zone in the region of the Middle East,

Conscious of the threat that all weapons of mass destruction pose to peace and security in the area and of the need to work towards the establishment in the Middle East of a zone free of such weapons,

Conscious also of the objective of achieving balanced and comprehensive control of armaments in the region,

Conscious further of the importance of achieving the objectives noted above using all available means, including a dialogue among the States of the region,

Noting that resolution 686 (1991) marked the lifting of the measures imposed by resolution 661 (1990) in so far as they applied to Kuwait,

Noting also that despite the progress being made in fulfilling the obligations of resolution 686 (1991), many Kuwaiti and third-State nationals are still not accounted for and property remains unreturned,

Recalling the International Convention against the Taking of Hostages, opened for signature in New York on 18 December 1979, which categorizes all acts of taking hostages as manifestations of international terrorism,

Deploring threats made by Iraq during the recent conflict to make use of terrorism against targets outside Iraq and the taking of hostages by Iraq,

Taking note with grave concern of the reports transmitted by the Secretary-General on 20 March and 28 March 1991, and conscious of the necessity to meet urgently the humanitarian needs in Kuwait and Iraq,

Bearing in mind its objective of restoring international peace and security in the area as set out in its recent resolutions,

Conscious of the need to take the following measures acting under Chapter VII of the Charter,

1. *Affirms* all thirteen resolutions noted above, except as expressly changed below to achieve the goals of the present resolution, including a formal cease-fire;

A

2. *Demands* that Iraq and Kuwait respect the inviolability of the international boundary and the allocation of islands set out in the "Agreed Minutes between the State of Kuwait and the Republic of Iraq regarding the restoration of friendly relations, recognition and related matters," signed by them in the exercise of their sovereignty at Baghdad on 4 October 1963 and registered with the United Nations;

3. *Calls upon* the Secretary-General to lend his assistance to make arrangements with Iraq and Kuwait to demarcate the boundary between Iraq and Kuwait, drawing on appropriate material including the maps transmitted with the letter dated 28 March 1991 addressed to him by the Permanent Representative of the United Kingdom of Great Britain and Northern Ireland to the United Nations, and to report back to the Council within one month;

4. *Decides* to guarantee the inviolability of the above-mentioned international boundary and to take, as appropriate, all necessary measures to that end in accordance with the Charter of the United Nations;

B

5. *Requests* the Secretary-General, after consulting with Iraq and Kuwait, to submit within three days to the Council for its approval a plan for the immediate deployment of a United Nations observer unit to monitor the Khawr Abd Allah and a demilitarized zone, which is hereby established, extending ten kilometres into Iraq and five kilometres into Kuwait from the boundary referred to in the "Agreed Minutes between the State of Kuwait and the Republic of Iraq regarding the restoration of friendly relations, recognition and related matters": to deter violations of the boundary through its presence in and surveillance of the demilitarized zone and to observe any hostile or potentially hostile action mounted from the territory of one State against the other, and also requests the Secretary-General to report regularly to the Council on the operations of the unit and to do so immediately if there are serious violations of the zone or potential threats to peace;

6. *Notes* that as soon as the Secretary-General notifies the Council of the completion of the deployment of the United Nations observer unit, the conditions will be established for the Member States cooperating with Kuwait in accordance with resolution 678 (1990) to bring their military presence in Iraq to an end consistent with resolution 686 (1991);

C

7. *Invites* Iraq to reaffirm unconditionally its obligations under the Protocol for the Prohibition of the Use in War of Asphyxiating, Poisonous or Other Gases, and of Bacteriological Methods of Warfare, signed at Geneva on 17 June 1925, and to ratify the Convention on the Prohibition of the Development, Production and Stockpiling of

Bacteriological (Biological) and Toxin Weapons and on Their Destruction, of 10 April 1972;

8. *Decides* that Iraq shall unconditionally accept the destruction, removal, or rendering harmless, under international supervision, of:

(*a*) All chemical and biological weapons and all stocks of agents and all related subsystems and components and all research, development, support and manufacturing facilities related thereto;

(*b*) All ballistic missiles with a range greater than one hundred and fifty kilometres, and related major parts and repair and production facilities;

9. *Decides also,* for the implementation of paragraph 8, the following:

(*a*) Iraq shall submit to the Secretary-General, within fifteen days of the adoption of the present resolution, a declaration on the locations, amounts and types of all items specified in paragraph 8 and agree to urgent, on-site inspection as specified below;

(*b*) The Secretary-General, in consultation with the appropriate Governments and, where appropriate, with the Director-General of the World Health Organization, within forty-five days of the adoption of the present resolution shall develop and submit to the Council for approval a plan calling for the completion of the following acts within forty-five days of such approval:

(i)   The forming of a special commission which shall carry out immediate on-site inspection of Iraq's biological, chemical and missile capabilities, based on Iraq's declarations and the designation of any additional locations by the special commission itself;

(ii) The yielding by Iraq of possession to the Special Commission for destruction, removal or rendering harmless, taking into account the requirements of public safety, of all items specified under paragraph 8 (*a*), including items at the additional locations designated by the Special Commission under paragraph (i) and the destruction by Iraq, under the supervision of the Special Commission, of all its missile capabilities, including launchers, as specified under paragraph 8 (*b*);

(iii) The provision by the Special Commission to the Director General of the International Atomic Energy Agency of the assistance and cooperation required in paragraphs 12 and 13;

10. *Decides further* that Iraq shall unconditionally undertake not to use, develop, construct or acquire any of the items specified in paragraphs 8 and 9, and requests the Secretary-General, in consultation with the Special Commission, to develop a plan for the future ongoing monitoring and verification of Iraq's compliance with the present paragraph, to be submitted to the Council for approval within one hundred and twenty days of the passage of the present resolution;

11. *Invites* Iraq to reaffirm unconditionally its obligations under the Treaty on the Non-Proliferation of Nuclear Weapons, of 1 July 1968;

12. *Decides* that Iraq shall unconditionally agree not to acquire or develop nuclear weapons or nuclear-weapon-usable material or any subsystems or components or any research, development, support or manufacturing facilities related to the above; to submit to the Secretary-General and the Director General of the International Atomic Energy Agency within fifteen days of the adoption of the present resolution a declaration of the locations, amounts and types of all items specified above; to place all of its

nuclear-weapon-usable materials under the exclusive control, for custody and removal, of the Agency, with the assistance and cooperation of the Special Commission
as provided for in the plan of the Secretary-General discussed in paragraph 9 (*b*); to
accept, in accordance with the arrangements provided for in paragraph 13, urgent
on-site inspection and the destruction, removal or rendering harmless as appropriate
of all items specified above; and to accept the plan discussed in paragraph 13 for the
future ongoing monitoring and verification of its compliance with these undertakings;

13. *Requests* the Director General of the International Atomic Energy Agency,
through the Secretary-General and with the assistance and cooperation of the Special
Commission as provided for in the plan of the Secretary-General referred to in paragraph 9 (*b*), to carry out immediate on-site inspection of Iraq's nuclear capabilities
based on Iraq's declarations and the designation of any additional locations by the
Special Commission; to develop a plan for submission to the Council within forty-five
days calling for the destruction, removal or rendering harmless as appropriate of all
items listed in paragraph 12; to carry out the plan within forty-five days following approval by the Council and to develop a plan, taking into account the rights and obligations of Iraq under the Treaty on the Non-Proliferation of Nuclear Weapons, for the
future ongoing monitoring and verification of Iraq's compliance with paragraph 12, including an inventory of all nuclear material in Iraq subject to the Agency's verification
and inspections to confirm that Agency safeguards cover all relevant nuclear activities
in Iraq, to be submitted to the Council for approval within one hundred and twenty
days of the adoption of the present resolution;

14. *Notes* that the actions to be taken by Iraq in paragraphs 8 to 13 represent steps
towards the goal of establishing in the Middle East a zone free from weapons of mass
destruction and all missiles for their delivery and the objective of a global ban on
chemical weapons;

D

15. *Requests* the Secretary-General to report to the Council on the steps taken to
facilitate the return of all Kuwaiti property seized by Iraq, including a list of any property that Kuwait claims has not been returned or which has not been returned intact;

E

16. *Reaffirms* that Iraq, without prejudice to its debts and obligations arising prior
to 2 August 1990, which will be addressed through the normal mechanisms, is liable
under international law for any direct loss, damage—including environmental damage and the depletion of natural resources—or injury to foreign Governments, nationals and corporations as a result of its unlawful invasion and occupation of Kuwait;

17. *Decides* that all Iraqi statements made since 2 August 1990 repudiating its foreign debt are null and void, and demands that Iraq adhere scrupulously to all of its obligations concerning servicing and repayment of its foreign debt;

18. *Decides also* to create a fund to pay compensation for claims that fall within
paragraph 16 and to establish a commission that will administer the fund;

19. *Directs* the Secretary-General to develop and present to the Council for decision, no later than thirty days following the adoption of the present resolution, recom-

mendations for the Fund to be established in accordance with paragraph 18 and for a programme to implement the decisions in paragraphs 16 to 18, including the following: administration of the Fund; mechanisms for determining the appropriate level of Iraq's contribution to the Fund, based on a percentage of the value of its exports of petroleum and petroleum products, not to exceed a figure to be suggested to the Council by the Secretary-General, taking into account the requirements of the people of Iraq, Iraq's payment capacity as assessed in conjunction with the international financial institutions taking into consideration external debt service, and the needs of the Iraqi economy; arrangements for ensuring that payments are made to the Fund; the process by which funds will be allocated and claims paid; appropriate procedures for evaluating losses, listing claims and verifying their validity, and resolving disputed claims in respect of Iraq's liability as specified in paragraph 16; and the composition of the Commission designated above;

F

20. *Decides,* effective immediately, that the prohibitions against the sale or supply to Iraq of commodities or products other than medicine and health supplies, and prohibitions against financial transactions related thereto contained in resolution 661 (1990), shall not apply to foodstuffs notified to the Security Council Committee established by resolution 661 (1990) concerning the situation between Iraq and Kuwait or, with the approval of that Committee, under the simplified and accelerated "no-objection" procedure, to materials and supplies for essential civilian needs as identified in the report to the Secretary-General dated 20 March 1991, and in any further findings of humanitarian need by the Committee;

21. *Decides* to review the provisions of paragraph 20 every sixty days in the light of the policies and practices of the Government of Iraq, including the implementation of all relevant resolutions of the Council, for the purpose of determining whether to reduce or lift the prohibitions referred to therein;

22. *Decides also* that upon the approval by the Council of the programme called for in paragraph 19 and upon Council agreement that Iraq has completed all actions contemplated in paragraphs 8 to 13, the prohibitions against the import of commodities and products originating in Iraq and the prohibitions against financial transactions related thereto contained in resolution 661 (1990) shall have no further force or effect;

23. *Decides further* that, pending action by the Council under paragraph 22, the Security Council Committee established by resolution 661 (1990) concerning the situation between Iraq and Kuwait shall be empowered to approve, when required to assure adequate financial resources on the part of Iraq to carry out the activities under paragraph 20, exceptions to the prohibition against the import of commodities and products originating in Iraq;

24. *Decides* that, in accordance with resolution 661 (1990) and subsequent related resolutions and until it takes a further decision, all States shall continue to prevent the sale or supply to Iraq, or the promotion or facilitation of such sale or supply, by their nationals or from their territories or using their flag vessels or aircraft, of:

(a) Arms and related *matériel* of all types, specifically including the sale or transfer through other means of all forms of conventional military equipment, including for paramilitary forces, and spare parts and components and their means of production for such equipment;

(*b*) Items specified and defined in·paragraphs 8 and 12 not otherwise covered above;

(*c*) Technology under licensing or other transfer arrangements used in the production, utilization or stockpiling of items specified in paragraphs (*a*) and (*b*);

(*d*) Personnel or materials for training or technical support services relating to the design, development, manufacture, use, maintenance or support of items specified in paragraphs (*a*) and (*b*);

25. *Calls upon* all States and international organizations to act strictly in accordance with paragraph 24, notwithstanding the existence of any contracts, agreements, licenses or any other arrangements;

26. *Requests* the Secretary-General, in consultation with appropriate Governments, to develop within sixty days, for the approval of the Council, guidelines to facilitate full international implementation of paragraphs 24, 25 and 27, and to make them available to all States and to establish a procedure for updating these guidelines periodically;

27. *Calls upon* all States to maintain such national controls and procedures and to take such other actions consistent with the guidelines to be established by the Council under paragraph 26 as may be necessary to ensure compliance with the terms of paragraph 24, and calls upon international organizations to take all appropriate steps to assist in ensuring such full compliance;

28. *Agrees* to review its decisions in paragraphs 22 to 25, except for the items specified and defined in paragraphs 8 and 12, on a regular basis and in any case one hundred and twenty days following the adoption of the present resolution, taking into account Iraq's compliance with the resolution and general progress towards the control of armaments in the region;

29. *Decides* that all States, including Iraq, shall take the necessary measures to ensure that no claim shall lie at the instance of the Government of Iraq, or of any person or body in Iraq, or of any person claiming through or for the benefit of any such person or body, in connection with any contract or other transaction where its performance was affected by reason of the measures taken by the Council in resolution 661 (1990) and related resolutions;

G

30. *Decides* that, in furtherance of its commitment to facilitate the repatriation of all Kuwaiti and third-State nationals, Iraq shall extend all necessary cooperation to the International Committee of the Red Cross by providing lists of such persons, facilitating the access of the International Committee to all such persons wherever located or detained and facilitating the search by the International Committee for those Kuwaiti and third-State nationals still unaccounted for;

31. *Invites* the International Committee of the Red Cross to keep the Secretary-General apprised, as appropriate, of all activities undertaken in connection with facilitating the repatriation or return of all Kuwaiti and third-State nationals or their remains present in Iraq on or after 2 August 1990;

H

32. *Requires* Iraq to inform the Council that it will not commit or support any act of international terrorism or allow any organization directed towards commission of such acts to operate within its territory and to condemn unequivocally and renounce all acts, methods and practices of terrorism:

I

33. *Declares* that, upon official notification by Iraq to the Secretary-General and to the Security Council of its acceptance of the above provisions, a formal cease-fire is effective between Iraq and Kuwait and the Member States cooperating with Kuwait in accordance with resolution 678 (1990);

34. *Decides* to remain seized of the matter and to take such further steps as may be required for the implementation of the present resolution and to secure peace and security in the region.

> Adopted at the 2981st meeting by 12
> votes to 1 (Cuba) with 2 abstentions
> (Ecuador, Yemen).

UN Security Council Resolution 1441 (November 8, 2002)

The Security Council,

Recalling all its previous relevant resolutions, in particular its resolutions 661 (1990) of 6 August 1990, 678 (1990) of 29 November 1990, 686 (1991) of 2 March 1991, 687 (1991) of 3 April 1991, 688 (1991) of 5 April 1991, 707 (1991) of 15 August 1991, 715 (1991) of 11 October 1991, 986 (1995) of 14 April 1995, and 1284 (1999) of 17 December 1999, and all the relevant statements of its President,

Recalling also its resolution 1382 (2001) of 29 November 2001 and its intention to implement it fully,

Recognizing the threat Iraq's non-compliance with Council resolutions and proliferation of weapons of mass destruction and long-range missiles poses to international peace and security,

Recalling that its resolution 678 (1990) authorized Member States to use all necessary means to uphold and implement its resolution 660 (1990) of 2 August 1990 and all relevant resolutions subsequent to resolution 660 (1990) and to restore international peace and security in the area,

Further recalling that its resolution 687 (1991) imposed obligations on Iraq as a necessary step for achievement of its stated objective of restoring international peace and security in the area,

Deploring the fact that Iraq has not provided an accurate, full, final, and complete disclosure, as required by resolution 687 (1991), of all aspects of its programmes to develop weapons of mass destruction and ballistic missiles with a range greater than one hundred and fifty kilometres, and of all holdings of such weapons, their components and production facilities and locations, as well as all other nuclear programmes, including any which it claims are for purposes not related to nuclear-weapons-usable material,

Deploring further that Iraq repeatedly obstructed immediate, unconditional, and unrestricted access to sites designated by the United Nations Special Commission (UNSCOM) and the International Atomic Energy Agency (IAEA), failed to cooperate fully and unconditionally with UNSCOM and IAEA weapons inspectors, as required by resolution 687 (1991), and ultimately ceased all cooperation with UNSCOM and the IAEA in 1998,

Deploring the absence, since December 1998, in Iraq of international monitoring, inspection, and verification, as required by relevant resolutions, of weapons of mass destruction and ballistic missiles, in spite of the Council's repeated demands that Iraq provide immediate, unconditional, and unrestricted access to the United Nations Monitoring, Verification and Inspection Commission (UNMOVIC), established in resolution 1284 (1999) as the successor organization to UNSCOM, and the IAEA, and regretting the consequent prolonging of the crisis in the region and the suffering of the Iraqi people,

Deploring also that the Government of Iraq has failed to comply with its commitments pursuant to resolution 687 (1991) with regard to terrorism, pursuant to resolution 688 (1991) to end repression of its civilian population and to provide access by international humanitarian organizations to all those in need of assistance in Iraq, and pursuant to resolutions 686 (1991), 687 (1991), and 1284 (1999) to return or cooperate in accounting for Kuwaiti and third country nationals wrongfully detained by Iraq, or to return Kuwaiti property wrongfully seized by Iraq,

Recalling that in its resolution 687 (1991) the Council declared that a ceasefire would be based on acceptance by Iraq of the provisions of that resolution, including the obligations on Iraq contained therein,

Determined to ensure full and immediate compliance by Iraq without conditions or restrictions with its obligations under resolution 687 (1991) and other relevant resolutions and recalling that the resolutions of the Council constitute the governing standard of Iraqi compliance,

Recalling that the effective operation of UNMOVIC, as the successor organization to the Special Commission, and the IAEA is essential for the implementation of resolution 687 (1991) and other relevant resolutions,

Noting that the letter dated 16 September 2002 from the Minister for Foreign Affairs of Iraq addressed to the Secretary-General is a necessary first step toward rectifying Iraq's continued failure to comply with relevant Council resolutions,

Noting further the letter dated 8 October 2002 from the Executive Chairman of UNMOVIC and the Director-General of the IAEA to General Al-Saadi of the Government of Iraq laying out the practical arrangements, as a follow-up to their meeting in Vienna, that are prerequisites for the resumption of inspections in Iraq by UNMOVIC and the IAEA, and expressing the gravest concern at the continued failure by the Government of Iraq to provide confirmation of the arrangements as laid out in that letter,

Reaffirming the commitment of all Member States to the sovereignty and territorial integrity of Iraq, Kuwait, and the neighbouring States,

Commending the Secretary-General and members of the League of Arab States and its Secretary-General for their efforts in this regard,

Determined to secure full compliance with its decisions,

Acting under Chapter VII of the Charter of the United Nations,

1. *Decides* that Iraq has been and remains in material breach of its obligations under relevant resolutions, including resolution 687 (1991), in particular through Iraq's failure to cooperate with United Nations inspectors and the IAEA, and to complete the actions required under paragraphs 8 to 13 of resolution 687 (1991);

2. *Decides,* while acknowledging paragraph 1 above, to afford Iraq, by this resolution, a final opportunity to comply with its disarmament obligations under relevant resolutions of the Council; and accordingly decides to set up an enhanced inspection regime with the aim of bringing to full and verified completion the disarmament process established by resolution 687 (1991) and subsequent resolutions of the Council;

3. *Decides* that, in order to begin to comply with its disarmament obligations, in addition to submitting the required biannual declarations, the Government of Iraq shall provide to UNMOVIC, the IAEA, and the Council, not later than 30 days from the date of this resolution, a currently accurate, full, and complete declaration of all aspects of its programmes to develop chemical, biological, and nuclear weapons, ballistic missiles, and other delivery systems such as unmanned aerial vehicles and dispersal systems designed for use on aircraft, including any holdings and precise locations of such weapons, components, sub-components, stocks of agents, and related material and equipment, the locations and work of its research, development and production facilities, as well as all other chemical, biological, and nuclear programmes, including any which it claims are for purposes not related to weapon production or material;

4. *Decides* that false statements or omissions in the declarations submitted by Iraq pursuant to this resolution and failure by Iraq at any time to comply with, and cooperate fully in the implementation of, this resolution shall constitute a further material breach of Iraq's obligations and will be reported to the Council for assessment in accordance with paragraphs 11 and 12 below;

5. *Decides* that Iraq shall provide UNMOVIC and the IAEA immediate, unimpeded, unconditional, and unrestricted access to any and all, including underground, areas, facilities, buildings, equipment, records, and means of transport which they wish to inspect, as well as immediate, unimpeded, unrestricted, and private access to all officials and other persons whom UNMOVIC or the IAEA wish to interview in the mode or location of UNMOVIC's or the IAEA's choice pursuant to any aspect of their mandates; further decides that UNMOVIC and the IAEA may at their discretion conduct interviews inside or outside of Iraq, may facilitate the travel of those interviewed and family members outside of Iraq, and that, at the sole discretion of UNMOVIC and the IAEA, such interviews may occur without the presence of observers from the Iraqi Government; and instructs UNMOVIC and requests the IAEA to resume inspections no later than 45 days following adoption of this resolution and to update the Council 60 days thereafter;

6. *Endorses* the 8 October 2002 letter from the Executive Chairman of UNMOVIC and the Director-General of the IAEA to General Al-Saadi of the Government of Iraq, which is annexed hereto, and decides that the contents of the letter shall be binding upon Iraq;

7. *Decides* further that, in view of the prolonged interruption by Iraq of the presence of UNMOVIC and the IAEA and in order for them to accomplish the tasks set forth in this resolution and all previous relevant resolutions and notwithstanding prior understandings, the Council hereby establishes the following revised or additional authorities, which shall be binding upon Iraq, to facilitate their work in Iraq:

- UNMOVIC and the IAEA shall determine the composition of their inspection teams and ensure that these teams are composed of the most qualified and experienced experts available;
- All UNMOVIC and IAEA personnel shall enjoy the privileges and immunities, corresponding to those of experts on mission, provided in the Convention on Privileges and Immunities of the United Nations and the Agreement on the Privileges and Immunities of the IAEA;
- UNMOVIC and the IAEA shall have unrestricted rights of entry into and out of Iraq, the right to free, unrestricted, and immediate movement to and from inspection sites, and the right to inspect any sites and buildings, including immediate, unimpeded, unconditional, and unrestricted access to Presidential Sites equal to that at other sites, notwithstanding the provisions of resolution 1154 (1998) of 2 March 1998;
- UNMOVIC and the IAEA shall have the right to be provided by Iraq the names of all personnel currently and formerly associated with Iraq's chemical, biological, nuclear, and ballistic missile programmes and the associated research, development, and production facilities;
- Security of UNMOVIC and IAEA facilities shall be ensured by sufficient United Nations security guards;
- UNMOVIC and the IAEA shall have the right to declare, for the purposes of freezing a site to be inspected, exclusion zones, including surrounding areas and transit corridors, in which Iraq will suspend ground and aerial movement so that nothing is changed in or taken out of a site being inspected;
- UNMOVIC and the IAEA shall have the free and unrestricted use and landing of fixed- and rotary-winged aircraft, including manned and unmanned reconnaissance vehicles;
- UNMOVIC and the IAEA shall have the right at their sole discretion verifiably to remove, destroy, or render harmless all prohibited weapons, subsystems, components, records, materials, and other related items, and the right to impound or close any facilities or equipment for the production thereof; and
- UNMOVIC and the IAEA shall have the right to free import and use of equipment or materials for inspections and to seize and export any equipment, materials, or documents taken during inspections, without search of UNMOVIC or IAEA personnel or official or personal baggage;

8. *Decides* further that Iraq shall not take or threaten hostile acts directed against any representative or personnel of the United Nations or the IAEA or of any Member State taking action to uphold any Council resolution;

9. *Requests* the Secretary-General immediately to notify Iraq of this resolution, which is binding on Iraq; demands that Iraq confirm within seven days of that notification its intention to comply fully with this resolution; and demands further that Iraq cooperate immediately, unconditionally, and actively with UNMOVIC and the IAEA;

10. *Requests* all Member States to give full support to UNMOVIC and the IAEA in the discharge of their mandates, including by providing any information related to prohibited programmes or other aspects of their mandates, including on Iraqi attempts since 1998 to acquire prohibited items, and by recommending sites to be inspected, persons to be interviewed, conditions of such interviews, and data to be collected, the results of which shall be reported to the Council by UNMOVIC and the IAEA;

11. *Directs* the Executive Chairman of UNMOVIC and the Director-General of the IAEA to report immediately to the Council any interference by Iraq with inspection activities, as well as any failure by Iraq to comply with its disarmament obligations, including its obligations regarding inspections under this resolution;

12. *Decides* to convene immediately upon receipt of a report in accordance with paragraphs 4 or 11 above, in order to consider the situation and the need for full compliance with all of the relevant Council resolutions in order to secure international peace and security;

13. *Recalls,* in that context, that the Council has repeatedly warned Iraq that it will face serious consequences as a result of its continued violations of its obligations;

14. *Decides* to remain seized of the matter.

Adopted by a 15–0 vote.

Appendix 2

A WHO'S WHO
OF THE IRAQI OPPOSITION

The following is excerpted from "What Lies Beneath," an Iraq backgrounder published by The International Crisis Group, October 1, 2002.

1. The Iraqi National Congress (INC)

Founded 1992
Led by Ahmad Chalabi
Base of Operations: London
Military Capabilities: Minimal

After the failure of the popular uprisings that followed the Gulf War, the Iraqi opposition organized a conference in Vienna in June 1992. Some 160 representatives created the INC, a broad-based grouping that included Kurdish organisations (the Kurdistan Democratic Party and the Patriotic Union of Kurdistan), major religious forces, former Iraqi military and security officials, and a variety of liberal and democratic movements. Claiming that Western powers were manipulating the initiative behind the scenes, some important Shiite groups such as the SCIRI and the Da'wa Party, along with the pro-Syrian Baathists distanced themselves from this embryonic organisation.

In October 1992, a broader conference was held in Salah ad-Din, in Iraqi Kurdistan. Following intense bargaining, some 234 delegates representing as many as 90 per cent of the opposition groups gathered, including representatives from the SCIRI, Da'wa, other Islamist groups and an increased number of Arab nationalists, although pro-Syrian Baathists continued to boycott. The delegates elected a three-man presidential council giving equal representation to Shiite, Kurdish and Sunni elements. It consisted of Muhammad Bahr al-Ulum, a senior Shiite religious scholar from Najaf; Masoud Barzani, the head of the Kurdistan Democratic Party; and Hassan Mustafa al-Naqib, a retired Sunni general.

The conference also decided that the northern Iraqi city of Erbil would serve as the INC's headquarters and the "provisional capital of Iraq." A 26-member executive council was formed to work as a cabinet. Ahmad Chalabi, a Shiite who continues to head the INC, was selected as president of the executive council.*

The International Crisis Group (ICG) is an independent nonprofit multinational organization with over eighty staff members on five continents, working through field-based analysis and high-level advocacy to prevent and resolve deadly conflicts.

* Chalabi has been dogged by charges that, while head of the Petra Bank in Amman, he siphoned off large amounts of money for his personal use. He was convicted in absentia in Jordan on charges of embezzlement. He has strongly and consistently denied these charges, claiming they are politically motivated.

The INC did not endorse any particular political program at Salah ad-Din. Rather, it presented itself as an umbrella organisation that "provides an institutional framework so that the popular will of the Iraqi people . . . can be democratically determined and implemented." With the overwhelming majority of Iraq's opposition parties represented on the executive committee, the organisation possessed a political legitimacy it found difficult to retain.

Indeed, the INC quickly became entangled in the increasingly complex and fractious politics of the Kurdish region—a problem that was particularly damaging given its Erbil base. The Kurdistan Democratic Party (KDP) and the Patriotic Union of Kurdistan (PUK) were at loggerheads throughout the early 1990s over a range of issues. The most important related to the distribution of customs duties levied at the Iraq-Turkey border and control of the regional government in Erbil. As relations deteriorated and parties on the left and in the Shiite movement picked sides, it became harder to sustain the fiction that the INC spoke with one voice. By late 1993 and into 1994, conflicts between the Kurdish parties erupted into open warfare. Both called on the INC to mediate, a role it could not perform effectively.

The INC also began to suffer a long series of defections. In September 1993 the Da'wa Party withdrew; in May 1995, one of the INC's three leaders, Muhammad Bahr al-Ulum, suspended his membership, followed by General al-Naqib. The latter claimed that the INC no longer represented Iraqi patriotic forces and had been reduced to serving as the "company of Ahmad Chalabi." Parties outside the INC and largely based in Syria and Europe, including Baathists, Arab nationalists and some Communists, expressed misgivings on the INC political platform, its procedures for selecting representatives, and its alleged dependence on the United States.*

A planned series of INC uprisings in northern Iraq in 1995–96 failed, in large part due to continuing infighting between Kurdish parties. In August 1996, the KDP invited Baghdad's forces back into the Kurdish region for help against the PUK, which enjoyed Iran's support. INC offices in Erbil, Salah ad-Din and elsewhere in the KDP-controlled territory were ransacked, and INC personnel either fled or fell to Iraqi security forces. The INC was forced to move its operations to London from where Chalabi quickly began an intensive and successful campaign to attract support in the United States.

Other opposition groups greeted Chalabi's success in Washington with a mix of distrust and envy. The two Kurdish parties objected to what they viewed as U.S. favouritism toward the INC. INC supporters bitterly complained that the U.S. administration, and particularly the State Department, were paying lip service to legislation authorising support of the Iraqi opposition while in reality undermining its intent by refusing to release the necessary funds.†

In an effort to rebuild its support, the INC elected a new, provisional seven-

---

* The Secretary General of the Communist Party in Erbil dubbed Chalabi "a hotel lobby opposition, with no popular support." Quoted in Nicholas Birch, "Iraq's Kurds Aren't Looking for a Fight," *The Washington Post*, 5 May 2002.

† Chalabi's lobbying was instrumental in getting the U.S. Congress to pass the Iraq Liberation Act in October 1998. This act authorised (though it did not require) the disbursement of U.S.$97 million to arm and train the Iraqi opposition. Seven groups were earmarked for funding: the INC, the KDP, the PUK, the Iraqi National Accord, the Islamic Movement of Iraqi Kurdistan and the Movement for Constitutional Monarchy. The Supreme Council for the Islamic Revolution in Iraq was also included but reportedly rejected U.S. military support. Sarah Graham-Brown, *Sanctioning Saddam: The Politics of Intervention in Iraq* (London, 1999), p. 12.

member leadership in March 1999 in Windsor. It included representatives from the two major Kurdish parties, the SCIRI, the Iraqi National Accord (INA) and three independents. Yet the Kurdish groups immediately refused to accept their appointments, and the SCIRI, the Communists, the INA and others soon suspended their membership in the INC completely. The INC has been further hobbled by allegations of fiscal mismanagement that led the U.S. government temporarily to suspend funding for it in December 2001 while the State Department's inspector general conducted an audit.

Over the years, the INC simultaneously has elicited great support and great scepticism. Views are polarized within both the Iraqi opposition and the U.S. administration. While it commands the loyalty of some Iraqi oppositionists and many in the West who believe it can help promote democracy and pluralism in Iraq, others view it as a group lacking in-country roots and overly dependent on Washington.* Some of the INC's staunchest defenders are high-ranking former and current members of the U.S. administration, which also includes some of its harshest critics. A source from the State Department noted, "The INC could still be a useful umbrella to bring other political forces together, but not as it is currently constituted. We need an INC that is more representative of all the forces in Iraq."

2. Kurdish Organisations

a) The KDP and the PUK

The Kurdistan Democratic Party (KDP)
Founded 1946
Led by Masoud Barzani
Base of Operations: Northwestern part of the
Autonomous Region
Military Capabilities (est.): 15,000 (KDP sources claim that they can count on 20,000 guerrilla fighters, in addition to a regular army of some 30,000 soldiers).

The Patriotic Union of Kurdistan (PUK)
Founded 1975
Led by Jalal Talabani
Base of Operations: Southeastern part of the
Autonomous Region
Military Capabilities (est.): 10,000

Drawing on a long history of resistance to the central government, the Kurdish nationalist movement represents a significant force in Iraqi politics. Today, it is noteworthy in that its components are among the very few that are able to operate both within Iraq (albeit not in areas under government control) and in exile. Yet questions about

---

* A senior official of the SCIRI said of the INC: "It is not an Iraqi opposition force, it's an employee of the Americans." Hamid Bayati, quoted in Daniel Williams, "Iraqi Exile Groups Wary of U.S., Each Other," *The Washington Post*, 2 June 2002.

their ability to mount an effective challenge to the regime persist. Though clearly the most militarily capable of the Iraqi opposition groups, they in all likelihood would be able to do no better than hold on to Kurdish territory currently under their control. Even then history suggests they would require massive outside support.*

In a region where the pull of tribal loyalty remains strong, two main nationalist political parties—the Kurdistan Democratic Party (KDP) and the Patriotic Union of Kurdistan (PUK)—dominate politics, each enjoying particular strength in its own geographic area.† The situation in Iraqi Kurdistan has been very much a function of the balance of power between these two organisations and of the willingness of their respective leaders to coexist peacefully. A far less significant Islamist movement and several parties defending the rights of ethno-religious minorities exist at the margins.

Founded in 1946, the KDP remains closely associated with the political fortunes of the Barzani clan. It currently is led by Masoud Barzani, the son of the legendary Kurdish leader Mullah Mustafa Barzani. The party's traditional stronghold is the Kurmanji-speaking northwest region of Iraq, an area that shares borders with Turkey and Syria and comprises two governorates (Dohuk and Erbil) that enjoy greater resources and host a slightly larger population than the PUK-controlled southern region. Approximately 125,000 civil servants work for the KDP-run administration; estimates of guerrilla fighters or *peshmerga* vary, with some sources saying 15,000 and KDP officials claiming 20,000 in addition to 30,000 regular soldiers. The KDP also possesses significant financial resources as a result both of the oil-for-food program and of customs duties levied on goods going into and coming from Turkey. The KDP draws its inspiration from deep tribal traditions and an aspiration to achieve Kurdish self-rule or autonomy short of outright independence. Within that overarching goal, the KDP seeks dominance for the tribes and families of the Iraqi northwest—including the Barzanis, the Zeibaris and others.

The KDP began its insurgency against the central Iraqi government in the 1960s. Following the Baathist coup in 1968, it turned to negotiations over Kurdish autonomy. The resulting agreement broke down over Kirkuk, and in the new round of fighting, the KDP enjoyed the material support of the United States, Israel and Iran. Yet when Iraq and Iran (then under the Shah) reached an agreement over the Shatt al-Arab waterway, Iran withdrew its support, and the Kurds were left to fend for themselves. Iraqi government forces roundly defeated the KDP and thousands of Kurds were killed as Iran closed the border and the U.S. failed to respond to requests for help.‡ The KDP leadership fled into exile in Iran.

Saddam Hussein's response to the KDP's decision to side with Iran in the 1980–1988 war was brutal. In 1983, Iraqi forces arrested several thousand members of the Barzani clan following a battle in which the KDP fought with Iranian troops inside Iraqi territory; they were never seen again. For the remainder of the war, KDP guerrillas were active throughout Kurdish territory, while its leadership retained its

---

* In particular, Kurdish troops were roundly defeated by the Republican Guard in 1991 and 1996.

† The KDP is strongest in the governorate of Dohuk (in the Kurmanji-speaking region of Badinan on the border with Turkey), while the PUK prevails in the primarily Surani-speaking governorate of Suleimaniyeh, adjacent to Iran. Both parties enjoy strong support in the Erbil and Kirkuk governorates.

‡ Taken to task for the U.S. failure to intervene, Henry Kissinger famously remarked that "covert action should not be mistaken for missionary work."

headquarters inside Iran. In 1986, the KDP joined forces with the other principal Kurdish opposition party, the PUK.

The Patriotic Union of Kurdistan was founded by Jalal Talabani on 1 June 1975 in Damascus. It was born in large part in reaction to the KDP's failed uprising strategy. Talabani blamed the Kurds' disastrous defeat in 1975 on Barzani's over-reliance on Iran and the United States. He also assailed the tribal structures of the KDP and declared that his PUK would be a more political, progressive organisation. Indeed, the PUK originally was made up of two major leftist groups, *Komala,* a Marxist organisation, and the Socialist Movement of Kurdistan. Many PUK cadres hail from urban areas.

PUK support is chiefly based in the Surani-speaking area between the Greater Zab and the Iranian border, including the Suleimaniyeh governorate, but also significant parts of the Erbil and Kirkuk governorates. The PUK employs 97,000 civil servants and has approximately 10,000 fighters.

During the Iran-Iraq war, the PUK first sought an accommodation with Baghdad but negotiations broke down over the perennial Kirkuk issue in 1985. The PUK rejoined the Kurdish insurgency, uniting with the KDP and smaller Kurdish parties in the Iraqi Kurdistan Front. As the war lumbered toward an end, the Front joined Iran in a last-ditch effort to gain territorial advantage and halt, or slow down, a vicious Iraqi counter-insurgency campaign that sought to depopulate the countryside through massive village destruction and resettlement. This triggered an even fiercer Iraqi response. In February 1988, the regime launched what it referred to as "the glorious Anfal" (spoils) campaign against the Kurds. Human Rights Watch has estimated that by its end in September 1988, Iraqi forces, extensively using poison gas, had destroyed several thousand villages and hamlets and caused the disappearance of some 100,000 Kurds, mostly civilians. The main KDP and PUK forces were driven across the border into Iran, returning only during the uprising that broke out after the Gulf War.

After their defeat in the post-Gulf War uprising, the Kurdish parties managed to stay in Iraqi territory, taking advantage of allied concern over the refugee flow spilling into Turkey. In late 1991, Iraqi forces withdrew unilaterally to a line roughly equivalent to the border marking the boundary of the Kurdish Autonomous Zone (i.e., excluding Kirkuk). This enabled a blossoming of Kurdish democracy.

In the 1992 parliamentary elections, the KDP captured 51 per cent and the PUK 49 per cent. The regional government that was put in place reflected a 50-50 power-sharing arrangement in which KDP ministers were shadowed by PUK deputy ministers and vice versa. The result was the emergence of two parallel Kurdish administrations. Although the leaders, Barzani and Talabani, remained outside both parliament and the government, they exerted considerable power and influence from their respective party platforms, making it all the more difficult to develop and sustain unified democratic institutions in the autonomous region. Political quarrels soon developed into financial quarrels over the distribution of income, international aid and commodity smuggling across the Iranian and Turkish borders. A fratricidal war produced some 3,000 victims and hundreds of displaced persons.

In August 1996, clashes between the two parties intensified. Feeling threatened, the KDP appealed to Baghdad and, aided by Iraqi troops, gained temporary control of most of Iraqi Kurdistan. However, the PUK soon regained most of its lost territory, save for Erbil, seat of the Kurdish regional government. Several countries, including

Iran and Turkey, engaged in mediation attempts and, after a number of aborted efforts, the U.S. and the UK finally secured a cease-fire in October 1996. Under intense U.S. mediation and pressure, and backed by a promise of U.S.$7.3 million in aid, the two parties agreed to a new power (and money) sharing settlement, the Washington Accord, in September 1998. Many of its provisions have remained dead letters.

The KDP controls the border crossings with Turkey and so is able to levy tens of millions of dollars of customs duties on all incoming goods and monopolise a major source of revenue. The PUK alleges that it has received only U.S.$4 million from the KDP since 1998 while the KDP is said to earn as much as $2 million daily from oil trafficking and other trade. In addition, elections contemplated in the Washington Accord have yet to be held. Still, the Accord was successful in one key respect: it has maintained peace since 1998. It also committed both parties to the territorial integrity and unity of Iraq, on the basis of a pluralistic, democratic and federal political structure. Since that time, the KDP and PUK leaderships reached agreement on a draft Iraqi constitution that contemplates a federal structure for the country.

KDP and PUK histories are testimony to the vagaries and risks of regional politics. Both dependent on and vulnerable to them, Kurdish organisations have had to navigate between Iran, Turkey, Syria and others. The PUK, at its origins critical of the KDP's over-reliance on Iran in the 1970s, gradually built a close relationship with Tehran during the latter years of the Iran/Iraq war. The KDP also has tried to strike an arrangement with Turkey, trading support in Ankara's fight against its own rebel Kurdish organization (PKK) for lucrative trans-border commercial deals. Yet both parties are aware that these alliances are tactical and short-lived, as both Iran and Turkey harbour their own fears about Kurdish national sentiment and have fought counterinsurgency campaigns against Kurds at home.

Nor has the relationship with the U.S. been trouble-free. Washington is seen as having embraced the Kurds in 1991 and again in 1996, only to abandon them to Saddam Hussein's fierce reprisals. As the prospect of a U.S. military intervention looms, they are caught between their hatred of the Iraqi regime, fear of losing the gains of the past few years in the aftermath of a war, apprehension of possible retaliation by the regime as the war unfolds, mistrust of Washington's long-term intentions in Iraq, and doubts that a new central government in Baghdad would accommodate key Kurdish demands concerning a federal arrangement and the status of Kirkuk.

b) Islamist and Other Movements

The Islamic Unity Movement of Kurdistan (IMK)
Founded 1986
Led by Sheikh Ali Abdel Aziz
Base of Operations: Halabja, Northern Iraq
Military Capabilities: minimal

A relatively weak and fragmented Islamist movement has developed at the margins of the nationalist Kurdish movement. Kurdish Islamists, particularly active in the area referred to as the "Halabja Triangle," are organised within several groups that include armed militias. Perhaps most noteworthy is the Islamic Unity Movement of Kurdistan (IMK). Founded in 1986, and having inherited some of the organisational structures

of the Muslim Brotherhood that existed in Kurdistan since the 1950s, the group declared holy war against "Saddam's unfaithful regime" during the Iran-Iraq war. Today,
it continues to play an important role particularly in the realm of social and charitable
work. Although it garnered minimal votes in the 1992 elections, the IMK performs
better in local and professional elections. While willing to see the United States assume a leading role in efforts to topple the regime, the IMK remains deeply suspicious
of the hegemonic ambitions of the more prominent Kurdish nationalist groups, the
KDP and PUK, with which it has clashed in the past. As an essentially Sunni group, it
also is concerned about the prospect that Iraqi Shiites would be given a decisive role
in the future, preferring to see a Sunni military figure become the next Iraqi president.

Some Kurdish veterans of the Afghan war have turned to far more radical alternatives, which are known under various and changing names such as Kurdistan Hizbul-
lah, Hamas, Tawhid, and Army of Islam. A grouping termed Ansar al-Islam, which
emerged in December 2001, is said to include several hundred members and to control a few villages in a tiny area bordering Iran above the town of Halabja. The group is
small in numbers though some claim it is now a force to be reckoned with. Mullah
Najm al-Din Faraj Ahmad, also known as Mullah Krekar, is a leading figure in this organisation, which, like many if not all of the Kurdish Islamist factions, is based on
tribal affiliations. The two main Kurdish parties traditionally have taken an ambivalent attitude toward the Islamist groups, apparently out of concern that they not alienate the regional powers said to support them—namely Iran (or certain factions within
the Iranian leadership) and Saudi Arabia, but the PUK did battle with Ansar al-Islam
forces in 2001 and 2002, and managed to hem them in their mountain strongholds.

The existence of possible links between the extreme Islamist elements in northern
Iraq and the terror-network al-Qaeda has become a matter of some concern, particularly in the United States. Yet beyond the reported relocation of individuals from
Afghanistan to Iraqi Kurdistan, claims of organised links with al-Qaeda remain un-
substantiated.* Allegations of a connection between Ansar and powerful factions inside the Iranian regime are more likely to be true. Given the group's location in a
corner of Iraqi Kurdistan hemmed in by Iran from three sides and the fact that Ansar
leader Mullah Krekar, who has legal residence in Norway, has been able to travel
abroad via Iran, it seems reasonable to conclude that Iran has offered the small Islamist group a measure of logistical support and relative freedom of movement, possibly even military support in the form of ammunition and light weapons.

Minority groups also have been allowed to organise in the autonomous Kurdish region. The Chaldeo-Assyrian minority features no political parties, but was represented
by five members in the elected parliament of 1992. The small Iraqi Christian community (roughly 4 per cent of Iraqis, and which includes Chaldeans, Assyrians and Orthodox) arguably has a stake in the survival of the current regime—which has basically left
it unharmed and allowed it to practice its religion—and fears the consequences of a
Shiite take-over. Chaldeans and Assyrians also are concerned about the prospect of increased power for the Kurds, with whom they traditionally have battled for land and resources in the North. Another minority in the region is the Turkoman. With an

---

* The two principal Kurdish parties arguably saw some advantage in exaggerating these purported links with
al-Qaeda as a means of limiting the influence of religious tendencies in Iraqi Kurdish politics and of gathering greater
U.S. support.

estimated 300,000 inhabitants in all of Iraqi Kurdistan (of whom only some 30,000 live in the autonomous area), it has several political parties. The Turkoman Front, established in 1995, is the umbrella organisation and receives solid financial and political support from Turkey. Yet it appears to enjoy little sympathy, whether among Kurds or Turkomans, many of whom view it merely as an extension of Turkish foreign policy. The Turkomans also claim Kirkuk based on their historical presence in the city.

3. Religious Forces

a) The Da'wa Party

The Da'wa Party
Founded 1957–58
Base of Operations: Iran, Europe, some
clandestine presence in Iraq
Military Capabilities: limited and clandestine

The Da'wa Party is the oldest of the currently active Islamist organisations in Iraq. Reports differ on when it was founded and by whom, but it is reasonable to assume that it was formally launched under that name in the late 1950s in the holy city of Najaf and that Sayyid Muhammad Baqir al-Sadr was the principal architect of its ideological and organisational structure. From the outset, the Da'wa was a clandestine movement organised around tightly knit secret cells (*halaqat*) and a strict hierarchy. It developed a comprehensive ideology based on the religious-philosophical and economic theories of Baqir al-Sadr. Its main objective is to preserve and fortify Shiite believers' religious identity against the influence of Western ideologies (in the Da'wa's earlier days, communism) through the renewal of Islamic thought and the reform and modernisation of religious institutions, including the hierarchically structured traditionalistic clergy. The party, which perceives itself as a religious and political vanguard, recruits its members from the Shiite intelligentsia of the modern urban middle class, students and professionals. But until 1978–1979 its influence was limited, as the bulk of Shiite believers continued to follow their old leadership, represented by the socially conservative and strictly apolitical high-ranking Shiite clergy.

In 1978–79, the Da'wa Party organised street demonstrations in several southern cities to protest the Iraqi government's repression of Shiites, which had intensified in the early 1970s. Indeed, by Saddam Hussein's own account, between 1974 and 1980 the Iraqi government put to death 500 Shiite activists, a majority of whom belonged to the Da'wa Party. The Da'wa initially refrained from taking up arms. However, when the more radical Organization of Islamic Action, its militant competitor for leadership of the politicised Shiite movement, resorted to violence in mid-1979, it followed suit. By then, the Islamic revolution in Iran had provided the Da'wa Party with a model it was eager to duplicate.

The Da'wa carried out attacks on government officials, centres and installations, prompting the Baath regime to enact a special decree in March 1980 retroactively making membership in the party a capital offence. In retaliation for the attacks by Shiite militants, the government began a vigorous counter-offensive and, in April 1980, the party's spiritual leader, Muhammad Baqir al-Sadr, and his sister were arrested and hanged. The regime's campaign and Baqir al-Sadr's death seriously damaged the

Da'wa Party. When the government began to expel some 30,000 Shiites to Iran in April 1980, numerous party members and leaders fled there, regrouped and helped establish an Islamic umbrella group, the Supreme Council for the Islamic Revolution in Iraq. The Da'wa continued to maintain clandestine cells in Iraq, especially in urban areas such as the largely Shiite Madinat Saddam in Baghdad and in cities in the South.

The exile in Iran and the ambivalent relationship with its host and supporter confronted the Da'wa with a new type of challenge throughout the 1980s. The Iranian government did not formally compel other Shiite opposition parties and organisations to disband. But Tehran made clear its support for the SCIRI and for the SCIRI's claim to be the sole legitimate political representative of the Shiite Iraqi opposition, which diminished the Da'wa's importance. In addition, the permanent pressure Iran exercised on the party led to internal divisions, splits and leadership changes. The last of the pro-Iranian wings fell away only in the wake of the Iran-Iraq War, allowing the more nationalistic Iraqi view once again to gain the upper-hand. Since then the party has been balanced and cautious towards Tehran.

Today, the party has branches in Tehran, Damascus and London. In an interview with ICG, a leader of the Tehran branch strongly emphasised that the Da'wa, despite avowed Islamic solidarity with Shiite brethren in Iran, considers its Iraqi-Arab identity to be the guiding principle of its political actions. Underscoring efforts to maintain political and financial independence during the exile in Iran, which has lasted since 1980, he explained that the priority on its national Iraqi orientation is the major dividing line with the SCIRI.

Unlike other Iraqi Islamist groups, the Da'wa possessed from the outset a defined political program based on a strict Islamic interpretation of the nation's history and social structure. Early on, it called for a government deriving its constitution and laws from *shari'a* law; later it attacked the Baath regime's secular character. At the same time, the Da'wa is a nationalistic party that claims to place the interests of Iraq (as it perceives them) above those of a putative Islamic *umma*. Like almost all opposition groups in exile, the Da'wai gradually embraced a more pragmatic ideology. It now accepts the need for free elections and the establishment of a democratic government in Iraq. Islamic rule no longer is seen as having to be imposed from the top down but rather as emanating from the popular will as expressed through voting. The Da'wa has been hostile toward a U.S. attack against Iraq, stating that the will of the Iraqi people, not that of foreign powers, should determine the country's fate.

b) The Supreme Council for the Islamic Revolution in Iraq

The Supreme Council for the Islamic Revolution in Iraq (SCIRI)
Founded 1982
Led By Ayatollah Muhammad Baqir al-Hakim
Base of Operations: Iran
Military Capabilities: 4,000–8,000 militia, the
Badr Brigade

The Supreme Council for the Islamic Revolution in Iraq (SCIRI) was founded in 1982 in Tehran under the leadership of Ayatollah Muhammad Baqir al-Hakim, who has lived in exile there since 1980. Baqir al-Hakim is the second eldest son of Grand

Ayatollah Muhsin al-Hakim, a leading spiritual guide of the Shia and one of the most respected clergy in its worldwide community. The organisation was culled largely from opposition Iraqi Shiites living in exile in Iran and prisoners of war. Prodded by Tehran, a number of Iraqi Shiite Islamic parties joined the SCIRI, among them the Da'wa and the Islamic Action Organisation. Originally designed as a loose organisation representing various Shiite parties and deriving its legitimacy principally from the stature of its leader, it was deeply influenced by (and dependent on) Iran. Hence its adoption of the principle of *velayet-e faqih* (Islamic rule under the direct leadership of a ruling Islamic jurist) developed by the late Ayatollah Khomeini.

In 1983, the SCIRI established a government-in-exile and set up a military unit, the Badr Corps, which fought against Iraq. It remains active in southern Iraq under the official guidance of the SCIRI. Estimates of its strength range from 4,000 to 8,000 fighters.

The SCIRI's first major action after the Iran-Iraq War was to participate in the February 1991 uprising against the Iraqi regime. However, as that uprising faltered and U.S. military backing failed to materialise, the government executed many of the Shiite community's political and religious leaders, destroyed mosques and expelled vast numbers of Shiites by draining the marshes in hopes of flushing out all resistance. These measures severely hurt SCIRI's capabilities, and only clandestine cells survived in southern rural Iraq.

The SCIRI's relationship with Iran has been a source of both strength and weakness. Tehran provides a logistical base and staging ground without which it would be unable to operate. At the same time, the close ties and the concerns they raised for many Iraqis—including Shiites—probably are a reason why the party failed to gain broad popular support during the 1991 uprising. The Iraqi regime consistently has invoked these links, accusing the organisation of being a pawn in Tehran's hands. Indeed, according to a former member of the Da'wa Party's collective leadership (Tehran wing), the SCIRI lacks effective control over its own military arm, the Badr Corps, which reportedly is commanded by officers of Iran's Islamic Revolutionary Guards Corps (IRCG). The relationship with Iran also has been the source of internal friction. During and after the Iran-Iraq War, a rift developed between the Da'wa Party and the rest of the SCIRI on this. The split effectively ended the SCIRI's status as a broad umbrella organisation. It now essentially represents Baqir al-Hakim's followers, and its relationship with other Islamic groups appears largely formal.

Over time, the SCIRI has sought to project the image that it has loosened ties with Iran, largely to broaden its domestic appeal. Baqir al-Hakim now holds himself up as a leader not only of Shiites but of all Iraqis, regardless of religion or ethnicity and the SCIRI has sought to moderate its concept of a post-Saddam government. In particular, it has suggested that it would tolerate a post-Saddam Sunni military interim government. That said, Tehran continues to provide the SCIRI with the vast bulk of its funding, weapons and training.

The closeness of the relationship is evidenced in strong personal ties. Two former SCIRI leaders, Ayatollah Ali al-Taskhiri and Ayatollah Mahmud al-Hashimi Shahrudi, are among the most trusted confidants and most influential aides to Iran's Supreme Leader, Ali Khamenei. Both belong to the Supreme Leadership Office, a centre of Iranian political power that includes only four members and that appoints the Leader's 2,000 clerical representatives entrusted with enforcing his authority throughout Iran (and beyond). In August 1999, Khamenei appointed al-Hashim Shahrudi as head of the judiciary, thereby making an Iraqi Arab the third most powerful official in Iran. The SCIRI leader, Baqir al-Hakim, has shown unwavering support for Khamenei, including during his abortive attempt in December 1994 to claim the post of supreme religious and political authority (*marja'-e taqlid-e motlaq*) for all Shiites of the world.

The SCIRI's ties with Iran inevitably have complicated relations with the United States. Nevertheless, by the late 1990s Washington began making overtures, presumably on the ground that it needed to build a bridge to the significant Shiite constituency. The SCIRI was designated a group eligible to receive support under the Iraq Liberation Act and was invited to the August 2002 opposition gathering in Washington. That the SCIRI chose to send Abdelaziz al-Hakim, the brother of its leader, despite renewed U.S.-Iranian tensions and official Iranian opposition to a U.S.-led war, probably is an indication of both the party's and Iran's growing anticipation of a military operation and their desire to enhance their position by securing positions of power for the SCIRI in a post-Saddam regime.

The role and influence of the SCIRI in Iraq is a matter of some debate. Although it attracts much international media attention, it is believed by many to lack both any credible following among the country's Shiite population and the capacity on its own to decisively affect the future course of political developments.

The SCIRI is ambiguous about a possible U.S. attack on the Iraqi regime while pursuing its contacts with Washington. These began in the context of the "Group of Four," which also includes the two principal Kurdish organizations and the Iraqi National Accord (INA) and have continued in the Washington gathering of the six opposition groups (the "Group of Four" plus the INC and the Constitutional Monarchy Movement). At times, al-Hakim has implied that he would support a U.S. operation that would nullify the regime's military advantage and facilitate the task of the opposition, though suggesting that any military action should not be unilateral. He has pointed to the Kosovo model—where NATO strikes supported Kosovo Liberation Army fighters on the ground—as a potential strategy for Iraq, arguing that Saddam Hussein must be deposed by a domestic mass uprising, but that U.S. support could be critical in preventing the regime from turning its heavy weapons against the rebels. At other times, al-Hakim has sounded a more critical note, explaining that "a political solution is necessary for a regime change in Iraq," the SCIRI is "against any attack or occupation," and its Washington contacts are designed to "keep off threats against Iraq."

c) The Organisation of Islamic Action

Founded 1965
Base of Operations: Iran, Europe, Syria,
some clandestine presence in Iraq
Military capabilities: very limited and clandestine

The *Munazzamat al-Amal al-Islami,* or Organisation of Islamic Action, was founded by Ayatollah Muhammad al-Shirazi in 1965 in Karbela. In the 1970s, it developed into a clandestine radical organisation, sending its members to Lebanon for military training during that country's civil war. The organisation also was able to recruit members outside Karbela, its original Iraqi stronghold, above all in the Gulf States, and particularly in Bahrain. Encouraged by the Iranian revolution, the group launched an unsuccessful armed struggle against the Baath regime in 1980. One of its most spectacular actions was the attempted assassination of Tariq Aziz, then the Iraqi deputy premier. In the early 1990s, the organisation split into two branches, with one in Damascus following Muhammad Hadi al-Mudarrasi, a nephew of Ayatollah al-Shirazi, and the other in Tehran, closer to Iran, under the leadership of Sheikh Qasim al-Husseini. Largely as a result of internal divisions regarding its relationship with Iran, the Organisation of Islamic Action has over the years lost ground relative to the SCIRI and the Da'wa.

d) The Iman al-Khoei Foundation

Founded Late 1980s
Base of Operations: London, plus worldwide presence
Military capabilities: None

The Iman Al-Khoei Foundation, which represents the traditionalist, apolitical Shiite believers, may exercise considerable influence over Iraq's future though it denies being a party and refrains from supporting other political forces. It has a political agenda, albeit one that is neither publicly announced nor clearly defined. Consistent with the world-view of its founder, the leading Shiite religious authority of the time, Grand Ayatollah Saiyyid Abolqasem al-Khoei (1899–1992), it rejects any active involvement in politics, abhors the use of violence and devotes much of its substantial financial resources and organisational capacities to cultural and educational works. It is respected by Shiite believers in Iraq (and beyond, in Lebanon, the Gulf States, Pakistan, and East Africa, and even Iran).

The foundation, which was established in the late 1980s, differs from other Shiite Iraqi organisations insofar as it perceives itself not as a political party but merely as an international charitable body that works for the propagation and spread of Shiite Islam worldwide. Since 1992 it has run its diverse activities, which also include humanitarian and disaster-relief for Muslims in distress and missionary work, from a centre in London. The foundation has schools and religious centres in New York, Paris, Swansea (UK), Karachi, Montreal and Bangkok and is a large donor to the UN. The source of its financial resources are religious contributions (*khoms*) of Shiite believers.

After the failed Shiite uprising in the wake of the Gulf War, the regime took reprisals against the religious centres of Najaf and Kerbala as well as against the traditionalist Shiite clergy in general. It kept Abolqasem Khoei under house arrest until his death and imprisoned or killed a number of his advisors in subsequent years. After his death, his successor as religious patron of the foundation and recipient of the religious donations was his former master-pupil Ayatollah Ali al-Sistani in Najaf. He has been under house arrest since 1994, and he and his closest collaborators have been targets of assassination attempts, for which Baghdad denies any responsibility. The secretary-general of the foundation until 1994 was the founder's eldest son, Muhammad Taqi al-Khoei, for whose death in a mysterious car-accident near Najaf the foundation holds the Iraqi government responsible. His successor was his younger brother, Majid al-Khoei, who supervises the foundation from London.

Since 1994 the al-Khoei Foundation has intensified its diplomatic and public relations activity (it publishes three Arabic and English journals in London) and has advocated Saddam Hussein's removal and the establishment of a vaguely defined democratic government. Although the foundation never articulates open opposition, it is also at loggerheads with Iran. Because the al-Khoei Foundation opposes the theocratic concept of *velayat-e faqih,* it presents a challenge to Iran's Supreme Leader's claim to religious and political leadership over Arab Shiites outside Iran.

4. Military and Nationalists

a) The Iraqi National Accord and the Iraqi Free Officers

The Iraqi National Accord
Founded 1990
Led by Ayad Alawi
Base of Operations: Amman
Military Capabilities: Minimal, independent
resources, relies on defections from Iraqi military

Iraqi Free Officers
Founded 1996
Led by General Najib Al-Salhi
Base of Operations: Washington
Military Capabilities: None

Formed with Saudi backing in 1990, the INA is composed largely of military and security officials who defected from Iraq. The group was founded by Ayad Allawi, a senior Iraqi intelligence official, who left in 1971, and Salah Omar al-Ali, a former senior member of the Baath Party and Minister of Information, who broke with Saddam Hussein over Iraq's invasion of Kuwait. After a brief stay in Damascus in the wake of the Gulf War, the INA settled in Amman where it has been headquartered since 1995. The INA's core strategy has been to attract dissident Baathists and Iraqi officers and encourage a conspiracy against the regime. Its natural constituency thus very much mirrors that of the regime itself—Sunni Arabs from central Iraq who dominate the Baath party, the security services and the officer corps. It is composed of strong Iraqi nationalists with a shared hatred of the current regime.

The INA's appeal among foreign countries intent on dislodging Saddam Hussein, particularly the U.S., rose after the failure of the 1991 uprising which seemed to show the limitations inherent in a "peripheral" approach—Shiites in the South and Kurds in the North seeking to squeeze the centre. The INA's attractiveness also was bolstered by the 1995 defection to Jordan of Saddam's son-in-law, Hussein Kamel, a key actor in Iraq's weapons program. Sensing the possibility of more significant haemorrhaging from Iraq, the United States in particular placed greater emphasis on the nationalist exile community located in Jordan and on its capacity to attract further defections within Iraq's military ranks.

In March 1996, General Nizar al-Khazraji, a former Iraqi chief-of-staff, fled and joined the INA, further enhancing its status. However, by that time the INA had been thoroughly penetrated by Iraqi security services and, in July, an attempted INA-backed coup against the regime failed. All the roughly 100 Iraqi officers and agents who had been involved in the plot were rounded up and executed. While the INA claims that its people continue to operate throughout Iraq, it is a greatly weakened organisation.

Nevertheless, its natural pool of recruits (disaffected Iraqi officers) has grown, a function of Iraq's general impoverishment and the collapse of the military's standard of living. For such disaffected officers, there are few alternatives to the INA, since most external opposition groups are viewed as both hostile to Sunni interests and overly subservient to foreign powers.

The view shared by many nationalists and members of the military who have joined the INA is that the army is not an unbreakable, monolithic entity, and defections can rapidly occur, perhaps in the face of a decisive U.S. attack. In their opinion, the regime quickly will lose two of its four key security supports—the army and the Republican Guard—in the face of a heavy external air attack, leaving only the Special Republican Guard and the personal Presidential Guard. They point to the fact that the regime has transferred units of the Republican Guard outside of Baghdad as evidence of its declining faith in them.

Many higher-ranking military defectors have pitched their support behind al-Khazraji, who lives in exile in Denmark and whom they consider capable of leading Iraq through a transitional period. A Sunni, General al-Khazraji is the highest-ranking officer to have defected and is considered a hero by many Iraqis at home and abroad for his conduct during the Iran-Iraq War. He has tried to remain above the fray and avoid involvement in disputes between opposition groups. However, he has been dogged by well-documented accusations that he was behind the ghastly use of chemical weapons against the Kurds.

Another exiled general, Najib al-Salhi, has been touted as a potential future president. A former chief of staff in the Republican Guard, he fled in 1995 and resided in Jordan before moving to the U.S. He established a secret network of colleagues both inside and outside of Iraq, the Free Officers' Movement. He has taken the position that Saddam Hussein can be removed through a combination of air attacks by an international coalition, U.S. special forces on the ground, domestic opposition groups and defecting Iraqi military units. In his view, once the Iraqi military becomes convinced that Washington is determined to overthrow Saddam Hussein, it will join the fight against him. Unlike al-Khazraji, he appears relatively untainted by previous military activities. Other ex-generals, such as Fawzi al-Shamari, a Shiite, and Wafiq al-Samarrai, former chief of military intelligence, also have their backers.* Many of the ex-generals claim strong contacts within the four central Iraqi governorates (Baghdad, Al-Anbar, Salah al-Din, Diyala) that so far have been loyal to the regime, unlike the remaining fourteen that joined the 1991 uprisings.

In July 2002, high-ranking Iraqi military living in exile (including Generals Najib Al-Salhi, Tawfiq al-Yassiri, and Saad Al-Obaidi) met in London and established a military council to prepare a political transition. They also agreed on a "Covenant of Honour" calling for a pluralist and demilitarised Iraq and committed to transfer power to civilians if a U.S.-led intervention led to Saddam Hussein's ouster.

---

* U.S. officials have been meeting with these and other exiled Iraqi generals in an effort to gauge how much support could be counted on within Iraq's military and how they envisage a post-Saddam Iraq. See Anthony Shadid, "U.S. Pursues Ex-Generals to Topple Saddam," *The Boston Globe,* 11 March 2002.

b) Pan-Arab and Baathist Parties

<u>The Arab Baath Socialist Party: Iraqi Command</u>
Founded 1963
Led by Fawzi al-Rawi
Base of Operations: Syria
Military Capabilities: None

<u>Also</u>: *The Iraqi Socialist Party, The Independent Group,*
The Arab Socialist Movement, The Unionist Nasserite Grouping,
The Democratic Pan-Arab Grouping, The National Reconciliation
Group and the Free Iraq Council.

The most important pan-Arab group is the Arab Baath Socialist Party: Iraqi Command, an organisation of Iraqi Baathists living in exile in Syria. While it still adheres to the old, quasi-socialist Baathist platform and continues to aspire to a United Arab Republic including Iraq and Syria, it gradually has been moving toward a more reform agenda, advocating pluralism and democracy. In its view change in Iraq will be carried out by disaffected elements of the existing power structure—the army, the security apparatus and dissident Baath members such as themselves—rather than by a popular uprising or foreign intervention. It is suspicious of plans to establish a federal structure, fearful that it could lead to the country's de facto partition. Other pan-Arab nationalist groups include the Iraqi Socialist Party, the Independent Group, the Arab Socialist Movement, the Unionist Nasserite Grouping, the Democratic Pan-Arab Grouping and the National Reconciliation Group.

5. Communists

<u>The Iraqi Communist Party</u>
Founded 1934
Base of Operations: Syria and Iraqi
Kurdistan
Military Capabilities: NA

Founded in 1934, the Iraqi Communist Party (ICP) is the oldest party on the political scene. From inception, it attracted young members of the Shiite community, and much of its recruitment and activity took place in southern Iraq. The Communists appealed to the educated and more secular minded—though often economically disadvantaged—members of the population, who welcomed its calls for political and social equality. Historically, it was one of the more effective parties, and to this day, it retains a degree of loyalty among Kurds and the Shiite urban population in the South, including possibly a presence on the ground, especially in urban centres like Baghdad.

The Communists faced repression until the monarchy was overthrown in 1958 but gained considerable influence during the 1960s. After the Baath Party seized power in 1968 and the new regime signed a "friendship agreement" with the Soviet Union in 1972, the pro-Soviet ICP joined the Baath-dominated National Progressive Patriotic Front in 1973. However, when Saddam Hussein took over the presidency and Baath Party leadership in 1979, the Front was brutally disbanded. The regime moved against the Communist Party and persecuted its members. As a result, the ICP took up arms, transferred its centre of operations to Kurdistan, and established close relations with the KDP and the PUK while fighting alongside their *peshmerga*. Following the 1987–88 campaigns against the Kurds, the ICP once more was forced to move, this time to Syria. After the Soviet Union's collapse, it kept its name, while shifting its ideological platform away from classical Marxism-Leninism.

While the Communist Party continues to hope that Saddam Hussein will be ousted by a mass uprising, it acknowledges the difficulties inherent in the absence of a unified opposition. It also has come to see the need for significant backing by the armed forces. Leery of a U.S.-led military intervention, it nonetheless has suggested that it could support it in order to overthrow the regime and establish a political system within which it once again could freely operate.

How significant a role the ICP might play in a future Iraq is debatable. Certainly its strong domestic roots, its legitimacy as a nationalist party, and its ability to attract sympathisers across religious lines provide it with relative strengths compared to a number of other opposition groups.

6. Democrats

The Union of Iraqi Democrats
Founded 1989
Led by Faruq Ridha'a
Base of Operations: London
Military Capabilities: None

Movement of the Democratic Centre
Founded 2000
Led by Adnan Pachachi
Base of Operations: London
Military Capabilities: None

The Constitutional Monarchy Movement
Founded 1993
Led by Sharif Ali Ibn Hussein
Base of Operations: London
Military Capabilities: None

Also: the Iraqi Democratic Party

While all opposition groups currently espouse democratic principles, this was the original premise of several. The last to be formed inside Iraq was the National Democratic Party, which existed from the 1940s until the Baath took power in 1968, at which point it was essentially disbanded, and most of its leaders went into exile. Since that time, only relatively small democratic parties have emerged, all established abroad. They include the Union of Iraqi Democrats, the Iraqi Democratic Party and the Movement of the Democratic Centre. While they lack genuine roots or a following in Iraq, they can claim a measure of success in helping shape the opposition's political discourse. Through their efforts, they have helped push to the fore issues of political pluralism, individual freedoms, civil liberties and government accountability.

In conversations with ICG, representatives of these groups expressed optimism regarding prospects for regime change in the aftermath of the events of 11 September 2001. A representative of the Union of Iraqi Democrats asserted that Saddam Hussein could be ousted only through U.S. intervention. Some members expressed the hope that their influence would increase in a post-Saddam Iraq with the return of some of the three to four million Iraqis living in exile, a majority of whom do not belong to any party and are both well-educated and accustomed to democratic systems. Yet at the same time, they appeared to harbour few illusions about their own role in a future Iraq.

The Constitutional Monarchy Movement (CMM) represents a slightly different tradition. It was founded in London in 1993 by Sharif Ali Ibn Hussein, a second cousin of King Faisal II, who was assassinated during the 1958 revolution. Ibn Hussein, who sees himself as a potential unifier for the opposition, is speaker of the Iraqi National Congress. He and his followers argue that after more than 40 years of turbulent politics and divisive government policies, the best solution for Iraq is a constitutional monarchy that would provide legitimacy and stability. The CMM believes that Iraqis should be asked to approve a constitutional monarchy through a referendum. It was invited by the United States to attend the August 2002 gathering.

Seymour M. Hersh for "A Case Not Closed," by Seymour M. Hersh, from the November 11, 2001, issue of *The New Yorker.* Copyright © 2001 by Seymour M. Hersh.

Joost Hiltermann for "The Men Who Helped the Man Who Gassed His Own People," by Joost Hiltermann. Copyright © 2002 by Joost Hiltermann.

Christopher Hitchens for "Why I Am for Regime Change" (Original title: "Chew on This"), from the January 16, 2003, issue of *The Stranger.* Copyright © 2003 by Christopher Hitchens.

Pervez Hoodbhoy for "American Dreams of Empire," by Pervez Hoodbhoy, from the January 26, 2003, edition of the *Los Angeles Times.* Copyright 2003 by Pervez Hoodbhoy.

Arianna Huffington for "We Don't Need No Stinkin' Proof," by Arianna Huffington, syndicated column, September 30, 2002. Copyright © 2002 by Christabella, Inc.

The Independent for "M16 and CIA: The New Enemy Within," by Paul Lashmar and Raymond Whitaker, from the February 9, 2003 edition of *The Independent.* Copyright © 2003 by *The Independent.*

International Crisis Group for "A Who's Who of the Iraqi Opposition," an excerpt from *Iraq Backgrounder: What Lies Beneath,* ICG Middle East Report Number 6, Amman/Brussels, October 1, 2002. Reprinted by permission.

Michael T. Klare for "Deciphering the Bush Administration's Motives," by Michael T. Klare, from *Foreign Policy in Focus* (http://www.fpif.org), January 16, 2003. Copyright © 2003 by Michael T. Klare.

Phillip Knightley for "Imperial Legacy," by Phillip Knightley (Original title: "Desert Warriors: Why Are We in Saudi Arabia? Blame It on Lawrence"), from the November 1990 issue of *M, Inc.* Copyright © 1990 by Phillip Knightley.

Charles Krauthammer for "The Unipolar Moment Revisited," from the Winter 2002/2003 issue of *The National Interest.* Copyright © 2002 by Charles Krauthammer. The essay includes material from "The Unipolar Moment," by Charles Krauthammer (*Foreign Affairs: America and the World,* 1990/91). Reprinted by permission of the author.

John le Carré for "The United States of America Has Gone Mad," by John le Carré, from the January 15, 2003 edition of *The Times* (London). Copyright © 2003 by John le Carré.

Nicholas Lemann for "The Next World Order," by Nicholas Lemann, from the April 1, 2002, issue of *The New Yorker;* and "The War on What? The White House and the Debate About Whom to Fight Next," by Nicholas Lemann, from the September 9, 2002, issue of *The New Yorker.* Copyright © 2002 by Nicholas Lemann.

Kanan Makiya for "Our Hopes Betrayed: The U.S. Plan for Post-Saddam Government" (Original title: "Our Hopes Betrayed: How a U.S. Blueprint for Post-Saddam Government Quashed the Hopes of Democratic Iraqis"), by Kanan Makiya, from the February 16, 2003, edition of *The Observer* (London). Copyright © 2003 by Kanan Makiya.

The Middle East Research and Information Project (MERIP) for "A Case for Concern, Not a Case for War," by Glen Rangwala, Nathaniel Hurd, and Alistair Millar, from

INDEX

Jane's Intelligence Review, 481

Japan: American military in, 544; and Bush Doctrine, 271, 273; and debate about going to war, 324, 333, 354; democracy in, 551; economy of, 399–400; as model for post-war Iraq, 548, 549, 551, 562–63; nerve gas used in, 452; and nuclear weapons, 508, 511, 521; number of American troops in, 435; oil reserves in, 404; and Pax Americana, 593, 594; and Persian Gulf War, 553, 636; post-World War II years in, 548, 549, 551, 558, 562–63; pre-emptive strike by, 511; and regime change, 399–400; and Schell's comments, 508, 511, 521; and unipolarity, 594; in World War II, 308, 347, 353, 511

Jawad, Mohammed, 158

Jennings, Peter, 123

Jerusalem, 10, 15, 59, 203

Jerusalem Brigade, 574

Jevons, W. S., 634

Jewish organizations: and anti-war movement, 488

Jews, 7, 15–16, 19, 24–25, 65, 202–4. *See also* Israel; Israeli-Palestinian conflict; Zionism; *specific person*

Jidda: oil meeting in, 69, 70

jihad, 197, 202–4, 240, 299, 389, 391, 616, 627

Jihad Group in Egypt, 202–4

Jihad Movement in Bangladesh, 202–4

Jihaz Haneen. *See* security service, Iraqi

Johnson, Lyndon, 284, 358

Joint Center for Political and Economic Studies, 495

Joint Chiefs of Staff, U.S., 548

Jones, Terry, 453–54

Jordan: and Byrd's speech, 484; and debate about going to war, 307, 308; and inspections and sanctions, 171, 172; Iraqi opposition in, 665; and legacy of imperialism, 15; and post-war Iraq, 549, 553; and regime change, 396, 404, 405, 406, 410; and sale of U.S. supplies to Iraq, 32

Joseph, Robert, 612

Joyce, Michael, 222–24

Judah, Tim, 568–79

Judt, Tony, 593

Jund al-Islam. *See* Ansar al-Islam

Justice Department, U.S.: and attempted assassination of ex-President Bush, 141, 144, 151, 153, 157, 160; and civil liberties, 229, 233–37, 627; and debate about going to war, 322; and impact of September 11, 229, 233–37; and Pax Americana, 630; and sale of U.S. supplies to Iraq, 34

Juwaibar, Khalil, 106

Kagan, Donald, 222–24, 350, 351, 352

Kagan, Robert, 199–201, 222–24, 243–49, 289, 601

Kakrak, Afghanistan, 320–21

Kalak checkpoint, 572

Kamel, Hussein, 118, 169, 175–76, 187, 412

Kamiya, Gary, 353, 355

Kang Sok Ju, 508

Kaplan, Lawrence, 608–13

Kaplan, Robert, 614–15

Karbala, Iraq, 105, 108, 388

Karimov, Islam, 397

Karsh, Efraim, 416, 417

Karzai, Hamid, 292, 312, 550, 551

Kashmir, 394, 395, 520

Kasuri, Khursid Mahmud, 236

Kazakhstan, 397, 450–51, 515

KDP (Kurdistan Democratic Party), 104, 109, 570, 572, 574, 576–78, 579, 655–58

Keith, Damon, 235

Kelly, James, 508

Kelly, John, 40, 54, 55, 57, 66

Kennan, George, 3, 258

Kennan Games, 286

Kennedy, Edward, 74, 599

Kennedy, John F., 270, 294, 497, 512

Kennedy, Paul, 593, 595–96, 634

Kennedy, Robert, 294

Kenya, 263, 477

Kerry, John, 286

Kessler, Gladys, 235

Khalil, Samir al-. *See* Makiya, Kanan

Khalizad, Zalmay, 199–201

Khan, Ayub Ali, 231, 232

Khan, Ayub Qadeer, 510

Khayrallah, Adnan, 20, 26

Khayrallah, Sajida (wife of Saddam Hussein), 22, 23

Khayrallah, Tulfah, 20, 21, 26

Republican Guard (*cont.*)
  Iraq, 575; and Saddam Hussein as
  survivor, 91–92, 101, 107; and Saddam
  Hussein's misreading of U.S., 77, 82,
  83, 84, 85; and U.N. debates, 466,
  472–73. *See also* military, Iraqi
Republican National Committee, 327
Republican Party, 248, 253, 279, 289, 294,
  319, 327, 336, 629, 631
Resolution 242 (U.N.), 311
Resolution 338 (U.N.), 311
Resolution 660 (U.N.), 380
Resolution 661 (U.N.), 380
Resolution 662 (U.N.), 380
Resolution 664 (U.N.), 380
Resolution 665 (U.N.), 380
Resolution 666 (U.N.), 380
Resolution 667 (U.N.), 380
Resolution 669 (U.N.), 380
Resolution 670 (U.N.), 380
Resolution 674 (U.N.), 380
Resolution 677 (U.N.), 380
Resolution 678 (U.N.), 379–80, 504
Resolution 686 (U.N.), 314
Resolution 687 (U.N.), 124, 165, 168,
  173, 186, 188, 314, 315, 380, 458, 499,
  504, 620, 621, 641–48
Resolution 688 (U.N.), 124, 165, 314, 380
Resolution 706 (U.N.), 169
Resolution 707 (U.N.), 186
Resolution 712 (U.N.), 169
Resolution 715 (U.N.), 458
Resolution 949 (U.N.), 380
Resolution 986 (U.N.), 169–70, 171
Resolution 1284 (U.N.), 167
Resolution 1373 (U.N.), 315
Resolution 1397 (U.N.), 311
Resolution 1409 (U.N.), 170
Resolution 1441 (U.N.), 451, 457, 462,
  463, 464, 465, 467, 469, 474, 478, 499,
  500, 501, 585–86, 648–52
resolutions, U.N.: and beginning of
  Operation Iraqi Freedom, 503; and
  Benn-Saddam Hussein interview, 464;
  and Bush Doctrine, 264; and Clinton-
  Project for the New American Century
  letter, 200; and Clinton's speech
  concerning Operation Desert Fox, 207,
  208; and debate about going to war, 305,
  311, 317, 318, 319, 326, 330, 347, 365,
  370, 371, 373, 378, 379–80, 381, 382;
  and inspections and sanctions, 175; and

Israeli-Palestinian conflict, 447; Israel's
  disregard for, 436; key, 641–52; and
  New World Order, 264; and Pax
  Americana, 599, 600; and regime
  change, 450; and U.N. debates, 457,
  458, 459, 465, 478, 499; and
  unipolarity, 599, 600; and yes-butters,
  490. *See also specific resolution*
retaliation, 419, 425–33, 485, 513
Reuters News Service, 72
Revolutionary Command Council, 24, 27,
  28, 70, 114, 566
Rhodesia, 171
Rice, Condoleezza: and Bush Doctrine,
  241, 253, 256–57, 262, 263; and debate
  about going to war, 281, 293, 324, 345;
  and genocide of Iraqi, 513; and Iraq's
  weapons of mass destruction, 461; and
  regime change, 420, 421, 437, 450–52
Richard, Mark, 150–51, 153, 155, 160–
  161
Richardson, Bill, 180
ricin (gas), 428, 475
Ridha'a, Faruq, 668
Riedel, Bruce, 76
Right, 225–28, 279, 322, 354
Ritter, Scott, 174, 177, 182–83, 187, 267
"The Road to Baghdad" (U.S. Army secret
  plan), 92
Robertson, Pat, 615
Robust Nuclear Earth Penetrator, 349
Rodman, Peter W., 199–201
Roe v. Wade, 629
Roethke, Theodore, 125
rogue states: and debate about going to
  war, 286, 288, 302, 376; and Pax
  Americana, 594, 597, 607, 609, 610,
  614; and regime change, 387, 430, 454;
  and unipolarity, 594, 597, 607
Rohde, David, 234
Romania, 474, 543
Roosevelt, Franklin D., 288, 361, 443,
  490, 518, 519
Rosen, Stephen P., 222–24
Rosenman, Samuel, 490
Ross, John Hume. *See* Lawrence (T.E.) of
  Arabia
Rove, Karl, 336
Rowley, Colleen, 229
Roy, Arundhati, 339–43
Royal Dutch-Shell, 583, 584
Ruba'i, Muwafak al-, 108

About the Editors

Micah L. Sifry is senior analyst at Public Campaign. He was the Middle East editor for *The Nation* and has written widely on the region for many publications. He also specializes in political reform issues, and last year authored *Spoiling for a Fight: Third-Party Politics in America*. He lives with his family in Hastings-on-Hudson, New York.

Christopher Cerf is an author, a multiple Grammy- and Emmy-winning composer and television producer, a co-creator of the PBS literacy education program *Between the Lions,* and a former senior editor at Random House. Among his many books are *The Experts Speak, The Pentagon Catalog,* and *The Official Politically Correct Dictionary and Handbook.* He lives in New York City.